Maurice Pinay

The plot

against the Church

MAURICE PINAY

THE PLOT

AGAINST THE CHURCH

1962

Published by

OMNIA VERITAS LTD

www.omnia-veritas.com

DEDICATION

To the Immaculate Heart of the Virgin Mary, Mother of God; to St. Joseph, Protector of the Universal Church; to St. Michael the Archangel, Prince of the Supernatural Host in the struggle against Satan, the first Naturalist; to St. Thomas Aquinas, the Catholic Church's Teacher of Order; and to St. Anthony of Padua, "Hammer of the Heretics."

* * * * * *

"In our time more than ever before, the chief strength of the wicked lies in the cowardice and weakness of good men... All the strength of Satan's reign is due to the easy-going weakness of Catholics. Oh! if I might ask the Divine Redeemer, as the prophet Zachary did in spirit: *What are those wounds in the midst of Thy hands?* The answer would not be doubtful: *With these was I wounded in the house of them that loved Me. I was wounded by My friends, who did nothing to defend Me, and who, on every occasion, made themselves the accomplices of My adversaries.* And this reproach can be levelled at the weak and timid Catholics of all countries." Pope St. Pius X, Discourse he pronounced on December 13, 1908 at the Beatification of Joan of Arc.

* * * * * *

O most powerful Patriarch, Saint Joseph, Patron of that Universal Church which has always invoked thee in anxieties and tribulations; from the lofty seat of thy glory lovingly regard the Catholic world. Let it move thy paternal heart to see the Mystical Spouse of Christ and His Vicar weakened by sorrow and persecution by powerful enemies. We beseech thee, by the most bitter suffering thou didst experience on earth, to wipe away in mercy the tears of the revered Pontiff, to defend and liberate him, and to intercede with the Giver of peace and charity, that every hostile power being overcome and every error being destroyed, the whole Church may serve the God of all blessings in perfect liberty. Amen.

Leo XIII. March 4, 1882.

INTRODUCTION TO

THE AMERICAN EDITION

This historically important book will, in all probability, be attacked as being anti-Semitic. Let nobody be led astray or distracted, however, from a serious and scientific consideration of the incontrovertible facts here set out. We are concerned with a major factor of history, and more especially of the history of the Christian Church. No crude, negative and destructive anti-Semitism comes into question. That the Jews have played a tremendous and not always beneficial role in the whole story of mankind is obvious; that their activities were not always friendly to Christianity and to the non-Jewish peoples is equally obvious, and there is an enormous fund of evidence from Jewish as well as other sources of unshakable authority to prove this.

This work of great erudition displays not alone a knowledge of events past, but shows also that its compilers had had knowledge of events to come in some immensely important respects. As readers will see from the foreword to a German-language edition, the first edition of this work, in Italian, began by stating that its authors knew that the purpose of calling the Second Vatican Council was to persuade it to declare that the Jews were not responsible for the Crucifixion of Our Saviour, i.e., they were not guilty of deicide, and this book appeared *before* the first session of the Council. Subsequently, as forecast, this proposal was put forward, great pressures were applied to get it accepted, and something, even if diluted, was agreed upon at the end.

Now it cannot be denied, even apart from the essence of the proposal itself, that the fact that any Jews, however representative or otherwise of most of their co-religionists and co-racialists, could do what they had done at the very highest levels of the Catholic Church, is a matter of tremendous significance to Catholics and all others, even to non-Christians.

And not only was it possible to find men at the summit of the Hierarchy to further this project, but the Council appeared to contain a large number of Bishops who, at the very least, did not seem to understand the importance of the problem.

None can sit in judgment on those concerned; it is understandable that the Jews want to "improve their image", especially as they have the power to do so. The lessons to be drawn are, surely, not that the Jews as such or any who have been misled should be the objects of severe criticism, but that the facts, the truth concerning all matters of great importance, and especially when they affect the purity and influence of the Church, should be made widely known. In this all Churches should help with a sense of urgency.

However, it should be pointed out to the Jews concerned that instead of trying to improve their reputation and increase their influence by fostering deceptions and attacking basic Christian traditions, they would serve their own true interests best by first setting their own hearts and attitude toward others aright. Again and again they have overreached themselves over the centuries, and then complained at the results for which they alone were responsible.

In particular, this recent initiative in Rome has merely served to draw the attention of intelligent and decent men to a matter of immediate concern to all. It is the obvious duty of all who may read this book to make its contents known and to encourage all their friends to acquire, read and spread it.

THE EDITOR

St. Anthony Press Los Angeles,
California February 15, 1967

INTRODUCTION TO

THE ITALIAN EDITION

The most infamous conspiracy is in progress against the Church. Her enemies are working to destroy the most holy traditions and thus to introduce dangerous and evil-intended reforms, such as those Calvin, Zwingli and other false teachers once attempted. They manifest a hypocritical zeal to modernise the Church and to adapt it to the present day situation, but in reality they conceal the secret intention of opening the gates to Communism, to hasten the collapse of the free world and to prepare the further destruction of Christianity. All this it is intended to put into effect at the coming Vatican Council. We have proofs of how everything is being planned in secret agreement with the leading forces of Communism, of world Freemasonry and of the secret power directing these.

It is intended to first carry out a probe and to begin with the reforms which encounter less resistance from the defenders of Holy Church, in order to then gradually extend the range, as weakening resistance allows this.

In addition, we have confirmation of what will still be unbelievable for those who are not initiated, namely that the anti-Christian forces have at their disposal, in the ranks of Church dignitaries, a veritable "Fifth Column" of agents who are the unconditional tools of Communism and of the secret power directing it. For it has been revealed that those cardinals, archbishops and bishops, who form a kind of progressive wing within the Council, will attempt to bring about a break through shameful reforms, whereby the good faith and the eagerness for progress of many devout Council Fathers will be deceived.

The assurance has been given that the Progressive block forming at the beginning of the Synod will be able to count upon the support of the Vatican, in which, so it is said, those anti-Christian forces possess influence. This appears unbelievable to us and sounds more like boastful arrogance by the enemies of the Church than sober reality. However, we mention this, so that one sees how far the enemies of Catholicism and of the Free World risk revealing themselves. Apart from the dangerous reforms in the doctrine of the Church and her traditional policy which stand in open contradiction to what was approved by the preceding Popes and Ecumenical Councils, it is desired that the Excommunication Bulls uttered by his Holiness Pope Pius XII against the Communists and their lackeys be declared nullified.

In this manner the effort is made to establish a peaceful coexistence with the Communists, which on the one side would be harmful to the regard for Holy Church in the eyes of Christians who fight against materialistic and atheistic Communism and on the other side weaken the morale of these fighters, hasten their defeat and would have as a consequence dissolution in their own ranks, in order in such a way to ensure the worldwide triumph of Red totalitarianism. Concern is taken that Protestants and Orthodox are in no way invited who fight heroically against Communism, but rather more only those Churches and Church counsellors who stand under the influence of Freemasonry, of Communism and the secret power directing them. In this manner the Freemasons and Communists disguised in priestly robes, who have usurped the leading posts in such churches, work together concealed and in a subtle way, but also very effectively, with their accomplices who have infiltrated into the Catholic clergy.

On its side the Kremlin has already decided to refuse known anti-Communist prelates an exit visa, and only to allow their unconditional agents or those who, without being the latter, have bowed out of fear of Red reprisals, to travel from the satellite states. Thus at the Second Vatican Council the Church will experience the silence of those who could defend her best of all and could enlighten the Holy Synod concerning what takes place in the Communist world.

This will undoubtedly seem incredible to those who read it; but the events at the Holy Ecumenical Council will open their eyes and convince them that we are speaking the truth. For it is there that the enemy intends to play a trump card, whereby it, so we are assured, will have on its side unconditional accomplices among the highest Church dignitaries. A further disastrous plan, which is being prepared, is that the Church shall contradict itself, so as a result to sacrifice its regard with the faithful; for later it will be broadcast that an institution which contradicts itself cannot be divine. With this proof they wish to desolate the Churches and achieve that the faithful lose their confidence in the clergy and abandon them.

It is intended to cause the Church to declare that what it has represented for centuries as bad, is now good. Among such manoeuvres spun for this purpose one particularly stands out on account of its importance, and refers in fact to the conduct of Holy Church towards the damned Jews, as Saint Augustine calls them; and this in reference both to those who nailed Christ to the cross, as also to their descendants, who are both archenemies of Christianity. The unanimous doctrine of the great Church Fathers, that "unanimis consensus Patrum" which the Church regards as a source of faith, condemned the unbelieving Jews and declared the struggle against them to be good and necessary.

For example, in this struggle, participated, as we will prove by means of irrefutable evidence, the following Saints: Saint Ambrose, Bishop of Milan, Saint Jerome, Saint Augustine, Bishop of Hippo, Saint John Chrysostom, Saint Athanasius, Saint Gregory of Nazianzus, Saint Basil, Saint Cyril of Alexandria, Saint Isidore of Seville, Saint Bernhard and even Tertullian as well as Origen, the latter two during the period of their indisputable orthodoxy. In addition, the Church fought energetically for nineteen centuries against the Jews, as we will likewise prove by means of reliable documents, and among which are found the following: Papal Bulls, Protocols of the Ecumenical and Provincial Councils as well as the highly renowned Fourth Lateran Council and many others, the teachings of Saint Thomas of Aquinas, of Duns Scotus and of the most important doctors of the Church. In addition we will quote Jewish sources of indisputable authenticity, like the official Encyclopaedias of Jewry, the works of famous rabbis as well as of the most well known Jewish historians.

The Jewish, Freemasonic and Communist plotters now have the intention at the coming Council of utilising, as they assert, the lack of knowledge of most clergy concerning the true history of the Church, to execute a surprise coup by adopting the standpoint at the assembled Holy Ecumenical Council that anti-Semitism must be condemned, as well as every struggle against the Jews who, as we will elaborate, are the wirepullers of Freemasonry and of international Communism. They would like the infamous Jews, whom the Church has regarded as evil for the course of nineteen centuries, to be declared good and beloved of God. As a result the "unanimis consensus Patrum" would be contradicted, which laid down exactly the opposite, as well as what also found its expression through various Papal Bulls and Canons of Ecumenical as well as Provincial Councils.

Since the Jews and their accomplices pillory every struggle within the Catholic Church against the wickedness of the former, as well as the plots directed against Christ Our Lord, as antisemitism, we will likewise reveal in this book that Christ Himself, the Gospels and the Catholic Church can be included among the sources of antisemitism, since they campaigned for nearly two thousand years against those who denied their Messiah.

With the condemnation of Antisemitism, which at times is called Antisemitic racialism, it is wished to attain that his Holiness the Pope and the assembled Council in condemnation of Antisemitism experience the catastrophic event that the Church contradicts itself, and therefore, without giving account to this, silently also condemn Christ Our Lord Himself, as well as the Holy Gospels, the Church Fathers and most Popes, among them Gregory VII (Hildebrand), Innocent II, Innocent III, Pius V, and Leo XIII, who as we will show in this book, have fought bitterly against the Jews and the "Synagogue of Satan".

With such condemnation it would be successful to simultaneously place countless Church Councils in the dock, among them the Ecumenical Councils of Nicaea and the Second, Third and Fourth Lateran Councils, whose Canons we will subject in this book to a thorough investigation, and which carried on an energetic struggle against the Hebrews. To put it in few words, the infamous plotters have the scheme in mind that Holy Church, by its condemning Antisemitism, condemns itself, whereby one can easily amplify the disastrous consequences.

It was already attempted at the last Vatican Council, even if in disguised form, to alter course in the traditional doctrine of the Church, when it was successful by means of a surprise manoeuvre and lasting pressure, to influence countless Church Fathers to signing "a Postulate in favour of the Jews". Misusing the Apostolic zeal of the devout prelates, it was first spoken of a summons to conversion of the Israelites, which regarded from the theological viewpoint is an intention without fault; but later they inoculated the secret poison in form of assertions, which, as we will reveal in the course of this work, stand in open contradiction to the doctrine which Holy Church has laid down in this respect.

But upon this occasion, when the "Synagogue of Satan" believed it had secured the approval of the postulate on the part of the Council, God, who always stands by His Church, prevented the mystical body of Christ from contradicting itself and fructifying the plots of its thousand years old enemy. The Franco-Prussian war broke out unexpectedly. Napoleon had to hastily withdraw the troops protecting the Pontificate, and the army of Victor Emmanuel prepared to take Rome. Therefore the 1st Holy Vatican Council had to be hastily dissolved, and the prelates returned to their dioceses, before a general discussion concerning the postulate in question was able to be begun.

This was, however, not the first time that divine providence held up such a misfortune by means of something extraordinary. History shows us that it has done it in numerous cases, whereby it mostly made use of the Popes and devout prelates as its medium; among the latter we include Saint Athanasius, Saint Cyril of Alexandria, Saint Leanero, Cardinal Aimerico, and even such humble monks as Saint Bernhard or Saint John of Capistranus. In other cases than those previously mentioned, it even made use of ambitious monarchs, as the example of Victor Emmanuel, the King of Italy, reveals.

When in the middle of the past year we experienced how the enemy was preparing renewed attempts to unleash a plot which would open the gates to Communism, prepare the collapse of the free world and deliver Holy Church into the claws of the "Synagogue of Satan", we began, without losing any time, to collect documents and to write the following work which is intended to be not so much a book with a certain disputed tendency, but rather an ordered summary of Council records, Papal Bulls and all kinds of documents and sources, from which we leave out those whose reliability or truthfulness is doubtful, and select those which possess indisputable truth.

In this book, not only is the plot uncovered which Communism and the "Synagogue of Satan" have entered upon against the 2nd Vatican Council, but also the preceding conspiracies, which were recorded in the course of nineteen centuries as cases of precedence, are subject to a thorough illumination. For what is intended to occur at the new assembled Holy Synod, has already occurred repeatedly in the past centuries. In order to grasp what will occur to the full extent, it is therefore essential to know the cases of precedence as well as the nature of that hostile "Fifth Column" infiltrated into the bosom of the clergy. This purpose is served by the extensive investigation of the Fourth Part, which rests upon a faultless proof of sources.

Since in addition attention is drawn to the possibility that the Holy See and the Second Vatican Council might abandon certain traditions of the Church in order to grant aid to the triumph of Communism and of Freemasonry, we lay at basis of the two first parts of this work a minute study, whereby we cite the two most serious sources concerning what one can call the quintessence of Freemasonry and of atheistic Communism, and investigate the nature of the secret power directing it. Even if the fourth part of this book is the most important, then nevertheless the first three and above all the third make comprehensible the plot threatening Holy Church in its entire circumference. This plot is not restricted to its activity during the coming universal Synod but extends far more to the entire feature of the Church. For the enemy has already calculated that, if for some reasons at the Holy Synod strong defensive forces awaken against its planned reforms and these should bring about the failure of its intentions at the Second Vatican Council, it will use at a later point any kind of opportunity to return to its plan, in which respect it would know how to utilise the strong influence which it pretends to have with the Holy See.

We are naturally convinced of the fact that, in spite of the intrigues of the enemy, the support which God always grants His Church will also cause their criminal machinations to fail this time. It is also written: "The Powers of Hell shall not triumph over it!"

Unfortunately, in writing this very documentary book, we have used more than fourteen months, and there remain only two until the opening of the Second Vatican Council. God will help us to overcome all resistance, in order to have ready the printing of this work either by the beginning of the Synod or at least before the enemy can cause the first harm. Though we are also aware that the Lord God will not permit a catastrophe, nevertheless we must keep before our eyes what an outstanding Saint expressed: that, although we know that all depends upon God, we should nevertheless act as if everything depended upon us. And as Saint Bernard said in a similar grave crisis to that of the present: "Pray to God and hit out with the stick."

Rome, the 31st August 1962.

The Author.

FOREWORD TO

THE AUSTRIAN EDITION

Due to the numerous requests that have reached us from the ranks of the Austrian and German clergy, we have decided to print the Austrian edition of the book "Plot Against the Church."

The Fathers of the Second Vatican Council, to whom this work was dedicated, had occasion to establish in the course of the Holy Synod that our warning voice with regard to the existence of a veritable plot against the most holy traditions of the Church and its defensive powers in the face of atheistic Communism found their full justification through the course of the first part of the Holy Council. This shows that our assertions correspond to a tragic truth.

The events of the coming months will provide our readers with the confirmation that our revelations rest upon an incredible but regrettable reality. The enemies of the Church renewed the attempt at the first sitting of the world-embracing Synod, by means of their accomplices in the high clergy, to abnegate or to narrow the tradition of the Church and its character as a source of revelation. This had already been striven for before them by the Waldenses, the Hussites and other Mediaeval heretics, as well as later by Calvin, Zwingli and additional false teachers; only that this time all this is fought for under the cloak of the high ideal, inspiring us all, of Christian unity, whereas the heretics of those times cited for substantiation of the same thesis further diverse and sophistic arguments.

To attempt that the Church deny the tradition of its character as a source of doctrine and to admit such an attribute only to the Holy Bible, more or less equates to the intention of causing it to contradict itself. This would accordingly mean that that which had been maintained for almost twenty centuries to be white was now declared to be black; and in fact with the devastating result that the mystical body of Christ, on grounds of contradiction, would forfeit its respect in the eyes of the faithful, since indeed an institution that contradicts itself in its essence can with difficulty be called divine.

A step of this kind would bring Holy Church into such an impossible situation that it could not be justified through the wishful image of the longed-for Christian unity, whose realisation at the moment would be very problematical. But should this dream become fact upon such an absurd basis, then this would signify that Holy Church recognises it has been caught up in error and its faithful would as a result turn in masses to Protestantism, whose essential postulate has always been from of old to recognise solely and alone the Bible as the source of true revelation and to refuse such a character to the tradition of the Catholic Church.

It is incomprehensible that the enemies of Catholicism and their accomplices in the high clergy have possessed the audacity to go so far. This also proves that what was prophesied in our book written before the Holy Council has found its confirmation through the launching of the same and that the enemy possessed infiltrated accomplices in the high clergy, who occupied the highest positions. As we in fact learned from well-informed sources, upon appearance of this book and after its distribution among the Council Fathers, the enemies first made a halt from bringing before the Council more daring proposals, which apart from the programme of the day they had kept in readiness for the last few days of the Council. Among such proposals was found that which had the aim of demanding the lifting of the Excommunication Bulls directed by Pope Pius XII against the Communists and their lackeys, as likewise the establishing of a peaceful coexistence between Church and Communism, and finally the condemnation of Antisemitism.

This step in retreat, which was forced by reason of the accusation in this book, may only be of partial duration. It is hoped that a careful propaganda worked out in agreement with the Kremlin will soften the resistance of those defending Holy Church in favour of the setting up of a peaceful co-existence with atheistic Communism. It is intended to attempt to weaken the defensive powers of the Church and of the free world, in which the support of the Red dictator can be relied upon, who in return would release the prelates imprisoned for many years, address letters of good wishes to his Holiness the Pope, and display further signs of visible friendship towards the Church. All this in order to bring weighty arguments in favour of the accomplices of the Kremlin, who have infiltrated into the high clergy, to give power to a lifting of the excommunication Bulls, and to bring about a pact of the Holy See with Communism.

In alliance with certain accomplices, who have nested themselves in the highest spheres of the Vatican, it is even planned in Moscow to take up diplomatic relations between Holy Church and the atheistic as well as materialistic Soviet State under the pretence that, as a result, an easing of the religious persecution in Russia could be introduced.

In reality it is the aim of the Kremlin and its agents from the ranks of the Church hierarchy to demoralise the Catholics as well as the heroic clergy who in Europe and the rest of the world fight heroically against Communism, in that they wish to provide the impression that the latter are in fact not so bad, after the Holy See has decided to take up diplomatic relations with the Soviet Union and other Communist states.

It is therefore also intended to cripple the fighting spirit of the North American Anticommunists; for through this step they would see themselves weakened in their struggle against the dark forces, which seek to draw even the United States into the Communist chaos. In a word it is intended, as we have already made clear in the introduction to the Italian edition, to cripple the defensive powers of the free world and to level the way for the final triumph of atheistic Marxism.

But the arrogance of Communism, of Freemasonry and of the Jews goes so far that they already speak of bringing the next Papal election under their control with the intention of placing one of their accomplices in the distinguished college of Cardinals on the throne of Saint Peter. Therefore they intend, with aid of the influence that they claim to have in the Vatican, to exercise pressure upon his Holiness the Pope, whose health is under much strain, in order to get him to appoint a large number of new Cardinals, even if the latter should exceed the highest number provided for. In this manner they will attain the necessary number of supporters, which is intended to secure the election of a Pontifex who will transform Holy Church into a satellite in the service of Communism, Freemasonry and the "Synagogue of Satan".

But the forces of the Antichrist do not reckon with the support which our Lord God will grant to His Church, in order to prevent that such a manoeuvre gains upper hand.

It suffices to recall that this is not the first time in history that such an attempt has been experienced. As we prove in this book by means of undoubtedly authentic documents, it was successful for the powers of the "devilish dragon" to enthrone a Cardinal as Pope who was directed by the forces of Satan and at times made it seem as though the latter might be the Lords of the Church. Christ, our Lord, who has never abandoned His Church, provided, however, such devout men as Saint Bernard, Saint

Norbert, Cardinal Aimerico, the Fathers of the Councils of Etampes, Rheims and Pisa as well as those of the Second Ecumenical Lateran Council, with the courage to act and armed their hands. They all divested Cardinal Pierleoni, this wolf in sheep's clothing who for many years was able to usurp the throne of Saint Peter, of his Papal dignity, excommunicated him and attributed to him the role of Anti-Pope, which fitted him.

The plans of the Kremlin, of Freemasonry and of the "Synagogue of Satan" are, however advanced they may seem, nevertheless nullified by the visible hand of God. For as in all times men will arise like Saint Athanasius, Saint John Chrysostom, Saint Bernard and Saint John Capistranus, who hold firm to the inspiration and strength which Christ, our Lord, chooses to provide them with, in order in this or that form to cause the disastrous plot to fail, which once again the dark forces of the Antichrist instigate to aid to victory the worldwide triumph of totalitarian Imperialism from Moscow.

We saw ourselves compelled, in the first Italian edition, to leave out eleven chapters of the fourth part from this book; and in fact by reason of the haste we had to distribute this work among the Fathers of the Second Vatican Council, before the beast could cast forth the first blows of its paws. But since we have more time at our disposal in the printing of this edition, we have added the eleven chapters in question, which are of fundamental importance for the better understanding of the devilish plot that threatens Holy Church in our days.

PREFACE TO

THE GERMAN EDITION

The following book was compiled by a group of Idealists, who are Catholics of strict belief and who, as Catholics, firmly believe that the Catholic Church is now passing through one of the most dangerous periods in its history.

In order to reveal, what dangers threaten the Catholic Church, in particular from International Communism and also from other International organisations, this Idealist group undertook the enormous task of compiling and editing this book, using numerous documents from the Middle Ages and recent times.

The Italian edition has already appeared and is already in the hands of the high clergy and other interested parties. Editions in other languages are in preparation.

The authors believe that it is vital that the German Catholic Church has this work in its hands, in order from the documents summarised in this work to be able to gain authentic information concerning historical facts from the struggle and life of the Catholic Church.

The authors must beg forgiveness that it was not possible to once again edit the German work stylistically. They know that the style in many chapters leaves much to be desired, and that repetitions also occur, which could have been prevented. The authors can only promise their highly esteemed readers that all these faults will be avoided in an eventual new edition. But they hope, nevertheless, that this work will find recognition and interest, and that their idealistic and selfless work for the well-being of our Catholic Church at least succeeds in informing the German leaders of the Catholic Church about historical facts that are certainly completely unknown to the public.

Madrid, 1963.

The Authors.

INTRODUCTION TO

THE SPANISH EDITION

A SENSATIONAL BOOK

The facts confirm that the term "sensational" applied to the book "Plot Against the Church" (Complot Contra La Iglesia) is not exaggerated. Following the first Italian edition, distributed in the Fall of 1962 among the Fathers of the Second Vatican Council, the press of different countries of the world began to make commentaries on this book, the reading of which is of capital importance not only for Catholics, but also for all free men.

It can be stated without fear of exaggeration that no book in the present century has been the object of so many commentaries in the world press; virulently unfavourable were those of communist newspapers and those controlled by Masons or Jews; and extremely favourable were those commentaries of some Catholic newspapers, which are independent of those obscure forces, and which have had, in addition, the courage and the possibility to express their points of view freely. Even one year after the distribution of the first Italian edition in the Vatican Council, the press of different countries of the world is still occupied with this extraordinary book — a thing truly unusual in matters of publicity.

In order that the reader may be informed of the importance of this work, we quote here some interesting paragraphs that the Rome correspondent of the Catholic newspaper *"Agora" of Lisbon*, edition of *March 1, 1963*, page 7, tells his readers:

"We are going to refer to a publication which came out some time ago in Rome. In addition to other information, we were able to obtain a copy of this book, which in two months became a bibliographic rarity... The book was printed in a Roman publishing house, but when the present authorities in Italy, the Christian Democrats, favourable to Marxism, took note of its publication, the copies of the thick volume of 617 pages had already been distributed among the Fathers of the Ecumenical Council. A fact which produced alarm both in the Vatican government as well as in the diplomatic world and in parties of the left. For several days the printing house was visited by the highest police authorities, who obtained only the statement that the printing of the book had been ordered, and that the cost of the edition had been paid in full. The leftist press attacked it furiously..."

"The exceptional importance of the book resides principally in one fundamental element, and that is, whether the book has one or several authors. Any person of elemental culture can divine that the compilation has been made by clerics. Naturally, the most diverse versions have appeared in respect to this matter. There are those that affirm that they (the authors) were Italian prelates, in collaboration with elements of English Catholicism; others speak of a group of priests including some bishops from an unidentified country of Southern America... This work, because of the enormous importance of its scrupulous, erudite, and minutely detailed documentation, is not just one more of those products of anti-Semitism based on the 'Protocols of the Learned Elders of Zion' (which are in no way used in the book). In conclusion, in the pages, in the arguments, and in the style of the book, is revealed the presence of Catholic clerics, in battle against the eternal heresy, which has always tended to subvert the religious, ethical, and historical bases of Catholicism, employing successively Simon the Magician, Arius, Nestor, the Albigenses, and in the present day the leftists of the Ecumenical Council."

So much for the quotations of the interesting commentary made about "The Plot Against the Church" by the Catholic Portuguese newspaper *"Agora"*.

Nevertheless, the version predominant in Rome as in the world press, is that the sensational book was prepared by no more or less than distinguished elements of *the Roman Curia*, which is, as is known, *the supreme government of the Church*, auxiliary of His Holiness the Pope in the highest functions. It is repeatedly affirmed that the work "The Plot Against the Church" is one of the greatest efforts of *the Roman Curia* to cause the destruction of those reforms which *the left wing of the Catholic clergy* is attempting to bring about, reforms which, if realized, would completely subvert *the bases* on which the Holy Church rests. There are newspapers which have been even more explicit, which affirm that it was the so-called *"Syndicate of Cardinals" who prepared the book*. It is necessary to explain that *the Masons, the communists, and their accomplices* have given the name "Syndicate of Cardinals" to the heroic group of Cardinals of the Roman Curia who are struggling in *the Second Vatican Council* to prevent *a group of the clergy* — which in a strange manner is found *at the service of Masonry and communism* — from imposing on the Holy Synod a whole series of theses, subversive, and some heretical, designed to cause the ruin of the Church. Such ruin will never be consummated, because it is written: "the gates of Hell shall not prevail against her", although the Apocalypse of Saint John also prophesises that such infernal forces will achieve great temporal triumphs, after which they will be conquered and destroyed.

So as not to prolong this Prologue, we will only transcribe in continuation that which an important Latin American newspaper has to say regarding Masonic and communist tendencies. We refer to the weekly "Tiempo" published in Mexico City by Mr. Martin Luiz *Guzman*, a distinguished *Hierarch of Masonry*, who says in referring to the Bishops called progressive: "The rebellion of the Bishops was considered as the beginning of heresy by Ottaviani and other Cardinals of the 'Syndicate'. Even the possibility that the Council would depose the Pope if it considered him a heretic, was mentioned in 'L'Osservatore Romano'. The 'Syndicate' (of Cardinals) then published, in October 1962, a libel entitled 'Plot Against the Church', having the pseudonym *'Maurice Pinay'*." *(Number 1119, Volume XIII, page 60, October 14, 1963)*. So much for the comment of the above mentioned newspaper.

What gives this book definite, provable worth is that it deals with a magnificent and imposing compilation of documents and sources of undeniable importance and authenticity, which demonstrates *with no room for doubt the existence of a great conspiracy*, which the traditional enemies of the Church have prepared against Holy Catholic Church, and against the Free World. These (enemies) are attempting to convert Catholicism into *a blind instrument in the service of communism, Masonry, and Judaism*, in order to weaken free humanity with it and to facilitate its ruin and, with this ruin, the definite victory of atheistic communism. The most useful instruments in this conspiracy are those Catholic clergymen who, betraying Holy Church, attempt to destroy her most loyal defenders, while at the same time they assist, in every way they can, *Communists, Masons and Jews* in their subversive activities.

In this edition, we attempt to alert not only Catholics, but also *all* the anti-communists of Venezuela and of Latin America, so that they may realize the grave dangers which at present threaten not only the Catholic Church, *but Christianity and the free world in general*, and so that they may offer all their support to that deserving group of Cardinals, Archbishops and Bishops who are now fighting in the Vatican Council and in their respective countries against the external and internal enemies of the Holy Church and of the free world; those enemies which, with satanic perseverance, are trying to destroy the most sacred traditions of

Catholicism, and to submerge us and our children in frightful communist slavery.

THE EDITOR,

Caracas, Venezuela, December 15, 1963.

PART ONE

THE SECRET DRIVING FORCE
OF COMMUNISM

CHAPTER ONE

COMMUNISM AS DESTROYER

Of all revolutionary systems, which throughout human history have been devised for the destruction of our civilised values, Communism is without doubt the most perfected, most efficient and most merciless. In fact it represents the most advanced epoch of the world revolution, in whose postulates it therefore not only acts to destroy a definite political, social, economic or moral institution, but also simultaneously to declare null and void the Holy Catholic Church as well as all cultural and Christian manifestations which represent our civilisation.

All revolutionary currents of Jewish origin have attacked Christianity in its different aspects with particular one-mindedness. Communism, spawned from this same revolutionary stream of thought, seeks to banish Christianity for the purpose of causing it to vanish from the face of the earth, without even the slightest trace remaining. The destructive fury of this satanic striving, which brings before the eyes of the world the most terrible pictures of terror and destruction which are possible to imagine, can only be based on the essence of Nihilism and the most evil, hate-filled rejection of everything hitherto existing. For otherwise, one would not be able to understand the indescribable insanity of its criminal acts and the spirit of destruction, of annihilation, of insult, of contradiction and of resistance by its leading personalities against everything, which represents fundamental features not only of Catholicism but of religion in general.

The purpose of Communism is, as we have indeed seen in Russia and in the other lands where it has been introduced, none other than to enslave the people in the economic, political, social, human and super-human sense, in order to make possible a minority rule through violence. From an international aspect, the goal cannot be clearer:

"To attain through violence world domination by an insignificant minority, which destroys the rest of humanity by means of materialism, terror and, if necessary, by death, completely indifferent to whether in the process the enormous majority of the population must be murdered."

The urge to murder, which has characterised the leading Soviet personages, is known well throughout the world. There are few, who upon learning of the bloody purges, which have been undertaken by the Marxists in Russia, will not be seized by shudders of horror. One needs only to recall a few details to fill the most stout hearts with fear and alarm.

"In its beginnings the Red Terror strove above all to exterminate the Russian Intelligentsia."[1] As proof of this assertion S.P. Melgunow affirms the following, in which he refers to the "Special Committees", which appeared in Russia in the first period of the Social revolution:

"The special committees are not organs of law, but of merciless extermination according to the decisions of the Communist Central Committee. The special committee is neither a commission of investigation nor a court of justice, but itself determines its own powers. It is an instrument of battle, which acts on the internal front of the civil war. It does not pardon whoever stands on the other side of the barricades, but kills them.

"It is not difficult to form ideas of how in reality this extermination proceeds, when in place of the nullified legal code only the revolutionary experience and conscience command. This conscience is subjective and experience allows complete free play to the will, which always, according to the position of the judge, takes on more or less furious forms."[2]

"Let us not carry on war against individual persons" – wrote Latsis – "but let us exterminate the Bourgeoisie as a class. Do not investigate, through study of documents and proofs, what the accused has done in words and deeds against the Soviet authority. The first question to be placed before him runs as to what class he belongs to, what is his origin, his education, his training and his profession."[3]

During the bloody dictatorship of Lenin, the Committee of Investigation under Rohrberg (Rohrberg, C.), which after the capture of

---

[1] Léon de Poncins, Las fuerzas secretas de la Revolución. Francmasoneria- Judaismo, Ediciones Fax, Madrid, 1932, p. 161.

[2] S. P. Melgunov, *La terreur rouge en Russie: de 1918 à 1923*, Payot, 1927.

[3] Latsis, "The Red Terror" of 19th November 1918.

Kiev entered this city with the White volunteers in August 1919, reported the following:

"The entire concrete floor of the large garage (this was the place where the provincial Cheka of Kiev had carried out executions) was swimming in blood, which did not flow but formed a layer of several inches; it was a grisly mixture of blood with brain and skull fragments, as well as strands of hair and other human remains. The entire walls, holed by thousands of bullets, were spattered with blood, and fragments of brain as well as head skin adhered to them.

"A drain ditch of 25 cm width and 25 cm deep and about 10 m long ran from the middle of the garage to a nearby room, where there was a subterranean outlet pipe. This drain ditch was filled to the top with blood.

"Usually, immediately after the massacre, the corpses were removed in lorries or horse-drawn wagons from the city and buried in a mass grave. In the corner of a garden we came upon an older mass grave, which contained about 80 corpses, in which we discovered signs of the most varied and unimaginable cruelties and mutilation. There were corpses from which the entrails had been removed; others had different limbs amputated and others again were cut into pieces. Some had had the eyes poked out, while the head, the face, the neck and the torso were covered with deep wounds. Further on we found a corpse with an axe in the breast, while others had no tongues. In a corner of the mass grave we discovered many legs and arms severed from the trunk."[4]

The enormous number of corpses, which have already been laid to the account of Communist Socialism and which increase terrifyingly all the while, will perhaps never be exactly known, but it exceeds everything imaginable. It is not possible to learn the exact number of the victims. All estimates lie below the real figure."

In the Edinburgh newspaper "The Scotsman" of 7th November, 1923, Professor Sarolea gave the following figures:

"28 Bishops; 1,219 priests; 6,000 Professors and teachers; 9,000 doctors; 54,000 Officers; 260,000 soldiers; 70,000 Policemen; 12,950 estate owners; 355,250 intellectuals and of the free professions; 193,290 workers and 215,000 peasants."

---

[4] S. P. Melgunov, op. cit., p. 161.

The Information Committee of Denikin on the Bolshevistic intrigue during the years 1918-1919 records in a treatise about the Red Terror in these two years "one million, seven hundred thousand victims."[5] In the "Roul" of 3rd August 1923, Kommin makes the following observation:

"During the winter of 1920 there existed in the USSR, 52 governments with 52 Special Committees (Chekas), 52 Special Departments and 52 revolutionary courts. Besides countless subsidiary Chekas, transport-networks, courts on the railways as well as troops for internal security, there were mobile courts, which were dispatched to mass executions in the places concerned."

To this list of courts of torture must be added the special departments, i.e., 16 army and divisional courts. All in all one must estimate 1000 torture chambers. If it is borne in mind that at that time district committees also existed in addition, then the number rises further. In addition the number of governments of the USSR increased. Siberia, the Crimea and the Far East were conquered. The number of Chekas grew in geometrical ratio.

According to Soviet data (in the year 1920 when the terror had still not ebbed and the reporting of news was not restricted) it is possible to establish an average figure for every court; the curve of executions rises from one to fifty (in the great cities) and up to one hundred in the regions recently conquered by the Red Army. The crisis of terror was periodic and then ceased; in this manner one can daily estimate the (modest) figure of five victims..., which, multiplied with the thousand courts, gives a result of five thousand, and thus for the year roughly one and a half million. We recall this indescribable slaughter, not because in its totality it was either the most numerous or the most merciless to arise from the special situation and inflamed passions consequent on the first victories of the Bolshevist revolution, but because today, forty-five years after these mass executions took place, all this might otherwise be obliterated from the present Communist picture, even for the persons who were contemporaries of the events and who today, still alive, have forgotten those tragedies with the ease with which people forget not only unpleasant events which do not directly concern them, but even those to which they fell victim.

Unhappily, time has shown us a truly demonic excess of Communism in its murderous activity, about which we give no details and do not present the monstrous statistics because all this is known to us. Several of

---

[5] Léon de Poncins, op. cit., p. 164-165.

these cruel bloodbaths have only taken place recently, so that one still seems to hear the lament of the persecuted, the death-rattle of the dying and the dumb, the terrible and haunting complaint of the corpses.[6]

It may suffice to recall the recent giant bloodbaths in Hungary, Poland, East Germany and Cuba as well as the earlier mass killings by Stalin and the annihilation of millions of Chinese through the Communist regime of Mao-Tse-Tung. But also the Communist attempts at revolution, which failed to achieve lasting permanence, such as that of Bela Kun who occupied Hungary in such a brutal way in the middle of 1919; of Spain in 1936, where the Bolsheviks gained control of Madrid and parts of the Spanish provinces and murdered more than 16,000 priests, monks and nuns, as well as 12 Bishops; further the happily unsuccessful attempt in Germany, its most successful realisation in the Red Republic of Bavaria in the year 1919. All these attempts were in fact orgies of 1918, which was directed by Hugo Haase, and which had blood and unrestrained bestiality.

One must also not forget that this Apocalyptic storm, which brings a flood of corpses, blood and tears, falls upon the world with the sole goal: to destroy not only the Catholic Church but the entire Christian civilisation.[7] Before this shattering picture the world asks itself with heavy heart: who can hate our Christian features in such a form and try to destroy them with such Godless fury? Who has become capable of instigating this bloody mechanics of annihilation? Who can with such insensitivity direct and order this monstrous criminal process? And reality answers us completely without doubt that the [Bolshevik] Jews are those responsible, as will later be proved.

---

[6] A complete statistical account of the victims of Communism has been published in the little volume "Rivelazione d'intéresse mondiale", Vermijon, Rome 1957, whose author for his part has taken information from the newspaper "Russkaja Mysl" of 30 November 1947, published in France.

[7] Traian Romanescu, *La gran conspiración judia*, 3rd ed., Mexico, D.F., 1961, p. 272.

CHAPTER TWO

THE CREATORS OF THE SYSTEM

There is absolutely no doubt, that the Jews are the inventors of Communism; for they have been the instigators of the dogma, upon which that monstrous system is built, which at present with absolute power rules the greatest part of Europe and Asia, which stirs up the lands of America and with progressive certainty floods over all Christian peoples of the world like a deadly cancerous growth, like a tumour, which steadily devours the core of the free nations, without apparently an effective means of cure being found against this disease.

But the Jews are also the inventors and directors of the Communist methods, of effective tactics of struggle, of the insensitive and totally inhuman government policy and of aggressive international strategy. It is a completely proven fact that the Communist theoreticians were all Jews, unheeded of what system the Jews lastingly use, as well as the theoreticians and the experienced revolutionaries, which has veiled from the eyes of the people, where they lived, their true origin.

1. Karl Heinrich Marx was a German Jew, whose real name was Kissel Mordekay, born in Trier, Rhineland, son of a Jewish lawyer. Before his famous work "Das Kapital" which contains the fundamental idea of theoretical Communism, whose concepts he strove with inexhaustible activity up to his death in the year 1887 to spread over the world, he had written and published with the Jew Engels in the year 1848 the Communist Manifesto in London; between 1843 and 1847 he had formulated in England the first modern interpretation of Hebrew Nationalism in his articles, as in the publication in the year 1844 in the periodical "Deutsch-Franzosische Jahrbücher" (German-French Year Books) under the title "Concerning the Jewish question", which shows an ultra-national tendency.
2. Friedrich Engels, creator of the "First International", and close collaborator of Marx, was a Jew and born in Bremen (Germany). His

father was a Jewish cotton merchant of the city. Engels died in the year 1894.

3. Karl Kautski, whose real name was Kraus, was the author of the book "The Beginnings of Christianity", in which he mainly combats the principles of Christianity. He was the most important interpreter of Karl Marx and in 1887 published "The Economic Doctrine of Karl Marx Made Intelligible for All." "The Bloodbath of Chisinaw and the Jewish Question", in the year 1903, "The Class Struggle", which for Mao-Tse-Tung in China was the fundamental book for Communist instruction; and the work with the title "The Vanguard of Socialism", in the year 1921. He was also the author of the "Socialist Programme" from Erfurt/Germany. This Jew was born in the year 1854 in Prague and died in 1938 in the Hague (Holland).

4. Ferdinand Lassalle, Jew, born in the year 1825 in Breslau. He had interfered in the democratic revolution of 1848. In the year 1863 he published his work entitled "Open Answers", in which he outlined a plan of revolution for the German workers. Since then he worked tirelessly for a "Socialist" crusade, which was directed at the rebellion of the workers. For this purpose he published a further work under the title "Capital and Labour."

5. Eduard Bernstein. A Jew born in Berlin in the year 1850. His principal works are "Assumptions concerning Socialism", "Forward, Socialism", "Documents of Socialism", "History and Theory of Socialism", "Social Democracy of Today in Theory and Practice", "The Duties of Social Democracy", and "German Revolution". In all his writings he expounds the Communist teaching and bases it on the views of Marx. In the year 1918 he became Finance minister of the German Socialist state, which, however, could fortunately only maintain itself a few months.

6. Jacob Lastrow, Max Hirsch, Edgar Loening, Wirschauer, Babe, Schatz, David Ricardo and many other writers of theoretical Communism were Jews. In all lands are found writers, almost exclusively Jewish, who preach Communism to the masses, although with many opportunities they strive to give the appearance in their writings of a feeling of humanity and brotherhood. We have indeed already seen in practice what this means.[8]

However theoretical all Jews mentioned may have been, they were not satisfied with setting up the doctrinaire bases, but each one of them was an experienced revolutionary, who busied himself in whatever particular land he found himself, to factually prepare the upheaval, to direct or to give it

---

[8] Data taken from Traian Romanescu, op. cit., pp. 19-23.

support. As leaders or members of revolutionary associations known only to one another, they took more and more active part in the development or Bolshevism. But apart from these Jews, who in the main were regarded as theoreticians, we find that almost all materialist leaders, who develop Communist tactics, also belong to the same race and carry out their task with the greatest efficacy.

As indisputable examples two movements of this type can be recorded:

A) In the year 1918 Germany was showpiece of a Communist, Jew directed revolution. The Red Councils of the republic of Munich was Jewish, as its instigators prove: Liebknecht, Rosa Luxemburg, Kurt Eisner and many others. With the fall of the monarchy the Jews gained control of the country and the German government. With Ministers of State Haase and Landsberg appear Kautsky, Kohn and Herzfeld. The Finance minister was likewise a Jew, had his racial fellow Bernstein as assistant and the minister of the Interior, likewise a Jew, and sought the collaboration of his racial brother, Doctor Freund, who helped him in his work.

Kurt Eisner, the President of the Bavarian Councils Republic, was the instigator of the Bolshevist revolution in Munich.

"Eleven little men made the revolution", said Kurt Eisner in the intoxication of triumph to his colleague, the Minister Auer. It is no more than right to preserve the unforgettable memory of these little men, who were, in fact, the Jews Max Lowenberg, Doctor Kurt Rosenfeld, Caspar Wollheim, Max Rothschild, Carl Arnold, Kranold, Rosenhek, Birnbaum, Reis and Kaisser. These ten with Kurt Eisner van Israelowitsch led the presidency of the Revolutionary court of Germany. All eleven were Freemasons and belonged to the secret lodge N.° which had its seat in Munich at No. 51 Briennerstrasse.[9]

The first cabinet of Germany in the year 1918 was composed of Jews.

1. Preuss, Minister of the Interior.
2. Freund, Minister of the Interior.
3. Landsberg, Finance Minister.
4. Karl Kautski, Finance Minister.
5. Schiffer, Finance Minister.

---

[9] Msgr. Jouin, *Le péril judéo-maçonnique.* (5 vols. 1919-1927). Vol. I, p. 161.

6. Eduard Bernstein, secretary of the State Treasury.

7. Fritz Max Cohen, director of the official information service. (This Jew was earlier correspondent of the Jewish "Frankfurter Zeitung").

The second "German Socialist government" of 1918 was formed of the following Jews:

1. Hirsch, Minister of the Interior.
2. Rosenfeld, Justice Minister.
3. Futran, Minister of education.
4. Arndt, Minister of education.
5. Simon, State secretary of finances.
6. Kastenberg, director of the department of science and art.
7. Strathgen, director of colonial department.
8. Wurm, secretary of food.
9. Merz, Weil, Katzenstein, Stern, Lowenberg, Frankel, Schlesinger, Israelowitz, Selingsohn, Laubenheim, etc., took up high posts in the ministries.

Among the remaining Jews who controlled the sectors vital to life of the German state, which had been defeated through the American intervention in the war, were found in the year 1918, and later:

1. Kohen, President of the German workers and soldiers councils (similar to the Soviet council of soldiers and workers of Moscow in the same year).
2. Ernst, police president of Berlin.
3. Sinzheimer, police president of Frankfurt.
4. Lewy, police president of Hessen.
5. Kurt Eisner, Bavarian state president.
6. Jaffe Bavarian finance minister.
7. Brentano, Industry, trade and transport minister.
8. Talheimer, minister in Württemberg.
9. Heimann, another minister in Württemberg.
10. Fulda, in the government of Hesse.
11. Theodor Wolf, chief editor of the newspaper "Berliner Tageblatt."
12. Gwiner, director of the "Deutsche Bank".[10]

---

[10] Traian Romanescu, op. cit., pp. 259-260.

B) Hungary in the year 1919. On 20th March 1919 the Jew Bela Kun (Cohn) took over power in Hungary and proclaimed the Hungarian Soviet republic, which from that moment on was submerged in a hair-raising sea of blood. Twenty-eight Commissars formed with him the new government and of these 18 were Israelites. That is an unheard of proportion, when one bears in mind that in Hungary lived one and a half million Israelites compared to 22 million inhabitants. The 18 Commissars held the actual control of rulership in their hands and the eight Gentile Commissars could do nothing against them.[11]

"More than 90% of the members of the government and the confidence men of Bela Kun were also Jews. Here follows a list of members of the Bela Kun government:

1. Bela Kun, general secretary of the Jewish government.
2. Sandor Garbai, "official" president of the government, who was used by the Jews as a Hungarian man of straw.
3. Peter Agoston, deputy of the general secretary; Jew.
4. Dr. E. Landler, Peoples commissar for internal affairs; Jew.
5. Bela Vago, deputy of Landler, a Jew with the name Weiss.
6. E. Hamburger, Agriculture Commissar; Jew.
7. Vantus, deputy of Hamburger; Jew.
8. Csizmadia, deputy of Hamburger; Hungarian.
9. Nyisztor, deputy of Hamburger; Hungarian.
10. Varga, Commissar for financial affairs; Jew by name Weichselbaum.
11. Szkely, deputy of Varga; Jew by name Schlesinger.
12. Kunftz, Education minister; Jew by name Kunstater.
13. Kukacs, deputy of Kunfi; a Jew, who in reality was chilled Lowinger and was the son of the director-general of a banking house in Budapest.
14. D. Bokanyi, Minister of labour; Hungarian.
15. Fiedler, deputy of Bokanyi; Jew.
16. Jozsef Pogany, War Commissar; a Jew, who in reality was called Schwartz.
17. Szanto, deputy of Pogany; a Jew named Schreiber.
18. Tibor Szamuelly, deputy of Pogany, a Jew named Samuel.
19. Matyas Rakosi, trade Minister; a Jew, who in reality was called Matthew Roth Rosenkrantz, present Communist dictator.
20. Ronai, Commissar of law; a Jew named Rosentstegl.
21. Ladai, deputy of Ronai; Jew.

---

[11] J. J. Tharaud, *Causerie sur Israël.* Marcelle Lesage, 1926, p. 27.

22. Erdelyi, Commissar of supply; a Jew named Eisenstein.
23. Vilmas Boehm, Socialisation Commissar; Jew.
24. Hevesi, deputy of Boehm; a Jew named Honig.
25. Dovsak, second deputy of Boehm; Jew.
26. Oszkar Jaszai, Commissar of nationalities; a Jew named Jakubovits.
27. Otto Korvin, political examining Commissar; a Jew named Klein.
28. Kerekes, state lawyer; a Jew named Krauss.
29. Biro, chief of the political police; a Jew named Blau.
30. Seidem, adjutant of Biro; Jew.
31. Oszkar Faber, Commissar for liquidation of Church property; Jew.
32. J. Czerni, commander of the terrorist bands, which were known by the name "Lenin youth"; Hungarain.
33. Illes, supreme police Commissar; Jew.
34. Szabados, supreme police Commissar; a Jew named Singer.
35. Kalmar, supreme police Commissar; German Jew.
36. Szabo, supreme police Commissar; Ruthenian Jew, who in reality was called Schwarz.
37. Vince, Peoples Commissar of the city of Budapest, who in reality was called Weinstein.
38. M. Kraus, Peoples Commissar of Budapest; Jew.
39. A. Dienes, Peoples Commissar of Budapest; Jew.
40. Lengyel, President of the Austro-Hungarian bank; a Jew named Levkovits.
41. Laszlo, President of the Communist revolutionary court; a Jew, who in reality was called Lowy.[12]

In this government which for a time held Hungary in thrall, the chief of the Hungarian Cheka Szamuelly, besides Bela Kun, distinguished himself through countless crimes and plunderings. While the latter rode through the land in his luxury automobile (with the symbol of a large gallows mounted on the vehicle, and accompanied by his capable Jewish woman secretary R. S. Salkind, alias Semliachkay), the former travelled through Hungary in his special train and sowed terror and death, as a contemporary witness describes:

"That train of death travelled snorting through the black Hungarian nights; where it stopped, one saw people hanging from trees and blood which ran on the ground. Along the railway line naked and mutilated

---

[12] Traian Romanescu, op. cit., pp. 203-205.

corpses were to be seen. Szamuelly dictated his judgements in his train, and whoever was forced to enter never lived to tell the tale of what he saw. Szamuelly lived constantly in this train. Thirty selected terrorists ensured his security. Selected executioners accompanied him. The train consisted of two saloon wagons, two first-class wagons, which were occupied by the terrorists, and two third-class wagons for the victims. In the latter executions were carried out. The floor of this wagon was stiff with blood. The corpses were thrown out of the windows, while Szamuelly sat comfortably in the elegant workroom of his compartment which was upholstered in rose-coloured damask and decorated with polished mirrors. With a movement of the hand he decided over life or death."[13]

---

[13] Cécile de Tormay, *Le livre proscrit*, Plon Nourrit, 1919, p. 204.

CHAPTER THREE

THE HEAD OF COMMUNISM

There exists therefore not the slightest doubt, that the Marxist theory (Communism) is a Jewish work, just as is also its every action, which aims at putting this doctrine into practice.

Before the final establishing of Bolshevism in Russia the directors and organisers of all Communist movements in their entirety were almost solely Jews, just as the great majority of the true organisers of the revolutions were to which they gave the impetus. But in Russia, as the first land where Bolshevism finally triumphed, and where it was and still is the fulcrum or driving force for the Communising of the world, the Jewish paternity of the system of organisation and of Soviet praxis also allows no doubt or error. According to the irrefutable data, which has been fully and completely proved and recognised by all impartial writers who have dealt with this theme, the Communist work of the Jews in the land of the Czars is so powerful that it would be useless to deny this disastrous triumph as their monopoly.

It suffices to recall the names of those who have formed the governments and the principal leading organs in the Soviet Union, in order to know what one has immediately to think of the clear and categorical proof of the evidence.

I - MEMBERS OF THE FIRST COMMUNIST GOVERNMENT OF MOSCOW (1918)

(Council of Peoples Commissars)

1. Ilich Ulin (Vladimir Ilich Ulianov or Nikolaus Lenin). President of the Supreme Soviet, Jew on mother's side. His mother was called Blank, a Jewess of German origin.

2. Lew Davinovich Bronstein (Leo Trotsky), Commissar for the Red Army and the Navy; Jew.
3. Iosiph David Vissarionovich Djugashvili-Kochba (Joseph Vissarianovich Stalin), Nationalities Commissar; descendant of Jews from Georgia.
4. Chicherin; Commissar for foreign affairs; Russian.
5. Apfelbaum (Grigore Zinoviev), Commissar for internal affairs; Jew.
6. Kohen (Volodarsky), Commissar for press and propaganda; Jew.
7. Samuel Kaufmann, Commissar for the landed property of the State; Jew.
8. Steinberg, law Commissar; Jew.
9. Schmidt, Commissar for public works; Jew.
10. Ethel Knigkisen (Liliana), Commissar for supply, Jewess.
11. Pfenigstein, Commissar for the settlement of refugees; Jew.
12. Schlichter (Vostanoleinin) Commissar for billetings (confiscation of private houses for the Reds); Jew.
13. Lurie (Larin), President of the supreme economic council; Jew.
14. Kukor (Kukorsky), Trade Commissar; Jew.
15. Spitzberg, Culture Commissar; Jew.
16. Urisky (Radomilsky), Commissar for "elections"; Jew.
17. Lunacharsky, Commissar for public schools. Russian.
18. Simasko, Commissar for health; Jew.
19. Protzian, Agriculture Commissar; Armenian.

In the Appendix at the end of this volume can be found the interesting and illustrative lists of the Jewish officials in all the government bodies of the Soviet Union, the Communist Party, the Red Army, the Secret Police, the trade unions, etc.

Of a total of 502 offices of first rank in the organisation and direction of the Communist revolution in Russia and in the direction of the Soviet State during the first years of its existence, no less than 459 posts are occupied by Jews, while only 43 of these offices have been occupied by Gentiles of different origin. Who then has accordingly carried out this terrible revolution? The Gentiles perhaps? Another statistic, which was published in Paris by the counter-revolutionary newspaper "Le Russe Nationaliste", after the victory of the Jewish Communists in Russia, reveals that of 554 Communist leaders of first rank in different offices the racial composition was as follows:

Jews   447

Lithuanians	43
Russians	30
Armenians	13
Germans	12
Finns	3
Poles	2
Georgians	2
Czechs	1
Hungarians	1

During the Second World War, and from then on up to our present time, the Jewish clique which rules the Union of Socialist Soviet Republics, continues to be very numerous, for at the head of the names stands Stalin himself, who for a long time was regarded as a Georgian of pure descent. But it has been revealed that he belongs to the Jewish race; for Djougachvili, which is his surname, means "Son of Djou", and Djou is a small island in Persia, whither many banished Portuguese "Gypsies" migrated, who later settled in Georgia.

Today it is almost completely proved that Stalin had Jewish blood, although he neither confirmed nor denied the rumours, about which mutterings began in this direction.[14]

Let us look at a list of the Soviet officials in the government of Stalin:

1. Zdanov (Yadanov), who in reality was called Liphshitz, foriner commander in the defence of Leningrad during the 2nd world war. Member of the Politbüro up to 1945 and one of the instigators of the decision which excluded Tito from the Cominform in the year 1948 and who shortly afterwards died.
2. Lavrenty Beria, Chief of the M.V.D. Police and of Soviet heavy industry, member of the Soviet Atom industry, who was executed upon orders of Malenkov, and in fact for the same reason for which Stalin liquidated Yagoda.
3. Lazar Kaganovich, director of Soviet heavy industry, member of the Politburo from 1944 to 1952, then member of the Presidium and at present President of the Supreme Presidium of the USSR.

---

[14] Bernard Hutton, French magazine *Constéllation*, March 1962, no. 167, p. 202.

4. Malenkov (Georgi Maximilianovich Molenk), member of the Politburo and Orgburo until 1952, then member of the Supreme Presidium, President of the Ministerial Council after the death of Stalin; Minister in the government of Bulganin since 1955. He is a Jew from Ornsenburg, not a Cossack, as is asserted. The name of his father, Maximilian Malenk, is typical for a Russian Jew. In addition there is a very important detail, which reveals the true origin of Malenkov and also of Khrushchev. The present wife of Malenkov is the Jewess Pearlmutter, known as "Comrade Schans chuschne" who was Minister (Commissar) for the fish industry in the Soviet government in the year 1938. If Malenkov had not been a Jew, it is extremely unlikely that he would have married a Jewess, and the latter would also not have married him. There exists no official description of the life of Malenkov. This is certainly to be attributed to the fact that he does not want his Jewish origin to be discovered.

5. Nikolaus Salomon Khrushchev, present chief (1963) of the Soviet Communist party, member of the Politburo since 1939, i.e. since the year when Malenkov was chosen member of the Orgburo. He is the brother of Madame Malenkov, i.e. of the Jewess Pearlmutter. Khrushchev is a Jew and his real name is Pearlmutter. Also, the present wife of Khrushchev, Nina, as well as the wives of Mikoyan, Voroshilov, Molotov, etc., are Jewesses.

6. Marshal Nikolaus Bulganin, at present first Soviet minister, former bank official, was one of the ten Jewish members of the Commissariat for the liquidation of private banks in the year 1919.

7. Anastasio Josifovich Mikoyan, member of the Politburo since 1935, member of the Supreme Presidium since 1952, Trade Minister and Vice-president in the Malenkov government. He is an Armenian Jew and not a true Armenian as is believed.

8. Kruglov, chief of the M.V.D. after Beria. Upon command of Kruglov the imprisoned Jewish doctors were released who had been imprisoned by Riumin, sub-chief of the police, during the rulership of Beria, in the year 1953. Likewise Jew.

9. Alexander Kosygin, member of the Politburo up to 1952, afterwards deputy in the Supreme Presidium and Minister for light industry and food in the Malenkov government.

10. Nikolaus Schvernik, member of the Politburo up to 1952, then member of the Supreme Presidium and member of the Presidium of the Central Committee of the Communist party; Jew.

11. Andreas Andreievich Andreiev, who was known as the "Politbureaucrat" of 3 A, member of the Politburo between 1931 and 1952, Jew from Galicia (Poland). He writes under a Russian pseudonym.

12. P. K. Ponomareno, member of the Orgburo in the year 1952; afterwards member of the highest Presidium and culture minister in the Malenkov government.

13. P. F. Yudin (Jew), deputy member of the highest Presidium and titulary of the Ministry for building material in the Malenkov government in the year 1953.

14. Mihail Pervukin, member of the Presidium of the central committee of the Communist party since 1953.

15. N. Schatalin, official in the sub-secretariat of the Central Committee of the Community Party.

16. K. P. Gorschenin, Justice minister in the government of Malenkov.

17. D. Ustinov (Zambinovich), Soviet ambassador in Athens (Greece) up to the second world war; defence minister in the Malenkov government.

18. V. Merkulov, Minister for state control at the time of Malenkov.

19. A. Zasyadko, Minister for the coal industry under Malenkov.

20. Cherburg, Soviet propaganda chief.

21. Milstein. one of the Soviet espionage chiefs.

22. Ferentz Kiss, Chief of the Soviet espionage service in Europe.

23. Postschreibitscher (Poschebicheve), former private secretary of Stalin, at present chief of the secret archives of the Kremlin.

24. Ilya Ehrenburg, delegate for Moscow in the Supreme Soviet, Communist writer; likewise Jew.

25. Mark Spivak, delegate from Stalino (Ukraine) in the Supreme Soviet of Moscow.

26. Rosalia Goldenberg, delegate from Birobudjan in the Supreme Soviet.

27. Anna E. Kaluger, delegate of Bessarabia in the Supreme Soviet, Her brother, not Koluger, but Calugaru in Rumanian, is a Communist official in the government of Rumania.

Also Kalinin, one of the great Soviet officials under Stalin who died some time ago, was a Jew.[15]

It is only too well known, that the Anti-Semitism of Stalin was a misrepresentation of the facts, and that the blood bath among the Jews

---

[15] Traian Romanescu, op. cit., pp. 174-176.

(Trotskyists) which he carried out in order to assert his power, was performed by other Jews. In the last instance the struggle between the Jew Trotsky and the Jew Stalin was a struggle between parties for control over the Communist government, which they created, it was purely a family dispute. As proof, the following list of Commissars for Foreign Affairs, during the period when Stalin got rid of some certain Jews, who had become dangerous for his personal power.

1. Maxim Maximovich Litvinoff, Minister for Foreign Affairs up to 1939, when he was replaced by Molotov. He afterwards occupied high offices in the same ministry up to his death in February 1952. He was born in Poland as son of the Jew Meer Genokh Moiseevich Vallakh, a bank clerk. In order to conceal his real name Maxim Moiseevich Vallakh, Litvinoff used various pseudonyms during his real career, among them Finkelstein, Ludwig Nietz, Maxim Harryson, David Mordecay, Felix, and finally, when he became an official in the Communist regime of Russia, he took on the name of Litvinoff or Litvinov. When this Jew was replaced by Molotov in the Year 1939, the Jews of the western world and the entire Jewish-Freemasonic press began to cry out that he had been removed by Stalin because he was a "Jew", but they kept quiet afterwards concerning the fact that up to his death Litvinov remained in the ministry. Why also say this, if it was not of interest for the conspiracy? In the Memoirs of Litvinov, which were published after his death, he wrote that in his opinion nothing would alter in Soviet Russia after the death of Stalin. In fact, Stalin died a year after Litvinov and nothing was altered in the Soviet's internal and external policies.

What the West calls change in the policy of the USSR, is simply nothing further than a skilled propaganda for the necessities of the plan for world rule through the Jews. Nothing has altered since the death of Stalin. A certain unrest may have arisen on account of the lack of a new leader of the stature of Stalin or Lenin, that is all. For this reason the Jewish- Freemasonic conspirators of the West wish to paint the Soviet-Communist black raven over with the glittering colours of "Pacifism", "Coexistence", "Human friendliness", etc., in order to introduce it to the world as something harmless, until a dictator with the same lusts of his predecessors arises.

When Litvinov asserted that nothing would alter with the death or Stalin, he knew very well, that this would be so, because Stalin was nothing more than one of the handymen of the Jewish band, which rules the

USSR, and because after him other Jews would be at hand, to carry on the plan of world domination, for which Bulganin, Baruch, Reading, Thorez, Mendes France, David Ben Gurion and many others are cooperating.

In continuing the list of Jews in the Ministry for Foreign Affairs of the USSR, we mention:

2. Andreas Januarevich Vishinsky, now dead, who was foreign minister of the USSR before the death of Stalin and afterwards permanent representative of the Soviet Union in the UNO. There he missed no opportunity to sling his obscenities against the non-Communist lands, exactly as in the times when he was "Peoples Judge." His Jewish name was Abraham Januarevin.
3. Jakob Malik, Soviet representative in the UNO and a great personality in the Soviet diplomatic hierarchy; Jew.
4. Valerian Zorin, for a time ambassador in London and likewise a great figure of Soviet diplomacy, who changes his post according to necessity.
5. Andrei Gromyko, diplomat, Minister for foreign affairs since 1958.
6. Alexander Panyushkin, former Soviet ambassador in Washington, ambassador in Peking during the year 1955, who is regarded as the actual dictator of Red China.
7. Zambinovich (Ustinov), ambassador in Athens up to 1940.
8. Admiral Radionovich, ambassador in Athens between 1945 and 1946, i.e., as the Communist coup d'état in Greece was prepared; Jew.
9. Constantin Umansky, ambassador in Washington during the Second World War and afterwards official in the Ministry for foreign affairs in Moscow.
10. Manuilsky, former representative in the Ukraine and in the UNO, at present President of the Ukraine; likewise Jew.
11. Ivan Maisky, ambassador in London during the war, afterwards high official of the Foreign Ministry in Moscow.
12. Madame Kolontay, ambassador in Stockholm until her death in March 1952; Jewess.
13. Daniel Solod, ambassador in Cairo in the year 1955. The latter, supported by a Jewish group which belongs to the diplomatic corps in Cairo, directs the Israelite conspiracy inside the Arab world under Soviet diplomatic protection, without the Egyptian government noticing this. This government should not forget that David Ben Gurion, first minister of Israel, as well as Golda

Meyerson, Israel's Minister in Moscow, are Russian Jews like David Solod.

At present, according to confirmed data, 80% to 90% of the key positions in all ministries in Moscow and the remaining Soviet republics are occupied by Jews.

"I do not believe that there can be any doubt of the origin of all those who occupy the highest posts in Moscow since the first moment of the revolution; for the Russians it is a lamentable fact that after all this course of time things are much worse, for the number of Jews who live in Russia has increased in frightening degree. All important leading positions are in their hands..."[16]

As in Russia the countries of Europe where Bolshevism has gained control, are also completely ruled by a Jewish minority; the latter always appears in the direction of the Communist government with an iron, criminal and merciless hand, so as to attain the utter enslaving of the native citizens through an insignificant group of Jews.

More convincing than any other proof is an exact surveying of the most principal leaders of the Bolshevist governments of Europe, which are always found in the hands of the Israelites. We will quote the most principal ones:

A - HUNGARY

1. The most important Communist leader since the occupation of this land by Soviet troops is Mathias Rakosi, an Israelite, whose real name is Mathew Roth Rosenkranz, and who was born in the year 1892 in Szabadka.
2. Ferenk Münnich, First Minister in Hungary in the year 1959 after Janos Kadar.
3. Erno Gero, Minister of the Interior until 1954.
4. Szebeni, Minister of the Interior before the Jew Gero.
5. General Laszlo Kiros, Jew, Minister of Interior since July 1954, simultaneously chief of the A.V.O., i.e. the Hungarian police, which corresponds to the Soviet M.V.D.

---

[16] Duque de la Victoria, *Israel manda*. Editora Latino Americana, S. A., Mexico, 1955, pp. 287-288.

6. General Peter Gabor, chief of the Communist political police of Hungary up to 1953, a Jew, who in reality was called Benjamin Ausspitz and was earlier a tailor in Satorai- Jeujhely, Hungary.

7. Varga, State secretary for economic planning; a Jew, who in reality is called Weichselbaum; former Minister of the Bela Kun government. He was also President of the supreme economic council.

8. Beregi, Minister for foreign affairs.

9. Julius Egry, Agriculture minister of the Hungarian Peoples Republic.

10. Zoltan Vas, President of the supreme economic council; a Jew, who in reality was called Weinberger.

11. Josef Reval, the editor of the Hungarian press and director of the Red newspaper "Szabad Nep" (The Free People); a Jew; who is really called Moses Kahana.

12. Revai (another), Minister for national education; a Jew named Rabinovits.

13. Josef Gero, transport minister; a Jew named Singer.

14. Mihaly Farkas, Minister for national defence; a Jew named Freedman.

15. Veres, Minister of State.

16. Vajda, Minister of State.

17. Szanto, Commissar for purging of enemies of the State, in the year 1951 sent by Moscow; a Jew named Schreiber; former member of the Bela Kun government.

18. Guyla Dessi, Justice Minister up to 1955; today chief of the secret police.

19. Emil Weil, Hungarian ambassador in Washington; he is the Jewish doctor who tortured Cardinal Mindszenty.

Among other important Jewish officials to be mentioned are:

1. Imre Szirmay, director of the Hungarian radio company.

2. Gyula Garay, judge of the Communist "Peoples court of Budapest."

3. Colonel Caspo, Sub-chief of the secret police.

4. Professor Laszlo Benedek, Jewish dictator for educational questions.

The sole important Communist of Gentile origin was the Freemason Laszlo Rajk, former minister for foreign affairs, who was sentenced and executed by his Jewish "brothers" for his "betrayal."

B - CZECHOSLOVAKIA

1. Clemens Gottwald, one of the founders of the Communist party in Czechoslovakia and president of the country between 1948 and 1953; a Jew, who died shortly after Stalin.
2. Vladimir Clementis, former Communist minister of Czechoslovakia for foreign affairs, "sentenced and executed" in the year 1952; Jew.
3. Vaclav David, present foreign minister of Czechoslovakia (1955); Jew.
4. Rudolf Slaski, former general secretary of the Communist party of Czechoslovakia, "sentenced" in the year 1952; a Jew by name of Rudolf Salzmann.
5. Firi Hendrich, present general secretary of the Communist party; Jew.
6. Andreas Simon, sentenced in the year 1952; a Jew named Otto Katz.
7. Gustav Bares, assistant of the general secretary of the Communist party; Jew.
8. Josef Frank, former assistant of the general secretary of the Communist party, "sentenced" in the year 1952; Jew.

C - POLAND

1. Boleislaw Bierut, President of Poland up to 1954; Jew.
2. Jakob Berman, general secretary of the Communist party of Poland; Jew.
3. Julius Kazuky (Katz), minister for foreign affairs of Poland, who is well known for his violent speeches in the UNO; Jew.
4. Karl Swierezewskv, former vice-minister for national defence, who was murdered by the Anti-Communist Ukrainian country population in south Poland (the mass of the people is not always amorphous); Jew.
5. Josef Cyrankiewicz, first minister of Poland since 1954, after Bierut; Jew.
6. Hillary Mink, Vice-prime minister of Poland since 1954; Jew.
7. Zenon Kliszko, minister of justice; Jew.
8. Tadaus Kochcanowiecz, minister of labour; Jew.

The sole important Polish Communist of Gentile origin is Wladislaw Gomulka who was removed from political leadership since 1949, when he lost his post as first minister. Sooner or later he will share the same fate as Rajk in Hungary.

D - RUMANIA

1. Anna Pauker, Jewess, former minister for foreign affairs of the "Rumanian Peoples Republic", and spy No. 1 of the Kremlin in Rumania up to the month of June 1952. Since then she has remained in the shadows in Bucharest up to the present day, naturally in freedom. This Jewish hyena, who was originally called Anna Rabinsohn, is the daughter of a rabbi, who came to Rumania from Poland. She was born in the province of Moldau (Rumania) in the year 1892.

2. Ilka Wassermann, former private secretary of Anna Pauker, at present the real directress of the ministry for foreign affairs.

3. Josef Kisinevski, the present agent No. 1 of the Kremlin in Rumania, member of the central Committee of the Communist party and vice-president of the council of ministers. He is a Jew and comes from Bessarabia; his correct name is Jakob Broitman. Also he is the real chief of the Communist party of Rumania, although "officially" the general secretary of the party is the Rumanian locksmith Gheorghe Gheorghiu Dez, who, however, only plays the simple role of a political front. Kisinevski took his present pseudonym from the name of the city of Kisinau in Bessarabia, where before the arrival of the Red Army he owned a tailor's workshop.

4. Teohari Georgescu, minister for internal affairs in the Communist government of Bucharest between 1945 and 1952; at the present time he has been reduced to a second-rank post, although he was "officially" "expelled" from the Communist party. He finds himself in the same position as Anna Pauker. His real name is Baruch Tescovich. He is a Jew from the Rumanian Danube harbour of Galatz.

5. Avram Bunaciu, likewise a Jew, is the present (1955) general secretary of the Presidium of the great national assembly of the "Rumanian peoples republic", i.e. the real leader of this assembly, for the "official" president Petru Groza is only an old Freemasonic marionette, who is married to a Jewess and plays only a purely static role. Avram Bunaciu is called in reality Abraham Gutman (Gutman translated into Rumanian is the corresponding name for "Bunaciu", i.e. the pseudonym taken on by this Jew).

6. Lotar Radaceanu, another Minister of the Communist government of Bucharest "deposed" in the year 1952, but who in 1955 reappeared on the honorary tribune. He is a Jew from Siebenbürgen and is called Lothar Würtzel. Since the "Würtzel" in Rumanian translates "Radicinu", this Jew has simply transferred his Hebraic name into Rumanian and is now called "Radaceanu".

7. Miron Constantinescu, member of the central Committee of the Communist party and minister for mining and petroleum. Now and then he changes his ministerial posts. He is a Jew from Galatzi (Rumania), who in truth is called Mehr Kohn, and as is customary among them, uses a Rumanian pseudonym.

8. Lieutenant General Moises Haupt, commander of the military district of Bucharest; Jew.

9. Colonel General Zamfir, Communist "security chief" in Rumania and responsible for thousands of murders, which this secret police has perpetrated. He is a Jew and comes from the Danube harbour of Braila. He is called Laurian Rechler.

10. Heim Gutman, chief of the civil secret service of the Rumanian Peoples republic; Jew.

11. Major-General William Suder, chief of the information service and of counter-espionage of the Rumanian Communist army. He is a Jew, by name Wilman Süder and former officer of the Soviet Army.

12. Colonel Roman, former director of the E.K.P. service (education, culture and propaganda) of the Rumanian army up to 1949, and at the present time Minister in the Communist government. His name as Jew is Walter.

13. Alexander Moghiorosh, minister for Nationalities in the Red government; Jew from Hungary.

14. Alexander Badau, chief of the Control Commission for foreigners in Rumania. He is a Jew who originates from the city of Targoviste whose real name is Braustein. Before 1940 his family in Targoviste possessed a large trading firm.

15. Major Lewin, chief of press censorship, Jew and former officer of the Red Army.

16. Colonel Holban, chief of the Communist "Security" of Bucharest, a Jew named Moscovich, former Syndicate (Union) chief.

17. George Silviu, general governmental secretary of the ministry for internal affairs; a Jew named Gersh Golinger.

18. Erwin Voiculescu, chief of the pass department in the ministry for foreign affairs. He is a Jew and is called Erwin Weinberg.

19. Gheorghe Apostol, chief of the general labour union of Rumania; he is a Jew named Gerschwin.
20. Stupineanu, chief of economic espionage; Jew by name Stappnau.
21. Emmerick Stoffel, Ambassador of the Rumanian Peoples Republic in Switzerland; a Jew from Hungary and specialist in bank questions.
22. Harry Fainaru, former legation chief of the Rumanian Communist embassy in Washington up to 1954 and at present official in the ministry for foreign affairs in Bucharest. He is a Jew named Hersch Feiner. Before the year 1940 his family possessed a grain business in Galatzi.
23. Ida Szillagy, the real directress of the Rumanian embassy in London; Jewess; friend of Anna Pauker.
24. Lazarescu, the "Chargé d'Affaires" of the Rumanian government in Paris. He is a Jew and is really called Baruch Lazarovich, the son of a Jewish trader from Bucharest.
25. Simon Oieru, State under-secretary of the Rumanian state; Jew with name of Schaffer.
26. Aurel Baranga, inspector general of arts. He is a Jew; Ariel Leibovich is his real name.
27. Liuba Kisinevski, president of the U.F.A.R. (Association of anti-Fascist Rumanian women); she is a Jewess from Cernautzi/Bukowina, and is called in reality Liuba Broitman, wife of Josif Kisinevski of the central Committee of the party.
28. Lew Zeiger, director of the ministry for national economy; Jew.
29. Doctor Zeider, jurist of the ministry for foreign affairs; Jew.
30. Marcel Breslasu, director general of arts; a Jew by name Mark Breslau.
31. Silviu Brucan, chief editor of the newspaper "Scanteia", official party organ. He is a Jew and is called Brükker. He directs the entire campaign of lies that attempts to deceive the Rumanian people concerning the true situation created by Communism. At the same time the Jew Brükker directs the fake "Antisemitic" campaign of the Communist press of Rumania.
32. Samoila, governing director of the newspaper "Scanteia"; he is a Jew; Samuel Rubenstein.
33. Horia Liman, second editor of the Communist newspaper "Scanteia"; Jew with the name of Lehman.
34. Engineer Schnapp, governing director of the Communist newspaper "Romania Libera" (Free Rumania), the second Communist newspaper on the basis of its circulation; likewise a Jew.

35. Jehan Mihai, chief of the Rumanian film industry, Communist propaganda by means of films; a Jew, whose name is Jakob Michael.
36. Alexander Graur, director general of the Rumanian radio corporation, which stands completely and solely in the service of the Communist party. He is a Jewish professor and is called Alter Biauer, born in Bucharest.
37. Mihail Roller, at present President of the Rumanian academy, is a sinister professor, a Jew, unknown before the arrival of the Soviets in Rumania. Today he is "President" of the Academy and in addition he has written a "new history" of the Rumanian people, in which he falsifies the historical truth.
38. Professor Weigel, one of the tyrants of the university of Bucharest, who directs the constant "purging actions" among Rumanian students who are hostile to the Jewish- Communist regime.
39. Professor Lewin Bercovich, another tyrant of the Bucharest university, who with his spies controls the activity of Rumanian professors and their social connections; an immigrant Jew from Russia.
40. Silviu Josifescu, the official "literary critic", who censures the poems of the best poets like Eminescu Alecsandri, Vlahutza, Carlova, etc., who all died centuries ago or more than half a century ago, and alters form and content, because these poems are "not in harmony" with the Communist Marxist ideas. This literary murderer is a Jew, who in truth is called Samoson Iosifovich.
41. Joan Vinter, the second Marxist "literary critic" of the regime and author of a book with the title "The problem of literary legacy" is likewise a Jew and is called Jakob Winter.

The three former secretaries of the General Labour League up to 1950, Alexander Sencovich, Mischa Levin and Sam Asriel (Serban), were all Jews.

E - YUGOSLAVIA

1. Marshal Tito, who with his real Jewish name is called Josif Walter Weiss, originates from Poland. He was an agent of the Soviet secret service in Kabul, Teheran and Ankara up to 1935. The true Brozovich Tito, in origin a Croat, died during the Spanis civil war in Barcelona.

2. Moses Pijade, general secretary of the Communist party and in reality the "grey eminence" of the regime, is a Jew of Spanish origin (Sefardit).

3. Kardelj, member of the Central Committee of the Yugoslav Communist party and minister for foreign affairs; is a Jew of Hungarian origin and is called in reality Kardayl.

4. Rankovic, member of the Central Committee of the Yugoslav Communist party and minister for internal affairs, is an Austrian Jew and was earlier called Rankau.

5. Alexander Bebler, member of the Central Committee of the Communist party and permanent representative of Yugoslavia in the UNO, is an Austrian Jew.

6. Ioza Vilfan (Joseph Wilfan), economic advisor of Tito, in reality the economic dictator of Yugoslavia, is a Jew from Sarajevo.

Since not so many Jews live in Yugoslavia as in other lands, we find a greater number of natives in the Communist government of this land, always however in posts of the second rank; for the abovementioned principal leaders in reality control the Yugoslav government completely and absolutely.[17]

---

[17] Countless Catholic writers have, similarly to those quoted in this chapter, made further statistical investigations, which always close with the categorical statement that Bolshevism is a Jewish work. The book *La Guerra Occulta* by Malinsky and de Poncins, Milan, 1961, contains an appendix with a study carried out in this respect, compiled by Msgr. Jouin. A further study worthy of mention is published in the periodical *Civilta Cattolica*, the organ of the famous Society of Jesus, in the city of Rome, which began its publication of this material from the end of the preceding century, and which has published a special work dealing with this theme under the title *La rivoluzione mondiale e gli ebrei*, which corresponds to pamphlet 1836 of the year 1922.

MAURICE PINAY

CHAPTER FOUR

THE FINANCIERS OF COMMUNISM

International Jewry strives in its entirety towards Communistic socialism in accordance with the doctrine of Marx, which has at present been realised by it in the Union of Socialist Soviet Republics and all its satellites. The direct goal of Communism is the striving for world domination and complete power over all peoples of the earth. This standpoint it has always manifested and from the beginning onwards striven for this goal. This Communist aim is understood with absolute unanimity by all Jews as their own goal, although many non-Jewish persons, who are lacking in knowledge and who are intentionally deceived, think that the great number of Jewish multi-millionaires which there are in the world and who even control world finance, must necessarily oppose this current, which attempts to snatch their wealth away from them.

At first sight there is nothing more self-evident than to see in a rich financier, a well-to-do trader or an important industrialist, the natural and keenest enemy of Communism. But if the industrialists, traders or financiers are Jews, there is not the slightest doubt that they are also Communists; for the Communistic Socialism of Marx has been created and carried out by them, and in fact not in order to lose their goods and chattels which they possess, but to steal everything which does not belong to them and to hoard together in their own hands the entire wealth of the world, which according to their assertion is unlawfully withheld from them by all who do not belong to the Jewish race.

The well-known Jewish (?) writer Werner Sombart says: "The fundamental characteristic feature of the Jewish religion consists in the fact that it is a religion which has nothing to do with the other world, but, as one might say, is solely materialistic. Man can experience good or evil only in this world; if God wishes to punish or reward, then he can do this only in the lifetime of man. Therefore the just man (righteous) must attain well-being here on earth and the Godless suffer."[18]

"It is useless to dwell upon the difference which derives from this contrast of two outlooks, relating to the attitude of the devout Jew and of the devout Christian, with regard to the acquisition of wealth. The devout Christian who has got into debt with the usurer, was tortured on his deathbed by pangs of regret (repentance) and was ready to abandon everything which he possessed; for the knowledge of the unjustly acquired goods consumed him. On the other hand the devout Jew, when the end of his life approached, regarded with contentment the trunks and cases filled to bursting-point, in which the profits were accumulated, which during his long life he had taken off the wretched Christians and also the poor Musulmans. It was a spectacle on which his devout heart could feast, for every roll of money which lay locked up there, he saw as a sacrifice brought to his God."[19]

Simultaneously, Jewish money (which at present represents the greatest part of the money in the world) is the most powerful tool of all, which in vast extent has made possible the financing of revolutionary movements without the help of which the latter would never have been able to triumph and be able in such manner to destroy Christian civilisation in all its appearances; be it whether the individual is materialistically influenced by it being taught that money is to be preferred to other-worldly values, or be it through the direct methods, which they know how to use so energetically, like bribery and embezzlement in public offices and taxation swindling as well as the general buying of consciences.

The Jewish idea of accumulating all the money in the world through Communism appears in all transparency with many famous Jewish writers like Edmond Fleg, Barbusse, Andre Spire and others; in particular most expressly in the well-known letter that the famous new Messianer Baruch Levy sent to Karl Marx, which was discovered in the year 1888 and published for the first time in the same year. The text is as follows:

"The Jewish people as a whole is its own Messiah. Its kingdom over the universe is obtained through the uniting of the other human races, through the suppression of frontiers and of monarchies, which are bulwarks for particularism and hinder the erection of a world republic where citizenship is everywhere recognised to the Jew. In this new

---

[18] Werner Sombart, *Les juifs et la vie économique*. Payot, 1923, pp. 277, 291.
[19] Werner Sombart, op. cit., p. 286.

organisation of mankind, the sons of Israel, who at present are scattered over the entire earth surface, will all be of the same race and of the same traditional culture, without, however, forming another nationality, and will be without contradiction the leading element in all parts, particularly if it is successful in laying upon the masses of workers a permanent leadership by some Jews. The governments of peoples all pass with the formation of the universal republic effortlessly into the hands of the Israelites in favour of the victory of the proletariat. Then the personal property of the rulers will be able to be suppressed by the rulers of the Jewish race who will everywhere govern over the property of the Peoples. Then the promise of the Talmud will be fulfilled, that when the time of the Messiah has come, the Jews will have the goods of all peoples of the world in their possession."[20]

If one follows these tactics of economic accumulation, then it is completely natural that we see how the richest financiers and the most important bankers of the world finance the Communist revolutions; it is also not difficult, bearing in mind the data mentioned, to explain a situation, which superficially studied appears senseless and absurd, namely that one always sees the richest Jews of the world united with the Israelite leaders of the Communist movements. If the explanations of the most well-known Jews suffice to show us this close connection with clarity, then the evident facts are still all the clearer, so that they wipe away even the slightest trace of doubt.

After the French defeat of 1870 and the fall of the Emperor Napoleon III, the Marxists, led by Karl Marx from London, formed the Commune from the 18th March 1871 onwards. During this period of more than two months, in Paris the National Guard, which had been transformed into an armed organisation, was through and through dependent on the Marxist International.

When the Commune could not resist the attack of the troops of the government, with its seat at Versailles, and the Communists saw their defeat as unavoidable, they devoted themselves to robbery, murder and incendiarism, in order to destroy the capital, in accordance with the plan already proposed by Clauserets in the year 1869:

"Ourselves or nothing! I promise you, Paris will belong to us or cease to exist."

---

[20] Salluste, *Les origines secrètes du bolchévisme: Henri Heine et Karl Marx.* Jules Tallandier, Paris, 1929, p. 23.

Upon this occasion was clearly revealed the joint guilt of the French Jewish bankers together with the Communists, when it is established how Salluste in his book "Les origines sécrètes du bolchevisme" alludes to the fact that Rothschild exercised pressure on one side in Versailles with Thiers, the President of the republic, in order to prevent a decisive fight against the Marxist Communists, by his talking of a possible understanding and agreements with the central committee of the Federals (Marxists), and on the other side enjoyed a total protection of his person as also of his property in the city of Paris, which was thrown into a horrible and bloody chaos.

In this respect Salluste tells us in his afore-mentioned work, page 137:

"It is certain that M. Rothschild had good reasons to hold a conciliation possible: his villa in the Rue Saint-Florentin was protected day and night by a guard troop of the Federals (Marxists), who had the task of preventing any plundering. This protective troop was maintained for two months, up to the moment when the great barricade, which was only a few paces away, was taken by the Versailles troops.

"While hostages were shot, the most beautiful palaces of Paris went up in flames and thousands of Frenchmen died as victims of the civil war, it is worth mentioning that the protection granted by the Communists to the great Jewish banker did not cease for a moment."

In the year 1916, the Lieutenant-General of the Imperial Russian Army, A. Nechvolodof, described secret information which had been received from one of his agents, which on the 15th February of the same year reached the supreme command of the Russian General Staff and read as follows:

"The first secret assembly, which reveals the beginning of the acts of violence, took place on Monday, the 14th February, in the East Side of New York. Of the 62 representatives gathered, 50 were veterans of the revolution of 1905, and the others new members. The greater part of those present were Jews and among them many educated people, as for example, doctors, writers, etc... Some professional revolutionaries were also found amongst them...

"The first hours of this assembly were almost exclusively devoted to testing the methods and the possibilities of carrying out a great revolution in Russia. It was one of the most favourable moments for this.

"It was stated that the party had just received information from Russia, according to which the situation was completely and absolutely favourable; for all previously agreed conditions for a favourable rising were present. The one serious hindrance was the question of money; but scarcely was this remark made, when several members at once answered that this circumstance should cause no reflection, for, at the moment when it was necessary, substantial sums would be given by persons who sympathised with the movement for freedom. In this connection the name of Jakob Schiff was repeatedly mentioned."[21]

At the beginning of the year 1919, the secret service of the United States of America provided high officials of the French republic who visited America with a memorandum, in which the participation of the most principal bankers in the preparation of the Russian Communist revolution was categorically revealed:

7-618-6   Provided by the General Staff
                                of the 20th Army.
No. 912-S-R.2.   *copy*

In February 1916 it became known for the first time that a revolution was being promoted in Russia. It was discovered that the following named persons and firms were involved in this work of destruction:

> 1. Jakob Schiff; Jew.
> 2. Kuhn, Loeb & Co; Jewish firm. Directors:
> Jakob Schiff; Jew.
> Felix Warburg; Jew.
> Otto Kahn; Jew.
> Mortimer Schiff; Jew.
> Hieronymus H. Hanauer; Jew.
> 3. Guggenheim; Jew.
> 4. Max Breitung; Jew.

At the beginning of the year 1917, Jakob Schiff began to protect the Jew and Freemason Trotsky, whose real name is Bronstein; the mission given to him consisted in the directing of the social revolution in Russia. The New York paper "Forward", a Jewish-Bolshevist daily paper, likewise protected him for the same purpose. Also he was aided financially by the Jewish firm of Max Warburg, Stockholm, the Rheinisch- Westfalische

---

[21] Esteban J. Malanni, *Comunismo y judaismo*. Editorial La Mazorca, Buenos Aires, 1944, pp. 54-55.

Syndicate, the Jew Olaf Aschberg of the Nye Banks, Stockholm, and the Jew Jovotovsky, whose daughter Trotsky married. In this manner relations were established between the Jewish multi-millionaires and the proletarian Jew.

"The Jewish firm of Kuhn, Loeb & Co. has links with the Rheinisch-Westphalian Syndicate, a Jewish firm in Germany; just as it has links with Lazard-Freres, a Jewish house in Paris, and also with the Jewish firm of Gunzbourg of Paris, and with the same Jewish firm of Gunzbourg of Petrograd, Tokyo and Paris; if we observe in addition that all affairs are likewise handled with the Jewish firms of Speyer & Co., London, New York and Frankfurt/Main, exactly as with the firms of Nye-Banks, who are the agents for Jewish-Bolshevist business affairs in Stockholm, then we can draw the inference from this that the banking firm has relations with all Bolshevist movements; one can see that in praxis it represents the true expression of a general Jewish movement, and that certain Jewish banking houses are interested in the organisation of these movements."[22]

In the pamphlet of S. de Baamonde we again find something new about the banking house of Kuhn & Co. Jakob Schiff was an Israelite of German origin. His father, who lived in Frankfurt, was in that city a modest local agent of the firm of Rothschild. The son emigrated to the United States. There he rapidly made a career which soon made him chief of the large firm of Kuhn, Loch & Co., the most important Israelite bank of America.

"In the Jewish banking world Jakob Schiff not only distinguished himself through his knowledge of business and the dare-devilry of his inventive power, but he also occasioned very resolute plans and intentions, even if neither new nor original, concerning the leading political activity that each banking System should exert over the fates of the world: 'The spiritual direction of human affairs.' "

Another of the constant concerns of this plutocrat was mixing at all cost in the political affairs of Russia, in order to bring about a change of regime in that land. The political conquest of Russia, which up to then had evaded the influence of Freemasonry thanks to its regime of reason, should be the best circle of effect to secure the power of Israel over the entire universe.[23]

---

[22] Duque de la Victoria, *Israel manda*, p. 312.
[23] Ibid., pp. 318-319.

In the spring of 1917, Jakob Schiff began to instruct Trotsky, a Jew, how he should carry out the social revolution in Russia. The Jewish-Bolshevistic newspaper of New York, "Forward", also concerned itself with the same theme:

"From Stockholm as centre, the Jew Max Warburg authorized Trotsky & Co., as did Rheinisch-Westphalian Syndicate, an important Jewish Company, as well as Olaf Aschberg of the Nye Bank of Stockholm, and Yivotousky, a Jew, whose daughter married Trotsky."[24]

"At the same time a Jew, Paul Warburg, was found to have such a close connection with the Bolshevists that he was not selected again to the 'Federal Reserve Board'."[25]

The "Times" of London of 9th February 1918 and the "New York Times" alluded in two articles by Samuel Gompers, which were published in the issues of 10th May 1922 and 31st December 1923, to the following:

"If we bear in mind that the Jewish firm of Kuhn, Loeb & Co. is connected with the Rheinisch-Westphalian Syndicate, a Jewish firm in Germany, with Lazard Freres, a Jewish firm of Paris, and also with the banking house of Gunzbourg, a Jewish firm in Petrograd, Tokyo and Paris, and if we in addition point out that the aforementioned Jewish trading firms maintain close relations to the Jewish firm of Speyer & Co. in London, New York and Frankfurt/Main, as likewise with Nye Banks, a Jewish-Bolshevist firm in Stockholm, then we can establish that the Bolshevist movement in itself is to a certain degree the expression of a universal Jewish movement, and that certain Jewish banking houses are interested in the organisation of this movement."[26]

General Nechvolodof alludes in his work "L'Empereur Nicholas II et Les Juifs" (1924) to the strong Jewish financing of the Communist revolution in Russia:

"During the years which preceded the revolution, Jakob Schiff had supplied the Russian revolutionaries with twelve million dollars. On their side the triumphant Bolshevists, according to M. Bakmetieff, the ambassador of the Russian Imperial government in the United States, who

---

[24] Esteban J. Malanni, op. cit., pp. 58-60.
[25] Esteban J. Malanni, op. cit., pp. 60-62.
[26] Esteban J. Malanni, op. cit., p. 63.

died some time ago in Paris, transferred six hundred million gold roubles between 1918 and 1922 to the firm of Loeb & Co."

According to these convincing proofs I do not believe that it occurs to anyone to arrive at the optimistic conclusion that there exist wicked Jews (the Communists) and good Jews (the Capitalists); further, that, while the ones strive to cut off the wealth of private persons and to cause private property to vanish, the others strive for the defence of both things, so as not to lose their enormous riches. To the misfortune of our civilisation the Jewish conspiracy shows features of unconditional unity. Judaism forms a monolithic power, which is directed at forcing together all riches of the world without exception, by means of Communist Socialism according to Marx.

At the present time one sees in our civilised world the admission of racial discrimination as the greatest sin into which man could fall. It is alleged to be a fault that leaves behind an eternal and ugly world of barbarity and animal nature, always presupposing that the Jewish people does not in practice commit this fault. Thanks to Jewish propaganda, which is controlled almost exclusively in the world by the Israelites (cinema, radio, press, television, publishing, etc.), anti-Semitism is the most disgraceful of all racial manifestations; for the Jews have made out of anti-Semitism a truly destructive weapon, which serves to nullify the efforts of countless persons and organisations who have clearly recognised who the real head of Communism is, in spite of the camouflage and cunning that this race uses to conceal its true activity. Particularly such persons and organisations that have tried to sound the alarm, since they were filled with horror at the fatal end which draws nearer and nearer.

This network of lies is so successful that the majority of anti-Communists who wish to make an end of the Marxist monster, direct their energetic and courageous attacks against the tentacles of the octopus and know nothing of the existence of the terrible head which renews the destroyed limbs, conducts its movements and brings the activities in all parts of its system into harmony. The sole possibility or destroying the Communist Socialism of Marx consists in attacking the head of the same, which at present is Jewry as the undeniable facts and irrefutable evidence of the Jews themselves allow to be discerned.

While the Christian lands are anti-racialist, because they build up their ideas on the concept of loving one's neighbour, the Jews were and are at present the most fanatical representatives of racial discrimination, which they base on ideas from the Talmud, because they proceed from the principle that the non-Jew is not even a human being.

However, this Christian opposition to racial discrimination is very skilfully utilised by the Jews; and in the shadow of the same they weld their devilish intrigues against the Catholic Church and all Christian order, by their forming the Communist system, where there is neither God nor church nor supersensual norms of any kind. As soon as they are attacked, they protest with crying lamentation and show themselves as victims of inhuman racial discrimination, only for the purpose of crippling that work of defence which opposes their destructive attacks.

In spite of this, one can regard the real defence against Communism, which must be forcefully directed against the Jews (against the head), in no manner as a sinful manifestation of a feeling of revulsion towards a definite race; for the characteristic of racial discrimination is completely alien to our culture and our Christian principles; however, one cannot avoid a problem of such weight and range out of fear of being described as an "Antisemite", which doubtless occurs with those who do not understand the present situation of the world.

Thus it is not a question of combating a race out of considerations of racial order. If one at present brings the problem under close inspection, the Jews alone must bear the responsibility of leaving us no other choice because of their racial discrimination in life and death, with their absolute disregard of all who are not of their race and with their greed for world domination.

For Catholics in particular, and for the civilised world in general, who still firmly believe in their established principles and other-worldly values, the confirmation cannot be simpler; for it is a problem of self-defence, which is accepted completely in the moral and just order, if the pure dilemma, which Judaism shows us, is the following: "Either Jewish-Communist domination or extermination."

CHAPTER FIVE

JEWISH TESTIMONY

In spite of their accustomed seclusion, and even in spite of their deceptive and clandestine manoeuvres, by which they have been successful in remaining concealed, so as not to reveal their Communist plan for world conquest, the Jews have had several weak moments, to which they have been induced either through optimism or excessive jubilation in the studying of their successes and which upon different occasions have called forth impetuous but highly factual declarations. Kadmi- Cohen, a highly regarded Jewish writer, affirms that:

"As far as the Jews are concerned, then, their role in world socialism is so important that one cannot pass quietly over it. Does it not suffice to recall the names of the great Jewish revolutionaries of the 19th and 20th centuries, such as Karl Marx, Lasalle, Kurt Eisner, Bela Kun, Trotsky and Leon Blum, so that in this manner it is clear who are the theoreticians of modern Socialism?"[27]

"What a brilliant confirmation do the strivings of the Jews find in Communism, apart from the material cooperation in party organisations, in the deep revulsion which a great Jew and great poet, Heinrich Heine, felt against Roman law! And the personal and passionate motives for the anger of Rabbi Aquila and Bar Kocheba of the years 70 and 132 after Jesus Christ, against the Roman peace and the Roman law which was understood personally and passionately and felt by a Jew of the 19th century, who had apparently preserved no bond with his own race."

"The Jewish revolutionaries and Jewish Communists, who dispute the basic principle of private property whose firmly established foundation is the civil law book of Justinian, of Ulpian, etc., only imitate their

---

[27] Kadmi-Cohen, *Nomades: essai sur l'âme juive*, F. Alcan, 1929, p. 80.

forefathers who opposed Vespasian and Titus. In reality it is the 'dead who speak'."[28]

The blasphemous Jewish writer Alfred Nossig tells us: "Socialism and the Mosaic law in no way oppose one another, but there exists on the contrary a surprising similarity between the basic ideas of both teachings. Jewish nationalism may not remove itself, as a danger that threatens the ideal, further from Socialism than the Jew from the Mosaic Law; for both parallel-running ideals must arrive in the same way at execution."[29]

"From the examination of the facts of the case it is revealed in a completely irrefutable manner that the modern Jews have cooperated in a decisive way and manner in the creation of Socialism; their own fathers were already the founders of the Mosaic Law. The seed of the Mosaic Law took effect over the centuries upon doctrine and command, in conscious manner for the one and unconsciously for the other. The modern Socialist movement is for the great majority a work of the Jews; the Jews gave it the stamp of their understanding; it was also Jews who had a striking share in the leadership of the first Socialist republics. In spite of this, the enormous majority of Jewish Socialist leaders were divorced from the Mosaic Law; for in an unconscious manner there took effect within them the racial principle of the Mosaic Law, and the race of the old apostolic peoples lived in their brain and in their social character. Present world socialism forms the first State in fulfilment of the Mosaic Law, the beginning of the realisation of the future World State, which was announced by the prophets."[30]

In his book "Integral Jews" he confirms this idea of Socialism as Jewish teaching, when he writes the following:

"If the peoples really wish to make progress, they must lay aside the Mediaeval fear of the Jews and the retrogressive prejudices which they have against the latter. They must recognise what they really are, namely the most upright forerunners of human development. At the present day the salvation of Jewry demands that we openly recognise the programme facing the world; and the salvation of mankind in the coming centuries depends upon the victory of this programme."[31]

---

[28] Kadmi-Cohen, op. cit., p. 86.
[29] *Westfällschen-Merkur*, Zeitung von Munster, no. 405 of 6 October 1926.
[30] Alfred Nossig, *Integrales Judentum*, L. Chailley, Paris, pp. 68, 71, 74.
[31] Alfred Nossig, op. cit., p. 79.

The reason for this Jewish revolutionary conduct is clearly explained by the well-known Jewish writer E. Eberlin in the following excerpt:

"The more radical the revolution is, all the more freedom and equality for the Jews comes about as a result. Every current of progress strengthens further the position of the Jews. In the same manner, every setback and every reaction attacks it in first place. Often, only a simple orientation towards the Right will expose the Jews to boycott. From this aspect the Jew is the pressure-valve for the social (steam) boiler. As a body the Jewish people cannot stand on the side of reaction; for reaction is the return to the past and means for the Jews the continuation of their abnormal conditions of existence."[32]

The ill-reputed Jew, Jakob von Haas, says to us in "The Maccabean" quite clearly that "the Russian revolution that we experienced is a revolution of Jewry. It signifies a change in the history of the Jewish people. If we speak openly, it was a Jewish revolution; for the Jews were the most energetic revolutionaries in Russia."

In the Jewish-French newspaper entitled "Le Peuple Juif" of February 1919, one can read the following: "The Russian Revolution, which we see at present, will be the exclusive work of our hands."

One finds the following passage in a book by the famous Jewish writer Samuel Schwartz with a foreword by Ricardo Jorge: "When we ascend from the heights of pure science to the place of battle, which the passions and the interests of men clash against each other, there rises before us the oracle of the new social-political religion, the Jew Karl Marx, the dogmatic leader of war for life and death. He finds in the head and in the arm of Lenin the realisation of his confession of belief and sees in him the forefighter for the Soviet State that threatens to overthrow the firm foundations of the traditional institutions of society."[33]

In the same way another Jew, Hans Cohen, confirms in the "Political Idea" that "the Socialism of Marx is the purpose of our striving and efforts."

In Number 12 of the newspaper "The Communist" which was published in Kharkov on the 12th April 1919, the Jew M. Cohen writes:

[32] Elie Eberlin, *Les juifs d'aujourd'hui*, Paris, 1928, p. 201.
[33] Ricardo Jorge, *Os cristãos-novos em Portugal no século XX*. Foreword by Samuel Schwartz. Lisbon, 1925, p. 11.

"Without exaggeration one can make the assurance that the great social revolution in Russia was carried out by the Jews. It is true that in the ranks of the Red Army there are soldiers who are not Jews. But in the committees and in the Society organisations, just as with the Commissars, the Jews lead the masses of the Russian proletariat to victory with courage."

"At the head of the Russian revolutionaries marched the pupils of the Rabbinic school of Lidia." Jewry triumphed over fire and sword, with our brother Marx, who had the mandate for the fulfilment of all that our prophets have commanded, and who worked out the suitable plan for the demands of the proletariat." All these sentences appeared in the Jewish newspaper "Haijut"of Warsaw of 3rd August 1928.

"The Jewish World", of 10th January 1929, expressed this blaspheming view: "Bolshevism, the very fact of its existence, and that so many Jews are Bolsheviks, further – that the ideal of Bolshevism is in harmony with the most sublime ideal of Jewry, which in part formed the foundation for the best teachings of the founder of Christianity, all this has a deep significance, which the thoughtful Jew carefully examines."

In order not to range too widely at this point, we quote in conclusion the allusions which the Israelite Paul Sokolowsky makes in his work, entitled "The Mission of Europe", where he boasts of the predominant role which the Jews played in the Russian Revolution and reveals details concerning the secret codes which they used to reach understanding with each other, even by means of the press, without the attention of the authorities being drawn to themselves, and how they distributed the Communist propaganda that they prepared through the Jewish children, whom they carefully schooled for these services in their settlements.[34]

The hellish, Jewish-Communist hate, which is chiefly revealed against Christian civilisation, is not unfounded, but it has its very deep causes, which can be judged with full clarity in this following excerpt from the "Sepher-Ha-Zohar", the holy book of modern Jewry, which represents the feelings of all Jews:

"Jesu (Jesus), the Nazarene, who has brought the world away from belief in Jehovah, who be praised, will each Friday be again restored. At daybreak of Saturday he will be thrown into boiling oil. Hell will pass, but

---

[34] Alfonso de Castro, *El problema judío*, Editorial Actualidad, Mexico, D.F., 1939, pp. 152-153.

his punishment and his tortures will never end. Jesus and Mohammed are those unclean bones of offal of which the Scripture says: 'Ye shall cast before the dogs. They are the dirt of the dog, the unclean, and because they have misled men, they are cast into Hell, from which they never again come out.' "[35]

---

[35] *Sepher-Ha-Zohar*, translated by Jean de Pauly. Ernest Leroux, Paris, 1907. Vol. II, p. 88.

PART TWO

THE POWER CONCEALED

BEHIND FREEMASONRY

CHAPTER ONE

FREEMASONRY AS ENEMY
OF THE CHURCH AND OF CHRISTIANITY

In view of the fact that the theme of this Second Book has been dealt with in such a masterly way and with such depth by outstanding and exactly instructed personages like his Holiness Pope Leo XIII, the High Dignified Cardinal Jose Maria Caro Rodriquez, Archbishop of Santiago de Chile, Monsignor Leon Meurin, S.J., Archbishop, Bishop of Port-Louis, and various other illustrious church and secular writers, we can restrict ourselves to writing down literally such authorised excerpts, without in the least enfeebling their great regard.

His Holiness Leo XIII says in his Encyclical *Humanum Genus* exactly as follows:

"The Popes, our forefathers, who bore conscientious concern for the spiritual salvation of the Christian peoples, soon knew very well who this deadly enemy was and what he wished, even if he hardly ever came out of the darkness of his secret conspiracy into the light, and accordingly, when he had spread his word of revolution, they exhorted princes and peoples to caution that they might not allow themselves to be caught by the malicious arts and traps which were prepared to deceive them. The first announcement of the danger was given in the year 1738 by Pope Clement XII (Constitution *In Eminenti*, 24th April 1738), which order Benedict XIV confirmed and renewed (Constitution *Providas*, 18th May 1751). Pius VII (Constitution *Ecclesiam a Jesu Christi*, 13th September 1821) followed the path of both, and Leo XII, who in the Apostolic Constitution *Quo Graviora* (Constitution given 13th March 1825) incorporated in this material the decrees passed by his predecessors, authorized and confirmed the same for ever. Pius VIII (Encyclical *Traditi*, 21st May 1829), Gregory XVI (Encyclical *Mirari*, 15th August 1835), and Pius IX (Encyclical *Qui Pluribus*, 9th November 1816; Allocution *Multiplices Inter*, 25th September 1865, etc.) naturally spoke repeatedly in the same sense.

"According to the example of our predecessors, we have now resolved to openly turn ourselves against the Freemasonic society, against the system of their doctrine, against their manner of feeling and acting, to ever more make clear their harmful power and thus to prevent infection by such a destructive plague.

"The good tree can bring forth no bad fruits, nor can the bad tree bring forth good fruits (Matth. Chapter VII. v. 18) and the fruits of the Freemasonry sects are harmful and in addition very sour. For, from the completely reliable proofs that we have mentioned previously, is revealed the ultimate and last and most principal of their intentions, namely: To destroy to their foundations every religious and civic order that has been erected by Christianity, and after their own manner to erect a new order with foundations and laws, which they took from the essence of Naturalism... The confusing errors, which we have enumerated, must already suffice in themselves to fill the States with anxiety and fear. For, if the fear of God and respect for the laws is abolished, if the authority of the princes is despised, if the madness of revolution is called good and is declared as lawful, if with the greatest unbridledness the passions of the peoples are unchained, without other hindrance than punishment, then universal upheaval and disorder must necessarily follow. And it is particularly this upheaval and disorder that is planned and put forward by many associations of Communists and Socialists, of whose plans it cannot be said that they are remote from the sect of the Freemasons, since they favour the latter's intentions in great measure and agree with them on the most fundamental principles...

"However this may be, worthy brothers, as far as concerns us in the face of such a heavy and already widespread evil, we must be diligent with our entire soul in seeking for aid. And since we know, that the best and foremost hope of aid is placed in the power of the divine religion, which is hated by the Freemasons in the same way as it is feared, we hold it to be essential that we stand in service of this healing power against the common enemy. Everything accordingly that all the Popes our predecessors have ordered to hold up the attempts and efforts of the Freemasonic Sects, everything which they praised to keep men away from such societies or entice them from them, we strengthen and confirm individually and entirely with our Papal authority."[36]

As one sees, both his Holiness Leo XIII as well as various earlier Popes are very clear in their condemnation of Freemasonry and recognise

---

[36] Pope Leo XIII, Encyclical *Humanum Genus*, 20 April 1884.

simultaneously the latter's intentions, in association with Socialists and Communists, to destroy Christianity. And who directs Freemasonry? As we wish to explain in the following chapters, it is the same who directs Socialism and Communism, i.e. the Jews.

MAURICE PINAY

CHAPTER TWO

THE JEWS AS FOUNDERS OF FREEMASONRY

"To unmask Freemasonry" — said Leo XIII — "means to conquer it." When we lift its mask, then every honest mind and every Christian heart will turn away from it with revulsion; and through this fact alone will it fall, completely destroyed and detested particularly by those who obey it. The learned scholar and Jesuit Monsignor Leon Meurin, S.J., Archbishop, Bishop of Port-Louis, shows us in his so very richly authenticated work, "Clarification of Freemasonry", with crushing authority that the Jews are the founders, organisers and leaders of Freemasonry, which they use to attain world domination, in order to destroy the Holy Catholic Church and the remaining existing religions. Among the attested literature that he presents in this connection appear several quotations, which we mention in the following:

"The First Highest Masonic Council was, as we have already said, formed on 31st May 1801 in Charleston, 33 degrees northern latitude, under the chairmanship of the Jew Isaac Long, who was made inspector general by the Jew Moses Cohen, and who had received his degree from Hyes, from Franken, and the Jew Morin."[37]

"The Jews were thus the founders of the First Great Council, which was to transform itself into the middlepoint of world Freemasonry. And they placed it in America, in a city chosen exactly on the 33rd parallel, Northern Latitude. The successive head has lived in Charleston since 1801. In the year 1889 this was Albert Pike, whom we have already mentioned in his circular letter of 14th July 1889, the famed anniversary and tercentenary.

"He assumes the title of each of the 33 degrees and in addition adds the following:

---

[37] Pablo Rosen, *Satán y Cía*, Buenos Aires, 1947, p. 219.

"Most mighty and all-highest Commander, Grand Master of the Supreme Council of Charleston, first highest council of the globe, Grand Master and preserver of the holy Palladium, all-highest Pontifex of world Freemasonry.

"With these pompous titles he published his circular letter in the one and thirtieth year of his Pontificate, supported by ten high dignitaries, most enlightened and most sublime brothers, rulers, grand-general inspectors, chosen magi, who form the most illustrious grand collegium of ancient Freemasons, the council of the chosen troops and of the holy battalion of the Order."[38]

"The circular letter enumerates the 23 highest councils, which previously were directly 'created' through that of Charleston and are dispersed over the entire world. Then it lists the hundred Grand Orients and Grand Lodges of all rites which are connected with the highest Council of Charleston as the all-highest power of Freemasonry; the exclusive rite of the Jews. For example, the Grand Orient of France, the General Council of the Rite of Mizraim, the Grand Council of the Freemason Oddfellows, etc. From the preceding we must conclude that Freemasonry all over the world is one in countless forms, however, under the supreme direction of the all-highest Pontifex of Charleston."[39]

JEWISH ORIGIN

"The rites and symbols of the Freemasons and of the other secret sects remind one constantly of the 'Cabbala' (secret Jewish mystique) and Jewry: The reconstruction of the temple of Solomon, the star of David, the seal of Solomon; the names of the different degrees, as for example, Knight Kadosh. 'Kadosh' means in Hebrew 'holy'; Prince of Jerusalem, Prince of Lebanon, Knight of the serpent of Airain, etc. And does not the prayer of the English Freemasons, which was recorded in an assembly held in 1663, recall Judaism in a most clear manner?"[40]

"Finally the Scottish Freemasons made use of the Jewish calendar; for example, a book, which was written by the American Freemason Pike[41] in

---

[38] Adolphe Ricoux, *L'éxistence des loges de femmes*. Paris, Téqui, 1891, pp. 78-95.
[39] Monsignor Leon Meurin, S. J., Archbishop, Bishop of Port-Louis, *Simbolismo de la masonería*. Madrid: Editorial Nos, 1957, pp. 201-202.
[40] "Revue Internationale des Sociétés Secrètes" (RISS). Paris, 1913, no. 2, p. 58.
[41] Albert Pike, *Morals and Dogma of the Ancient and Accepted Scottish Rite of Freemasonry*, Anno mundi 5641 (1881).

the year 1881, is dated 'Anno mundi 5641'. At present this calendar is retained only in the highest degrees, while the Freemasons in general add four thousand years to the Christian calendar, and not 3760 like the Jews."[42]

The clever Rabbi Benamozegh writes the following:

"Those who wish to make the effort to examine the questions of relations between Jewry and philosophic Freemasonry, between Theosophy and the secret doctrines in general, will lose a little of their arrogant despisal of the Cabbala (Jewish Mysticism). They will cease to smile contemptuously at the idea that the 'Cabbalistic' theology perhaps has to fulfil a mission in the religious re-shaping of the future."[43]

"Who are the true leaders of Freemasonry? This is one of the secrets of the sect, which is very carefully kept; but one can assert that Freemasonry all over the world develops in agreement with one and the same plan; that its methods are always and in all parts identical, and that the aims pursued are permanently the same. This occasioned us to believe that a uniform middlepoint exists, which directs all movements of the Sect.

"Further on we will touch upon this question; however, here let us recall that 'Carta de Colonia', dated 24th June 1935, speaks of a director of Freemasonry: the Grandmaster or patriarch, who, although known by very few brothers, exists in reality; and Gougenot des Mousseaux points out that 'this choice of the Order, these real directors, whom only a very few initiates know, exercise their function in useful and secret dependency upon the Israelite Cabbalists (Mystics)' (page 338-339) and that the true directors of Freemasonry are the friends, the helpers and the vassals of the Jew to whom they do homage as their highest Lords. The same judgment is shared by Eckert, Drumont, Deschamps, Msgr. Jouin, Lambelin and other savants of Freemasonic and Jewish questions".[44]

Let us leave the dogmatic teachings of the Freemasons and Jewry to one side and let us examine the alliances between both from the purely practical and realistic standpoint. If one proceeds logically, one cannot avoid drawing the conclusion which is formulated by L. de Poncins in "The Secret Powers Behind Revolution."

---

[42] Maurice Fara, *La masonería en descubierto*. Buenos Aires: La hoja de roble, 1960, p. 23.
[43] Rabino Benamozegh, *Israel y la humanidad*. Paris, 1914. p. 71.
[44] Gougenot des Mousseaux, *Le juif, le judaïsme et la judaïsation des peuples chrétienne*. Paris, 1869, pp. 338-339.

"The manifoldness of Freemasonry, its permanence, the inalterability of its goals, which are completely explicable since it is a question of a Jewish creation to serve the Jewish interests, would be completely incomprehensible if its origin were of a Christian nature.

"Even the purpose in itself of Freemasonry, namely the destruction of Christian civilisation, reveals to us the Jew, for only the Jew can draw advantage from it, and the Jew alone is inspired by a sufficiently violent hatred towards Christianity to create such an organisation."

"Freemasonry", continues de Poncins, "is a secret society and is directed by an international minority. It has sworn Christianity an irreconcilable hatred. These three characteristics are exactly the same as those that describe Jewry and represent the proof that the Jews are the leading element of the lodges."[45]

Already in 1867 the "permanent international league for peace" came into existence, and its secretary, the Jew Passy, outlined the ideas of a court of justice, to settle all conflicts between the nations without appeal.[46]

The newspaper "The Israelite Archive" dreamed of a similar court of justice in the year 1864. "Is it not natural and necessary" — wrote a certain Levy Bing — "that as soon as possible we see erected an additional court of justice, and in fact a highest court of justice, to whom the great open conflicts and the quarrels among the nations are submitted, which in the last instance passes judgment, and whose last word is given powerful weight? This will be the word of God, which is uttered by his first-born sons (the Hebrews), and before which the general rest of mankind will bow in respect before our brothers, our friends and our pupils."[47]

These are the dreams of Israel. As always they accord with those of Freemasonry. The "Freemasons calendar" writes:

"When the Republic has been set up in the whole of old Europe, Israel, as ruler will rule over this old Europe."[48]

At the world congress of Jewish youth, which was held on 4th August 1928, H. Justin Godard announced that the Jews were the firmest

---

[45] León de Poncins, *Les forces secrètes de la Révolution*, pp. 139-140.
[46] "Revue Internationale des Siciétés Secrètes" (R.I.S.S.), 1926, no. 8, p. 269.
[47] "Archivos Israelitas", 1864, p. 335.
[48] *Freimaureralmanach*, Leipzig, 1884.

supporters of the League of Nations, which had to thank its existence to them."[49] The Jew Cassin gave more exact information:

"The rebirth of Zionism is the work of the League of Nations. Through it the Jewish organisations place themselves as defenders of the League of Nations, and therefore Geneva swarms with representatives of the 'chosen people'."[50]

The most venerable Cardinal Jose Maria Caro R., Archbishop of Santiago and Primate of Chile, also proves, in his authoritatively supported work "The Secret of Freemasonry", that it is the Jews who direct this sect, in order to rule the world and to destroy Holy Church. In connection with its origin he affirms:

"The Freemasonic rite clearly betrays its Jewish origin: the symbols, which begin with the Bible itself; the coat of arms upon which an attempt is made to explain the different forms of the Cherubim described by Ezekiel in his second poem, an ox, a man, a lion and an eagle; the two pillars of the Freemasonic temple in remembrance of the temple of Solomon; the rebuilding of the temple which is the work of the Freemasons, etc. The reading matter and the handbooks, which in greater part are taken from the Bible, they turn almost always towards Freemasonic taste, especially the legend of Hiram, which plays an important role in the Freemasonic rite.

"The customary words and expressions, like the names of the pillars 'Boaz' and 'Jachin', the words of knowledge and of admittance: Tubalcain, Shibboleth, Giblim or Moahon, Nekum or Nekam, Abibalc, etc; the importance, which is allotted to numbers, a matter very original to the Cabbala, all these are further proofs of the Cabbalistic influence on Freemasonry.

"Finally the facts, the rule of terror, the outbreak of Satanic hatred against the Church, against our Lord Jesus Christ, the terrible blasphemies against God that the revolutionary Freemasons perpetrated in France, are nothing more than the expression and the fulfilment of the Cabbalistic and secret sects, which already for several centuries have fought secretly against Christianity. What the Jewish Bolshevists to greatest part do in Russia against Christianity, is only another edition of the deeds of the Freemasons in the French revolution. The executioners are others;

---

[49] *Les Cahiers de l'Ordre*, 1926, nos. 3-4, pp. 22-23.
[50] Maurice Fara, op. cit. p. 111.

however the doctrine that motivates and empowers them and the supreme leadership are the same."[51]

---

[51] Cardinal Jose Maria Caro. R., Archbishop-Bishop of Santiago, Primate of Chile: The Secret of Freemasonry, Difusion Publishers, page 258.

CHAPTER THREE

THE JEWS AS THE LEADERS OF THE

FREEMASONS

The famous and learned Jesuit, Monsignor Leon Meurin, Archbishop of Port-Louis, confirms in his authoritatively substantiated work "Philosophy of Freemasonry" the following:

"The first degrees of Freemasonry are intended for the purpose, as we will see further below, of transforming the 'laymen' into 'real men' in the Freemasonic sense; the second section, which passes from the 12th to 22nd degree, is intended to dedicate men to the 'Jewish Pontifex', and the third section of the 23rd to 33rd degree must dedicate the Pontifex to 'the Jewish king' or 'Cabbalistic Emperor'.

"The first thing that surprises the new disciple of a lodge is the Jewish character of everything which he finds there. From the first to the thirtieth degree he hears only talk of the 'great work' of rebuilding the temple of Solomon; of the murdering of the architect Hiram Abiff; of the two pillars Boaz and Jachin (III, Kings VII, 21); of a host of secret symbols (signs) and Hebrew holy words; and of the Jewish calendar, which adds 4000 years to our own, so as not to honour the birth of the divine Saviour."

"After the Jews had set up Freemasonry in different lands, they secured themselves predominance in the 'Grand Orients' by number and in influence. On the other hand, they set up a great number of lodges exclusively for Jews. Even before the revolution of 1789, the brothers Ecker and Eckhoffen had founded in Hamburg the 'Lodge of Melchizedek', which was reserved for Jews. The Hebrews von Hurschfeld and Cotter founded towards end of the 18th century in Berlin the 'Lodge of Tolerance'.

"Since that time, the Jews used the trick of bringing Jews and Christians closer, to ideologically and politically control or lead astray the later. However, at that time they had to take their refuge in the 'Secret Leagues' since the laws and customs of the Christian states of Europe revealed satisfactory measures which had the aim of protecting the Christians against cheating by the Jews. The secret Freemasons' paper of Leipzig said in their October number of 1864 that the middlepoint of the Jewish lodges in Paris was under the direction of Cremieux and the Grand Rabbi."

THE DOCTRINES, SIGNS AND DEGREES OF FREEMASONRY COME FROM JEWRY

The famous Archbishop-Bishop of Port-Louis says, when he speaks of the Jewish origin of Freemasonic doctrines, the following:

"The doctrines of Freemasonry are those of the Jewish Cabbala (Mysticism) and in particular those of their book 'Sohar' (Light). This is not recorded in any Freemasonic document; for it is one of the great secrets, which the Jews preserve so that only they themselves know it. Nevertheless we have been able to discover it, when we followed the traces of the Number 11. Here we have discovered the fundamental doctrines of the 'Jewish Cabbala' which were taken up into Freemasonry."[52]

In the preceding chapters there remained always a certain number of Freemasonic signs that were more or less inapplicable. All this, which plays a role in Freemasonry and its history, allows itself to be applied with astonishing ease to the Jewish people. What exists in reality in Freemasonry, is all completely, exclusively, and passionately Jewish from beginning to end.

What possible interest have the other peoples in rebuilding the temple of Solomon? Do they do it on their own account or an account of the Jews? Have these peoples or the Jews a use therefrom? What advantages does the fact represent that one destroys the other, so that, in the end all over the world, the "Princes of Jerusalem" (16th degree), "the Heads of the Tabernacle" (23rd degree) or "The Princes of the Tabernacle" (24th degree) triumph? Have the peoples become united, so as to serve the Jews

---

[52] Monsignor Leon Meurin, S. J., Archbishop-Bishop of Port-Louis: Philosophy of Freemasonry, 1957, pages 30, 211, 212, 41 and 42.

as a footstool? (Psalm 109) Why do they hurry to set upon their head the crown (Kether) and to lay the kingdom (Malkuth) at their feet?"

It is so evident that Freemasonry is only a tool in the hands of the Jews, which only they in reality lead, that one feels tempted to believe that the non-Jewish Freemasons, on the same day when their eyes are bound for the first time, lose their understanding and their power of judgement.[53]

THE FREEMASONIC RESPECT FOR THE JEWS

The most dignified Cardinal Caro says in his work "The Secret of Freemasonry":

"In Freemasonry a great and quite special respect is always shown for the Jews. If there is talk of superstition, the Jewish religion is never mentioned. Upon outbreak of the French revolution, French citizenship was urgently demanded for the Jews. Although it was rejected on the first occasion, it was expressly urged that it be granted, and it was allowed. The reader will recall that in those days the Catholics were persecuted to death. When the 'Commune' ruled in Paris and it was necessary to protect the cash of the bank of France against plundering, no one threatened the Jewish banks. (La Franc. Mas. Secte Juive 60.)

"Freemasonry has regarded Antisemitism with revulsion, and in fact so much so that an Antisemitic brother, who believed honourably in the tolerance of political opinions by Freemasonry, once placed himself as candidate for the Chamber of Deputies in France and was even elected. When the question of re-election arose, instructions were expressly given to the lodges that war was to be waged against him. Such instructions, which one almost never hears openly in the lodges, had to be followed."

THE JEWISH PREDOMINANCE IN THE LODGES

In the year 1862 a Berlin Freemason, who noticed the Jewish predominance in the lodges, wrote in a Munich paper: "There exists in Germany a secret sect with Freemasonic forms, which is subject to 'unknown leaders'. The members of this association are in their great majority 'Israelites'... In London, where, as one knows, the revolutionary

---

[53] Monsignor Leon Meurin, S. J., Archbishop-Bishop of Port-Louis: Symbolism of Freemasonry, 1957, page 34.

herd are found around the Grandmaster Palmerston, there exist two
Jewish Lodges that have never seen Christians cross their threshold; it is
there that are combined all the threads of the revolutionary elements
which nestle in the Christian lodges. In Rome there is a further lodge,
'which consists completely of Jews', and where all threads as well as plots
instigated in the 'Christian lodges' unite: 'the supreme court of justice of
the revolution.'

"From there outwards the other lodges are directed as by secret
leaders, so that the greater part of the Christian revolutionaries are only
marionettes who are set in motion by Jews by means of the secret leaders.

"In Leipzig exists by occasion of the Fair, which a part of the high
Jewish and Christian merchants of all Europe attend, a 'permanent secret
Jewish Lodge' in which a Christian Freemason is never accepted. This
opens the eyes of more than one of us... There are secret envoys, who
alone have admittance to the Jewish lodges of Hamburg and Frankfurt.

"Gougenot des Mousseaux reports the following occurrence, which
confirms the ensuing statements: 'With the breaking out again of the
revolution of 1848, I had connections with a Jew, who out of vanity
betrayed the secrets of the secret societies of which he was a member. The
latter instructed me eight or ten days in advance of all revolutions that
would break out in any point of Europe. I have to thank him for the
unshakeable conviction that all these great movements of 'repressed
peoples, etc.' were instigated by half a dozen persons who imparted their
instructions to the secret societies of the whole of Europe. The ground
under our feet is through and through undermined, and the Jewish people
provided an entire contingent of these subterranean agitators.'

"In the year 1870 de Camille wrote in 'Le Monde' that he met a
Freemason upon a round trip through Italy, one of his old acquaintances.
To his question how things went with the order, he answered: 'I have
finally left the lodge of my Order for I have gained the deep conviction
that we were only the tools of the Jews, who drive us to the total
destruction of Christianity.' (La F.M. Secte Juive, 43-46).

"As confirmation of the above I will reproduce a report, which is
found in the 'Revue des Sociétés Secrètes' (p. 118-119, 1924):

1.) The Golden International (International Plutocracy and High
Finance), at whose head are found:

a) In America: J. P. Morgan, Rockefeller, Vanderbilt and Vanderlip.

b) In Europe: the firm of Rothschild and others of second rank.

2.) The Red International or international association of Social Democratic workers. This comprises:

a) The Second International (that of Belgium, Jew Vandervelde).

b) The International No. 21/2 (that of Vienna, Jew Adler).

c) The Third International or Communist International (that of Moscow, the Jews Apfelbaum and Radek). This hydra, with three heads, which works separately for better effect, has at its disposal the 'Profintern' (International bureau of professional associations), which has its seat in Amsterdam and which dictates the Jewish word to the Syndicates that have still not been incorporated into Bolshevism.

3.) The Black International or combat organisation of Jewry. The chief roles in it are played by: the world organisation of Zionists (London); the Israelite world league, which was founded in Paris by the Jew Cremieux; the Jewish order of the B'nai-Moiche (Sons of Moses) and the Jewish societies 'Henoloustz', 'Hitakhdoute', 'Tarbout', 'Karen- Haessode', and a hundred more or less masked organisations, which are dispersed over all the lands of the Old and New world.

4.) The Blue International or international Freemasonry. This unites all Freemasons in the world through the 'United Lodge of Great Britain', through the 'Grand Lodge of France' and through the Grand Orients of France, Belgium, Italy, Turkey and the remaining lands. (The active middlepoint of this association is, as readers know, the great 'Alpina-Lodge'.)

5.) The Jewish Freemasonic Order of 'Bnai-B'rith', which, contrary to the principles of the Freemasonic lodges, accepts only Jews, and which numbers over the world more than 426 purely Jewish Lodges, serves as links to all the above enumerated Internationals. The leaders of the 'B'nai-B'rith' are the Jews Morgenthau, former ambassador of the United States in Constantinople; Brandeis, supreme judge in the United States; Mack, Zionist; Warburg (Felix), Banker; Elkus; Kraus (Alfred), the first president; Schiff, already dead, who supported the movement for emancipation of the Jews in Russia with financial contributions; Marshall (Louis), Zionist.

" 'We know definitely', says Nesta Webster, 'that the five powers, to which we have referred — the Freemasonry of the Grand Orient, Theosophy, Pan-Germanism, International finance and the social revolution — have a very real existence and a very definite influence on the destinies of the world. Hereby we do not proceed from assumptions but from facts, which can be authoritatively substantiated.'

"Since the revolution, the Jews have most of all appeared in connection with Freemasonry. Jewish Encyclopaedia."[54]

"In order to attempt to overthrow the Christian religion and in particular the Catholic, the Jews took their refuge in work of agitation, by that they despatched others imperceptibly and they themselves hid behind, in order not to reveal their intentions, so greatly are they despised by all: to bring that fortress to collapse in the name of freedom. It was therefore necessary to undermine its granite foundation and to destroy the entire building of Christianity. And they set about the work of this enterprise and placed themselves at the head of this concealed world revolution by means of Freemasonry, which they had controlled.

"The emancipation of Jewry in France was the gain, pursued in secret, of the revolution, which invented its famed human rights (rights of man) in order to place the Jews upon equal rights with all Christians. To this and nothing else extends the much-praised freedom, in whose name that terrible revolution was instigated."[55]

---

[54] Jose Maria Cardinal Caro R., Archbishop-Bishop of Santiago, Primate of Chile: The Secret of Freemasonry. Publishers: Difusion. Pages 263, 264, 265 and 266.
[55] Prato: Della questione judaica in Europa, 1891, page 53.

CHAPTER FOUR

CRIMES OF FREEMASONRY

Concerning the monstrous crimes of this master work of modern Jewry, which Freemasonry represents, the most dignified Cardinal Caro says:

"The reading of the Freemasonic ritual allows it to be discerned, at least in the highest degree, that it prepares its disciples for revenge, revolution and hence for crime.

" 'In all these rites', says Benoit, 'the Freemasons are subjected to an education which teaches them cruelty in theory and practice. They are told that the Freemasonic order follows the aim of avenging the death of Hiram Abiff or his three faithless companions, or the death of de Molay on his murderers, the Pope, the King and Nogaret.'

"In the First Degree the beginner tests his courage on neck and head, which are dressed about with blood-filled entrails. In another degree, he who is accepted, must throw about heads which are placed upon a snake; or also kill a lamb (30th degree of the Scottish rite A.A.), with which action he believe that he kills a man. Here he must carry on bloody fights with foes who dispute his return to the fatherland; there are heads on a pole or a corpse in a coffin and the brothers in mourning vow revenge. The murdering of Rossi, the minister of Pius IX, through his former conspiratorial brothers is well known.

"In the year 1883 four Italians, Emiliani, Scuriatti, Lazzoneschi and Adriani, members of 'Young Italy' who had fled to France, were betrayed to Mazzini and his helpers as traitors.

"On 22nd October 1916, Count Stürck, the chancellor of Austria, was murdered. The murderer, Fritz Adler, was a Freemason and son of a Freemason, as well as member of a lodge with high Freemasonic dignitaries in Switzerland. In his declaration he defended the right to exercise justice with his own hand.

"In France occasioned by the Dreyfus affair the following persons were murdered: Captain d'Attel, who gave evidence against him, the deputy Chaulin-Servinière, who had received from d'Attel the details of Dreyfus's confession; the district captain Laurenceau, who revealed sums of money which had been sent from abroad to the friends of Dreyfus, in his opinion for bribery, and the prison warden Rocher, who claimed to have heard how Dreyfus partially confessed his crime. Captain Valerio, one of the witnesses against Dreyfus, and President Faure who had opposed a revision of the trial, also vanished soon afterwards. All defenders of Dreyfus were Freemasons, and in addition Jews.

"In Sweden the brother of Gustav III was murdered by H. Ankerstrom, secret envoy of the grand lodge, which Condorcet directed, in accordance with the agreement of the Freemasons who have assembled in 1786 in Frankfurt/Main.

"In Russia Paul I was murdered, a Freemason, who although he knew the danger from the brotherhood, strictly forbade it. For the same reason his son, Alexander I, suffered an identical fate, who was murdered in 1825 at Taganrog. The murderers were in their entirety Freemasons. ('The great criminals of Freemasonry.' Trans.)

MURDERS OF LAYMEN

"In France the death of Louis XVI is attributed to them. Cardinal Mathieu, Archbishop of Besançon, and Monsignor Bessan, Bishop of Nimes, have reported in letters, which are known all over the world, of the revelations which were made to them concerning the resolution taken in the convent of Wilhelmsbad to murder Louis XVI and the king of Sweden. These revelations were made to them by two former members of this convent... The murder of the Duke de Berry... the murder of Lew, the great patriot and enthusiastic Catholic of Lucerne/Switzerland were resolved upon and carried out by members of the sect.

"In Austria the famous crime of Sarajevo, which was the cause of the First World War, was arranged by the Freemasons, announced in advance and carried out at the given time. A high Freemasonic dignitary, of Swiss nationality, expressed himself in 1912 in this connection in the following manner: 'The successor to the throne is a personality with much talent; a pity that he is condemned; he will die on the way to the throne.' Madame de Tebes predicted his death already two years previously. Those principally guilty were in their entirety Freemasons.

" 'All this', says Wichtl, 'is no mere suspicion, but legally proven facts, which have been intentionally concealed.'

"In Germany Marshal Echhorn and his adjutant, Captain von Dressler, were murdered on 30th July, 1918. The day before, the Paris Freemasons newspaper 'Le Matin' wrote that a patriotic secret society had offered a high price for the head of Echhorn. One can certainly imagine what kind of society supplied this information to 'Le Matin'.

"In Italy Umberto I was murdered by the anarchist Pressi, who as a Freemason belonged to a lodge in Paterson, New Jersey, United States, even though he himself had not been to America. Thus the declaration that, in certain Degrees, arrogant men gave of the inscription on the cross, was transformed into its opposite: I.N.R.I. = Justum necare reges Italiae: it is just to murder the kings of Italy.

"On 26th March 1885, the Duke Carl III was murdered in Parma; the assassin, Antonio Carra, had the day before been chosen and incited at a secret session, whose chairmanship Lemmi performed; Lemmi was later all-highest Grandmaster of Italian Freemasonry, and as it appears, also of world Freemasonry. A certain Lippo had prepared a doll in order to illustrate how the most deadly dagger thrusts could be given, and the executioner was chosen by lots.

"On 22nd May, Ferdinand II of Naples died; he was given a poison in a slice of melon, which caused his terribly painful death. The instigator of this king's death was a Freemason who belonged to one of the most criminal branches of this sect, to that of the so called 'sublime and perfect Masters'. He was a disciple of Mazzini and one of the most respected persons of the royal court. Margiotta does not risk giving his name. (Marg.

A   L. 21-34) With this author one can read about further countless crimes that were committed by Freemasonry in Italy. In Portugal, King Charles and his son Louis were murdered. The Freemasons prepared the fall of the monarchy. The venerable H. Magalhaes de Lima travelled in December 1907 to Paris, where he was solemnly received by H. Moses, the member of the Grand Lodge. Magalhaes held lectures, in which he announced 'the fall of the monarchy in Portugal' and the 'imminent foundation of the republic'. The well-known opponent of Freemasonry, Abbé Tourmentin, wrote then that the Freemasons were clearly preparing a blow against the Portuguese royal family. He gave expression to his fear that within a short time King Charles would be driven out or murdered. Ten weeks later Tourmentin's fears were fulfilled, and he openly and clearly accused the Freemasons of this murder. The latter preferred to keep silent. In America, one can read various details by Eckert concerning the persecution and murdering of Morgan in the United States, because he wished to publish a book revealing the secrets of Freemasonry; further, concerning the destruction of printing works and the persecution of the printer as well as other hateful crimes that followed upon this murder; concerning the public alarm that broke out when it was learned what favour the authorities, who as a rule were Freemasons, afforded the murderer and the support with which the Lodges regarded them (Eckert, II, 201 and sequel). Also known is the murder of the President of Ecuador, Garcia Moreno.

BLOODBATHS, SUMMARY EXECUTIONS AND PLUNDERINGS

"It is necessary to read the description of the freethinker Taine, in order to have an idea of what happened in France, when in the year 1789 and the three following years the Freemasons conducted the government: more than 150,000 refugees and fugitives were imprisoned; 10,000 persons were killed without trial in a single province, that of Anjou; there were 500 dead in only one province of the west. In the year 1796, General Hoche wrote to the Ministry of the Interior:

" 'The present ratio to the population of 1789 is one to twenty. There have been up to 400,000 prisoners at once in the prisons. More than 1,200,000 private persons have suffered injury to their person and several millions, with property, in their goods and chattels.' " (Taine, mentioned by Benoit, F.M. II. 268, remark.)[56]

Whoever desires more information should read the work of the most dignified Cardinal Caro, "The Secret of Freemasonry."

---

[56] Jose Maria Caro R., Cardinal Archbishop of Santiago, Primate of Chile: The Secret of Freemasonry. Publishers: Difusion. Pages 190, 191, 193, 194, 195, 196, 197, 198, 201.

CHAPTER FIVE

FREEMASONRY AS SPREADER OF THE JACOBIN REVOLUTIONS

The Archbishop of Port-Louis, Monsignor Leon Meurin, says in his work "Philosophy of Freemasonry":

"In the year 1844, Disraeli placed the following words in the mouth of the Jew Sidonia (Coningsby VI. XV.): 'Since English society has begun to stir and its institutions are threatened by powerful associations, they see the formerly so faithful Jews in the ranks of the revolutionaries... This mysterious diplomacy, which so disturbs the western powers, is organised by Jews and for the greatest part also carried out by them... the monstrous revolution, which is prepared in Germany, and whose effects will be still greater than those of the Reformation, is carried out under the protectorate of the Jews. Leading its preparations and effects in Germany I see a Lithuanian Jew, in the Spanish Senor Mendizabal, I see a Jew from Aragon; in the President of the French Council, Marshal Soult, I recognise the son of a French Jew; in the Prussian minister, Graf Arnim, I see a Jew. As you already see, dear Coningsby, the world is ruled by personages who are very different from those who are regarded as ruling and do not work behind the scenes.'

"During the revolution of 1848, which was led by the Grand Orient of France, its grandmaster, the Jew Cremieux was minister of Justice. In 1860 this man founded 'the Israelite International League' and announced with incomprehensible insolence in the year 1861, in the 'Israelite Archives' (page 651), 'that in place of Popes and Caesars, a new kingdom, a new Jerusalem, will arise.' And our good Freemasons with their blind eyes help the Jews in the 'great work' of building up this new temple of Solomon, this new Caesarean-Papal kingdom of the Cabbalists!

"In the year 1862, a Berlin Freemason had a leaflet of eight pages printed, in which he complained about the predominance of Jews in the lodges. Under the title 'Signs of the Time', he alludes to the dangerous character of the Berlin elections of 28th April and 6th May of the year in question. 'An element', he said, 'has appeared on the scene and has exercised a dangerous influence which causes disintegration on all sides: the Jew. The Jews are leading in their writings, words and deeds; they are the most principal leaders and agents in all revolutionary undertakings, even in the building of barricades. One has seen this very clearly in Berlin in the year 1848. How is it possible that, in Berlin, 217 Jewish candidates were elected, and that, in two districts, only Jews were elected with the exclusion of any Christian candidates?'

"This position of things has worsened more and more. The Jews form the majority in the city government, so that Berlin with justice could be called the capital of the Jews.

"In the press the Jews speak of the 'people' and of the 'Nation', as if there were only Jews and no Christians existed. The explanation for this could be given by the 'Freemasonic inciters' who, following Brother Lamartine, introduced the revolutions of 1789, 1830, 1848, etc. This explanation is confirmed by 'Brother Garnier Pages', a minister of the Republic, who, in the year 1848, publicly declared that the revolution of 1848 represents the triumph of the norms of the Freemasons league, so that France was dedicated to Freemasonry, and that 40,000 Freemasons had promised their help to conduct to an end the glorious work of the erection of the Republic, which had been chosen to spread out over the whole of Europe and in the end over the entire earth."

"The high peak of all this is the political and revolutionary power of the Jews, according to the words of J. Weil, leader of the Jewish Freemasons, who in a secret report said: 'We exercise a powerful influence on the movements of our time and of the progress of civilisation in the direction of the Republicanising of the peoples.'

"The Jew Ludwig Boerne, another Freemasonic leader, said likewise in a secret document: 'We have with mighty hand so much shattered the pillars upon which the old building rests that they groan and crack.' Mendizabal, likewise a Jew and the soul of the Spanish revolution of 1820, set through the capture of Porto and Lisbon, and in 1838, by means of his Freemasonic influence, realised the revolution in Spain, where he became Prime Minister."

And his Excellence, the Archbishop, goes on to say:

"The Jew Mendizabal had promised as minister to improve the insecure financial position of Spain; but in a short time the result of his machinations was a frightful increase of the national debt and a great diminishing of the State incomes, while he and his friends accumulated enormous riches. The sale of more than 900 Christian institutions of a religious and charitable kind, which the 'Cortesa', upon the instigation of the Jews, had declared to be national property, created for them a magnificent opportunity for the unparalleled increase of their personal property. In the same manner church property was dealt with. The unskilful mockery of religious and national feelings went so far that the mistress of Mendizabal dared to flaunt herself in public with a wonderful necklace, which a short time previously had served to decorate an image of the Holy Virgin Mary in one of the churches of Madrid."

"The Berlin Freemason, whom we mentioned at the beginning, said further: 'The danger for the throne and the altar, which are threatened by the Jewish power, has reached its highest point, and it is time to sound alarm, just as the leaders of German Freemasonry did when they said: 'The Jews have understood that 'the kingly art' (the Freemasonic art) was a principal means to erect their own secret kingdom... The danger threatens not only our Order, Freemasonry, but the State in general... The Jews find manifold opportunities in the lodges, to exercise their old familiar systems of briberies; by their sowing confusion in many affairs. If one bears in mind the role that the Jews played in the crimes of the French revolution and the illegal Corsican seizure of property, if one also bears in mind the tenacious belief of the Jews in a future Israelite kingdom which will rule over the world, as well as their influence on a great number of ministers of State, one will recognise how dangerous their activity can become in

Freemasonic affairs. The Jewish people forms a tribe, which hostilely opposes the entire human race, and which believes the God of Israel has only chosen one people, to whom all others must serve as 'footstools.'

"Let it be borne in mind that among the 17 million inhabitants of Prussia there are only 600,000 Jews; let it be borne in mind with what convulsive zeal this people of Oriental and irrepressible activity works to attain the overthrow of the State with all means; to occupy the higher teaching institutions, even by means of money, and to monopolise the government offices in its favour.

"Carlile, one of the most authoritative Freemasonic personages, says (page 86): 'The Freemasonry of the Grand Lodge is at present through and through Jewish.'

"The 'Kreuz-Zeitung', the principal organ of the Prussian conservatives, published, from 29th June to 3rd July 1875, a series of articles, in which it elaborated that the chief ministers in the German and Prussian government, not excluding Prince Bismarck, found themselves in the hands of the Jewish kings of the Bourse, and that the Jewish bankers were those who in practice ruled Prussia and Germany. These facts caused the Jew Gutzkow to assert: 'The true founders of the new German Reich are the Jews; the Jews are the most advanced in all sciences, the press, the stage and politics.'

"In the year 1860 M. Stamm wrote a book on this theme, in which he proves that the kingdom of all-embracing freedom on earth was founded by the Jews. In the same year, Sammter published a long letter in the 'Volksblatt', in order to demonstrate that the Jews would very soon take up the place of the Christian nobility; the rule of the nobility was falling and will lose its place in this epoch of all enveloping light and of all embracing freedom, to which we have drawn so near.

" 'Do you not understand', he writes, 'the true meaning of the promise, which was given by the Lord God Sabaoth to our father Abraham? This promise, which will be fulfilled with certainty, namely that one day all peoples of earth will be subject to Israel. Do you believe that God referred to a universal monarchy with Israel as King? Oh no! God scattered the Jews over the entire surface of the globe, so that they should form a kind of leaven over all races, and in the end, as the chosen, which they are, extend their rulership over the former."

" 'It is not likely that the terrible repression that the Christian peoples of Europe have suffered — who have been made poor through the usurers and the greed of the Jews and lament about this, so that the national wealth is accumulated in the hands of the great bankers — will be satisfied with isolated anti-Semitic upheavals. The monarchies, whose firm foundations are still not shattered through the Freemasonic hammer and whose ruling houses are still not at the position of the ragged and barefooted Freemasons, who have their eyes bound, will join together against this vile sect and destroy the ranks of the Anarchists.' "

"Carlile, himself a fanatical Freemason, horrified at the fate of mankind in the hands of the Jews, says: 'When the legislators busy themselves again with the secret societies, they would do well to make no exception in favour of Freemasonry.'

"The privilege of secrecy is allowed to the Freemasons according to law in England, France, Germany and, according to our recognising it, in most countries. The fact that all revolutions emanate from the depths of Freemasonry would be inexplicable, if we did not know that, with the present exception of Belgium, the ministries of all lands are found in the hands of leading Freemasons, thus fundamentally, of the Jews."[57]

One of the most interesting proofs is undoubtedly that of the "Freemason" Haugwitz, who was inspector of the Lodges of Prussia and Poland. In the year 1777 he wrote in his Memoirs:

"I took over the direction of the lodges of Prussia, Poland and Russia. There 1 have gained the firm conviction that everything which has occurred since 1789 in France — in a word, the revolution — was at that time not only arranged, but was also prepared by means of meetings, instructions, oath-taking and signs, which leaves the intelligence in no doubt as to who thought it all out and directed it."[58]

As far as the murder of Louis XVI is concerned, we likewise possess the evidence of the Jesuit father Abel:

"In the year 1784", he declared, "there took place in Frankfurt an extraordinary assembly of the Grand Eclectic Lodge. One of the members placed for discussion the condemning of Louis XVI, the king of France, and Gustav III, the king of Sweden. This man was called Abel and was my grandfather."[59]

After this gathering, one of the participants, the Marquis de Visieu, declared as follows:

"What I can say to you is that a finely spun and a most deep-reaching conspiracy has been instigated, so that your religion and governments will succumb."[60]

"The existence of this conspiracy and its plan to murder the king of France and the king of Sweden, are likewise confirmed by the greatest number of authors, who have made serious investigations into the

[57] Monsignor Leon Meurin S. J., Archbishop-Bishop of Port-Louis, Philosophy of Freemasonry, 1957, pages 212, 213, 214, 215, 217 and 218.
[58] Von Haugwitz: Memoiren.
[59] P. Abel: Die Neue Freie Presse, Vienna, 1898.
[60] Barruel: Memoirs of the History of Jacobinism.

Freemasonry question,[61] and the tragic events do the same. On 21st January King Louis XVI died, executed through the guillotine, after a mock trial, at which the majority of judges were Freemasons. A year later, King Gustav III of Sweden was murdered by Akustrem, a pupil of Condorcet. In the same year the Emperor Leopold vanished in a mysterious manner.

"In order to live, France must not sacrifice what is most rational in its existence: the philosophical, political and social ideals of its predecessors of 1789; it must not extinguish the torch of its revolutionary spirit, with which it has illuminated the world."

The same speaker adds:

"The worst humiliation for France would occur if the work of the revolution were cursed... at least it should be possible to perpetuate it without the loss of its ideals."[62]

"One must never forget that it was the French revolution which realised the principles of Freemasonry, which were prepared in our temples", said a speaker at the congress of Freemasons of Brussels.[63] In an assembly of the Lodge of Angers, which took place in 1922, one of the brothers proclaimed: "Freemasonry, which played the most important role in the year 1789, must be ready to supply its fighting groups for an always possible revolution."[64]

Let us pass over the stage of participation of the Jews in revolutions in general. Already in the year 1648 the great revolutionary leader Cromwell was supported by the Jews; a deputation, which came from remotest Asia and was led by the Rabbi Jakob ben Azabel, appeared before the English dictator. The results of the conversations which took place were not long in coming and "Cromwell used his entire power in order to abolish the laws that placed restrictions upon the Jews in England."[65] One of the closest collaborators of Cromwell was the Rabbi of Amsterdam, Manasse ben Israel.[66]

---

[61] P. Deschamps, Cardinal Mathieu, Monsignor Besson and others.

[62] Maurice Fara: Freemasonry exposed. Publishers: La Hoja de Roble, Buenos Aires, pages 62 and 63.

[63] International Congress of Brussels, 1910. Memorial. Page 124.

[64] Official state journal of France, October 1922, page 281.

[65] Leon Halevy: Zusammenfassung der Geschichte der Juden. Short History of the Jews.

[66] R. Lambelin: Die Siege Israels, page 44.

Ernest Renan, who cannot be accused of Antisemitism, wrote the following:

"In the French revolutionary movement, the Jewish element plays a chief role and it is very difficult to deny this. It is true that around 1789 the Jews went to work with much caution and concealed themselves behind the Freemasonic organisations and the philosophical associations; however this did not prevent several of the sons of Israel from taking an active part in the revolutionary events and making use of these from the material standpoint. The first shot against the Swiss Guard of the Tuilleries was fired, on the 10th August 1791, by the Jew Zalkind Hourwitz Land."[67]

But since this zeal for war carries with it many dangers, the Jews prefer to devote themselves to other, less dangerous and above all rewarding activities. The old Hebrew, Benoltas, a millionaire of this city (Cadiz), was from now on named as General Treasurer of the Order and already reckoned to possess a disposable capital of three hundred thousand Thalers. (Rule 44 of the Grand Spanish Orient of 10th April 1824).[68]

The supplying of the Republican armies was carried out through the Israelites Biderman, Max Beer, Moselmann and others. This gave occasion to the complaints which were made by Colonel Bernanville of the army of the Moselle, because for the troops he had been supplied with boys' shoes with cardboard soles, children's stockings and completely moth-eaten sailcloths for tents.[69]

Soon after, the laws that restricted the rights of the Jews were lifted, thanks to the mediation of Abbot Gregoire, Mirabeau, Robespierre and others (this is done on the first occasion by all revolutionary governments), and soon afterwards, when the ideas of 1789 gained the upper hand, a veritable flood — according to the words of Capefigues — of foreigners discharged themselves over France from the banks of the Rhine.[70] Then appeared in the political arena such names as Klotz, Benjamin Veitel Ephraim, Etta Palm, etc. "The Messiah has arrived for us on 28th February 1790 with the Rights of Man",[71] wrote the Jew Cohen, "and in fact the awarding of all rights of citizenship to the Jews was one of

---

[67] Leon Kahn: Die Juden von Paris wahrend der Revolution.

[68] Maurice Fara: Freemasonry exposed. Publishers: La Hoja de Roble, Buenos Aires, page 83.

[69] P. Gaxotte: The French Revolution. Pages 279-280.

[70] Capefigue: "Las Grandes Operaciones Financieras."

[71] "Archivos Israelitas", VIII, 1847, page 801.

the great victories of Israel." "The revolution of 1830", says the Jew Bedarride, "has only perpetuated these happy results."

When, in the year 1848, the rule of the peoples reached its last limits, the same author cynically added that Israelite names appeared in the highest realms of power. These chosen ones, these representatives of the people, often took on such French names as Fould, Ceriber, Cremieux, etc. The custom of there being at least one Jewish representative in the government of the Republic is something that, apart from rare exceptions, has been preserved up to our days.

However, not only in France did the Jewish people play a predominant role, but with all revolutionary movements. "The revolution that shook central Europe in the year 1848", writes Lambelin, "was spread and supported by the Jews, as the countless facts and documents prove."[72]

Among the instigators of the revolution of 1870 and among the members of the Commune appear likewise the Jews, who were represented through Ravel Isaac Calmer, Jacob Pereyra, and others. The afore-mentioned author remarks of the presence of 18 Jews among the principal leaders of the Commune.[73] It is interesting to establish that, during the burning of Paris in the year 1871, the revolutionaries left untouched the 150 buildings that belonged to the Rothschild family.

If we proceed with the study of these movements in Europe, we again find Jews, the poet Heine, Karl Marx, Lasalle and many others.

"In order to destroy the former society, which rejected him", writes Drumont, "the Jew has understood how to place himself at the head of the democratic movement. Karl Marx, Lasalle, the most principal Nihilists, all leaders of the worldwide revolution are Jews. In this manner the Jews represent the leadership of the movements, which suits them."[74] Let us not forget that the founders of the International in the year 1864 were the Jews Marx, Neumeier, Fribourg, James Cohen, Aaron, Adler, Franckel, and the sole non-Jew (?) Gompers.

In order to direct the revolutionary movement in France, the so-called newspaper "L'Humanité" was founded. For this purpose a subscription was opened, which brought in the sum of 780,000 Francs. Let us mention

[72] Bedarride: "Los Judios en Francia, en Italia yen Espaira". Pages 428-430.
[73] R. Lambelin: Op. cit., pages 10 and 62.
[74] E. Drumont: Jewish France.

the names of the twelve contributors who "by chance" were all Jews: Levy Brul, Levy Bram, A. Dreyfus, L. Dreyfus, Eli Rodriquez, Leon Picard, Blum, Rouff, Kasevitz, Salmon Reinach and Sachs.

After one has read the preceding, one cannot wonder that, at the Jewish Synod of Leipzig on 29th June 1869, the following resolution was accepted:

"The Synod recognises, that the development and carrying through of modern (read: revolutionary) principles are the firmest guarantee for the present and the future of Jewry and its members. They are the most important conditions of life for the expanding existence and the greatest development of Jewry."[75]

"In many respects the revolution has only been the application of the ideal that Israel has brought to the world", as Leroy Beaulieu,[76] writes, an author who is in no way accused of Antisemitism. One must give him justice, for the importance of Jewish infiltration in the revolutionary work cannot be denied.

THE ORGANIZATION OF THE LEAGUE OF NATIONS

We have seen the League of Nations, which was founded and maintained by the same secret forces, which we have already encountered, when it was a matter of destruction; today Freemasonry, their helpers the Left Parties, and, behind everything, the Jewish people, attempt to destroy national feeling and the sovereignty of the state through the creation of an international super-government and at the same time to demoralise the peoples with an anti-militarist and pacifistic propaganda. If national feeling is lost, we will see those peoples standing completely defenceless against this secret and cunning power, as the "Jewish-Freemasonic striving for power" can be described.

Brother Eugen Bertraux has recently proposed to the "Grand Lodge" of France that Article 17 of the Constitution of the said "Grand Lodge" should be abolished, which prescribes to all its disciples that they should obey the "laws of the land in which they have permission to freely assemble, and that they be ready for all sacrifices which their country

---

[75] Gougenot des Mousseaux: The Jew, Jewry and the Judaisation of the Christian Peoples, page 332.
[76] Leroy Beaulieu: Israel among the Peoples, page 66.

desires of them"; for, "according to the principles of a universal morality, every Freemason is by definition an essentially free man, who only acts according to his conscience, and our Freemasonic conscience cannot compulsively demand of its disciples that they be ready for all sacrifices which the country desires." The abolition, which he proposes, will suffice in value in protecting the individual conscience; whereby is to be understood that, in the case of an increase in tragic conflicts, those individual consciences, according to their own responsibility, will obey or disobey the call of their reason and their belief in the highest truth.[77]

THE JEWISH-FREEMASONIC ACTION
IN THE FACE OF CATHOLICISM

The most dignified Cardinal Caro assures us in this connection, that: "It is beyond doubt that the activity of Freemasonry against the Catholic Church is only the continuation of the war against Christ that has been waged by Jewry for 1900 years, naturally adjusted to the situation of the Christian world, by which the former has to conduct itself by means of secrecy, cheating and sanctimoniousness."

"Let us not forget that Rabbinic Jewry is the declared and irreconcilable enemy of Christianity", says Webster. "The hatred against Christianity and against the person of Christ is no occurrence of recent date, nor can one regard it as the result of persecution: it forms an important component of Rabbinical tradition, which has arisen before any kind of persecution of Jews through the Christians took place, and which lasted in our land very much later than after this persecution ended."

On its side, "The British Guardian" (13th March 1925) makes this assertion: "The Christian Church is being attacked as never for centuries, and this attack is almost exclusively the work of the Jews." (Rev. of S.S. Sacr., p. 430, 1925). For the rest, the relations of Freemasonry or of Jewry with Bolshevism and Communism in Mexico, in Russia, in Hungary,

---

[77] Maurice Fara: "Freemasonry Exposed". Publishers: La Hoja de Roble, Buenos Aires, page 115.

persecuting the Catholic Church and with it the whole of Christianity (and the threat of doing this all over the world), are a universal occurrence."[78]

---

[78] Jose Maria Caro R., Cardinal, Archbishop of Santiago, Primate of Chile: The Secret of Freemasonry, [The Mystery of Freemasonry Unveiled], Publishers: Difusion. Pages 267 and 268.

CHAPTER SIX

FREEMASONRY FAVOURS AND SPREADS

COMMUNISM, WHICH IS A JEWISH CREATION

Among the abundant documentation which his most Reverend the Cardinal Caro quotes, to show that Jews and Communists spread Communism, we select the following:

"According to the 'Russian Tribune' which appears in Munich in the Russian language, Jewry in its fight maintains, according to various plans, the following combat organisations, all for the purpose of preparing the triumph of the Third International."

1. The Golden International; see Chapter III.
2. The Red International; see Chapter III.
3. The Black International or Combat Association of Jewry.[79]

"A very similar work is performed by Russian Jewry. We, the emigrant Russians, have seen with our own eyes the enormous number of Jews who play a role in the ranks of the instigators of revolution."

If we pass over the work of preparation of this revolution and the events of 1905, we will at once see what the Vienna Jewish paper "Der Hammer" wrote on occasion of the Beylis Affair (an affair of ritual murder in Kiev). The judgment in favour of Beylis, through the jury, amounted to his exoneration; but the character of the ritual murder was proven.

"The Russian government had resolved to declare war on the Jews of Kiev. Now, they must know that, upon this war, the fate, not of the Jews, for the Jewish people is unconquerable, but of the Russian people depends. For the Russian government it is a question of life and death. Its

---

[79] Jose Maria Caro R., Cardinal, Archbishop of Santiago, Primate of Chile: The Secret of Freemasonry. Publishers: Difusion. Page 265.

victory in this affair will be the beginning of its collapse. May the Russian rulers exercise caution! We will provide proof to the whole world that one cannot meddle unpunished with the Jews, whether the latter are of Kiev or any other place." (Der Hammer, No. 254, 1911. Mentioned by General Nechovolodof in "Czar Nicholas II and the Jews"; and by Msgr. Jouin in "The Jewish-Freemasons Danger" and "The United Front", 1927, edition of "Petit Oranais".) Unfortunately for Russia and the entire civilised world, this threat was not without consequences. Six years later it was turned into a fact. We will quote some figures. The first Workers and Soldiers Council (Soviet) was composed of 23 members, of whom 19 were Jews; the Council of Peoples Commissars of 1920 had 17 Jews among its 22 members; among the 43 high officials of the War Commission, 34 were Israelites; on the Commissariat of the Interior there were 54 Jews among the officials; in that for foreign affairs, 13 Jews and 17 members. In the financial department of the government the percentage of Jews rose to 86% and in the court system up to 95% etc.

In order to briefly summarise this statistic, let us remark that, among the 545 most principal agents of the Russian revolution in question, 447 belonged to the "chosen people", 68 to different nationalities (Latvians, Germans, Poles, etc), and only 30 were of Russian nationality.

These figures, which are taken from Bolshevist information sources, appeared in a pamphlet under the title "Who Rules in Russia?" which was published in New York in 1920. (See Msgr. Jouin, "The Jewish-Freemasonic Danger", II, page 108 and seq.) We should add that, at present, there are 16 Jews among the 22 trade agents of the Soviets abroad. "Report of the Urbe Agency", of 25th August 1927, which was quoted by R. Lamelin in "The Victory of Israel," page 170.[80]

In his book "Il manganello e l'aspersorio", the lay writer Ernesto Rossi disputes violently with the already mentioned periodical "Civilta Cattolica", from which he reproduces the following paragraph, with the intention of refuting it:

"We see 'heroes' of the sect, who are not able to resist a gift of two millions, perpetuated in all cities through statues. We see the sons of these 'heroes', who pocket large sums while despising the dominant misery. Mazzini involved himself with the synagogue, whose fruits of love are very well known in the Campidoglio of Rome; Garibaldi, Cavour, Farini,

---

[80] Maurice Fara: Freemasonry exposed, Publishers: Hoja de Roble, Buenos Aires, Pages 81 and 82.

Depretis were modest servants of the synagogue, and so are still many of those 'great men' to whom the good will of the peoples has erected and still erects memorial stones, busts and monuments, in order to glorify their love of 'freedom' and of the 'Fatherland'."[81]

Many writers of the most different directions have asserted that the Jewish question in Italy did not represent the features of a national disorder. We do not share this opinion and limit ourselves only to recalling that those who introduced Communism into our land, Modigliani, Treves, Della Seta, Musatti, Momigliano, Donati, etc, were Jews.[82]

"And did not the renowned Togliatti, the leader for many years of the Italian Communist party, marry the Jewess Montagnana? And was not her brother, Mario Montagnana, in the directorship of the newspaper "L'Unita" in its Milan edition? It should be known, in addition, that likewise those who directed the Communist press in Italy were Jews: Longo (Vie Nuovo), Alatri (L'Unita of Rome), Tedeschi (L'Unita of Milan); Cohen directs the 'Paese Sera', Levi the 'Lotta Sindicale', and Jachia the paper 'Republicia', who came from there into the directing of the press of the Communist party."[83]

---

[81] Ernesto Rossi: II Manganello e l'Aspersorio. Florence. Page 336 and volumes of the "Civilta Cattolica" of September, November and December 1889.

[82] The Jew Salvatore Jona writes in reference to Treves and Modigliani: "... they were the men at the head of Italian Socialism; even if they were men with weak Jewish belief, one cannot deny that they devoted themselves with Semitic passion and with tenacity to the following of their ideal." From the work: Gli ebrei in Italia durante il fascismo, Milan 1962, page 9.

[83] Excerpt from the little volume already mentioned: Rivelazione d'interesse mondiale.

PART THREE

THE SYNAGOGUE OF SATAN

CHAPTER ONE

JEWISH STRIVING FOR POWER

The Hebrew people was chosen by God as preserver of the true religion, to whose preservation it was entrusted in the midst of the idolatrous peoples until the arrival of the promised Messiah, in whom the prophecies of the Old Testament should be fulfilled. However, even before the coming of Christ, the Jews began to distort the said prophecies by giving them a false, racial and ambitious interpretation.

The promise of a kingdom of the true God upon earth, i.e. a spiritual Kingdom of the true religion, the Jews interpreted as a material kingdom of their race, as the promise of God of world domination to the Israelites and an enslaving of all peoples on earth through them. As examples of these false interpretations one can quote the following: In Genesis, Chapter XXII, Verse 17 and 18, the angel of the Lord says to Abraham:

"That in blessing I will bless thee, and in multiplying I will multiply thy seed as the stars of the heaven, and as the sand which is upon the seashore; and thy seed shall possess the gate of thine enemies." "And in thy seed shall all the nations of the earth be blessed."

The Jews, lusting for power, have given these verses a materialistic interpretation and think that God has offered them, as the full-blooded descendants of Abraham, that they have power over the gates of their foes: that only in them, as the Jewish race, all peoples of earth be blessed. On the other hand, Holy Church interprets these prophecies in a spiritual sense:

"This is the victory that the spiritual children of Abraham (i.e. the Christians) shall obtain through the power of Jesus Christ and the gifts of an everlasting righteousness concerning the visible and invisible foes of their salvation. And so was fulfilled according to Scripture this prophecy with the erecting of the Church, when all peoples of the world subjected themselves to Jesus Christ and received from Him blessing and salvation."[84]

In Deuteronomy, Chapter II, Verse 25, the Lord says:

"This day will I begin to put the dread of thee and the fear of thee upon the nations that are under the whole of heaven, who shall hear report of thee, and shall tremble, and be in anguish because of thee."

This passage is also given a restricted interpretation by Holy Church which differs completely from the ambitious Jewish feeling, which degenerated throughout history into frightful actions, which prove the practical application of this false interpretation. Also, wherever during the Middle Ages the heretical movements directed by Jews triumphed, although these victories were locally limited and of transitory nature, they were always accompanied by crime, fear and terror. The same occurred with the Freemasonic revolutions, such as those of 1789 in France or that of 1931-1936 in Spain. And yet it is said that one must not speak of Jewish-Communist revolutions! In the Soviet Union, where the Hebrews were successful in introducing their totalitarian dictatorship, they have sowed fear and death in such a cruel manner, that the poor enslaved Russians, have now only to hear the word "Jew" to tremble with terror.

Another example of this kind is obtained for us through the false interpretation by the Jews of Verse 16, in Chapter VII of Deuteronomy, which says:

"And thou shalt consume all the people which the Lord thy God shall deliver unto thee; thine eye shall have no pity upon them; neither shalt thou serve their gods; for that will be a snare unto thee."

While Holy Church likewise gives this passage a limited spiritual interpretation, the Jews understand it in the sense that God has provided them with the right to consume all peoples of earth and to gain power over their riches. We already saw, in the 4th Chapter of this work, what the Rabbi Baruch Levi wrote to his pupil, the young Jew Karl Marx, as the later founder of what was badly described as "scientific Socialism", where he quoted apparent theological principles to justify the right of the Jews to appropriate to themselves the riches of all peoples on earth through Proletarian Communist movements, which are controlled by Jewry.

---

[84] Authorized commentaries on the Bible, Scio, Madrid 1852, Volume 1, p. 59.

The 24th verse of the same Chapter VII of Deuteronomy runs as follows: "And he shall deliver their kinds into thine hand, and thou shalt destroy their name from under heaven; there shall no man be able to stand before thee, until thou have destroyed them."

This prophecy, which Holy Church relates to the sinful kings who ruled in the land of Canaan, the Jews interpret as having universal character. They therefore regard all their revolutions and conspiracies against the Kings of recent time as holy enterprises, which they perform in fulfilment of the Biblical prophecies, which they assume further as useful means to obtain domination over the world, which they likewise accept as commanded by God in the Holy Scripture.

The constant distortion of the true meaning of the prophecies of the Bible through the Jews we find renewed in reading of Verse 27 of chapter VII of the prophecy of Daniel:

"And the kingdom and dominion, and the greatness of the kingdom under the whole heaven, shall be given to the people of the saints of the Most High, whose kingdom is an everlasting kingdom, and all dominions shall serve and obey him!"

While Holy Church interprets this prophecy by accepting it as referring to the eternal rule of our Lord Jesus Christ, the Jews regard it as meaning that a flock is to be formed with a shepherd who naturally comes from the tribe of Israel, that their race shall attain eternal rulership in the world over the other peoples.

The prophecy of Isaiah LX, Verses 10-12 relates:

"10. And the sons of strangers shall build up thy walls, and their kings shall minister unto thee. 11. Therefore thy gates shall be open continually; they shall not be shut day nor night, that men may bring unto thee the riches of the Gentiles, and that their kings may be brought. 12. For the nation and kingdom that will not serve thee shall perish; yea, those nations shall be utterly wasted."

This prophecy alluding to the spiritual kingdom of Christ and his Church[85] takes on for the Jews a completely altered meaning, which crystallises in clearly recognisable actions. Wherever the Jewish

---

[85] Ibid. Volume IV, page 115.

dictatorship was set up, as for example in the Terror in France in the year 1789 or in the Jewish- Communist dictatorship in the lands which have fallen into the claws of the monster, whoever did not serve the Jews or dared to rebel against their slavery, has been destroyed. The Jews exist only as owners; for they gain power over the wealth of these nations. So one could go on in this way, to quote verses of the Old Testament that have been falsely interpreted by Jewish Imperialism. One must bear in mind that many of the prophets were murdered by the Jews, only because they contradicted them and blamed their perversion. However, the most dangerous of these false interpretations of the prophecies of the Bible was that in connection with the arrival of the Messiah as the redeemer of the human race, who would set up the rule of the true God in this world. Here it was that the Jews departed in the worst possible way from the true reality, by their giving the most sublime promises in relation to the Messiah a racial and imperialistic character.

Already in the times of our Lord Jesus Christ this false interpretation was so general among them that the majority of Hebrews imagined they saw in the promised Messiah a king or warlord who, with the help of God, would conquer all nations of the earth through bloody wars, and in the end Israel would in fact rule the whole world. When, therefore, Jesus was faced with such demands, and rejected all shedding of blood and revealed that His kingdom was not of this world, the Jewish Imperialists felt that all their hopes and demands were being destroyed. They began seriously to fear that the teaching of Christ might in the end even convince the Hebrews, and they might recognise Him as the promised Messiah.

When Jesus preached the equality of all men before God, the Jews thought, and they did so with good reason, that Christ with His teachings would render null or void their false views concerning Israel, as a people chosen by God to actually rule the world. Simultaneously He would declare null and void the idea of a people which is superior through the will of God to the others, and which is destined through the commandment of God to subjugate the remaining peoples and gain control of their wealth. Therefore the leaders of Jewry in that time, priests, scholars and Pharisees, etc, feared that Jesus threatened the glorious future that was predestined the people of Israel as future master of the world, for, if all peoples are equal before God, as our Lord Jesus Christ preached, there was no reason upon earth to choose one as preferential in the future and to rule over mankind.

In order to defend the ambitious Jewish thesis, Caiaphas, the high priest of Israel, alluded to the suitability that one man should die, namely Jesus Christ, in order to save a people.

After the blackest and most world-denying crime that was ever committed in the history of mankind, i.e. the murder of the Son of God by the Jews, the latter stood stiff-necked upon their demands for power and attempted in a new Holy Book to compile their false interpretations and to justify these. So appeared the "Talmud," which is damned by Holy Church and in which, as the Jews assert, the most perfected interpretation of the Old Testament is contained through divine inspiration. Afterwards appeared the collection of the "Jewish Cabbala", which means 'Prophecy.' In this was explained, likewise according to the Jews, through divine inspiration, the secret interpretation, i.e. the concealed and true interpretation of the Holy Scriptures. In the following we will quote some passages from these Secret Books of Jewry.

"You, Israelites, are called men, while the peoples of the world do not deserve the name of men but that of beasts."[86]

"The generation of a stranger is like the generation of beasts."[87] In the previously quoted passages the false interpreters of the Holy Scripture take a step of great weight: namely to deny the Christians and Gentiles, i.e. all peoples of earth, their human capacity, by ranking them among the breed of beasts.

To do justice to the importance of this criminal step, one must bring to mind that according to the "Divine Revelation" of the Old Testament, all animals and beasts have been created by God for the service of men, who eat their flesh, use their skins as clothing, kill them and in general can do with them as they please. On the other hand, He compelled men to keep His commandments in relation to other men.

According to the false interpretation of the Holy Scripture, both the Christians as well as other Gentiles are to the Jews simple beasts and not human beings. Therefore the Hebrews have automatically no duty to keep the commandments towards them and feel themselves at the same time completely in their right to kill, fleece and rob them of everything that they possess, like any kind of beast. Never upon earth has there existed or does there exist today, such an irreconcilable and totalitarian striving for power

---

[86] Talmud, Baba Metzia, Fol. 114, Section 2.
[87] Jebamoth. Fol. 94, page 2.

as that of the Jews. This far-reaching view that the other peoples are beasts, explains in clear form the irreconcilable, cruel and despicable ignoring of every human law, such as one can observe with the high Jewish personages of International Communism.

Their disdain towards other peoples goes so far as to assert: "What is a prostitute? Every woman who is not a Jewess."[88] This explains the fact, as different writers of diverse nationalities have recently shown, that the Jews have everywhere been the most unscrupulous traders in girls and the most zealous defenders of the disintegrating teachings of free love and of race mixing, while in their own families they maintain strict discipline and morality. Since Christians and Gentiles are in fact beasts, it is no wonder that they should live in immorality and intermixing.

As far as the murderous instincts of the Jews are concerned, which they have displayed over the centuries, they see themselves encouraged by what they hold to be the divine inspiration of the "Talmud" and of the "Cabbala," but which according to Holy Church is nothing more than a devilish interpretation.

"Kill the best among the Gentiles."[89] If God commanded them such – whereby it is a question of a cruel and bloodthirsty people, as the sufferings and death of Christ, the tortures and bloodbaths of Communist Russia, etc, prove –, how can it still surprise us that, wherever the Jew can, all those are murdered who oppose in any form his godless intrigues? This devilish hatred, this sadism, which the Jews have always shown towards other peoples, has its origin likewise in the false interpretation of divine revelation, i.e. in the "Cabbala" and in the "Talmud."

May the next example serve as an illustration:

"What does Har Sinai, i.e. Mount Sinai, mean? It means the mountain from which the Sina, i.e. hatred towards all peoples of the world has radiated."[90]

One must recall that upon Mount Sinai God revealed to Moses the Ten Commandments. But the modern Jews are of the opinion, equally false and disgusting, that there the religion of hate was revealed which they have preserved up to our days, that Satanic hatred towards all other peoples

---

[88] Eben Ha Eser, 6 and 8.
[89] Aboda Sara, 26 b Tosephot.
[90] Shabbath. Fol. 89, page 2.

which found its most extreme manifestation in the tortures and bloodbaths that have been perpetrated by International Communism.

The "Cabbala", which is reserved for the high initiates of Jewry and not the Plebs, carried out the division between Jews and Gentiles (among whom Christians were included) to the most disgusting and extreme limits. While on the one side the Gentiles are denigrated to the category of simple beasts, the Jews on the other are elevated to the category of Gods, by placing them equal to the Godhead himself. To such a degree have the Jews falsified the meaning of the "Pentateuch" and the Old Testament in general!

The blasphemous passage, which is quoted in the following, is highly enlightening in this connection:

"God places himself for display upon earth in the likeness of the Jew — Judas, Jevah or Jehovah are the same and unique being. The Hebrew is the living God, the God become flesh, the heavenly man, the Adam Kadmon. The other men are earthly and of inferior race, and only exist to serve the Hebrew; they are little beasts."[91]

It is therefore natural that this mode of thought has led the Jews to the conclusion that everything that exists upon earth belongs to them, including the beasts (among whom they include us, the rest of mankind) and also everything which belongs to these beasts.

The falsifiers of the Holy Scriptures attempted, both in the "Talmud" as in the "Cabbala", to strengthen the Jewish striving for power, by their giving these steps the feature of a divine dispensation. The following passages prove it:

"The All-highest spoke thus to the Israelites: 'You have recognised me as the sole ruler of the world and therefore I will make you into the sole rulers of the world.' "[92]

"Wherever the Hebrews settle, they must become the Lords; until they possess absolute rulership, they must regard themselves as banished and

---

[91] Kaballa ad Pentateucum, Fol. 97, Col. 3.
[92] Chaniga, Fol. 3-a, 3-b.

captives. Even if they are successful in ruling peoples, they may not, until they rule all, cease to cry: 'What torture! What indignity!' "[93]

This false divine revelation, which is found in the "Talmud," is one of the theological principles of the politics of modern Jewry, which in fact believes it is following the will of God through the literal translation into deeds.

As soon as the Christian and Gentile peoples in magnanimous manner opened their frontiers to the immigrant Jews, they could never have imagined that, in comparison with the migrations of other peoples, they granted shelter to eternal conspirators, who are always ready to work in the shadows and restlessly, until they rule the naive people that kindly opened its gates to them.

The "Talmud" remarks, however, that the Jews will not be able to rest, until their rule is unrestricted. The Hebrews have grasped that Democracy and Capitalism, which have allowed them to rule the peoples, have not obtained for them that unrestricted rulership commanded to them by God of which the "Talmud" speaks; therefore the Jews Karl Marx and Friedrich Engels invented a totalitarian system, which guaranteed to them to take from the Christians and Gentiles all their wealth, all their freedoms, and in general all their human rights, in order to place them on the level of the beasts. The dictatorship of Communist Socialism of Marx allows the Jew to attain this tyranny; and therefore, since its introduction in Russia, they have worked ceaselessly to destroy the Capitalist form of government, which admittedly they themselves had created, but which was incapable of allowing them to arrive at the desired goal. As the "Talmud" reveals, it does not satisfy the Jews to rule over some peoples, but they must control them all; and as long as they are not successful, they must cry out: "What torture! What an indignity!" This also explains the circumstance why the Jewish-Communist hunger for power is insatiable; and reveals how absurd it is to believe in an upright and peaceful coexistence or in the possibility that Communism will abandon its demand to conquer all the peoples of earth. The Jews believe that God has commanded them to lay upon all peoples their absolute tyranny, and that this absolute tyranny can only be successful for them through the unrestrained Socialist dictatorship of Communism. As this tyranny must extend to all peoples, they do not rest until they have laid Communist slavery upon all peoples of earth.

---

[93] Talmud Bab. Sanhedrin. Fol. 104, Col. 1.

It is unavoidably necessary that the Christians and Gentiles should fully grasp this giant tragedy. The existence of an imperialistic and cruel totalitarianism, which is spurred on by a group of mystics, fanatics and madmen, and which will perform all its crimes and all its perversions in the firm belief that they fulfil faithfully the commands of God, is an unhealthy reality. Their wickedness extends to such a degree that they hold it to be morally permissible to allow denial of God and for Communist materialism to triumph in the whole world, while they, the pious and faithful, are successful in destroying hated Christianity and the other "false" religions, for the purpose of permitting the present religion of Israel to rule on the ruins of all others, who recognise the right of the Jews to control the world and recognise through divine right their character as the chosen race to rule over mankind in the coming times. On the other hand, the "Talmud" says that it gives the Jews the truthful version of the Biblical promises about the Messiah! "The Messiah will give the Hebrews rulership over the world and to them all peoples will be subject."[94]

One could quote passages from the different parts of the "Talmud" and the Jewish "Cabbala," which are equally as informative as these, which allow us to understand the extent and importance of the present religion of the Jews and the danger which it signifies for Christianity and the rest of mankind. The deeper one penetrates into this material, all the clearer will one recognise the abyss that has opened between the original and true religion, which was revealed by God to the Hebrews through Abraham, Moses and the Prophets, and the false religion, which these Jews, who crucified our Lord Jesus Christ, have worked out, as well as their descendants, on grounds of the consciously false interpretation of the Holy Bible, above all with the appearance of the "Talmud" of Jerusalem and Babylon and of the latter completion of the Cabbalistic books, "Sepher-ha-Zohar," and "Sepher-Yetzirah," holy books, which are the foundations for the religion of modern Jews.

If an abyss exists between the religion of Abraham and Moses and of modern Jewry, then the same is unfathomable between Christianity and modern Jewry. One could say of the latter that it is the contrast and the denial even of the Christian religion, against which it desires hatred and urges its destruction in the holy books and in its secret rites. The centuries-long struggle of Holy Church against the Jewish religion and its rites had not, as is falsely said, the religious intolerance of Catholicism as the cause, but the enormous infamy of the Jewish religion, which represents a deadly

---

[94] Talmud. Bab. Schabb. Fol. 120, Section I and Sanhedrin, Fol. 88, Section 2 and Fol. 89, Section I.

threat for Christianity. This compelled the Church, which at first was so tolerant, to adopt a positive attitude for defence of the truth of Christianity and of the entire human race. Erroneous and deceitful is consequently the view of some clergy, who call themselves Christians but work together with the Jews in a thoroughly suspicious way, asserting that it is not admissible to fight against Jewry; for the true Jews, the believing Jews have a religion related and similar to Christianity.

What the Jews strive for in reality, when they put before Catholics this thesis of unlawfulness of struggle against the criminal Jewish sect, is the obtaining of a new permit for freebooting, which allows them, without exposing themselves to direct counter-attacks, to continue in their Freemasonic or Communist revolutionary movements until they are successful in the destruction of Christianity and the enslavement of mankind. The Hebrews and their accomplices within Christianity wish to secure in a comfortable manner the victory of the Jewish hunger for power, for if the Christians abandon attacking and conquering the head of the whole conspiracy, by restricting themselves only to attacking the Freemasonic, anarchistic, Communist or any other branch, the head, which is free of attacks, i.e. Jewry, preserves its whole power, while its Freemasonic and Communist tentacles devote themselves with all their branches in a merciless manner, as they have done previously, to the attack upon the religious, political and social institutions of Christianity over the whole world.

CHAPTER TWO

MORE CONCERNING THE JEWISH RELIGION

In the present chapter something will be learned concerning the teachings of belief of the so-called honourable Jews, in order to be able to prove with all the greater clarity that no relationship or kinship exists between the latter and the religion of the Christians. The first thing which one must bear in mind with the studying of modern Jewish religion is the fact that it is a question of a secret religion, in contrast to the remaining religions, whose dogma, teachings and customs have a clear character and therefore could be learned by anyone at choice, even those standing to one side.

After the crucifying of the Lord, the Jews kept concealed over centuries from the Christians and the Gentiles all those teachings and customs which, because they represented a threatening of other men, had to be concealed. They rightly feared that, if people knew their teachings, they would answer with violence against the Jews.

In the text of the "Talmud" one can read the following:

"To communicate anything of our law to a Gentile means the death of all Hebrews; for if the Goyim (Gentiles) knew what we teach about them, they would exterminate us without mercy."[95]

The lie has been the most principal weapon of those whom Christ, the Lord, already in His time called the "Synagogue of Satan." With lies and deceit they have controlled the peoples with their Freemasonic revolutions, and with lies and deceit they lead the latter to the Communist revolutions. It may suffice to mention that they even make use of lies for matters not concerned with their own religion.

---

[95] Divre in "Dav". Fol. 37.

131

They cheated the Christians and Gentiles in that they made the latter believe that the present Jewish religion is exactly the same as all the others. That they have restricted themselves to worship God, our Lord, to establish norms for morality and to defend spiritual values. But at the same time they pay very great attention to concealing from the world that their religion is in reality a secret sect, which pursues the purpose of destroying Christianity, which in addition hates Christ and his Church to the death, and which attempts at first to control the remaining peoples of the earth and then to enslave them.

It is therefore not to be wondered at that, in their holy hook, the Talmud, they confirm that, if the Gentiles (among whom they number the Christians) "knew what we teach about them, they would exterminate us without mercy."

History shows us how clever this caution of the "Talmud" is. When Holy Church discovered what the Masters or Rabbis taught their believers in secret, they ordered upon various occasions the confiscation and destruction of the books of the "Talmud". In view of the danger that their teachings signified for the Jews, namely for those who in very violent religious manner accept unconditionally and with zeal of belief the teachings of the "Talmud" and of the "Cabbala." A further Jewish deceit was useless, which consisted in preparing false texts of the "Talmud", which were then brought before the civil and church authorities without the passages whose reading was regarded as dangerous for the Christians. For frequently both Holy Church as well as the civil governments also discovered the authentic texts and the general indignation was often revealed in violent reactions against the religious sects of Jewry, whose authentic holy books already contained the plans for the conspiracy, which they have developed against the whole of mankind.

The Jewish writer Cecil Roth speaks abundantly in his work, "Storia del Popolo Ebraico", of the condemnation of the "Talmud" by Pope Gregory IX and his successors up to that of Pope Leo X in the 16th century which had its origin in an intimation to Cardinal Carafa, according to which the work was destructive and blasphemous. This revelation was made by the Jew Vittoria Eliano, who was the nephew of the Jewish scholar Elia Levita, and had as its consequence the public burning of the work in the autumn of 1553 on the "Campo dei Fiori" of Rome.[96]

---

[96] Cecil Roth: Storia del Popolo Ebraico, Milan 1962. Pages 327 and 408.

In the trials of the Inquisition, which were conducted against the concealed Jews, whom Holy Church called "Jewish heretics", can be found another richly informative source about the secret and factual religious doctrines of belief of the Jews. Those who would like to penetrate deeper into this study should use for this purpose the archives of the Inquisition of this capital of the Catholic world, that of Carcassonne and Narbonne and other cities of France; those of Simancas in Spain and those of La Torre do Tombe in Portugal; for those of Mexico, "Trials of Luis de Carbajal" (El Mozo), from which one can appreciate the mode of thought of the Jews and obtain knowledge of certain very informative religious doctrines. Relative to this is an edition by the government of Mexico from the "Main Archive of the Nation", of the year 1935, which was an official publication. In it are found the original handwriting with the corresponding signatures of the accused Jews, the Inquisitors, witnesses, etc. The validity of the document is beyond doubt and the contemporary Jews themselves have not been able to deny it.[97]

The content of this document is something most horrible – monstrous blasphemies against our Lord Jesus Christ and the most Holy Virgin Mary, a Satanic hatred against Christianity, a hatred that has nothing to do with the law given to the real Moses by God on Mount Sinai, but which represents the nature of the secret religion of modern Jewry itself, a religion of hatred, of wild hatred, which calls for a bloodbath of the Christians and persecutions of Holy Church, and which has been unleashed as an unbridled and disastrous evil explosive in all places where the Jewish-Freemasonic and Jewish-Communist revolutions have been victorious. From the second trial against Luis de Carbajal, which began towards the end of the 16th century, in the year 1595, we will, with true regret, take leave of same. For it is urgently necessary that we again conciliate our Lord Jesus Christ and the most Holy Virgin Mary for the blasphemies uttered by the Jews; and further it is urgently necessary to prove the untruthfulness of this strange thesis, which at the present time is represented by some clergy. The latter assert that it is improper to fight against Jewry, since a relationship nevertheless exists with the Christians religion, an assertion which borders on insanity and which can only prosper among those who, in ignorance of the problem, have fallen into the trap as victims of Jewish lies.

---

[97] Trials of Luis de Carbajal [El Mozo], edition of the Mexican government, 1935, official publication of the General archive of the nation, pages 127 and 128.

CHAPTER THREE

CURSES OF GOD AGAINST THE JEWS

Jewish Freemasonry, Communism, and the various political forces that control both, have brought countless attacks against the temporal policy of the Holy Catholic Church. One of the most frequent attacks is made with reference to the Inquisitional Court and the publicly made judgment of the religious court, which some clergy, out of lack of knowledge of history or as a result of propagandistic, Freemasonic-Liberal influence, have been duped to the degree that they think that Holy Church has erred in its Inquisitorial policy; and things have come to such a pass that they attempt to avoid this question with verbal disputes or with an unconscious feeling of guilt.

This shameful conduct stands in contrast to the personal behaviour of some Jewish historians, who, as believers in truth, approve some positive points of the Inquisitorial system, like Cecil Roth, who in his work "Storia del Popolo Ebraico" says:

"... One must admit that, from its standpoint, the Inquisition was just. Only rarely did it take steps without a reliable foundation; and when a matter was in progress, the ultimate purpose consisted in obtaining a complete admission, which, united with the feeling of repentance would redeem the victims from the terrors of eternal torment. The punishments laid down were never regarded as such, more as a redeeming sacrifice."[98]

In this much disputed matter, which the enemies of Catholicism have regarded as the "Achille's heel" of the Church, one must not lose sight of reality in the midst of the host of lies, falsification and historical deceit, which conceal the truth as if with a dense undergrowth, which was intentionally woven for this purpose by the Jews and their accomplices. The Inquisitorial policy of Holy Church, far from being something punitive or anything of which the Church should be ashamed, was not

---

[98] Cecil Roth: Storia del Popolo Ebraico, Milan 1962, page 477.

only theologically justified, but of the greatest value for mankind, which, thanks to the Holy Inquisition, described by the Popes, Councils, Theologians and Saints of the Church as holy, then saw itself freed of the catastrophe that now threatened them, and which would already have occurred several centuries ago.

We are not of the opinion that in the present one should attempt to force religion upon anyone by violence, nor that anyone should be persecuted on account of his ideas; for the truth will be able to establish itself without the necessity of resorting to compulsory methods; in fact we know that Holy Church, tolerant and good-willed in its early times, had to adjust itself in the face of an extraordinary situation. There was the deadly threat that International Jewry had planned for all Christianity in the twelfth century. This threat in its gravity can only be compared with that which at present is represented for free mankind by Jewish Communism.

In order to save Christianity from this danger, Holy Church had to take refuge in the most extreme methods, whose justification is already proven solely through the circumstance that the misfortune, which now threatens mankind, was delayed by several centuries. In their thousand-year long struggle against the Church of Christ the Jews used, as their principal weapon of battle, the "Fifth Column", which arose as thousands and thousands of Jews all over the world were converted in a hypocritical manner to Christianity.

The already mentioned Jewish historian Cecil Roth confirms in his previously quoted work "Storia del Popolo Ebraico", page 229, Milan 1962, that "... naturally the conversions were for the most part a pretence..." They were baptised and remained nevertheless just as much Jews in secret as before, although they have given themselves Christian names, went to Mass and frivolously received the sacraments. They then used their new position as seeming Christians to set up false teachings, which developed into underground movements. This would have brought about the dissolution of Christianity and secured the rule by Jewry over all peoples, as will be elaborated on later with irrefutable proofs.

It was soon seen that the whole of Christianity was threatened by death, unless the necessary measures were seized upon to command a halt to the secret organisations of Jewry and the secret societies which the concealed Jews formed among the true Christians. The conclusion was reached that Holy Church could only defend itself and mankind from destruction by setting up a similar secret organisation. There remained no other choice than to oppose the secret anti-Christian organisations with equally secret counter-bodies. So arose the very effective organisation of the Inquisition court.

An often alluded to fact of the Inquisition is the burning of the secret Jews or their execution through the garrotte, in which respect it is difficult to establish the exact number of those executed who were Judaised heretics, as the Church described those who in appearance were Christians but in secrecy practised Judaism. Many estimate at thousands, and others at tens of thousands, the number of underground Jews who were killed by the Inquisition; however, whatever number it may be, the enemies of the Church have directed unjustified attacks against it on account of this procedure. The mitigation of responsibility that has been granted the Church, on the grounds that it did not directly execute those found guilty but handed them over to the worldly authority, is easily refuted by the enemies of Catholicism. They say that, although the Church did not directly condemn and kill them, then nevertheless it gave its approval to the Inquisitorial procedures and to the laws that punished the backsliding Jewish heretics with death. In addition it had given its agreement for six centuries to these executions. Another weak proof of the defenders of the Church has been the assertion made that the Spanish and Portuguese Inquisitions were devices of the State and were not directed by the Church; but this thought process is powerless, for one cannot apply it to the Papal Inquisition, which was in progress over three centuries in the whole of Christian Europe, and which was directed by none other than his Holiness the Pope, who personally appointed the Grand Inquisitor. The remaining Franciscan or Dominican Inquisitors exercised their functions as papal delegates with full papal authority. It is certain that the Papal Inquisition sent thousands of secret Jews to be burned at the stake, who, although they were executed through the worldly arm of authority, died with the approval of Holy Church. The latter for its part had itself approved the procedures used to judge them, the laws which condemned them and the executions. If the Church had not been in agreement with the death sentences against the Jews, it would have prevented the same through a command. Even with the Spanish and Portuguese Inquisitions, which were State institutions and where the Grand Inquisitor was appointed by the King and not by the Pope, Holy Church authorised the Dominican order in the setting up of Inquisition courts, to prosecute and seek out the Jews, to imprison them and to conduct the whole process up to the handing over of them to the worldly power of authority. Also in these cases the Church had given its agreement to the laws that empowered the worldly arm of authority to burn these malefactors or to strangle them with the garrotte.

In order to establish an effective and convincing defence of Holy Church and the Inquisition, one much possess the courage to take refuge in the truth and only in the truth. Holy Church will never need to fear it, for its actions are always determined by justice and fairness. Therefore with the truth, which always wins in the end, and which is expressly elaborated in the book with the title "The Jewish Fifth Column in the Clergy", a truthful defence of the Holy Catholic Church is asserted in relation to its Inquisitorial policy.

First we will begin with the proof that the Jews are not untouchable people by virtue of the fact that at one time they were the chosen people of God, but, on the contrary, God predicted to them that, in the event of their not keeping His commandments, they would be very severely punished. From this consideration, the policy of the Church towards the Jews with regard to the Inquisition has a broad theological foundation. The Jews still boast at present of being the chosen people of God, which they tend to substantiate based upon certain passages of the Holy Bible, of which they give a false and ambitious interpretation. However, in so doing, they are very careful to avoid other Bible passages, in which God clearly and unequivocally linked this privilege to the condition that they faithfully fulfilled the commandments and other commands of God under the threat that, if they would not do so, the distinction of being the chosen people would be withdrawn and they would be transformed into an accursed people who would encounter diverse punishments, which were expressly indicated to Moses by God. However, the Jews attempted to conceal this position of things, just as certain Christian clergy attempt to do, whose apparently inexplicable conduct more favours Jewry and its revolutionary plans than the Holy Church of Christ. In Deuteronomy of the Holy Bible, Chapter XXVIII, Verses one and two, Moses, who conveys the divine will to the Hebrews, describes quite clearly this situation.

"1. And it shall come to pass, if thou shalt hearken diligently unto the voice of the Lord thy God, to observe and to do all His commandments which I command thee this day, that the Lord thy God will set thee on high above all nations of the earth:

"2. And all these blessings shall come on thee and overtake thee, if thou shalt hearken unto the voice of the Lord thy God."

From the foregoing it is perfectly clear that the distinction of Israel, as a people chosen and blessed of the Lord, is clearly linked to the fact that it keeps all His commandments and obeys the voice of the Lord. It is therefore completely false to assert that God regards it in a final and unconditional manner as a chosen people. He gave it the possibility of retaining this privilege; however, since the Jewish people had neither kept nor keeps the Commandments, nor listens to the voice of the Lord, it trampled upon the obligation that was laid upon it in order to preserve this exceptional position, and drew the divine imprecations upon itself. One must recall that after Moses mentions all the blessings that God would grant to the Israelites, if they kept all his commandments and would listen to the voice of the Lord, he records the terrible curses that would strike them, if they did the opposite. Whoever wishes to learn these completely, can take the Bible, for proof, in Deuteronomy, Chapter XXVIII, and Leviticus XXVI. Here we will only restrict ourselves to quoting some of the most important passages:

In the chapter of Deuteronomy mentioned, Moses says in conveying the Commandments of God:

"15. But it shall come to pass, if thou wilt not hearken unto the voice of the Lord thy God, to observe to do all his Commandments and His statutes which I command thee this day, that all these curses shall come upon thee, and overtake thee:

"16. Cursed shalt thou be in the city, and cursed shalt thou be in the field.

"17. Cursed shall be thy basket and thy store.

"18. Cursed shall be the fruit of thy body, and the fruit of thy land, the increase of thy kine, and the flocks of thy sheep.

"19. Cursed shalt thou be when thou comest in, and cursed shalt thou be when thou goest out.

"20. The Lord shall send upon thee cursing, vexation, and rebuke in all that thou settest thine hand unto for to do, until thou be destroyed, and until thou perish quickly; because of the wickedness of thy doings, whereby thou hast forsaken Me.

"21. The Lord shall make the pestilence cleave unto thee, until He have consumed thee from off the land, whither thou goest to possess it.

"22. The Lord shall smite thee with a consumption, and with a fever, and with an inflammation, and with an extreme burning, and with the sword, and with blasting, and with mildew; and they shall pursue thee until thou perish.

"24. The Lord shall make the rain of thy land powder and dust; from heaven shall it come down upon thee, until thou be destroyed.

"25. The Lord shall cause thee to be smitten before thine enemies; thou shalt go out one way against them, and flee seven ways before them; and shall be removed into all the kingdoms of the earth.

"43. The stranger that is within thee shall get up above thee very high; and thou shalt come down very low.[99]

"45. Moreover, all these curses shall come upon thee and overtake thee, till thou be destroyed; because thou hearkenedst not unto the voice of the Lord thy God, to keep His commandments and His statutes which He commanded thee:

"48. Therefore shalt thou serve thine enemies which the Lord shall send against thee, in hunger and in thirst, and in nakedness, and in want of all things; and He shall put a yoke of iron upon thy neck, until He have destroyed thee. (First a fearful prophecy of enslaving and then of destruction of the Jews, through foes which God himself will lay as punishment and curse over them.)

"54. So that the man that is tender among you, and very delicate, his eye shall be evil toward his brother, and toward the wife of his bosom, and toward the remnant of his children, which he shall leave.

"55. So that he will not give to any of them of the flesh of his children whom he shall eat; because he hath nothing left him in the siege, and in the straitness wherewith thine enemies shall distress thee in all thy gates.

"62. And ye shall be left few in number, whereas ye were as the stars of heaven for multitude; because thou wouldest not obey the voices of the Lord thy God!"[100]

---

[99] The fathers of the Church understand by this prophecy the calling of the heathen to faith, who for this reason are gloriously preferred to the Jews. San Cipriano, Contra Judae. Book I, Chapter 21. Annotation of Scio, Bible, Volume I, page 477.
[100] Deuteronomy. Chapter XXVIII, Verses cited.

In Chapter XXVI of Leviticus the reward is likewise mentioned, which is offered by God to the Jewish people, whereby He promises that it will be His chosen and blessed people, if it observes His commandments, and will be cursed, if it does not keep them. In addition, He prophesies the punishments with which He will punish its bad behaviour. Of the curses, which God in this last case casts directly against the Israelites, we quote only those which we regard as of the highest importance. Those who wish to learn them all, we refer to the Holy Bible, which served as source in this matter.

"14. But if ye hearken not unto Me, and will not do all these commandments; 15. And if ye shall despise My statutes, or if your soul abhor My judgments, so that ye will not do all My commandments, but that ye break My covenant: (Here God the Lord plays upon the fact that the Jews with their sins have broken and made invalid the agreement of bond which God has concluded with the said people.)

"16. I also will do this unto you; I will even appoint over you terror, consumption, and the burning ague, that shall consume the eyes, and cause sorrow of heart; and ye shall sow your seed in vain, for your enemies shall eat it!

"17. And I will set My face against you, and ye shall be slain before your enemies; they that hate you shall reign over you; and ye shall flee when none pursueth you. (A further prediction of destruction). (It is of import to establish how the collective persecution mania from which the Jewish people suffers at present, agrees in surprising manner with this divine curse.)

"18. And if ye will not yet for all this hearken unto me, then I will punish you seven times more for your sins!

"38. And ye shall perish among the heathen, and the land of your enemies shall eat you up.

"39. And they that are left of you shall pine away in your enemies' lands; and also in the iniquities of their fathers shall they pine away with them."

The word of God speaks for itself. God gave Israel a very great privilege, but not in order to use it as a common law, which could allow it to commit unpunished every kind of sins and crime and to violate the divine commandments and statutes. For this very reason God, who is justice itself, linked the existence of this privilege and this blessing to very strict conditions, which were intended to secure the good use of the same by the Jews. As a condition He laid upon them that they should not only heed a few, but expressly all the commandments, as is stated very clearly in various verses of "Deuteronomy" and of "Leviticus." He also commanded that they hear the divine ordinations, treasure the wisdom contained in them, and observe the laws made by God (Leviticus, Chapter XXVI, Verses 14 and 15), otherwise the agreement or alliance which God had granted the people in question would become invalid. What have the Jews in fact done over three thousand years? Instead of fulfilling the commandments and other conditions made by God, they killed the greater part of the Prophets, denied God's Son, slandered and killed Him. They sinned against the first commandment which commands us to love God above all things, against the fifth which commands us not to kill, and against the eighth which forbids bearing of false witness and lying. In addition, they murdered various disciples of Christ, soiled their hands in bloody revolutions, during which opportunity they killed millions of human creatures, plundered the wealth of Christians by first robbing the latter through usury, afterwards through Communism, and thereby in terrible manner blasphemed the name of God in the Communist lands, without there being any foundation to the claim, which they make in their secret assemblies, that they would do this only transitorily for some centuries, until the destructive machine of Communist Socialism had destroyed all false religions, in order to erect on the ruins of the same the completely distorted religion of the God of Israel and His chosen people, who would be the future family of mankind. It must be remarked that the blasphemies and the denial of God through materialistic Communism are not directed against this or that religion regarded as false, but against God, against all universal spiritual values. Neither the insanity of the "Synagogue of the Devil" nor its demonic lust for power will ever be able to justify the monstrous blasphemies that are cast against God in the states subjected to the Socialist dictatorship of Communism, even if one may say that we are concerned with a purely passing situation of a few hundred years.

To put it briefly, instead of observing the commandments and everything which God made as a condition of their being His chosen people, they have violated all this systematically in the most far-reaching form, above all through committing murder of God, that terrible crime, which consists in the killing of the Son of God, and which represents the horrible peak of many crimes and violations of the commandments, which they have in addition carried out for two thousand years and even up to our days. So they have deserved all the curses and punishments with which

God threatened them, when they, instead of observing the commandments, refused to obey them. The curses and punishments prophesied by God the Lord they have fulfilled to the letter, even the most terrible, which consist in mass destruction and murder. If one reads once again the aforementioned verses from the Bible, which speak of this destruction, and one compares them with the bloodbaths carried out among Jews in Europe when occupied by the Nazis, it will be proved that yet once again in history the curses and punishments predicted by our Lord God centuries ago have been fulfilled. Clearly the Creator has even used the Pagan peoples, such as the Chaldaeans, the Romans and others as implements of divine providence, in order to punish the misdeeds and sins of the Jewish people, and to fulfil the curses prophesied by God Himself. If the Hebrews or their agents within Christianity, in the reading of these lines, feel themselves afflicted, they must nevertheless recognise that we neither may nor can alter the divine order. In the following chapter we will see how the Biblical Prophets in conveying the will of God were even clearer than Moses in reference to the punishments that would scourge the Jews by reason of their sins and crimes.

CHAPTER FOUR

MASSACRES OF JEWS ORDERED BY GOD AS PUNISHMENT. BIBLE.

The terrible punishments ordered by God against the Jews are also continually spoken of by the Prophets in the Holy Bible. In the prophecy of Isaiah, God predicts through the mouth of the former various punishments against the Israelites, which would be too involved to describe. Therefore we will limit ourselves only to these two verses of Chapter LXV of said prophecy, while referring those who wish to delve deeper into this theme to the Holy Scriptures:

"11. But ye are they that forsake the Lord, that forget My holy mountain, that prepare a table for that troop, and that furnish the drink offering unto that number. 12. Therefore will I number you to the sword, and ye shall all bow down to the slaughter; because, when I called, ye did not answer; when I spoke, ye did not hear; but did evil before Mine eyes, and did choose that wherein I delighted not!"[101]

The prophet Ezekiel relates that the Lord, angered at the worship of idols by the Jews (How will He not now be angered at the new kind of idolatry of the Socialist states and other fetishes that the Jews have set up again in the Communist hells?), had revealed to him: Chapter VIII, Verse 18:

"Therefore will I also deal in fury: Mine eye shall not spare, neither will I have pity; and though they cry in Mine ears with a loud voice, yet shall I not hear them."

Chapter IX, Verse 1:

---

[101] Bible, Prophecy of Isaiah, Chapter LXV. Verses 11 and 12.

"He cried also in mine ears with a loud voice, saying, cause them that have charge over the city to draw near, even every man with his destroying weapon in his hand. 5. And to the others He said in mine hearing, Go ye after him through the city and smite; let not your eye spare, neither have ye pity. 6. Slay utterly old and young, both maids and little children, and women; but come not near any man upon whom is the mark; and begin at My sanctuary. Then they began with the ancient men which were before the house. 7. And He said unto them, Defile the house, and fill the courts with the slain; go ye forth. And they went forth, and slew in the city. 8. And it came to pass, while they were slaying them, and I was left, that I fell upon my face, and cried, and said, Ah, Lord God! wilt Thou destroy all the residue of Israel in Thy pouring out of Thy fury upon Jerusalem? 9. Then said He unto me: The iniquity of the house of Israel and Judah is exceedingly great, and the land is full of blood, and the city full of perverseness; for they say, The Lord hath forsaken the earth, and the Lord seeth not. 10. And as for Me also, Mine eye shall not spare, neither will I have pity; but I will recompense their way upon their head."[102]

The word of God, our Lord, speaks for itself. We cannot, without blaspheming, contradict Him or criticise Him. This is the divine justice, just as Holy Scripture reveals it to us, not in the manner of the enlightened Jews or even those clergy who pretend to be Christians but who act as if they were Jews, falsifying and therefore working together with the "Synagogue of the Devil."

In the Prophecy of "Hosea" the crimes of Israel and Judah are spoken of, and the punishments which God will lay upon them: Chapter IV, Verse. 1:

"... There is no truth, no mercy, nor knowledge of God, in the land. 2. By swearing, and lying, and killing, and stealing, and committing adultery, they break out, the blood toucheth blood."

Chapter V, Verse 2: "They will not frame their doings to turn unto their God; for the spirit of whoredoms is in the midst of them, and they have not known the Lord. And the pride of Israel doth testify to its face; therefore shall Israel and Ephraim fall in their iniquity; Judah also shall fall with them."[103]

---

[102] Bible, Prophecy of Ezekiel, Chapter VIII, last verse, and Chapter IX, the verses quoted.
[103] Hosea. Chapter IV and V, verses cited. Amos, Chapter VIII.

At the same time that God refers to the shameful deeds of Israel, He brings, in the prophecy of "Amos", His resolution to expression, that He will not allow the continuation of these misdeeds: Chapter VIII, Verse 2. "And He said, Amos, what seest thou? And I said, a basket of summer fruit. Then said the Lord unto me, The end is come upon my peoples of Israel; I will not again pass by them any more." Chapter IX, Verse 1. "I saw the Lord standing upon the altar; and He said, Smite the lintel of the door, that the posts may shake, and cut them in the head, all of them; and I will slay the last of them with the sword: he that fleeth of them shall not flee away, and he that escapeth of them shall not be delivered."[104]

In the prophecy of Daniel the latter mentions what the archangel Saint Gabriel revealed to him concerning the death of Christ. He reported that the people which scorned him would no longer be the chosen people of God, but that devastation would come over Israel and the end of the world.

Chapter IX, Verse 25: "Know, therefore, and understand, that from the going forth of the commandment to restore and build Jerusalem, unto the Messiah the Prince, shall be seven weeks, and threescore and two weeks; the street shall be built again, and the wall, even in troublous times. 26. And after threescore and two weeks shall the Messiah be cut off, but not for Himself; and the people of the prince that shall come shall destroy the city and the sanctuary; and the end thereof shall be with a flood, and unto the end of the war desolations are determined. (i.e. until the end of the world.)"[105]

It is unbelievable that clergy who regard themselves as good Christians, but who are more concerned with the defence of Jewry than with Holy Church, risk asserting in our days that this God-murdering people is still the chosen people of God, in spite of all its crimes and the passages in the Holy Scripture that prove that it is far removed from being the "chosen people" in the present, such as it was before Jesus Christ; rather is it far more a people cursed by God, because all curses which the Lord has cast against this people, in the event of its not obeying his commandments, have now been fulfilled. These curses have with justice fallen upon the Jews, indeed with all the more justice, because they have committed the most revolting and punishable crime of all times: "of denying the Son of God in person, martyring and crucifying Him."

---

[104] Hosea. Chapter IV and V, verses cited. Amos, Chapter VIII.
[105] Bible, Prophecy of Daniel, Chapter IX, Verse 25, 26 and 27.

It is very difficult to comprehend the whole truth concerning this event, the naked truth, particularly in a world that has been influenced over generations by a host of lies and Jewish fables, which even words of St. Paul elaborate.[106] These fables have distorted the truth about the Jewish question even in the minds of Catholics. It is therefore urgently necessary that someone dares to speak openly, even if it is unpleasant for all who feel themselves offended in Christianity in their own flesh. Let us recall that Christ, our Lord, said to us clearly Himself that only the truth would make us free.[107]

On the other hand, the previously quoted word of God proves to us that, just as God was energetic and irreconcilable in His struggle against Satan, so He was also irreconcilable against the forces of Satan upon earth. This leaves without prospect of success the attempts of the enemy to bind the hands of Christians with a destructive and cowardly morality which supports itself upon the ideas of a pretended Christian love of one's neighbour, which they shape according to their whim and whose application they prescribe, in order to make clear the way for the powers, already alluded to, of the Devil upon earth, a morality which clearly stands in contradiction with the combating and energetic mode of action of God, our Lord, in these cases.

In the preceding passages of the Old Testament, which contain what God revealed to the world through the mediation of Moses and the Prophets, the myth is destroyed that the Jewish people is untouchable, that no one can combat its crimes because it is a kind of holy people; for we have already seen that God ordained the punishments that He would cause to fall upon them, if, instead of the commandments being kept by this people, they trampled upon them. When Holy Church gave its agreement to the restricting policy of the Inquisition courts, it acted in accordance with what God had foreseen in the Old Testament and defended the whole of mankind, by in this way holding up for several centuries the progress of the bloody conspiracy, which is on the point of sinking the world into chaos and into the most monstrous slavery of all times. We are sincere enemies of bloodshed, our greatest longing consists in the hope that wars may vanish from the face of the earth. But the Jews must understand that these terrible bloodbaths, which they have suffered over the centuries, apart from the fact that they are announced in the Old Testament as divine punishment, have been to the greatest part the

---

[106] Paul in his letter to Titus, Chapter I, Verses 13 and 14, said: "And do not listen to the Jewish fables nor to statutes of men who deny the truth."
[107] Apostle John, Chapter VIII, Verse 32.

consequence of the criminal conduct which the Israelites have shown in the lands of other peoples, who in magnanimous manner allowed them to immigrate and offered them heartfelt hospitality.

If the Hebrews, in every land which receives them with open arms, repay this friendly reception by their beginning a traitorous war of conquest, by their organising conspiracies, causing revolutions to break out and killing thousands of citizens of that nation, it is only natural that they suffer the consequences of their criminal acts. And if we deeply regret the shedding of Israelite blood, then we do this all the more with shedding of Christian and Gentile blood, which the Jews, with their disturbances or by means of the Red Terror, have caused to flow in torrents. We honestly invite the Jewish youth to reflect impartially concerning this problem and to lay to one side the fake historical texts concerning Jewry, with which the Rabbis deceive them by their wishing to make the youth believe that the Hebrews are always innocent victims of the other nations, in order to give the young Jews a diabolic hatred towards mankind and an insane thirst for revenge.

CHAPTER FIVE

ANTISEMITISM AND CHRISTIANITY

In all their ambitious and revolutionary undertakings the Jews have always used the same tactics, in order to deceive the peoples. They have used abstract and hazy concepts or playing with words of malleable importance and contents, which can be interpreted in a twofold manner and used in a different way.

For example, there appear the ideas of all-embracing liberty, equality and fraternity, and above all that of "Anti- semitism", a word of enormous stretching power. They give this generalisation diverse meanings and uses, which have the aim of laying the Christian and Gentile peoples in chains, with the intention of preventing their defending themselves against the Jewish striving for power and the destructive effect of their anti-Christian forces.

This deceitful behaviour one can summarise as follows:

First Step: The condemning of "Antisemitism", by means of skilled campaigns and to attain persistent influences adjusted to each other and of diverse energy, which are exercised either by Socialist forces", which Jewry controls, or which are carried out by their secret agents who have smuggled themselves into the Christian institutions, into their churches or into their governments. In order to be able to do so and attain this first step, so that one after another of the religious and political leaders condemns "Antisemitism", they give this first step its importance:

A) As a racial discrimination of the same kind as is carried on by the whites in different lands against the negroes, and conversely by the negroes against the whites. Also they represent "Antisemitism" as a racial consciousness, which regards other races as inferior, and which therefore resists the instruction and teaching of the martyr of Golgotha, who on His part established and confirmed the equality of men before God.

B) As pure hatred towards the Jewish people, which stands in contradiction with the highest principle of Christ: "Love one another."
C) As an attack upon or condemnation of the people which gave its blood to Jesus and Mary. The Jews have described this argument as irresistible.

By giving these or other such interpretations to "Antisemitism", the Jews or their agents who have penetrated into Christianity have wrong-footed the charity, goodness and good faith of many Christian rulers and even highly-regarded religious personages, be it those of the Catholic Church or of the Protestant churches and other dissidents.[108] For, when the latter yield to such well-organised, murky and persistent influences, abstract and sweeping criticisms or condemnations of Antisemitism begin to be formulated which lack any specifics as to what in reality is being condemned and what actually this censured Antisemitism means. And when the real object of the condemnation is thus left so imprecise and vague, there is every danger that the Jews and their agents within Christianity will become the sole interpreters of such weighty decisions.

If the high religious personages who are exposed to indescribable pressure would at least pay heed to describing exactly what they understand by this "Antisemitism" which they condemn, the danger is lesser; for in condemnation expressions should be exactly defined, which one condemns; for example, "racial discrimination" or hatred towards a particular people.

If the Jews also possess the boldness to raise a claim for a final all-embracing definition of "Antisemitism", in order to skilfully enlarge the radius of effect of its condemnation, it is easier to prove the sophistry of their approach.

Second Step: After the Jews or their secret agents have attained these condemnations, they give the words a different meaning than was intended, in order to preserve these judgments. Then "Antisemites" will be described as:

I. Those who protect their countries from the attacks of the ambitious Jewish striving for power, in that the former make use of the natural right, which all peoples possess, to defend independence and freedom.

---

[108] We refrain from using more severe terms to describe the Protestant and schismatic churches, because we hold to the desire of his Holiness the Pope, John XXIII, to promote a daily greater association among the whole of Christianity before the Communist threat.

II. Those who exercise criticism of the disintegrating activity of the Jewish forces, which destroy the Christian family and degenerate the youth, and who combat these effects.

III. Those who in any kind of form censure or combat hatred and racial discrimination, but which the Jews believe they have the right to exert against the Christians, although they hypocritically attempt to conceal it; and those who in any kind of form broadcast the misdeeds, offences and crimes that were committed by the Jews against the Christians, and demand deserved punishment for this.

IV. Those who snatch away the mask from Jewry as leader of Communism, of Freemasonry and other underground movements, and attempt to attain that necessary measures are put in force to prevent disintegrating activity in the circle of the Christian family.

V. Those who in any kind of form resist the Jewish activity that has the aim of destroying Holy Church and Christian civilisation in general.

This dirty game is apparent: to attain the censure or condemnation of an "Antisemitism" which they equate with a racial discrimination or with an outbreak of hatred against peoples, which is exercised against the Jews — both, however, contrary to Christian teaching, — in order to afterwards give the word new meanings, and to attempt to bring it about that those who defend Holy Church, their nation, their family or their natural rights against the attacks of Jewish hunger for power, are bound hand and foot and are thus incapable of carrying out such a justifiable defence. In order to attain this, the open and secret Jewish forces set up a loudly resounding apparatus of propaganda and of lamentation, by setting up a complaining outcry about the Antisemites who make use of the right of self-defence.

They cry themselves hoarse with their assertion that the Catholic Church condemns Antisemitism; and in the name of the Church they condemn such leaders who, so they assure us, no believer may support in this "Antisemitic" work of defence of his people, his family and of Holy Church against the revolutionary activity of the Jewish striving for power. A clumsy manoeuvre, but it succeeds in sowing confusion and calling forth disorder and weakening the activity of these estimable leaders in the defence of their peoples and of Christian civilisation. This is the securest form which they have conceived, in order to obtain the victory of the Jewish- Freemasonic or Jewish-Communist revolutions. These procedures have secured the triumph of Jewry in recent time, and called forth the corresponding catastrophe that threatens the Christian world. For this reason, this matter must be studied and thought over fundamentally by us all, who are obligated to defend Holy Church and our country against the anti-Christian striving for power that modern Jewry represents.

An example of this incredible manoeuvre is shown to us by the following case: the highly-regarded Catholic writer Vincente Risco describes to us how certain organisations, which were founded for the conversion of the Jews, are more effective in their defence of the Jewish race than in their conversion. The Lehmann Brothers, for example, used the devout zeal of Holy Church more for defending the Jewish people than for attaining successful results in conversion. When, therefore, the Catholic writer Drumont revealed in the past century, in his "France Juive", the Jewish conspiracy that attempts to destroy Christianity and to rule the French people, Peter Lehmann answered in defence of his race and hence contributed to the defeat of the Catholics in France and to the victory of Jewish-Freemasonry. The same occurs with the Order of our Virgin of Zion, which was founded by newly converted Jews, and which dedicated itself more to the purpose of defending the Hebrews who are members of the "Synagogue of the Devil", than converting them to the truth. In the present century another association was founded in order to accept the Jews into the Church by means of their conversion. Such a devout ideal was very popular, and it was successful in arranging countless demonstrations of confidence by clergy and laymen. The educated historical writer Vicente Risco says about this:

"To it belonged countless influential and rich believers, bishops and even cardinals. They carried on propaganda and published a pamphlet speaking for the Jews under the title: 'Pax super Israel'. This association began to advocate strange teachings, which stood on the fringe of the unfalsified spirit of the Catholic Church and gradually separated themselves from the tradition of instruction by the Popes and from the Liturgy, as a Catholic journal says:

" 'They said that one might not speak of the 'conversion' of the Jews, but of their 'reception' into the Church, as if the Jews in fact need not give up their false belief. They rejected the epithet 'God-murdering' people, which was applied to the Jews, and 'God-murdering' city applied to Jerusalem, as though the Jews had not contributed to the death of Jesus, and as though Church language had not called them 'traitors'."

They accused the Popes, because "they had not understood the Jewish people", as though the latter were not guilty of voluntarily remaining in Judaism.

"Finally they maintained the Jewish nationality of Jesus Christ and alluded to the fact that the Christians, by means of Holy Communion, unite with the Jews and enter into blood relationship with them.

"Naturally this was going too far. The Church could not tolerate it, and the Inquisition court saw no alternative than to intervene. Since among such arrogant 'Friends of Israel' there were many honourable believers, bishops and cardinals, the court, in its decree of the year 1928, spoke no formal punishment, but, resolute in this, banned the association and the pamphlet 'Pax super Israel' which had been the cause of the intervention of the Church court."[109]

Divine support became evident a further time, when this recent conspiracy was destroyed, which had reached into the highest circles of Holy Church. This example is very actual; for as we have experienced, the Israelites planned far more weighty acts against the second Vatican Council (1963), when they use the holy zeal of faith for Christian unity and talks with the Jews, in order to attempt to attain that decisions were made relating to the Hebrews that would not only contradict the doctrine that has been defended by Holy Church over centuries but would also, in almost imperceptible form for the great majority of the Council fathers, represent a silent condemnation of the policy that had been maintained over 1500 years by the earlier Popes and Councils.

It is illuminating and understandable that, with the realisation of their Satanic intentions, the conspirators would be successful in achieving that Holy Church contradicted itself and from this would result the most unwholesome consequences that one can possibly imagine. But what the Jews and their agents within Christianity do not reckon with is the support of God for His Church, which He allows to triumph a second time against the forces of hell.

With reference to the Jew-friendly association, which cardinals, bishops and believers belonged to, and to their pamphlet "Pax super Israel", their condemnation through the Inquisition court by means of edict of dissolution in the year 1928 was no easy matter. There was a bitter struggle in the highest spheres of the Church, as one learns from reliable sources; and when their members saw coming the unavoidable dissolution of the association and the resultant following ban, they prepared a desperate counter-attack, in which they made renewed use of Christian love of one's neighbour and the true-heartedness of the high personages of the Church, in order to attain that Antisemitism would also be banned. They regarded it as a manifestation of race hatred, which is in contradiction with the sermons of our Lord Jesus Christ, which are based upon the guiding motive: "Love one another." In this manner they were so successful that,

---

[109] Vicente Risco: Historia de los Judios. 3rd edition, 1960. Pages 430 and 431.

after exerting all influence and manifold pressure, the Inquisition Court, which dissolved the association friendly to the Jews, passed an order which affirmed as a result, "that, just as Holy Church disapproves of all hatred and bitterness between peoples, so it also condemns hatred against the people chosen by God in His time: that hatred which today is generally described with the word 'Antisemitism'."

As usual Jewry was successful, by means of the condemned "Pax super Israel" group, in also attaining the condemnation of "Antisemitism", in that the latter was equated with hatred towards a definite people, a hatred, which is incompatible with the preachings of love of our Lord Jesus Christ. Later, Jewry attempted to cause this condemnation to fall on Catholics who defend Holy Church, their country and their children from the Jewish conspiracy, by applying to the word "Antisemitism" a different meaning from that which served as foundation for its condemnation.

If, with this procedure, a Catholic in the United States demands the punishment of Jews, because they have supplied atomic secrets to Russia, to provide Communism with the power for subjection of the world, it is said that this is the "Antisemitism" condemned by the Church, and that one must keep silent. If someone pillories the Jews as leaders of Communism and of Freemasonry and lays bare their intentions, namely that of destroying the Church, then he is likewise condemned as an "Antisemite". The result of these subtleties and intrigues consists in that the Jews are regarded as untouchable, so that they commit every kind of crime against the Christians, instigate the most destructive crimes against the Church and Christian countries and can carry out the most devastating Freemasonic or Community revolutions, without anyone being able to act, punish and still less curb their activity, because otherwise he will be accused of "Antisemitism" and hence incur the condemnation of the Inquisition Court. If the leaders of this serviceable institution, which the Jew-friendly organisation "Pax Super Israel" represented, had taken account of what misuse Jewry and its agents would exercise with the Edict which condemned hatred towards people, and hence also against the Jewish people, they would have been filled with horror. If one wishes to see still clearer the lies spun by Jewry in this connection, it suffices to take a very evident example, which allows the hatefulness of this truly dialectic sophistry to be discerned, which the Hebrews and their accomplices pretend with the word "Antisemitism".

What would the Jews have said, if proceeding from the basis that Holy Church condemns hatred between the peoples, one had come to the conviction during the last war that this universal condemnation also includes hatred towards the German people, which analogously was called anti-Germanism, so as accordingly to declare every struggle against the Nazis as impermissible; for the latter were Germans and to fight them is a manifestation of anti-Germanism which was also fundamentally condemned by the Church court? Would the Jews have accepted such a mode of thought, which, under protection of such playing with words, allowed Nazi Germany to be declared as untouchable? With such a rational conclusion, the Jews, like their forefather Caiaphas, would have rent their clothes and have protested against the criminal playing with words, which does not prevent the Hebrews from utilising the same with all calm and cynicism, in order to prevent Christians from being able to defend themselves.

In reference to the condemning of racial discrimination something similar occurs. First of all the Israelites and their accomplices within the clergy give a restrictive meaning to the word "racial discrimination", by equating it with the demand of one specific race to regard the other races as inferior and to rob them of their natural rights; or by equating it with an Antisemitic racial discrimination which, in blasphemous manner, draws our Lord Jesus Christ, the most Holy Virgin or the Apostles into their critique, so as with such impressive arguments to attain a completely universal condemnation of racial discrimination, which then allows them, as fighters against racial discrimination, to accuse all those who fight for protection of the Church or their nations against the Jewish onslaught, in order to attain their condemnation.

In addition we must bring to mind that a condemnation of racial discrimination is very dangerous for the Catholic Church itself; for there exist orders of his Holiness Paul IV and other Popes that forbid admittance to the honorary offices of the Church to Catholics of Jewish origin, or which confirmed this ban. We will study this order later on. Therefore a condemnation of racial discrimination will be the evil-willed occasion for asserting that Holy Church contradicts itself, and, what is still more weighty, it tacitly condemns several of its most famous Popes who recognised and confirmed the natural rules of the purity of blood.

CHAPTER SIX

CHRIST OUR LORD, THE SYMBOL OF

ANTISEMITISM, SO THE JEWS ASSERT

So that the well-meaning Catholic clergy can form an idea of how dangerous this affair of "Antisemitism" is, they must know that the Hebrews at different periods have regarded our Lord Jesus Christ, the Apostles, various Popes, the Councils and Saints of the Church as hostile to the Jews. It is natural that they have done this, for they regard everything as hostile to the Jews that blames or combats their crimes or their conspiracies against mankind; and both our Lord Jesus Christ as well as the Apostles and the other mentioned Catholic authorities censured and fought on different occasions against the blackmail of the Jews. The New Testament of the Holy Scripture, the Church laws of the Councils, the Bulls and Papal despatches, and the trustworthy testimonies of the Saints who were canonised by the Church, as well as the confessions which in part were made by the Jews themselves, prove this in an unmistakeable manner.

So that Catholics may not have the slightest doubt of the testimonies which are recorded, we translate with special care what the outstanding Zionist writer Joseph Dunner writes in his book "The Republic of Israel", in which he asserts the following:

"For every sect believing in Christ, Jesus is the symbol of everything that is healthy and worthy of love. For the Jews he is from the 4th century onward the symbol of 'Antisemitism', of slander, of violence and of violent death."[110]

If the Israelites regard our Lord Jesus Christ as a symbol of "Antisemitism", or better expressed, of "Anti-Judaism", then they are completely right; for if they describe as "Antisemites" those who blame

---

[110] Joseph Dunner: The Republic of Israel, Edition of October 1950, page 10.

and combat their disgraceful deeds, then our Divine Redeemer was the first who did this. When our Lord Jesus Christ had a discussion with certain Jews, He began the following dialogue, as the Gospel of John relates:

Chapter VIII, Verse 39: "They answered and said unto him, 'Abraham is our father.' Jesus saith unto them, 'If ye were Abraham's children, ye would do the works of Abraham. 40. But now ye seek to kill me, a man that hath told you the truth, which I have heard of God; this did not Abraham. 41. Ye do the deeds of your father.' Then said they to him, 'We be not born of fornication; we have one father, even God.' 44. 'Ye are of your father the devil, and the lusts of your father ye will do. He was a murderer from the beginning, and abode not in the truth, because there is no truth in him. When he speaketh a lie, he speaketh of his own; for he is a liar and the father of it. 47. He that is of God heareth God's words; ye therefore hear them not, because ye are not of God.' 48. Then answered the Jews, and said unto him, 'Say we not well that thou art a Samaritan, and hast a devil?' 49. Jesus answered, 'I have not a devil; but I honour my Father, and ye do dishonour me.' " And this passage of the Gospel ended with the following verses: "57. Then said the Jews unto him, 'Thou are not yet fifty years old, and hast thou seen Abraham?' 58. Jesus said unto them, 'Verily, verily, I say unto you: Before Abraham was, I am.' 59. Then took they up stones to cast at him; but Jesus hid Himself, and went out of the temple, going through the midst of them, and so passed by."[111]

In the preceding passage of the Gospel of John, one sees how Christ, our Lord, upbraids the Jews for their murderous intentions, and calls them children of the devil. He likewise proves that the Hebrews of that time were unable to carry on discussions in a calm and honourable form, exactly as today, without bringing in insults, slanders or violent actions, always according to its suiting them. And if with our Divine Redeemer they used lies and insults and attempted to dishonour Him, as He Himself gives evidence in Verse 49, or strove to end the discussion with stone-throwing, what could we poor human creatures then expect?

In Chapter XXIII of the Gospel of Matthew, our Lord Jesus, in reference to the Jewish leaders who opposed him so much,[112] describes the latter as hypocrites (V. 13, 14, 15, etc), "full of iniquity" (Verse 28), foolish, blind (Verse 17); clean outside, but within full of extortion and excess

---

[111] Gospel of St. John, Chapter VII, Verses quoted.
[112] Our Divine Redeemer here reprimands the scribes, pharisees and Rabbis, all persons who formed the spiritually leading strata of the Jewish people.

(Verse 25); whited sepulchres, which indeed appear beautiful outwards, but within are full of dead men's bones and of all uncleanness (Verse 27); children of them which killed the prophets (Verse 31). The said chapter of the Holy Gospels ends with this express complaint of our Lord Jesus Christ against the Jews, who denied their Messiah and resisted him; and which, because of its importance, we quote completely here:

"Verse 33. Ye serpents, ye generation of vipers! How can ye escape the damnation of hell? 34. Wherefore, behold, I send unto you prophets, and wise men and scribes: some of them ye shall kill and crucify, and some of them shall ye scourge in your synagogues, and persecute them from city to city. 36. That upon you may come all the righteous blood shed upon the earth, from the blood of righteous Abel unto the blood of Zechariah son of Barachiah, whom ye slew between the temple and the altar. 36. Verily I say unto you: All these things shall come upon this generation. 37. O Jerusalem, Jerusalem, thou that killest the prophets, and stonest them which are sent unto thee, how often would I have gathered thy children together, even as a hen gathereth her chickens under her wings, and ye would not!"[113]

Better than any other, Christ, the Lord, here reveals to us the murderous and cruel instincts of the Jews. This is understandable, because, in the revelation which He made to His favourite disciple, and which the latter has written down in the "Apocalypse", he called the Jews, who denied their Messiah, the Synagogue of Satan",[114] an equally appropriate as well as divine description, which, in the ensuing centuries, was often used by the Holy Catholic Church as a description for criminal and conspiratorial Jewry, which since its murder of the Son of God has not ceased to commit every kind of crime against God and mankind. In the present book we used on our side this expression "Synagogue of Satan" in order to frequently identify modern Jewry; for one would with difficulty find a more fitting appellation than this, which was already thought of by Christ, our Lord. Only with difficulty will one find among the leaders who have combated Jewry in the Christian era, someone who has used such hard words against the Jews as Jesus Christ himself. It is therefore not to be wondered at that the Jewish writer Joseph Dunner, in his work mentioned, gives the assurance that the Jews regard Christ as the "Symbol of Antisemitism", all the more as many Christians and Gentiles have been accused of "Antisemitism" on account of far milder attacks. It is therefore dangerous that good-willed Christian clergy allow themselves to be torn

[113] Gospel of Matthew, Chapter XXIII, Verses cited.
[114] Apocalypse, Chapter 2, Verse 9; Chapter 3:9.

away by those who are not. Dangerous again for them to let loose general and unclear condemnations of "Antisemitism" – which exposes them to the danger of condemning even Christ our Redeemer, His Apostles, the Saints and Popes, described by the "Synagogue of Satan" as "Antisemites" –, because the Jews afterwards attempt to use such condemnations as a new carte blanche that justifies them in furthering every kind of crime, offence and conspiracy against mankind and secures freedom from punishment for themselves, so that the former cannot even effectively defend themselves against them.

It is necessary to keep before our eyes that in every land or every institution in which Jewry gains sufficient influence, be it through its open activity or be it in secret manner through its "Fifth Column", it seeks first of all to attain the condemnation of "Antisemitism", which on occasions prevents every attempt at defence. When they have been successful, by means of their cheating, in creating such a situation contrary to order, then any kind of conspiracy, any kind of treachery, any kind of crime or offence can only be punished if it was committed by a Christian or a Gentile, but not if committed by one or more Jews. And should anyone wish to lay punishment upon those responsible, one will at once hear the outcry of the press, of the radio and of letters that are artificially organised, in the form of angry protests against the beginnings of "Antisemitism", which has appeared like a hated plague.

This is in every respect unjust, unbelievable and insane, for the Jews have not the right to demand a special privilege that allows them to commit crimes unpunished, to betray peoples who grant refuge to them, and to instigate conspiracies and unrest, in order to secure domination over the others.

Without discrimination of race or religion, every person or organisation that is responsible for the committing of this kind of crime must receive the deserved punishment. This truth cannot be more open or simpler, and, if the Jews do not wish to believe it, the latter is nevertheless fully and completely in force for them also. It very frequently occurs that the Jews, apart from the fact that they use the condemnation of "Antisemitism" in the form already elaborated, also use another kind of cunning for the same purpose. This malice is founded upon the sophistry that is spun by the Jews themselves and is supported by Catholic and Protestant clergy who consciously or unconsciously work together with them, and solemnly assert in dogmatic form: "That it is illegal to fight against the Jews, because they are the people which gave its blood to Jesus."

Such clumsy quibbling is very easy to refute. One needs only to quote the passage from the Gospels, where Christ, our Redeemer, after He calls the Jews, who fight against Him, once again a "generation of vipers",[115] clearly and distinctly rejects the consequence of blood relationship and recognises only the spiritual. In fact one reads in this passage the following:

Matthew XII. "47. Then one said unto him, 'Behold, thy mother, and thy brethren stand without, desiring to speak with thee.'[116] 48. But He answered and said unto him that told him, 'Who is My mother? And who are My brethren? 50. For whosoever shall do the will of My Father, which is in heaven, the same is My brother, and sister, and mother.' "[117]

In spite of the fact that Jesus, on His mother's side, was blood-related with the ancient Hebrew people of Biblical times, it is evident that for the future He only recognised the spiritual relationship, in that He looked over and beyond the blood- related links with His relatives, and, with even more justice, beyond those with the Jewish people who rejected Him as the Messiah, denied Him, martyred Him and murdered Him after a long and cruel torture, committing the most monstrous crime of all time and transforming itself into the God-murdering people.

But if Christ called the Jews, who slandered Him, children of the devil and generation of vipers, He confirmed that He is God's Son and allows it to be discerned that no kind of relationship binds Him with the Jews, that indeed none can exist between God's Son and the children of Satan, nor can a connection exist between good and evil.

The thesis that the "Synagogue of Satan", i.e. modern Jewry, had given Christ His blood and therefore must not be combated, is therefore completely false and even heretical. If this most disgraceful thesis were true, neither Christ Himself, nor His apostles, nor many saints, the Councils and the Popes, would have combated it.

It is foolish to equate with the later Jews the original Hebrew people, in which Abraham, Isaac, Jacob, Moses, the most Holy Virgin Mary and the Apostles are included, who received the divine privilege of being the chosen people of the Lord. The later Jews violated the condition laid upon them by God of being the chosen people, and therefore deserved, on

---

[115] St. Matthew's Gospel, Chapter XII, Verse 34.
[116] It is customary in Biblical language to describe the closest relatives as brothers.
[117] St. Matthew's Gospel, Chapter XII, the verses quoted.

account of their crimes, their rebelliousness and misdeeds, the title of "Synagogue of Satan."

The privilege of the chosen people has been inherited by the Holy Church of Christ, which is the real spiritual successor of the original Hebrew people of Biblical times.

Into the same confusion, into which those Christian clergy have fallen who cooperate with the "Synagogue of Satan", fell certain radical circles of Hitlerite Nazism who, in their zeal to combat international Jewry, invented an absurd, nay blasphemous, racial doctrine that identified the chosen people of Abraham, Isaac, Moses, the most Holy Virgin Mary and the Apostles with the "Synagogue of Satan", i.e. with modern Jewry, and in identical manner rejected the one as the other as members of an undesirable race, thereby maintaining a thesis unacceptable to Christians.

The Anti-Communist Germans, who at present fight in such a heroic manner against the Soviet strivings for power, should calmly reflect about this affair, so that those who combat devilish Jewry do not commit anew the errors of the Nazis, which leads to that foolish and anti-Christian confusion of a racist kind, which, apart from the fact that it is unjust, false and blasphemous, would call forth the indignation of Christians at the moment when the unity of all honourable people in the world, all who believe in God and the good cause, is necessary in order to fight the Jewish-Communist monster, which advances unceasingly and thirsty for blood, threatening all mankind equally, without discrimination of race or religion.

In order to give a striking proof of how dangerous it is to formulate condemnations of "Antisemitism", we will in conclusion quote an irrefutable document, and in fact one of the official and most important works of contemporary Jewry: "The Spanish-Jewish Encyclopaedia", which was published in 1948 by the Jewish Encyclopaedia Publishers, Mexico, D.F., and in whose preparation the following collaborated: Ben Zion Uziel, Grand Rabbi of the Holy Land; Max Yogupsky, of the Latin-American section of the "American Jewish Committee" of New York; Professor Dr. Hugo Bergmann, professor and former rector of the Hebrew university of Jerusalem; Isidore Meyer, librarian of the "American Jewish Historical Society" of New York; Haim Nahoun Effendi, Grand Rabbi of Egypt; Dr. Georg Herlitz, director of the Zionist central archive of Jerusalem; and many other leading personalities and men of science of world Jewry.

The most important thing is how the said Jewish Encyclopaedia defines the word "Antisemitism", and what the Hebrews regard as such, asserting among other things the following: "In the Middle Ages: With the establishment of the Christian Church as the State religion and its spreading into Europe began the persecution of the Jews; the motives for this were at first of a purely religious nature.

"The spiritual power of the Church was only very imperfectly established. In the measure that heresy raised its head, so the persecution became more intensive and in general fell always upon the Jews as a convenient scapegoat. In the face of the propagandist strivings of the Church the Jew was the constant denier. A great part of Christian 'Antisemitism' is to be attributed to the reforming of the religious rituals, which the Church had accepted from Jewry and which it transformed into anti-Jewish symbolism. The Jewish feast of the Passover was linked with the crucifixion... And in the sermons the Jews began to be denounced as traitors, as bloodthirsty, etc, and the feelings of the people stirred up against them. They were said to have magical and maleficent powers owing to their alliance with Satan. The Catholic world came to believe that the Jews knew that the Christian teaching was the truthful one, but that they refused to accept this truth and falsified the Biblical texts to prevent a Christological interpretation being applied to them. The Jewish alliance with Satan was not some kind of mediaeval-minded allegory, nor the invention of a fanatical priesthood. The Gospel itself (John VIII, Verse 44) said that the Jews are children of the devil. The servants of the Church constantly stressed the Satanism of the Jews and called them disciples and allies of the devil.

"The constant ecclesiastical accusation of deicide, of their thirst for Christian blood, their symbolic scourging of the crucifix, their lack of reason and their evil instincts produced a too frightening picture for it not to exert the deepest effects upon the human masses. Although the Church attempted, by means of Papal Edicts and Encyclicals, to contain the popular hatred, which it itself had produced, the anti-Jewish mentality of the time took effect in excesses of the mob, in bloodbaths among the Jews, in expulsions and compulsory conversions, etc...

And after the Hebrew Encyclopaedists have quoted the Jew-hostile laws of certain Christian rulers, of which some were apparently inspired by various Church fathers like Ambrose and Chrysostom, they concluded with the assertion:

"However, the most hostile legislation came from the side of the Church itself, from its councils, from Papal agreements and from Canon Law, whose severity constantly increased from the 4th to the 16th century."[118]

One of the most recent revelations of Jewish literature that supports the thesis that the Church had been unjust towards the Jews, are the books of Jules Isaac: "Jésus et Israël" and the recently published "L'Enseignement du Mépris", which was praised by the writer and politician Carlo Bo.[119]

The lasting pressure of those who serve the interests of Jewry within Holy Church and which has been directed towards attaining ambiguous condemnations of "Antisemitism", can have no other disastrous purpose than to seek to attain that the Church in the end passes judgment on itself. For the Jews, who more than anyone else feel themselves authorised to define Antisemitism, regard Holy Church, as one can see from the preceding, as principally responsible for an unbridled Christian "Antisemitism".

---

[118] Enciclopedia Judaica Castellana, Mexico, D.F., 1948. Word: "antisemitism". Vol. I, pages 334-337.
[119] Carlo Bo: "E ancora deficile dire ebreo." Article from the periodical L'Europeo of 26th August 1962.

CHAPTER SEVEN

THE DEICIDE PEOPLE

Let us recall that an association under the name "Friends of Israel", to which even cardinals and bishops belonged, was dissolved by his Holiness Pope Pius XI, by means of the Sacred Congregation of the Holy Office, in the year 1928; and that among the assertions condemned, assertions which the said association spread, was that the Jewish people were not the murderers of God, which contradicts what the Church has maintained for nearly twenty centuries. Condemned by the Church, this association was dissolved through the Edict mentioned. No one imagined that its adventures would be re-enlivened, until it was established to great astonishment that, after more than thirty years, the Jews had founded the same association again and it was supported by a numerous group of clergy, who nevertheless defiantly contradict the condemnation expressed by the Holy Office and assert that it is completely false that our Lord Jesus Christ was killed by the Jews and that those really responsible for the murder were the Romans; consequently it is unjustifiable to describe the Jewish people as murderers of God. The audacity of the new Friends of Israel verges on the limits of the incomprehensible; for they not only dare to contradict the Apostles of the Lord, but Christ Himself, as will be proved in what follows by means of texts from the New Testament, which reveal:

I. That Christ accused the Jews and not the Romans of wishing to kill him.

II. That the Jews and not the Romans were those who had the intention of killing Jesus, and who upon different occasions attempted to destroy him before his Passion and Death.

III. That the Jews and not the Romans were the instigators and truly responsible for the crime.

IV. That the Apostles accused the Jews and not the Romans of the death of Jesus.

First Thesis: Christ accused the Jews and not the Romans of wishing to kill him. Proof:

In the Gospel of John, Chapter VIII, the Apostle relates that Jesus, in a verbal dispute with some Jews, said to them (Verse 37):

"I know that ye are Abraham's seed; but ye seek to kill Me, because My word hath no place in you."

And afterwards, as the Apostle alludes in verse 40 of the same chapter, Jesus Christ, our Lord, says anew to the Jews:

"But now ye seek to kill Me, a man that hath told you the truth, which I have heard of God; this did not Abraham."[120]

And in another chapter of the said Holy Gospel (in the VIIth), the favourite disciple points out that Jesus, having gone on a certain day to the temple in order to preach, said to the Jews:

"19. Did not Moses give you the law, and yet none of you keepeth the law? Why go ye about to kill Me?"[121]

In no passage of the Holy Apostles does it appear that Christ, our Lord, said that the Romans wished to kill him, but on the contrary he accused the Jews of wanting to do it. Do then the clergy who represent this new kind of (Jew-friendly) thesis believe that Christ, our Lord, was wrong and that now, in this century, they have just discovered that our Lord Jesus Christ could not foresee that it was the Romans and not the Jews who wished to kill Him?

Second Thesis: It was the Jews and not the Romans who repeatedly planned and attempted to kill Jesus, even before His Passion and Death.

Proofs: The Gospel according to Matthew, Chapter XXI, relates to us that Christ our Lord,

"23. When He had come into the temple, the chief priests and the elders of the people came unto Him as he was teaching and said, 'By what authority doest thou these things? And who gave thee this authority?' "

---

[120] Gospel of John, Chapter VIII, Verses 37-40.
[121] Gospel of John, Chapter VII, Verses 19-20.

The Apostle then tells further of the discussion which Jesus conducted with such high leaders of the Jewish people, to close the passage with these two verses:

"45. And when the chief priests and Pharisees had heard His parables, they perceived that He spake of them. 46. But when they sought to lay hands on Him, they feared the multitudes because they took Him for a prophet."[122] This passage shows that the intentions of attack did not emanate from irresponsible Jews, but from the respected leaders of the Jewish people, who were then the chief priest as well as the Pharisees, who had a decisive influence in the government of that nation.

In the Gospel according to Mark, Chapter III, one reads the following: "1. And He entered again into the synagogue; and there was a man there which had a withered hand. 2. And they watched Him, whether He would heal him on the Sabbath day; that they might accuse Him. 5. And when He had looked around about on them with anger, being grieved for the hardness of their hearts, He saith unto the man, 'Stretch forth thine hand.' And he stretched it out, and his hand was restored whole as the other. 6. And the Pharisees went forth, and straight away took counsel with the Herodians against Him, how they might destroy Him."[123]

One thus sees that the leading strata of the Jewish people plotted against Jesus to cause His death, and in fact long before He was led before Pilate, without there being in the Gospels one passage which alludes to an intention or a plan of the Romans to do this.

John remarks that, because Jesus had healed the lame man on the Sabbath, the Jews persecuted Him. In Chapter V, he says:

"18. Therefore the Jews sought the more to kill Him, because He not only had broken the Sabbath, but said also that God was His Father, making Himself equal with God."[124]

In the Gospel according to Luke, the disciple tells us how Christ was in Nazareth and went on the Sabbath into the synagogue, began to preach and aroused opposition in many of those present with his preaching. In verses 28 and 29 of the fourth chapter the evangelist says:

---

[122] Gospel of Matthew, Chapter XXI, Verses 23, 45 and 46.
[123] Gospel of Mark, Chapter III, Verses 1, 2, 5 and 6.
[124] Gospel of John, Chapter V, Verse 18.

"28. And all they in the synagogue when they heard these things, were filled with wrath. 29. And they rose up, and thrust Him out of the city, and led Him unto the brow of the hill whereon their city was built, that they might cast Him down headlong."

If they attempted to kill Him in His own city, this means that the intention of murdering Him was universal and not only restricted to the Jewish leaders of Jerusalem.

Saint John further reveals in Chapter VII, Verse I: "After these things Jesus walked in Galilee, for he would not walk in Judaea because the Jews sought to kill Him."

This passage cannot be clearer. Throughout the whole of Judaea the Jews sought Jesus in order to kill Him; but since His hour had not yet come, He preferred not to go into this region.

If there were various preceding intentions and conspiracies to kill Jesus, then it was also the Jews and not the Romans who hatched the final conspiracy that was to result in His death.

Third Thesis: The Jews and not the Romans were the instigators and those really responsible for the crime – Proofs:

In the Gospel according to Saint Luke, Chapter XXII, the disciple says: "1. Now the feast of unleavened bread drew nigh, which is called the Passover. 2. And the chief priests and scribes sought how they might kill Him."[125]

In Chapter XI of the Gospel according to Saint John, for its part, is found the following passages:

"47. Then gathered the chief priests and the Pharisees a council, and said, 'What do we? for this man doeth many miracles?' 49. And one of them, named Caiaphas, being the high priest that same year, said unto them, 'Ye know nothing at all. 50. Nor consider that it is expedient for us that one man should die for the people, and that the whole nation perish not.' 53. Then, from that day forth, they took counsel together for to put

---

[125] Gospel of Luke, Chapter XXII, Verses I and 2.

Him to death. 54. Jesus therefore walked no more openly among the Jews."[126]

Saint Luke says that it was the Jews and not the Romans who bribed Judas to hand Christ over to them (Chapter XXII):

"3. Then entered Satan into Judas surnamed Iscariot, being of the number of the Twelve. 4. And he went his way, and communed with the chief priests and captains, how he might betray Him unto them. 5. And they were glad, and covenanted to give him money. 6. And he promised, and sought opportunity to betray Him unto them in the absence of the multitude."[127]

Chapter XVIII: "1. When Jesus had spoken these words, He went forth with His disciples over the brook Cedron, where was a garden, into the which He entered, and His disciples. 2. And Judas also, which betrayed Him, knew the place, for Jesus oft-times resorted thither with His disciples. 12. Then the band and the captain and officers of the Jews took Jesus, and bound Him. 13. And led Him away to Annas first; for he was father- in-law to Caiaphas, which was the high priest that same year.

14. Now Caiaphas was he which gave counsel to the Jews that it was expedient that one man should die for the people. 24. Now Annas had sent Him bound unto Caiaphas the high priest. 28. Then led they Jesus from Caiaphas unto the hall of judgment; and it was early; and they themselves went not into the judgment hall, lest they should be defiled; but that they might eat the Passover. 39. 'Ye have a custom that I should release unto you one at the Passover. Will ye therefore that I release unto you the King of the Jews?' 40. Then cried they all again, saying, 'Not this man, but Barabbas.' Now Barabbas was a robber."[128]

In Chapter Nineteen, he relates further that, after Pilate had had Jesus scourged (as the Bible annotation of Scio Vol. V, page 255 explains) and Jesus was seen in a condition which would have moved to pity even the wild beasts and softened their hearts:

4. "Pilate therefore went forth again, and saith unto them, 'Behold, I bring Him forth to you, that ye may know that I find no fault in Him. 5. Then came Jesus forth, wearing the crown of thorns, and the purple robe.

---

[126] Gospel of Saint John, Chapter XI, Verses 47, 49, 50, 53 and 54.

[127] Gospel of Saint Luke, Chapter XXII, Verses 3-6.

[128] Gospel of Saint John, Chapter XVIII, Verses 1, 2, 12, 13, 14, 24, 28, 39 & 40.

And Pilate saith unto them, 'Behold the man!' 6. When the chief priests therefore and officers saw Him, they cried out, saying, 'Crucify him, crucify him.' Pilate saith unto them, 'Take ye him, and crucify him: for I find no fault in him.' 7. The Jews answered him, 'We have a law, and by our law he ought to die, because he made himself the Son of God!' 15. But they cried out, 'Away with him, away with him, crucify him.' Pilate saith unto them, 'Shall I crucify your King?' The chief priests answered, 'We have no king but Caesar.' 16. Then delivered he Him therefore unto them to be crucified. And they took Jesus, and led Him away. 17. And He bearing His cross went forth into a place called the place of a skull, which is called in the Hebrew, Golgotha: 18. Where they crucified Him, and two others with Him, on either side one, and Jesus in the midst."[129]

Pilate, like others also who did not belong to the "generation of vipers", to use the actual words of Christ, could not imagine to what degree the cruelty of the Jews would reach, for it is something extraordinary in the history of mankind. By their denying their God and Lord, they fell into the deepest abyss. If they did even with Jesus what they have done, then we can no longer be surprised at the terrible ritual crimes that the Jews practised for several centuries, concerning whose monstrous occurrences indisputable evidence is at hand, even from the saints of the Catholic Church. These ritual crimes consisted, as is known, in capturing an innocent Christian child and, on Good Friday subjecting it to all tortures of the Passion, and causing it to suffer the same cruel death that they had prepared for Christ our Lord. In the unfortunate child they cold-bloodedly repeated the Passion and Death of Jesus. The veneration that is shown in Italy to the child Blessed Simon of Trent and the child Blessed Lorenzino de Marostica has in fact its origin in that both were martyred by the Jews.

All this would seem incredible to us, if irrefutable proof of their actual execution were not available, not only during the Middle Ages, but also in recent times.

Only a "generation of vipers", as the Son of God called them, a cold-blooded and merciless race, the murderers of Jesus Christ, could arrive at such uttermost limits of insanity, which today we still experience in the Communist lands, where they tortured and killed millions of Christians and Gentiles with all application of cruelty. As long as the beast, according to the expression used in the Apocalypse of Saint John, lay in chains for a thousand years, i.e. from the fifth to the fifteenth century, it limited itself

---

[129] Gospel of Saint John, Chapter XIX, Verses 4, 5, 6, 7, 15, 16, 17, & 18.

to crucifying defenceless children, to polluting crucifixes and images of the Holy Virgin Mary, to degrading sacred objects, to dirtying the holy memory of Jesus and Mary with blasphemies and terrible slanders. But when the beast made itself free at the beginning of the 16th century, it finally rolled over the whole world in the 19th and 20th century.

Then it no longer restricted itself to only spitting upon and shamefully polluting the crucifixes or the images of the Holy Virgin Mary, or in slandering in horrible manner the memory of the latter. It was no longer necessary, due to a lack of other objects, to concentrate their entire hatred and their entire cruelty upon innocent children; the horrible monster, freed of its chains and free of ecclesiastical and civil laws, which had kept the Jews locked in the ghettos and separated from the Christians, free of the ban of occupying leading posts in Christian society, stormed loose in order to now bring everything into its possession, in order to destroy one after another of the Christian institutions and to unleash their diabolic hatred against the whole of Christianity, which is being systematically destroyed in the Communist lands.

The Jewish writer Salvatore Jona confirms the foregoing, when he says: "Once the Hebrews were out of the Ghetto, they flung themselves upon the conquest of all those material and spiritual positions which had been forbidden to them in the past centuries."[130]

Only the hand that martyred Jesus Christ could be capable of organising Chekas and secret police, in order to commit horrible crimes in frightful number, which have not their like in history.

Saint Mark reports to us in Chapter 14 of his Gospel:

"1. After two days was the feast of the Passover, and of unleavened bread: and the chief priests and the scribes sought how they might take Him by craft, and put Him to death. 10. And Judas Iscariot, one of the twelve, went unto the chief priests, to betray Him unto them. 11. And when they heard it, they were glad, and promised to give him money. And he sought how he might conveniently betray Him."

It is necessary to establish that Judas did not attempt to betray Him to the Romans, but to the Jews, because they and not the Romans were interested in killing Christ.

---

[130] Salvatore Jona, Gli Ebrei in Italia durante il Fascismo. Milan, 1962, page 7.

Saint Mark continues with a passage which proves that it was the spiritual and civil leaders of the Jewish peoples, and not the Romans, who had Jesus taken prisoner:

"43. And immediately, while He yet spake, cometh Judas, one of the twelve, and with him a great multitude with swords and staves, from the chief priests and the scribes and elders.

44. And he that betrayed Him had given them a token, saying, 'Whomsoever I shall kiss, that same is he: take him, and lead him away safely.' 46. And they laid hands on Him, and took Him. 53. And they led Jesus away to the high priest: and with him were assembled all the chief priests and the elders and the scribes (i.e. the leaders of the Jewish people; the most far-reaching representatives of Israel). 55. And the chief priests and all the council sought for witness against Jesus to put Him to death; and found none. 56. For many bare witness against Him, but their witness agreed not together. 59. But neither so did their witness agree together. 60. And the high priest stood up in the midst, and asked Jesus, saying, 'Answerest thou nothing? What is it which these witness against thee?' 61. But He held his peace, and answered nothing. Again the high priest asked Him, and said unto Him, 'Art thou the Christ, the Son of the Blessed?' 62. And Jesus said, 'I am, and ye shall see the Son of man sitting on the right hand of power, and coming in the clouds of heaven.' 63. Then the high priest rent his clothes, and saith, 'What need we any further witnesses? 64. Ye have heard the blasphemy; what think ye?' And they all condemned Him to be guilty of death. 65. And some began to spit on Him, and to cover His face, and to buffet Him, and to say unto Him, 'Prophesy'; and the servants did strike Him with the palms of their hands."[131]

For two thousand years long the whole world has been filled with horror at the cruelty and hardness that has been displayed by the Jews in the torturing of their own God; this cruelty and this sadism has later always revealed itself, where they have intervened, especially in those lands where they were successful in introducing their totalitarian dictatorship, i.e. in the so-called Socialist or Communist states.

The Holy Gospels show us clearly three of the weapons that have been the favourites of Jewry in its struggle against Christianity and still are: deception, slander and crime; these three were even used mercilessly against our God and Lord. Later they used the same against the whole of

---

[131] Gospel of Saint Mark, Chapter XIV, Verses 1, 10, 11, 43, 44, 53, 55, 56, 59-65.

mankind, so that it has brought them the name which they bear so rightly as "fathers of deceit and calumny."

With these despicable weapons they easily discourage even the most resolute defenders of our belief, who are subjected without remedy to the treacherous attacks of the agents of Jewry smuggled into the Church.

The supreme ruler and leader of Israel, the high priest Caiaphas, the chief priests, the elders, the judges, scribes, Herodians and even the influential Pharisees were responsible for the murder of God; for at first the popular mass followed Christ, and those who planned His death, feared the people. However, gradually the priests and leaders poisoned the climate and led the people against Jesus, until finally they were successful in bringing the masses into opposition with their Messiah, as the following passage of the Gospel according to

Saint Matthew proves:

Chapter XXVII: "1. When the morning was come, all the chief priests and elders of the people took counsel against Jesus to put Him to death. 2. And when they had bound Him, they led Him away, and delivered Him to Pontius Pilate the governor. 15. Now at that feast, the governor was wont to release unto the people a prisoner, whom they would. 16. And they had then a notable prisoner, called Barabbas. 17. Therefore, when they were gathered together, Pilate said unto them, 'Whom will ye that I release unto you? Barabbas, or Jesus which is called Christ?' 20. But the chief priests and elders persuaded the multitude that they should ask for Barabbas and destroy Jesus. 21. The governor answered and said unto them, 'Whether of the twain will ye that I release unto you?' They said, 'Barabbas.' 22. Pilate saith unto them, 'What shall I do then with Jesus which is called Christ?' They all say unto him, 'Let him be crucified.' 23. And the governor said, 'Why, what evil hath he done?' But they cried out the more, saying, 'Let him be crucified.' 24. When Pilate saw that he could prevail nothing, but that rather a tumult was made, he took water, and washed his hands before the multitude, saying, 'I am innocent of the blood of this just person: see ye to it.' 25. Then answered all the people, and said, 'His blood be on us, and on our children.' 26. Then released he Barabbas unto them; and when he had scourged Jesus, he delivered Him to be crucified."[132]

This passage alone already represents a proof of the complete guilt of the Jews for the murder of Jesus Christ, Our Lord. It also proves the

---

[132] Gospel of Saint Matthew, verses quoted.

responsibility that the Jewish people had for this crime; for even if its religious and civil leaders and its legal representatives had previously conceived, prepared and completed it, then nevertheless the mass of the people could have prevented it at the last hour, asking for Jesus instead of Barabbas; instead of that it demanded the freeing of the latter and the crucifying of Jesus, even though as a result the blood of the Son of God would descend upon them and their descendants.

CHAPTER EIGHT

THE APOSTLES CONDEMN THE JEWS
FOR THE MURDER OF CHRIST

ourth Thesis: The Apostles accused the Jews and not the Romans of the death of Christ. Proofs:

In the Holy Scriptures, in the Acts of the Apostles (Chapter II), Saint Peter, addressing his words to the Jews of different lands who were gathered in Jerusalem, where each (after the descent of the Holy Ghost) heard the words of the Apostle in his mother tongue, said:

"14. Ye men of Judaea, and all ye that dwell at Jerusalem, be this known unto you, and hearken to my words! 22. Ye men of Israel, hear these words: Jesus of Nazareth, a man approved of God among you by miracles and wonders and signs, which God did by Him, in the midst of you, as ye yourselves also know. 23. Him, being delivered by the determinate counsel and foreknowledge of God, ye have taken, and by wicked hands have crucified and slain."[133]

Peter thus clearly lays responsibility for the murder on the entire Jewish people and does not accuse the Romans. Do the clergy, who in such incredible manner assert the contrary, perhaps assume that Peter lied when he said to the Jews who were come from other provinces: "Men of Israel, ye have crucified and slain Him"?

In the third chapter of the aforementioned work we find the passage relating to the healing of the man lame from birth:

"11. And as the lame man which was healed held Peter and John, all the people ran together unto them, in the porch that is called Solomon's, greatly wondering. 12. And when Peter saw it, he answered unto the

---

[133] Acts of the Apostles, Chapter II, verses quoted.

people, 'Ye men of Israel, why marvel ye at this? or why look ye so earnestly on us, as though by our own power or holiness we had made this man to walk? 13. The God of Abraham and of Isaac, and of Jacob, the God of our fathers, hath glorified His Son Jesus; whom ye delivered up, and denied Him in the presence of Pilate, when he was determined to let Him go. 14. But ye denied the Holy One and the Just, and desired a murderer to be granted unto you; And killed the Prince of life, whom God hath raised from the dead; whereof we are witnesses!"[134]

In this passage of the New Testament, where the entire people was assembled, Saint Peter upbraids the Jews for having killed Christ.

In addition we find in the "Acts of the Apostles" (Chapter V) a passage where not only Saint Peter, but also the remaining Apostles, categorically accuse the Council of Elders of Israel, which was summoned by the priests, of the death of Christ:

"29. Then Peter and the other Apostles answered and said, 'We ought to obey God rather than men. 30. The God of our fathers raised up Jesus, whom ye slew and hanged on a tree.' "[135]

We have thus here a common evidence of the Apostles, which accused the Jews and not the Romans, of having killed Christ. If all this will still not suffice, we will quote in addition the evidence of Saint Paul and Saint Stephen, the first martyrs of Christianity.

Saint Paul, in his First Epistle to the Thessalonians (Chapter II), says with reference to the Jews:

"15. Who both killed the Lord Jesus, and their own prophets, and have persecuted us; and they please not God, and are contrary to all men."[136]

In this verse Saint Paul describes the Jews in convincing manner as "contrary to all men." This is a truth that can be doubted by no one who has thoroughly studied the mode of thought and the illegal activities of the Jewish people.

However, it is very probable that, if Paul had lived today, he would have been condemned as an enemy of the Jews, since he publicly

---

[134] Bible, Acts of Apostles, Chapter III, Verse 11-15.
[135] Bible, Acts of Apostles, Chapter V, Verses 29, 30.
[136] First Epistle of Saint Paul to the Thessalonians, Chapter II, Verse 15.

announced a truth that may never be announced to any one, owing to the Jews and their accomplices within the clergy. When, on his side, the protomartyr Saint Stephen turned to the Jews of the Synagogue of the Freedmen, the Cyreneans, the Alexandrians and then to those of Cilicia and Asia, i.e. to Jews from different parts of the world, he said to them in the presence of the high priest, the spiritual leader of Israel:

"51. Ye stiff-necked and uncircumcised in heart and ears, ye do always resist the Holy Ghost; as your fathers did, so do ye.

52. Which of the prophets have not your fathers persecuted? and they have slain them which shewed before of the coming of the Just One; of whom ye have been now the betrayers and murderers!"[137]

The evidence of Saint Stephen thus agrees with that of the Apostles and with that of Saint Paul, when he regards the Jews in general, i.e. both those of Jerusalem and the remaining parts of Judaea, as well as those who live in other parts of the world, as a people responsible for deicide. All this is recorded in Holy Scripture, where one does not find a single verse that accuses the Romans of the murder.

In short, the preceding revelations of Christ Our Lord, as well as the evidence of the Apostles, including Saint Paul, represent an irrefutable proof that Holy Church, far from having erred over nineteen centuries, was completely right to regard the Jewish people as murderers of God; whereas to attribute responsibility for the crime to the Romans lacks any foundation.

Since this doctrine, which asserts that the Romans and not the Jews were responsible for the murder of our divine Redeemer, stands in contradiction to the evidence of Christ and the Apostles, it is proven in clear manner to be false and even heretical. At first sight, it seems absurd and inexplicable that a group of zealous Catholic clergy should be so emboldened to support such an apparent error in our days, which, if it were to prosper, would deny the truth of that which is said in the Holy Gospels, with all its unimaginable consequences. But such godless intrigues are explained, if one bears in mind that the "Synagogue of Satan", as well as the clergy who stand in its service, are disturbed by the struggle that devout Christians from different parts of the world are conducting against Communism and against its father and instigator, the Jewish striving for power, and that they under all circumstances wish to reform

---

[137] Bible, Acts of the Apostles, Chapter VI, Verse 9; Chapter VII, Verses 51, 52.

the Church in such a manner as to allow them to use it henceforth as a serviceable tool of the Synagogue, in order to crush Catholics who fight heroically against it for the defence of Christendom and its threatened and oppressed nations. In order to attain this, it must in the first place destroy the Jew-hostile teachings of the Church Fathers, of the Popes and Councils. In their indescribable insolence they go so far as to demand the setting up of new doctrines, such as those which represent the Romans and not the Jews as responsible for this despicable murder. As long as Christians continue to regard the Jewish people as the murderers of God, every assertion that has the aim of regarding them as good, holy and untouchable, is condemned to failure. However, the Hebrews fight bitterly to force upon Christianity a false doctrine, which declares them as the beloved, sacred and untouchable of God and then allows them to carry out free and without contradiction all their conspiracies and crimes. We will study later, how many other reforms, which the so-called Liberals and progressive clergy plan, have no other purpose than to destroy the traditions of the Church as sources of our teaching, in order to render easier the destructive plans of Communism and of Jewish hunger for power.

CHAPTER NINE

MORALITY OF STRUGGLE

AND NOT DEADLY DEFEATISM

One of the most godless intrigues, which has yielded the Jews a magnificent result in their struggle against Christianity, has been the utilisation of the idea of Christian morality and love of one's neighbour, which they shape according to their whim and use with crushing precision as a destructive weapon against Christianity. It appears incredible that such noble things as morality and Christian love of one's neighbour should be transformed under this disastrous influence into dangerous intrigues. But the Jews have attained this skilled and death-bringing transformation with such harmful results for Holy Church, that it is necessary to sound the alarm and to show the danger in all clarity, in order to prevent Christians from falling into this fatal deception.

For a better understanding of this matter, one can resort to comparisons which, if a little crude, are nevertheless very clear: Let us assume that at a boxing match a boxer is forced at the decisive moments of the match to fight on with one hand bound, leaving him only the possibility of using one hand for striking his opponent, while the latter uses his two hands. What would be the result of such a fight? It would not be surprising if the unfortunate boxer whose one hand is bound were beaten in the fight. Well now, this is exactly what upon different occasions treacherous Jewry has been successful in achieving with the poor Christians, in that Christian charity and Christian morality were distorted and afterwards used to bind the Christians by hands and feet, in order in this manner to attain their defeat.

Every time, therefore, when the Christians react with an attempt to defend themselves against the "Synagogue of Satan" and to protect Holy Church or their country or to preserve the natural rights that they possess as persons, as family fathers, etc, the Jews and their aides, whenever the former are on the point of gaining the victory, of overthrowing and punishing them, always appeal to Christian neighbourly love. They attempt to touch the believers hearts with this appeal, so that they may give up the struggle or refrain from pushing to its conclusion the victory that they are on the point of winning.

They also resort to such cunning in order to prevent appropriate punishment being laid upon them as criminals or as being responsible for a repelled attack. All this for the purpose of re-establishing, under protection of this armistice or of forgiveness which they receive by reason of a misuse of Christian neighbourly love, the necessary power to begin anew the overwhelming, merciless, destructive and irremediable aggression, after whose victory one will be able to expect neither moral acts nor Jewish charity.

In order to carry through their intentions of laying the Christians in chains and preventing them from defending themselves, the Israelites and their agents use wordplay and hair-splitting terminology. For example they say: "If God pardons every sinner who repents of his sins before his death, why do you Christians not imitate your God and Lord?" They thus proceed from a true premise, from the Christian teaching of the forgiveness of sin, and then attempt to use it in hair-splitting form and to draw false conclusions from it.

In this manner they conclude for example, with reference to the said promise, that Christians are obligated to allow Jewish criminals who murder a King, the President of the Republic, or any Christians, to go unpunished. It is also logically concluded from this that Catholics are obligated to allow freedom to spies who have supplied a foreign power with secrets vital to the life of the nation, so that they are able to continue their traitorous activity and render easier the defeat of the country. Likewise the conclusion is reached that Christians are obligated to allow to go unpunished, indeed even to allow to walk in freedom, the conspirators who instigate a bloody revolution and carry it out, so that they, free and unpunished, can carry out further conspiracies, until they have set up the Jewish-Communist dictatorship in the land with their whole bloody apparatus of repression and tyranny. With hair-splitting wordplay like this, they surprise the good faith of many, who fall easy victim to deceit and give to the Jewish conspirators or their helpers the possibility of victory of their devilish intentions.

Nevertheless it is perfectly clear that if the Catholic Church accepts the forgiveness of sins, this does not imply a recognition that criminals and malefactors or conspirators should escape human justice or even the divine justice.

Some writers, who describe themselves as Christians, but who prove through their activity that they are in the service of the "Synagogue of Satan" use such clumsy sophisms as those which we give in the following: The Jew-friendly Italian Ernesto Rossi makes a summons to Christians in a chapter of his book, which is written for defence of the Hebrews, and attempts to support his defeatist thesis with the words of the Evangelist Saint Matthew:

"Then Peter neared and said to him: 'Lord, how many times must I forgive my brother, who has sinned against me? Up to seven times?' And Jesus answered him: 'I say unto you, not seven times, but up to seventy times seven.' "[138]

And Julian Green, who is quoted by Carlo Bo, says in the article to which we have referred:

"One can strike no Jew, without at the same time touching him who in the truest sense of the word is the man par excellence and the flower of Israel, Jesus Christ; dry the tears and the blood of your Jewish brother and the face of Christ will shine."

A great cynicism is needed to make the attempt to equate Christ Our Lord with those who nailed him to the cross and continue to oppose him up to our days. Frequently the Hebrews and their accomplices possess the shamelessness to use this cunning utilisation of Christian morality and neighbourly love, in order to prevent believers in Christ from defending themselves or their peoples and institutions from the conspiracies and attacks which emanate from the "Synagogue of Satan". For this purpose they always use Catholic or protestant clergy, who describe themselves as good Christians but who work together with Freemasonry, Communism or any other Jewish enterprise. These kinds of clergy even go as far as to remind Christians of the Sermon on the Mount and other sermons of our Lord Jesus Christ about the forgiveness of sins or love for one's enemies in order to touch believers and even to spiritually exercise a pressure, by means of similar cunning, for the purpose of weakening or even crippling the struggle, which the latter have undertaken against the powers of evil. The activity of these clergy has frequently to great part been responsible for Freemasonic or Communist triumphs.

---

[138] Ernesto Rossi, Il Manganello e L'Aspersorio, Florence, p. 356.

We can without doubt give the assurance that these Godless intrigues largely allow the "Synagogue of Satan", at least hitherto, to alter the course of history in disastrous form for the forces of Good and in favourable manner for the hosts of evil. Holy Church was able for a thousand years long, up to the end of the fifteenth century, to overthrow the "Synagogue of Satan" in all conflicts which it had to withstand year for year against the same. Christianity was then on the point of carrying off the final victory, which would have preserved Christianity from the Protestant schism, from the bloody religious wars, from the Freemasonic upheavals, in which streams of blood were shed, and from the even bloodier and more threatening Communist revolutions. The court of the Inquisition, so slandered by Jewish propaganda, which was founded for the purpose of fighting and conquering Jewry as well as the underground movements which it used in the form of false teachings in order to divide Christianity and make it disunited, would have been able with the means at its disposal to attain a final victory for Holy Church, if the treacherous Jews had not been successful in preventing this by using deceit and malice, which we will investigate, particularly in the decisive moments of that struggle, and by employing sophisms about Christian charity (which the Jews never practise), in order to move the Christian, ecclesiastical and civil leading personages through sympathy, in order to obtain their protection from the watchful Inquisitors and even the universal pardoning of the criminals.

Instead of being thankful, Jewry used this forgiveness only in order to strengthen anew its forces in secret, in order afterwards to take up the struggle with new false doctrines again and again. Finally, at the beginning of the 16th century, the international Jews were successful in breaking the unity of Christianity and in opening the breach, through which they stormed to attack the Christian citadel with the disastrous consequences that we can all observe in the present. They therefore cunningly used the goodness of Christians and used the measures of forgiveness and the armistice which they had attained through cheating in every possible way, in order to alter the course of history in a favourable sense for the forces of Satan and his Synagogue. Holy Church can measure the greatness of the catastrophe, if one bears in mind the millions and millions of souls who have been lost to Catholicism through the Protestant division, the Freemasonic upheavals and above all through the Communist revolutions of our days.

It is necessary to establish this characteristic coincidence: in those periods of history in which the leading Christian personages, civil or ecclesiastical, have most tolerated and protected the Jews, the "Synagogue of Satan" has attained greater progress in its struggle against Holy Church and overwhelming victories.

On the other hand, those other historical epochs, in which the Popes, the Ecumenical councils and the Catholic rulers had pursued an energetic and effective policy against Jewry, were victorious for Holy Church in its struggle against the Hebrews and against the false doctrines which these set up and broadcast. These victories were at times gained with force of arms and allowed millions of Christian souls to be saved. It is not our intention to criticise or to censure the leading religious and civil personages, because they committed political faults in good faith, by their granting protection to the enemy, which made possible eventually his triumph over Christianity; for what occurred in reality was that the Christians were subjected to the skilful deceits of the "Synagogue of Satan", by their being attracted by those fearful "Jewish fables" about which Saint Paul talked. One must recall that Satan is the father of lies and master in the art of deceiving men. This art was inherited by his spiritual children, the modern Jews, of whom Christ Our Lord said that they are "children of the devil."

It is not the suitable moment to criticise anyone, nor for useless lamenting about what others could have done and did not; but what is urgent is that we act with speed and energy before it is too late. It is urgent that we Catholics break off our sleep and awaken to the present reality.

In Russia, with the introduction of the socialist dictatorship thousands of archbishops, bishops, dignitaries and priests were thrown into dirty prisons, where they languished for years until their death; many others were tortured and murdered in a cruel manner; millions of Christians of all classes were subjected to indescribable tortures and thrown for years into dark and dirty prisons; further millions suffered a horrible annihilation through the merciless Jews, who do not forgive, but who destroy and enslave.

These terrible dangers threaten the whole world in the same manner. Communism will be victorious over the entire planet, if we do not act together to prevent it; for God does not help those who do not help themselves. Then cardinals, archbishops, bishops, ministers, priests and monks are thrown for years long into dark prisons and interned, tortured and finally murdered in terrible concentration camps. As for example, in Russia, Communist China and all remaining lands, where the all-destroying avalanche of Jewish Communism has triumphed.

Karl Marx, Engels and Lenin, whose doctrines the Communists follow, said it clearly in their works: "The clergy of the different religions, but above all those of the Christian, must be exterminated; the bourgeois class must be destroyed and totally annihilated." By "bourgeois class" is to be understood the owners of private houses in the city and estates on the land, of factories, of public enterprises, of workshops and businesses.

All shall be murdered without discrimination of outlook, irrespective of whether they are members of the parties of the Right, the Centre, or the Left; for it is not a question of the destruction of this or that bourgeois section, but of the whole of the bourgeois class. So it is arranged by the founders and leading personages of Communism.

The only ones who escape the slaughter are naturally the Jews, although they can belong to any one of the condemned classes. Not even the bourgeois Freemasons of Christian origin are saved, but they also are murdered. With this, Jewry proves its ingratitude a further time towards those who aid it, whom it makes use of as long as it needs them, in order to afterwards eliminate them.

But also the workers and peasant class are not spared from the misfortune, who are used by Jewry as a means of setting up the socialist dictatorships. For the Russian and Chinese experiments have clearly shown that the social classes mentioned were not only enslaved in a cruel manner, but also decimated through the murder of millions of their members, who had committed the grave crime of protesting against the deceit to which they had fallen victim to their harm and against those who had promised them a paradise, but given them a hell.

This is the frightful truth. It is useless that they attempt to conceal the same, to diminish its importance or even to deny it. The existence of members of this "Enemy Fifth Column", who have penetrated into the ranks of Christianity, we will elaborate in the fourth part of this work with palpable and irrefutable proofs. These false Catholics of the "Fifth Column" in service of the enemy attempt to make it believed that the danger does not exist or at least to diminish its importance and its close imminence, which is a reality, in order to lull us all to sleep and to prevent us from effectively defending ourselves.

When the skilled exploitation, ill-intentioned and sophistic, of charity and Christian morality, is added to the above, one can form an idea of the crushing aids which are at the disposal of the enemy, in order to disarm us and to prevent us from fighting against atheistic Communism and the

"Synagogue of Satan". One must not forget that Christian charity carries the obligation of protecting the good from the corruption of the bad, but not of protecting the bad and allowing them free rein, so that they can seduce, rob and enslave the good, at the same time as the powers of the good are chained hand and foot with a fake morality, so that the latter can be subjected to compulsion by the forces of Bolshevism.

If we express ourselves completely and unconditionally for the declarations of their Holinesses the Popes and the power of their authoritative dignity, as well as hold to the Ecumenical Councils, it is clearly evident that every interpretation put forward concerning morality and Christian charity which results in facilitating the victory of the forces of evil over the powers of good, is false; for Our Lord God created morality and charity in order to obtain the triumph of good over the bad, and not the converse. The words of the Lord, which are used in the third chapter of this part of the work as heading, give account of how God in His struggle against the devil or against the Jews, who followed the path of the former, was energetic and not weak, strong and not defeatist.

It is no use resorting to cunning appeals, as the members of the "Fifth Column" do who assert that Christ Our Lord preached love of one's enemies and forgiveness, setting up an apparent and fallacious contradiction between what the Son of God says in the New Testament and what is commanded by God the Father in the Old Testament. The theologians know very well that these contradictions are not present, and that the love and forgiveness towards enemies, this sublime teaching of our divine Saviour, refers to the enemies of a personal and private kind which arise at every moment in our social relations, not in fact to the evil-natured enemy, Satan, nor to the forces of evil that are led by him. Christ never preached either love or forgiveness for the Devil and his works, but completely the opposite.

When Jesus, like his eternal Father, attacked the forces of evil, They were both equally as unequivocal as energetic. One would attempt in vain to find a contradiction in the mode of action between the two.

As far as concerns the Jews who denied their Messiah, they were described by Christ himself as the "Synagogue of Satan". Jesus treated them in energetic and implacable manner in various passages of the Gospels, above all, according to the Apostle Saint Matthew, when He expressed himself verbally - Chapter VIII:

"11. And I say unto you, that many shall come from the east and west, and shall sit down with Abraham, and Isaac, and Jacob, in the kingdom of heaven. 12. But the children of the kingdom (i.e. the Hebrews) shall be cast out into outer darkness; there shall be weeping and gnashing of teeth."[139] Against the forces of evil Jesus was as strict as God the Father. There exists an agreement and harmony between the mode of action of both Persons of the same God. Therefore our struggle against the forces of the Devil must be energetic enough and effective enough to allow us to overthrow them. The Jews and the clergy who cooperate with them would like to see our behaviour so weak and defeatist that it permits the triumph of the forces of hell, even if this were only temporary and involved the loss of millions of souls for Holy Church, just as occurs in the lands where, through our weakness and our lack of energetic activity, atheistic Communism continues its conquests.

L'Osservatore Romano quotes an important publication and says: "The weekly journal 'Time' mentions, in its issue of 6th March 1956, that in China, after five years of Communist rule, 20 million persons have been murdered and a further 25 million thrown into concentration camps."[140]

To conclude: let us hold valid the authority of the great Church Fathers and the meaning that they gave to Christian charity. As our source we will use the "History of the Catholic Church" that was written by three Jesuit fathers, Llorca, Garcia-Villoslada and Montalban. It cannot in any respect be suspected of anti-Judaism, for which reason we prefer to use it in this case, since it limits itself to following the unanimous current of the historical writers of Holy Church.

In this connection the work says: "5. Great figures of Christian charity in the East.- In the midst of this very Christian climate, it is not surprising, that several figures distinguish themselves by their pure charity for the poor and needy, who on their side powerfully contributed to promote this same spirit. In the impossibility of recording them all, we select several of them, who distinguished themselves most of all in the 4th to the 7th centuries." After the Jesuit fathers refer to Saint Basilius, they go on to describe the figure of the great Church Father, Saint John Chrysostom, and say: "No less illustrious is Saint John Chrysostom as the great promoter of Christian charity". As an appendix the authors continue with their report of a succession of deeds, which represent Chrysostom as an example of Christian charity, and then refer to two other great Church

---

[139] Gospel according to Saint Matthew, Chapter VIII, Verses 11, 12.
[140] L'Osservatore Romano of 19th April 1956, pages 877-878.

Fathers, to Saint Ambrose, Bishop of Milan, and Saint Jerome. Of the first they assert among other things:

"6. Great figures of charity in the West.- Saint Ambrose is always the model of a Catholic bishop. Therefore it is not remarkable that he is also the most perfect example of charity and charitable works." Additionally, the Jesuits go on to relate deeds that prove their assertion that Saint Ambrose is in fact the most perfect example of Christian charity.

Referring to Saint Jerome, the studious priests remark that "Saint Jerome, who so profoundly knew the high society of Rome with all its light and dark sides, has presented us with the most remarkable examples of Christian charity..."[141]

In this connection the Jesuits mentioned quote from the words of Liese and Saint Gregory Nazianzen, the great Father of the Church, who are irreproachable as sources and Christian authorities.

Now we will see what the classical Israelite historical writer Graetz, whose works are regarded as completely trustworthy in Jewish circles, asserts concerning Saint John Chrysostom, Saint Ambrose and Saint Jerome, who, as we have already seen, are regarded by Catholic historians as models of Christian charity and worthy of imitation.

In his work "History of the Jews", whose possession the educated Hebrews regard as an honour, Graetz says literally with reference to the terrible struggle that took place between Holy Church and Jewry: "The chief fanatics against the Jews in that time were John Chrysostom of Antioch and Ambrose of Milan, who attacked them with great excess."

Then Graetz records in detail the actions of Saint John Chrysostom against the Hebrews, to whom he devotes a quarter of the book. Referring to the activity of Saint Ambrose: "Ambrose of Milan was an impetuous officer, who was ignorant in theology, and whose renowned violence within the Church had elevated him to the rank of a bishop. He was in fact the most malicious towards the Jews."[142]

---

[141] B. Llorca, S.J., R. Garcia-Villoslada, S.J. and F. J. Montalban, S.J., *Historia de la Iglesia Catolica*. Madrid: Biblioteca de Autores Cristianos, 1960. Volume I, pages 927-928.
[142] Heinrich Graetz, History of the Jews, Edition of the Jewish Publication Society of America, 5717. Philadelphia, 1956. Volume II, pages 613-614.

And in the index of the said second volume, pages 638 and 641, Graetz summarises the purpose of each section in very expressive form: "Ambrose, his fanaticism against the Jews", and "Chrysostom, his fanaticism against the Jews."

As far as concerns the other great Church Father, the symbol of Christian charity, Saint Jerome, Graetz who stands in such authority in Hebrew circles, says, in order to stress the orthodoxy of this saint, as follows:

"And if it is a requisite to despise the individual persons and the nation, then I abominate the Jews with a hatred which is impossible to express."

The highly regarded Jewish historical writer comments immediately afterwards:

"This confession of belief, in respect of hatred towards the Jews, was no personal opinion of an isolated writer, but the oracle for the whole of Christianity, which hastily accepted the writings of the Church Fathers, who were revered as Saints. In later times this confession of faith armed the kings, the people, the crusaders and the spiritual shepherds against the Jews. Implements for their torture were discovered and the gloomy fires of the stake erected in order to burn them."[143]

As one sees, these symbols of Christian charity, who were Saint John Chrysostom, Saint Ambrose of Milan and Saint Jerome, left behind to us a clear description of the same and give us to recognise that they do not exclude energetic and ruthless action against the Jews and against the "Synagogue of Satan". They transformed this struggle into a very important part of their holy life. They also teach us that Christian love of one's neighbour is not practised in favour of the forces of evil, which they principally equate with Jewry. On the other hand, it is true what the Israelite Graetz says, when he asserts that this was the unanimous teaching of the Church Fathers. Those who are interested in penetrating deeper into this theme, can do this directly in the works of the Fathers. There they can establish that all energetically condemned the Jews and fought courageously, without hesitation, against those enemies of mankind, as Saint Paul so aptly called them. We Catholics know that the unanimous opinion of the Church Fathers regarding this teaching is in many cases a binding rule of conduct for all believers and in every case is without exception an example worthy of imitation. Only the complex of Judas

---

[143] Graetz, Ibid., the same edition. Volume II, pages 625-626.

Iscariot can explain the fact that many clergy, who describe themselves as Catholics, serve the "Synagogue of Satan" better than the Church, and attempt to give us false rules of morality and of Christian charity, in order to bind our hands and to prevent us from fighting with all energy and efficacy against Jewry and its accomplices, "Freemasonry" and "Communism."

CHAPTER TEN

THE JEWS KILL THE CHRISTIANS AND
PERSECUTE THE APOSTLES

Since the origin of the Church, Jewry has declared a war of life and death upon Christianity without any grounds, without provocation, and without the Church in the first three centuries answering violence with violence. The Jews abused in cruel form the gentleness of the first Christians, who restricted themselves to combating their deadly enemies simply with well-founded discussions, in return for which they had to suffer the degrading slanders of the Jews, their imprisonments, their murders and every kind of persecution. These begin with the unjust and cruel murder of Christ Our Lord; there follows the killing of Saint Stephen, which is related to us by the Holy Bible in the Acts of the Apostles, in all its horror, from the planning of the crime in the bosom of the Synagogue, passing to the use of bribery, so that some slandered and cast poisonous accusations against him, up to the use of false witnesses to confirm these accusations, and finally the murder of the Saint by the Jews, which was completed by stoning in a cruel manner, without Stephen having committed any misdeed other than to preach the true religion.[144] He was the first martyr of Christianity, and the Israelites had the honour of being the first to have shed Christian blood after the murder of Jesus.

The Bible itself, in the Acts of the Apostles, Chapter XII, reveals, how the Jewish King Herod stretched forth his hands...

"1. ... to vex certain of the church. 2. And he killed James the brother of John with the sword. 3. And because he saw it pleased the Jews, he proceeded further to take Peter also."[145]

---

[144] Bible, Acts of the Apostles, Chapter VI, Verses 7-15; Chapter VII, Verses 54-59.
[145] Bible, Acts of the Apostles, Chapter XII, Verses 1-3.

However, the Hebrews, not satisfied with their having begun the murder of the leading Saints of nascent Christianity, fell upon the carrying out of cruel persecutions, which degenerated into terrible bloodbaths, as the Bible relates to us in the Acts of the Apostles, and which gave Heaven its first martyrs. In these persecutions, Saul, the future Saint Paul, took part before his conversion,[146] and in fact with a zeal which he himself describes in his letter to the Galatians in the following manner:

Chapter I, Verse 13: "For ye have heard of my conversation in the past in the Jews' religion, how that beyond measure I persecuted the church of God, and wasted it."[147] The Jews do not accept God, asserts Paul. The Hebrews persecuted with particular tenacity, as is natural, the Apostles and the first leaders of the Church, of which Saint Paul lays witness in his First Letter to the Thessalonians, and in which he categorically asserts that the Jews do not accept God. He says literally: "14. For, ye, brethren, became followers of the churches of God which in Judaea are in Christ Jesus: for ye also have suffered like things for your own countrymen, even as they have of the Jews; 15. Who both killed the Lord Jesus, and their own prophets, and have persecuted us; and they please not God, and are contrary to all men."[148]

It is therefore false to say that the Jews, who have denied Christ as the Messiah, are pleasing to God, as those clergy assert who work together with them for the purpose of crippling the defence of the Catholic peoples against the Jewish striving for power and its revolutionary activity. How can it be possible that these Jew-friendly priests lay claim to be right, and that Saint Paul lied when he assured us that the Jews are not pleasing to God? Nevertheless, one sees completely clearly that the powers of evil, the children of the Devil – as Christ called them – and an integral part of the "Synagogue of Satan", could not be acceptable to God. The Jews frequently imprisoned the Apostles. In the Acts of the Apostles it is, confirmed that the Jewish priests, the Sadducees and the officials of the temple laid hands on Saint Peter and Saint John and threw them into prison.[149]

In Chapter V the following is related: "17. Then the high priest rose up, and all they that were with him (which is the seed of the Sadducees), and were filled with indignation. 18. And laid their hands on the apostles,

---

[146] Bible, Acts of the Apostles, Chapter VIII, Verses 1-3; Chapter XXVI, Verses 10, 11; Chapter XXII, Verses 4, 5.
[147] Bible, Letter of Saint Paul to the Galatians, Chapter I, Verse 13.
[148] Bible, First Letter of Paul to the Thessalonians, Chapter II, Verses 14, 15.
[149] Bible, Acts of the Apostles, Chapter III; Chapter IV, Verses 1-3.

and put them in a common prison."[150] Among the persecutions unleashed by the Jews against the first leaders of the Church stand out those on account of their mercilessness which were directed against Saint Paul. It is remarked in the Acts of the Apostles — Chapter IX:

"22. But Saul increased the more in strength, and confounded the Jews which dwelt at Damascus, proving that this is the very Christ. 23. And after that many days were fulfilled, the Jews took counsel to kill him."[151] Afterwards when Saint Paul and Saint Barnabas had discussed religious questions with the Jews in Antioch, the latter ended the discussion with their usual fanaticism and their intolerance and used the argument of violence. The Acts of the Apostles quotes this — Chapter XIII:

"50. But the Jews stirred up the devout and honourable women, and the chief men of the city, and raised persecution against Paul and Baraabas, and expelled them out of their coasts."[152]

Afterwards, in the 14th chapter of the Bible book mentioned, it is confirmed what occurred in the city of Iconium after a further theological discussion by Saint Paul and Saint Barnabas with the Hebrews:

"4. But the multitude of the city was divided: and part held with the Jews, and part with the Apostles. 5. And when there was an assault made both of the Gentiles, and also of the Jews with their rulers, to use them despitefully, and to stone them,

6. They were aware of it, and fled unto Lystra and Derbe, cities of Lycaonia, and unto the region that lieth round about. 19. And there came thither certain Jews from Antioch and Iconium, who persuaded the people, and, having stoned Paul, drew him out of the city, supposing he had been dead."[153]

One thus sees that even in those days the division was very clear: on the one side the supporters of the Apostles, i.e. the Christians, and on the other, the Jews.

The New Testament of the Holy Bible already makes use in these books of the word "Jews" in order to describe the members of the ancient

---

[150] Bible, Acts of the Apostles, Chapter V, Verses 17, 18.
[151] Bible, Acts of the Apostles, Chapter IX, Verses 22, 23.
[152] Bible, Acts of the Apostles, Chapter XIII, Verses 44-50.
[153] Bible, Acts of Apostles, Chapter XIV, Verses 1-6 and 18.

chosen people who murdered God's Son and fought against His Church; for those who had converted to the faith of the Redeemer were not Jews, but Christians. The Jews, who in our days persecute the Church still further and threaten to rule and enslave mankind, are in fact the descendants of these Jews, who are described by the New Testament as the worst enemies of Christ and His Church. They have nothing in common spiritually with the old chosen people of Biblical times. The chosen people was loved by God. However, the Jews who denied their Messiah, who murdered Him and who fought against Christianity and continue to fight against it, and who stiff-neckedly grant support to their criminal organisations in our days, are, as Saint Paul said, not acceptable to God.

In Chapter XVII of the aforementioned book of the New Testament, it is said that Saint Paul and Silas came to Thessalonia, where there was a synagogue of the Jews.

"5. But the Jews which believed not, moved with envy, took unto them certain lewd fellows of the baser sort, and gathered a company, and set all the city in an uproar, and assaulted the house of Jason, and sought to bring them out to the people. 6. And when they found them not, they drew Jason and certain brethren unto the rulers of the city, crying, 'These that have turned the world upside down are come hither also. 7. Whom Jason hath received: and these all do contrary to the decrees of Caesar, saying that there is another king, one Jesus.' 8. And they troubled the people and the rulers of the city, when they heard these things. 9. And when they had taken security of Jason, and of the other, they let them go."[154]

The passages quoted of the Holy Scripture prove clearly that the Jews were the only enemies of nascent Christianity and that everywhere they not only directly persecuted the Christians, but attempted with slanders to stir up the Gentile peoples against them, and, what is still more weighty, the authorities of the Roman Empire. In the preceding passage of the Acts of the Apostles it is evident how they used slanders, in order with criminal intent to thrust the whole power of the then invincible Roman Empire against Holy Church, by their more or less accusing the Christians of recognising another king in place of Caesar, an outrage which infuriated the Roman emperors and their collaborators to the extreme; for this form of treachery to Caesar invited immediate punishment of death upon them. Thus it is beyond doubt what the Israelites strove for, who for many years afterwards applied the whole poison of their slanders and intrigues.

---

[154] Bible, Acts of the Apostles, Chapter XVII, Verses 1, 5-9.

However, they were not successful in letting loose the Roman Empire against the Christians. Only on the basis of much pressure did they attain this with Nero. An attempt also took place to stir up the rulers of Rome against Saint Paul, as the following passage of the New Testament proves:

Chapter XVIII: "12. And when Gallio was the deputy of Achaia, the Jews made insurrection with one accord against Paul, and brought him to the judgment seat, 13. Saying, 'This fellow persuadeth men to worship God contrary to the law.' 14. And when Paul was now about to open his mouth, Gallio said unto the Jews, 'If it were a matter of wrong or wicked lewdness, 0 ye Jews, reason would that I should bear with you:

15. But if it be a question of words and names, and of your law, look ye to it; for I will be no judge of such matters.' 16. And he drove them from the judgment seat. 17. Then all the Greeks took Sostheness, the chief ruler of the synagogue, and beat him before the judgment seat. And Gallio cared for none of those things."[155] This passage of the Holy Bible allows us to recognise: On the one side the religious tolerance of the Roman authorities and the absolute lack of interest in attacking Christians; on the other side it was the Hebrews who constantly sought for means in order to repeatedly unleash, even if unsuccessfully, the rulers of the Roman Empire against the Christians. In conclusion, when such an infamous attempt had failed, the Jews as madmen ended the affair with a general and furious free fight. Here Sosthenes, the superintendent of the Synagogue, became the unlucky object of Hebrew rage and madness. Naturally, we cannot doubt the truthfulness of these facts, for it is a matter of a literal passage from the New Testament.

It is therefore certainly explicable that, when this mob of wolves, in addition with all full powers, was unchained with the victory of the Communist revolutions, it carried out unbelievable bloodbaths and caused Christian and Gentile blood to flow in torrents, until in the end both in the Soviet Union, as also in the Satellite States, they cut one another to pieces, without respect for anything, not even of Rabbinical dignity, as in the case of that poor Sosthenes who is mentioned in the preceding passage of the Bible. It is completely beyond doubt that they are and remain always the same.

In the Acts of the Apostles the disciple Saint Luke tells us of further persecutions undertaken by the Jews against Saint Paul. In his description about the behaviour of the Hebrews in those times, one could say that he

---

[155] Bible, Acts of the Apostles, Chapter XVIII, Verses 12-17.

might be writing to us in the present day. Nothing seems to have altered in nearly two thousand years. He relates of the stay of the Saint in Jerusalem: Chapter XXI: "27. And when the seven days were almost ended, the Jews which were of Asia, when they saw him in the temple, stirred up all the people, and laid hands on him.

28. Crying out, 'Men of Israel, help: this is the man, that teacheth all men everywhere against the people, and the law, and this place; and further, brought Greeks also into the temple, and hath polluted this holy place.' 30. And all the city was moved, and the people ran together: and they took Paul, and drew him out of the temple: and forthwith the doors were shut. 31. And as they went about to kill him, tidings came unto the chief captain of the band, that all Jerusalem was in an uproar. 32. Who immediately took soldiers and centurions, and ran down unto them; and when they saw the chief captain and the soldiers, they left beating of Paul."[156]

This passage of the New Testament shows us how the Jews accused Saint Paul of "teaching all men everywhere against the people", i.e., they caused him in slanderous manner to appear as an enemy of the people, in order to justify his killing. More than nineteen centuries afterwards, when the Jews in the Soviet Union and other Communist lands wished to kill someone, they accused him of being an enemy of the people and an enemy of the working classes. The methods have remained the same. They have not altered in approximately two thousand years. They also slanderously accused Saint Paul of preaching against the temple, just as in the mock trials of Communist lands they accuse the future victims of having carried out a conspiracy against the Soviet Union or the proletarian state. Finally they also accuse Saint Paul of having brought Gentiles into the temple and thus defiled the holy place; for in those days the Jews regarded the temple as closed to Gentiles, just as they now regard Jewry as closed to men of other races. Then they only allowed new converts as far as the door of the temple, thus only to the outside door. Now they accept, so they say, Gentiles and Christians in some lands into Jewry, but also only to the outside door, in that by deceit they only allow the latter into the peripheral organisations and never to enter the real synagogues and communities of the Jewish people. In this, their methods have also remained the same. The book of Holy Scripture mentioned further relates that, when the captain allowed Paul to address his words to the angry Jews, in order to calm them, this occurred (Acts of the Apostles, Chapter XXII):

---

[156] Bible, Acts of the Apostles, Chapter XXI, Verses 27-32.

"22. And they gave him audience unto this word, and then lifted up their voices, and said, 'Away with such a fellow from the earth: for it is not fit that he should live.'

23. And as they cried out, and cast off their clothes, and threw dust into the air...".[157]

We see here the veritably possessed Jews, who, centuries later, in the midst of the Jewish-Communist terror, were to cut their unfortunate victims into pieces with all their application of cruelty.

This passage from the New Testament goes further (Acts of the Apostles, Chapter XXII):

"30. On the morrow, because he (i.e. the Roman captain) would have known the certainty wherefore he was accused of the Jews, he loosed him from his bands, and commanded the chief priests and all their council to appear, and brought Paul down, and set him before them."

(Chapter XXIII) "6. But when Paul perceived that the one part were Sadducees, and the other Pharisees, he cried out in the council, 'Men and Brethren, I am a Pharisee, the son of a Pharisee: of the hope and resurrection of the dead I am called in question.' 7. And when he had so said, there arose a discussion between the Pharisees and the Sadduccees: and the multitude was divided. 8. For the Sadducees say that there is no resurrection, neither angel, nor spirit: but the Pharisees confess both. 9. And there arose a great cry: and the scribes that were of the Pharisees' part arose, and strove, saying, 'We find no evil in this man: but if a spirit or angel hath spoken to him, let us not fight against God.'".[158] A magnificent lesson in how, for the cause of Good, the internal differences of opinion of the Jewish parties and sects could be used. One can do this in effective form, if one knows the secret interior of Jewry, which permits deception through false combat manoeuvres, which are frequently pretended among one another, in order to attain definite political goals.

After the violent struggle that was inflamed between the Jewish leaders mentioned and which compelled the Roman captain to use his soldiers, the Apostle continues his report (Acts of the Apostles, Chapter XXIII):

---

[157] Bible, Acts of the Apostles, Chapter XXI, Verses 35-40; Chapter XXII, Verses 19-23.
[158] Bible, Acts of the Apostles, Chapter XXII, Verse 30; Chapter XXIII, Verses 1-9.

"12. And when it was day, certain of the Jews banded together, and bound themselves under a curse, saying that they would neither eat nor drink till they had killed Paul. 13. And they were more than forty which had made this conspiracy. 14. And they came to the chief priests and elders, and said, 'We have bound ourselves under a great curse that we will eat nothing imtil we have slain Paul. 15. Now, therefore, ye with the council, signify to the chief captain that he bring him down unto you tomorrow, as though ye would inquire something more perfectly concerning him: and we, or ever he come near, are ready to kill him.' "

The foresight of the captain, who knew the Jews only too well, frustrated their criminal plans. Therefore he sent Paul away under the guard of two hundred soldiers and two officers. Verse 25 explains that the Roman captain did this because he feared that the Jews could snatch away Paul with force and kill him. Also he feared that afterwards they would slander him by saying that he had accepted their money.[159] This enlightening passage of the New Testament clearly explains that the Jews as swindlers and inventors of the "hunger strike" already put into practice in the times of Saint Paul, when they swore neither to eat nor to drink until they had succeeded in killing him. The Acts of the Apostles does not explain whether, after the salvation of Saint Paul through the caution of the Roman captain, the fasting Jews kept their oath until death. However, the silence of the Apostle allows us to assume that with the Jews then as with the "hunger strikes" of our days, the Hebrew comedians, as soon as they could not achieve their goal, found a suitable excuse to halt the strike.

On the other side, one sees that, even in those distant times, they applied the system of murdering a prisoner on the road, when the latter was brought from one place to another. One further observes that even the Romans had anxiety before the slanders of the Jews, whom they doubtless knew as masters of this disastrous art.

In order to gain knowledge of the wicked activity of Jewry and its mode of action, one scarcely needs to read the famed "Protocols of the Elders of Zion". The teachings of the Holy Bible as well as other reliable and undisputed documents suffice, which often originated from the most unhoped-for Hebrew sources.

After Saint Paul was led before the deputy (governor), the Acts of the Apostles continues in Chapter XXV:

---

[159] Bible, Acts of the Apostles. Chapter XXIII, Verses 12-25.

"2. Then the high priest and the chief of the Jews informed him against Paul, and besought him. 3. And desired favour against him, that he would send for him to Jerusalem, laying wait on the way to kill him. 4. But Festus answered, that Paul should be kept at Caesarea, and that he himself would depart shortly thither. 5. Let them therefore, said he, which are able, go down with me, and accuse this man, if there be any wickedness in him. 7. And when he was come, the Jews which came down from Jerusalem stood round about, and laid many and grievous complaints against Paul, which they could not prove. 8. While he answered for himself, 'Neither against the law of the Jews, neither against the temple, nor yet against Caesar, have I offended any thing at all.'"[160]

In order to understand this terrible tragedy, one must bear in mind that Saint Paul was a devout man and illuminated by the grace of God, to such an extent that he is worthy of being regarded as one of the greatest saints of Christianity. Nevertheless, the Jews, with their natural falsity and their insane tenacity, fell into a fury with him in the manner described in the preceding passages of the Holy Bible. The problem was sharpened still more as a result that not only the Jews from Palestine, but also those from the most different parts of the world, exposed their murderous and godless instincts, and that not only the sect of the Pharisees but also the Sadducees, who were opponents of the former. It was not individuals, isolated and without representation, who oozed such maliciousness, but the high priests, the scribes, the leading personages and most illustrious men of Israel; all cut from the same cloth.

The passages of the New Testament teach us to recognise the danger that modern Jewry represents for mankind, whose infamy exceeds the boundaries of everything which other peoples could possibly imagine. Therefore the Popes and Councils repeatedly called them "perfidious Jews", which words, together with other eloquent expressions, figure in the Liturgy and the rites of Holy Church, and which the Israelites would like to see removed completely and utterly, in order to thrust us Catholics into still greater uncertainty about the monstrous perversity of our thousand-year-old enemies and in order to compel us all the easier by their using their deceitful manoeuvres and usual surprise blows.

The most significant thing is that, in the description of the falsity of this generation of vipers, as Christ Our Lord called them, the New Testament of the Holy Bible coincides perfectly with the writings that were composed hundreds of years later by the Church Fathers, with the

---

[160] Bible, Acts of the Apostles, Chapter XXV, Verses 1-8.

ideas that are contained in the Koran of Mohammed, with the prescriptions of different Church Councils, with the trials of the Holy Inquisition, and with the opinion of Martin Luther, as well as with the accusations that have been made in different countries by savants of the problem, and in fact by Catholics, Protestants, Russian Orthodox, Mohammedans, and even by unbelievers like Voltaire and Rosenberg. All these have, without previous agreement, agreed during the last thousand years to denounce the high degree of falsity and malice among the Jews. This proves that unfortunately this wickedness and falsity, very dangerous for the remaining peoples, correspond to a confirmed and undisputed reality.

The Apostle Matthew spread the word of God far and wide, at first in Macedonia and afterwards in Judaea and converted many to belief in Jesus Christ through his sermons and his miracles. It is said, that the Jews could not suffer this, therefore they laid hands upon him, stoned him to the point of almost killing him, and finally he was decapitated on the 24th February.[161]

---

[161] Saint Jerome, quoted in the catalogue of Adricomio and also mentioned in the Bible of Scio, Page 670, Section II. Another different reading, concerning the death of this apostle (Saint Matthew), also quotes the source that records the place of his death in Egypt or Ethiopia. In face of the persecution unleashed by the Jews against the Christians all over the world, the first reading appears to us in fact very possible and the source, which we record, quotes it in first place.

CHAPTER ELEVEN

THE ROMAN PERSECUTIONS
WERE CALLED FORTH BY THE JEWS

We have already studied, in the preceding chapter, the various attempts that the Jews made in order to incite the Roman authorities against Saint Paul. They accused him of being against Caesar and recognising another King in his place, by which they meant Jesus. Concerning these intrigues and slanders, an undisputed document, i.e. the New Testament of the Holy Bible, provides us with knowledge. These attempts to incite the might of the Roman Empire against nascent Christianity followed frequently upon one another, even if for some time without success. It is a historically proven fact that the Romans in religious matters were tolerant and also in no way hostilely disposed towards the Christians, as is proved by the conduct of Pilate in the case of Jesus and the favourable interventions of the Imperial authorities in the persecutions unleashed by the Jews against Saint Paul and the first Christians. The following fact is very revealing and is recorded by Tertullian and Orosius, who remark that, before the Hebrew attempts at persecution arose against Christians, the Emperor Tiberius had a law published that threatened with death those who accused Christians.[162]

In the ninth year of his government, Claudius commanded all Jews to leave Rome because, according to the evidence of Flavius Josephus, they had caused Agrippina, his wife, to take on Jewish customs; or also, as Suetonius writes, because frequent upheavals gave the impetus to the persecutions of Christians.[163]

One sees that the pagan Emperor Claudius was tolerant in the extreme towards Christians. When he became tired of the mutinies that the Jews

---

[162] Tertullian: Apologeticum, Book V; Orosius, Book VII, Chapter II.
[163] Chronological Tables after Scio. Bible edition quoted, page 662, Section II, taken from Adricomio.

caused, he expelled them from the city of Rome. The Acts of the Apostles also report this expulsion.[164] One sees here the Jewish tendency to cause their influence to rise up to the steps of the throne, by their controlling the Empress in order to exert influence on the Emperor. In so doing, they held to the completely distorted teachings of the Biblical book of Esther, giving this an ambitious interpretation. Esther, a Jewess, was successful in transforming herself into the Queen of Persia and in exercising a decisive influence on the King, in order to destroy the enemies of the Israelites. However, in the case of the Emperor Claudius, the attempt openly failed, which did not occur with Nero, with whom it was successful in bringing close to him a Jewess named Poppaea, who soon transformed into the lover of the Emperor, and, according to some Hebrew chronicles, into the real Empress of Rome. She was successful in exercising a decisive influence upon this ruler.

Tertullian, one of the Church Fathers, says in his work "Scorpiase": "The synagogues are the places from whence the persecutions against Christians emanate." And in his book "Ad Nationes", the same Tertullian writes: "From the Jews come the slanders against the Christians."[165]

During the rule of Nero, tolerance at first reigned towards the Christians; however, the Emperor finally gave way to the persistent intrigues of his Jewish lover Poppaea, who is described as the originator of the idea of laying the blame for setting fire to the city of Rome upon the Christians, based on which the first cruel persecution of Christians that was carried out by the Roman Empire was justified.

The Jesuit fathers R. Llorca S.J., R. Garcia-Villoslada S.J. and F. J. Montalban S.J. have established the following in connection with the Christian persecutions by pagan Rome against the weak and defenceless Christians by Nero:

"The Jews were the most active elements in the promotion of the climate of hatred against the Christians, whom they regarded as the falsifiers of the Mosaic Law... This activity of the Jews must have exercised a notable influence, for it is known to us that they already enjoyed great regard in Rome at the time of Nero and that, on the occasion of the martyrdom of Saint Peter and Saint Paul, some had hinted at the idea that the latter were killed out of the jealousy of the Jews.

---

[164] Bible, Acts of the Apostles, Chapter XVIII, Verse 2.
[165] Tertullian, *Scorpiase* and *Ad Nationes*, quoted by Ricardo C. Albanes in *Los Judios a través de los siglos*, Mexico, Pages 432 and 435.

"Given this climate of violence incited by the hatred of the Jews, one can easily understand the persecution by Nero. Since they are capable of every crime, it was simple for them to denounce the Christians as the incendiaries of Rome. It needed no great effort for the people to believe it."[166]

In fact, they accused the Christians in a slanderous manner that they had even committed the disgusting crime of eating children at their ceremonies,[167] which naturally called forth alarm among the authorities and the Roman people. It is only too understandable that this constant intrigue, this persistent work of slander and blasphemy, which the Hebrews always unleash against those who disturb their plans, and which was carried out by thousands of individual persons in the Roman Empire month by month, year by year, finally attained its goal and unleashed against nascent Christianity, which they alone could not destroy, the enormous power of the Roman Empire in a destructive fury never previously known in human history.

In order to defend the truth, we will quote the reliable evidence of an authorised Jewish source: "Rabbi Wiener, who, in his work "The Jewish Food Laws", confesses that the Jews were the instigators of the Christian persecutions in Rome, observed that under the rule of Nero, in the year 65 of our calendar, when Rome had the Jewess Poppaea as Empress and a Jew as prefect of the city, the era of martyrs began which was to extend for over 249 years."[168]

In these instigations of the Hebrews to call forth the Roman persecutions against Christianity, participated even those Rabbis outstanding in the history of the synagogue, such as the famed "Rabbi Jehuda, one of the authors of the Talmud (the sacred books and the source of the religion of modern Jewry), [who was] was successful in the year 155 of our calendar in obtaining a command, according to which all Christians of Rome were to be sacrificed, and on the grounds of which many thousands were killed. The executioners of the martyrs and Popes, Cayo and Marcelino were in fact Jews."[169]

---

[166] B. Llorca, S.J., R. Garcia-Villoslada, S.J.and F. J. Montalban, S.J. *Historia de la Iglesia Catolica*, edition quoted, Volume I, pages 172, 173.

[167] Ricardo C. Albanes, op. cit., page 435.

[168] Rabbi Wiener: *Die Jüdischen Speisegesetze*, quoted by Ricardo C. Albanés, op. cit., page 435.

[169] August Rohlieng, Catholic priest, *Die Polemik und das Manschefenopfer des Rabbinismus*, quoted by Ricardo C. Albanés, op. cit., page 435.

During three centuries, the Christians showed heroic resistance, without answering violence with violence. In fact it is understandable that, after three centuries of persecutions, when Christianity had gained a complete victory in the Roman Empire through the conversion of Constantine and the acceptance of the Christian religion as the state religion, that it was finally decided to answer violence with violence, in order to defend the victorious Church – as well as the peoples who had placed their faith in it and who also saw themselves continually threatened by the destructive and annihilating activity of Jewish imperialism – against the lasting conspiracies of Jewry.

On the other side, it is necessary that the cowards, who, given the present position, think of capitulating to the "Synagogue of Satan", out of fear of its persecution, power and influence, bear in mind that the terrible threats of our days are far removed from being so grave as those which Christ our Lord, then the Apostles and after them the first Christians faced. They had to expose themselves not only to mighty Jewry, but to the then apparently unconquerable power of the Roman Empire, the greatest and strongest of all times. To these two deadly dangers were added those which arose through internal dissension, which the Jews, by means of their "Fifth column", had called forth in the bosom of Christianity, along with Gnosticism and other false destructive doctrines.

One must bear in mind that, despite the fact that that situation was far graver and more tragic than that of the present, Holy Church could only save itself if it achieved a complete victory over its deadly enemies. If it was successful in this, then it is because it was able to rely upon spiritual shepherds who never despaired, never lost courage, nor entered into shameful alliances with the powers of the Devil. At no moment did they think of seeking situations of cooperation, nor of peaceful coexistence, nor of diplomatic capitulations, which are always quibbles used by the cowardly clergy and accomplices of the enemy, who in our days strive to achieve that Holy Church and its spiritual shepherds deliver the sheep, whose careful protection Christ our Lord entrusted to them, into the claws of the wolf, for the disadvantage of the Church itself and of the trust that true Catholics have placed in it.

PART FOUR

THE "JEWISH FIFTH COLUMN"
IN THE CLERGY

CHAPTER ONE

THE OCTOPUS STRANGLING CHRISTIANITY

The Freemasonic-Jacobin revolution was successful in ruining the whole of Christianity, according to the same method that now triumphs in overwhelming form in the Jewish-Communist revolution: for the Holy Catholic Church and the whole of Christianity have only been able to fight against the arms of this octopus (the Communist party, revolutionary groups and in a few cases, as in Spain, Freemasonry), although its powerful head has remained untouched. For this reason the monster has been able to renew and restore the limbs which were occasionally cut off it, in order to use them anew and still more effectively, until gradually it has been successful in enslaving half the Christian world (Russia and the East-European states), and now has the plan of enslaving the rest of mankind.

The lasting victory of the Jewish-Freemasonic and Jewish- Communist revolutions since the end of the 18th century up to our days is also to be attributed to the fact that neither the Holy Catholic Church nor the separated Churches[170] have fought effectively against the "Jewish Fifth Column", which has smuggled itself into their bosom.

This "Fifth column" is formed by the descendants of the Jews, who in earlier centuries were converted to Christianity and seemingly held in enthusiastic manner to the religion of Christ, while in secret they preserved their Jewish belief and carried out clandestinely the Jewish rites and ceremonies. For this purpose they organised themselves into communities and secret synagogues, which were active centuries-long in secret. These apparent Christians, but secret Jews, began centuries ago to infiltrate into Christian society, in order to attempt to control it from within. For this reason they sowed false doctrines and differences of opinion and even attempted to gain control of the clergy in the different churches of Christ.

---

[170] Here we avoid using hard words against those churches, in order to support the wish of our Holy Father, John XXIII, of attaining a drawing closer together of the Christian Churches.

With all this, they applied the cunning of introducing crypto- Jewish Christians into the seminaries of the priesthood, who could gain admission into the honorary offices in the Holy Catholic Church and then into the dissident churches, upon whose division these secret Jews had so much influence.

While the Church of Rome, their Holinesses the Popes and the Ecumenical Councils fought effectively through the thousand years of the Middle Ages against Jewry and above all against the "Fifth Column", the revolutionary movements that were organised for the division and destruction of Christianity were completely conquered and destroyed. So it occurred from Constantine until the end of the fifteenth century. Unfortunately afterwards Holy Church, for reasons which we will study later, could no longer attack in an effective manner the "Fifth Column", which was formed by secret Jews who had been smuggled in as believers, as priests and even as dignitaries. Then the power of the Jewish revolutionary movement became ever stronger, until, at the end of the eighteenth century, it took on the character of an irresistible avalanche.

In the 20th century, when Jewish cunning had reached its uttermost limits of causing Catholics to forget the gigantic struggle of several centuries, which had taken place between Catholicism and Jewry, the latter attained its greatest progress in its plans for the control of the world. For it has already been successful in enslaving a third of mankind under the Jewish- Communist dictatorship.

In the Middle Ages, the Popes and the Councils were successful in destroying the Jewish revolutionary movements which appeared within Christianity in the form of false teaching and which were introduced by those who were Christians in appearance but Jews in secret. The latter then recruited upright and good Christians for the arising heretical movement by persuading the latter in a crafty way.

The secret Jews organised and controlled in secret manner the movements, which were the creative and driving force of wicked false teachings, such as those of the Iconoclasts, the Cathars, the Patarines, the Albigensians, the Hussites, the Alumbrados and others.

The work of these Jews smuggled as a "Fifth Column" into the bosom of the Church of Christ was made easier through their hypocritical conversion to Christianity or that of their forefathers. In addition, they laid aside their Jewish surnames and took on very Christian names, which were embellished with the surnames of their godfathers. Thus they were successful in mixing with Christian society and taking possession of the names of the leading families of France, Italy, England, Spain, Portugal, Germany, Poland and the other lands of Christian Europe. With this system, they were successful in penetrating into the bosom of Christianity itself, in order to conquer it from within and to destroy the core of the religious, political and economic institutions.

The network of secret Jews existing in Mediaeval Europe passed on in secret manner the Jewish belief from fathers to children, even if all openly led a Christian life and filled their houses with crucifixes and images of Catholic saints. In general they observed Christianity in an ostentatious manner and appeared most devout, in order not to arouse any suspicion.

Naturally this Jewish system of converting themselves in hypocritical manner to Christianity, in order to take the Christian citadel and to make easier the loss of its unity, was finally discovered by Holy Church to the corresponding scandal and alarm of the Holy Fathers, the Ecumenical, the provincial councils and those clergy steadfast in their faith. However, what called forth most scandal was the fact that these secret Jews introduced their sons into the established clergy and monasteries, and in fact to such good effect that many of them attained the dignity of canon, bishop, archbishop and even cardinal.

The Ecumenical and provincial councils of the Middle Ages combated Jewry violently as well as the "Jewish Fifth Column" which had penetrated into the ranks of the Catholic clergy; there thus remains a copious set of canonical legislation, which was provided for the purpose of obviating the cunning of the enemy.

In order to combat not only the tentacles of the octopus, which the heretical revolutions in the Middle Ages represented, but the head itself, the Holy Catholic Church resorted to different methods, amongst which the Holy Office of the Inquisition, so slandered by Jewish propaganda, stands out on account of its importance,. This organisation was intended to eliminate the false doctrines and to give the death blow to the secret power of Jewry, which directed and stirred up the same. Thanks to the Inquisition, Holy Church was able to overthrow Jewry and for several centuries to hold up the catastrophe that now hovers threateningly over mankind; for several of the so-called false doctrines were already revolutionary movements of the same kind of scope and pretensions as those of recent times, and they not only fought to destroy the church of Rome, but also to destroy all princes and to destroy the existing social order in favour of Jewry, which was the concealed director of those earlier heretical movements and later of the Freemasonic-Jacobin and Jewish-Communist ones of the present time.

Those Catholic clergy who are horrified at mention of the word Inquisition because they are influenced by the age-old propaganda of International Jewry and above all by the "Jewish Fifth Column" introduced into their ranks, should understand that, if so many Popes and Councils, whether Ecumenical or provincial, defended for six hundred years first the Papal European Inquisition and later the Spanish and Portuguese Inquisition, there must have been well-founded motives for this. Catholics, who are shocked and horrified when they hear talk of the Inquisition court, do not recognise the facts that have just been mentioned above and whose truthfulness will be proved in later chapters, with credible verification and indisputable sources.

CHAPTER TWO

THE ORIGIN OF THE "FIFTH COLUMN"

In order to prove some of the facts that were mentioned in the preceding chapter, we fall back upon the evidence of that contemporary Jewish historian who is very authoritative in his material, the careful and painstakingly exact Cecil Roth. The latter is rightly recognised in Israelite circles as the most outstanding contemporary Jewish historical writer, above all on the subject of crypto-Jewry.

In his celebrated work "History of the Marranos", Cecil Roth provides some very interesting details about how the Jews, thanks to their apparent but false conversions, entered Christianity and publicly acted as Christians, but all the while secretly held to their Jewish religion. He also shows us how this secret belief was passed on by parents to children, cloaked with the appearance of an outward Christian militancy.

In his "History of the Marranos", published by Editorial Israel of Buenos Aires, 1946, Jewish Year 5706, he says:

"Introduction: The Early Life of Crypto-Jewry. Crypto-Jewry is in its various forms just as old as the Jews themselves. At the time of Greek rule in Palestine, those weak of character attempted to conceal their origin, in order to avoid arousing derision at athletic exercises. Likewise under Roman discipline the evasions increased so as to avoid payment of the special Jewish tax, the 'Fiscus Judaicus', which was introduced after the fall of Jerusalem. The historian Suetonius gives a lively report of the indignities that were exercised upon a ninety year old man to establish whether he was a Jew or not.

"Official Jewish conduct, as this finds expression in the judgments by the Rabbis, could not be clearer. A man can and should save his life, if it is in danger, by every means, excepting murder, incest and idolatry. This maxim came into use in those cases in which a public abandonment of faith was required. The simple secrecy of Jewry, on the other hand, was

213

something very different. The strict doctrinaires demanded that the typical priestly garments should not be renounced, if these were imposed as a measure of religious suppression. Such a rigid fidelity to principles could not be demanded of all people. The traditional Jewish law makes exceptions for cases where, as a result of legal compulsion, it is impossible to keep the commandments (*'ones'*) when the whole of Jewry is living through hard times (*'scheat-ha-schemad'*). The problem became a reality at the close of the Talmudic period, in the 5th century, during the Zoroaster persecutions in Persia. However, it was solved more on grounds of an enforced neglect in the following of tradition than of a positive concordance with the ruling religion. Jewry became in a certain manner subterranean and only obtained years later its complete freedom.

"With the increase of Christian teachings, which were finally introduced in Europe in the fourth century, there began a very distinct phase of Jewish life. The new faith demanded for itself the exclusive possession of the truth and inevitably regarded proselytising as one of its greatest moral obligations. The Church admittedly disapproved of compulsory conversion. Baptisms, which were undertaken under such conditions, were regarded as invalid. Pope Gregory the Great (590-604) repeatedly condemned them, although he gladly received in a friendly and heartfelt way those who were attracted by other means. The majority of his successors followed his example. Nevertheless, heed was not always paid to the Papal ban. Naturally it was recognised that compulsory conversion was not canonic. In order to circumvent it, the Jews were threatened with expulsion or death, and they were given to understand that they would save themselves through baptism. At times it happened that the Jews submitted to a hard necessity. In such cases their acceptance of Christianity was regarded as spontaneous. In this manner a compulsory mass conversion took place in Mahon, Minorca (418) under the auspices of Bishop Severus. A similar episode took place in Clermont (Auvergne) on the morning of the day of the Ascension of Mary in the year 576; and, despite the disapproval of Gregory the Great, the example spread into different places in France. In the year 629, King Dagobert commanded all Jews of the land to accept baptism under threat of banishment. The measure was imitated a little later in Lombardy.

"Obviously, the conversions obtained by such measures could not be sincere. Insofar as it was possible, the victims continued to practise their Jewish beliefs in secret and used the first opportunity to return to the belief of their forefathers. One such notable case took place in Byzantium under Leo the Isaurian, in the year 723. The Church knew this and did what it could to prevent the Jews maintaining relations with their rebellious brothers, irrespective of the methods by which conversion had been obtained. The Rabbis called these reluctant rebels 'Anusim' (compelled) and treated them very differently from those who abandoned their belief out of their own free will. One of the first manifestations of Rabbinical wisdom in Europe was represented by the book of Gerschom, of Mainz, 'The Light of Exile' (written round about the year 1000), which forbade harsh treatment of the 'compelled' who came back to Judaism. His own son had been a victim of the persecutions. Although he died as a Christian, Gerschom was in mourning, as though he had died in the faith. In the Synagogue service there exists a prayer that implores divine protection for the entire house of Israel and also for the 'compelled' who find themselves in danger, be it on land or on water, without making the least distinction between the two. When the martyrdom of medieval Jewry began with the massacres of the Rhine during the first crusade (1096), countless persons accepted baptism to save their lives. Later, encouraged and protected by Salomon ben Isaac of Troyes, the great French- Jewish scholar, many returned to the Mosaic faith, even if the ecclesiastical authorities regarded with a baleful eye the loss of those precious souls that had been gained by them for the Church.

"However, the phenomenon of Marranism went beyond forced conversion and the consequent practice of Judaism in secret. Its essential characteristic is that it was a clandestine faith passed down from father to son. One of the reasons put forward to justify the expulsion of the Jews from England in 1290 was that they seduced newly-made converts and made them return to the 'vomit of Judaism'. Jewish chroniclers add that many children were seized and sent to the north of the land, where they continued for a long time to practise their former religion. It is owing to this fact, reports one of them, that the English accepted the Reformation so easily; it also explains their preference for Biblical names and certain dietetic peculiarities which are preserved in Scotland. This version is not so improbable as would seem at first sight, and constitutes an interesting example of how the phenomenon of crypto-Jewry can appear in places which seem obviously so little suited to it. In the same way, some malicious genealogists discovered that, after the Jews had been driven out of the south of France, some proud ancestral families, as a result of rumours, carried on Judaism in their homes as the remnant of the bloodline of those Jews who preferred to remain as public and confessing Catholics.

"There are similar examples from much earlier times. The most remarkable is that of the 'neofiti' (neophytes or new converts) of Apulia, recently brought to light after many centuries of oblivion. Towards the end of the 13th century, the Angevins, who ruled in Naples, induced a general conversion of Jews in their lands, located in the neighbourhood of the city of Trani. Under the name of 'neofiti', the proselytes continued to live for three centuries as crypto-Jews. Their secret loyalty to Judaism was one of the reasons why the Inquisition became active in Naples in the 16th century. Many of them met their death at the stake in Rome in February 1572; among others, Teofilo Panarelli, a scholar of reliable repute. Some were successful in escaping to the Balkans, where they joined the existing Jewish communities. Their descendants in south Italy still preserve some vague memories of Judaism up to the present day.

"This phenomenon in no way remained restricted to the Christian world. In various parts of the Mohammedan world, ancient communities of crypto-Jews are found. The 'Daggatun' of the Sahara continued to practise Jewish rules for a long time after their formal conversion to Islam, and their present sons have still not completely forgotten it. The 'Donmeh' of Salonica originate from the adherents of the pseudo-Messiah Sabbetai Zevi, whom they followed in his rebellion. Even if they were in public complete Moslems, they practised at home a messianic Judaism. Further to the east there are still other examples. The religious persecutions in Persia, which began in the 17th century, however, left countless families in the land, especially in Meshed, who in private observed Judaism with punctilious scrupulosity while outwardly they appeared devout disciples of the dominant belief system.

"But the classic land of crypto-Jewry is Spain. The tradition there has been so durable and universal that one can only suspect that a Marranian predisposition is present in the atmosphere of the land itself. Even at the time of the Romans the Jews were numerous and influential. Many of them asserted that they were descended from the aristocracy of Jerusalem, who had been deported by Titus or by earlier conquerors into banishment. In the 5th century, after the attacks of the barbarians, their situation improved very much: for the West Goths (Visigoths) had taken on the Arian form of Christianity and favoured the Jews, both because they believed in one God, as also because they represented an influential minority, to secure whose support was worth the effort. However, after they were converted to the Catholic faith, they began to reveal the traditional zeal of neophytes. The Jews immediately suffered the unpleasant consequences of such zeal. In the year 589, when Reccared came to the throne, the Church legislation was at once applied to them down to the smallest detail. His successors were not so strict; but when Sisebutus ascended the throne (612-620), a very stiff-necked fanaticism prevailed. Perhaps he was incited by the Byzantine emperor when in 616 he published an edict which ordered baptism for all Jews of his kingdom under threat of expulsion and of loss of their entire property. According to the Catholic chroniclers, ninety thousand accepted the Christian faith. This was the first of the great misfortunes that distinguished the history of the Jews in Spain.

"Until the time of the rule of Roderick, the 'last of the Visigoths', the tradition of persecution was faithfully continued apart from a few short interruptions. During a great part of this period the practice of Judaism was completely forbidden. However, as the watchfulness of the government relaxed, the newly-converted used the opportunity to return to their original belief. Successive Councils of Toledo, from the fourth to the eighteenth, devoted their powers to the discovery of new methods that would prevent a return to the synagogue. The children of suspects were removed from their parents and educated in an unspoilt Christian atmosphere. New-converts were compelled to sign a declaration, as a result of which they obligated themselves in the future to respect no Jewish rites with exception of the ban on eating of pork, for which they, so they said, felt a natural aversion. But, in spite of such measures, the notorious unfaithfulness of the newly converted and their descendants continued to be one of the great problems of Visigoth policy until the invasion of the Arabs in the year 711. The number of Jews who were discovered by the latter in the land proves the complete failure of the repeated attempts to convert them. The Marrano tradition had already begun on the peninsula.

"With the arrival of the Arabs, the golden era began for the Jews of Spain, at first in the Caliphate of Cordoba, and after its fall (1012) in the small kingdoms that arose on its ruins. Jewry became considerably stronger on the peninsula. Its communities exceeded in number, culture and wealth over those of Jews of the other lands of the West. However, the long tradition of tolerance was interrupted by the invasion of the Almoravids at the beginning of the 12th century. When the puritanical Almoravids, a North African sect, were summoned to the peninsula in the year 1148, in order to hold up the advance of the Christian armies, there arose a violent reaction. The new rulers introduced intolerance into Spain, which they had already shown in Africa. The practice of Judaism as well as of Christianity was forbidden in the provinces which continued to remain under Musulman rule. Upon this the greater part of the Jews fled into the Christian kingdoms of the North. In that time began the hegemony of the communities of Christian Spain. The minority, who could not flee and saved themselves from decapitation or sale as slaves, followed the example that their brothers in North Africa had given in earlier years, and took on the religion of Islam. In their deepest innermost heart they nevertheless remained always true to the belief of the ancients. In a new way one came to know on the peninsula the phenomenon of the dishonest proselytes who paid lip service to the ruling religion and within their houses kept to the Jewish traditions. Their unfaithfulness was evident."[171]

So much for the complete text of the Jewish historian quoted, Cecil Roth, who proves:

1. That crypto-Judaism or concealed Judaism is in its different forms as old as the Jews themselves and that the Jews even in the times of pagan antiquity already used cunning to conceal their real nature as such, so as to appear as ordinary members of the (pagan) people in whose region they lived.
2. That in the 5th century of the Christian era, during the persecutions in Zoroastrian Persia, Jewry went to a certain extent underground.
3. That with the period of flowering of Christian teaching in the 4th century a new phase began in Jewish life, in that the latter claimed for itself the new faith and exclusive possession of the truth, inevitably regarding proselytism as one of its greatest moral obligations.

Although the Christian Church condemned the compulsory conversions or those attained with force and attempted to protect the Jews against these, it nevertheless accepted that they should be subjected to difficulties and pressure, so as to make them more inclined to conversion. In this case they were judged as acting from their own impulse. The author then cites conversions of this kind that were carried out on Minorca, in

France and Italy in the 5th and 6th century of the Christian calendar, going on to conclude from this that such conversions of Jews to Christianity could not be sincere and that the new converts continued to practise their Judaism in secret.

He observes how in Byzantium something similar had already happened in the times of Leo the Isaurian, in the year 723, and proves that even in the eighth century of the Christian calendar, i.e. more than two hundred years earlier, the infiltration of the Jews into the bosom of the Church, by means of false conversions had become universal practice from France to Constantinople, from one end of Christian Europe to the other. In this manner there arose alongside Jewry, which openly practised

---

[171] Cecil Roth, *History of the Marranos*, Israel Publishers, Buenos Aires, 1946. 57506, pp. 11-18.

its religion, a subterranean Judaism, whose members were only Christian in appearance.

4. That in Marranism, besides the hypocritical conversion and the practice of Judaism in secret there exists a deeply-rooted tradition, which obligates the Jews to transfer this inclination from parents to the children. The author cites the events in England and Scotland since 1290, where one of the reasons presented for the expulsion of the Jews was that they misled the newly converted to practise Judaism, and that many children were stolen by them and brought into the north of the land, where they continued to practise the old religion i.e. the Jewish. It must be pointed out that after 1290 the Jews were banished from England and no one could be domiciled in the land if he were not a Christian.

In this connection a very interesting reference is made by the renowned Hebrew historian to the assertion of a Jewish chronicler, viz. that to the presence of crypto-Judaism is to be attributed the fact the English so easily accepted the Reformation as well as their preference for Biblical names. It was thus a false conversion of the Jews to Christianity that allowed that "Fifth Column" to arise within the Church of England and made easier its severance from Rome.

It is also evident that these false conversions of Jews in England, far from obtaining for the Church the expected salvation of souls, brought it instead the loss of millions of souls, when the descendants of these false proselytes promoted the Anglican schism.

There are still other very outstanding cases of false conversions of Jews to Christianity, among them that of the *"neofiti"* in the south of Italy, as recorded by Cecil Roth, who were persecuted by the Inquisition and of whom many were burned at the stake in Rome.

It is important to mention the fact that the Inquisition which functioned in Rome was, of course, the Holy Papal Inquisition whose serviceable activity was successful in the Middle Ages in holding up the progress of the apocalyptic beast of the Antichrist for three hundred years.

5. That the phenomenon of Crypto-Judaism was not merely confined to the Christian world. One still finds in different parts of the Musulman world, communities of Crypto-Jews, as Cecil Roth observes, who records several examples of Jewish communities in which the Hebrews,

who outwardly were Musulmen, are in secret still Jews. This means that the Jews have also introduced a "Fifth Column" into the bosom of the Islamic religion. This fact perhaps explains the many divisions and the uproar which has occurred in the world of Mohammed.

CHAPTER THREE

THE "FIFTH COLUMN" IN ACTION

The renowned Jewish writer Cecil Roth explains, as we have already seen earlier, that Crypto-Judaism, i.e. the conduct of Hebrews who conceal their identity as such by covering themselves with the mask of other religions or nationalities, is as old as Judaism itself.

This infiltration of the Hebrews into the innermost heart of religions and nationalities, whilst still preserving their former religion and their organisations in secret, has really formed Israelite "Fifth Columns" in the bosom of the other peoples and the different religions; for if the Jew has gained entrance into the citadel of his enemies, he is active there, follows orders and carries on an activity which was planned in the Jewish secret organisations. This aims at controlling the people from within, whose conquest was resolved upon, as well as the control of its religious institutions, and to attempt to attain the decomposition of the same. It is evident that as soon as they have gained control of the power of a religious confession from within, that they have then always used the same to favour their plans of world domination. In so doing they above all use their religious influence to destroy the counter-defence of the threatened people or at least to weaken it. It is necessary that we mark well these three chief goals of the "Fifth Column", since for two centuries they have represented their essential activity, whether they present themselves in the bosom of Holy Church or in the other Gentile religions. This explains how the work of crypto-Jews as members of the "Fifth Column" has been all the more effective, the greater the influence it acquired in the religion in which it concealed itself; therefore one of the most important activities of the crypto-Jews has been that of smuggling themselves into the ranks of the clergy itself, in order to ascend the ecclesiastical hierarchy of the Christian Church or of a gentile religion which they control, reform or wish to destroy.

An activity of primary importance also consists for them in creating worldly saints, who in this realm can control the masses of the faithful with a definite political goal, which is useful for the "Synagogue of Satan". In the plan of playing along with and of mutual aid with the religious personages who belong to the "Fifth Column" and who work for the same purpose, the religious leaders always receive a valuable and frequently decisive aid in the face of spiritual authority, with which it was successful for these religious, crypto-Jewish personages to first of all provide themselves.

In this manner the priests and church dignitaries, with aid of the political and religious leaders, can disintegrate the real defenders of religion and of the threatened peoples by their weakening or even destroying the defence of both, and promote the victory of Jewish Imperialism and its revolutionary undertaking.

It is important to indelibly imprint this truth, for in these few lines is summarised the secret of success of the Imperialist and revolutionary Hebrew policy for some centuries. The defenders of religion or of their threatened country must therefore bear in mind that the danger comes not only from the so-called Left or from revolutionary Jewish groups, but from the bosom of religion itself or from the circles directed to the Right, from Nationalists and Patriots, always according to how the case lies; for it is a thousand year old policy of the Jews, to infiltrate secretly into particularly these sectors and religious institutions, in order by means of slanderous intrigue, which is well organised, to eliminate the true defenders of the country und of religion, above all and particularly those who, because they know the Jewish danger, might have the possibility of saving the situation. With these methods they eliminate the latter and replace them with false apostles, who cause the failure of the defence of religion or of the country and make possible the triumph of the enemies of mankind, as Saint Paul so strikingly called the Jews. In all this the great secret of the Jewish triumphs, especially in the last five hundred years, has taken root.

It is necessary that all peoples and their religious institutions seize upon suitable defence measures against this internal enemy, whose driving force is formed by the "Jewish Fifth Column", which has infiltrated into the Christian clergy and into the remaining Gentile religions.

If Cecil Roth, the Flavius Josephus of our days, assures us that almost the entirety of all conversions of Jews to Christianity were pretended, we can ask ourselves if it is possible to believe that the said Jesus Christ, our

Lord, who attempted to convert them, could be deceived. The answer has to be negative; for no one can cheat God; in addition the facts prove, that Jesus placed a greater trust in the conversion of the Samaritans, of the Galileans and the remaining inhabitants of Palestine than in that of the Jews properly speaking, whom the others despised because they had a low opinion of them although they likewise observed the law of Moses.

In fact, Jesus did not trust in the honesty of Jewish conversions; for He knew them better than anyone else, as the following passage of the Gospel according to Saint John proves:

Chapter II. "23. Now when He was in Jerusalem at the Passover, in the feast day, many believed in His name, when they saw the miracles that He did. 24. But Jesus did not commit himself unto them, because He knew them all."[172]

Jesus Himself despised the Jews, because He was a Galilean. Unfortunately, the Samaritans, Galileans and the other inhabitants of Palestine were ruined by assimilation into modern Jewry, with the exception of those who had already previously been converted to the faith of our Divine Redeemer.

This rule of distrusting the conversions of the Jews was also heeded by the Apostles; and later by the various hierarchies of the Catholic Church. If precautionary measures were not always enforced to clearly prove the honesty of the conversions, the results were disastrous for Christianity; for these conversions served only to increase the destructive crypto-Jewish "Fifth Column", which had infiltrated into Christian society.

Another passage of the Gospel contained in Chapter VIII, Verses 31-59, shows us, how various Jews, who according to Verse 31, had believed in Jesus, afterwards attempted to contradict His sermons and even to kill Him, as Christ Himself confirms this in verses 37 and 40.[173] The Lord has first to conduct with them a verbal dispute for the defence of His teaching and afterwards to conceal Himself, so that they did not stone Him; for His hour was not yet come. The Gospel of Saint John shows us here something further of the classical tactics of the Jews falsely converted to Christianity and their descendants: misrepresentation of belief in Christ, in order to afterwards attempt to destroy His church, exactly as they then attempted to kill Jesus Himself.

---

[172] Bible, Gospel of Saint John, Chapter II, Verses 23-24.
[173] Bible, Gospel of Saint John, Chapter VIII, Verses 31-59.

In the Apocalypse appears another very revealing passage in this connection:

Chapter II. "1. Unto the angel of the Church of Ephesus write... 2. I know thy works, and thy labour, and thy patience, and how thou canst not bear them which are evil: and thou hast tried them which say they are apostles, and are not, and hast found them liars."[174]

This is a clear allusion to the necessity of examining the honesty of those who give themselves out to be apostles; for from these examinations results that many are false and lying. The Holy Scripture proves to us that Christ and His disciples not only knew the problem of false new converts and of fake apostles (the Bishops are regarded as successors of the Apostles), but that they expressly warned us to be cautious of them. If Christ, our Lord, and the Apostles had wished to avoid this topic out of fear of a scandal, as so many cowards now wish to do, they would not also have remarked the danger in such express form and would not have referred so clearly to such dreadful deeds as the betrayal of Christ through Judas Iscariot, one of the twelve disciples.

Even more, if Christ had not held as advisable the public exposing of these false Apostles, who are so richly represented in the clergy of the twentieth century, it would have been possible for Him as God to avoid that the instigator of the greatest betrayal might be one of the twelve Apostles. If He did this and publicly exposed him, so that the greatest betrayal is remarked in the Gospels for the knowledge of all until the end of the world, then a quite special reason existed for this. This fact shows to us that Christ, our Lord, as well as the Apostles, regarded it as the lesser evil to unmask the traitors at the right time, in order to prevent them causing the Church further deadly harm, and that it is worse to cover them out of fear of a scandal by allowing them to continue to destroy the Church and to conquer the peoples who have placed their faith and their trust in this Church. This explains the reason why Holy Church, every time an heretical or estranged bishop or cardinal or a false pope appeared, regarded it as indispensable to unmask them publicly, in order to prevent them dragging the faithful further into misfortune.

A priest who makes easier the triumph of Communism in his country, with all its deadly danger for Holy Church and for the rest of the clergy, must immediately be accused before the Holy See, and in fact not only in one but in various ways in case one fails, so that with recognition of the

---

[174] Bible, Apocalypse, Chapter II, Verses 1-2.

danger, the means are removed from him of causing further harm. It is monstrous to have to think that the confidence placed by the nations in the clergy is utilised by Judases, in order to lead the said peoples into the abyss.

If this had been done in time, the catastrophe of Cuba would have been prevented, and the Church, the clergy and the Cuban people would not have fallen into the bottomless abyss in which they find themselves at present; for the destructive and traitorous work of many clergy in favour of Fidel Castro was the decisive factor for his victory. It influenced the majority of clergy, who were not conscious of deceit and who with good faith encouraged a people involuntarily to suicide, to favour Fidel Castro; a people who had particularly placed its faith in these spiritual shepherds.

We observe this circumstance with absolute clarity, so that all may realise the gravity of the problem, in view of the fact that clergy of the "Fifth Column" are attempting to drive more Catholic states, such as Spain, Portugal, Paraguay, Guatemala and various others towards Communism. They use as means the most subtle deceptions and even cloak their activity with equally sanctimonious false zeal, by pretending to defend religion itself, which they wish to destroy in its innermost heart. These traitors must be quickly discovered and charged in Rome, in order to nullify their activity and hence to prevent their destructive work which opens the doors to the Freemasonic or Communist victory. If those, who have the possibility of doing this, maintain silence out of cowardice or indifference, they are in a certain respect just as responsible for the catastrophe breaking out as the clergy of the "Fifth Column".

Before Saint Paul upon one occasion travelled to Jerusalem, he called together in Ephesus the bishops and presbyters of the Church and spoke to them:

Chapter XX. "18. And when they were come to him, he said unto them, 'Ye know, from the first day that I came into Asia, after what manner I have been with you at all seasons. 19. Serving the Lord with all humility of mind, and with many tears and temptations which befell me by the lying in wait of the Jews. 28. Take heed therefore unto yourselves and to all the flock over the which the Holy Ghost hath made you overseers, to feed the church of God, which He hath purchased with his own blood. 29. For I know this, that after my departing shall grievous wolves enter in among you, not sparing the flock.

30. Also of your own selves shall men arise, speaking perverse things, to draw away disciples after them. 31. Therefore watch, and remember, that by the space of three years I ceased not to warn every one night and day with tears.'"[175]

Saint Paul thus held it as imperative to open the eyes of the bishops and to warn them that raging wolves would come among the flock and would not spare them, as well as that even among the bishops men would appear, who spoke godless things, in order to bring the disciples onto their side. This prophecy of Saint Paul's has fulfilled itself literally in the course of centuries, even up to our days, where it takes on a tragic actuality. And so must it come; for Saint Paul spoke with divine insight; and God cannot err, if He predicts future things. It is also interesting that this martyr and apostle of the Church, far from concealing the tragedy out of fear of scandal, wished to warn all of the same and recommended the bishops present to be constantly watchful and to bear it in mind; to fail to remember these things, as Christians often do, has largely made possible the victories of the "Synagogue of Satan" and its destructive Communist revolutions.

On the other hand, it is worth noting that, if the Apostles had held it to be unwise or dangerous to speak of the wolves and traitors who should appear even among the bishops, this frightening passage of the Bible in the Acts of the Apostles would have been left out; but, as it is remarked there, it shows that, far from regarding their knowledge as scandalous or unwise, they held it as indispensable to perpetuate it and to broadcast it to the end of time, so that Holy Church and Christians could be ever watchful against this inner danger, which in many cases is more destructive and deadly than those which the enemies from without represent.

As we will show in the course of this work with irrefutable proofs, the gravest dangers that have appeared against Christianity come from those wolves about whom the prophecy of Saint Paul speaks so clearly. The latter, in disgraceful alliance with Jewry and its false destructive doctrines and revolutions, made easier the victory of the Jewish cause. Always, when Holy Church set about at the right time to bind the hands of these wolves and to destroy them, it was able to triumph over the "Synagogue of Satan", which on its side began from the 16th century onwards to carry off victories of ever greater importance, when in a large part of Europe the watching-over through the Papal Inquisition was suppressed. This was constantly expressed in the ranks of the clergy itself and among the

---

[175] Bible, Acts of the Apostles, Chapter XX, Verses 18-19 and 28-31.

bishops; in fact, the latter allowed themselves to be mercilessly crushed, when the wolf in sheep's clothing appeared in their ranks.

Jewish activity also began to show decisive successes in the Spanish and Portuguese Empires, when, at the end of the 18th century, the hands of the State Inquisitions were bound in both Empires. Then the wolves in sheep's clothing were able to make possible first the Jewish-Freemasonic triumphs and afterwards the Jewish-Communist ones, which fortunately were of limited extent. However, these become greater in number day by day if one allows these wolves who have penetrated into the high clergy to use the power of the Church in order to crush the true defenders of the same, the patriots who defend their peoples and those who fight against Communism, Freemasonry or Jewry.

Saint Paul mentions clearly and distinctly this work by members of the "Fifth Column," when he says in Chapter II of the "Letter to the Galatians": "1. Then, fourteen years later, I went up again to Jerusalem with Barnabas, and took Titus with me also. 3. But neither Titus, who was with me, being a Greek, was compelled to be circumcised. 4. And that because of false brethren unawares brought in, who came in privily to spy out our liberty which we have in Christ Jesus, that they might bring us into bondage. 5. To whom we gave place by subjection, no, not for an hour; that the truth of the gospel might continue with you."[176]

A very evident allusion to the false brothers, i.e. the false Christians, who attempt to bind us in slavery and distort the true teaching of Christ and the Gospels. Neither Saint Paul nor his disciples ever allow themselves to be subjected to this slavery.

Saint Paul, the leader of the Church, alludes also in his letter to Titus to the vain gossips and liars, for the most part Jews, who cause so much misfortune and says in this connection:

Chapter I. "10. For there are many unruly and vain talkers and deceivers, especially they of the circumcision."[177]

In the later centuries the facts have proved that from the false converts from Judaism and from their descendants have emanated the boldest talkers and flatterers or "vain talkers" as Saint Paul calls them. In his

---

[176] Bible, Letter of Saint Paul to the Galatians, Chapter II, Verses 4-5.
[177] Bible, Letter of Saint Paul to Titus, Chapter I, Verse 10.

Second Epistle to the Corinthians he lets us clearly see the outward show, which the false Apostles would take on in the future. He says:

Chapter XI. "12. But what I do, that I will do, that I may cut off occasion from them which desire occasion; that wherein they glory, they may be found even as we. 13. For such are false apostles, deceitful workers, transforming themselves into the apostles of Christ. 14. And no marvel; for Satan himself is transformed into an angel of light. 15. Therefore it is no great thing if his ministers also be transformed as the ministers of righteousness; whose end shall be according to their works."[178]

In this passage of the New Testament Saint Paul describes with prophetic words and with divine insight some of the fundamental characteristics of the clergy of the "Fifth Column" in the service of the "Synagogue of Satan", the fake apostles of our days, for according to Holy Church the bishops are the successors of the apostles. These religious personages, who simultaneously stand in concealed but effective collusion with Communism, Freemasonry and Judaism, attempt like the Devil to disguise themselves as true angels of light and to take on the outward appearance of servants of justice. However, one must not judge them according to what they say, but according to their works and their real link with the enemy. The prophetic words of Saint Paul are also very worthy of being borne in mind, when he accuses them in the Verse 12 mentioned of glorifying themselves as standing like the true Apostles. It is curious that those who glorify themselves most of all for their investiture in the clergy, are particularly those who aid Communism, Freemasonry or Judaism; for it is necessary for them with their high churchly authority to crush those who defend their country or Holy Church against these sects. The latter they command in private, as prelates, to cease their much justified defence. They make use of their authority as bishops and use it to favour the victory of Communism and its dark forces, which direct and drive it on. But if in spite of such shameful misuse of their authority as bishops, the defenders of Catholicism and of their country fight on, they accuse them of being rebels against churchly authority, as rebels against the high personages and against the Church itself; they are even excommunicated in some cases, so that the faithful refuse them their aid and the defence fails, whereby they in great measure make use of that vain talk of which Saint Paul speaks, and which is so very harmful for our Holy Religion.

---

[178] Bible, Second Letter of Saint Paul to the Corinthians, Chapter II, Verses 12-15.

Finally, we also quote the Second Epistle of the Apostle Saint Peter, the first Pope of the Church, who says:

Chapter II: "1. But there were false prophets also among the people, even as there shall be false teachers among you, who privily shall bring in damnable heresies, even denying the Lord that bought them, and bring upon themselves a swift destruction. 2. And many shall follow their pernicious ways; by reason of whom the way of truth shall be evil spoken of. 3. And through covetousness shall they with feigned words make merchandise of you: whose judgment now of a long time lingereth not, and their damnation slumbereth not."[179]

In the course of the following chapter we will see how this prophecy of the first deputy of Christ upon earth has been fulfilled; Peter reveals in another passage of the Epistle in question:

Chapter II. "21. For it had been better for them not to have known the way of righteousness, than, after they have known it, to turn from the holy commandment delivered unto them. 22. But it happened unto them according to the true proverb: The dog is turned to his own vomit again (Proverbs XXVI, 11) and the sow that was washed, to her wallowing in the mire."

We allude to this for many Hebrews have criticised the harsh expressions, which were used by various Councils of Holy Church against the Hebrews, who with the water of baptism were washed clean of sins and then returned to the vomit of Judaism. It is thus worthy of mention that the Holy Synods used only the words of Peter when they quoted the Bible verses in this connection.

With the passages of the New Testament mentioned one can thus confirm that both Christ the Lord as well as the Apostles distrusted the sincerity of the conversions of the Jews. Since they realised what the false new converts and the false Apostles would do, they warned the faithful against this deadly danger, so that they could defend themselves.

---

[179] Bible, Second Epistle of Saint Peter, Chapter II.

CHAPTER FOUR

JEWRY, THE FATHER OF THE GNOSTICS

The first false teaching to bring the life of the nascent Church into danger was that of the Gnostics. The latter was formed not by one but by various secret societies, which began to carry out a really destructive work within Christianity. Many Gnostic sects pretended to give a further significance to Christianity because, as they revealed, they linked it with the oldest religious teachings. The idea was transferred from the Jewish "Cabbala" to Christianity that the Holy Scriptures had a double meaning, an *exoteric* one, i.e. outwardly and literally according to the text visible in the Holy Scripture; and an additional *esoteric* or concealed meaning, which is only accessible to the high initiates, the experts in the art of deciphering the secret meaning of the text of the Bible. As we have seen, many centuries before the appearance of the Cabbalistic works "Sepher-Yetzirah", "Sepher-ha-Zohar" and others of lesser importance, the oral "Cabbala" was practised among the Hebrews, above all in the secret sects of the higher initiates, whose false interpretations of the Holy Scripture contributed very greatly to turning the Hebrew people away from the truth revealed by God.

Concerning the real origins of Gnosticism, the renowned historians John Yarker and J. Matter agree that Simon the Magician, a Jew converted to Christianity, was the true founder of Gnosticism. Apart from the fact, that he was a mystic cabbalist, he favoured magic and occultism. With a group of Jews he founded a priesthood of "Mysteries", in which his own teacher Dositheus and his pupils Menandro and Cerinthus figure, who represented a section of his collaborators.[180]

Simon the Magician, founder of the false Gnostic doctrine – the first to disrupt early Christianity – was also one of the pioneers of the Jewish "Fifth Column" that penetrated into the bosom of Holy Church. The

---

[180] John Yarker, *The Arcane Schools*, pp. 167, 365.

Holy Bible tells us in the Acts of the Apostles how this Jew obtained admittance to Christianity:

Chapter VIII. "9. But there was a certain man, called Simon, which beforetime in the same city used sorcery, and bewitched the people of Samaria, giving out that himself was some great one. 12. But when they believed Philip preaching the things concerning the kingdom of God, and the name of Jesus Christ, they were baptised, both men and women. 13. Then Simon himself believed also: and when he was baptised, he continued with Philip, and wondered, beholding the miracles and signs which were done. 14. Now when the Apostles which were at Jerusalem heard that Samaria had received the word of God, they sent unto them Peter and John: 15. Who, when they were come down, prayed for them, that they might receive the Holy Ghost: 16. (For as yet He was fallen upon none of them; only they were baptised in the name of the Lord Jesus.) 17. Then laid they their hands on them, and they received the Holy Ghost. 18. And when Simon saw that through laying on of the Apostles' hands the Holy Ghost was given, he offered them money. 19. Saying, 'Give me also this power, that on whomsoever I lay hands, he may receive the Holy Ghost.' 20. But Peter said unto him, 'Thy money perish with thee, because thou thought that the gift of God may be purchased with money.'[181]

And after Peter had blamed Simon, the latter answered: "24. Then answered Simon, and said, 'Pray ye to the Lord for me, that none of these things which ye have spoken come upon me.'"[182]

This passage of the New Testament reports to us, how the "Fifth Column" of falsely converted Jews arose and what their mode of thought was. Simon the Magician is converted to Christianity and receives the water of baptism; but then, even in the bosom of the Church, he strives to destroy it and attempts nothing more or less than to buy the favour of the Holy Ghost. After the failure of this attempt in the face of the incorruptibility of the apostle Saint Peter, the supreme head of the Church, he pretends repentance in order afterwards to introduce the inner division of Christianity with the heretical schism of the Gnostics. Upon this as also on other occasions the Holy Bible raises its warning cry and shows us what would happen in the future, if the Jews belonging to the "Fifth Column" within the Church and the clergy followed the example of Simon the Magician, by being converted to Christianity in order to attempt to destroy it by means of Simony, to divide it through heretical teachings and

---

[181] Bible, Acts of the Apostles, Chapter VIII, verses mentioned.
[182] Bible, Acts of the Apostles, Chapter VIII, Verse 24.

then to strive to attain the highest honorary offices of the Church by the most diverse means, including that of buying the favour of the Holy Ghost.

As we will see later, the Councils of Holy Church occupied themselves with energetically suppressing the bishops who wished to buy a place by means of money; and the Holy Inquisition confirmed that the clergy of Jewish origin were the most principal spreaders of simony and of false doctrine. A further classical example is revealed to us by the Holy Evangelists; it is that of the first Christian personage of Jewish origin who betrayed Christ and sells him to the Hebrews for thirty pieces of silver. And the latter was even more than a bishop or a cardinal; for he was one of the twelve Apostles: Judas Iscariot, who had been chosen by Jesus himself to such high dignity. Why did our Divine Redeemer do such a thing? Did He err when He made the choice and Himself invested Judas with the highest dignity of the nascent Church after Jesus Christ Himself? It is clear that Christ, because He is God Himself, could never err. If He did such a thing, then it was only because it was convenient for Him to do it, in order to let His Holy Church clearly recognise whence the greatest danger would come for its existence; in other words, He wished to warn it of the enemies who would appear among its own ranks and especially in the highest hierarchies of the Church, because if a Judas arose amongst those chosen by Christ Himself, then it is obvious, with all the more reason, that they would appear amongst those appointed by Christ's successors.

The faithful should therefore never vex themselves about this and still less lose their faith in the Church when they learn, through history, of those cardinals and bishops who were heretics and schismatics and brought the life of Holy Church in danger; even less so, when they realise that in the struggle of our days there are still cardinals and bishops who themselves help Freemasonry, Communism and Jewry itself in their work of destroying Christianity and enslaving all peoples on Earth.

If we come back to Gnosticism, which was originated by the newly converted Jew, Simon the Magician, it is necessary to establish that many years later Saint Irenaeus, described Valentinus, a Jew from Alexandria, as the leader of the Gnostics.[183]

J. Matter, the renowned historian of Gnosticism reports to us that the leading Jewish personages, the Alexandrian philosophers Philo and

---

[183] William Thomas Walsh, *Philip II*. Espasa Calpe, p. 206.

Aristobulus, who were completely and utterly true to the religion of their fathers, resolved to deck themselves out with the remains of other systems and make a way clear to Jewry for enormous conquests; both were also leaders of Gnosticism and Cabbalists. The said author explains: "That the Cabbala predates Gnosticism, is a viewpoint that Christian writers little understand, but which the scholars of Judaism profess with true certainty"; they also assert that Gnosticism was not exactly a falling away from Christianity but a combination of systems in which several Christian elements were taken up.[184]

After diligent study of the material, the learned English writer Nesta H. Webster comes to the conclusion that "the goal of Gnosticism was not to adapt the Cabbala to Christian practice, but to adapt Christianity to Cabbalist practices, by mixing its pure and simple teaching with theosophy and even with magic."[185]

This attempt to adapt Christianity according to Cabbalist practices, the Jewish Cabbalists have repeated as often as they could. After the Gnostic failure, they introduced it into the Manichaean sects, then into the Albigensians, the Rosicrucians, Freemasonry, theosophical societies, spiritualists and other sects of different eras which are said to have practised Occultism, which is nothing other than the Hebrew Cabbala with all its derivations.

In his confirmation that Cabbalists founded Gnosticism, the famous historian of Freemasonry, Ragon, reports that: "The Cabbala is the key to the secret sciences. The Gnostics emanated from the Cabbalists".[186]

The "Jewish Encyclopaedia" asserts that Gnosticism had a "Jewish character" before it was transformed into a Christian one."[187]

An interesting coincidence is the fact that the principal centre of Gnosticism at the time of its apogee was Alexandria, which at that time was the most important centre of Jewry outside Palestine, until Saint Cyril, the bishop of said city – centuries later – gave this breeding ground of infection for Christianity a deadly blow by expelling the Jews from Alexandria. The evidence of the Church Fathers completes the total

---

[184] J. Matter, *Histoire du Gnosticisme*. Ed. 1844. Vol. I, pp. 12, 44.
[185] Nesta H. Webster, *Secret Societies and Subversive Movements*, pp. 27-29.
[186] Ragon, *Maçonnerie Occulte*, p. 78.
[187] "Was Jewish in character long before it became Christian." Jewish Encyclopaedia, word "Cabbala".

picture of proofs, which we have laid before the reader, in order to show that Gnosticism was the work of Jewry; for they name several of the leaders of the Gnostic schools as Jews.[188] On the other hand the "Jewish-Castilian Encyclopaedia" indicates that: "The fact that the original Gnosticism, both the Christian as well as the Jewish, used Hebrew names in its system and that it even based its opposition upon Biblical ideas, points to its Jewish origin."

It says in addition that it influenced the later development of the Cabbala.[189]

After it is proved that Gnosticism is of Hebrew origin and was directed by Israelites, of whom some had infiltrated into Christianity through baptism, we will see what its extent has been in the Christian world. The most dangerous thing about Gnosticism is its appearance as a science; for it is necessary to establish that the word "Gnosticism" means science, knowledge.

As one sees, the system of the Jew Karl Marx and other Israelites to attempt to dress its false and destructive teachings with a scientific exterior is not new, in order to set the unsuspecting in astonishment and to capture them; for almost two thousand years ago their predecessors, the Gnostics, did the same with very good results. One thus sees that also in this respect the Jewish tactics are always the same.

In addition they had no kind of scruples about introducing into Gnosticism ideas of Persian dualism; and above all of the Hellenistic culture, in which the Jews of Alexandria who have been the decisive factor in the spreading of Gnosticism, were educated. It is necessary to recall that also in this respect, the Jewish tactics have not altered, for they introduced into the teachings, customs and symbols of Freemasonry – as well as Cabbalist and Jewish elements – elements of Greco-Roman and Egyptian-Oriental origin, in order to deceive Christians concerning the real origin of the brotherhood.

On the other hand, it is evident that only the Jews already dispersed all over the world could work out so easily this highly-coloured mixture of Jewish, Christian, Platonic, Neo-Platonic, Egyptian, Persian and even Hindustani ideas, of which Gnosticism is composed, which, similarly to

---

[188] Jewish-Spanish Encyclopaedia, edition quoted, Volume V. Word "Gnosticism", p. 84, Collection 1.
[189] Jewish-Spanish Encyclopaedia, Work quoted.

the Hebrew Cabbala, was founded as an esoteric teaching for chosen people and was spread in the form of secret societies according to Jewish style. These increased in number and deviated each time more among each other in their doctrines. The attempts made like those of the Cabbala to find a concealed meaning in the Holy Scriptures, were so made that each gave different interpretations of the Gospels, just as later happened with the free inquiry of Protestantism, which split it into an infinity of Churches, which were at times even rivals. The principle of the existence of concealed meanings, deviating from the literal text of the Bible, made it possible for the Gnostics to turn away completely from the real Christian doctrine. With their multiplicity of sects they represented a veritable cancer, which threatened to disintegrate the whole of Christianity in its innermost.

The Gnosis proceeded from the basis of the existence of a good God and of matter regarded as the origin of evil. This God, as Highest Being created through emanation of intermediary beings called aeons, who are connected with one another and who, united with the Highest Being, represented the kingdom of light. According to the degree, in which they removed themselves from God, they were less perfect, although even the lowest aeon possessed particles of the divinity and were therefore incapable of creating matter, bad by nature.

They explained the creation of the world through one of these aeons, whom they called Demiurge. The latter claimed to be like God and rose against him, for which reason he was cast out of the kingdom of light and thrown into the abyss. There he created our universe, gave form to material and created man, whose soul, as a particle of light, remained enchained in matter. Then God, in order to redeem the souls of the ruined world, sent another aeon, named Christ, upon earth, who was truly devoted to the Highest Being, and who never had a real body, for matter is intrinsically evil. The various Gnostic sects gave diverse interpretations to this complete mechanism, sometimes going so far as to identify Jehovah with the evil Demiurge. For some Jehovah was the Supreme Being and for others he was only an aeon faithful to the latter. Manichaean Dualism took over from Gnosticism the form of a struggle between the world of the spirit and that of matter.

The redemption of the souls incorporated in matter took place, according to this host of sects, through the Gnosis, i.e. the knowledge of the truth, without need of morality or good works. This had the disastrous consequence, in many sects, of calling forth the most repellent immorality and dissoluteness of morals and practices.

The most dangerous of all these secret sects for Christianity was directed by the crypto-Jew Valentinus, a classic "Fifth Columnist." For he was outwardly active as a true Christian and sowed disintegration in Holy Church by extending his disastrous sect. At first he had the city of Alexandria as his principal bastion, but towards the middle of the second century he went to Rome with the intention of undermining Christianity in the capital of the Empire itself. The Valentinians seriously threatened to disintegrate Holy Church from within, which finally, in order to nullify the disastrous work of this false Christian, a true Jew of the "Fifth Column," cast him out of its bosom.

Gnosticism spread doctrines, which are now fundamental in many subversive Jewish movements of modern times. For example, the sect of the Carpocratians attacked all then existing religions and only recognised the Gnosis – knowledge of which was provided by the great men of every nation, such as Plato, Pythagoras, Moses and Christ – which "frees one from all that the vulgar call religion" and "makes man equal to God." Gnosticism in its purest forms strove to give Christianity the widest possible meaning by linking it with the oldest religious doctrines. The learned historical writer, Matter, assures us in connection with the Gnosis, that "the belief that the divinity has revealed itself in the religious institutions of all nations" leads to the idea of a kind of universal religion, which contains the elements of all.[190] Many of these concepts we find at present in the secret doctrine of the Freemasons and the theosophical societies.

N. H. Webster in her diligent study of the material finds that the Gnostic sect of the Carpocratians of the second century "arrived at much the same conclusions as modern Communists with regard to the ideal social system. Thus Epiphanus held that, since Nature herself reveals the principle of the community and the unity of all things, human laws which are contrary to this law of Nature are so many culpable infractions of the legitimate order of things. Before these laws were imposed on humanity, everything was in common – lands, goods, and women. According to certain contemporaries, the Carpocratians returned to this primitive system by instituting the community of women and indulging in every kind of licence."[191]

As one can see from this, the subversive movements of modern Jewry are to the greater part a repetition of the doctrines of the great Gnostic

---

[190] Matter, op. cit., Volume II, p. 188; Volume I, p. 44.
[191] Nesta H. Webster: *Secret Societies and Subversive Movements*, pp. 30-31.

revolution, although they emanate from a contrary philosophic foundation. For modern Communism is materialistic, while the Gnosis itself regarded matter as bad and objectionable. However, the facts prove to us that the Jews have been very skilled in using the opposing philosophical system to attain similar political results.

The Gnostics possessed mysteries and initiations. "Tertullian, a Father of the Church, assures us that the sects of the Valentinians perverted the mysteries of Eleusis and made a 'sanctuary of prostitution' out of them."[192] And we must not forget, that Valentine – the false Christ and crypto-Jew from Alexandria – was revealed by Saint Irenaeus to be the leader of the Gnostics, whose sects, according to some, were directed by one and the same power. It is thus evident that the Hebrews are the same as eighteen hundred years ago and spread immorality and prostitution in Christian society in order to ruin it and to make easier its destruction.

Some Gnostic sects reached the highest degree of perversion in their doctrines. Thus Eliphas Levi assures us that certain Gnostics introduced into their rites the profanation of the Christian Mysteries, which were made to serve Black Magic,[193] whose principal propagators have also been the Hebrews. Dean Milman says in his "History of the Jews" that the Ophites worshipped the serpent because the latter had rebelled against Jehovah, "to whom they referred using the Cabbalist expression of the Demiurge."[194]

It is thus evident that this glorification of evil, which is so important to modern revolutionary movements secretly controlled by the Synagogue of Satan, is likewise nothing new. It was already unleashed as poison by the Gnostic Jews into the nascent Christian society of more than eighteen centuries ago.

E. de Faye in his work "Gnostics and Gnosticism," as well as Matter in his already mentioned work "History of Gnosticism", both assure us that another secret Gnostic sect, called Cainites on account of the cult in which they worshipped Cain, represented the latter, Dathan and Abiram, the homosexual inhabitants of Sodom and Gomorrah and Judas Iscariot

---

[192] Matter, op. cit., p. 365.
[193] Eliphas Levy, *History of Magic*, p. 218.
[194] Dean Milman: *History of the Jews*, Everyman's Library, Edition II, p. 491.

himself as noble victims of the Demiurge, i.e. of the malicious creator of our universe according to their perverse teachings.[195]

Apparently, these Gnostic sects were the forerunners of the Bogomils, of the Luciferians, of Black Magic and of certain small satanic masonic circles, which all, apart from rendering homage to Lucifer, regarded as good everything that Christianity holds to be evil and vice versa. Voltaire himself regards the Jews during the Middle Ages as the spreaders of Black Magic and satanism. The Marquis De Luchet reports in his famous work "Essai sur la Secte des Illuminés" that the Cainites, incited by their hatred towards all social and moral order, "called upon all men to destroy the work of God and to commit every kind of infamy."[196]

The great leader, who appeared in the Church in order to combat Gnosticism and to triumph over it, was in fact Saint Irenaeus, who thoroughly studied its disastrous sects and their dark teachings and mercilessly fought them in word and deed. Simultaneously he attacked the Jews, whom he described as the leaders of this disintegrating subversive movement,[197] whose strongest and most dangerous sect for Christianity was that of the Valentinians, which was led by Valentinus, behind whose false Christianity Saint Irenaeus discovered the Jewish identity.

Thanks to the virile and ceaseless labour of Saint Irenaeus, Holy Church was successful in triumphing over the Gnosis, which for nascent Christianity was a more threatening internal danger than the grave external snares then represented by the frontal attacks of the Synagogue and its intrigues, which managed, as we have already observed, to unleash the whole power of the Roman Empire and its terrible persecutions against the nascent Church, resulting in so many martyrs for Christianity. These facts prove that, from its first beginnings onwards, the activity of the Jewish "Fifth Column" which had penetrated into its interior, was far more dangerous for Holy Church than that of its external foes. Naturally, the existence of a devout and very combative clergy, to whom indulgence disguised with the cloak of peaceful coexistence, dialogue or diplomacy was unknown, had the effect that Holy Church emerged victorious from this terrible struggle, in which it completely overcame its foes: Jewry, Jewish Gnosticism and Roman paganism.

---

[195] E. de Faye: *Gnostiques et Gnosticisme*. Ed. 1913, p. 349, and Matter, ibid, Volume II, p. 171.

[196] De Luchet: *Essai sur la Sectes des Illuminés*, p. 6.

[197] His work *Adversus Haereses* is especially important.

Never has the situation been so grave for the Church as in that time; for Christianity then was much weaker than in the present and the difference in strength between the Church and its enemies was immeasurably greater in favour of the adversary. If Holy Church was able then to triumph over its enemies who were relatively stronger than they are now, it should now be able to do so even more; always presupposing that it is successful in fighting and eliminating the destructive and perfidious activity of the crypto-Jewish "Fifth Column" which has infiltrated the clergy; and with the presupposition that within the religious hierarchies leaders appear who imitate Saint Irenaeus and sacrifice everything in order to defend the faith of Christ and the cause of mankind, which is threatened by a cruel servitude; leaders who are likewise able to overcome the resistance presented by cowards and conformists who, however sincere in their beliefs, think more about not compromising the ecclesiastical preferments they hanker after and of living a peaceful and financially safe life than in defending Holy Church and humanity in these times of mortal danger.

Finally, let us examine another of the teachings of the gnostic revolutionary movement. The Jews who sowed poison in Christian society were careful to ensure that said poison did not end up poisoning the poisoners themselves. The Synagogue had to face up to this grave danger for the first time. It is very difficult to disseminate poisonous ideas without running the risk of being infected by them. It is true that the Gnosis, which the Hebrews at first spread in the Synagogue, was in the main a collection of mystic interpretations of Holy Scripture, which stood in close connection with the Cabbala. But the accumulation of stupidities, contradictions and perverse actions which the Hebrews smuggled into the Christian Gnosis, formed a serious danger for the synagogue itself, but which the latter certainly guarded against by energetically combating every possibility of infection among the Jews.

Eighteen hundred years later the same phenomenon appears; the Hebrews as spreaders of atheism and of Communist materialism among the Christians, Mohammedans and the other Gentiles, take every kind of precautionary measure to prevent the materialistic cancer from infecting the Israelite communities, which they have been better able to achieve at present than in the times of Gnosticism; for the experience of eighteen centuries in this kind of service has made these destroyers into true masters in the art of handling poisons and of spreading them throughout the world without the poison infecting the Jews themselves. At all events even still in our days the Rabbis must be constantly on guard, in order to prevent materialism, with which they have immersed half the surrounding world, from causing damage in the Hebrew families. They constantly seize upon measures of different kind, in order to present this. The atheistic and materialistic poison is only destined for the Christians and Gentiles, in order to render their domination easier; for Jewry must preserve itself with its mystique purer than ever. They know that it is mysticism which makes men who fight for an ideal invincible. Just as the Hebrews had no scruples at other times when they spread teachings against Jehovah himself and advocated the cult of Satan, which is so common in Black Magic, so they now have no scruples in spreading the atheistic materialism of the Jew Marx, although the latter denies the existence of God of Israel himself. The end justifies the means. This maxim the Hebrews observe down to its most unbelievable consequences.

With the conversion of Constantine, the victory of Holy Church over Paganism, Gnosticism and Jewry was complete.

When once Holy Church was controller of the enormous power of the Roman Empire, the Jews lacked any possibility of persecuting it further and attacking it directly or inciting persecution through pagan emperors against Christianity, as they had done previously. However, the "Synagogue of Satan" did not give way before such a bleak picture. It clearly understood that, in order to destroy the Church, only one aid remained of the three which we have studied. It directed its special attention to its "Fifth Column" of false new converts who were smuggled into Christianity, in order through Church divisions and internal underground movements to be able to attain the desired goal, the destruction of the Church of Christ. The fact that in some points the Christian doctrine was not well defined made the task far easier for them.

CHAPTER FIVE

THE JEW ARIUS AND HIS HERESY

Arianism, the great heresy, which split Christianity over three and a half centuries, was the work of a concealed Jew, who outwardly practised Christianity; a striking and infamous example of the descendants of Judas Iscariot, like all those priests who, as members of the "Jewish Fifth Column", have infiltrated into the Catholic Church.

The well-known American writer, William Thomas Walsh, who is outstanding for his zealous Catholicism and has well documented works, says to us, referring to the mode of action of the Jews who infiltrated into Christianity, the following: "Arius, the Catholic Jew (Father of the heresy) treacherously attacked the divinity of Christ, and he was successful in dividing the Christian world for centuries."[198]

From the trials by the Inquisition against the crypto-Jews, who were called the Judaising heretics, one can conclude that the Trinity is one of the Catholic dogmas which the Jews reject most violently; for what repels them most of all in their deadly hatred towards Christ, is the fact that Jesus Christ is regarded as the second person within the Holy Trinity; this means that God is One in essence and Three in person. It is therefore illuminating that the Jews, after they had infiltrated into the Church through their pretended conversion to Christianity, afterwards strove to alter the dogma of the Church in such a way as to regard God as one in person and hence to deny the divinity of Christ.

Arius was born in Libya, which at this time was under Roman rule. Already as a youth he joined himself to the schism of Melesius, who usurped the office of the Bishop of Alexandria; however, after the cause of Melesius had suffered severe setbacks, Arius was reconciled with the Church. It is well known how the Jews make use of such reconciliations

---

[198] William Thomas Walsh: *Philip II*. Ed. Espasa Calpe, p. 266.

with the Church, of which they say themselves that such were performed as true comedies, exactly as suits them.

The always universally kind Holy Church, which is fundamentally ready to pardon the repentant sinner, sanctioned the reconciliation with Arius, by taking him anew into its holy bosom, while this secret Jew merely made use of this kindness, like all who belong to his race, in order to later cause it inconceivable harm which could easily have caused such misfortune as that which threatens us today.

After Arius had consoled himself, he had himself consecrated as Catholic priest and presbyter of the Bishop Alexander of Alexandria, by whom he was entrusted with the church of Baucalis. Various outstanding Church historians attribute to Arius an extraordinary and impressive asceticism as well as a remarkable mysticism; to which are added his great talents as a preacher and a convincing dialectic skill, which allowed him to convince the great mass of believers and even the hierarchies of Holy Church.

The basic principle of the Arian doctrine was the Jewish thesis of the absolute unity of God, denying the Trinity and representing Christ solely as the most exalted of all creatures, but in no way as possessing divine nature. This was one of the first serious attempts to provide Christianity with a Jewish stamp.

He neither attacked Christ nor criticised Him, as the professing Jews did; for then his mission would have failed, because no Christian would have supported him. In order to arouse no suspicion, he rather praised Jesus beyond all measure. So he gained the sympathy and interest of the faithful and then in the midst of all these speeches of praise he allowed his poison to seep in with the cunning denial of the divinity of Jesus Christ, since it is the point which encounters the most stiff-necked rejection by the Jews.

It is curious that, fourteen hundred years later, the Jews strike the same note when they deny the divinity of Christ and simultaneously praise Him in their doctrines and instructions in order to provoke no strong reactions amongst Christians introduced into the sect.

A further innovation which the Arian heresy brought with it, was the attempt to alter the doctrine and policy of the Church in relation to the Jews. While Christ damned them and upon various occasions attacked them in the sharpest possible way, and the Apostles did the same, as did the Church in general in its beginnings, Arius and his heresy strove to effect a true reform in this respect, in that they carried out a pro-Jewish policy and strove for an accommodation to the "Synagogue of Satan."

Like John Huss, Calvin, Karl Marx, and other Jewish revolutionary leaders, Arius was a man of strong dynamism, of extraordinary perseverance as well as an artist of words and with the pen, who wrote pamphlets and even books,[199] in order to convince the Church hierarchies, the civil governors and other outstanding personalities within the Roman Empire. The first important assistance was given to him on the part of Bishop Eusebius of Nicomedia, who on grounds of his great friendship with the Emperor possessed the boldness of wishing to win the latter for the Arian heresy. Even if he was not successful in this, he nevertheless succeeded unfortunately in leading Constantine astray, by making him believe that it was simply a question of discussions between different orthodox viewpoints. Under this assumption the Emperor sought in vain to introduce a settlement between Arius and the Bishop of Alexandria. He sent his advisor, Hosius, the Bishop of Cordova, so that the latter might bring about an understanding between the two parties. No result was attained. As if it had merely been a personal dispute between Bishop Alexander and Arius!

In the course of these negotiations Hosius and the Church reached the conviction that here it was not a simple dispute between different schools or persons, but rather a conflagration which threatened to scorch the whole of Christianity.

This is worthy of being remarked, since it is the classical technique with which the Jews begin a revolutionary movement. Upon many occasions they give themselves out to be harmless, good-willed, of small influence and without any kind of danger, so that the institutions threatened by the revolutionary germ do not allot to the latter its true importance and therefore look away from applying their whole force against it, which is imperative if it is to be rapidly and effectively destroyed.

Lulled through this outward conduct, the Christian or Gentile leading personages are accustomed to avoid such measures, by reacting in a modest way. This is utilised by Jewry, in order to treacherously kindle the conflagration, so that, when combative measures are finally resolved upon,

---

[199] His work *Thalia* was of great importance for the spreading of heresy.

it already possesses such an overwhelming force that it is impossible to halt it.

It is interesting to remark that, after Arius had finally been excommunicated by the Synod called in the year 321 by the Prelate of Alexandria and attended by over a hundred bishops, the heretic at first went to Palestine, in order to win disciples. And it is further worthy of note that the first Synod to support Arius by betraying Catholicism was precisely that of Palestine, as well as that of Nicomedia, where Eusebius, Arius' right-hand man, was Bishop. It is illuminating that it was Palestine where, in spite of the repressive measures of Titus and Hadrian, the most compact Jewish population was found, and where the "Jewish Fifth Column", which had infiltrated into the Church, was very powerful. It is therefore not strange that Arius, declared outlawed through excommunication and in a desperate position, sought his salvation in flight, in order to seek support with his brothers in Palestine. He was so successful in this intention that an entire Synod of Bishops and high-ranking clergy, as was the Synod of Palestine, decided upon support of him and gave new power and prestige to his cause, which, after its condemnation by the Synod of Alexandria, seemed condemned to failure.

In the same manner another Synod, which was assembled in Nicomedia, supported Arius and imparted to him, like that of Palestine, its approval to return to Egypt. In such a way did Arius and his fellow travellers set one Synod against the other and thus divide the episcopate of the Catholic world.

The study of this giant struggle which lasted for centuries, is extremely valuable, since it allows us to clearly recognise that the "Jewish Fifth Column" which has seeped into the clergy of Holy Church, was then already effective with the same methods as centuries later, when it was successful by means of a crypto-Jew, Cardinal Pierleoni, in usurping the dignity of Pope. These are likewise the same methods which, a thousand years later, were combated by the Holy Inquisition, and the same of which we are witnessing in our days.

Arius and the Arianist Bishops intrigued against the clergy who defended Holy Church. They persecuted and feuded against them and even attacked the venerable Bishops and all priests, without regard for their rank, who had appeared to the fore through their zeal in the defence of Catholicism. They persecuted and fought them by means of secret and poisonous intrigues and by means of false accusations, until they were rendered harmless or destroyed.

By means of a well-organised action the Arians on their side strove to bring under their control the Bishops' offices when they fell vacant, and they were successful in occupying them with clergy of their own way of thinking and of preventing true Catholics from finding admittance to this office.

These infamous manoeuvres were set in motion above all after the Ecumenical Council of Nicaea. At this council Arius and his heresy were condemned in spite of the opposition of a minority of heretical bishops, who participated with them in the Council and who vainly attempted to bring about the victory of their viewpoints which were just as novel and contrary to the traditional Catholic doctrine as those which some bishops wish to make prevail at the present Ecumenical Council of Vatican II.

In the campaign instigated by the heretical bishops against the Catholics, the uproar that they set in motion against Eustasius, the Bishop of Antioch, is particularly notable. The latter was accused by them of pretending to observe the agreement of the Council of Nicaea, but in reality sowing the Sabellian heresy and discord. With these and other accusations the traitorous clergy were so successful that he was deposed and an Arianist bishop named in his stead. In addition, they were successful in deceiving Constantine, who, in the belief that he was offering the Church a service, exiled the devout bishop of the land and allowed the hypocritical heretics to enjoy his support, since he regarded them as the true defenders of the Church.[200]

But more important still is the conspiracy that they instigated in order to destroy Saint Athanasius, who had succeeded Alexander, after the latter's death, in the Patriarchate of Alexandria. Already at the Council of Nicaea he had demonstrated that he was one of the bulwarks in the defence of Holy Church. This had cost him the hatred of the Arian clergy, who recognised the necessity of making him harmless. In order to gain the Emperor to their side, they accused Saint Athanasius of cultivating relations with certain rebels of the Empire. This is the classical manoeuvre of Jewry in all times; if it is wished to remove any kind of leading personage from the sphere of the head of State, then at the suitable moment a conspiracy is instigated, in order to make the latter believe that the former conspires against him and is secretly allied with his enemies. In this manner they succeed in getting the head of State to remove leading personage who hinders the Jewish plans. In such a manner they accused

---

[200] Cavallera: *Le Schisme d'Antioche*. Sellers. R.V. "Eustasius of Antioch and his place in the early doctrine of Christ." Cambridge 1928.

Saint Athanasius of having humiliated the clergy by laying upon them a linen tax, as well as sowing discord in the ranks of the Church.

This slander is also a classical method of the "Fifth Column," which, when it is seen that a conspiracy is instigated against Holy Church and someone denounces it or rushes to the defence of the institution, sends its crypto-Jewish clergy into the field to accuse the defenders of the Church of undermining the unity of the Church and of sowing discord among Christianity. In reality it is they, the enemies of Christ who have infiltrated into the clergy, who with their conspiracies and dark machinations provoke those schisms and divisions, and not the true Christians upon whom lies the duty of defending Catholicism and preventing the former from winning ground.

So it occurred in the case of Saint Athanasius; the heretical clergy were in reality those, who through their mode of action conjured up the schism. But they possessed the insolence to accuse Saint Athanasius of sowing discord, because he attempted to defend Holy Church in the face of the machinations of heresy.

The blow was additionally directed higher up; for Arius and his followers knew very well that the unity of the Church lay before the eyes of Constantine as the highest goal, and thus they hoped to bring down Saint Athanasius with a typical accusation of provoking discord.

Later, the Melesian heretics, working together with the Arians, accused Saint Athanasius of having murdered one of the collaborators of their leader; however, Athanasius was successful in discovering the whereabouts of the man whom he was falsely alleged to have murdered, so that the slanders were exposed.

Since up to then all intrigues had failed, they now took refuge in one last manoeuvre. In Tyre they summoned a Synod of Bishops, at which they accused Saint Athanasius of having seduced a woman; however, he was also successful in refuting this slander.

However, the Arian Bishops were successful in bringing under their control the Synod of Tyre and resolved upon the deposition of Saint Athanasius as Patriarch of Alexandria. Concerning this, an inflammatory note was despatched to bishops all over the world, so that the latter should break off all relations with Saint Athanasius, who was accused of various crimes. Constantine, who highly respected the decisions of the Synods of

Bishops, was highly impressed. This together with another skilfully launched slander campaign, which accused Saint Athanasius of selling grain to the Egyptians in order to prevent it reaching Constantinople and in this manner to create a food shortage in the capital of the Roman Empire, made the Emperor furious. He banished the unfortunate Saint, whom at this time he regarded as the most dangerous disturber of public order and the unity of Holy Church.

While the Arian bishops first gained the sister of the Emperor, Constance, who exercised a strong influence upon him, and other confidants, to their side, they continually gave the hypocritical appearance of watching with zeal over the unity of the Church and of the Empire, which was so strongly desired by Constantine, and they accused the Catholics of endangering this unity with their exaggerations and eccentricities. They thus attained that Constantine, who had supported orthodoxy at the Council of Nicaea, carried out a deviation towards Arians and approved the solemn reacceptance of the latter into the bosom of the Church. This would have been without doubt the apotheosis and the highest triumph of the Jew Arius, who already played with the idea of demanding the Papal dignity of the Holy Catholic Church, which, regarded by modest human understanding, did not seem impossible; for he could already count upon the friendly approval of the Emperor and on the support of a daily growing number of bishops within Christianity. However, in the face of the support which God allows his Holy Church to enjoy, all human calculations must fail. The Church, will certainly be persecuted, but never conquered; and Arius died on the threshold of his victory in such a mysteriously tragic manner, as Saint Athanasius himself has recorded for posterity. It is very interesting to quote what the "Castilian Jewish Encyclopedia", an official Jewish document, asserts about this great Church Father and Saint, Athanasius:

"Athanasius (Saint), Church Father (293-373), Patriarch of Alexandria, resolute opponent of the Arian teachings which approach a pure Monotheism and hence the Jewish doctrines. Athanasius polemicised against the Jews from dogmatic grounds, but the situation of the Jews worsened everywhere so that the teachings of Athanasius triumphed over the Arian doctrines, as was the case with the Visigoths in Spain."

Like other Church Fathers, Saint Athanasius fought bitterly not only against the Arians, but also against the Jews. As one sees, the latter attribute such an importance to his teachings that the Jewish Encyclopaedia categorically admits, that "the situation of the Jews worsened where the teachings of Saint Athanasius triumphed." It is therefore understandable that the powers of evil unleashed a satanic hatred against the Patriarch of Alexandria.

If Saint Athanasius and other great Church Fathers had lived in our time, the "Jewish Fifth Column", which has infiltrated into the clergy, would certainly have done all in its power so that the Church condemned them on account of Antisemitism.

As far as the Bishop of Cordova, Hosius, is concerned, he had been another Paladin of the Church in the struggle against Arianism and was the soul of the Council of Nicaea, and was an active fighter against Jewry. After he had distinguished himself at the Council of Elvira, which under the name Illiberian Council was held in the years 300 to 303, he exercised a decisive influence upon the approbation of canons tending to effect a separation between Christians and Jews, in order to counter the nefast influence of the latter over the former. Since at that time the harmful fraternising of the Catholic clergy with the Jews was the order of the day, the Illiberian Council accordingly strove to counter this evil state with drastic measures. In this respect the following rules are interesting:

Canon L (50). "Should a priest or one of the faithful sit at table with Jews, then for his amendment he shall be excluded from Communion."

Canon XLIX (49). "It has been found good to thoroughly admonish teachers that they should not suffer their fruits received from God to be blessed by Jews, so that our distribution of blessings does not become weak or valueless. Should anyone be presumptuous enough to do this, after it has been forbidden, then he should be excluded from the Church."

Canon XVI (16). "It is determined among other things that the Jews, and likewise heretics, must not be permitted Catholic wives. So that there may be no communion between the faithful and unfaithful."

This last Canon is clear and sharp. Any communion between Christians and Jews is regarded as dangerous.

The Illiberian Council had a great importance, since its disciplinary measures were to a great part incorporated in the general legislation of the Church.

After Constantine's death, his three sons took over the government of the Empire: Constantine II and Constans in the west, and Constantius in the East. The first two were passionate Catholics, while Constantius was admittedly a good Christian, but was very influenced through friendship with his father's friend, the Arian Eusebius of Nicomedia. After the death of Constantine, however, both Constantius as well as his two brothers approved of the return of Saint Athanasius and other orthodox bishops from banishment, who had been expelled from the land through the intrigues of the Arians. In addition, after the death of Eusebius of Nicomedia, in the year 342, this bad influence upon Constantius vanished, who, under the influence of his brother Constans and of Pope Julius, finally supported Catholic orthodoxy.

Extremely alarmed over the progress of Jewry, Constantius applied against the latter the measures that the Jews call the first great persecution on the part of the Christians.

For the course of twelve years, up to the death of Constans and of Pope Julius, the Catholics were successful in almost overcoming Arianism. Under the imprint of the sermons and the great regard for Saint Athanasius as well as Bishop Hosius of Cordova, it seemed destined to perish. Constantius had a long and extremely heartfelt conversation with Saint Athanasius in Antioch, during which the Emperor of the Orient showed him the greatest deference. And finally the illustrious Father of the Church made his entrance into Alexandria in a kind of veritable apotheosis.

When Ursacius and Valente, the leaders of Arianism, recognised imminent defeat and were alarmed by the firm conduct of Constantius in favour of orthodoxy, they bowed to the situation and went so far as to beg from the Pope their reconciliation with the Catholic Church.

This was one further example of the classical tactics of the foe, which the Jew Stalin called "strategic withdrawal." This consists in yielding in the moment of defeat, in abandoning the struggle outwardly, in order to avoid defeat, and in conspiring in the background until one is sufficiently strong to risk a new attack as soon as the possibility of triumph appears.

If things went badly with Arianism, then it was worse still for Jewry; for when Constantius had convinced himself of the danger that it represented for the Empire and Christianity, he began, as the great Jewish historian Graetz proves, to expel the Jewish doctors of laws from the land. In consequence of this decree, many of them had to emigrate to Babylonia. The persecutions worsened to such a degree that the leading Jews were threatened with death, which resulted in an even greater flow of

251

emigration, particularly from Judaea. This development caused the decline of the Jewish Academy of Tiberiades. The very frequent marriages between Jews and Christians were punished by Constantius with death, whereby he went beyond what was laid down in this respect by Canon 16 of the Illiberian Council.

As shown by the Israelite Graetz, the Jews were called "the murderers of God" by Catholics in that time. In answer to this, the Jews instigated isolated rebellions against the Empire, which, however, were nipped in the bud.

But all these setbacks did not discourage me enemy, who lurked in the background and awaited the first favourable opportunity to assert themselves again. This favourable opportunity began to show itself when first Constans and then Pope Julius died, whose beneficial influence had caused Constantius to hold firm to Catholicism.

The Arian leaders Valente and Ursacius, who had hypocritically implored their reconciliation with orthodoxy, took up their intrigues anew, while they sought at all costs to estrange Constantius from orthodoxy. For this purpose they flattered his selfishness and made use of his utterly violent reactions towards everything which might lessen his authority or his prestige. In the background the Arians instigated a true conspiracy, in order to distance Constantius from Saint Athanasius and thus obtain his withdrawal with them from orthodoxy. Among other slanders they accused him of disseminating defamatory rumours against the Emperor, by which he was alleged to represent the Emperor as a heretic and as excommunicated. In this manner they attempted to cause the people to withdraw their support from Saint Athanasius and at the same time to lyingly present him as an enemy of the Emperor. The Arians represented themselves as his most loyal subjects.

These sinister machinations against Athanasius and the Catholics infuriated Constantius. More and more he inclined to the side of the Arians, until finally in common with them he attempted to persuade Liberius, the new Pope, to divest the illustrious Church Father of his dignity.

It is incredible, how Jewry frequently manages to transform its sworn opponents into unconscious allies, whereby, as in this case, it makes use of the most subtle means in order to attain its goal. In history there have been several examples like that of Constantius.

The Holy Father, pressed by the Emperor, pointed out the necessity of calling a new Council to attempt to put an end to this dispute. With the agreement of the Emperor the Council of Arles was called, which took place in the year 353 in the presence of two Papal Legates. Great were the expectancies which the good placed upon the Council for the obtaining of Christian unity; but the bishops, led by Valente and Ursacius in the service of the "Fifth Column", were able to instigate such intrigues and such pressures that the Council finally yielded to the demands of the Arians, who were granted support through the implacable pressure of Imperial power. Even the two Papal Legates yielded and, as a disastrous consequence, the unjust condemnation of Saint Athanasius was resolved upon.

The sole Bishop, who voted against the resolution, was Paulinus of Trier, who for this reason was expelled from the land. But when Pope Liberius received the knowledge of its disastrous outcome, he raised objectives and proposed summoning another Synod, which was held in Milan in the year 355. But this Synod also was the target of countless conspiracies and exposed to the pressure of the heretical bishops who enjoyed the support of the Emperor. Finally they were successful. This new Synod composed of 300 Bishops condemned Saint Athanasius once again. Thus Arianism gained a complete triumph and was able to again ban the highly regarded Saint. Since the Pontifex Maximus refused to yield to the demands of the Arians and of Constantius, the Emperor banished the Pope as well, a banishment which lasted quite some time.

However, the efforts of Athanasius, that Saint and Father of the Church, that iron and dynamic man, who revealed so much courage and tenacity in the face of the enemy, finally bore fruit. After three centuries of struggle Holy Church finally triumphed over Jewry and its heresy. What the Church and men of today urgently need are men who possess the hardness, the courage and the energy of such as Saint Athanasius, to counter the Jewish-Communist threat, which, exactly as in the case of the Jewish-Arian heresy, has brought Catholicism to the edge of the abyss.

We are certain that in this situation, as also in similar situations, the Lord God shows us His mercy so that among the hierarchies of Holy Church new Athanasiuses will appear, which the Church needs for its salvation. This is the maxim of our time in which the modern instruments of Jewry within the Church, such as false apostles, play into the hands of Communism and the "Synagogue of Satan." They cripple the defensive powers of the Church, in order to mislead the truly faithful and to make possible the triumph of the worldly foe, just as they intend to do at the present Ecumenical Council Vatican II, called by John XXIII.[201]

Finally we must point out that the inconstancy of Constantius is also revealed in his conduct towards Jewry. In contrast to his hostile policy, he decreed measures which favoured it; thus the law that equated the Jewish patriarchs and officials working in the service of the synagogue with the Christian clergy, exempted them from the severity of the law, as the Israelite historian Graetz himself reports to us.

THE WICKED ARE HELPED

AND THE GOOD EXCOMMUNICATED

What occurred to Saint Athanasius more than sixteen hundred years ago, occurs in the 20th century in greater or larger measure with many excellent defenders both of Holy Church as also of the Free World, be they clergy or laymen. Some cardinals and bishops who in a suspicious manner favour the principal enemies of Christ and his Church, namely the Jews, take them under their protection or favour the development and the triumph of the political or social movements controlled by Freemasonry and Communism, and, while they show the forces of Antichrist so much favour and support, are at the same time enraged concerning the cardinals, prelates or priests who fight with more resolution and efficacy against the beast. The activity of the "Fifth Column" of the descendants of Judas Iscariot has altered little since the time of Arius up to our days. If any Catholic regent or political leader fights so effectively against the forces of Jewry, Freemasonry or Communism that he defeats them, then these Prelates and even Cardinals appear upon the scene, in order once more to play into the hands of the hellish forces and make possible their victory which normally is beyond their reach. If the Jewish-Freemasonic or Jewish-Communist forces see themselves conquered in practice by direct action through the Catholic leaders or regents, then the "Fifth Column", which has infiltrated into the highest honorary offices of Holy Church,

---

[201] Books which have been referred to in this Chapter: Graetz, *History of the Jews*, Philadelphia 1956, Volume II, Chapters XXI and XXIII. *Acta Conciliorum et Epistolae Decretales* etc. Johannis Harduini, S.J., Paris, 1715, Volume I, p. 255. Jewish-Spanish Encyclopaedia. St. Athanasius: *Historia Arianorum ad Monachos. Contra Arianos.* Eusebius: *Vita Constantini.* Cevatkin: *Studies of Arianism.* Batiffol: *Les sources de l'histoire du Concile de Nicée.* Echoes d'or. 28th edition, 1925. Sokrates: *Church history.* St. Athanasius: *Epistola de morte Arii.* St. Hilary: *History 2.20 Fragm.* Ch. J. Hefele, Volume I. Sozomeno: *Church History,* Chapter I, St. Epiphanius Haeret. Waud: *The Four Great Heresies,* 1955.

hits upon the plan of unleashing a wild campaign of intrigues and Church censures, to set the entire clergy against those leaders or regents, who represent a serious hindrance for the Freemasonic or Communist triumph. And if this campaign of slander and defamation alone does not suffice to destroy the support of the said leaders or regents with the Catholic masses, then those false Apostles, of whom Saint Paul speaks, send forth a fulminant excommunication as their sharpest weapon. Thus, by undermining the prestige of such regents or leaders, they gain the support of the mass of the people in their favour to make possible as a result the triumph of Freemasonic or Communist forces. This is the secret of many victories of the forces of evil.

CHAPTER SIX

THE JEWS AS ALLIES

OF JULIAN THE APOSTATE

In the year 360, Julian, a cousin of Constantius, was proclaimed Roman Emperor by the army. Constantius, who had prepared for battle against him, died on the way; this made easier the final victory for Julian and his proclamation as Emperor of the Orient and Occident.

The policy of Julian had three principal aims: 1. To renew paganism and to again declare it a state religion of the Empire, so that Rome, which according to his view had declined through Christianity, might return to its old glory. 2. To destroy Christianity. 3. To concede to Jewry its old positions, from which it had been expelled by Constantine and his sons; even the rebuilding of the Temple of Solomon was to be arranged.

From the beginning the Jews were his unconditional allies, which once again proves that, when it suits them, they are capable of fighting for paganism and the cult of idols, even indeed against monotheism, whenever this allows them to work for the destruction of the Church, even though they are inwardly monotheists and enemies of the cult of idolatry.

While the Jews allied themselves with Julian and allowed him to enjoy their help, they supported the restoration of idolatry, although they say that they are so greatly repelled by it. However, in order to obtain their goal, namely the destruction of Christianity, they prove that they are capable of everything, even of utilisation of the atheistic and materialistic teachings of modern Communism, although they remain deeply religious and spiritual.

The famous Jewish historian Graetz says of Julian:

"The Emperor Julian was one of those strong characters who imprint their names indelibly on the memory of men. Only his early death and the hatred of the ruling Church were responsible for his not being provided with the title 'Julian the Great'" He adds that Julian paid great admiration to the Jewish religion, and confirms that "the period of government by Julian, which lasted just two years (November 361 to June 363), was a time of extreme felicity for the Jews of the Roman Empire."

Graetz likewise establishes that the leader of Jewry in the Empire, the Patriarch Hillel, was expressly called by Julian "his respected friend", and that he promised him in an autographed letter to make an end of the misdeeds committed by the Christian Emperors against the Jews.

Further, Julian made all necessary preparations in order to begin the rebuilding of the Temple of Jerusalem. He addressed a letter to all Jewish congregations of the Empire, in which he spoke in friendly way of the leader of Jewry in the Empire, the Patriarch Julos (Hillel), as his brother. He promised the abolition of the high taxes laid upon the Israelites by the Christians, guaranteed that in future none should accuse them of blasphemy, promised freedom and security, and promised to have Jerusalem rebuilt at his expense, as soon as he returned victorious from the Persian war.

For the rebuilding of the Temple of Jerusalem Julian commissioned his best friend, Alypius of Antioch, to whom he gave instructions to spare no expense, and commanded the governors of Palestine and Syria to assist with everything necessary.

In his zeal to restore paganism, Julian also prepared all means for the reconstruction of the pagan temples. He reorganised the worship of idols and gave them a hierarchy similar to that of the Church. He renewed the pagan cult with great splendour and celebrated the pagan feasts in ancient pompous manner.

Labriolle and Koch provide us with information concerning the zeal of Julian to provide paganism with new strength by means of the creation of welfare institutions which were similar to the Christian ones. Hospitals, hostels for children and old men, charitable institutions and others of the like were erected; at the same time he made efforts to add to paganism a kind of religious order, which resembled that of the Christian monks.

It was not only a question of the re-establishment of the idolatrous cult, but of the creation of a reformed and strengthened paganism with methods copied from the Christians.

The threat, which drew over Holy Church, could thus scarcely be graver. The Emperor, paganism and Jewry joined themselves together closely, in order to face Christianity with a struggle for life or death.

Although in principle Julian gave the assurance of maintaining religious tolerance, since he recalled the bad results which the violent persecutions through the Roman Emperors had produced, he nevertheless applied all means in order to achieve the annihilation of Christianity. As Saint Gregory Nazianzen reports to us, who describes the period of Julian's government "as the cruellest of all persecutions", martyrdoms unleashed through the fury of the unbelievers were the order of the day.

Among the measures decreed by Julian against Catholicism, the following stand out: the renewed expulsion of Saint Athanasius, who was regarded as the bulwark of orthodoxy; the removal of all Christian symbols on coinage and the cancelling of rights accorded to the clergy through the Catholic Emperors; as well as the elimination of Christians from public offices, unless they recanted. And with all this it was pretended that these were measures necessary for the maintenance of religious freedom and of equality for believers of all confessions in the Roman State. His Jewish allies had thus in Julian a good master, just as in our own time they applied the same methods with identical hypocrisy in order to cause their Freemasonic Liberal revolutions to triumph, through which, under the pretence of introducing freedom of conscience, they robbed the Church of all her rights.

But the true intentions of the Emperor were revealed when he announced that the Galileans (disciples of Christ) must vanish, because they were enemies of Hellenism; the books he personally wrote to combat Christianity also prove what hatred the Emperor felt for the Church.

The fact that the rebuilding of the Jewish temple among other things failed as a result of mysterious flames shooting up out of the earth and burning those that worked there, has all the elements of a confirmed historical event; Christian historians also confirm the latter, and it is also accepted by such prestigious Hebrew historians as Graetz. Only that the latter, instead of attributing the occurrence to a miracle, as Catholics do, assumes a natural cause. According to his explanation, the cause was gases compressed in subterranean passages, to which an outlet was blocked, and which, becoming free and making contact with the air, unleashed those fires, which among other reasons caused Alypius to stop the works.

As the Catholic historians report in that time it was not only pagan hordes who martyred and slaughtered the Christians. The Jews, enjoying the protection and friendship of the Emperor, likewise attacked and began to destroy the churches in Judea and the neighbouring regions as well as to cause Christians every conceivable harm. The Jew Graetz naturally calls these versions malicious slanders.

For those who have experienced what deeds the Jews are capable of against Christianity if they are allowed a free hand, it cannot be remarkable that in the time of Julian they used all their power in order to destroy Catholic churches. They did this in the same manner in the Middle Ages, when they were supported by some heretical sects; and so have they acted in our days, in order to secure the triumph of their Freemasonic and Communist revolutions.

Much of that which they perform in the present is a repetition of what they learned in the times of Julian the Apostate, whose period of rule, if it had lasted longer, would have taken a catastrophic course for Christianity.

Fortunately, Julian died before he could cause Christianity greater harm, struck by a deadly arrow in a decisive battle against the Persians. It is said that, before he died, he addressed our Lord Jesus Christ, calling out: "Thou hast conquered, Galilean!"

Through the death of Julian the Apostate, Holy Church was spared from the threatening destruction which had faced it since the last pagan persecutions.

As far as the Israelites are concerned, then the following commentary of the Jewish historian Graetz, speaks for itself:

"The death of Julian close to the Tigris (June 363) robbed the Jews of their last ray of hope for a peaceful and untroubled life."

And the Jewish-Castilian Encyclopaedia remarks under the word "Julian" the following:

"He particularly valued the Jews. He had extensive knowledge of the Jewish cause and refers in his writings to various religious institutions of the Jews. It appears that he wished to found among the Jews of Palestine a Patrician Order (called "Aristoï" in the Talmud), which was to exercise judicial functions. He attributed a higher value to Judaism than to Christianity, although he regarded it as inferior to the pagan philosophy. With his death, the short period of tolerance was at an end, which the Jewish community enjoyed between the setting-in of Christian persecutions."[202]

---

[202] Books used in this chapter: Graetz: *History of the Jews*, Volume II, Chapter XXI, Jewish-Spanish Encyclopaedia. W. Koch: *Comment l'empereur Juliana tacha de fonder une Eglise païenne.* Articles in the *Revue de Philosophie de l'Histoire*, 6th Year 1927-1935 and 7th 1928-485. Labriolle: *La réaction païenne.* P' 1934. St. Gregory Nazianzen: *Oratio I en Julianum.*

CHAPTER SEVEN

SAINT JOHN CHRYSOSTOM AND SAINT AMBROSE CONDEMN THE JEWS

The first dissensions to occur within Arianism were apparently produced by the increasingly moderate tendencies of the bishops, who though in error nevertheless acted in good faith; they therefore clashed with the extremists who were undoubtedly controlled by the "Fifth Column."

This gradually weakened the heresy in the Roman Empire. Upon the death of Julian the army proclaimed General Jovian as Emperor. The latter was a Catholic, so that orthodoxy almost controlled the situation.

The new Emperor summoned Saint Athanasius back out of banishment and appointed him his advisor. Unfortunately and unexpectedly, however, Jovian died the next year and Valentinian I was proclaimed as new Emperor. The latter appointed his brother Valens as Regent for the Eastern part of the Empire. Thus it came about that, while the former allowed religious freedom, Valens, who was a zealous Arian, made efforts to resurrect this heresy at least in the eastern part of the Empire. Meanwhile the heretics used the situation in order to exert influence on the Germanic tribes who threw themselves into the arms of Arianism and thus in the Jew-friendly direction.

Valens unleashed a new persecution of Catholics and once again banished the now aged Saint Athanasius. At the same time he began, as the Catholic historian Theodoretus reports, to grant the Jews and pagans all kinds of guarantees. Also he was not satisfied with persecuting the Christians, but included the moderate Arians, whom he, without wishing it, drove into the arms of Holy Church.

The Jewish historian Graetz agrees in this regard, when he alludes to the fact that Valens was "Arian and had had to suffer so much from the

Catholic party that he now became intolerant towards the latter. He allowed the Jews to enjoy his protection and heaped honours and distinctions upon them."

It is therefore evident that the resurgence of Arianism in the East coincided with the persecutions of Catholicism and with a preferential treatment of Jewry.

With Gratian set in years of deadly struggle between Pagans and Christians. The outcome remained changeable until the Spanish general Theodosius took over the Emperorship both in the east as well as the west.

Theodosius the Great dealt paganism as well as Arianism, which had risen to new life in the east under the protection of Valens, deadly blows and hence provided Catholicism in the Empire with the final victory. It was to be hoped that he would also combat Jewry, but the Hebrews knew how to gain his tolerance at the right hour, under which they wished to extend anew their influence in Roman society. This activity was so dangerous for Holy Church that both the Bishop of Milan, Saint Ambrose, as well as Chrysostom, another of the great Fathers of the Church, saw themselves necessitated to conduct an energetic struggle against the Jews as well as against those Christians who secretly furthered the protection of the Jewish cult. Concerning this struggle, the Israelite historian Graetz, to whom we will hand over at this point, reports:

"On Saturdays and the Jewish festivals, many Christians, especially of the female sex, both women of noble birth as well as those of lowly status, were regularly to be encountered in the synagogues. They listened devoutly to the trumpet call on the day of the Jewish New Year, were at the solemn cult of the Day of Atonement and took part in the celebration of the Feast of Tabernacles. The fact that they performed all this behind the back of the Christian clergy and therefore had to beg their neighbours not to betray them, made the matter still more attractive. Against this spontaneous honouring by Christians of Jewish institutions, Chrysostom directed his violent monkish sermons and used all kinds of harsh expressions against them, by his preaching that the synagogues were disgraceful exhibitions, dens of thieves and even worse."[203]

This great Father of the Church undoubtedly expressed great truths; in fact if he had uttered them in our days, then he would have been

---

[203] Graetz, op. cit., Volume I, pp. 613-614.

condemned as an Antisemite by the Jews as well as by the Christian clergy who play into the latter's hands.

On the other hand one sees from this how widespread even in Rome the core of Christians was who outwardly appeared Christian, but in secret practised the Jewish cult. The Jew Graetz describes to us how these kinds of Christians attended the synagogues behind the back of the Catholic clergy, and how they were concerned that their neighbours did not betray them, if they noticed this most suspicious activity. It is therefore natural that the great Father of the Church, Chrysostom, thundered against these false Christians; for Holy Church had still not created the institution for their combating and prosecution, namely the Holy Office of the Inquisition.

Saint Ambrose, Bishop of Milan, one of the great Saints and illustrious Church Fathers, who exercised such a decisive influence upon the Emperors Gratian and Theodosius I, and to whom belongs thanks for the final triumph of Holy Church in the Roman Empire, was at that time the most restless and most energetic fighter against the "Synagogue of Satan". Upon different occasions he condemned the Jews and attempted to prevent them gaining control of the Roman Empire. It was also his heart's wish to prevent them being successful in destroying Holy Church; above all when the usurper Maximus temporarily revealed himself to be lord of half the Empire. As Saint Ambrose himself provides evidence, Maximus was a Jew and had attained his crowning as Emperor of Rome by murdering the devout Catholic Gratian.

As was to be expected, Maximus supported anew the Jews and pagans who gathered around him. However, he was fortunately defeated by Theodosius in the year 378, as a result of which the hope of the Jews of this time gaining control of the Imperium of the Caesars vanished.

In order to form an idea of the anti-Jewish zeal and Catholic saintliness that formed the quintessence of Saint Ambrose, we will again allow Graetz, the official and classical historian of Jewry, who enjoys so much prestige and authority with the Hebrews, to speak. With dismay he confirms:

"Ambrose of Milan was a violent official, who had not the slightest inkling of theology. Particularly for this reason, because he was notorious within the Church as violent, he was elevated to the rank of Bishop... On a certain occasion, when the Christians of Rome had set on fire a synagogue and the usurper Maximus had ordered that the Senate should rebuild it at state expense, Ambrose called him a Jew. When the Bishop of Callinicus in North Mesopotamia had caused a synagogue there to be burned by monks, Theodosius commanded that it should be erected at his expense, and punished those who had participated in this deed (388). Ambrose broke out into a violent rage over this and, in the letter he sent to the Emperor upon the occasion, used the harshest and most provocative turns of phrase, so that the Monarch saw himself obliged to rescind the command. Ambrose accused the Jews of disregarding and deriding the Roman Laws. In connection with this he abused them by saying that they might not provide either Emperors or governors from their ranks; that they were refused admittance to the army or Senate and they did not even possess the right to sit at table with nobility. The Jews were thus only there to pay high taxes."[204]

Apart from other extremely interesting things, the outstanding Israelite Graetz tells us something which awakens our main interest, namely that Saint Ambrose "on account of his reputation for being violent", was elevated to the dignity of Bishop. Graetz himself confirms his violence with details which prove his energy in combating Jewry. As we will later expressly prove, the honorary offices of the Church during the times of the apogee of Holy Church, as with those in the times of Saint Ambrose, were entrusted to those who defended the Church most zealously and energetically, especially against its principal enemy, Jewry. This gives an exact explanation for the glorious period of Catholicism in such times. A combative hierarchy, which is conscious of the enemy on the other side, guarantees the possibilities of triumph, whilst a largely non-combative hierarchy, which does not recognise the true danger, coincides exactly with the epochs of weakness and decline of Holy Church. The epochs of Saint Athanasius and the Arianist triumphs coincide with the unmistakeable fact that the honorary Church offices were bought by indifferent representatives and even by members of the "Fifth Column". The true defenders of the Church were at that time pressed to the wall, disregarded and even persecuted. So it occurred with Athanasius, the great Father of the Church, and with all the bishops and clergy who followed him.

The same occurs in many places in our time. A great number of clergy and religious dignitaries, who have stood out through their adherence to Christ and their energy in the defence of Holy Church, see themselves humiliated and even persecuted through other clerics who provide Communism and Freemasonry with every assistance. Those clergy, who serve the interests of Jewry, strive to purchase the offices of bishops and

---

[204] Graetz, op. cit., p. 614.

cardinals when these become vacant, in identical manner as their predecessors in the time of Arius.

This concealed manoeuvre has made possible the Freemasonic and Communist triumphs, so that it already seems as if no one can any longer stop them.

By means of these deceptive tactics, of slandering the good and pressing them to the wall, in order to purchase the honorary Church offices for the wicked, which fortunately has not been successful in many places, although in others far more so, the "Fifth Column" has been able to bring under its control in recent years many positions, which in fact form a minority within the clergy of Holy Church, but have a decisive influence. They form the principal cause why in some lands a more or less considerable part of the Catholic clergy has promoted the revolutionary Freemasonic or Communist movements. As a result the defence of Catholic governments has been completely crippled, or at least the good patriots frustrated, by being robbed of the support of great sectors of Catholicism and being unconsciously driven into the Freemasonic or Communist revolts.

The most recent case of Cuba, in America, speaks volumes in this respect and should be for all the occasion of a deep reaching study and investigation, since it represents a typical example. The Communist and persecutor of the Church, Fidel Castro, was, when he was about to suffer shipwreck, protected by Catholic bishops, and his revolutionary movement was supported by the clerics and bishops with an enthusiasm and zeal which would have been worthy of a better cause. It was this circumstance that in the first place motivated the deeply orthodox Cuban people to commit itself unreservedly to the cause of the Communist leader. Thus the latter carried off a triumph, whose desolating result we all know.

It is understandable that Saint Ambrose, Bishop of Milan and a great Church leader in his time, was dismayed that Theodosius allowed the Jews to overstep the laws of Rome, which blocked admission for them to the Senate as well as allowing them no admittance to the army and to government positions; for he was conscious of the great harm which they could cause Christianity and the Empire, if they gained control of the government. A further important fact must be mentioned. The Jews were the initiators and propagandists of the Arian heresy, to which sect many Germanic barbarians from the frontier regions also belonged, of whom the majority, which was an open secret, were inspired by the wish to attack and conquer the Roman Empire. If Saint John Chrysostom had lived in our times, then undoubtedly the Jews and their satellites within Christianity would have thrown against them the accusation of being Nazis and disciples of Hitler, just as they do the same with all zealous Catholics who at present wish to protect the Church from the Jewish threat. The Jew Graetz says, as we have already quoted elsewhere, in reference to the role which both played in that period of open struggle of Holy Church against the Jews:

"The chief fanatics against the Jews in that time were John Chrysostom of Antioch and Ambrose of Milan, who attacked the Jews with most extreme violence."[205]

Naturally, before Holy Church was able to carry through its final triumph over the "Synagogue of Satan" and Arianism, it had to withstand such critical moments as in our days. We are given vivid details of this in the letter which was signed by thirty-three of the most well-known bishops. Among these are found the first president of the Ecumenical Council of Constantinople, Saint Meletius of Antioch; the great Church Father Saint Gregory Nazianzen, who presided over the said Ecumenical Council after the death of Meletius; Saint Basil, likewise Father of the Church; and other outstanding personages through their reputation and their holiness. From this letter we quote word for word the following paragraphs:

"The dogmas of religion are distorted and the laws of the Church are turned upside down. The ambition of those who do not fear the Lord reaches out for the honorary offices of the Church, and the office of bishop is offered as prize for the most subtle infamy and in fact with such craft that he who utters the gravest blasphemies is held to be most capable of all for leading the people as bishop. The seriousness of the bishop's office has been lost.

"There is a lack of shepherds, who conscientiously guard the flock of the Lord. The property of the poor is permanently used by the ambitious for their own advantage and used for gifts to aliens. The true following of the Canon has come into forgetfulness... concerning all this the unbelievers laugh, and those weak in faith hesitate; the faith itself has become doubted. Uncertainty has poured itself over souls; for those who

---

[205] Graetz, Ibid.

mocked the word of God in their maliciousness, reflect the true state of affairs, and the voice of the devout is silent."[206]

What finds expression by the aforementioned bishops in this memorable letter can in fact be applied to what occurs at present in some dioceses, even if fortunately not in all. However, there are dioceses, above all such in which the "Fifth Column" predominates, in which the Semitophilic Prelates are at work in perceptible alliance with Freemasonry and Communism to secure themselves in boldest manner the bishop's office, exactly as the Saints quoted reveal. They interfere in the internal affairs of other dioceses, in which devout bishops officiate, and only await their death in order to stretch out their feelers in Rome. By means of deceptive manoeuvres and misrepresentations they strive to buy the successors of the vacant dioceses and in fact not only for the most capable, but for the accomplices of the "Fifth Column". In such a way they trample upon the right of those, who on grounds of their virtue and services should occupy bishop's chairs.

But in that epoch these Saints, who have now been canonised by the Church, managed to save the situation. If they also on their side revealed unnecessary caution and hesitancy, then they nevertheless resolutely opposed the powers of evil and unmasked them publicly. They also pilloried all evil conditions, as we clearly recognise by means of the letter quoted, because as these saintly Church Fathers say, the silence of the Good makes possible the victory of the Evil. As a result of such clear as well as energetic conduct, Holy Church was able to carry off the triumph over Jewry, paganism, Arianism and other heresies.

However, the Saints who saved Catholicism in such different times, had to pass along a painful path of suffering; and in fact not only from the side of Jewry, against which they fought with such resolution, but also from the side of those within the clergy, who consciously or unconsciously served the interests of the Jews. We have already seen that Saint Athanasius was persecuted by the bishops adhering to the heresy of the Jew Arius, as also by the Emperors standing under the heretical influence. Even two Church Councils did not call a halt to this, but these that had actually been summoned for the salvation of Catholicism, transformed themselves, once they were controlled by the Arians and turned against the Orthodoxy, into veritable heretical Councils.

---

[206] St. Basil and St. Gregory Nazianzen: Church Fathers, Letter published in works of John Chrysostom. Library of Christian authors. La Editorial Catolica. S.A. Introduction, p. 7.

And in order to complete the picture, which shows how those Saints had to suffer, who like Saint Chrysostom opposed Jewry and heresy with energy and resolution, we take over literally what the biographers of the Saints mentioned say. As sources we quote Chrysostom himself as well as the Catholic historians John Cassian, Martirius and others:

"What is most astonishing and incomprehensible for us, as for John Cassian and the obscure eulogist of the 7th century, Martirius, is, that he (Saint John Chrysostom) was not banished or finally condemned to death by a governor of Decius or Diocletian, but by a band of ambitious and ill-willed bishops…

"On the other side there were bishops who, while whispering to the weak Arcadius and the raving Eudoxia that John was guilty of insulting their majesty, which meant nothing less than demanding his head, protested that they could not intervene and that the Emperor would in fact know what was to be done in such a case, for which naturally no small punishment existed. And why should one not recall the terrible scenes at Caesarea in Cappadocia, when the Saint, coming from distant Cocusus, trod the soil there. Tired, exhausted and delirious, with high fever, he was almost torn to pieces by a horde, as he called them himself, of wild monks who were incited by the Bishop. And what was worse, they belonged to the protective troop, which should have accompanied the poor banished Saint. And while the people wept and as a result showed that it was better that its shepherds, the envy of the local Bishop mercilessly pursued the outlawed Saint into his refuge, where the magnanimous neighbourly love of a noble woman granted him a roof. And they compelled him to continue his march on a night without moonlight over treacherous mountain paths."[207]

These were the men, who made Christianity great; who allowed Holy Church to triumph, and saved them from the cunning of their outer and inner foes. At present the same type of Catholics, clergy and laymen, are needed in order to save Christianity and the whole of mankind, who are threatened by Communism, Freemasonry and the Synagogue of Satan which has instigated the whole conspiracy.

The high dignitaries of the Church and the worldly political leaders, who fight for the salvation of Catholicism under such difficult conditions, must be prepared to suffer not only all kinds of attacks from the side of

---

[207] *Sources Chrétiennes*, Volume 13, p. 142 and FF, quoted as works of John Chrysostom, Library of Christian authors. Editorial Catolica. SA. Madrid, 1958.

the revolutionary forces of Jewry, but also from the side of the descendants of Judas Iscariot. The latter play within the clergy in this or that form the cards of the forces of Satan; and it is they, who through their high and arrogantly usurped struggle within Holy Church can instigate the most violent, destructive and painful attacks against those who fight for the defence of a Catholicism and their gravely threatened nations. May the Lord God provide faith, resolution and strength to them who, in imitation of Christ, take up the cross in order to follow Him in this decisive hour for the fate of the world.

CHAPTER EIGHT

SAINT CYRIL OF ALEXANDRIA CONQUERS NESTOR AND EXPELS THE JEWS

After the death of Theodosius I, his sons Honorius and Arcadius inherited the throne of the already divided Empire; the first in the West and the second in the East. Their policy towards the Jewish enemy was weak, since they completely disregarded the norms of an energetic struggle, such as had been preached by Saint John Chrysostom and by Saint Ambrose. In addition, Arcadius in the East surrounded himself with corrupt advisors, who sold their protection to the Jews Rufinus and Eutropius, who, according to Graetz, "showed the Jews most extreme favour". Rufinus was avaricious, and the Jews had already discovered the magic power of gold in order to thaw out the most hardened hearts. As a result various laws favouring the Jews were announced. Among these laws is found that which had already been put in force again through Constantius and confirmed, concerning which Graetz asserts:

"The Patriarchs and likewise all Synagogue servants were placed equal to the Christian clergy, by their being freed from the heavy burden of the magistracy."[208]

What the renowned Jewish historian stresses here, is in fact of the highest importance; for it shows that the Jews had already discovered the power of gold, in order to bribe the Christian and pagan leaders. In reality they had already found this out much earlier, as the example of the Jew Simon the Magician proves, who even wished to bribe Saint Peter; or that of the Jewish superintendents, who were successful in buying one of the Twelve Apostles, that he might betray Jesus. In the course of history the Jews have systematically used the power of gold in order to buy political and religious leaders and to maintain a policy favourable to Jewry. The

---

[208] Graetz, op. cit. Vol. II, pp. 615-616.

successors of Judas Iscariot have caused the Church and mankind grave harm by means of this method, and they are to a great part guilty of the misfortune which stands before our door.

The protection in the East and tolerance in the West allowed the Jews to collect sufficient strength, which was extremely dangerous, if one takes into consideration that they were the sworn enemies of the Church and of the Empire. Even in our times Jewish evidence has been handed down to us, which provides us with information about the hatred that the Jews fostered against ancient Rome.

In the east of the Empire Theodosius II, the successor of Arcadius, was attentive to the danger at the correct time and seized upon a series of measures, in order to counteract them and to ward off the Jewish danger in a resolute manner. However, the Jewish historians always record these defensive measures of the Christian states as persecutions which were unleashed through the fanaticism and the anti-Jewish tendency of the Catholic clergy.

The Jew Graetz speaks about these events as follows:

"The Middle Ages began for Jewry with Theodosius II (408-450), a very talented Emperor, but guided by monks, and whose weakness granted freedom from punishment to the fanatical zeal of some bishops and fostered cruelty. Edicts of this Emperor forbade the Jews to build new synagogues, to celebrate on Thursdays the synagogue service communally for Jews and Christians, and to keep Christian slaves. In addition they contained some other bans of lesser importance. Under this Emperor the Patriarchy finally fell."[209]

The Patriarchy was an institution which for a long time performed the representation of Jewry in the Roman Empire and in many other places; it had its seat in Jerusalem.

What Graetz does not mention is the reason the Catholic clergy had for reacting in such a violent manner against the Jews. As in all cases, so here also, the Jewish historians give information concerning the measures that Holy Church or the Catholic monarchs entered upon against them; however, they never mention the occasions the Jews gave to provoke these reactions.

---

[209] Graetz, Ibid.

In the struggle of the Church against Jewry of that time one must mention the decisive appearance of Saint Cyril of Alexandria. He was the leading spirit in the defence of Catholicism against a new heresy which was led by Nestor and which was on the point of dividing the Church in exactly the same way as the Arian heresy had done.

Saint Cyril, the Patriarch of Alexandria, plays at these moments the same role against Nestorianism which previously the great Church Father, Athanasius, had taken up in the struggle against Arianism. Like the latter, Saint Cyril applied himself actively in the defence against Jewry, by his condemning the Jews upon different occasions and combating all their false machinations.

The heresy of Nestor divided the Episcopate, since various bishops made common cause with the heretical patriarchs. After along drawn-out struggle, however, Saint Cyril was successful in obtaining the condemnation of Nestor from his Holiness the Pope. At the Third Ecumenical Council which took place later at Ephesus, the heretical bishops were fully defeated and Catholicism triumphed. The spirit of the Council in question was naturally Saint Cyril of Alexandria, who had to fight further against the remnants of the heresy, until he could destroy them.

In order to obtain knowledge of the conduct of Saint Cyril towards the Jews, let us refer to the words of the Jewish historian Graetz, which repeat faithfully the feelings of Jews towards the Fathers and Saints of the Church:

"During the rulership of Theodosius in the East and Honorius in the West, the Bishop of Alexandria, Cyril, who was remarkable for his quarrelsomeness, his violence and his impetuosity, tolerated the bad treatment of the Jews and expelled them from the city. He aroused the Christian rabble and incited them against the Jews. His excessive fanaticism called his attention to the synagogues, of which he seized possession in the name of Christianity. He drove the Jewish inhabitants half-naked out of the city, which had previously served them as home. Without his being able to be hindered, Cyril gave their property free for plundering by the mob, as indeed the latter always thirsts for enrichment."[210]

---

[210] Graetz, Works, Volume II, pp. 618-619.

In its turn, the "Jewish-Castilian Encyclopaedia" already quoted states under the word Cyril in this reference:

"Cyril (Saint) of Alexandria, Patriarch (376-444). Was practically the master of Alexandria, from whence he drove out the non-Christian populace. In the year 415 he commanded the expulsion of the Jews, in spite of the protests of the Imperial Prefect, Orestes."[211]

All Church histories agree with one accord, that, although Saint Cyril had a fighting nature, he nevertheless possessed a moderate and conciliatory nature. He was, in the complete meaning of the word, an absolutely virtuous man and therefore deserved to be canonised.

What the Jewish historians who, like Graetz or the official encyclopaedists of Jewry, stand in such high regard with the Jews, say about all those who dare to fight against the destructive activity of the Israelites, provides an idea to what degree they degrade and pollute the memory even of the most magnificent Saints of the Church. That Saint Cyril drove the Jews half-naked out of Alexandria and is said to have left their goods to the mob for plundering, sounds improbable for all those who know the history of this Saint well. The fact was that Alexandria had long been transformed into the principal centre of the Jewish conspiracy against Holy Church and the Empire. This city was the principal centre of Jewish Gnosticism, and from there radiated every kind of subversive idea directed against the existing order. It cannot therefore be remarkable that Saint Cyril, who was conscious of the Jewish threat, resolved to extirpate this cancerous tumour. So he expelled the Jews from the city, just as after him in other lands excellent defenders of Christianity have had to do.

If one knows the events as well as the blameless leadership of the Saint, then it appears more credible that he made all necessary provisions that this expulsion should take place under humane conditions; and that he disapproved of every excess and abuse which was committed by the masses on grounds of Jewish perfidy.

The Jewish historian describes further the bloody episodes in the struggle conducted by Saint Cyril and the Christians against the Jews. Among other things Graetz asserts:

---

[211] Jewish-Spanish Encyclopaedia, Edition mentioned, Volume II, p. 30.

"The Prefect Orestes, who was very concerned at the barbaric treatment of the Jews, lacked the power to protect them. He merely pulled himself together to lay complaint against the Bishop. However, Cyril won the case before the court of Constantinople. What now occurred after the expulsion of the Jews in Alexandria, gives a proof of how great the fanaticism of this Bishop was. Not far from the city there was a mountain, which was called Mount Nitra, where lived an order of monks whose desire to acquire the crown of martyrdom had transformed them into a pack of wild beasts. Goaded by Cyril, these monks threw themselves upon Orestes and stoned him as punishment for his not having approved the expulsion of the Jews; only when they had half killed him did they leave off attacking him. The same fanatical band cut up into pieces the body of the celebrated philosopher Hypatia, who had astonished the world through his deep knowledge, his eloquence and his purity."[212]

The Catholic clergy at this time, who certainly knew what importance the terrible Jewish problem had, and who possessed an exhaustive knowledge of the Jewish conspiracy against the Church and the Empire, threw themselves without hesitation into the fight in order, as good shepherds, to defend their sheep against the cunning of the wolf. But the Jews always exaggerate in their history books what had occurred by inserting hair-raising passages with the aim of discrediting Catholicism and the Saints defending the Church.

As we have seen in addition, all these stories described in exaggerated and striking terms, serve to educate the Jewish youth and to inoculate into them from birth onwards a satanic hatred towards the Church and its clergy. Thus they breed an unquenchable lust for revenge, which expresses itself at the first opportunity offered in the burning down of monasteries, destruction of Churches, cruel slaughtering of priests and all kinds of violence against the Christians.

It is beyond doubt that, if Cyril had lived in our time, then he would not only have been condemned on account of Antisemitism, but he would also have been abused of being a war criminal, Nazi and the like.

The Jews believe that they possess the right to agitate against the peoples, to cause them to bleed in civil wars and to commit every kind of crime and infamy, without receiving the deserved punishment for this. But if anyone restrains them with the energy of such as Saint Cyril and punishes their excesses in a just manner, then they heap imprecations on

---

[212] Graetz, op. cit., Volume II, p. 619.

him and attempt to lower his respect before men. Not even after death do they pardon him, as the example of this excellent Saint of the Catholic Church teaches us.

It is interesting to read the description by Graetz of how the Israelites at that time celebrated the feast of Purim of Queen Esther:

"On this day the Jews were accustomed, in the midst of the joyous feast, to hang up on a stage the figure of Haman, their arch-enemy, and his gibbet, which, after their burning of him took on accidentally or intentionally the form of a cross. Naturally, the Christians complained that their religion was being profaned, and Emperor Theodosius II commanded the provincial governor to bring about a cessation of this activity. In spite of severe punishments threatened for this, it was nevertheless not successful in preventing such acts. Upon one occasion this carnival entertainment, as it is reported, had terrible consequences. The Jews of Inmestar, a small place in Syria, which is situated between Antioch and Chalcis, had erected one of these gallows for Haman. The Christians at once accused them of having hanged a Christian child, crucifying him on it and whipping him to death. The Emperor gave the command, in the year 415, to punish those responsible."[213]

This, the highly renowned, authorised Israelite historian Graetz, standing in such high regard with the Jews, calls enjoyment and carnival entertainment!

One can easily imagine the alarm that was caused by such kind of Jewish conduct among the Christians. Just as at present in the Soviet Union and other Communist lands, the sacrifices, blasphemies and political assassinations committed by Communist Jews would provoke the Christians there, had they not been enslaved and made incapable of defending themselves.

In contrast to the temples of other religions, the synagogues do not restrict themselves to holding religious services; they are far more assembly places, in order to discuss and approve political decisions. They are the chief centres of the Jewish conspiracy, from whence every kind of measures take their outlet, which aim at the conquest of peoples which with goodwill grant them hospitality. In these measures the exerting of economic pressure is also planned, in order to rob the Christians and Gentiles of their wealth, which the Jews believe belongs to them by divine

---

[213] Graetz, Ibid, Volume II, pp. 620-621.

right. How right the great Church Father John Chrysostom was to call the synagogues "infamous exhibitions, thieves' dens and even worse." The aforementioned Israelite historian does not dare to mention this. It is therefore understandable that the Catholic clergy at that time, conscious of the danger that they represented for Christianity and the Empire, accordingly strove to close down those centres of conspiracy and infamy.

Besides the measures already referred to, which the clergy introduced for this purpose, it is worth mentioning what occurred on the island of Minorca, which at that time was a Roman possession, and of which Graetz says, that:

"Severus, the Bishop there, set on fire the synagogues on the island and drove the Jews through the streets with blows, as a result of which he was successful in leading many of them to Christianity."[214]

This last mentioned measure was a grave error, since the conversions, as the renowned Israelite historian Cecil Roth elaborates, were pretended, and the Jews secretly adhered to their old religion. Thus the number of underground Jews was increased, who certainly practised the Christian religion outwardly, but in truth formed the Jewish "Fifth Column" in the bosom of Holy Church. It was the cause of most heresies, to which it provided aid and stimulation.

A further, very holy opponent of the Jews was at that time the famous ascetic and Saint Simon Estilita (Simon Stylites), wh0, 0n account of the rigorous penances he observed during all his life, was very well known. Hanging for several years on a pillar, he mortified himself and did penance out of love of God. His example and his preachings had the consequence that several nomad tribes originating from Arabia confessed to Christianity. On account of his saintliness he stood in high esteem with Emperor Theodosius II, with whom he always made intercession for all those persecuted. In the controversies between the Catholic Church and the heretics he made his influence felt in favour of orthodoxy.

How great must have been the malice of the Jews and the intrigues of their synagogues, if this man, who represented the incarnation of neighbourly love and was in the extreme a mediator and protector of the persecuted, who was canonised by the Church as a saint and was famed on account of his penances as well as representing a model for youth, made an exception in his peaceful life concerning Judaism and intervened

---

[214] Graetz, Ibid.

energetically in the decisive struggle unleashed against the "Synagogue of Satan"!

In connection with this Saint, Graetz informs us that, when the Christians of Antioch took away their synagogues from the Jews, which occurred as requital on account of the Christian child killed by the Jews at Inmestar at the feast of Purim, the Prefect of Syria described to the Emperor this expropriation of the synagogues in such an impressive manner that he succeeded in getting Theodosius II, despite his "priestly fanaticism", to order the inhabitants of Antioch to return the same, which greatly vexed Saint Simon Stylites.

On this matter the noted Jewish historian Graetz expresses himself as follows:

"This decision was, however, disputed by Simon Stylites, who led the life of a rigorous asceticism in a kind of stall not far from Antioch. From the top of his pillar he had rejected the world; however, his hatred of the Jews was sufficient to move him to interfere in earthly things. Scarcely had he received knowledge of the command of Theodosius relating to the return of the looted synagogues, than he immediately addressed an arrogant letter to the Emperor, in which he informed him that he recognised God alone, and no other, as Lord and Emperor, and begged him to lift the Edict. Theodosius could offer no resistance to such intimidation. In the year 423 he revoked his command and even displaced the Syrian Prefect, who had raised his voice in favour of the Jews."[215]

What has been elaborated in the last chapters, gives us proof of the capability of the clergy and of the Saints of the Church, who made possible the triumph of Christianity in the face of the deadly enemies of the Church and mankind. The present Ecumenical Council of Vatican II will therefore offer a splendid opportunity for the success of the present clergy in moving at the same heights as those who in those times were capable of saving Holy Church in the midst of so many catastrophes, and who allowed it to triumph in the face of so many enemies. This is extremely urgent, since in fact the Communist danger, which threatens to drag everything with it, can only be banished if and when the clergy of Holy Church and the temporal leaders attain that moral fighting courage and that spirit of sacrifice which inspired the Catholic hierarchies during the first centuries of Christianity. If one does not react energetically in this sense, then it is completely possible that God may punish us with the

---

[215] Graetz, Ibid, Volume II.

worldwide triumph of Communism and the resultant catastrophe for Christianity.

SAINT AUGUSTINE, SAINT JEROME AND OTHER CHURCH FATHERS CONDEMN THE JEWS

Saint Jerome, the great Church Father, wished to study the Bible in its original sources and therefore undertook seriously to acquire a deep knowledge of the Hebrew language. So he came into contact with such outstanding Jews as Bar Canina; but in spite of the personal friendship that the Saint had with distinguished Hebrews, his conduct towards Jewry rested upon complete rejection.

One can say the same of the most illustrious Church Father and Bishop of Hippo, Saint Augustine.

Our information will be taken from the texts of Jewish authors of undisputed authority in Jewish circles, so that there is no risk of these sources being branded antisemitic. With reference to Saint Jerome and Saint Augustine, the Israelite historian Graetz expressly states the following (initially referring to Saint Jerome):

"After his enemies had accused him on grounds of his Judaic studies of being infected with heresy, Jerome proved to them his orthodoxy, by affirming his hatred for the Jews. 'If I had to give expression to my contempt for individuals and the nation, I would detest the Jews with a hatred difficult to put into words.' But Jerome was not the only one who thought thus. His views were shared by a younger contemporary, the Church Father Augustine. This confession of belief with regard to hatred towards the Jews was not the opinion of a definite author but an oracle for the whole of Christianity, which hastily accepted the writings of the Church Fathers, who were revered as Saints. In later times this mode of thought led to that practice by kings who invented instruments of torture for the Jews and erected the stake in order to burn them."[216]

Here Graetz gives a resumé of the policy that was followed by Holy Church and Catholicism more than a thousand years ago. What he is naturally silent about is what the grounds were that compelled the Church,

---

[216] Graetz, op. cit., Volume II, pp. 625-626.

its more outstanding Saints, the Church Fathers, Popes and Councils, to take refuge in this kind of defence.

Whoever has experienced the slaughtering of Christians and the desecrations of the Church that have been carried out by pagans and heretics instigated by the Jews; whoever has been eyewitness of the crimes committed by the Jews themselves; and as we know of the crimes, which have been perpetrated by the Israelites in Soviet Russia and the Communist lands — it is not difficult for us to imagine, that in the face of such an extremely dangerous and criminal foe, against a foe who threatens humanity as well as religion, and both Holy Church as well as other civilised institutions, the right of self-defence exists, and that one seizes upon such extraordinary measures as the infamy of the enemy in fact demands.

CHAPTER NINE

THE BARBARIAN INVASION:
A TRIUMPH OF THE ARIAN JEWS

The renowned Jewish historian Narcisse Leven in his work "Fifty Years of History: The Universal Jewish Alliance" – to which we will refer later in more depth – points out among other things that, when the Church triumphed in the Roman Empire and was transformed into the official religion, "it guided the forces of the Empire against the Jews", and that it persecuted the Jews who openly confessed their religion as well as those who had passed over to Christianity through baptism. He says further:

"Honorary rights (*jus honorum*) were taken from them, and even the baptised were excluded from the higher offices and a military career. Upon pain of death they were forbidden to carry on trade with Christians and town slaves, even if the latter were pagans... Justinian went so far as to not recognise the evidence of Jews against Christians as proof in the courts of law." In conclusion the Israelite historian says that these orders were summarised "in the Codices of Theodosius II and Justinian, but that they lost their power with the barbarian invasion. The East Empire preserved and renewed them... in the Western Empire the barbarian invasion halted the persecution."[217]

The interesting part about the legislation enacted in Catholic Rome lies in the fact that the hierarchies of the Empire and of Holy Church were in harmony, to exclude not only the declared Jews, but also those baptised, from the higher offices and a military career. This reveals that the Jews and their descendants who had gone over to Christianity were excluded from leading positions of state and the army despite their baptism.

---

[217] N. Leven, *Cinquante ans D'Histoire Israelite Universelle.* [1860-1910]. Paris 1911, Volume I, pp. 3-4.

The grounds for such measures become evident, if one takes into consideration that other authorised Jewish historians like Graetz and Cecil Roth openly admit that the conversions of the Hebrews to Christianity were feigned. Although they confessed outwardly to the said religion, they were secretly just as much Jews as before; and among these false Christians the secret cult of Judaism was passed on by father to son, although the latter were baptised and outwardly lived like Christians.

On the basis of such facts it is understandable that the Imperial authorities, who certainly knew that the conversion of the Jews was in almost all cases only a farce and baptism the same, included in their measures the descendants of Jews, even if they had received water of baptism. These defensive measures without doubt formed a distant forerunner of the famous laws or statutes for ethnic purity, by means of which in some lands Catholics of Jewish origin were removed from the leading positions of the State and honorary offices of the Holy Catholic Church. These laws for ethnic purity were approved by Popes Paul III, Paul IV and others. These were approved as means of preventing the false Christians, who were secretly Jews, from infiltrating further into the clergy. This means that these false Christians were regarded as a Jewish "Fifth Column" introduced into the bosom of the Church, the principal cause of the triumph of heresy and subsequently of the Freemasonic and Communist revolutions, as we shall when the opportunity presents itself.

The position of the Jews on the eve of the decline of the Roman Western Empire is described to us by the Israelite Graetz as follows:

"The fanaticism of Theodosius II was also alive in the Emperor of the Western Empire, Honorius and his absurd laws. Both placed the Jews in that abnormal position in which the then developing, new Germanic states found them. It was already no longer permitted the Jews, as was previously the case, to occupy public offices or to obtain military ranks."[218]

The historian and great friend of the Jews, José Amador de los Rios, says, in commenting upon the situation of the Jews in the Empire after the Illiberian Council:

"The situation that the Fathers of the Illiberian Council created by virtue of such legal ideas, could not be more awkward and distressing for the sons of Israel. Inspired without doubt by the same spirit that is reported to us at the end of that century, as the 'Lyre of Prudence' reveals,

---

[218] Graetz, Ibid, Vol. II, p. 622.

these Church Fathers gave a striking example of the regrettable animosity which that host of unfortunate Jewish believers all over the world encounters, upon whose shoulders rests the terrible accusation of deicide."[219]

Such Jewish and Semitophilic historians lament the situation of the Jews in the last days of the Roman world. However, they are careful not to mention the true reasons which placed them in that situation. It is worthy of note that Catholicism attained its complete triumph in the Empire exactly at that time when the Jewish beast was enchained, a highly significant coincidence.

Therefore the invasion of the Teutonic Arians was for the Jews a great triumph, albeit it only a temporary one.

The Northern Teutonic tribes, standing under the influence of the Arian sects, in fact pursued a policy of friendship and alliance with the Israelites, which was opposed to that observed by the triumphant Catholics in the Roman Empire.

On the basis of this circumstance, the situation of the Jews and Catholics in the Western Empire altered with the invasion of the barbarians into the Western Empire. The former clambered once more upon the ladder of power and of influence, while the Catholics, especially in some districts, had to suffer the cruellest persecutions.

Some assure us that the Jews encouraged the Teutonic leaders, to fall upon the Empire, and that they were even helpful to them with the carrying out of the conquest. We have had no time to set up an exact investigation concerning this point, but in the "Jewish-Castilian Encyclopaedia" we find something very interesting. Under the reference word "Arianism", which refers to the good treatment of the Jews on the part of the Arian intruders, the following is stated:

"As a consequence of the tolerant treatment shown them by the invaders, the Hebrews declared their solidarity with them (the Arians) in their wars against the Catholic monarchies. Thus they took an active part

---

[219] José Amador de los Rios, *History of the Jews in Spain and Portugal*, Madrid, 1875, Vol. I, p. 75.

in the defence of Arles (508) against Clovis, the king of the Franks, and in that of Naples (537) against Justinian."[220]

The Jewish historian, Graetz, remarks in addition that: "In Italy, since the time of the Republic, the existence is known of Jews, who enjoyed full political rights until these were taken away from them by the Christian Emperors. They (the Jews) probably viewed the fall of Rome with great satisfaction and were delighted when they saw that the city, which had guided the fates of the world, was transformed into the booty of the barbarians and subject to the derision of the whole world."[221]

It is evident that the Jews are not willing to admit that they bear a great part of the guilt for the destruction of the Roman Empire and for the catastrophe that this signified for civilisation. But the pleasure they felt at the fall of Rome, and the general confirmation that they felt a solidarity with the Arian barbarians "in their wars against the Catholic monarchies", reminds us that the principal Catholic monarchy against which the Teutonic disciples of Arius fought was in fact the Roman Empire of the West.

In order to illuminate the historical truth and define the responsibilities, one must strive to gain a profile of this and at the same time take into consideration that the destruction of the then prevailing order and its replacement by one that favoured them suited no one more than the Jews.

Almost all Teutonic tribes penetrating into the Empire were Arian. Among the few exceptions stand out the Franks, who embraced Christianity from the beginning.

Speaking of the political change that took place with the invasions of the barbarians, the Philosemite J. Amador de los Rios says the following in relation to the Iberian peninsula:

"It was in this way that, when Arian tolerance had made the way free to a hitherto unknown prosperity the Israelite community on Iberian soil became stronger during the first epochs of the Visigoth rule. Thanks to their intelligence and their wealth they attained no less favour and

---

[220] Jewish-Spanish Encyclopaedia. Edit. mentioned. Vol. I, Word "Arianism".
[221] Graetz, Ibid, Volume III, p. 27.

importance and came to enjoy the exercise of public offices, which provided Jewry with an usual regard within the Republic."[222]

In his turn, the Jewish historian Cecil Roth refers to the fact, that the Arian Visigoths favoured the Jews, in contrast to the Catholics, whom they persecuted.[223]

The Jewish historian Graetz gives us an example which proves what good conditions the Jews enjoyed in the lands conquered by the Nordic Arians, in contrast to that under which they lived in the Catholic kingdoms. He relates to us at first that, in the then Catholic Byzantine Empire, one of the Emperors drove the Jews out of their synagogue and converted it into the Church of "The Mother of God", and that in the midst of such persecutions the Jews had then to drag the sacred vessels of the Temple of Solomon from one place to another, until they were conveyed to Carthage, which was then under the rule of the Arian Vandals. Graetz then continues:

"They remained there almost a century, and it was with great sorrow that the Jews of the Byzantine capital witnessed their translation to Constantinople by the conqueror of the Vandal kingdom, Belisarius. With triumphant cries, the Jewish trophies were dragged away together with Gelimer, the Prince of the Vandals and grandson of Genseric, as well as the treasure of the unfortunate monarch."[224]

During the disintegration of the Roman Western Empire by the Arian barbarians, the Jews devoted themselves in great style to the slave trade. In this respect the Jew Graetz affirms that:

"The repeated invasion of the barbaric tribes and the countless wars caused the number of prisoners to rise, and the Jews carried on a lively slave trade, although they were not the only ones to do so."[225]

It is worth noting that the Jews played a main role in the slave trade in the course of history and that in the 17th and 18th centuries they were the principal traders in this disgraceful business. They seized the unfortunate negroes in Africa and mercilessly dragged them away from their

---

[222] J. Amador de los Rios, Ibid, Volume I, p. 79.
[223] Cecil Roth, *History of the Marranos*, pp 15-16.
[224] Graetz, Ibid, Volume III, p. 26.
[225] Graetz, Ibid, Volume II, pp. 28-29.

homesteads, in order to sell them in various parts of the world, especially in America, as slaves.

CHAPTER TEN

CATHOLIC VICTORY

The conquest by the East Roman Empire of great territories controlled by the Arian barbarians, as well as the conversion to Catholicism of all Teutonic princes who previously belonged to the sects of the Jew Arius, once again altered the situation in Europe. With the triumph gained by Catholicism over this heresy there naturally arose a new situation for the Jews, which brought with it the loss of their privileged position and prevented them from further harassing the Christians.

It must be remarked, that Arian control over the immigrant Teutonic tribes was weak, since it fundamentally depended upon the conversion and loyalty of their leaders to the heresy. When the latter were now gained for Catholicism through the restless evangelising labour of Holy Church, Arianism received its death blow. It is hardly surprising that, following all the abuses and excesses committed by the Jews while they were protected by the heresy, its collapse led to a truly anti-Jewish reaction in the lands newly conquered for the Church of Rome.

Even José Amador de los Rios, who was so favourable to the Jews – after mentioning the fact that the Jews in the Arian epoch scaled the government posts and were able to obtain an unusual influence allowing them, contrary to the decision of the Illiberian Council which had been made a dead letter by the Arians, to keep Christian slave girls and concubines – says the following:

"Such esteemed prerogatives, denied to the Spanish-Latin people by the Visigoths, in flat contradiction to the decisions of the Illiberian Council, may have flattered the pride of the descendants of Judah for a while, demonstrating their superiority, but they nevertheless gravely endangered their future when Catholic doctrine arose victorious over the errors of Arius."[226]

On the other hand, the Jews attempted in every manner to prevent the triumph of the Catholic armies. Thus, in the case of the Ostrogoth Empire established in Italy, where the Jews had already begun to have conflicts with Theodoric, we see how, at the threat of an invasion by the Catholic Emperor Justinian, they resolutely stood by their Arian friend, King Theodatus, Theodoric's successor, with tenacity and fanaticism. Later, when the armies of Justinian attacked Naples, the inhabitants of the city divided into two parties, of which one wished for capitulation and the other war. In this case the party resolved upon war was not willing to sacrifice itself for the Ostrogoths, who according to Graetz were hated throughout Italy. And on this point the Jewish historian stresses:

"Only the Jews and two legal scholars, Pastor and Asclepiodotus, who had risen high thanks to the influence of the Ostrogoth kings, opposed the surrender of the city to the Byzantine general. The Jews that were rich and patriotic, offered their lives and their property for the defence of the city. And to dispel any concern about the shortage of provisions, they promised to supply Naples during the siege with every necessity."[227]

Given the extensive nature of this work, it is not possible for us to quote further examples of this kind; but there is no doubt that the Jews everywhere desperately attempted to prevent the triumph of Catholicism over Arianism.

In relation to what occurred after the decisive victory of Holy Church, events in the Visigoth kingdom speak for themselves. It had been the most mighty monarchy that the Arian barbarians had managed to found, it had been regarded as the principal bastion of Arianism, and it had been there, as we have seen, that the Hebrews had succeeded in rising to government posts and gaining such privileged influence.

The Jewish historian Cecil Roth notes that, after the Visigoths had gone over to Catholicism, "they began to show the traditional zeal of neophytes. The Jews immediately suffered the unpleasant consequences of such zeal. When, in the year 589, Reccared came to the throne, ecclesiastical legislation began to be applied to them down to the smallest details. His successors were not so strict, but when Sisebutus ascended the

---

[226] J. Amador de los Rios, Ibid, Volume I, pp. 79-80.
[227] Graetz, Ibid.

throne (612-620), a narrow-minded fanaticism predominated. Perhaps goaded by the Byzantine Emperor Heraclius, he passed an edict in the year 616, in which he commanded all Jews of the kingdom to take baptism under threat of banishment and the loss of all their goods. According to the Catholic chroniclers, ninety thousand embraced the Christian faith."[228]

In the Byzantine Empire, measures were also approved which aimed at converting the Jews to Christianity. The "Jewish-Castilian Encyclopaedia" says that Justinian "… ordered the reading of the 'Torah' (Bible) in Greek, hoping for the conversion of the Jews by this method, and in 532 he declared null and void every testimony made by a Jew against a Christian. This measure was later raised to a law almost everywhere in Christendom, having as its logical foundation the fact that the Jews, feeling themselves justified in lying to Christians and Gentiles, provided such widespread false witness that it would have been puerile to give credit to them. For this reason, any testimony made by a Jew against a Christian was denied judicial validity, as it had been proved in the course of centuries that lies and deception are one of the Jews' most utilized and effective weapons.

All these measures, which the Christian states introduced, in order to achieve the conversion of the Jews, ranging from peaceful persuasion to force, originated from the apostolic fervour of Holy Church, eager to guide unbelievers to the true religion. Simultaneously both Holy Church as well as the Catholic states recognised the vital necessity of putting an end to the "Synagogue of Satan", which was in fact a group of foreigners infiltrated into the Christian states, ever conspiring against both Church and state; it was a permanent danger both for the stability of its institutions as also for the defence of those peoples against their external foes. And this especially as the Jews have always shown themselves quick to betray any country kind enough to offer them hospitality, providing support to foreign invaders and undermining the very heart of the unfortunate nation that offered them shelter, should it suit their selfish interests.

One way of solving such a tremendous problem seemed to be that of eliminating the unwholesome sect of Jewry by converting them to the Christian faith. As a result of their ceasing to be Jews and joining the people in whose lands they lived by incorporation into the Catholic religion, not only would that strange "Fifth Column" disappear, which represents a danger for every nation, but the salvation of their souls would also be attained by faith in our Divine Redeemer. These were the grounds that moved the very Catholic Visigoth king Sisebutus to order the Jews in

---

[228] Cecil Roth, Ibid, p. 16.

his kingdom to receive baptism under pain of banishment and confiscation of their goods. These were the same motives that inspired the no less Christian Byzantine Emperor, Basil I, the Macedonian (867-885), when he compelled the Jews to accept the waters of baptism, offering those who agreed to this demand all kinds of honours and tax exemptions.[229]

Unfortunately all these measures failed, since the Jews, as the Israelite historian Cecil Roth assures us, only feigned the conversions, in order in secret to continue to adhere to the Jewish religion. Because of this, the contingent of the "Fifth Column" within the bosom of Holy Church was vastly augmented.

The Jewish Encyclopaedia says that with the conversion carried out in the times of the Emperor Basil:

"More than a thousand communities saw themselves compelled to accept baptism; however, after the death of the Emperor, they returned to their primitive religion."[230]

The conversion of the Jews in the Visigoth kingdom, which was carried out at the time of Sisebutus to a massive extent, provided no better results. The Jew Cecil Roth says:

"The notorious infidelity of the newly converted as well as their descendants continued to form, up to the Arab attack in the year 711, one of the greatest problems of Visigoth policy."[231]

All measures were also in vain, which were introduced against the unfaithfulness of those converted from Judaism and their descendants. Naturally, these false Christians were subjected to a strict attention on the part of the government offices, which, as the same Jewish historian assures us, went so far as "to separate those suspect from their sons, so as to bring the latter up in an unpoisoned Christian atmosphere. As soon as the watchfulness of the government was relaxed, the recently converted seized the opportunity to return to their original belief."

---

[229] Concerning this compulsory conversion in the Byzantine Empire see: Jewish-Spanish Encyclopaedia, term "Bizantino Imperio".
[230] Jewish-Spanish Encyclopaedia, Volume II, term "Bizantino Imperio".
[231] Cecil Roth, Ibid, p. 16.

Roth ends these observations by concluding that all these occurrences initiated the Marrano tradition on the Iberian peninsula, in other words, the tradition of clandestine Jewry in Christian dress.[232]

The Popes and many Christian kings were alarmed by these insincere converts who were on the point of overwhelming Holy Church, and therefore introduced various measures in order to prevent and prohibit Jews from being forcefully converted. Among others, we can quote those which the "Jewish-Castilian Encyclopaedia" refers to, which says the following in this connection:

"Leo VI the Philosopher (Byzantine Emperor), son of Basil, re-established religious freedom for the purpose of preventing the appearance of false Christians."[233]

Pope Saint Gregory recognised this problem in all its magnitude as well as the extraordinary danger that false converts represented for Holy Church. He therefore passed a definite prohibition of the persecution of the Jews or of compelling them to become converted in any kind of form. The bishops followed these instructions and opposed everything that might signify a compulsory conversion of the Jews, albeit reducing the latter to powerlessness, so that they could not infiltrate and poison Christian society. The Jewish historian Graetz makes an interesting commentary in connection with these measures:

"But the tolerance even of the most liberal bishops had no great significance. They merely abstained from any proselytism that involved threats of banishment or death, because they were convinced that by these means the Church would be populated with false Christians who would curse it in their innermost heart. But they did not hesitate to chain and harass the Jews, nor to place them on the same level as slaves on the social ladder. This kind of behaviour appeared completely justified and pious to almost all representatives of Christianity during the centuries of barbarism."[234]

Here the Jewish historian summarises one of the aspects of the new policy that several Popes of Holy Church were to pursue during the Middle Ages. Convinced of the fact that it was dangerous to compel the Jews to conversion by means of persecution or threats, they strove to

---

[232] Cecil Roth, Ibid, pp. 16-17.
[233] Jewish-Spanish Encyclopaedia. Volume II, term 'Bizantino Imperio".
[234] Graetz, Ibid, Volume III, pp. 25-26.

prevent such enforced conversions. They even declared it as anti-canonical. At the same time they undertook energetic measures against the false converts and their descendants: the false judaizing Christians. Some Popes and kings permitted the Jews to practise their religion openly, treating them tolerantly and even granting them protection against unjust attacks; but this kind of new policy also failed against the malice and perfidy of Jewry, which, far from thanking the goodness of such Popes, did not hesitate to exploit this leniency, in order to plan and prepare every kind of conspiracy against the Church and the State. This stiff-neckedness soon forced the Popes to alter their policy and to try to prevent the unleashed Jewish beast from devastating everything. Thus they attempted to enchain the latter anew, so that the Jews could cause no further harm. This is the true explanation of that which might seem to be a contradictory policy with respect to the Jews, which the various Popes have carried out.

It is therefore understandable that, when it was revealed that the measures of tolerance towards the foe revealed catastrophic results, they recognised the urgent necessity of seizing upon energetic measures to save Christianity from the cunning of the "Synagogue of Satan." Unfortunately, this fluctuation in the policy of the Christian hierarchies was in the long run harmful to Holy Church Christianity.

If they had followed without interruption the energetic action directed against Judaism by the Fathers of the Church as well as by many Popes and Councils, then perhaps in time the threat of Jewish imperialism, which at present threatens to overwhelm everything, would have been banished.

CHAPTER ELEVEN

THE THIRD COUNCIL OF TOLEDO REMOVES
THE JEWS FROM PUBLIC OFFICES

With the conversion of the Visigoth king Reccared from Arianism to Catholicism, the sect of the Jew Arius received a decisive blow, since, as already stated, the Visigoth empire was the bastion of the heresy.

At that time the tragic memories and wounds opened by the bloody persecution unleashed by the Arian Leovigild against the Catholics were still felt. In this persecution the Jews had participated in a cruel way, so that in Gothic Spain there was a widespread resentment of the Catholic people against the congregation of Israel. It is understandable therefore that, after the Visigoth princes had abjured the Arian heresy and adopted Catholicism, a series of corresponding measures were seized upon, in order to command a halt to the dominating expansion of Jewry. The judaeophile historian José Amador de los Rios recognises in this respect that:

"The doors to the public offices stood open to the Hebrews, the occupying of which they had to thank the Arian kings for. Through marriage they could infiltrate into the Christian family, which considerably improved their position and their wealth and in the future secured them no small influence within the state. Made dizzy by their prosperity and their power, they had perhaps taken some part in the last and most painful persecution carried out by the Arians against the Catholics during the reign of Leovigild. The fear of the Toledo Fathers, who knew of the importance of the Catholic triumph and the cause represented by them, was therefore no objectionable and childish suspicion. Inspired by the example of the

Illiberian synod, they set themselves to bridle the Jews, reducing them to impotence against the Christians..."[235]

Among the canons passed by the Third Council of Toledo for this purpose, canon XIV stands out an account of its importance, which states the following concerning the Jews:

"No public offices shall be conferred on them by virtue of which they could impose penalties on Christians."[236]

This statute of the Holy Catholic Church has its complete justification, since the Jews always misuse the government posts that they acquire within peoples who have offered them hospitality, in order to cause the Christians damage in this or that form. It is completely beyond doubt that, if the metropolitans and bishops of the said Toledo Council had lived in our days, they would have been accused of a cruel antisemitism by the "Jewish Fifth Column" which has crept into the Catholic clergy.

The Prelates of the Third Council of Toledo likewise ordained that "if Christians have become polluted with the Jewish rite or circumcision, the former should be reinstated without any kind of reprisal into a position of freedom and in the Christian religion."

The aforementioned historian J. Amador de los Rios, commenting upon other anti-Jewish statutes of the Holy Council, says the following:

"In recommending these repressive measures to Reccared, as a principal point and one of major importance, the Council Fathers were seeking to follow the intentions of the Council of Elvira, denying the Hebrews any alliance and mixing with the Hispanic-Latin race, just as with the Visigothic people previously and for a long time afterwards mixing was not permitted to the peoples ruled by them."[237]

Among the statutes passed by the said Toledo Council were found those that refused the Jews the right to buy Christian slaves. They agree perfectly with the statutes passed by his Holiness Pope Saint Gregory the Great. This Pope not only violently opposed the forcible conversions of

---

[235] J. Amador de los Rios, Ibid, Volume I, p. 82.

[236] Acts of the Third Council of Toledo. Canon XIV, compiled by Juan Tejada y Ramiro, *Collection of laws of all Councils of the Church in Spain and South America*, Madrid, 1859. Volume II.

[237] J. Amador de los Rios, Ibid., Volume I, p. 83.

Jews and any kind of oppression that could force them to convert as false Christians, but decisively forbade them to buy Christian slaves. He also energetically combated every manifestation of clandestine Judaism practised by those who passed themselves off in public as Christians. In this respect, the Jewish historian Graetz quotes a very interesting case; writing about Pope Saint Gregory, he says:

"Having learned that a certain Jew named Nasas had erected an altar in Elijah (probably a well-known synagogue under that name) on the island of Sicily, and that Christians met there to celebrate the divine services (Jewish), Gregory commanded the Prefect Libertinus to tear down the building and to impose corporal punishment on Nasas for this offence. Gregory ruthlessly persecuted the Jews who bought Christian slaves or possessed them. In the Empire of the Franks, where fanaticism had still not taken root, there was no ban forbidding the Jews to take part in the slave trade. Indignant at this, Gregory wrote to King Teodoric (Dietrich) of Burgundy, King Teodobert of Austrasia, and likewise to Queen Brunhilde, whereby he gave expression to his astonishment that they allowed the Jews the possession of Christian slaves. With great zeal he admonished them to alter this evil state and to liberate the true believers from the violence of their foes. The Visigoth King Reccared, who had subjected himself to the Holy See, was flattered by Gregory in such grand style that he promulgated an edict of intolerance."[238]

One sees from this that the measures for restraining the Jews that were approved by the Visigoth Reccared were, according to the Jew Graetz, inspired by no less than Pope Saint Gregory the Great, who attempted for a time in vain to gain the Jews through kindness and tolerance. It is likewise interesting to note that Pope Saint Gregory the Great, whilst rejecting forced conversions, cherished the hope of evangelising the Hebrews by peaceful means. Although he knew that in general the conversions were feigned and insincere, he hoped at least that the children of the *conversos* might be sincerely rooted in Christianity. In this respect our Jewish historian clearly states concerning Saint Gregory:

"However, he was not deceived into thinking that converts obtained in this way were loyal Christians, but he reckoned upon their descendants. 'If we do not gain them, then we will at least gain their sons'."[239]

---

[238] Pope St. Gregory the Great. Quoted by Graetz, Ibid, Volume III, pp. 33-34.
[239] Graetz, Ibid, Volume III, Page 33.

As our writer said, and it is highly worthy of note, even Pope Saint Gregory the Great – of such illustrious memory in the history of the Church – knew that the conversions of the Jews to Christianity were insincere, and what he aimed at with them was to win over their already Christian-educated sons.

Unfortunately, the malice and perfidy of Jewry always causes the most apparently logical calculations to fail. As we have already seen in Chapter II of Part Four, the Jewish historian Cecil Roth confirms that "Marranism" i.e. clandestine Judaism, is characterised by the transmission by parents to children of the secret Jewish religion, hidden under the appearances of a Christianity practised in public by the Marranos. For this reason, the calculations of all the hierarchies of the Church and of the Christian states – based on the idea that even if the conversions are pretended and false, one could nevertheless convert the descendants of the *conversos* into good Christians – have failed lamentably throughout the centuries, as we shall analyse further in good time.

CHAPTER TWELVE

THE FOURTH TOLEDO COUNCIL DECLARES THE BISHOPS AND CLERGY SUPPORTING THE JEWS TO BE BLASPHEMERS AND EXCOMMUNICATES THEM

One of the principal reasons for the slow but constant triumph of Jewish Imperialism in the last nineteen hundred years has been the short memory of Christians as well as pagans, who were always inclined to forget the past, and did not take into consideration that history is the instructor of life. The Jews were always able to gain control of the government offices and obtain great influence within Christian society, if they were successful by application of their indescribable skill in deceiving their neighbours, in attaining the confidence of Christian potentates, whether churchly or worldly.

This so greatly desired power was used by them in order to cause harm to those of generous heart, who had opened door and gates to them, since now they conspired with greater prospect of success against Holy Church or the Christian states. Thus we see that, once Reccared had died and the motives had been forgotten which justified the exclusion of Jews from public offices, the latter were again permitted to exercise these and they were permitted to fall back again into their wicked practices, which had brought about the just punitive measures of the Third Toledo Council.

In this manner they represented anew a grave problem in the Gothic kingdom. When therefore in the year 612 Sisebutus was elected through the votes of the Visigoth potentates and with approval of the Episcopate, he first attempted to call a halt to the abuses of the Jews by putting into effect the Canon of the 3rd Toledo Council, which, because of neglect or yielding by the previous government, was no longer practised, and by likewise most energetically refusing the Jews the right of being able to buy Christian slaves.

J. Amador de los Rios confirms as follows: "Sisebutus, firm in his efforts to separate the Jewish race from the Christian, by his removing every power of the former over the latter, commanded that the crown should permit the return of all incomes, gains or presents which they had accumulated through deceiving the Kings before him."

The historian in question reveals that Sisebutus with his zeal to put into application the statutes of Reccared in their entire extent, "gained for himself the approval of the Episcopate and the applause of Catholics"[240] and, conversely, the tenacious opposition of the Israelites, "who already showed the hard attributes of Jewish infamy." Finally, Sisebutus resolved to grasp the evil by its roots, and to remove from the Imperium this community of disgraceful aliens, who left in peace neither the Visigoth nation nor the Hispanic-Latin believers and hence represented a lasting threat for church and state. He therefore announced a fulminant edict, which uttered the expulsion of all members of the Jewish race from the kingdom. However, he committed the cardinal blunder of excluding from this statute those who confessed to Catholicism, so that the majority preferred to remain and allow themselves to be baptised. As the Jewish historian Cecil Roth has reported, such conversions were pretended and consequently only served to replace Judaism practised in public as their religion by one cultivated in secret, as a result of which a strengthened "Fifth Column" grew up which represented a much more dangerous organisation than that of open Jewry.

The Jesuit historian Mariana says, when he speaks about this general conversion of Iberian Jews, that a great number of Jews had themselves baptised with proclamation of this decree, "of which some were conversions from conviction and the majority hypocritical." Mariana further elaborates that the Jews who received water of baptism, in order to evade the edict of Sisebutus, "followed anew and with greater zeal the confession of belief of their elders" upon the latter's death in the year 621.[241]

The faulty memory of Christian rulers, which has been so grave in its consequences and of such advantage for the Jews, brought with it the fact that the Christians and pagans in the course of history, forgot the lessons

---

[240] J. Amador de los Rios, Ibid, Volume I, pp. 85-86.
[241] Mariana: General history of Spain. Book VI. Chapter II.

of the past and fell into the old faults of wishing to bring the terrible Jewish problem towards a solution through conversion. Thus they admittedly ordered the expulsion of the "Fifth Column", but at the same time left the escape valve of conversion open, so that things were merely made worse. For the majority preferred to remain and to falsely convert themselves into good Christians, whereby a "Fifth Column" grew up, which refined itself more and more, took effect in secret and therefore became more dangerous.

The expulsion of all Jews from the Gothic kingdom would have signified a solution of the problem, if it had been carried out totally, and the possibilities had not been made clear for the Jews to retain a loophole through their apparent conversions.

The expulsion would have been justified on the other side; for the owners of a house have always the right to show a guest the door, who, far removed from giving thanks for the hospitality enjoyed, sets himself to rob his hosts of their property or to cause them difficulties.

The commentary which the Jew Graetz makes, referring to the expulsion edict of Sisebutus, is characteristic in this respect, when he says, that "Sisebutus, by means of this fanatical persecution, cleared the way for the dissolution of the Visigoth kingdom."[242] Undoubtedly he here refers to the fact that the complicity of the Jews favoured the triumph of the Mohammedan invaders. The fact is that the Jews had not ceased, since the conversion of the Visigoths to Catholicism and their abjuration of Arianism, to conspire against the new position of things. If there existed a fault on the part of Sisebutus or his successors, then it was that of not expelling completely the conspiratorial aliens who had infiltrated into the land, which in fact favoured from within outwards the Arabic conquest. Without Jews on Gothic soil this service of espionage would not have been able to be performed and the handing over of fortified places as well as the desertion of troops in the army of Roderich would not have been able to be effected, as the Jews were successful in doing. It was the fault of the Goths that the possibility was left open to the "Jewish Fifth Column" by means of a pretence of a false conversion to remain further on their soil; for it is always dangerous to allow the activity of any kind of "Fifth Column".

It is very important to establish that Sisebutus was certainly conscious of the lack of strength on the part of the Christians, of pursuing

---

[242] Graetz, Ibid. Volume III. Page 49.

throughout history a firm policy towards their enemies, as well as the faulty memory of the peoples in relation to the lessons of the past. Therefore he did everything humanly possible to prevent his successors falling into the traps of the skilled deceptive manoeuvres on the part of cunning Jewish diplomacy and renouncing the laws which he had enacted for defence of the Church and of the State. The legislation created by him for this purpose, which was incorporated in the "Fuero Juzgo", was impressed upon the hearts of his successors by Sisebutus himself, so that the latter applied all strictness in the following of the anti-Jewish laws; with the punishment of seeing themselves deprived of rights for lifetime, as well as with death, to be thrust out of the host of believers in Christ and cast among the Jews so that the raging flames of Hell licked them eternally.[243]

And Sisebutus, who well knew the chronic faults of the Christian dignitaries, did not err in this. Scarcely was he dead, than the new King Swintila soon fell a victim to the smooth diplomacy of the Jews, who have the special gift of injecting confidence in their future victims, by their lulling them through an extremely hearty treatment and hypocritically pretending to show a friendship and loyalty, which covers their black plans and allows them to appear as victims of the most disgraceful injustices.

With their classical methods of deception they were successful in winning Swintila for themselves, who disregarded the admonitions of Sisebutus to his successors not to alter the anti-Jewish laws for the defence of the kingdom, and who did not know how to cast his curse against those who disavowed the said laws. He lifted the entire anti-Jewish legislation and with it the edict of expulsion of the Jews, so that the untrue converts, if they wished, could again publicly practise their Jewish cult, as well as return to the land from which they had been driven out.

The Jew Graetz, who is better acquainted in the internal matters of Jewry than Father Mariana, says in this connection the following: "In spite of baptism the converted Jews had not given up their religion." He thus does not make Mariana's allusion, that, although the majority pretended conversion, there were nevertheless some who did it from inner conviction. On the other hand, Graetz further elaborates that in the epoch of the Semitophile Swintila "the act of baptism was regarded as sufficient,

---

[243] Forum judicium, Book XII. Tit. II. Laws 14. Formula of cursing against those Kings who did not heed the anti-Jewish laws: [Sit in hoc saeculo ignominiosior cunctis hominibus... Futuri etiam examinis terribile quum patuerit tempus, et metuendus Domini adventus fuerit reservatus, discretus a Christi grege perspicuo, ad laevam cum hebraeis exuratur flammis atrocibus..." etc.]

and none bothered to make enquiry as to whether the converts retained their old habits and practices. The noble King Swintila was naturally dethroned through a conspiracy of the nobility and clergy, who placed Sisenand in his place, who was a willing tool of theirs."[244] Here the Jew Graetz mentions a condition, which represents the ideal for the false converts from Jewry and which consists in that they already transformed themselves into true Christians through baptism, without anyone bothering to investigate whether the converts and their descendants still adhered in secret to the Jewish cult. This is exactly the situation today of the descendants of the false converts, who enjoy freedom of action as powerful "Fifth Column" within the Church and cause Christianity colossal harm, without anyone setting up a real investigation, in order to establish who practises Judaism in secret.

Conversely, at other epochs of the Visigoth monarchy, watch was kept with Argus eyes over the converts and their descendants, in order to discover who of them still carried on Judaism. It is natural that, under the protection and shield of Swintila, the Jews again accumulated great power within the kingdom and brought the Christian Church anew into danger. This explains and justifies the secret measures of the Catholic clergy, in order to overthrow the traitorous monarch, who, as is to be expected, is praised as good and liberal by the Jews.

Leader in this new struggle against the "Synagogue of Satan" was Saint Isidore of Seville, another of the most renowned Fathers of the Church, who, after the fall of the unfaithful Swintila and the crowning of Sisenand, organised and directed the Fourth Toledo Council, which was highly authorised in Church doctrine.

The greatest difficulty in this situation was that those who had gone over to Judaism, and their descendants, followed their old tradition and allowed their sons to enter into the Catholic priesthood, as a result of which they could even rise and occupy the bishops' chairs, which thus served to provide the Jews with aid in their conspiracies against the Catholic faith. This is the typical case of activity of the "Jewish Fifth Column" which had infiltrated into the Church, whose destructive activity can be traced up to our days.

In other cases the Jews took refuge in that system which had commenced with their predecessor, the Jew Simon the Magician, by buying the favour of the clergy who, although they were not secret Jews,

---

[244] Graetz, Ibid. Volume III. Page 49.

sold their support to the cause of the Devil; exactly as their forerunner Judas Iscariot had done as one of the chosen Twelve. The treachery which had made itself noticeable up into the highest offices of Holy Church, called forth the alarm of the Fourth Toledo Council and its leader, Saint Isidore of Seville. Upon the Metropolitans and Bishops assembled there fell the task of laying down in the Holy Canons a series of statutes which not only had the aim of countering the Jewish threat at this time, but also of banning and punishing the treachery in the high clergy, which was most dangerous of all for Holy Church and the Christian states.

Thus among the Canons passed for this purpose the following stand out: "Canon 58. Concerning those who show support and favour to the Jews against the faith of Christ. The avarice of some is so great that they therefore separate themselves from the faith, just as the Apostle expressed it; just as even many among the clergy and laity accept presents from the Jews and aid their perfidy, in that they allow them to enjoy their protection; to those, of whom one knows not without reasons, that they belong to the body of the Antichrist, since they work against Christ. Every bishop, priest or layman, who in the future grants support to them (the Jews) against the Christian faith, be it through briberies or favours, shall be regarded as profane and blaspheming God. He shall be excluded from the Communion of the Catholic Church and be regarded as not belonging to the kingdom of Cod; for it is no more than right that those who reveal themselves as protectors of the enemies of the Lord be separated from the body of Christ."[245]

The threat which had arisen for the Church and Christian society, must have been very great on grounds of the complicity of the Bishops and Priests with the Jews, these eternal enemies of Christianity. This is the reason, why the wise Saint Isidore of Seville had to expose them before the Council which consisted of Metropolitans and Bishops, in this quoted Canon, and called those Bishops and Priests who supported the Jews profane and blasphemous, whereby they at the same time threatened them with the punishment of excommunication.

May this be borne in mind by all those clergy and highest dignitaries of the Church, who, instead of serving Holy Church, at present prefer to give free rein to the Jews, these principal enemies of Christ, or to Jewish enterprises like Freemasonry and Communism. And they should give

---

[245] 4th Council of Toledo, Canon 58, compiled by Jaun Tejada y Ramiro. Page 305. *Collection of Canons of all Church councils in Spain and South America*, Volume II.

account concerning the great responsibility, which weighs upon them, as well as the grave sins, which they commit as a result.

As is known, the Toledo Councils enjoyed great regard within the Holy Catholic Church, and their edicts even found entry into civil law. Thus the statutes and penalties of the aforementioned Canon were taken over in the "Fuero Juzgo", which was proclaimed with approval of Holy Church. In article XV, Title II, Book XII of Law 15 it is stated:

"So that the cheating by the Jews does not have the power to broaden itself in any kind of form and to govern according to its choice; over which we have always to watch. Therefore we stipulate in this law that no man of any religion, or spiritual order, or any dignity, or of our Court, either great or small, nor any kind of people, nor any kind of line, neither princes nor potentates should strive accordingly, to protect the Jews, who will not allow themselves to be baptised, in order to hold firm to their beliefs and their customs. Nor those who have been baptised but return to their perfidy or their bad customs. None should risk to defend them in their malice with his strength in any kind of way. No one should attempt to help them, neither by means of arguments nor deeds, so that they may not be able to agitate against the holy belief of Christians. Neither shall anyone in secret or in public undertake anything against the faith. Should anyone accordingly risk this, whether he be bishop, priest, member of an order or lay brother, and if proof is shown against him, then he shall be separated from the community of Christians, excommunicated by the Church and a quarter of his property declared to be confiscated in favour of the King."[246]

In this form in those critical times Holy Church as well as the Catholic State enacted sanctions and in fact the former with the approval of the first-named, against the accomplices of Jewry within the Church and the high dignitaries of the clergy itself.

In order to come back now to the Fourth Toledo Council, we now reproduce, what Canon 59 orders, which refers directly to the Jews, who after their going over to Christianity were revealed in their secret practices of Jewish belief. About this the Canon in question expressly states: "Many Jews took on the Christian faith for a certain time and now give themselves, by slandering Christ, not only up to the Jewish rites, but even

---

[246] *Fuero Juzgo* [Collection of Visigoth Laws in old Castilian tongue] in Latin and Castilian, provided by the Real Academia Espanola with the oldest most magnificent handwritings, Madrid, 1815.

go so far as to carry out the repellent act of circumcision. In reference to these Jews and upon proposal of the highly devout and highly religious Lord, our King Sisenand, this Holy Council decrees that the said converts, after they have been purified through the Papal authority, are again conducted into the care of the Christian dogma; but those, who do not better themselves from their own decision, should be restrained by clerical punishment. And relating to the circumcised, it is ordered that, if it is a matter of their own sons, then they shall be separated from their parents; but if it is a matter of slaves, then they shall be granted freedom on account of the injury done to their body."[247]

Although both Cecil Roth as well as other Jewish authors assure us that the conversions were, according to their nature, pretended, and in this they agree with the Jesuit historian Mariana and with what is laid down in various mediaeval documents of undoubted proof, then the Church at least in the early periods held every converted Jew to be a serious Christian, as long as it was not proved that he practised Jewish rites in secret.

Later, all Israelites were under suspicion of crypto-Judaism who had gone over to Christianity as well as their descendants, since proof could be provided that with few exceptions all pretended their conversion and transferred their secret religion from father to son. It therefore in no way astonishes us that, in the aforementioned Canon 59, measures were seized upon, in order to prevent the crypto-Jews, i.e. the untrue converts, from transferring Hebrew rites to their sons, and the latter were separated from them for this purpose. For the same purpose the Council in question passed its 60th Canon, which according to its compiler, Tejada Ramiro, refers to the so-called backsliding Jews, i.e. to the Christians, who fell back into the crimes of secret practice of Jewish belief. The said Canon elaborates:

"It is ordered that the sons and daughters of Jews, so that in the future they may not fall into the error of their fathers, be separated from their parents and entrusted to a monastery or to Christian men and women, who fear God, so that in their education they learn the cult of the faith and, better instructed, make progress in customs and beliefs."[248]

---

[247] Fourth Council of Toledo, Canon 59. Compiled by Juan Tejada y Ramiro, same edition, Volume II, Page 103.
[248] Fourth Council of Toledo. Canon 60. Compiled by Juan Tejada y Ramiro, same edition, Volume II. Page 306.

As one can recognise, these Canons were chiefly conceived in order to destroy the "Jewish Fifth Column" which had infiltrated into the Church, be it by means of punishments of the false crypto-Jewish Christians or through the attempt to prevent the latter handing on the secret rites to their sons. It was and remains highly dangerous for the Church to have in its ranks members of the Jewish sect who, disguised as good Catholics, make efforts to destroy Christianity. For this means to have the foe in their own ranks, and no one has called into question the right that every human society possesses to render harmless the espionage service of enemy powers or to get rid of saboteurs. The measures seized upon by Holy Church, in order to ward off Jewish infiltrations, which attempted to undermine it externally, were fully justified, even if they may also appear very strict; exactly the same as those, which every modern nation seizes upon, in order to eliminate espionage or sabotage of a hostile power.

History has proved, that even if open Jewry was expelled and despised in many nations, that crypto-Jewry nevertheless lived on under the mask of Christianity. It was always held to be logical, that the intercourse of converted Jews with those who practised their cult in public, was harmful, since the latter could influence the first-named to fall back into Judaism.

Canon 62 of the Holy Council mentioned deals with the banning of this danger: "Concerning the baptised Jews, who have dealings with the false believing Jews. If association with the bad often in fact destroys the good, with how much more probability will the former be destroyed by the latter, who incline to blasphemy. Therefore, from now on, the Jews converted to Christianity must carry on no association with those who still adhere to the old Rite, so that they do not become perverted by them. Whoever in consequence does not avoid this association, will be punished as follows: if he is a baptised Jew, he shall be handed over to the Christians, and if he is not baptised, he shall be publicly whipped."[249]

Canon 64 rejects the capacity of giving witness and in fact here not by the open Jews, but by the crypto-Jewish Christians.

Up to then the Christian law had solely refused the open Jews the right of bearing witness against Christians, but Canon 64 forms an innovation, since it also denies to Christians still practising the Jewish cult in secret, the capacity of bearing witness: "Canon LXIV. Whoever has been untrue to God, cannot be faithful to men. Therefore the Jews, who became

---

[249] 4th Council of Toledo, Canon 62. Compiled by Juan Tejada y Ramiro, same edition, Volume II. Pages 306-307.

Christians and again fell away from the faith of Christ, shall not be permitted as witnesses; and not even then if they declare to be Christians. Just as one mistrusts them relating to the belief in Christ, so shall one suspect them else in earthly evidence..."[250]

More logical the proof given by the Council Fathers could not be; for it is logical that, if they lie in things of God, they likewise speak untruth in earthly things. On the other side, one sees clearly that both Saint Isidore of Seville as well as the Metropolitans and Bishops of the Council knew best of all the lasting distortions and falsities that had become second nature of the false crypto-Jewish Catholics. The same one can say of many today, who swear to be Catholics but act as Israelites.

In spite of this violent defensive struggle on the part of the Church and of the Christian state against the dangerous infiltration by the "Jewish Fifth Column", the latter must have obtained further government offices. Particularly during the desolate period of government of the Semitophile Swintila this development attained such a dangerous degree that both the Catholic Monarch on the throne and also the Holy Toledo Council resolved to make an end of the situation. So in their Holy Canons they uttered the express ban, which refused the Jews the right to occupy public offices within Christian society.

Canon 65 says: "Upon command of our illustrious Lord and King Sisenand, this Holy Council lays down that the Jews, or those who are of their race, may occupy no public offices, because through this they would insult the Christians. Therefore the judges in the provinces in common with the priests should make an end to these cunning deceptions and forbid them to occupy public offices. But if, in spite of this, a judge grants his approval to anything of the like, then he shall be excommunicated as a blasphemer and be accused of 'fraud' and be publicly whipped."[251]

Canon 66 expressly calls the Jews "Servants of the Antichrist", just as another already quoted Canon said of the bishops and priests who helped the Jews that they formed part of the body of the Antichrist.

---

[250] 4th Council of Toledo. Canon 64. Compiled by Juan Tejada y Ramiro, same edition, Volume II. Page 307.
[251] 4th Council of Toledo. Canons 65 and 66. Compiled by Juan Tejado y Ramiro. Same edition. Volume II. Page 308.

It is worthy of note that Canon 65 adds an innovation to the laws of the Catholic Church in that admittance is not only blocked to declared Jews to government offices, but to all those who belong to their race.

This must not be interpreted as racial discrimination; for Holy Church regards all men as equal before God, without discrimination of race. But since the conviction, repeatedly substantiated through facts, predominated that Christians of Jewish race with few exceptions secretly practised the Jewish cult, it was logical that one attempted to prevent the infiltration of crypto-Jews into the government offices. This was a vitally important defensive measure by the Christian state, since, if the latter had once been ruled by its deadly enemies, who are simultaneously the principal foes of Holy Church, both institutions would have come into gravest danger. To block the door to government of the state to aggressive or converted Jews, was not only prudent but indispensable to protect it from the powerful "Fifth Column" which at a given moment could cause its collapse. Thus it came about in catastrophic degree when a weak-minded leader of the state, who violated these Laws of the Church and those announced by his predecessors, cleared anew the possibility for the Israelites to gain control of the leading posts in the Gothic kingdom. This law of public security is without doubt the predecessor of further most energetic and far-reaching laws, which Holy Catholic Church passed many hundreds of centuries later.

It is interesting to establish that Saint Isidore of Seville in his struggle against Judaism wrote two books against the Hebrews, which, according to Graetz, were compiled "with that lack of taste and feeling that distinguished the Fathers of the Church from the beginning in their warring polemics against Jewry".[252] It is entirely natural that the anti-Jewish books of the Church Fathers do not please the Jews, but one must understand that the Israelites obscure the historical truth. Also they attempt to destroy the honour of all those who have fought against them, even if it is a question of such holy, learned and excellent men as the Church Fathers are.

It is completely beyond doubt that, if Saint Isidore of Seville as well as the Metropolitans and Bishops of the Fourth Toledo Council had lived in our days, they would immediately have been accused of antisemitism or criminal racism; and in fact not only by the Jews, but also by the clergy, who give themselves out as Christians, but in reality stand in the service of Jewry.

---

[252] Graetz, same work, Volume III. Page 50.

CHAPTER THIRTEEN

CONDEMNATION OF KINGS AND CATHOLIC CLERGY WHO ARE NEGLIGENT IN THEIR STRUGGLE AGAINST CLANDESTINE JEWRY

As we were able to observe, the Holy Church laws of the 4th Council of Toledo should have finally destroyed the "Jewish Fifth Column" in Christian society. Its decisions would have been more effective, if the Jews had not always been from of old so skilled in politics and diplomacy and knowing how, through flattery, perfected false loyalty, false arguments and confidence-giving comedies, to deceive. In addition, they know how to sow discord among their opponents, in order to keep the upper hand. They ally themselves first with the one in order to destroy the other, then defeat their first allies with the aid of the other, and finally destroy them all. This was one of the great secrets of their victories, and the clergy and politicians of all mankind must bear this in mind, in order to protect themselves from such Machiavellian manoeuvres.

Another ground for their successes was their great courage to accommodate themselves to an unfortunate situation, their resolution to never surrender to their enemies and to combat the cowards in their own ranks, since the latter could make a transitory into a final defeat.

In the supreme hierarchy of Christianity there are such cowards. They are responsible for so many defeats and compromises in recent times and are cynical enough to conceal their cowardice and their egoism behind apparent clear and conciliatory arguments. It means nothing to them that their cowardice handed over entire peoples to Communist slavery, and they say to themselves: let us live comfortably at the expense of the beast, even if the peoples, whom we lead, perish! That is the supreme wisdom of their false prudence and compromises.

If the Jews had been like this, they would finally have been defeated in the Gothic kingdom, when Christianity brought defeat to them and triumphed at the 4th Council of Toledo. However, they did not think of surrendering – as today the cowards – they fought on with zeal and fanaticism and prepared the moment when they could conduct a new battle, in which they could triumph. With their accustomed tenacity they began to circumvent the laws, which the Holy Council of Toledo had passed in order to make them powerless, supported the rebellious spirit of the nobles against the King and worsened it through their intrigues. When hearts were sufficiently aroused, they then served as effective protagonists of the demands of the rebellious nobility.

If the King, Holy Church and the Visigoth nobility had been united, they could not have been conquered by the Jews. It was thus necessary to break this unity and to divide the enemy, in order to weaken him. This was not difficult, since the nobles frequently showed the tendency to rebel against the authority of the king. The Jews made use of this tendency, utilised the arising frictions in order to sharpen the struggles, and gradually attained their goal. At first they made efforts in order to obtain the protection of certain aristocrats, in order to circumvent the Toledo Church laws and the laws of the monarch. The nobles – deceived by the Jewish falsehood – had fallen into the trap and held them for valuable allies in their struggle against the King. For this the Jewish converts and their descendants were principally to be thanked, who pretended to be loyal Christians and who thus easier gained the confidence of the Visigoth aristocrats.

The Jewish historian Graetz comments: "These resolutions of the 4th Council of Toledo and the persecutions by Sisesand against the converted Jews do not appear to have been carried out with the planned strictness. The Spanish-Visigoth nobles took the Jews more and more under their protection and against them the royal authority had no power."[253] One thus sees that the converted Jews skilfully discovered the weak point of the Visigoth kingdom and effectively utilised it, just as they also understood a thousand years later in England how to conquer the nation, by their utilising the struggles of the parliamentary nobility against the King and sharpened these even more.

In the midst of increasing internal struggles, which began to weaken the heroic Visigoth kingdom dangerously, Chintila attained power. At the

---

[253] Graetz, same work, Volume III. Page 51.

beginning of his period of government the 6th Council of Toledo[254] took place. The lack of constancy by non-Jews in their struggle against the principal enemy was also chronic and made easier the latter's successes, even in the case of the Catholic Visigoth monarchs, who were thus conscious of the threat of the Jews and who wished to exterminate them. Therefore the archbishops and bishops at the Council sought to prevent this evil. In Canon III it is stated:

"Through devoutness and superior power, the unbending falsehood of the Jews seemed to decrease, for through devotion to God, we know that the illustrious Christian prince in his zealous faith has resolved together with the priests of his realm, to make impossible from the start their violations of duty and not to allow non-Catholics to live in his kingdom... But for our caution and great watchfulness, with it our zeal and our labour – which often fall asleep – which must not be abandoned, we pass further edicts. We therefore announce with one heart and one soul – a unanimous judgment, which must please God and which we also simultaneously approve, with the approval and reflection of his nobles and aristocrats – that anyone who in future strives for supreme power in the kingdom will not become King if he does not promise, among other things, not to allow the Jews to dishonour this Catholic faith (i.e. the Jews apparently converted to Christianity), so that he in no way supports their faithlessness, or through neglect or greed[255] gives way to violation of duty which leads to the abyss of faithlessness. He must therefore ensure that in the future he continues to stand firm, which in our time has required so much effort, for the good has no effect if it does not proceed with constancy. If he afterwards breaks his promise, may he be accursed in the presence of the eternal God, may he burn in everlasting fire and with him all priests or Christians who share his error. We add this and confirm the preceding determinations of the general Synod concerning the Jews, for we know that in this all necessary measures are laid down for the salvation of their souls. Therefore the appertaining prescriptions should be valid."[256]

This polemic against the kings and Catholic clergy who would not participate in the struggle, not only against the open Jews, but also against the betrayal by Christians of Jewish origin, who were described as friendly to the Jews, could not be sharper. It is worthy of note that, while hitherto

---

[254] Concerning the year in which the Council met, there are differences of opinion. Some, as for example Cardinal Aguirre, assert, that it was the 2nd year, on the other hand Tejada y Ramiro is of the opinion that the gathering took place in the 3rd year.

[255] *Neglectu et cupiditate.*

[256] 6th Council of Toledo. Law 3. Compiled by Juan Tejada y Ramiro, same edition. Volume II. Pages 333-334.

the condemnations and penalties of the Holy Church Councils only hit at bishops and priests who supported the Jews and were their accomplices, now also those priests were threatened with immediate excommunication who were not constant or were neglectful in the struggle for life and death which Holy Church conducted against clandestine Jewry. One thus sees that the Archbishops and Bishops of the Holy Councils not only exactly knew the faithlessness of the Jewish enemies, but also the weaknesses and the lack of constancy of the civil and clerical members of Christianity in such a just struggle.

It is strange that at this Council they still restricted themselves to combating the negligence of the priests without alluding to the Bishops. This is perhaps to be attributed to the circumstance that particularly the bishops passed those statutes and did not dare to include themselves among those who deserved this punishment. However, the negligence of the Prelates themselves in the time following must have been so serious that, at a later Council, they even proceeded with alarm and uttered severe penalties against the guilty, just as they had previously declared for godless and excommunicated those who supported the Jews to the harm of Christianity.

It is likewise worthy of note that in this law those are again mentioned who out of avarice or forgetfulness of duty gave way to the converted Jews. Without doubt the Simony briberies played a major role in the Jewish intrigues, which appears to be confirmed in Law IV in which among other things it is stated: "Therefore, whoever imitates Simon, the instigator of the Simonist heresy, in order to acquire Church offices, not in the usual way, but through gifts, offerings, etc."[257]

The Jew Simon Magus introduced this policy of bribery into Holy Church, which was called Simony after him. In the course of centuries it could be proved that the converted Jews and their descendants, who already belonged to the priest class and the hierarchy of Holy Church, had learned very much from their predecessor Magus and bought Church dignities or on their side sold Church goods, as the Holy Inquisition and the Church authorities repeatedly revealed. Worthy of note is also the commentary of the Jewish historian Graetz concerning the command of King Chintila, which was greeted by the 6th Council of Toledo, to admit no non-Catholics in the Gothic kingdom. This statute is directed only against the Jews: "For the second time the Jews were compelled to

---

[257] 6th Council of Toledo. Canon 4. Compiled by Juan Tejada y Ramiro, same edition. Volume II. Pages 3 and 4.

emigrate, and the converts who had remained true to Judaism in their innermost hearts had to sign a confession and obligate themselves to practise the Catholic religion and follow it without reserve. But the confession of men whose sacred conviction was a matter of honour, could not be honest and it also was not. They resolutely hoped for better times, so that they could allow the mask to fall, and the constitution of the elected monarchy of the Visigoth kingdom made this possible to them. The present condition lasted only four years under the rulership of Chintila (638-642).[258]

The historian could not be clearer concerning the false Christianity of the converted Jews and the invalidity of their confessions and promises. Graetz further observes that the converted Jews broke their promise not to practise the Jewish rite in order to become honest Christians, and Chintila accordingly condemned them "to be burned or stoned."

The historian Amador de los Rios shows the practical consequences of all these measures: However, notice must be taken that this immoderate severity of the lawmakers was not sufficient to suppress the impatience of the Jews. When fifteen years had passed and Recceswinth ruled, the Fathers saw themselves compelled to repeat the demand which obligated the elected King to swear "that he would defend the faith against Jewish faithlessness". This occurred at the 8th Council of Toledo and is laid down in Canon X.[259] As Graetz has said, the Jews were successful after the death of Chintila in introducing, on grounds of the elected monarchy, a favourable change for their interests with the new King. Here we have another example of that chronic malady from which we Christians and also the pagans suffer: we are incapable in the face of this foe of maintaining a firm lasting conduct over several generations of rulers. With us Christians and also with the pagans the rulers strive so much for innovations that the edicts of their predecessor are always made useless and no united policy towards Jewry is possible. If the Jews without doubt also influence this change in policy, nevertheless our own inconstancy and our lack of tenacity is principally guilty of this.

During the period of rule by Recceswinth, the converted Jews and their descendants in Toledo handed to him a very interesting petition, in which they demanded of him: "Since the Kings Sisebutus and Chintila had compelled them to give up their law and they lived in all things like Christians, without deceit or cunning, he might allow them not to eat pork.

---

[258] Graetz, same work, Volume III. Pages 51-52.
[259] J. Amador de los Rios, same work, Volume II. Pages 95-96.

They said that they begged this far more because their belly would not stand it, since it was not accustomed to such flesh, than from stings of conscience."[260] It must, however, already be anticipated that centuries later, when the prosecution through the Inquisition threatened to exterminate clandestine Jewry, the Christians who were secret Jews had to eat pork very much to their sorrow, for the Inquisition and all the people in general suspected the Christian who ate no pork of being a secret Jew, even if he swore only to do this out of disinclination. From then up to today the clandestine Jewry abolished the religious statute of eating no such flesh, in order to arouse no suspicion among their neighbours. Therefore a Secret Jew eats everything today, and no one suspects that he is a Jew on grounds of his diet. Only one or two fanatics among the Jewish Christians still maintain this statute.

Unfortunately no effective barrier was erected so that the converted Jews and their descendants could not introduce themselves into the clergy. The more they joined themselves to it, all the more increased the cases of Simony, which grew to such frightening extent that the 8th Council of Toledo had to energetically fight this vice of Jewish origin. In its Canon III it is therefore stated that many "wished to buy the grace of the Holy Ghost for a shabby price, in order to fully receive the sublime Papal blessing and forgot Peter's words to Simon Magus: 'Thy money be cursed with thee, for thou wouldst have the gift of God for money.'"[261] Upon this follow the punishments for this crime.

The Jewish historian Graetz writes that the King, when he noticed that the European nobles of the land showed protection to the Jews and allowed them to practice their Jewish religion in secret, "passed an edict which forbade all Christians to protect the secret Jews." Whoever did not follow this command should be punished. And it is further stated: "These measures and statutes, however, had not the desired results." "The secret Jews – or, as they were called officially, the Jew-Christians – could not force Judaism out of their heart. The Spanish Jews, threatened by the danger of death, had from of old exercised themselves in the art of remaining true to their religion in their most secret hearts and of evading the sharp gaze of their enemies. In addition, they celebrated the Jewish feasts in their houses and despised the festivals of the Church. In order to make an end to this condition, the representatives of the Church passed a law which was intended to take from these unfortunate people their home

---

[260] Amador de los Rios, same work, Volume I. Page 95.
[261] Council of Toledo. Canon 3. Compiled by Juan Tejada y Ramiro. Same edition, Volume II. Page 375.

life. From now on they had to observe the Jewish and Christian festivals under the scrutiny of the clergy, since it was wished to compel them not to observe the Jewish festivals and to maintain the Christian."[262]

Here the Jewish historian forgets all evasions and calls the Christians of Jewish origin by their name: secret Jews or Jew-Christians, i.e. Jews who practised the Jewish religion in secret. In addition, he quotes interesting feasts in their homes, since as apparent Christians they could not do this in ordinary synagogues. Simultaneously the famous historian, so respected in Jewish circles, explains the reason for the decision of the 9th Council of Toledo that the Jews should spend the Jewish and Christian festivals under scrutiny of the Catholic clergy.

In Canon 17 of the 9th Council of Toledo, to which Graetz openly refers, it is expressly stated: "The baptised Jews should spend the festivals with the bishops." "The Jews baptised anywhere and at any time can assemble. But we determine that they must come together on the chief festivals laid down through the New Testament and on those days which were once sacred for them according to their ancient law, in the cities and public assemblies with the highest priests of God, so that the Pontifex learns their life and their faith and they become really converted."[263] In this law it becomes clear that the bishops of the Council doubted – and with good reason – the sincerity of the Christianity of the Jews converted to our holy faith.

After the death of Recceswinth, Wamba was elected as King. The Jews utilised anew the disunity of the nobility and attempted to alter the existing order to their favour. José Amador de los Rios mentions that the 10th Council of Toledo had almost ignored the Jews and comments: "The spiritual legislators perhaps believed in the honesty of the almost universal conversion of the Jews and hoped that, if they were all Christians, the internal struggle with them would find a happy end. But their hope was in vain. Scarcely had Wamba ascended the throne of Reccared than the rebellion of Hilderich and Paul gave them opportunity to reveal their secret grudges and to place themselves openly on the side of the rebels. As a result many Jewish families who had been expelled from the kingdom at the time of Sisebutus returned into the Visigoth kingdom and especially into the region of Gothic Gaul (Southern France) where the rebellion had its outlet. But the rebels were defeated in Nimes and destroyed, and

---

[262] Graetz, same work, Volume III. Page 104.
[263] 9th Council of Toledo. Canon 17. Summarised by Juan Tejada y Ramiro, same edition. Volume II. Page 404.

several edicts were published for the punishment and penalising of the Jews. The latter were expelled anew in large numbers from Gothic Gaul."[264]

The Jesuit Pater Mariana also confirms that, after the defeat of the rebels, "many edicts were passed against the Jews, who were expelled from the whole of Gothic Gaul."[265]

The Jew Graetz gives us interesting details in this respect and reports that after the death of Recceswinth: "The Jews participated in a rebellion against his successor, Wamba (672-680). Count Hilderich, governor of the Spanish province of Septimania, refused to recognise the newly-elected king and hoisted the flag of rebellion. In order to obtain support and followers, he promised the converted Jews a place in his own province where they could freely practise their religion. The latter accepted the offer and followed him in great numbers. The rebellion of Hilderich in Nimes took on enormous extent, and at first the hope existed of an easy victory, but the rebels were finally destroyed. Wamba appeared with an army at Narbonne (France) and drove the Jews from the city."[266]

However much one watches over the "Fifth Column", it nevertheless always utilises the first opportunity to overthrow the government, which does not suit it. Once again it becomes clear that disputes and personal lust for power gave the Jews the opportunity of coming on top. Fortunately the rebellious Count in this case lost the battle and could not alter the existing order, which would have been disastrous for the Church. Thus Christianity triumphed fully over Jewry and its egoistic opportunist allies.

At the same tune, however, when the visible recognised foe was decisively conquered, the "Fifth Column" slowly gained ground. For the more the Jewish infiltration took roots in the bosom of the Church, Simony – an evil of Jewish origin – increased and the false converted Jews and their descendants in the clergy utilised it.

The 11th Council of Toledo, which took place during the period of rule under Wamba, laid special emphasis on the combating of Simony and made efforts to prevent the cunning, which is utilised by those, who wish

[264] J. Amador de los Rios, same work, Volume I. Page 97.
[265] Mariana, Ibid, Book VI. Chapter XIII.
[266] Graetz, Ibid, Volume II. Pages 104-105.

to buy the "Bishops' dignities" (offices) so desired by the Jews of the "Fifth Column".

CHAPTER FOURTEEN

THE CHURCH COMBATS SECRET JEWRY. EXCOMMUNICATION OF NEGLIGENT BISHOPS

Fifty years had passed since a great number of Jews in the Gothic kingdom had been converted to Christianity and three decades since the time when the historian Amador de los Rios spoke of an almost universal conversion. The kingdom of Reccared was nevertheless flooded and undermined by false Christians who secretly practised the Jewish religion and plotted in secret to destroy the Church and the State. In the year 681, when Ervigio entered the government, the situation was so serious that the high Catholic clergy and the monarch together worked out common civil and church laws in order to destroy the "Jewish Fifth Column" in Christianity. Everyone who, as a Christian, observed in secret the rites and customs of the Jews and supported these false Christians or concealed them in any kind of form – even without exception of the bishops who made themselves guilty of this crime – was severely punished. These laws were at first approved by the monarchs in collaboration with respected members of the clergy and later laid before the 12th Council of Toledo for approval. There these laws were approved as church authority by archbishops and bishops and were entered into the laws of the Synod mentioned.

In order to understand the basis of the canons, both of the Ecumenical as well as the provincial Holy Church Councils, which wished to solve the terrible Jewish problem and especially that of the "Fifth Column" in Christian society, one must bear in mind that both then as today no land tolerated that a group of foreigners might abuse the magnanimously given hospitality and betray the land in question, which had naively opened its doors to them, through espionage and sabotage.

321

Then these spies and saboteurs were without exception punished with death by all peoples, as also in general still in modern times. There is additionally the fact that the "Jewish Fifth Column" in Christian and pagan nations, besides carrying on espionage and sabotage, has also exercised and provoked in the course of centuries an inner attempt at conquest and has provoked civil wars which cost millions of men their lives, and which has murdered in their own house those who opened the frontiers to them, robbed them or attempted to enslave them. Undoubtedly the so-called Jewish colonies in the Christian and pagan lands are more dangerous and harmful for the states afflicted than the usual espionage and sabotage organisations. If the members of these organisations are punished without regard to race, religion or nationality, why should an exception be made to the most dangerous, harmful and criminal "Fifth Column"? What privilege do the Jews enjoy, that when they commit high treason, espionage or sabotage or plot against the people which houses them, they are forgiven and not punished like spies of other races and nationalities?

All peoples have a natural right of justified defence, and if a pair of alien immigrants violate the hospitality granted them, they bring these peoples into a dilemma of life and death. These disgraceful aliens are solely responsible for the measures which the betrayed, threatened people seizes upon against the "Fifth Column."

So did Holy Church and the Christian monarchs conceive things, and at several Councils – as we will see later – it is made clear that these criminals should be punished with death. But instead of passing in this case the customary and completely justified judgment, Holy Church and the Christian kings made an exception with the Jews and presented them with life a hundred times over. As a result they endangered their future and their right to live in peace and freedom in their own land. With such exceptionally good will a series of measures, instead of radically suppressing them, were seized upon in order to prevent the "Jewish Fifth Column" from being able to cause all too much harm and so that it did not injure the people which sheltered them. But since they were granted life, the measures were ineffective. Therefore the various Councils of the Church and the Papal Bulls passed a series of norms and laws, laying down, for example, that the Jews should wear a sign, so that they were distinguished from the other inhabitants of the land in which they lived. This should enable it to be easier to safeguard oneself from the revolutionary activity of the Jews against Church and State. These signs varied; they had to have a mark on their heads, they had to wear a special cap, a dress or another distinguishing mark.

In other cases it was ordered in the Church laws and the Papal Mandates that they must restrict themselves to certain parts of the city, so-called Ghettos, and that they might occupy no government or Church offices, which made it possible for them to continue their activity of conquest and their domination over the people which in unfortunate manner had opened its frontiers to them.

The backsliders were often executed, but in most cases these were spared their lives, and it was limited to confiscating their goods, to expelling them from the land or by applying lighter punishments, such as whipping, no longer customary today, which was then the practice in all lands of earth.

Since this dangerous "Fifth Column" again and again plotted against the Christian peoples and "Holy Church", the Church attempted, instead of seeking the final way out and applying the death penalty – as all peoples do with professional spies and saboteurs – to suppress them by gentler methods, by removing their authority from the grown-ups and bringing the children into monasteries and honourable Christian families. In this manner they wished to attain that, after two or three generations, the threat from the "Fifth Column" would be eliminated, without carrying out mass executions of these masters of espionage, of sabotage and of betrayal.

However, it must be recognised that this extraordinary good-will by Holy Church, by Christian monarchs, and also by the high personages of the Islamic world, was of no avail. The repressive measures against the "Fifth Column" were not only hated, but the Jews also made use of countless subterfuges in order to evade the measures which tied their hands and which were intended to prevent them from doing too much evil. They made use of bribery and bought with gold the bad civil and church personages so that the latter caused the valid civil and Church laws to become dead letters, or they spun countless intrigues in order to free themselves from this control, which was intended to restrict their power. They called forth fresh revolts, plotted more and more dangerous conspiracies and abused the goodness of the Church and Christian peoples, until they were successful in modern times in breaking the chains which had prevented them from causing greater harm, in invading Christian society, and threatening it with complete destruction.

In order to grasp the justification of all Church laws which we investigate in this work and all measures to preserve the peoples from the conspiracy of these harmful aliens, we must recall all the preceding. We understand among this that Holy Church acted in no way cruelly – as the Jews assert – but in an extremely good-willed way with them. And perhaps this most extreme good-will was particularly responsible for the great progress that the Jews with their conquest and enslaving of the peoples could make, as is the case today in the unfortunate lands in which the totalitarian dictatorship of Jewish socialism rules. This is a catastrophic situation, which would have already come into existence many centuries before, if the Church had not at least carried out the precautionary measures which we will investigate in the ensuing chapters of this work.

After these justified elaborations concerning the defence of doctrine and policy which Holy Church followed in course of the centuries, we will now occupy ourselves with the corresponding statutes of the 12th Council of Toledo.

In the letter which the King laid before the Holy Synod it is stated as follows: "Hear, honourable Fathers and respected priests of the heavenly ministries... I come with tears in the eyes to your honourable paternal gathering, so that through the zeal of your court the earth will be freed from the infection of wickedness. Arise, I beg thee, arise, unmask the guilty, censure the repellent customs of the evildoers, show the whip of your zeal towards the faithless, and make an end to the bite of the arrogant, make easier the burden of the oppressed, and above all exterminate the Jewish pest thoroughly which each day reaches out more rapidly around itself (*et, quod plus his omnibus est, judaeorum pestem quae in novam semper recrudescit insaniam radicitus exstirpate*). Investigate also very thoroughly the laws, which you passed a short while ago against the falsity of the Jews, strengthen these laws still more and compile them in a statute, in order to bridle the blasphemy of the faithless."[267]

It is interesting that, among the evil conditions which were brought to the notice of the Synod, the Jewish pest, which day by day increased in alarming measure, is held to be the worst.

In Canon IX of this Holy Council the laws approved against clandestine Jewry were confirmed, i.e. against the Jews who pretended to be Christians and who were described both by the monarchs as also by the Synods simply as Jews, since one was certain that, as descendants of the Jews, they secretly practised their Jewish religion. Of the law mentioned,

---

[267] 12th Council of Toledo. Records. Visit of King. Compilation by Juan Tejada y Ramiro, same edition. Vol. II. Pages 454-455.

which comprises the entire anti-Jewish legislation, we will repeat only the most interesting parts.

"Canon IX. Confirmation of the laws against the wickedness of the Jews (*quae in judaeorum nequitiam promulgatae sunt*) arranged according to the different titles as they are recorded in this law."

"We have read the titles of the different laws which the famous prince has recently passed against the monstrous falsehood of the Jews and have approved them after strict examination. And since they were approved by the Synod with justice, they will be irrevocably applied in future against blasphemy. Among these fall..."[268] Now follow the laws which, after their approval, belong to Law IX. On account of their importance we have emphasised the following statutes. In the first law it is mentioned that the great falsity of the Jews and their dark errors "become very subtle and they perfect themselves in their wicked art and in deceit." For they pretended to be good Christians and always attempted to evade the laws which forbade to them their secret subterranean Judaism. In the IVth and Vth Canon the punishments for the secret Jews are cited who celebrate the Jewish rites and festivals, and who attempt to bring Christians away from their faith in Christ. Here it is not a question of the rites and ceremonies of an alien religion, but of punishing the false Christians who, in spite of their hypocrisy, still practised the Jewish religion in secret. The repressive measures were thus aimed at destroying the "Jewish Fifth Column" in the bosom of Holy Church and of the Christian State.

In the VIIth Canon, the Jews who pretended to be Christians are forbidden to practise the Jewish religious customs relating to meat. However, it is elaborated that the good Christians must eat no pork. One sees that these false Catholics still always deceived the clergy and the King with their apparent disinclination against pork.

In Canon IX the revolutionary activity against the Christian faith is forbidden and severe penalties laid upon malefactors. In addition, punishments are even provided for Christians who conceal the Jews or support them. Concerning this it is expressly stated: "If anyone hides them in his house or aids them to flee, he shall, if that is proved... receive a hundred lashes of the whip, his goods fall to the King, and he will be expelled forever from the land." Thus those who supported the Jews or concealed them are punished in a terrible way. By this the bishops of the

---

[268] 12th Council of Toledo. Canon 9. Compilation by Juan Tejada y Ramiro, same edition, Vol. II. Pages 476-477.

Council and the monarch himself wished to be rid of those who supported the Jews and their accomplices in the struggle against Christianity.

Without doubt more than ever today must effectiveness be given to these statutes of this Holy Law. For only thus can we hope to conquer the Jewish-Communist beast, which has success because the seeming Christians are ready to support the Jews and Communists and to make their victory easier.

Also in the Xth Law, without regard to class or position, punishments are ordained against those who support Jewry, and it is stated among other things: "When, therefore, a Christian of any origin, class or rank, man, woman, priest or layman, accepts a gift in order to help a Jew or Jewess against the law of Christ, or accepts any kind of present from them or their agents, or in return for any kind of gift does not guard and hold high the Commandments of the Law of Christ (simple passivity in the face of the foe), so... All who allow themselves to be bribed with a gift or conceal a fault of a Jew and do not exemplarily punish his wickedness, will be penalised by the statutes of the Holy Fathers in the decrees and must, if it is proved against them, pay double to the state treasury of the King of what they received from the Jew or Jewess."[269]

As one sees, the Jews have always understood in a masterly way how to buy the Christians and Gentiles with gold, since the latter frequently suffered from a chronic avarice and sold themselves to the "Synagogue of Satan".

The Israelite ambassadors and embassies in various lands of the world have handed over to archbishops and high dignitaries of the Catholic Church suspicious invitations and seduced them with an interesting, expense-free journey with a skilfully drawn-up route of travel, exactly as in the case of travels in the Soviet Union. This they do on the eve of the next Ecumenical Council and wish with this, as we have experienced, to buy support for their proposal condemning anti-Semitism, which the international Jews hold in readiness and which their agents of the "Fifth Column" intend to set through at the Council. We hope that this kind of bribery – gratis journeys to Palestine – fails and that no imitator of the Apostles commits the sin of Judas and sells himself for thirty pieces of silver.

---

[269] Fuero Juzgo, Ed. Realacademia Espanola, 1815. Pages 186-192.

Holy Church has always made efforts to find the motive which binds secret Jewry, the converts and their descendants. A reason lies in the Jewish books which these false Christians secretly read and whose doctrines were inherited from father to son. In Canon XI it is proposed to punish this offence severely, and it is ordered, among others, that the secret Jew, who is found with such books in his house or which are found on him, shall be marked on his head and upon the first occasion receive a hundred lashes of the whip. In addition, he must sign in the presence of witnesses that he will never again read such books or possess them. If he afterwards becomes back-sliding, his property shall be made responsible to the Baron, whom the King has appointed and he shall be expelled from the land. If a teacher is trapped thereby in spreading this error, and continued to teach what is forbidden, then he shall experience the same punishment as his pupils when they are older than twelve. If they are younger, they are not punished in this manner...”[270]

As one sees, the utmost effort was made in this regard, in order to prevent false Christians transmitting secret Judaism through instruction in their doctrine and secret books handed down from father to son. Simultaneously a vain attempt was made to prevent the guilty from backsliding and they were made to give before witnesses a formal written promise that they would not do it again. This promise was valueless, for the Jews have neither upon this nor upon other occasions kept their promises or solemn pacts, as the facts have proved in the ensuing years.

In Canon XIII it is ordered: “If a Jew, through cheating or deceit or from fear of losing his wealth, asserts that he keeps to the morals and laws of the Christians and fulfils the words according to the law of Christ and says he will retain his Christian servants because he is a Christian, so... we have reflected upon what manner he shall prove what he has said, so that from now on he may not cheat or hold back what he has said. Therefore we ordain that all Jews in the province of our kingdom can sell their Christian servants, as we have ordered in the preceding law. If they wish to keep them, they must declare themselves to be Christians as we have declared in this book. For we give them an opportunity not to further render themselves suspect and to wash themselves free of all doubts in the time of sixty days, from 1st February to 1st April of this year.” Accordingly, they are obligated through this law to go to the bishop of the province, and to promise openly before witnesses to give up all Jewish customs which they condemned, and that “they never more fall back into their old unbelief and maintain all other statutes which we explain in this

---

[270] Fuero Juzgo, same edition. Pages 192-193.

chapter; that they under such circumstances confess and openly admit not to preserve in their heart the opposite of what they proclaim with their mouth, and not to hypocritically adopt Christianity outwardly and in their hearts preserve Judaism"... "And if one of them gives himself out as a Christian and, after the evidence mentioned and the oath, holds again to the law of the Jews, believes in it and thus breaks his promise and does not hold it, and has falsely spoken in God's name, and falls back into the unbelief of the Jews, his goods are confiscated in favour of the King, he shall receive a hundred lashes of the whip, be marked on the head, and banished to the uttermost ends of the world."[271]

With this determination, which belongs to the collection of laws mentioned that were approved and empowered in the Church Canon IX of the 12th Council of Toledo, the archbishops and bishops of the Holy Synod wished to prevent the secret Jews controlling Christian servants and gave them the opportunity of remaining Jews openly, without expropriating them. By the uttermost caution with which the Prelates and the King proceeded, it is clear that the Jews, in order to retain their Christian servants, pretended to be bound to the Christian faith whilst they remained Jews in secret and belonged to that destructive "Jewish Fifth Column" in Christianity. Therefore they were threatened with severe punishments if they were discovered in the act, and a vain attempt was made to attain the honest conversion of the Jews and their descendants, and to destroy the dangerous "Fifth Column".

Unfortunately, neither Holy Church nor the Christian monarch could attain their goals. They only attained that the false Christians became more and more successful in concealing their subterranean Judaism based on their experience and because they knew that lack of reflection and lack of caution could betray them. As a result, they perfected their deceptive methods and in the course of centuries attained the greatest possible perfection in this art.

On the other hand, the Holy Synod already concerned itself with a problem which was intended to draw the attention of Christian and Mohammedan peoples: that the Jews should wear a special distinguishing mark that distinguished them from the rest of the people, so that the latter could protect themselves from their deceit and their revolutionary activity. Here the Holy Synod determined that they should be marked on the head. As a result they were perhaps distinguished in a more effective way as dangerous, secret Jews than they were later by other Christian and

---

[271] Fuero Juzgo. Same Edition. Canon XIII.

Mohammedan devices and lastly by the Nazi device of the renowned star of Judah on their clothing. They could remove their caps, their special dress or their stars, but only with difficulty the distinguishing mark on their heads. A similar determination would alarm us in the 20th century, if a Holy Church Council passed it. But whoever knows the deadly danger which this Jewish band of criminals has always represented for the rest of the world and still represents will be more tolerant and understand. These signs, which were used at different times, were an effective method, so that the false Christians of the "Jewish Fifth Column" were recognisable and the real disciples of Christ could protect themselves from their destructive activity. If we could recognise them at the time in our days, then it would not have been possible for them to commit so successfully their betrayal and deceit, through which so many peoples were handed over to murderous Communism.

We will come back again later to the Holy Council of Toledo. To the Laws which were approved through the Church Canon IX belong the Canons XIV and XV, which contain the wording for the conspiracy of Judaism and simultaneously the oath of loyalty to Christianity. Both were unfortunately used within the framework of an unfruitful attempt to secure the honesty of this false conversion.

In spite of all measures to prevent this, the Jew attempts, in every land which opens its gates to him, to exercise a rule over those who afforded him hospitality. Through Canon XVII it is attempted to make an end to a part of this activity by forbidding the Jews, among other things, to "have power over a Christian or control him" and ordering that they "in no manner command Christians, sell them, or have any kind of power over them." For the Jews who overstep this law and also for the nobles and barons in public offices who violate it and give the Jews power over the Christians, penalties are ordered. Unfortunately, the Jews spurred on the rebellious spirit of the Visigoth nobles against the monarch, in order to secure their protection and thus made the efficacy of these laws largely worthless.

Another measure of the Holy Council for destruction of the "Fifth Column" is cited in Canon XVIII, which established a veritable espionage against Christians of Jewish descent within their very homes, by compelling their Christian servants to denounce their Jewish practices and offering them their freedom in exchange. In the law mentioned it is stated concerning the servants: "That at each time he who says and swears he is a Christian, and reveals the unbelief of his master and reveals his error, shall be set free." Perhaps this measure for the destruction of clandestine Jewry in the bosom of Christian society was the most effective of all those previously cited. At that time it was logical that a servant who was almost a slave had interest in receiving freedom, if he revealed the secret Jewish practices of his masters who were only seeming Christians. In this respect the Prelates of the Holy Council really undertook a decisive step, for now the members of the "Fifth Column" in their own homes had to take heed before their own servants, who could any moment discover and report their secret Judaism. Unfortunately, the false Jewish Christians found ways and means in order to conceal their secret Judaism even in their own homes, and the measure was not sufficient in order to destroy the "Fifth Column". Clandestine Jewry was only more resolute and concealed, as we shall see in later chapters.

BANISHING OF BISHOPS AND PRIESTS WHO GIVE POWER TO THE JEWS

This Holy Council concerned itself again with the condemnation of bishops and clergy who supported the Jews in a harmful way and manner. In addition it is stated in Canon XIX, which was approved in Church Law IX: "And when a bishop, priest or deacon provides a Jew with power, in order to somehow control the Church or to destroy the affairs of Christians, he must give so much of his property to the king as the Church affairs are worth which he entrusted to the Jew. If he has no property, in order to pay, he shall be expelled to the furthermost ends of the earth, so that he does repentance and realises his wicked act."[272]

The Prelates of the Council also approved laws intended to prevent Christians of Jewish origin travelling from one city to another in order to secretly exercise their Jewish religion, when they were no longer subject to the control of the clergy where they currently were. Therefore it is stated in Canon XX: "When they travel from one place to another, they must reveal to the bishop, priest or burgomaster their place of arrival. They must not remove themselves from this priest, so that the latter can provide proof that they have not celebrated the Sabbath and have not maintained the customs of the Jews. They shall have no opportunity to preserve their error and to hide themselves in order to remain in it. For the same reason they should pay heed to the laws of Christianity"... It is further stated that when they pretend to travel from one place to another: "They must not leave the priests without permission, to whom they come, before the

---

[272] Fuero Juzgo, Edition of the Real Academia Espanola, 1815. Page 200.

Sabbaths have passed and before the priests know that they do not observe the Sabbaths. And the priest of their place should write a letter to those of the other place through which these Jews come, in order both with the period of stay or also with the journeys, to avoid deceit. And they are instructed to carry this out exactly. If anyone does not follow our command, the bishop, priest or burgomaster of the place can order a hundred lashes of the whip. For we do not tolerate that they return home without the letters of the bishops or priests of the place which they visited. In the letters the days must be remarked, which they spent with the bishops of that city, how they have come there, when they leave it and have come home."[273]

Without doubt the obligation was difficult for Christian servants to denounce their masters, who were also Christians but who practised the Jewish religion in secret, but it made it difficult for the secret Jews even to maintain in their homes the rites of the Sabbath and of the Jewish festivals. There therefore remained no other choice for them than to pretend a journey and to perform these rites in a secret unwatched-over place. After this cunning had been seen through, the Holy Council and the Christian monarch sought ways and means to control these journeys by secret Jews down to the last detail, in order to prevent that the official Christians as a result practised the Jewish religion. The Law XI perfects the preceding ones and renews the old law that the Jews must spend the Jewish feast days with a bishop or priest or – if that is not possible – with good Christians of the place, so "that they prove together with them that they are good Christians and live correctly." In this manner they sought to deprive Christians of Jewish origin of even the smallest possibility of keeping the Jewish feast days, in order to see if they would in the long run become honest Christians and no longer adhere to secret Judaism.

CLERGY FORBIDDEN TO PROTECT THE JEWS

Through the Law XXIII the priests receive power, in order to carry out these laws, and the strict command is given them: "Not to protect the Jews or to cite grounds for their defence which give them the possibility of remaining with their error and their law." Clearly the problem of the Judases among the clergy was already then so great that the approval of this law through the Holy Synod was also justified.

---

[273] Fuero Juzgo, Book XII. Tit. III. Canon XX.

EXCOMMUNICATION OF NEGLIGENT BISHOPS

Canon XXIV is still more definite in this respect: "The priests of the Church must avoid falling into the sin, of leaving the peoples in their error... and therefore we add, in order to shake them out of their negligence, that a bishop who gives way to avarice or a bad idea and hesitates to fulfil these laws, if he knows their errors, their conceit and their folly and does not compel and punish them, will be banned for three months and must pay the King a pound in gold. If he does not possess this, he will be banned for six months, so that his negligence and weakness be punished. And we give every bishop who zealously serves God the power to check and restrain the error of those Jews and to correct their follies, and he does this in place of the negligent bishop and he completes what the other overlooked. If he does not do this, if he is negligent like the other bishop, fails to serve God zealously and is not conscientious, the King shall make good their error and punish them on account of their sin. The same which we have ordered for those bishops who are negligent in their task of correcting the error of the Jews, is valid also for all believers, priests, deacons, clergy..."[274]

When the Council approved this law in its sacred Canon IX, it was declared that it was not only deadly sin if one supported the Jews, but also if the bishop, priests or cleric is negligent in the fulfilment of his duties in the struggle against Jewry, and this deadly sin would be punished with the excommunication of the guilty. Here one could now ask: How many prelates and high dignitaries of the Church would be excommunicated today if Canon IX of the aforesaid Sacred Council were applied, since the committing of this deadly sin to support the Jews in any kind of form is so widespread among our present-day clergy?

In Canon XXVIII a very effective measure is ordered. The honesty of the Christian belief of Catholics of Jewish origin should not only be proved through the witness of the bishops, priests or burgomasters of the land, but also through the actions of the Christians themselves. It no longer suffices that they give the assurance of being honestly converted, but they must prove it through deeds. This law, however, deals even more strictly with Christians who, having already been unmasked as secret Jews and pardoned on demonstrating their repentance in words and deeds, were soon to be discovered again practising the Jewish religion. Concerning these recidivists it is stated in the law mentioned: "That one will never

---

[274] Fuero Juzgo, Book XII. Tit. III. Law XXVII.

more pardon them and they should suffer punishment without any kind of sympathy, be it now the death penalty or a lesser one which they deserve."[275]

When this Canon was approved by the Holy Council, the doctrine of the Catholic Church in this respect was also firmly laid down. For, although Our Lord God is ready to forgive every sinner before his death, it is quite another matter to hold that the Jews, who represent a constant threat for the Church and mankind, must be punished by the civil authorities on account of their crimes. It is not permissible for them, in order to escape their justified punishment, to quote Our Divine's Saviour's sublime doctrine concerning the forgiveness of one's enemies, for He referred to forgiving the offences committed by one individual against another individual, not to the crimes or offences of an evildoer to the harm of society or of the nation.

The clergy who today stand in the service of Jewry, draw in this respect sophistical conclusions and attempt in a blasphemous way and manner to use the sublime teachings of love and forgiveness of Our Redeemer Jesus Christ, since they wish to prevent peoples threatened by Jewish enslavement from making use of their natural right to a just defence and from fighting against the criminal Jewish conspirators and allotting them a just punishment. Moreover, one should not forget the great authority that Holy Church has always given to the Councils of Toledo regarding the definition of ecclesiastical doctrine and regarding the measures taken against the Jews by the 12th Council; their vigour, as doctrine of Holy Church, is even greater in view of the fact that, in the year 683, a new Council of Toledo, number XIII, not only confirmed, in its Canon IX, the laws approved in the previous Synod, but also ordered that they should be eternally in force and constant, giving them the perennial character of a doctrine of the Church. To this end the aforesaid Canon IX of the 13th Council of Toledo says: "Although the synodal acts of the 12th Council of Toledo, which took place in the first year of government of our illustrious Prince Ervigio, were arranged and fixed by the unanimous judgment of our agreement in this royal city, we now add with firm resolve that these resolutions, as they are written or ordered, shall have eternal force and validity."[276]

---

[275] Fuero Juzgo, Book XII. Tit. III. Law XXVII.
[276] 13th Council of Toledo, Law 9. Compilation of Juan Tejada y Ramiro, same edition, Vol. II. Page 505.

CHAPTER FIFTEEN

THE 16ᵀᴴ COUNCIL OF TOLEDO HOLDS THE DESTRUCTION OF THE "JEWISH FIFTH COLUMN" TO BE NECESSARY

As we have already said, the Visigoth kingdom, after the almost universal conversion of the Jews to Christianity, had to fight tenaciously against a far more dangerous kind of Judaism: clandestine Jewry. The efforts of the 12th and 13th Synods of Toledo to destroy this powerful block of Jews in the bosom of Holy Church had completely failed. The all-embracing, energetic anti-Jewish collection of laws, which were approved by both Councils, was ineffective to destroy the dangerous "Fifth Column," since they did not have the effect that the Christians of Jewish origin gave up their secret Jewish practices and became true Christians. The proof of this is that ten years later, when Egica already ruled, the 16th Council of Toledo concerned itself anew with this fearful affair. Already in the first law it is stated:

"Canon I. In the face of the falsehood of the Jews. – Although there are countless judgements of the old Fathers concerning the falsehood of the Jews and in addition many new laws, nevertheless, as per the prophetic prediction relating to their stiffneckedness, the sin of Judah is written as with an iron pen on a diamond, harder than stone in its blindness and obstinacy. It is therefore very necessary that the wall of their unfaithfulness is combated through the machinations of the Catholic Church more thoroughly, so that they may either improve themselves against their will or be destroyed in such a way that they perish for ever by judgment of the Lord."[277] After clarifying this point of doctrine, the Holy Council enumerates in the canon cited additional measures that should be immediately applied against the Jews.

---

[277] 16th Council of Toledo. Canon 1. Compilation by Juan Tejada y Ramiro. Same edition. Vol. II. Pages 563-564.

This definition of the doctrine of Holy Church against the Jews served centuries later as basis for the later Popes and Councils asserting the death penalty for the secret Jews in the bosom of Catholicism. For defence of these doctrines and of the policy of Holy Church we have already cited that all states of the Christian and pagan world have always approved similar measures against spies or saboteurs of hostile nations and they also still approve them today.

It has never occurred to anyone to criticise a government because it executes members of the "Fifth Column" and traitors to the country. The whole Jewish propaganda is, however, already directed against the Church, because they, like all other lands of the world, held the death penalty for the Jews in the bosom of Christian society as justified, who carried on espionage in Christian society and wished to destroy or conquer it. It is, of course, regrettable to kill a man. But if the peoples have the right to defend themselves, then Holy Church has it also, which defends not only herself but also the peoples who believe and trust in her, especially when we reflect that the Jews in the bosom of Holy Church not only organise an all-embracing network of the usual espionage and sabotage, but represent the most destructive "Fifth Column" in the same land, whose institutions they unfortunately also utilise. Thus without doubt action was taken against them on account of the State and for defence of Holy Church, whereby Holy Church and the Christian state directed themselves with one accord against them.

The ideal solution would be that the Jews voluntarily leave the land which generously accepted them and return to their homeland, that they should recognise the independence of every people, and not commit the crime of the worst espionage and sabotage as members of the most dangerous "Fifth Column" which has existed in the world. No one would then trouble them and the remaining nations could live in peace. If in addition they commit crimes for which the supreme penalties exist, they are solely responsible for the just punishment they have received for such crimes in the course of history. In addition, they have in fact their own land, which has been allotted to them in the Soviet Union and in Israel. During the centuries when they had no homeland, they could have behaved like other immigrants, lived in peace with the peoples and recognised the religions which they accepted. Then nothing would have happened to them. However, they betrayed the nations which allowed them hospitality, attempted to conquer them, to rob and destroy them, and did everything possible in order to destroy Christianity from its beginning 0nwards. They accepted it and attempted to disintegrate it from within through heresies. They gave impetus to the bloody Roman persecutions and furthered them. Through their crimes they called forth universal rejection and defence, not only from the side of the Church and Christian peoples, but also on the part of Islam and the peoples ruled by it.

The Jews themselves through their criminal, ungrateful and treacherous mode of action called forth the bloody repressive measures which the threatened peoples seized upon against them by making use of their right to justified defence. They complain about this repression but conceal the motives. It is the same as if the Romans, who wished to conquer Gaul and who had to mourn many thousands of dead in the battle, had been cynical enough to accuse the attacked Gauls of being murderers and persecutors of the Romans. Or if the Japanese, in the last war when they conquered China and suffered hundreds of thousands of losses, had possessed the insolence to describe the Chinese as murderers or persecutors of the Japanese. Then we could say: If the Romans had not fallen upon Gaul, they would also not have needed to lament that the Gauls killed thousands of Romans. And if the Japanese had not attacked China, they would also not have had to lament the death of their fellow-citizens.

While these and other peoples, however, have never struck upon the idea of lamenting over the losses and injuries which they suffered on grounds of their battles of conquest, the Jews for centuries have secretly and hypocritically begun the cruellest, most totalitarian and bloodiest war, and were cynical enough, to make a great outcry if religions or peoples justifiably defended themselves and killed Jews or robbed them of their freedom in order to prevent them from causing further harm. If Jews in the future wish not to bear the consequence of their stiff-necked, cruel universal struggle for conquest, they must abandon it. If they do not do this, they should at least be so brave and adapt themselves in a dignified way to the consequences as the other conqueror peoples of the world have done.

CHAPTER SIXTEEN

THE 17TH COUNCIL OF TOLEDO PUNISHES
THE JEWISH CONSPIRACIES WITH SLAVERY

In the year 694, when Ervigio still ruled, the widely- branched conspiracy of false Christians was discovered, who secretly practised the Jewish religion and who had many aims. On the one side they wished to bring the Church into disorder and conquer the throne, one the other side to betray the country and destroy the Visigoth state.

At that time St. Felix, the archbishop of Toledo, had summoned a new Council, in which participated all prelates of the kingdom and only some from Gallia Narbonensis, since a plague prevented the others from coming. When the Holy Synod was already assembled, it learned about and received proofs of the secret Jewish conspiracy which was instigating a revolution in all classes and was thus so dangerous for Christianity and the Christian state that the Holy Synod condemned it. The Holy Synod had assembled in the Church of Santa Leocadia de la Vega in Toledo, and St. Felix performed the presidency in this terrible struggle and was the new leader of Christianity against the Jews.

The protocols of this Holy Synod are one of the most valuable documents and give details concerning what the "Jewish Fifth Column" in the bosom of the Church and also in the realm of a Christian or pagan people is capable of doing. We hold this document to be important not only for Catholics, but also for all men of whatever people or whatever religion who have to compete with the threat of Jewish Imperialism.

Most interesting in this Council is Canon VIII, in which it is expressly stated: "Concerning the condemnation of the Jews. – And since it is known that the Jewish people with wickedness, blasphemy, and the shedding of the blood of Jesus Christ, in addition through the violation of the oath (because, among other things they had sworn to be true

Christians and not to honour Judaism in secret) they are polluted, so that the wickedness has no end, they therefore must weep that they have committed such a serious, horrible sin, who on account of their wickedness wished not only to destroy the Church, but have also attempted with tyrannical bravado to ruin the fatherland and the nation, and had rejoiced because they held their time to have come, and to have caused harm to Catholics. Therefore must this cruel, astonishing arrogance be done penance with a still more cruel punishment. So must judgment against them be all the stricter, and whatever is established of infamy must be everywhere punished. In connection with other affairs we here at this Council have learned of their conspiracy. Thus not only on account of breaking their promise have they polluted, through belonging to their sects, the garb (tunica) of faith with which Holy Church had invested them with holy baptism, but wished also to gain control of the royal throne through the conspiracy. Since we have learned through their own confessions of this disastrous wickedness, they should be punished with irrevocable censure through the condemnation of our decree. Upon command, namely of our devout religious prince Egica, who serves the Lord zealously and is strong in Holy Faith, should not only the mocking of the cross of Christ but also the planned destruction of his people and country be avenged, against which they proceeded so cruelly. They shall proceed more strictly against them and their property be confiscated, which then falls into the state treasury. In addition they themselves, their women, children and other descendants in all provinces of Spain live in eternal servitude. They must leave their homeland, must be driven apart from one another and must serve whosoever the King so commands... Over their children of both sexes we shall dispose, so that, as soon as they are seven years old, they be separated from their parents and no relationship be allowed to them. Their own masters shall give them over to true Christians for education, so that the men marry with Christian women and conversely. As we had already said, it is allowed neither the parents nor the children to celebrate the ceremonies of Jewish superstition or to fall back upon any occasion again into unbelief."[278]

As first commentary to this Holy Canon of the 17th Council we can make the assurance that, if this Synod of the Catholic Church had taken place in our time, both the archbishop St. Felix, who was president, as well as the entire Holy Council would have been condemned as Anti-Semites and Nazi war criminals by those cardinals and bishops who today more serve the "Synagogue of Satan" than Holy Church. These would impose

---

[278] 16th Council of Toledo, Canon 8. Compilation by Juan Tejada y Ramiro. Same edition, Vol. II. Pages 602-603.

censures and condemnations against those Catholics who defend the Church and their country against the Jewish threat. These Church dignitaries cause the real Catholics and patriots to be condemned and disapprove of attacks upon the Jews, which are by far milder than those of the Holy Council which was led by the renowned Saint Felix, the archbishop of Toledo, whom the Church has canonised. On the other hand, through the dangerous conspiracy which the converted Jews and their descendants instigated, it is clear that the false Christians and secret Jews could proceed successfully against the laws directed against them of the preceding Councils and were strong enough in order to organise such an extensive plot.

In the face of the great danger, the Christian state and Church armed itself for defence and seized upon the most extreme measures, to enslave all Jews and to take away from them their seven-year old children, so that separated from their parents they received a Christian education and the possibility was removed from them of being attracted to the organisations of secret Jewry. By this it was wished to avoid that Judaism was passed on by parents to children, even if the parents in secret continued to be bound to Judaism. Thus it was wished to attain that in the following generations the "Fifth Column" of the false Christians, who secretly adhered to the "Synagogue of Satan" would be completely destroyed. The fact that the children of the new generation should marry as grown-ups with good Christians or Christian women, was doubtless intended to give a further guarantee that the third generation of "Fifth Column" in question would be completely destroyed and the descendants of the Jews would be honest Christians. As we will see later, however, this kind of attempt failed, for the non-identified secret Jews could again and again secretly introduce the Christian children of Jewish origin into Jewish customs.

On the other hand the skilled intrigues of the Jews broke through all plans of the Holy Council and again condemned to failure the strict measures which the Church and the very Christian Visigoth monarchy had seized upon in defence against the Jewish threat.

In the records of this Holy Council we find a very interesting fact, from which emerges already at that time, thus almost 1200 years ago, several Jewish revolts had broken out against the Christian kings. This fact is confirmed to us by King Egica in his letter to the Holy Synod: "On several places of the earth they (the Jews) rebelled against their Christian princes, who killed many of them, according to the just judgment of God."[279]

With these revolts against the princes they had clearly only success, when after hundreds of years experience they understood that they had to make the Christian peoples themselves, even if unconsciously, into their allies. In addition, the Jewish leaders pretended to be Christians and appeared as redeemers of these peoples and organisers of liberal and democratic movements, to give the mass of the people the seductive promise that they would rule themselves and free them from the yoke of the monarchy.

One must bear in mind that the terrible punishments which the 17th Council uttered against the secret Jewish conspirators found application in the entire realm of rule of the Gothic kingdom, with exception of the province of Gallia Narbonensis. This district was "nearly depopulated" – as it is said in a letter from the prince – through a deadly epidemic and for other reasons. Therefore the Jews were to be allowed to live there as earlier "with all their property, under the duke of this land, so that they might be of use to the public income."[280] It is thus highly possible that the Duke of Gothic Gaul mentioned exerted pressure so that the Jews living in his district remained spared from the punishments imposed against the rest of the Jews in the kingdom by the Holy Council. As a result not only were these false Christians saved, but also many others from the affected districts fled from the threat of slavery and other punishments to Gallia Narbonensis. As a result the percentage of secret Jewish population in South France increased, where a second Judaea arose.

Admittedly they were only tolerated and protected in Gallia Narbonensis under the condition that they became honest Christians and did not secretly practise the Jewish religion. In other cases the severe punishments of the Holy Synod were applied to them. But, as was established in later centuries, these false Christians in no way gave up their Judaism and practised it so secretly that South France was famed in the Middle Ages as the most dangerous secret Jewish nest. The Jews skilfully pretended an apparent honest Christianity and erected in this region the headquarters of the destructive revolutionary heresy which by a hair's breadth would have destroyed the Church and the whole of Christianity in

---

[279] 16th Council of Toledo. Records. Visit of the King. Compilation by Juan Tejada y Ramiro. Same edition. Vol. II. Page 593.

[280] 16th Council of Toledo, Records, Visit of the King. Compilation of Juan Tejada y Ramiro, same edition. Vol. III. Page 594.

the Middle Ages. From this the catastrophic consequences became clear, which leniency and good-will in the face of such an infamous enemy as Judaism represents brings with it.

The Jewish revolt which Egica energetically repressed, whereby he was supported by the severe penalties of the 17th council of Toledo, had increased in great measure and was close upon destroying the Christian state and replacing it through a Jewish one. In order to understand this, we must investigate some preceding events:

The Catholic writer Ricardo C. Albanes writes concerning the situation of the Jews in the Visigoth monarchy: "The Jews had increased as astonishingly in Gothic Spain as previously in ancient Egypt and here also gained great importance and wealth, so that they were valuable to the Visigoth conquerors. They particularly devoted themselves to trade, the arts and industry. Almost all doctors were Jews and there were also many Jewish lawyers. They chiefly had a monopoly in trade with the east, whereby their origin and language were very much to their favour. As important owners of businesses they had also many Christian servants, whom they treated badly. But the Jews gained control not only of the Gothic land, but did not cease where they could, from undermining the Christian faith. The fact that they supported the heretics, at first the Arians and later the Priscillians, and the activity of the Jew-Christians, made difficult the conflict between Christianity and Judaism in Spain, which led to both the Councils as well as the Kings themselves very soon seizing upon strict anti-Semitic measures."[281]

Apart from this enormous power which they had gained, the policy of Holy Church and the Christian Kings of heaping with honours the Jews who had honestly been converted to Christianity, giving them valuable positions and even nobility titles, and opening to them the doors to the priestly office and high church posts, while at the same time prosecuting the false converts pitilessly – which, however, did not have the desired result of honestly converting them all –, had not the desired results. For then already they hypocritically pretended to be honestly converted, in order to have advantages and to obtain valuable positions which were given to the honestly converted. Thus they could more and more gain a foothold in the religious and political institutions of Christian society and obtain the highest power.

---

[281] Ricardo C. Albanes: The Jews in the course of centuries. Pages 167-168.

This position gave them hope of being able to conduct to victory a well prepared revolt, in order to destroy the Christian state and to replace it with a Jewish one. In addition they secured at the right time the military support of powerful Jewish centres in North Africa, which should fall upon the Iberian peninsula, when the general revolt of the false Christians, who practised the Jewish religion in secret, broke out.

The renowned Spanish historian Marcelino Menendez Pelayo declares the following: "Since they wished to spread Christianity more rapidly and to establish peace between the two races, the 12th and 13th Council of Toledo permitted the Jews really unusual privileges (*Plena mentis intentione*), elevated them to nobles and freed them from the head tax. However, all was in vain. The Jew-Christians (Christians, who were secret Jews), who were rich and numerous under Egica, plotted against the security of the State... Danger threatened. This King and the 17th Council of Toledo took refuge in a last hard resort, confiscated the property of the Jews, declared them to be slaves and took away from them the children, that they might be brought up as Christians."[282]

One can already discern how the Jews for twelve centuries have laughed at the noble efforts of Christians for peace and unity between the different races, in order to utilise this devout striving and to gain valuable positions, which permit them to destroy the Christian society and to subject the people which naively opened to them its frontiers. Today they still successfully utilise the noble wish for unity of the peoples and brotherhood of the races with similar infamous aims.

The renowned Dutch historian Reinhardt Dozy provides interesting details concerning the conspiracy investigated by us, which on the other side are also confirmed by the Jewish- Spanish Encyclopaedia authorised by Jewry. This historian writes about the Jews in the Gothic kingdom: "Towards 694, seven years before Spain was conquered by the Musulmans, they planned a general revolt together with their brothers in belief on the other side of the Straits of Gibraltar, where several Berber tribes practised the Jewish religion and those expelled from Spain took refuge. Probably it was intended that the revolt should break out in several places at once, when the Jews from Africa had landed on the Spanish coast. But before it came to this the government was given knowledge of the plot. King Egica at once seized upon the necessary measures. Later he called a Council in Toledo and instructed his spiritual and worldly leaders

---

[282] Marcelino Menendez Pelayo: *History of the heterodox Spaniards*, Printer F. Marato e Hijos. Vol I. Page 627.

concerning the punishable plans of the Jews and ordered them to punish this accursed race. Some Jews were sent to trial, and it was revealed that through the plot Spain was to be made into a Jewish state. The Bishops foamed with rage and alarm and condemned all Jews to the loss of their property and of their freedom. The king intended to hand them over to the Christians as slaves, indeed even to those who had previously been slaves of the Jews and who were emancipated by the king..."[283]

This is a typical example of how the "Jewish Fifth Column" proceeds against the nations which has accepted them.

---

[283] Reinhard Dozy: *Histoire des musulmans d'Espagne*, Leiden 1932, Page 267, and Jewish-Spanish Encyclopaedia, same edition, Vol. IV. Word "Spain".

CHAPTER SEVENTEEN

CHRISTIAN-JEWISH RECONCILIATION.
PRELUDE TO COLLAPSE

After the death of Egica there occurred what so often happens to Christian and pagan states: the new rulers forgot to follow the wise policy of their predecessors further, and attempted to introduce all possible kinds of innovations, which in a short time nullified the years of conscientious work – the result of great experience. One of the reasons for the superiority of the Jewish devices, in comparison to our own, was that they have understood how to conduct over centuries a unified definite policy towards those whom they regard as their foes. On the other hand neither we Christians nor the pagans were capable of carrying out a constant policy towards Jewry lasting more than two or three generations, even if it was so arranged and founded on the basic right of self defence.

Witiza, the son of Egica, who followed him on the throne, began to nullify everything which his father had done, both the good as well as the bad. He was a very passionate man who in fact inclined to worldly contentment, but at first had good intentions and ascended the throne with the wonderful wish to forgive all enemies of his father and to attain the unity of his subjects. In the Chronicle of Pacense, Witiza is described as a conciliatory man who wished to make good past injustice and who went so far as to burn documents falsified in favour of the state treasury.

The false Jewish Christians, who then lived in arduous slavery, after their monstrous conspiracy had failed, saw in the conciliatory intentions and the just striving for unity of the realm, which they attributed to Witiza, the means of freeing themselves from the terrible punishment and of regaining their lost influence. They attained that he release them from the sorrowful servitude and – at least for the moment – placed them equal with the rest of his subjects. Witiza fell into the trap like others and believed the Jewish problem could be solved through Christian-Jewish reconciliation, which, on the foundation of mutual respect, equal rights, greater understanding and even brotherly and friendly coexistence of Christians and Jews, would make an end to a century-long struggle and would secure the internal peace of the kingdom.

Such reconciliation can be a wonderful, desirable solution, but is only possible when both sides really wish it. But if the one side acts in good faith and sacrifices for reconciliation its justified defence, it destroys its own means of defence and must trust powerlessly in the honesty of the other side. The latter on the contrary only utilises the magnanimous conduct of its former opponent and awaits the moment to give it its death thrust. Then the apparent reconciliation and the false brotherhood are only a prelude to death, or at least to collapse.

This has always occurred when Christians and pagans allow themselves to be deceived by the skilled diplomatic manoeuvres of the Jews and believed in their friendship and loyalty. For the Jews unfortunately only utilise these subtle requests in order to disarm those whom they secretly regard in their deepest hearts always as deadly foes, in order then, when they have once been lulled asleep through the aromatic nectar of friendship and brotherhood and are disarmed, to easily enslave or destroy them. The Jews have always followed the norm, if they are weak or dangerously threatened, of giving themselves out as friends of their foes, in order to be able to easier rule them. Unfortunately, they have had success with this manoeuvre in the course of centuries and still also today.

Jewish diplomacy is classic: In order to arouse sympathy, they describe the persecutions, slavery and murders, which their people has suffered, in the blackest colours, but carefully conceal the motives through which they themselves called forth these persecutions. If they have been successful in inoculating pity, they attempt to transform it into sympathy. Accordingly they fight without pause, in order to attain all possible advantages on grounds of this pity and sympathy. These advantages have always been directed at destroying the defence erected against them by Christian or pagan clergy or civil authorities, so that the Jews can set their plans for conquest over the unfortunate state into fact, which has naively destroyed the walls which earlier rulers had erected for defence against Jewish conquest.

Gradually, the Jews gain greater influence in the land through this manoeuvre, which affords them hospitality, and they go from being the persecuted to become merciless persecutors of the real patriots, who attempt to defend their religion or their land against the rule and destruction of the undesired aliens, until the Jews finally rule or destroy the Christian or pagan state, always according to what is planned.

Thus it also occurred under the rule of Witiza. At first the Jews were successful in arousing his pity and inoculating him with sympathy, so that he freed them from the hard servitude which the 17th Council of Toledo and King Egica had imposed upon them as defence against their plans of conquest. The defence of Holy Church and of the Visigoth monarchy against Jewish imperialism was thus demolished. Witiza placed them equal with the Christians as brothers, in order to later go still further, as is revealed by the renowned Chronicles of the 13th century, which were written by the Archbishop Roderich (Rodericus Toletanus, "De rebus Hispaniae") and Bishop Lucas de Tuy ("Chronicle of Lucas Tudensis"). Here it is described to us that, when the Jews had once gained the sympathy of the monarch, the latter protected and favoured them and allotted them greater honours than the churches and prelates.

As one sees they were successful, after their liberation and the granting to them of equal rights, in occupying higher positions than the prelates and Churches. All these measures naturally aroused the dissatisfaction of the Christians and clergy who zealously defend the Church. It is well possible that this increasing resistance finally influenced Witiza to strengthen the position of his new Jewish allies. As the Bishop Lucas de Tuy writes in his Chronicle, he caused those to be summoned back whom the Councils and the previous kings had banished from the Gothic kingdom. These returned in great number into their new promised land, in order to enlarge and strengthen their growing power in the Visigoth kingdom.[284]

The historian of the previous century, José Amador de los Rios, who is known on account of his skilled defence of the Jews, admits, however, that Witiza, in relation to the Jews, undertook exactly the opposite of what his father and his predecessors had done: At a new national Council Witiza revoked the old Church laws and the laws which had been enthusiastically accepted by the nation, in order not to have to confess to the Catholic faith. He released those baptised from their oath, and finally placed many members of this despised race in high positions. The consequence of these tumultuous incomprehensible measures was soon to be seen. In a short time the Jews had attained a really dangerous predominance and utilised all opportunities for their advantage. And perhaps out of revenge they welded

---

[284] Rodericus Toletanus: De Rebus Hispaniae, Book II. Chapter 15 and 16. Cronicon [short chronicle]. Lucas Tudensis: "Cronicon", Hispania Ilustrata. Vol. IV.

new plans and secretly prepared to avenge themselves also for the humiliation under the Visigoth rule.[285] This historian, whom no one can accuse of Anti-semitism and who in general is regarded by the Jewish historians as reliable source, has described to us with few words the terrible consequences which the policy of King Witiza, with its enticements to free the repressed Jews and later to attain the Christian-Jewish reconciliation and the reconciliation of both peoples – at the beginning of his period of government – had for Christians.

The Jesuit father Juan de Mariana, a historian of the 16th century, writes concerning the terrible transformation of Witiza: "Witiza in fact at first seemed a good prince, who wished to return to innocence and to suppress wickedness. He lifted the exile which his father had imposed upon many, and as this were not enough, he gave them back their property, their dignities and offices. In addition he ordered the documents and trial records to be burned, so that no trace might remain of the crimes and disgrace which they had been accused of and for which they had been condemned in that unruly time. This would have been a good beginning, if things had proceeded further and everything had not altered. It is very difficult to tame unbridleness and power with reason, virtue and moderation. The first step to chaos was made when he listened to flatterers." The Jesuit historian reports in the following concerning all the unskilled dispositions of Witiza, which he had approved by this obscurantist Council of which Amador de los Rios speaks. The commentary of Father Mariana concerning the laws, which openly allowed the Jews to return to Spain, is worthy of note: "In particular – contrary to the old determinations – it was allowed the Jews to return to Spain and to live there. From that time onwards everything came into disorder and began to decay."[286]

It is only natural that everything fell into disorder and went awry when the Jews were left government offices and the expelled Jews allowed to return. This occurred almost always in the course of history when Christians or pagans magnanimously extended the hand of friendship to the Jews and allowed them influence and power. For far removed from thanking this gesture of great-heartedness, the Jews have turned everything into an upheaval and cast into the abyss, to use the apt expression of Father Mariana.

---

[285] J. Amador de los Rios. Same work. Vol. I. Pages 102-103.

[286] Father Juan de Mariana, S.J.: General History of Spain. Valencia, 1785. Vol. II. Chapter XIX. Pages 369-371.

The Catholic historian Ricardo C. Albanés describes the transformation in Witiza in the following manner: "The energetic Egica had understood how to hold within bounds the rebelliousness of the Jews and the plots against the state by the Moslems. But his son and successor Witiza (700-710) became, after a brief period of praiseworthy conduct, a despotic and deeply blasphemous monarch. He threw himself into the arms of the Jews, provided them with honours and public offices..."[287]

We find an impressive description of the lamentable perversity of Witiza in the valuable chronicle from the 9th century, which is known as the "Chronicon Moissiacense". The black swamp of vice is described, into which Witiza and his court plunged, and it is asserted that a harem was erected in his place. In order to legalise this situation, he allowed polygamy in his kingdom and permitted – to the horror of all Christianity – even the Christian clergy to have several women. This condition is described in the brief "Chronicle of Sebastian de Salamanca", who asserts in addition that Witiza furiously attacked the clergy who opposed his enormities. He even went so far as to dissolve Councils and to prevent by force that the Holy Church Laws were observed and placed himself openly against the Church.[288]

But Witiza did not only dissolve a Council which condemned him, but also caused a new one to be called by the clergy who followed him unconditionally, which – as the Bishop Lucas de Tuy in his mediaeval chronicle, the renowned Jewish historian Juan de Mariana and other no less renowned chroniclers and historians report – took place in the church of Saint Peter and Paul in Toledo, in the city quarter, in which a Benedictine monastery was found. This Council approved the errors against the traditional doctrine of the Church and was therefore in fact a heretical Council, whose laws were illegal.

As the chroniclers and historians mentioned assert, at this heretical Council at first the doctrine and the canons of Holy Church were contradicted, which condemned the Jews and which commanded Christians, and in fact particularly the clergy, under threat of ban, to neither support the Jews nor to be neglectful in their struggle against them. At the heretical Council, in contradiction to the preceding, protective statutes were passed for the Jews and the return approved of those expelled under earlier kings. In addition monogamy was abolished and even the clergy allowed to have not only one but several wives. The

[287] Ricardo C. Albanes. Ibid. Pages 171-172.
[288] Chronicon Moissiacense and Chronicon Sebastiani: Holy Spain, Chapter XIII, Page 477.

records of the heretical Council were lost. Through the chroniclers mentioned we have only knowledge of some matters regulated there. Various chroniclers of the Middle Ages even assert that Witiza became furious because his Holiness the Pope disapproved of his outrages, refused him obedience and called forth a scandalous schism, which, in order to lend this division validity, was authorised by the heretical Council in question.[289]

The clergy faithful to Holy Church were so severely persecuted that many finally abandoned the monarch out of cowardice or convenience. Father Mariana writes, among other things, the following: At that time Gunderico, the successor of Felix, was archbishop of Toledo, who would have been a personage of great spiritual gifts and qualities, if he had had the courage to combat such great wickedness. There are people who in fact are displeased by wickedness, but who are not courageous enough to oppose him who commits it. In addition there remained still various priests who held high and kept pure the memory of the preceding time and did not approve of the excesses of Witiza. These he had persecuted and tortured in all ways until they were of his will, as happened with Sinderedo, the successor of Gunderico, who went with the current of the time and was so subservient to the king, that Oppas, the brother or – as others assert – the son of Witiza, was replaced by the Church in Seville, where he was archbishop and sent to Toledo. As a result a new disorder arose; for it was against the Church laws that in this city two prelates should simultaneously be in office.[290]

In this as in many other cases, it was possible for the Jews through the pity which later became sympathy and pro-Semitism – under the pretence of an apparent reconciliation or Christian-Jewish brotherhood – to first free themselves from servitude and later to influence the monarch, so that he allowed them high government posts. With this as also with other affairs these facts go with the disorder and perversity of the Christian State, the upward rise of evil and the persecution of the defenders of Church and nation together. Unfortunately at the time of Witiza there was no Saint Athanasius, Saint John Chrysostom or Saint Felix who could have saved the situation. On the contrary the archbishops and bishops were more concerned to live comfortably than to fulfil their duty, and they finally submitted themselves to the tyrant and went with the times. Such a situation had to lead to a terrible catastrophe for Christian society and the

---

[289] Lucas Tudensis; Cronicon in Hispania Ilustrata, IV Father Juan de Mariana, S.J. Ibid, Vol. II. Chapter XIX. Other historians doubt that it went so far as to separate the Visigoth Church from Rome.
[290] Father Juan de Mariana, S.J. Ibid. Vol. II. Pages 372-373. Chapter XIX.

Visigoth church, which after a short time was subjected to a bloody devastating struggle.

The situation which we investigate here, is particularly important because it is so similar to the present situation. Holy Church is threatened with annihilation by Communism, Freemasonry and Jewry and unfortunately nowhere appears a new Saint Athanasius, Saint Cyril of Alexandria or Saint Felix in order to save the situation. The wicked concern themselves with destroying the defence of the Church, to alter its rites, to bind the hands of the Christians and to hand them over as in the past to Jewish imperialism. The good are cowardly, for at the moment it is still not clear which cardinals or prelates will effectively defend Holy Church and mankind, which today more than ever are threatened by Jewish imperialism and its Communist revolution.

We recommend ourselves zealously to our Lord God, that he may send in this as in other cases a new St. Athanasius or St. Bernhard to save the Church, Christianity and mankind from the terrible catastrophe which threatens them.

The high dignitaries of the Church must bring before their eyes that they, if they go with the times and vacillate like the higher clergy at the time of Witiza, are just as responsible for the catastrophe which then falls upon the Christian world as the Jews themselves. They are then as guilty as the majority of those prelates and clergy who, in the last days of the Visigoth kingdom, through their cowardice and love of comfort, made easier the cruel destruction of Christianity on the frontiers of the kingdom, which the Musulmans conquered with the effective and decisive support of the "Jewish Fifth Column".

The government of Witiza is another classic example of what happens to a nation which the Jews wish to destroy and which, lulled asleep and deceived by the apparent wish of founding the Christian-Jewish reconciliation, the unity of peoples, the equality of men and similar ideals which are too beautiful to be honest, concede to the Jews, who are out for destruction and conquest, high positions in the nation. History shows us that in such cases the Jews spread immorality and perversion by all attainable means, for it is relatively easy to destroy a land weakened by these two vices, because it cannot properly defend itself. It is a strange coincidence that even in the case of the Gothic kingdom, when Witiza conceded to the Jews high positions in the government and society, all possible perversions and immoralities spread out there and even the king and his closest advisors did not remain spared by this. This king abandoned himself to ignoble Jewish counsellors and advisors.

The perverted morals which distinguished the government of Witiza and the short rule of Roderich, are described to us vividly by the Jesuit Father Mariana: "Everything consisted in banqueting with rare foods and wines which consumed the energies, and in perverted immorality, for which the nobles gave an example; and the majority of the peoples lived immoderately and disgracefully. They were suited to make revolts, but very unskilled in the art of reaching for arms and acting resolutely against the foe. The government and the high esteem which had been attained through bravery and effort, went down in superfluity and contentment – as usual. All strictness and effort, through which they had grown great in war and peace, perished through the vices, which also destroyed military discipline, so that there was then nothing more perverted than morals in Spain, and the people as nowhere else was to be had for a gift."[291] The commentary of the cautious historian José Amador de los Rios to these lines is also very interesting: " It is impossible to read these lines, which we take from a very highly regarded historian, without attaining the conviction that a people reduced to such a state stood on the brink of a great catastrophe. No noble, great-hearted feelings had survived this violent storm. Everything was mocked and disgracefully slandered. These crimes and errors had to be atoned for and punished. And only a few years passed before the places of pleasure were soaked with Visigoth blood and the palaces were consumed by Musulman fire, which the effeminate successors of Ataulf had built."[292]

We must allude to two important coincidences: First there was then in Christianity no more perverted society than that of the Gothic kingdom. This coincides with the fact that in Christianity there was also no other kingdom where the Jews had such great influence. For the rest remained true to the traditional doctrine of the Church and continued to fight more or less against Jewry. Secondly such perversity came about particularly when the chains were removed from the Jews, which had prevented them from doing evil, and they obtained high positions in the Visigoth society.

Twelve hundred years after these events, the methods of Jews have still remained essentially the same. They wish to overthrow authority in the USA, England, and other western states and therefore spread immorality and perversion there. Many patriotic writers have accused the Jews as

---

[291] Father Juan de Mariana. S.J., same work. Vol. II. Chapter XXI. Page 375.
[292] J. Amador de los Rios, same work, Vol. I, Pages 103-104.

being principal agents of white slavery, of trading with heroin and the dissemination of pornographic, destructive theatres and cinemas. All this harms the American, English and French youth and the other lands, whose decline Jewry has resolved upon. As one sees, the methods have little altered in twelve hundred years.

MAURICE PINAY

356

CHAPTER EIGHTEEN

THE JEWS BETRAY THEIR MOST LOYAL
FRIENDS

Witiza, who threw himself into the arms of the Jews and surrounded himself with Jewish advisors, filled the measures of madness in that he – according to our opinion – followed a suicidal policy. As some assert, under the pretence of being peace-loving and in the opinion of others in order to be able easier to suppress the opponents of his absurd policy, who from day to day increased in number and strength, he had weapons turned into ploughshares and the walls of many cities with their powerful fortresses levelled to the ground, which would have made difficult the invasion by the Musulmans. Meanwhile, the Jews betrayed their truest friend Witiza and aided the invasion from North Africa, in order to destroy the Christian state and if possible the entire European Christianity forever.

The Archbishop Rodericus Toletanus and Bishop Lucas de Tuy describe, in their above-mentioned chronicles, how the government of Witiza tore down the city walls, destroyed the fortresses and had the weapons transformed into ploughs.[293]

Marcelino Menendez Pelayo, the renowned Spanish historian of the previous century, writes concerning the treachery of the Jews: "The indigenous population would have been able to show resistance to the handful of Arabs who crossed the Straits, but Witiza had disarmed them, levelled the towers to the ground and had the lances turned into harrows."[294] While the Visigoth kingdom disarmed under the influence of the Jewish advisors and friends of Witiza, dismantled its defence and

---

[293] Lucas de Tuy: Cronicon Era 733. Rodericus Toletanus: Rerum in Hispania Gestarum. Book III. Chapters XV and XVI.
[294] Marcelino Menendez Pelayo: History of the heterodox Spaniards. Edition of Consejo Superior de Investigaciones Cientificas [Supreme Council for Scientific Research], 1946, Vol. I. Chapter III. Page 373.

destroyed its war power, the Jews encouraged the Musulmans to fall upon the Christian kingdom and to destroy it. Great preparations were made in North Africa for this.

Into the land which the Jews wished to destroy they introduced pacifism, and into the land which should serve them as a tool to destroy the other, a warlike spirit. These classical tactics the Jews have applied in the course of centuries in different states and use them today with a perfection, in which they have attained experience in the course of centuries. It is worthy of note that at the present time the Jews preach – directly or with the help of freemasonic or theosophical organisations, Socialist and Communist parties, secret infiltration in different Christian churches, press, radio, and television controlled by them – Pacifism and disarmament in the free world, while in the Soviet Union and the other states under the totalitarian dictatorship they incite the peoples to war. While towards the end of the last war the USA and England disarmed in a dangerous way, they handed over to Communism vitally important positions, simultaneously destroyed the basic defence of these two great powers, and even traitorously betrayed to the Soviet Union and other Communist lands armed to the teeth the very weapons which they had stolen from the other countries. The "Fifth Column" has controlled the governments in Washington including atomic and rocket secrets. The tactics are fundamentally the same as twelve hundred years ago.

If the American and English people do not open their eyes at the right time and diminish the power of the "Jewish Fifth Column" in their states, they will soon find their lands desolated and ruled by a Bolshevist-Jewish horde, who will enslave them, as it did more than twelve centuries ago with the Christian Visigoth kingdom. It is curious to observe that the Jews always use the same tactics down to the last details.

In the USA we have witnessed in different places the fulfilment of the words of the Bible passage "weapons shall be turned into ploughshares." But this sublime ideal is only capable of being carried out if "all" disputing parties do it simultaneously. Today the Jews utilise it, as twelve hundred years ago, in order to introduce Pacifism and disarmament into the lands whose decline they plan, i.e., the peoples of the world, who still do not live under their totalitarian Communist dictatorship. For in the Socialist states where they have already erected this dictatorship, which serves for enslaving the free world, they have in no way transformed their weapons into ploughshares, but created the most gigantic destructive armaments industry of all times. Thus on one side the peoples of the Free World are lulled asleep with pacifistic sermons, immorality and disunity, which the

"Jewish Fifth Column" carries on. However, on the other side of the Iron Curtain the destructive invasion is prepared, which will suppress the free peoples after its victory, if they allow the traitorous "Fifth Column" of the Jews in their land to exist further, which makes easier the victory of Communism at a given hour, as it also at a suitable moment made easier the destruction of the Christian state of the Visigoths.

Around the year 709 the dissatisfaction of the nobility and of the people with Witiza had become so great that his position became untenable. At this moment the Jews gave us a new lesson in their high politics. A method was used which after twelve centuries has been very successfully perfected. When they believe their cause is lost, they allow before the defeat elements to appear in the enemy camp, so that afterwards, when his victory is unavoidable, these Jews fight always to remain on top and, if possible, to reach the head of the new government. So it is the same whichever side wins, they are always masters of the situation. With scientific mystery they apply the principle that the sole way to guess a card is that of placing them all simultaneously.

This was one of the great secrets of the constant victory of Jewish imperialism in the course of centuries and as a result the Jews arrived at world domination. Therefore all religious and political leaders of mankind should be conscious of this classic manoeuvre of high Jewish policy (diplomacy) in order to meet the deceit in advance and not to fall into the trap.

When the cause of the protector and true friend Witiza was practically lost, the Jews had no scruples about betraying him, in order at the right time to conquer decisive positions in the enemy camp, which made it possible for them to control him after the victory. The following details for which we have to thank the energetic research of the learned historian Ricardo C. Albanés, are very informative: "This degeneration and despotism called forth a great dissatisfaction, which since the beginning of the year 710 burdened the dynasty of Witiza. The renowned Eudon, a Jew – so it is asserted – who concealed his race, placed himself at the head of the Spanish or Roman party, since he was threatened through the reintroduction of the burdening racial law abolished by Recceswinth, and gained control of Witiza by means of a rapid and skilfully carried out plot. In an assembly (Roman Senate) the rebels conceived the idea of electing Roderich, the grandson of the great Recceswinth, to whom the Roman Spaniards had so much to thank, because he abolished the hated Gothic privileges (which had subjugated the Spanish-Latin race conquered by the Goths) as King. Roderich, who led a homely life, rejected the crown which the plotters offered him, but finally gave way and accepted the throne. He at once rewarded Eudon and appointed him as Conde de los Notarios, i.e., as minister of state, who possessed the full royal confidence.[295]

After the conspiracy was successful, the agreement of the majority of the powerful of the Visigoth kingdom, who were already dissatisfied, apparently legalised the rule of Roderich.

On the other hand Witiza died a natural death soon after his fall, so some assert, but according to others, cruelly tortured by Roderigo who had his eyes cut out. This last version is probable if one bears in mind that Witiza also had the eyes of Roderigo's father cut out a couple of years before and had him murdered. Witiza thus had nothing good to expect of the son of Teodofredos, who was tortured in the described manner and way.

In this manner international Jewry repaid the great good deeds of Witiza, who not only released the Jew-Christians of the kingdom from slavery, but also called back the Jews from exile, allowed them all to freely practise the Jewish religion, appointed them to high positions and displayed complete trust in them in relation to Christian-Jewish reconciliation and the brotherhood of the peoples.

For the Jewish imperialists the friendship of Christians or pagans is only a means, in order to have advantages which make easier the task of Jewry to destroy its foes through the destruction of their inner defence and to conquer the remaining peoples. All in all they also finally betray and in a cruel manner and way the simpletons who throw themselves into their arms or unconsciously join in their game. Woe to the wretches who allow themselves to be deceived through the proofs of friendship and the countless examples for the tragic end of those who childishly believed in such friendship and allowed themselves to be bluffed through such proven diplomacy.

The decisive influence which the Jew Eudon, the minister of state of King Roderich, must have had on this man, who did not even wish to be king and only agreed after the repeated visits of the Jews, is easily understandable. For in the first place the originator of a new political situation has at least for a time influence accordingly, and there is no sign that the weak Roderich, who had also given himself up to vice and debauchery, would have attempted to shatter the power of his minister of

[295] Ricardo C. Albanes, same work, Page 173.

state. On the other side the policy of Roderich was already so suicidal that it clearly was influenced by those who planned his destruction and hence the destruction of Christianity with the declining Visigoth kingdom. The favourable influence which Relayo, the leader of the royal guard, might have been able to exert is not to be traced, and it is clear that others determined the policy of the weak monarch, who transferred the command over a part of his army to the archbishop Oppas. The latter was not only a close relative of Witiza's, but also his right hand in the leadership of the catastrophic church policy of the monarch. In addition King Roderich, particularly as the Musulmans with aid of the Jews undertook the invasion of the kingdom from the south, was occasioned to undertake a campaign in the north to conquer the Basque land, which the Goths had never been able to conquer.

The historian Ricardo C. Albanés alludes to the fact that Tarik ben-Ziyad in those days was able to push forward the front by four thousand Saracens up to present-day North Morocco and he goes on: "At that time the traitorous Count Julan, the governor of Ceuta and one of the conspirators, surrendered to him this valuable key position to the Straits of Gibraltar, encouraged him to immediately move over to Spain, and offered himself as leader. At the court in Toledo these events were attributed no importance and they were shelved as risky enterprise, which could easily be prevented by Teodomiro, the duke of Bética (Andalusia). On the contrary, the king was even persuaded to move with his army to Northern Spain, in order to conquer the land of the Basques, which even the most mighty Gothic monarchs had not succeeded in doing. And to make this mobilisation final, Pamplona rebelled – caused through the intrigues and the gold of the powerful old Jewish organisation in this city. Meanwhile Tarik at the head of the Berbers crossed over the Straits of Gibraltar and defeated the armies of the loyal Teodomiro in the Bética. This war-skilled general then wrote the famous letter to Roderich – which was found in the Basque land – in which he anxiously begged for help."[296]

When the sons of Witiza and the treacherous archbishop Oppas had already concluded a secret alliance with the Jews and Musulmans, Roderich committed the deadly fault of transferring to them the command over an important part of the army, which was to supply the decisive battle against the invading Musulmans. On the eve of the battle, which the Spaniards call the Guadalete, the sons of Witiza treated with the Gothic nobles and the Jewish conspirators. This is reported in the Arabic Chronicle "Abjar Machmua" and laid in the mouth of the nobles: "This son of a dog,

---

[296] Ricardo C. Albanes, Ibid. Pages 173-174.

Roderich, has gained power over our kingdom, although he does not belong to our kingly family and is rather one of our lowly. These tribes from Africa do not come in order to settle in our land but solely and only in order to get plunder. When they have attained their intention, they will withdraw again and leave us alone. Let us flee in the moment of struggle, and this misery will be conquered.[297]

The twelve thousand Musulmans sent by Tarik fought on the next day against the hundred thousand of Roderich, the Christians led by archbishop Oppas and by the sons of Witiza. The battle naturally developed favourably for the Visigoths. But at a convenient moment the traitorous archbishop and the two sons of Witiza did not flee but went over with their armies to the Islamic side and destroyed – as the Arab Chronicler "Al-Makkari" reports – the rest of the troops who had remained loyal to King Roderich.[298]

As most historians assert, Roderich lost his life in this decisive battle. In different regions of Spain the memory still lives on today of the treachery of archbishop Oppas, who, as worthy imitator of Judas Iscariot, betrayed Christ and Holy Church and worked decisively with the latter's enemies for the destruction of Christianity in the once glittering Visigoth kingdom. As a great friend of the Jews, like his relative Witiza, he finally betrayed, together with the Jews, his country and the Church in a fateful way. The Jews now utilised the almighty power of pagan Rome.

Unfortunately in the present time there are in the upper clergy many who act exactly in the same way as archbishop Oppas and in secret alliance with Jewry make easier the successes of Communism and of Freemasonry, while hampering the clergy as well as the worldly leaders who defend Holy Church or their country, which are threatened by Jewish imperialism and its Freemasonic or Communist revolutions, exactly as the archbishop Oppas attacked in the back the army of Rodrigos, who defended Christianity in these decisive moments.

May our Lord Jesus stand by Holy Church and mankind against the treachery of the Oppases of the 20th century!

In the Spanish Encyclopaedia "Espasa Calpe" there is a report based on Christian Chronicles concerning the treachery of archbishop Oppas:

---

[297] Abjar Machmua. Translation by Emilio Lafuente y Alcantara. Collection of Arab works on history and geography. Publication of the Real Academia de la Historia, Madrid, Vol. I.
[298] Al-Makkari, quoted by Ricardo C. Albanes in his quoted work. Pages 175-176.

"After the troops of Tarik had been reinforced through 5,000 Berbers – whom Murza had mustered – many Jews and the Christian supporters of Witiza (a total of about 25,000 against 40,000) took on the battle. This lasted two days, and on the first day the Visigoths were at au advantage, because the Berbers had no cavalry. Then Sisberto and Oppas committed treachery and went over to the enemy. Although the centre of the army under the king fought bravely, it was defeated (19th and 20th June 711)."[299]

Concerning the treachery of the archbishop Oppas, who lost a great empire for Christianity, the Jesuit historian of the 16th century, Juan de Mariana, reports. He describes how this prelate at first aided the sons of Witiza in the preparations for the black conspiracy, and then he writes about the role which Oppas played in the decisive battle: "The victory was doubtful almost the entire day, undecided. Only the Moors showed weakness, and it appeared as if they wished to turn back and flee, when – oh, unbelievable wickedness! – the archbishop Oppas, who until then had kept concealed his treachery – as he intended – suddenly went over to the side of the enemy with his men. He joined forces with Julian, who had gathered around him a great number of Goths, and attacked our men at their weakest place. The latter were astonished at such a great treachery and were too exhausted by the fight to withstand this new onslaught, so that they could easily be defeated and driven to flight."[300]

It is only natural that there are differences in the figures given by Christian and Musulman historians for both armies. But without doubt the Christian army was in all cases numerically larger than the Saracen and only through the betrayal of Archbishop Oppas and the conspiracy principally directed by the "Jewish Fifth Column" could such a great kingdom be conquered so quickly by a small army. With justice King Roderich scarcely attached importance to the Islamic army, for this consisted only of a small contingent of the invading army. But he did not reckon with the secretly planned treachery and also not with the extraordinary power of the "Jewish Fifth Column," which – as we shall later prove – played a decisive role in this struggle. May with God's will the nations of the free world learn from history and, if they also hold themselves far stronger than the nations ruled by Communism, they should nevertheless still keep before their eyes that in a war all their calculations could be fatefully false, if one permits the "Jewish Fifth Column" to secretly undermine the free states. For at the given moment

---

[299] Encyclopedia Espasa Calpe, Vol. XXI. Word "Espana", Page 906.
[300] Father Juan de Mariana, S.J. same work, [Ibid]. Vol. II. Chapter XXI. Page 377.

they can bring the defence to a complete collapse and aid Communism to an easy victory.

In order to complete these proofs for the destruction of a Christian state more than twelve hundred years ago and its responsibility through the "Jewish Fifth Column" by the foes of Christianity, we will quote different historical evidence by Christians, Musulmans and Jews, from which it is revealed with certainty that the Jews in the Gothic kingdom and outside it stood in close connection with the Musulman invasion and supported it in different ways. All sources which we quote are undisputed and originate from respected chroniclers and historians. In addition, it is improbable that in the midst of this centuries-long deadly war between Christians and Musulmans both parties would have united in blaming the Jews for the betrayal of the state in which they lived. The Jewish authors are, however, likewise of one opinion with that previously quoted concerning this historical event.

The renowned Marcelino Menendez Pelayo, the world- renowned historian of the past century, writes the following: "It is proved that the Jews living in Spain infamously supported the invasion of the Arabs and opened to them the gates of the most important cities."[301]

Reinhart Dozy, the Dutch historian descended from the Huguenots, who enjoyed such high regard in the last century, gives in his masterwork "History of the Musulmans in Spain" a series of details from which is revealed that the Jews gave the Saracens valuable aid and made easier to them the conquest of the Gothic kingdom.[302]

Dr. Abraham Leo Sachar, the American Jewish historian and director of the Hillel Foundation for the Universities in the USA, stresses among other things, in his work "History of the Jews," that Arab armies had crossed over the Straits separating them from Spain and taken control of the land. In so doing the decadent position of the Visigoth kingdom and also without doubt the sympathetic conduct of the Jews were of value.[303]

The Committee for Jewish education of the United Synagogues, which has its seat in New York, officially published the work of Deborah Pessin "The Jewish People," in which it is stated: "In the year 711 Spain was

---

[301] Marcelino Menendez y Pelayo, same work, Vol. I. Chapter III. Pages 372-373.
[302] Marcelino Menendez y Pelayo, same work, Vol. I. Chapter III. Pages 372-373.
[303] Abraham Leo Sacher: History of the Jews, Edition Ercilla. Santiago de Chile, 1945. Page 227.

conquered by the Musulmans, and the Jews greeted them with jubilation. From the lands to which they had fled, they returned to Spain. They stormed towards the conquerors and helped them to capture the cities."[304] This official Jewish publication briefly summarises the activity of the Jews, which is proved to reveal two aspects: On the one side the Jews in North Africa, who had emigrated from Spain a century before, joined together with the invading Musulman armies. On the other side the Jewish inhabitants of the Gothic kingdom, the "Fifth Column", opened the gates of the kingdom to the invaders and destroyed the defence from within.

The Jewish-German historian Josef Kastein writes in his work "Geschichte und Schicksal der Judan" (History and Destiny of the Jews), which he dedicated with deep respect to Albert Einstein: "The Berbers helped the Arab movement with their expansion to Spain, while the Jews supported the enterprise with money and men. In 711 the Berbers led by Tarik crossed the Straits and took Andalusia, The Jews provided pickets and garrisons for the district."[305]

This Jewish historian thus reveals to us the valuable fact that the Jews financially supported the invasion and conquest of the Visigoth kingdom.

The Jewish historian Graetz mentions that the Jews in North Africa and in Spain were active in the conquest of the Visigoth kingdom through the Musulmans and states further: "After the battle of Jerez (July 711) and the death of Rodrigo, the last king of the Goths, the victorious Arabs advanced further, and everywhere they were supported by the Jews. In every conquered city the Musulman generals could leave behind a small garrison of their own troops, for they needed their men in order to subject the land. Therefore they authorised the Jews with guarding the captured places. Thus the Jews, who had once lived in servitude, became masters over Cordoba, Malaga and many other cities."[306]

The rabbi S. Raisin alludes to the fact that the invasion in Gothic Spain was carried out by an army "of twelve thousand Jews and Moors", which was led by a Jew converted to Islam, the son of Cahenas, a heroine who belonged to a Jewish Berber tribe and was the mother of Tarik-es-Saids. It is then further revealed: "In the battle of Jerez (711) the Visigoth king

---

[304] Deborah Pessin: "The Jewish People, Book II. Edition United Synagogue Commission on Jewish Education, New York 5712-1952. Pages 200-201.
[305] Josef Kastein: History and Destiny of the Jews, translated from the German by Buntley Paterson, New York, 1953. Page 239.
[306] Graetz, Ibid, Vol. III. Page 109.

Rodrigo was defeated by one of the generals of Cahenas Tarif-es-Said", a Jew of the tribe of Simon. "Therefore the island was given the name Tarifa. He was the first Moor who trod upon Spanish soil."[307]

It is strange that this rabbi, although he writes that Tarik- es-Said had gone over to the Mohammedan faith, calls him a Jew of the tribe of Simon. Whoever knows how to value the conversion of the Jews to another religion can easily explain this, for, apart from rare exceptions, these conversions were always false.

The Arab historians mention in their Chronicles that the Jews assisted in the invasion and conquest of the Visigoth kingdom. In a Chronicle consisting of a collection of traditions, which was compiled in the 11th century and is known as "Abjar Machmua", among other things the conspiracy of the Jews against Rodrigo is mentioned.

These Jews joined together on the eve of the decisive battle in the Visigoth camp with the sons of Witiza and the dissatisfied Gothic nobles. Still further details are known about the complicity of the Jews living in Spain, for, as it is stated, the Musulmans, if many Jews lived in a city, leave the guarding to the latter, together with a company of Musulmans, while the main army moved on. In other cases they entrusted the guarding of conquered cities solely to the Jews, without leaving behind an Islamic detachment. Thus it is stated in the Arab Chronicle mentioned, concerning the capture of Cordoba: "Moguits assembled the Jews in Cordoba and entrusted them with the guarding of the city", and concerning Seville, "Muza entrusted the guarding of the city to the Jews." The same is reported of Elvira (Granada) and other cities.[308]

The Saracen historian Al-Makkari gives us no less interesting details concerning this matter and writes concerning the invading Musulmans: "They usually assembled the Jews with some Musulmans in the fortresses and authorised them with the guarding of the cities, so that the rest of the troops could move on to other places."[309]

The Islamic Chronicler Abn-el-Athir provides us with various details in his Chronicle "El Kamel" concerning the Musulman invasion in the Gothic kingdom and the Jewish complicity in this. These details are also

[307] Rabbi Jakob S. Raisin, same work. Page 429.
[308] Abjar Machmua, Publication quoted, Vol. I. Page 23 ff.
[309] Al-Makkari, quoted by Vicente Risco, History of the Jews, Surco Publishers, Barcelona, 1960. Page 212.

later confirmed by the Musulman historian "Ibn-Kahldoun" born in Tunis in 1332 in his renowned "History of the Berbers". From him we take over the following details, because it is of great importance, in order to make clear what the Jews understand by Christian-Jewish reconciliation or brotherhood.

Ibn-Khaldoun bases himself upon Ibn-el-Athir and writes that, after the Musulmans had captured Toledo, "the remaining detachments conquered the other cities to which they had been sent, and that Tarik left behind in Toledo Jews with one or others of his companions and used them..."[310]

And what happened to the Christian civil population when the latter was delivered to the Jews?

Can it be possible that the Christian-Jewish reconciliation and friendship, which the Jews betrayed, as we have already sufficiently proved, now when they had already bound their victims, served to allow mildness and tolerance to govern?

The Chronicle of Bishop Lucas de Tuy provides us with revealing details in this respect. The representation of the events is later repeated by almost all Toledo historians. When the Visigoth capital was occupied by Tarik-ben-Zeyad, "the Christians left the city, in order to celebrate in the nearby Basilica of Santa Leocadia the passion of the Saviour on Palm Sunday (715). The Jews utilised their absence, delivered the throne of Leovigild and Reccared to the Musulmans, and the Christians were murdered partly in the open air and partly in the Basilica itself."[311]

The Jewish historian Graetz gives a version, which agrees with the preceding. He writes, that, when Tarik appeared before Toledo, this city was guarded by a small garrison and that, "while the Christians prayed in the church for the salvation of their land and their religion, the Jews opened the gates to the victorious Arabs on Palm Sunday 712, received them with applause and thus avenged the misery, which they had had to suffer in the course of a century at the time of Reccared and Sisebutus."[312] Naturally this Jewish historian does not mention the murders of

---

[310] Ibn-el-Athir: Chronicle El Kamel and Ibn-Khaldoun: Histoire des Berbederes. Translation from the Arabic into the French by Baron Freiherr von Salane. Algerian edition. 1852. Vol. I.
[311] Chronicle of Lucas Tudensis. Hispania Ilustrata. Vol. IV.
[312] Graetz, Ibid, Vol. III. Page 109.

Christians, which then followed and which the Bishop Lucas de Tuy expressly describes in his Chronicle and the majority of the ancient historians from Toledo. For this there exists an interesting case of precedence: Approximately a century before, the Byzantine Emperor Heraclius had urged the Visigoth monarchs to drive the Jews from Spain since their presence in Christian states represented a danger for the latter's existence. He quotes the fact that the Jews "bought 80,000 captive Christians from Cosroes, whom they killed without pity."[313] Unfortunately Sisebutus in no way exterminated the dangerous deadly "Fifth Column" at its root, but had the Jews choose between expulsion and conversion. As a result he caused the majority to apparently convert themselves to Christianity and thus made the "Jewish Fifth Column" in the Christian State into a "Fifth Column" in the church itself, as a result of which they became still more dangerous.

Without doubt Musulmans and Jews must have participated in the murders of Christians, even if on the one side the mildness and tolerance of the Arab conquerors in Spain is even recognised by Jewish writers, and on the other side the facts prove that the Jews always, when they could satisfy their hatred on the Christians, organised murders and then had them carried out by the pagans in Rome. On the other side a victorious heresy or revolution led by Jewry has often degenerated into murder of Christians, not to speak of Jewish-Communist revolutions of our days, where mass murders are the order of the day.

In face of the recognised tolerance of the victorious Arabs in Spain and of the facts which we investigate, one can easily imagine who were the chief instigators of the massacre of Christians in the subjugated Gothic kingdom.

However this may be, one thing is clear: The Christian- Jewish policy of reconciliation, which Witiza began in the Visigoth kingdom, had catastrophic consequences, for in the long run it brought the destruction of a Christian state, the loss of the independence of the country and even cruel murder of countless Christians.

In conclusion we will quote what the great friend of the Jews, José Amador de los Rios, who cannot be accused of Antisemitism, writes about the Musulman invasion: "And how in the meantime did the Jewish people behave? Did it perhaps arm for defence of its chosen fatherland? Or did it remain neutral in the midst of such devastations when no resistance could

---

[313] Encyclopedia Espasa Calpe, Vol. XXI. Word 'Espana'.

be offered further against the onward storm of the victors? The love of one's country, i.e., the love of the earth, where one was born and gratitude for the last Statutes of the Goth Kings certainly ought to have occasioned that people to put together all its powers with those of the Visigoth nation, in order to ward off the foreign invasion, and also at the same time to open its gold coffers, in order to satisfy the urgent needs of the state. But against these reflections stood the ancient hatred and the lively memory of a disgraceful past. On the other side the situation brought to the Jews as a people which had its home in all corners of earth, their general and special interests, their customs and a permanently erroneous mode of life, the wish and striving for what was new, while their powerful religious fanaticism impelled them to turn against their hated hosts as enemies of their faith, in order to hasten their destruction and ruin. Thus the Musulman conquest on the entire Iberian peninsula was furthered and spread. Noble cities, in which the wealthy Jewish race was represented in great number and which would without doubt have cost the armies of Tarik and Muzas much blood, were handed over to them by the Jews, who later expected them and joined in brotherhood with the Africans."[314]

Finally we will quote two very interesting details, which the official monumental work of Jewry, the Jewish-Spanish Encyclopaedia, makes. Under the word "Espana" (Spain) it is expressly stated: "It is undisputed that Muza, who in spite of the convincing demands of the party of Witiza was still unresolved to send his armies to Spain, decided finally only upon the secret information of the Spanish Jews who reported to the Emir concerning the military incapacity of the crown, the ruinous condition of the castles, the exhausted state treasury and the embitterment of the nobility and of the people at the general oppression." Then it is stated further: "On 19th July 711, Tarik[315] annihilated the Visigoths in the battle of Jana, or on the Guadalete, in which Rodrigo apparently lost his life. At this historic encounter one saw many Jews from North Africa fight on the side of the victor. Immediately their Spanish fellow believers rebelled everywhere, and placed themselves at the disposal of Tarik and Muza..."[316]

In this chapter, we wished to provide an idea of how, twelve hundred years ago, Jewish imperialism and its "Fifth Column" in the bosom of the Church destroyed a Christian state. But we can give the assurance that experience in twelve centuries has helped Jewish Imperialism and its "Fifth Column" to perfect their methods down to the last detail.

---

[314] J. Amador de los Rios, same edition, Vol. I. Pages 105-106.
[315] The differences in the orthography of the word "Tarif", "Tarik", "Taric", etc. are to be traced back to the different quoted sources, whose text was taken over liberally.
[316] Jewish-Spanish Encyclopaedia. Word "Spain". Vol. IV. Page 144.

CHAPTER NINETEEN

THE CHURCH COUNCILS FIGHT JEWRY

In face of the repeated false conversions of the Jews to Christianity, Holy Church attempted to seize upon various precautionary measures, which were approved at the individual Councils.

The Council of Agde – a city in South Gaul – which took place in the year 506 under the protection of Saint Caesarius, the primate of the province of Arles, and was tolerated by Alaric, ordered the following: "Law 34. Concerning the acceptance of Jews who wish to be converted. Since the falsehood of the Jews often breaks out again, they shall, if they wish to be converted to Catholic law, be catechism pupils for eight months, and if it is revealed that they come in purity of faith, they shall be baptised after this period"...[317] The facts show, however, that this term of trial had no value for the guarantee of the honesty of their confessions.

At the Trulanian Council, in the year 692, which is authoritative as a supplementary Council to the 5th and 6th Ecumenical Councils, it was announced that the heresy of Nestorius was renewing Jewish godlessness, and in Canon 1 it is stated: "We also simultaneously recognise the doctrine which two hundred divine fathers spread in Ephesus, who prosecuted the foolish division of Nestorius as deviating from the divine destiny, who declared that Jesus Christ was a man for himself, and thus renewed the Jewish blasphemy." In Canon XI the priests were threatened with deposition if they maintained close relations with the Jews. Thus one sees that in such distant times the clergy who entered into dangerous friendships with the Jews were a veritable nightmare for Holy Church and it was necessary to order punishments – even the deposing of Jew-friendly clergy. Concerning this it is stated in Canon XI: "No priest or layman shall eat the Matzo of the Jews, maintain intimate relationship with them, visit them when they are ill, receive medicines from them, or bathe in their

---

[317] Council of Agde, Canon 34. Compilation by Juan Tejada y Ramiro, same edition, Vol. I. Page 403.

company. Whoever acts against this statute, will be deposed if he is a priest and if layman expelled from the Church."³¹⁸

Through this measure, Holy Church did not turn away from its Christian neighbourly love, which it has always fought for, with, among other things, the noble custom of visiting the sick. The universally proven fact was known to the prelates of this Holy Council that the Jews always even utilised the most magnanimous works of Christian neighbourly love in order to gain influence upon the Christians and to undermine our holy religion. Thus the prelates regrettably saw themselves compelled to forbid everything which could have led to dangerous friendship between Christians and Jews and brought the Christians into the danger of being delivered to the ancient wolves. Undoubtedly Holy Church was in the right when it threatened the clergy with deposition and the Jew-friendly laymen with exclusion from the Church, for these intimacies are, the closer they become, proven to be always to have been a deadly danger for Christianity. What would happen if this Holy Church Canon were applied to the present day clergy, who are so intimate with the Jews and closely befriended and are united with them in those so-called Jewish- Christian brotherhoods? If this canon were applied to them, one would advance a great step forward with the salvation of the Church from the deadly sabotage of the "Jewish Fifth Column" in the clergy.

THE 2ND ECUMENICAL COUNCIL OF NICAEA (787)
AND THE SECRET JEWS

The plague of the false Christians, who were Jews in secret, had become so dangerous for Christianity at the end of the 8th century and especially after the Visigoth kingdom had fallen into the hands of the Musulmans, that it was resolved at the 2nd Ecumenical Council of Nicaea that it was to be preferred that the Christians who secretly practised the Jewish religion, should be Jews openly and not false Christians. The anti-Christian activity of the Jews in the bosom of Holy Church, who soon spread revolutionary heresies, conspired against the Kings, or made agreements with the Musulmans and delivered the Christian states to them, had called forth such grave concern in Christianity, that Holy Church preferred to see that they were known publicly as Jews and were not false Christians. Thus the Church preferred to have the enemy outside

---

³¹⁸ Trulanian Council, Canon I, Compilation by Juan Tejada y Ramiro, collection quoted. Volume III.

and not in its own ranks. The measures passed by the Holy Synod in this sense could not have been bolder. But unfortunately the great advantages were already known to the Jews, which they possessed through their infiltration into the bosom of the Church and Christian society.

In Canon VIII of the 2nd Ecumenical Council of Nicaea it was expressly stated: "And because some Jews pretended to be Christians, but remained Jews in secret and celebrate the Sabbath, we dispose that they be not admitted to the Communion, prayer or to the Church, but live as real Jews, do not baptise their children, and it shall not be allowed to them to buy or to own slaves. But if someone is converted in purity and honesty... then shall he and his sons be admitted and baptised, whereby caution is commanded that he does not allow himself to be again led astray. But if they do not conduct themselves so, they shall not be admitted."[319]

The Ecumenical Council mentioned by us also condemned the heresy of the Iconoclasts. For the Jews there is nothing more hateful than the Catholic images of saints, which they describe as pictures of idols. Always when they had influence on a certain realm of Christianity, they have therefore attempted to abolish these images. The heresy of the iconoclasts was instigated by the Jews, for the false converts lived pleasantly with a Christianity without images, since it cost them effort to show the latter even the simplest honour. But practical as they are, they have nevertheless, when it was to their advantage, and in order not to offend the feelings of the Christian population, had to tolerate the cult of Saints and even decorated their dwellings with such images.

According to the Church historian Juan Tejada y Ramiro, a Jewish conjurer incited the Iconoclastic ideas with the Byzantine Emperor Leo the Isaurian. This monarch accepted these tendencies with great fanaticism and for a start had the image of our Lord Jesus Christ pulled down, which had been arranged high over the gate of Constantinople. According to this learned collector of Church canons, this image "was worshipped by the people to the embitterment of the Jews for many years."[320]

At the Ecumenical Council mentioned by us measures were taken against heresy, among others, the deposing of those bishops, priests or deacons was ordered, who concealed the books with iconoclastic ideas. Thus it is ordered in Canon IX: "All the childish mockeries, harmful

---

[319] 2nd Council of Nicaea, Canon 8. Compilation by Juan Tejada y Ramiro, same collection. Vol. III. Page 819.
[320] Juan Tejada y Ramiro, same collection. Vol. III. Page 808.

deviations and writings, which are falsely directed against the venerable images of Saints, shall be handed over to the Bishop of Constantinople so that they may be placed with the books of other heretics. But if anyone conceals these things, he shall, whether bishop, priest or deacon, be deposed, and if he is monk or layman, excommunicated."[321]

Holy Church proceeded not only against the secret Jews and heretics, but also very energetically against the bishops and other clergy who supported the heresy and Jewry.

When the destructive activity of the "Fifth Column" increased, the defence of Holy Church was driven more and more to extremes. Already at this Holy Ecumenical Council of Nicaea, those bishops and clergy are threatened with deposition, who simply conceal the heretical books. What punishment then do the high clergy of the present day deserve, who not only conceal Freemasonic or Communist books, but actively collaborate, so that the Freemasonic and Communist heresies can destroy Christianity.

However, we come back to the iconoclastic Emperor Leo the Isaurian. In this connection it is worthy of note that the Jews experienced the same with him as with Martin Luther. At first he allied himself with them against the orthodoxy. But when he recognised the enormous danger which they represented for his kingdom, he attempted to evade this danger. He therefore seized upon the same lamentable methods as the Catholics and compelled the Jews to be converted to Christianity. He laid before them the choice of being converted or severely punished.

Concerning the honesty of this new general conversion of the Jews in Greece, the Balkans, a part of Asia Minor and the remaining regions of the Byzantine kingdom, the Jewish historian Graetz writes the following: "Leo the Isaurian, a farmer's son, whose attention the Jews and Arabs directed to the idolatrous cult of saintly images (icons) which was practised in the churches, therefore fought to eliminate these images. Since he was accused by the clergy before the ignorant masses, who revered these holy images, of being a heretic and Jew, Leo again began to take his orthodoxy seriously and persecuted the heretics and Jews. He ordered in a decree, that all Jews of the Byzantine kingdom and of the mountains of Asia Minor, under threat of severe punishments, should accept the Christianity of the Greek Church (723). Many Jews fitted themselves into this Edict and allowed

---

[321] 2nd Council of Nicaea. Canon 9. Compilation of "Acta Conciliorum et epistolas decretales, ac constitutione Summorum Pontificium", Study by P. Johannis Harduini, S.J., Paris 1714.]

themselves to be baptised against their will. They were thus less constant than the mountain dwellers, who in order to remain true to their conviction, assembled in their house of prayer, set it on fire and perished in the flames. The Jews who allowed themselves to be baptised were of the opinion that the storm would soon pass and he would then allow them to return to Judaism. Therefore they certainly converted themselves outwardly to Christianity, but in secret they held to the Jewish rites..." And the renowned Jewish historian closes with the following, very interesting comment: "Thus the Jews of the Byzantine kingdom vanished before the constant persecutions and for a time they remained concealed from the eyes of history."[322]

This vanishing on the part of Jewry, in order to remain hidden from the eyes of history – to use this fortunately chosen expression of Graetz's – was always the most dangerous thing in the affair, since they grew from a visible "Fifth Column into a secret force, an invisible power, which is more difficult to combat as such. In the course of time the Balkans were completely undermined by this secret power and were later to become the most dangerous centre of the secret sects of the Cathars and later of the treacherous "Fifth Column," which delivered the Christian kingdom to the Mohammedan Turks. In modern times the Balkans had become a breeding ground for the conspiratorial and terror organisations which had such great influence on the unleashing of the world war of 1914-1918. We will see later still how a similar vanishing act by Jewry, in order to remain concealed from the eyes of history, took place in the whole of France, England, Russia, Spain, Portugal, in isolated districts of Italy, Germany and other Christian countries, and in the long run had catastrophic consequences for these nations and the rest of mankind. Concerning the terrible struggle by Holy Church and the Christian monarchs against Jewry in France, we allow the Jewish historian Graetz to speak, who cannot be accused of antisemitism, and who is so respected in Jewish circles. He writes concerning King Sisismund of Burgundy: "This king was the first (in France) to set up barriers between Christians and Jews. He confirmed the resolution of the Council of Epaone, which took place under the presidency of the bloodthirsty Bishop Avitus, and at which it was even forbidden to laymen to participate in Jewish banquets (517). The hostility towards the Jews gradually spread from Burgundy to the other French provinces. Already at the 3rd and 4th Councils of Orleans (388 and 545) strict determinations were passed against them... At the Council of Macon (581) several resolutions were determined and the Jews allotted a subordinate position in society. They were forbidden to be judges and tax-

---

[322] Graetz. same work. Vol. III. Pages 122-123.

collectors, and they were excluded from all positions which would have given them power over the Christian population. They were compelled to show the Christian priests the highest deference... Although King Chilperic was not very favourable to the Catholic clergy, he nevertheless followed the example of Avitus. He also forced the Jews in his kingdom to be baptised, and he personally went to the baptismal font as Father of the newly-converted. However, he was satisfied with the mere appearance of conversion, and he was not hostile to the Jews, when they continued to celebrate the Sabbath and followed the Jewish Laws."[323]

This was a deplorable error on the part of this monarch who on the one side pressed the Jews to be converted and even served them as baptismal Father, but on the other side permitted the new Christians to continue to practise the Jewish religion in secret. Thus he furthered the creation and strengthening of this secret power, which was to call forth in France in the coming centuries so much disunity and revolutions.

Concerning this conversion of the Jews at the time of Chilperic, St. Gregory the Bishop of Tours reports to us – who with full right is called the father of French history – that among those compulsorily converted belonged Priscus – the royal treasurer, an office which today corresponds to that of chancellor of the exchequer[324] – who, because he refused to be converted, was imprisoned and was later murdered by another converted Jew. The latter in turn was killed by a relative of the former royal chancellor of the exchequer.[325] The case of Priscus was a hard blow for the Jews, who preferred to have one of themselves as state treasurer, in order to thus exert a decisive influence upon the Christian monarchs and utilise the reputation of the Jews and false Jewish Christians as good financiers. Concerning Clotaire II and the Holy Council of Paris, Graetz writes: "The last kings of the Merovingians were always more fanatical in their hatred towards the Jews. Clotaire II, who ruled over the whole of France, was, however, regarded as a model of religious devoutness. He approved the resolutions of the Council of Paris, which excluded the Jews from authoritative offices and from the army." (615)[326]

Here Graetz not only uses the traditional method of sullying the memory of the rulers who acted against the Jewish danger, but also then expresses a great truth: that a Christian, the more fanatical he is, must also

---

[323] Councils of Epaone, Orleans, Third and Fourth of Macon, quoted by Graetz, same work, Vol. III. Pages 37, 38 and 39.
[324] St. Gregory, Bishop of Tours; Historia Francorum, Vol. VI. Page 17.
[325] Rabbi Jakob S. Raisin, same work. Page 440.
[326] Council of Paris, quoted by Graetz, same work, Vol. III. Pages 39 and 40.

be against the Jews (the Jews describe a Christian as fanatical, who defends his religion and his fatherland). This is nothing extraordinary, if one reflects that the Jews are the chief enemies of Christianity and of the human race and understands, that the defenders of the Church, of the fatherland or of mankind, must also energetically oppose the greatest enemy, if they do not wish to be subjected in defence. Therefore, the great father of the Church, Saint Jerome has said that, if it were necessary to abhor the Jews and Judaism in order to be a good Christian, then he would do it in exemplary form. Only the false Christians, who secretly practise the Jewish religion, will not recognise this traditional doctrine of the Church and attempt to make us believe that it is a sin to oppose the Jews and their satanic imperialism, in order as a result to cripple the defence of the Church and Christian people.

In connection with this bitter struggle between Holy Church and the Synagogue, the Rabbi Jakob S. Raisin writes that, even in Gaul during the time of Clovis who destroyed Arianism, Bishop Avitus stirred up the masses on Ascension Day to destroy the Synagogue.[327] We have already seen that the Jewish historian Graetz describes this prelate as a "bloodthirsty bishop".

As one sees, this Holy Synod also wished to avoid that secret Jewry continued to exist, which could also have been avoided if it had been attained that the Christians of Jewish origin had not been introduced into Jewry. In order to avoid this, the Holy Council suspended the punishment of confiscation of property against the transgressors. One sees that the prelates of the Council knew the problems well.[328]

The Jewish historian Josef Kastein affirms in connection with the then hard struggle between Holy Church and the Jews: "The Christian Church, be it now in Italy or Gaul, in France or Spain, declared war on Jewry."[329] In our time Holy Church would doubtless have been condemned by the accomplices of the Synagogue in the ranks of Christianity on account of race hatred or anti-Semitism. The zealous and passionate Rabbi Raisin reports how then, later in Toulouse, three times a year, at first all Jews of the city and afterwards only their rabbis were whipped through the streets,

---

[327] Rabbi Jakob S. Raisin, same work. Page 438.
[328] 4th Council of Orleans. Quoted by Rabbi S. Raisin, same work, Page 439.
[329] Josef Kastein, same work. Page 229.

"under the pretext that the Jews had once attempted to deliver the city to the Moors."[330]

This attempt by the "Jewish Fifth Column" in France is very well known, which, just as with the "Jewish Fifth Column" in the Gothic kingdom, wished to deliver this other Christian kingdom to the Musulmans. Luckily Charles Martell condemned this criminal attempt to failure forever. After the Christian murders in Spain, the alarm of the inhabitants of Toulouse against the Jews is understandable. It is very regrettable that the Jews therefore had to accept a whipping several times a year. But one must reflect that in all nations of the world not only whipping but the death penalty exists for this kind of betrayal.

With Dagobert I, the Merovingian monarchy attained its highest peak. Its possessions stretched from the Elbe to the Pyrenees and from the Atlantic up to the frontiers of Bohemia and Hungary. Dagobert I, the son of Clotaire II, had, as long as he was not of age, Arnulf, the Bishop of Metz, as guardian, and then left important government offices to highly respected Saints recognised by the Church, as for example, St. Ovanus, whom he made chancellor of Neustria and who later became Bishop of Rouen, and St. Eloy, whom he appointed state treasurer, and who was chosen as bishop of Noyon when he withdrew from the world.

The situation of Christianity in this realm was extremely serious, for it was completely permeated by false Christians, whose hypocrisy Chilperic had tolerated, as we already described. Dagobert I led a disorderly sexual life, and his renowned counsellors could not prevent him from doing this. But on the other side he recognised – perhaps on account of the education taught him and upon the advice of these holy men – the danger which the Jews represented in his realm of rule. Many then pretended to be Christians and therefore he attempted to apply a radical method: In the year 629 he passed a decree, in which it was stated that the Jews in the kingdom must be converted by a fixed day honestly to Christianity or be regarded as enemies and be condemned to death.

Dagobert interpreted the problem thus, because he regarded the Jews as enemies, which rested upon the centuries-old truth of how Saint Paul himself, with divine insight, described them as enemies of all men. The most serious thing about the matter was that they were once again given the possibility in France and South Germany of escaping with their skins. This cardinal error was made centuries later by all Christian monarchs, for

---

[330] Rabbi Jakob S. Raisin, same work.

the Jews always swore and promised, in order to save themselves, to be in future honest true Christians and simultaneously concealed with still greater skill their secret Judaism. It would have been better if Dagobert had expelled them in masses – in the same way every harmful foreign conspirator is expelled from the land, whose hospitality he betrays – and thus had given them the possibility to be honestly converted to Christianity in other lands. Thus would France and Germany have freed themselves from the terrible "Fifth Column" and the destructive secret power, which has finally controlled the whole of France to the harm of Christianity and of the French.

Jewry again vanished once more for a time from the surface, in order in dangerous form in all realms of the Frankish kingdom, in the clergy and at the court, to gain admittance, and called forth years later the terrible decline of Christianity at the time of Louis (Ludwig) the Pious.

In conclusion let us say something about the origin of the German Jews, whose blond hair and blue eyes stand in contrast to the other types of Jews. Graetz explains the origin of the Jews in South Germany in the following way: "A large number of German soldiers took part with the legions in the destruction of the temple of Jerusalem. Many of them chose from the great number of captives the most beautiful women and took them with them to the banks of the Rhine and Maine. The children of these unions were half Jews and half Germans and were introduced by their mothers to Judaism, for their father raised no objections in this regard."[331] If one reflects that the apparent conversions of the Jews to Christianity began in the German possessions of the Merovingians already at the time of Chilperic and Dagobert I, one will understand, that the "Jewish Fifth Column" in Germany already existed a very remote time ago, and that therefore the Nazis committed the gravest fault when they believed all secret branches of Jewry could be identified through a genealogical investigation of only three generations.

---

[331] Graetz, same work, Vol. III. Pages 40 and 41.

CHAPTER TWENTY

AN ATTEMPT TO BRING THE HOLY ROMAN GERMANIC EMPIRE UNDER JEWISH RULE

The following facts are of great importance for the religious and political leaders of all times, for Jewry, especially its clandestine form, represents a concealed power, whose danger under certain circumstances is not discernible even for the most talented leaders in its whole extent. Thus the skilled diplomacy of the synagogue can occasion them to commit faults which could have catastrophic consequences for their nation and often for the entire world.

What happened to one of the greatest political geniuses of the Christian era should draw the attention of all those leaders or personages who, underestimating the wickedness and danger of the Jews and attracted by the monetary advantages so alluringly offered to their collaborators, start playing with fire and believe they will not get themselves burned. In this they are perhaps influenced by that natural tendency to regard themselves as all-powerful, a trait so often found – and often with good reason – among the great men of mankind.

Charlemagne, who built up again the western Roman Empire and protected Holy Church, who gave an impetus to science, the arts and trade, and was one of the most important political geniuses of all times had, however, one weakness: He was subjected to the skilled deceit and diplomacy of Jewry, which utilised in its favour the characteristic wish of the grandson of Charles Martel for unity of the peoples and races, his inborn sympathy with the oppressed and persecuted and the correct desire on the other side of the monarch, to enlarge and strengthen his kingdom through the extension of trade. Thus he released the beast which the Merovingians, with good reason and insight, had laid in chains, and gave back to it freedom of movement, without taking into regard that as a result he violated the canons of Holy Church, to whom on the other side he conceded all possible advantages.

With their skill tested in the course of centuries the Jews understood how to arouse the inborn sympathy of the Emperor for the oppressed, and attained that he allowed them all possible freedoms. As usual they were able to transform this pity into sympathy and to convince him that the greatness of the kingdom could only be secured with their economic power, and that again could be achieved with the development of a flourishing trade. Since the Jews had then almost a monopoly, they convinced the Emperor of the utility of using them to extend the trade of the Holy Empire to the whole world. One can easily imagine how attractive such a prospect was at a time when the nobility devoted itself exclusively to the art of war, the slaves cultivated the land, and the Jews or secret Jewish Christians were almost the sole ones who carried on trading activity.

Concerning the new policy of Charles the Great in the face of the Jews, the Jewish historian Graetz confirms: "Although Charlemagne was a protector of the church and helped to establish the supremacy of the Papacy, and Pope Hadrian, a contemporary of the Emperor, was absolutely no friend of the Jews and had repeatedly summoned the Spanish bishops to ensure that the Christians did not have relations with the Jews and pagans, Charlemagne in no way shared the prejudices of the clergy towards the Jews. Against all statutes of the Church and the resolutions of the Councils the first Frank Emperor favoured the Jews in his kingdom... The Jews were in that time the principal representatives of world trade. While the nobles turned to war affairs, the plebs to crafts, and the farmers and slaves turned to agriculture, the Jews were not allowed to perform military service and possessed no hired land, but directed their attention to the import and export of goods and slaves, so that the favour of Charlemagne was in certain respect a privilege for the trading folk."[332]

The Jewish historian Josef Kastein writes about Charlemagne: "He knew exactly how to evaluate the Jews as a principal support of international trade. Their connections stretched from France as far as India and China. Their communities in the whole world functioned as agencies. They knew many languages in an admirable way and were astonishingly well suited as linking-parts between East and West."[333]

If the Jewish historians elaborate their possibilities so emphatically to us today, then one can easily imagine how they introduced their plans to Charlemagne in order to gain his support.

---

[332] Graetz, same work, Vol. III. Chapter V. Page 142.
[333] Rabbi Josef Kastein, same work, Page 4. Page 252.

But they not only attained this support in trade, but also applied their traditional tactics and attempted, when they had once attained this position, to conquer a further one, afterwards the next, later another, etc. The Jew Sedechias became confiding doctor of the Emperor, as a result of which the Jews gained admittance to the court, and one soon sees them there in important posts of the diplomatic service of Charlemagne. The latter sent Isaak the Jew as ambassador to the court of Harun al Raschids,[334] under whose government the Caliphate of Baghdad reached its highest point. On the other side the Caliph was justly alarmed at the increasing power of Jewry in the Islamic lands and undertook defensive measures against this. Among other things he compelled the Jews to wear a sign which distinguished them from the Musulmans. These measures stood in unmistakeable contradiction to the protection which the Christian Emperor granted them.[335]

The Jew Graetz asserts that the protection of Charlemagne made easier the appearance of the Jews in North Germany and their penetration into the Slavic lands.

The activity of the Jews at the time of Charlemagne shows us how the Jews applied new tactics, which consisted in conducting themselves well and serving the Christian monarch loyally, so that the latter removed the chains which hampered them in their freedom of movement and then gradually gained high positions in the Christian state. At that time they withheld themselves from all revolutionary activity, as long as the genial powerful monarch lived, who would doubtless have overthrown them at the first false step, enjoyed in the meantime the Imperial protection, and gained more and more in power, in order at the suitable moment to carry out the treacherous blow. This occurred after the death of the Emperor, when a mediocre, weak-willed, irresolute and easily influenced man followed him on the throne.

When Charlemagne died, his son Ludwig (Louis) succeeded him, who, on account of his extreme piety during his first years of rule, received the surname of the Pious. Unfortunately, he was an untalented, weak-willed man, who easily fell into the hands of flatterers and those who knew how to handle him.

When he ascended the throne, he began to expel his half-brothers and later the ministers of his father from the land. He had the eyes cut out of

---

[334] Rabbi Jakob S. Raisin, same work. Page 441.
[335] Graetz, same work, Chapter V. Pages 141 and 142.

Bernhard, the king of Italy, who had risen against him. All these facts show that the so-called piety of the monarch did not extend as far as it appeared.

When his first wife died, he married Judith, who appeared at the court with a retinue of Jews and, as the new Empress, exerted, together with the royal chancellor (treasurer) Bernhard, a decisive influence upon the monarch. The latter allowed declared Jews and Christians of Jewish origin at the court, which is not further to be wondered at, if one reflects that he had seen from youth onwards how his father protected the Jews and entrusted high offices to them.[336]

If now Christian, anti-Jewish leaders with insuperable energy had not fought against the Jewish beast, the Holy Roman German Empire would perhaps have been subjected eleven centuries ago to Jewish Imperialism. If this kingdom had fallen, which was the mightiest of the then world, Jewry would perhaps have been successful in conquering the whole earth in a short time.

The Rabbi Jakob S. Raisin writes about Ludwig the Pious: "Ludwig the Pious (814-40) went still further than his father. He informed the bishops, abbots, counts, prefects, governors and others, that the Jews stood under the protection of the Emperor and might be disturbed neither in the practising of their religion nor in their business trade." He then enumerates further privileges, which Ludwig allowed the Jews, and it is further stated: "And since the Jews made no business on the Sabbath, the market day was transferred to Sunday. Ludwig also appointed a special judge for the defence of the Jews against the intolerance of the clergy." And concerning the struggle of Agobard, the archbishop of Lyon, and St. Bernhard, the archbishop of Vienna, against the Jews, the zealous Rabbi says: "The reaction of the Church to the measures of Ludwig to lift certain legal restrictions laid on the Jews, found expression through Agobard, the archbishop of Lyons (779-840), who, together with St. Bernhard, the archbishop of Vienna, deposed the Emperor, who on his side deposed them. In four letters to the king they complained about these people (the Jews), 'who invested themselves with the Curse as with a dress', and boasted of being highly valued by the king and by the nobility, so that on the other side the women observed the Sabbath with the Jews, worked on Sunday, shared their fast foods, and that the Jews not only concerted the pagan slaves, but in their capacity as tax-collectors bribed the fanners and seduced them to confess to Judaism, by their lessening these taxes or

---

[336] Graetz, work mentioned, Chapter V. Pages 141 and 142.

excusing them therefrom."[337] As one sees, the Jews utilised to a great extent the protection of the Emperor and of the nobility and even their position as tax collectors, in order to press the Christian peoples to confess to Judaism and to give up their own belief. Then without doubt the Synagogue wished to rule the peoples through conversion at the gate. The methods have been different at different times and in the individual lands, but the purpose was always the same, i.e. the conquest and ruling of the peoples who naively tolerated the Jews in their realm.

St. Bernhard, the archbishop of Vienna, and Agobard, the archbishop of Lyon, fought in common this struggle for life and death. For those who wish to investigate the Jewish problem, Agobard's book against the Jews makes interesting reading, and was written with the valuable cooperation of St. Bernhard of Vienna.

The Jewish historian Josef Kastein writes, that Ludwig the Pious "took not only individual Jews but entire communities under his personal protection and allowed them rights and a Magister Judaeorum, who was to ensure that these rights were respected."[338]

In order to provide ourselves with a better idea of the serious position of Christianity under this disastrous government, we once again allow the highly-regarded Jewish historian Heinrich Graetz to speak. He writes concerning the conduct of the Emperor towards the Jews: "He took them under his special protection and defended them against the injustices of the barons and of the clergy. They had the right of dwelling everywhere in the kingdom. In spite of countless laws that forbade this, they could not only employ Christian workers but also import slaves. The clergy were forbidden to baptise the slaves of the Jews and to give them the possibility of regaining their freedom. On their account the market was changed from Saturday to Sunday... In addition they were freed from the severe fire and water tests. They were also tax collectors and had through this privilege a great power over the Christians, even if this was also contrary to the Church Canons."[339]

These facts reveal to us in what measure the Jews had dominance in the Holy Roman Empire. For on the one side the Christians were subjected to the then customary fire and water tests, while the Jews had the special privilege of being freed therefrom. Since the Christians at that

[337] Rabbi Jakob S. Raisin, same work. Chapter XVI. Pages 441 and 442.
[338] Rabbi Josef Kastein, same work. Page 252.
[339] Graetz, same work, Vol. III. Chapter VI. Page 261.

time celebrated Sunday very strictly, the market was held on Saturday, and it was unheard of that things then went so far to grant the Jews the pleasure of changing market day from Saturday to Sunday, so that they and not the Christians could celebrate their festival. Not once in the world of today, so favourably inclined to Jewry, have things come to this.

This proves who the real rulers at the Court of Ludwig and Judith were, where the worst of all the Jews were also even tax-collectors and utilised this valuable position, in order to economically oppress the farmers and to occasion them to deny Christianity and to take on Judaism, by their either putting into effect or lessening the oppressive tax burdens. Now it was the Jews who attempted to compel the true Christians in a Christian monarchy to give up their belief. The roles had been changed in a couple of years of philosemitic policy.

This regrettable situation was already prepared at the time of Charlemagne himself through the contact and living- together of Jews and Christians. This is revealed to us by the lamentations of Pope Stephen III, whom the learned Jewish historian Josef Kastein quotes literally: "Pope Stephen III had made a complaint to the bishop of Narbonne in south France: "with great sorrow and deadly anxiety we have heard that the Jews... have in a Christian land the same rights as the Christians and possess Allodial goods in the city and suburbs, which they describe as their city. Christian men and women live under the same roof with these traitors and defile their soul day and night through blasphemies."[340]

Pope Stephen III described the Jews as traitors and with this hit a sore place. In our days he would have been destined, if he still lived, to be condemned on account of race hatred and antisemitism. On the other hand, we must, in order to understand another motive for the lament of the Pope, explain that then interest on loans had to be paid for family goods, with exception of the Allodial goods, which were a real privilege of some nobles, but which the Jews possessed in Narbonne, while the Christian people did not have such privileges.

Graetz reveals that the chief reason for the protection which the Jews enjoyed, was that "the Empress Judith, the second wife of Ludwig, was very favourable to the Jews. The beautiful clever woman, whom her friends admired, just as her enemies hated her, had a great respect for the ancient Jewish heroes. When the learned Abbot of Fulda, Rhabanus Maurus, wished to win her favour, he could find no more effective means

---

[340] Pope Stephen III. Quoted by Rabbi Josef Kastein, same work. Page 252.

than to dedicate to her his works on the biblical books of Esther and Judith and to compare her with these two Jewish heroines. The Empress and her friends and probably also the state treasurer Bernhard, who in reality ruled the kingdom, became protectors of the Jews, since the latter were descended from the patriarchs and prophets. 'They must be honoured for this reason', she said to her friends at the court, and her opinion was supported by the Emperor."[341]

But as usual the protection of the Jews and Semitophilism turns into the domination of the Jews over the Christians and to anti-Christian activity. The additional report by Graetz is very illuminating in this respect: "Learned Christians delighted in the writings of the Jewish historian Joseph and of the Jewish philosopher Philo and preferred their works to those of the Apostles. Well-educated court ladies openly confessed that they valued higher the founder of the Jewish Law than of the Christian Law (i.e. Moses higher than Christ). They went so far as to beg a blessing from the Jews. The Jews had free access to the court and direct contact with the Emperor and his confidants. The relatives of the Emperor gave the Jews valuable presents, in order to show them their favour and respect. And since such distinctions were granted them in the highest circles, it was only natural that towards Jews of the Frankish kingdom, which also comprised Germany and Italy, far-reaching tolerance was practised, as perhaps in no other time in their history. The hated church laws were quietly annulled. The Jews were allowed to build synagogues, to openly speak to Christians about Judaism, and even to assert that 'they were descendants of the patriarchs', 'the race of the righteous' (i.e. Christ) and 'the sons of the Prophets'. Without fear they could give expression to their opinions concerning Christianity, the miracles of the Saints, the relics and the cult of the holy images. The Christians attended the Synagogues and were attracted by the method of how the Jews practised worship of God and they took in even more the tectures of the Jewish preachers (Darshanim) than the sermons of the clergy, even if the Darshanim were hardly in the position to reveal the deep content of Judaism."[342]

"The clergy were then not ashamed to take over their explanations of the Holy Scriptures from the Jews. The Abbot Rhabanus Maurus of Fulda admitted that he had learned much from the Jews, which he used in his commentary on the Bible dedicated to Ludwig the German – who afterwards became Emperor. As a consequence of these marks of favour

---

[341] Graetz, same work, Vol. III. Chapter VI. Page 162.
[342] As we will investigate later, the deep content of Judaism, its doctrines and its secret policy were never revealed to the new converts at the threshold, but only to the hereditary good of the blood descendants of Abraham, i.e. of the people chosen by God.

towards the Jews at the Court, many Christians felt themselves drawn to Judaism and regarded it as the true religion."[343]

This description by the highly regarded Jewish historian Graetz makes clear to us that the present day arguments – that, for example, the Jews are untouchable, because they are descended from the Patriarchs and more of the like – with which they attempt to deceive the Christians and wish to prevent them defending themselves against the Satanic Imperialism of the Synagogue, are the same which the Jews used centuries ago for similar purposes, who then infamously fought to destroy Christianity and to bring the Holy Roman German Empire under Jewish rule. The tricks, subtle deceptions or Jewish fairy tales, as Saint Paul would say, are still always the same after eleven centuries.

But our Lord Jesus saved Holy Church once again from the Jewish falsehood and such desolation. This time it was the Paladine Abogard, the archbishop of Lyons and later his pupil and imitator in the episcopal see, Amolon. They fought for the salvation of the Church from Jewry.

In a recently published official work of the Jewish- Argentinian society, Agobard and Amolon, the two archbishops of Lyons, are described as fathers of Antisemitism in the Middle Ages.[344] This accusation seems terrible, since the Jews attribute to Mediaeval antisemitism the greatest harm to Jewry which a Christian mind can imagine.

This welcome reaction is commented upon by the classical Jewish historian Graetz, as follows: "Those who held firmly to the discipline of the Church, saw in the violation of the Church laws, in the favour shown to the Jews and in the freedoms allowed to them, the downfall of Christianity. Envy and hatred were at the back of this righteousness. The protectors of the Jews at the court with the Empress at their head were hated by the Church party... The advocate of Church righteousness and of hatred for the Jews of the then time was the restless enthusiastic Archbishop of Lyon, Agobard, whom the Church has canonised.[345] He slandered the Empress Judith, rebelled against the Emperor and drove the princes to rebellion... The bishop wished to restrict the freedom of the

---

[343] Graetz, same work, Vol. III. Chapter VI. Pages 162-164.
[344] The Jews, their history, their contribution to culture. Publication of the Jewish association of Argentina. Buenos Aires, 1956. Page 186.
[345] He was veritably revered for a long time in Lyon and was known as St. Aguebald. In the breviary of Lyon he had his own service of God. But we have no proofs that Holy Church approved this canonisation. Under these circumstances, it is explicable that Graetz, who was so cautious, held him for a real saint.

Jews and to bring them back to the low position which they occupied under the Merovingians."[346]

Graetz further writes, that the struggle of the Archbishop Agobard against the Jews lasted many years and as its basis "had the maintenance and defence of the Church Laws against the Jews, so that he directed his attention to the representatives of the Church party at the court, of whom he knew that they were enemies of the Empress and of her Jewish favourites. He urged them to influence the Emperor, so that he would restrict the freedom of the Jews. Apparently they also proposed something similar to the Emperor. But simultaneously the friends of the Jews at the Court sought for new ways and means, in order to spoil the plans of the clergy." And Graetz continues: "Agobard gave anti-Jewish sermons and ordered his flock to break off every connection with the Jews, to carry on no business with them and not to enter into their service. Fortunately the protectors at the court supported the Jews actively and condemned the intentions of the fanatical clergy to failure. As soon as they learned of his activity, they had themselves protective letters (indiculi) written by the Emperor and sent them, provided with his seal, to the Bishop in which he was ordered, upon threat of severe penalties, to cease his anti-Jewish sermons. In the year 828 a second letter went to the governor of the district of Lyon, which requested him to allow the Jews to enjoy every possible support. Agobard did not heed these letters and added contemptuously that the Imperial edict was certainly forged and could not be true."[347]

The worthy archbishop Agobard fought ceaselessly. He directed letters to all inhabitants of the Bishopric and requested them to participate actively in the struggle against the Jews. He aided the rebellion against the Emperor and Judith and, with the support of the sons of Ludwig from the first marriage, he fought bitterly to save the Holy Empire and Christianity from the ruin threatening them.

The authorised historian Graetz comments on the conduct of Agobard as follows: "Although the deep hatred of Agobard for the Jews must be regarded as having sprung principally from his own feelings, one cannot deny that he acted completely in accord with the Church doctrines. He referred himself simply to the assertions of the Apostles and the Church Laws. The inviolable decrees of the Councils were also on his side. Agobard was in his dark hatred strictly orthodox, while the Emperor

---

[346] Graetz, same work, Vol. III. Chapter VI. Page 164.
[347] Graetz, same work. Vol. III. Chapter VI. Pages 165 and 166.

Ludwig with his tolerance tended to heresy. Agobard, however, did not risk openly asserting this. He rather more hinted at that he found it difficult to believe that the Emperor would betray the Church in favour of the Jews. His complaints found an echo in the hearts of the Church princes."[348]

This commentary of Graetz's concerning the true teaching of the Church existing over many centuries in relation to the Jews, could not be more balanced and more realistic, even if these lines were written by the renowned historian in the previous century, when the "Synagogue of Satan" was still not in the position, as today, to attempt the complete falsification of the true Catholic teaching with regard to the Jews. But one sees clearly that Graetz had already essentially grasped the problem. He was one of the most important men of Jewry of his time. His historic works, especially the works which we quote, had an enormous influence upon the Jewish organisations and their leaders.

In addition it was universally evident that the Church laws and anti-Jewish resolutions of the Holy Ecumenical and provincial councils were the chief hindrance for the traitors in the Church itself, which her principal enemies, the Jews, furthered. For whoever made such attempts, had to reckon upon being deposed, with excommunication and the other penalties laid down in the Holy Church Canons. Hence it was the chief concern of the new traitors to remove this troublesome hindrance. But how was it possible to abolish with one blow the thousand-year-old Church Laws, the Papal Bulls and the teachings of the Church Fathers? How were these to be abolished so that the secret Jewish clergy could serve their Jewish masters without fear of being deposed and excommunicated and even attempt to falsify the doctrine of the Church in relation to the Jews, and as a result to promote its final defeat and the victory of its century old foe?

In the course of centuries the Jews and their "Fifth Column" in the clergy have repeatedly made the attempt to abolish the anti-Jewish Laws and to achieve that the Papal Bulls and the anti-Jewish theses of the Church Fathers should not fall under these laws. They have for this purpose, always according to the given possibilities, taken the most diverse paths. At the beginning of this century they have utilised the praiseworthy wish of Pope Pius X to summarise the most important Church Law determinations in one Codex; for in the turbulent time of the first world war of 1914-18 all attention was directed to the apocalyptic struggle and so

---

[348] Graetz, same work, Vol. III. Chapter VI. Page 167.

they attained that from the Church legal Codex the voluminous collection of Laws was excluded which represented the most effective defence of Holy Church against the secret Jewish infiltration and its destructive activity in the bosom of this institution. It is noteworthy that this occurred a few years after the Jewish historian Graetz, – the oracle of the then Jewish leaders – wrote the previously quoted lines. As a result it becomes evident that the anti-Jewish Church Legislation was the chief hindrance for attempts to bring Catholicism as well as the Holy Empire under Jewish rule. On the other hand it is clearly revealed in the Church Law Codex mentioned, that fundamentally the old Church legislation has not been altered. But in actual praxis the anti-Jewish and anti-heretical Laws were carefully left out, which represented the best defence of the Church against the centuries-old enemy. This differentiating, painfully exact omission, must certainly have been undertaken by a person very interested in the matter, who without doubt stood in the service of the organisation which from this veritable purging of anti-Jewish and anti-heretical laws, which took away from Holy Church a defence which it had built up in hundreds of years of experience, drew such great advantages. It is generally known that Pope Pius X did not work out the Codex himself, but left its editing to committees, whose presidency was conducted by Cardinal Gasparri and to whom without doubt those joined themselves, who undertook so carefully the suspicious editing of the Laws. If, as a result, the anti-Jewish Church Laws of the Holy Councils still remained in force (for the old Synods' legislation was still valid despite the omissions of the Codex), the omission of the Holy Church Laws which ordered severe punishments and deposing for clergy and Church dignitaries, nevertheless made it possible at the time of Pius XI for that Jew-friendly association of clergy and laymen to be founded, whose heretical theses were only the prelude for those of present-day priests and church dignitaries in the service of the Synagogue of Satan."

Another method which Jewry and its "Fifth Column" have always used again in the course of centuries, in order to cause the vanishing of Bulls and anti-Jewish theses of the Church Fathers, was the organisation of heretical movements, which did not recognise the doctrine of Holy Church and asserted that the Holy Bible is the sole source of revelation. Put briefly, these heretics make the assurance – as we will investigate later – that not tradition but only the Holy Scriptures are the source of revelation. These kinds of heretical movements, which – as we shall still see – were led by Jewry, began in the 11th century and were repeatedly combated by the orthodoxy, until in the 16th century Protestantism conducted these theses to success, abolished tradition as doctrine and source of revelation and recognised only the Holy Bible as such. The Jews, who in most cases directed and influenced these movements, were in reality concerned with eliminating the Holy Church Laws of the Ecumenical Councils, the Papal Bulls and the doctrine of the Church Fathers, who condemn Jewry and its accomplices in the clergy, as doctrine of the Church and source of the truth revealed by God. For if this defence were destroyed, the Jews in the higher clergy could carry out unpunished their treacherous disintegrating activity. But today they are exposed to the danger on grounds of these Church traditions, which they wish to abolish at every price as source of divine revelation, of being discovered and condemned. As one sees, the struggle of the clergy in service of Jewry which has lasted nine centuries has very deep roots and should solve for them the problem of destroying the Church unpunished or being able to cause it in priestly garb the greatest injuries and to favour Jewry and its revolutionary movements, without needing to fear the judgments or threat of deposition laid down in the Church Laws, Bulls and the doctrine of the Fathers. Naturally they cloak their offence against tradition in flattering, seemingly righteous arguments, which do not allow the poison of these manoeuvres to be discerned. Among other things, they say that the Church must adapt itself to the new times and fight with progress for Christian unity. These are great truths with which we are all perfectly in agreement. But we cannot accept what is being attempted under this pretence, viz. the destruction of the best defence of Holy Church, which could preserve it through centuries from the cunning of its most infamous and stiff-necked foes.

CHAPTER TWENTY-ONE

THE COUNCIL OF MEAUX COMBATS OPEN
AND SECRET JEWS

In the face of the deadly danger that threatened the Church and the
new western Roman Empire, several archbishops and bishops
assembled in the year 829 in Lyon. At this gathering they were
concerned – as the Jewish historian Graetz reports – with "humbling the
Jews and threatening their peaceful existence. They (the Bishops) also
discussed how the Emperor could best be influenced, so that he made
appropriate decisions. It was resolved at the assemblies to write a letter to
the Emperor which would draw his attention to how godless and
dangerous the favouring of the Jews was and to enumerate individually the
privileges which should be taken from them (in the year 829). The letter, in
its still preserved form, is signed by three Bishops and has as its heading:
'Concerning the superstition of the Jews.' Agobard wrote the foreword
and in it elaborated his position in the struggle. Accordingly he accuses not
only the Jews, but also makes their friends responsible for the evil. The
Jews, he says, have become bold through the support of the influential,
who believed they were not really so bad and were valued by the
Emperor." And he reports further: "From the standpoint of belief and of
the Church Canons, the argument of Agobard and the other Bishops is
irrefutable, and the Emperor Ludwig the Pious should, on the basis of
such logic, have exterminated the Jews completely and utterly. But
fortunately he felt himself not to be interested, perhaps because he knew
the character of Agobard or because the letter with the complaint did not
even come into his hands. The fear of Agobard that the letter could be
intercepted by the friends of the Jews at court was certainly well
founded."[349]

It is thus certainly highly possible that the theft of this letter through
the Jews was decisive in this struggle. Jews usually prevent complaints

---

[349] Graetz, same work. Vol. III. Chapter VI. Pages 167 and 168.

against them penetratingto the highest religious or civil authorities. If then the secret Jewish infiltration intercepts a complaint on the way or cripples its effect, it thus nevertheless at all events attains its aim in other ways.

One of the most important facts in the process of the Judaisation of the Holy Roman German Empire was the conversion of one of the Christian Semitophilic bishops to Judaism, who enjoyed a great confidence at the court of the Emperor and was one of his chief advisors. Concerning these prelates, the Jewish historian Graetz writes: "The Emperor had promoted him and, in order to always have him at his side, he made him into his confessor."[350] The struggle became even more terrible, for under the intimate advisors of the Emperor, who promoted his absurd Semitophilic policy, were found bishops of Holy Church. Also in our days there are those who support the interests of the Jewish enemies of Christianity.

But the case of Bodo was gravest of all. Many clergy of that time served, although they apparently remained of the true faith, the interests of the "Synagogue of Satan", as a result of which they without doubt caused greatest harm. They must certainly have held themselves to be very powerful, in order to allow themselves the luxury of introducing one of their most influential men, the confessor of the Emperor, who publicly boasted of denying Christianity, of confessing Judaism and proclaiming that this was the true religion.

Concerning the effect of this devastating blow at the Christian people, Graetz writes: "The conversion (to Judaism) of Bishop Bodo, who up to then occupied a high position, then aroused great attention. In Chronicles it is reported of this event, as if it were an extraordinary phenomenon. The event had without doubt special accompanying circumstances and struck devout Christians a heavy blow."[351]

We have not sufficient material at our disposal, in order to reveal whether it was a matter of a secret Jewish Bishop, who completed his theatrical conversion for propaganda purposes and wished to strike a blow which should hasten the decline of morals and the attempt at a Judaisation of the Empire, or whether it was really a Bishop who fell away through dangerous Semitophilism, became rebellious and admitted to Judaism. Whatever the truth may be then, it is nevertheless undeniable that, with the difficult situation of Holy Church in the Holy Roman Germanic

---

[350] Graetz, same work, Vol. III. Chapter VI.
[351] Graetz, same work. Vol. III. Chapter VI. Page 168.

Empire, the event must have been extremely harmful for Christianity. If Charlemagne had risen again and could have seen the catastrophic consequences of the unchaining of the beast - which the Church Canons had placed in chains – but which he had freed out of pity for the oppressed Jews and from the wish to make their valuable services of use for the Empire, he would have been able to recognise that he had fallen victim to the skilled deceit of those who have proven themselves as the most skilled swindlers in the world. All religious and political leaders should thus draw a lesson from this painfully rich tragedy; for if the Jews, with their skilled diplomacy, could deceive one of the greatest political geniuses, then it is not further remarkable that, with their traditional tactics of manipulating the desire of every virtuous man to show human pity, to protect the oppressed, or to defend the sublime demand for equality of peoples and races, they were able to deceive and outwit in the course of history the good faith of many popes, kings and political or religious leaders of mankind, and are still able to do this today. Only the absolute knowledge of Jewish wickedness and their traditional tactics of deceit can keep awake the good against the Jewish lies, of which Saint Paul warned us in his wisdom. Only thus can the danger be diminished that the good fall into the net of the masters of lies and distortion.

In the face of this catastrophic situation, the tireless courageous Archbishop Agobard took part in a conspiracy against the Empress Judith and supported Ludwig's sons from his first marriage in their struggle to dethrone the disastrous Emperor. Agobard was deposed as archbishop and the Empire fell into a succession of civil wars, in which now one, now the other side was victorious. The death of Ludwig, however, gave Jewry a decisive blow, but the heroic archbishop also died without having experienced the victory and the success of his struggle.

The new policy of Ludwig, who was falsely named the Pious, and who placed the Jews under the protection of the crown, had catastrophic consequences for mankind; for in the ensuing centuries it was imitated by many Christian kings, who gave the foe protection in the midst of his terrible conspiracies. They bore in mind thereby that the Jews are very useful as tax-collectors, in addition contribute in difficult times to balancing the budget through loans, that they are a decisive factor for the progress of trade and with their punctual payment of taxes effectively contribute to maintaining the state capacity. Admittedly they instigate conspiracies, spread heresies and rebellions, but the mediaeval monarchy held itself to be strong enough to be able to overcome this danger. The monarchy and the nobility of the Middle Ages were also really so powerful that they were able to achieve this for a long time. However, the moment came when the descendants of those optimistic kings and aristocrats had to bitterly lament the faults of their forefathers and the whole of mankind still suffers under this today.

When Ludwig died, the Empire fell to pieces and was divided among his four sons. As was to be expected, the Jewish dominance existed only in the realm of Charles the Bald, Judith's son, who had inherited from her the sympathy for the Jews, even if he did not go too far in this respect. But different Jews had additional influence at the court, among others, Zede Kish, the physician of the king and particularly a favourite whom the monarch called "my faithful Judas" on account of his political services. The Jew Graetz makes a remarkable observation about South Europe at that time: "South Europe, which was disturbed by anarchy and ruled by a fanatical clergy, was not a suitable ground for the development of Jewry."[352]

The dominance of Jewry in France was in addition in every respect such a serious danger for Christianity that Amolon, the new bishop of Lyon, took in hand the defence of the Church and the peoples and continued the struggle of his teacher and predecessor Agobard. Amolon could count thereby on the support of the greatest part of the bishops, including that of the rebellious Hincmar, the bishop of Rheims, who knew how to gain the full confidence of King Karl (Charles), and so partly counteracted the bad influence of the Jewish favourites.

The worthy archbishop Amolon was without doubt a tool of divine providence for the defence of Holy Church and France against the destructive activity of the Jews. He not only fought energetically against them, but also fought with the pen and wrote his famous tractate against the Jews, in which he openly pilloried their infamous crimes against Christianity and called upon the clergy and laymen to combat this principal foe.[353]

Under the leadership of Amolon, the French bishops began an important struggle against the Jews at the Holy Council, which took place in the year 845 in Meaux, in the neighbourhood of Paris. This Synod approved a series of anti-Jewish measures, which were relayed to the King for carrying out. Among these fell Church Canons which had been valid since Constantine, the laws of Theodosius' II, who forbade the Jews to

---

[352] Graetz, same work, Vol. III. Chapter VI. Page 170.
[353] Amolon, Tractate against the Jews. Published in the Library Patrum Maxima, Vol. XII and XIV.

occupy public and honorary offices, the edict of the Merovingian king Childebert, who excluded the Jews from the positions of judge and tax-collector and commanded them to respect the clergy.

The problem of the secret Jewish Christians who originated from false converts, which became more and more grave in France, naturally attracted the special attention of the Holy Synod, which drew into the list Church Canons approved at Synods of other lands, the anti-Jewish Church Laws of the Councils of Toledo against the baptised who remained Jews in secret, and the Church Canons which ordered that their children be taken from them, in order to be brought up as Christians.[354]

As we have already seen, these measures were to prevent secret Jewry from being passed on eternally in secret from one generation to the other. As one sees, this Holy Council of the Church wished to free France from the Jews – to fight great evil through great healing methods – and combated both open as well as secret Jewry to life and death.

Unfortunately Charles the Bald – doubtless still influenced by his mother's education – when he received knowledge of the resolutions of the Synod, in no way had a high opinion of the decisions, but had the Council dissolved by force, although his advisor and friend Hincmar had taken part in this Council. This proves that at that time the Jews still retained a decisive influence at the French court.

However, archbishop Amolon did not allow himself to be intimidated through this act of the king, and began again from anew. He sent the clergy a pastoral letter which, according to the report of Graetz, "was poisonous and slandered the Jewish race." He then writes further that "the poisonous letter was just as unsuccessful as that of Agobard and the Edict of the Council of Meaux. But gradually the poison spread from the clergy to the people and the princes."[355]

The Jewish historian Josef Kastein writes about this event and asserts that the Church "with the battle cry that the Christian religion was threatened, set in operation the most dangerous weapon, namely the uneducated masses of the nation. To minds which easily allowed themselves to be impressed by every cause, they constantly presented the same argument, which they had sooner or later to take up. The consequence of this was that the masses, who lived together with the Jews,

---

[354] Council of Meaux. Quoted by Graetz, same work. Vol. VIII. Chapter VI. Page 173.
[355] Graetz, same work, Vol. III. Chapter VI. Pages 172 and 173..

became their enemies. As a result the Church secured the great advantage of altering the conduct of the rabble in the desired manner. This occurred independently of political conditions at a given moment."[356]

Kastein, as well as Graetz and the other important Jewish historians, regard the Church as the actual mother of mediaeval antisemitism, in which respect they are without doubt also right, for they regard every movement as antisemitic which defends Christianity against Jewish imperialism and its revolutionary activity. On the other hand it is understandable that, with more or less semitophilic governments and such an influential Jewry as in France at that time, the most effective way and means to preserve Christianity from Jewish control consisted in convincing the people and revealing to it the extent of the Jewish danger and its threat to religion and the people itself. This conviction had success at that time, as the Jewish historians themselves confirm to us when they complain that it was successful for Holy Church to cause that Semitophilic conduct of the people in the France of Ludwig the Pious and of Charles the Bald to change later into a hostile behaviour towards Jewry. This shows us also that this decisive battle, which the Jews nearly won, ended with the victory of Holy Church and the defeat of the "Synagogue of Satan."

When the Jewish historians assert that the Church applied the most effective weapon, the uneducated rabble, then in this they are incredibly cynical, for this was particularly the weapon which the Jews have always used and still use even today.

This work of personal enlightenment, which the Church then undertook, opening the eyes of the people about the Jews and alluding to the danger, can alone today also save the world in its present situation. It is thus urgently necessary to imitate what the Church did in that difficult time, and short but clear pamphlets must be printed for the working masses and books for the educated classes, which must be distributed for the greater part gratis to individual households and to individual persons, so that all the world is enlightened about the danger of Jewish imperialism and its revolutionary activity.

This work of enlightenment must be directed especially at the leaders and officers of the army, navy and airforce, soldiers, rulers, teachers, political leaders, financiers, journalists, academicians, the personnel of radio and television, the working masses and the youth of all strata of

---

[356] Rabbi Josef Kastein, same work, Pages 252 and 253.

society. And especially to the members of the clergy of the Catholic and the other Christian churches, which, unlike our clergy, usually, on grounds of a series of circumstances which we will investigate later, do not recognise the danger. The convincing and making known of the Jewish danger must proceed at the fringe of political activity, among the members of all political parties and of all religious confessions, so that from all these domains the natural defensive movements emanate, which must be coordinated.

If the majority of the peoples and the domains which have in their hand the vital forces of a nation as well as the means of propaganda, open their eyes and recognise the danger of enslavement threatening us all and the enormous wickedness of Jewish imperialism and its dark intentions, the way to freeing of this nation and of the whole world is prepared.

The method of writing books in order to sell them in bookshops, so that a few persons obtain knowledge from them, is insufficient, for this alarm cry should be accessible to all houses and all men. The pamphlets or books should be distributed in the houses and given into the hand or, if possible, sent through friends to the recipients.

The clergy, the rich and all others who have money, should lay aside their chronic, sinful greed and work at the financing of this work of enlightenment, for if they do not help, there awaits them – according to the doctrines of Marx, Engels and Lenin, which predict the destruction of the clergy and of the Bourgeoisie – execution or concentration camps, should the Socialists dictatorship of Communism triumph.

CHAPTER TWENTY-TWO

JEWISH TERROR IN CASTILE
IN THE 14ᵀᴴ CENTURY

After the treachery of the Jews which led to the fall of the Christian Visigoth kingdom and its conquest through the Musulmans, began the so-called "Reconquista". It was introduced by the Christians who had become powerful in the mountains to the north of the peninsula under the Visigoth Pelayo. This fight for freedom was to extend over nearly eight centuries and naturally began with bloody retaliatory measures against the Jews, who were held responsible for the fall of the Christian states and for the murder of Christians after this catastrophe.

This anti-Jewish outlook lasted through several centuries. Resulting from this, the Jews understood how on basis of their own slyness and skill to use all opportunities to dissipate these reproaches, in that they especially provided valuable services to the Christian kings of the peninsula, when they made Spain into a place of refuge for the Israelites, who fled from the whole of Europe. At first they were persecuted by the Christian monarchs and later by the Holy Papal Inquisition, which reacted violently when the "Synagogue" attempted to conquer the Catholic states and to dismember Christian society.

In addition, the Jews at the beginning of the 10th century practised treachery on the Musulmans, whose allies they had once been, began to introduce the decomposition of Islamic society, and attempted to control it through secret organisations and false doctrines. The most important of these organisations were the criminal sects of murderers – undoubtedly a forerunner of modern freemasonry – whose secret power extended to the entire region of Islam and even to Christian Europe, until it was finally destroyed chiefly through the invasion of the Mongols. At all events the Musulman kingdom in the 12th century was facing a dangerous decline which is partly attributed to the manifold revolutionary activity of the

Jews. The dynasty of the Almohades, which in North Africa and in Islamic Spain followed upon that of the Almoravides, wished to save Islam from a catastrophe and began to wage a war of life and death against Jewry. This resulted as usual in thousands of seeming conversions to Islam and the flight of many Jews from Christian Spain in consequence.

The monarchs of the Iberian peninsula, who were occupied with the driving out of the Saracens from their territory, forgot the former treachery of the Jews and used them in the Reconquista as money-lenders, tax-collectors and even as spies. Now the roles were exchanged. The Jews represented in Islamic Spain the "Fifth Column" in favour of Christian Spain and thus practised treachery on their former allies. Once again a historical event was repeated: the Jewish population of a Musulman monarch became a dangerous "Fifth Column" favouring the external enemies of this state – then the Christian kingdom of Iberia (Spain), which, on the grounds of the valuable services which they provided it, promoted the Jews to government members and even to ministers or royal state treasurers. As a result they violated the decisions of the Holy Church Councils, which excluded the Jews from government offices.

The Jews turned back once again to their traditional tactics, to gain their enemies through seeming good conduct and effective services, thus obtaining valuable offices which made it possible to them to later conquer the states which had offered them protection.

They therefore left no opportunity unused in order to get into their hands control over this Christian kingdom, which had already become a second Palestine to them, into which they streamed ready and willing.

The Jews came to Castile at a time when they had reached the high point of their power. Peter the Cruel was then king, and for several years they controlled his government. The manner in which they conquered this Christian kingdom is extremely interesting.

Peter the Cruel ascended the throne in 1350, as a child of 15 years, and was soon subject to the influence of the Jewish leader Samuel Ha-Levi Abulafia. The latter incited the passions of the young prince and flattered him. Thus he was successful in eliminating the king's guardian, Juan Alfonso de Alburquerque and also the favourable influence of the queen mother. At first he was appointed as royal treasurer and in fact later to

THE PLOT AGAINST THE CHURCH

supreme minister of the kingdom.[357] As a result this Jew attained a political power like no other Jew before him in a Christian kingdom. In the ensuing time the influence of the Jewish counsellor on the monarch increased to such an extent that he was regarded by many as dangerous.

Even in the first years the outrages which the young king committed on the instigation of his wicked advisors called forth a general rebellion in the kingdom. The queen mother, the half-sister of the monarch, his aunt Leonora, Queen of Aragon, and many powerful nobles formed a league which made it its task to withdraw the young king from the influence of the Jewish counsellors and the evil-willed clique surrounding him. To the latter also belonged the relatives of his mistress, Maria de Padilla, on account of whom he had left his wife, the young Bianca of Bourbon, sister of the Queen of France.

When Peter saw himself abandoned by most of the nobles of the kingdom, he agreed to place himself under the guardianship of his mother. He therefore betook himself to Toro in the company, among others, of Samuel Ha-Levi – as Pero Lopez de Ayala, a Chronicler of this time, reports – who, according to the assertions of this Chronicler, "was his great favourite and advisor."[358]

There his mother and his aunt prepared him a hearty reception, at which, however, the taking captive of his retinue and also of the influential Jewish minister Samuel Ha-Levi took place.

The death of Juan Alfonso de Alburquerque, who, so it is asserted, was poisoned,[359] was a heavy blow for the league, for this magnate represented the connecting-link between very unusual men and interests. In the following we now give a summary of the report by Prosper Merimee, the famous French historian of the last century. He shows us how Samuel Ha-Levi understood how to utilise the new situation and skilfully created disputes, in order to destroy the league, by his offering the Infanta of Aragon castles and rich districts in the name of the King in exchange for her releasing him. In addition the sly Jewish counsellor offered estates and knighthoods to numerous magnates until such time as he was successful in

---

[357] Gutienre Diez de Gamez: Chronicles of Pedro Nino, Count of Buelna. This chronicle was written in the year 1495. The details are taken from the edition of Madrid, 1782. Chronicle of King Pedro by Pero Lopez de Ayala, Year I, II, III, IV ff. This Chronicle was hand-written by its author in the second half of the 14th century. Jose Amador de los Rios, History of the Jews in Spain and Portugal, Madrid 1876. Vol. II. Page 220 ff.
[358] Pero Lopez de Ayala: Chronicle of King Pedro, 5th Year. Chapter XXXIV and XXXV.
[359] Others hold this version not to be true.

destroying the league and one day could flee with the young monarch when they were at the hunt.[360]

J. Amador de los Rios, another historian of the past century, reports to us the following concerning this crafty enterprise: "Thanks, however, to the clever action of Samuel, it was successful for the son of Alfonso XI to obtain again the freedom which his mother and sisters had taken from him. Thanks to the gold which he knew how to distribute, and thanks to the promises in the name of the King, he had carried mistrust and disunity into the league and rendered null the plans of the Bastard. The King was soon surrounded by powerful servants who promised him eternal loyalty. Samuel had gained the absolute confidence of the king."[361]

Through the regard of the Jewish minister, the Jews gradually gained more and more influence in the kingdom. Concerning this the Jewish historian Bedarride gives us exact details, asserting that the Jews had reached "the high point of their power" under Peter the Cruel in Castile.[362]

Unfortunately, however, history proves to us that every time the Jews in a Christian or pagan state attain "the high point of their power", a terrible wave of murders and terror is unleashed, and Christian or pagan blood flows in streams. Thus it also occurred under Peter from the moment when the Jews obtained decisive influence upon education and government.

This intelligent child – who later showed himself as far-sighted, had great illusions and possessed enormous energy – would perhaps have been one of the most important monarchs of Christianity, if he had not been destroyed in his youth through the bad example and the still worse advice of his Jewish favourites and counsellors. The people held them guilty for the wave of crimes and ambushes which were unleashed under this bloody government. The Jews attained high regard and the synagogues prospered, while the Churches decayed and the clergy and the Christians were disgracefully persecuted.

Many contemporary and later Chroniclers report concerning the decisive influence of the Jews on the young monarch and their malicious power in relation to the cruelties during this stormy time of government.

---

[360] Prosper Merimee: Histoire de Don Pedro. Edition of Paris 1848. Pages 182 and 183.

[361] J. Amador de los Rios, same work, same edition. Vol. II. Chapter I. Pages 223 and 224.

[362] Bedarride: Les Juifs en France, en Italie, et en Bretagne. 12th edition, Paris, 1861. Michel Levy-Freres Editeurs. Page 268.

The French contemporary Cuvelier asserts that Henry, the half-brother of the king, "was begged and implored by the Spanish nobles to once again bring to the notice of the King that he acted badly in allowing himself to be counselled by the Jews and to expel the Christians"... "When Henry came into the royal palace of his brother, the latter was just having a council with several Jews. No Christians were present." "Henry implored Peter, nevertheless, not to listen to the counsels of the Jews." The Chronicler reports in addition of a Jew named Jacob who was present and clearly stood very close to Peter.[363] Paul Hay de Chartelet, another well-known French Chronicler, adds further to this episode in reference to the aforementioned counsellor of King Peter, that Henry of Trastamara could not conceal his anger "when he saw a Jew named Jacob", who enjoyed the full confidence of Peter and whom was held to be the instigator of all his cruel actions.[364]

Concerning the terrible crimes during the bloody period of government of Peter the Cruel report the "Prima Vita Urbani V", the Italian contemporary Chronicler Matteo Villani, and the Mohammedan Chronicler – likewise contemporary – Abou Zeid-Ibn Khaldoun, who makes the assurance among others, "that Peter cruelly oppressed the Christian people and on account of his tyranny made himself so greatly hated that they rebelled against him." In the Chronicle from the time of Peter of Aragon the criminal action of this government is described in a hair-raising manner, and in his renowned Chronicle of reminiscences the Frenchman Jean Froissard mentions not only the cruelty and tyranny which were characteristic of this government, but particularly stresses the hostile conduct of Peter the Cruel towards the Church and the Papacy.[365]

In the Annals and Chronicles written towards the end of the 15th century by Nicolas Gilles, Peter the Cruel is called "the great tyrant" and "rebel against the religion of Jesus Christ and his tragic end attributed to

---

[363] Cuvelier, Histoire de Monseigneur Bertrand du Guesclin, Manuscript of the Chronicler in verse. In the year 1387, Estoneville was given the task of writing them in prose. Spanish translation: Berenguer. Madrid, 1882, Pages 108 and 110.

[364] Paul Hay, Seigneur de Chartelet: Histoire de Monseigneur Bertrand du Guesclin, Paris 1666.

[365] Prima Vita Urbani V. Editio Bosqueti. Col. cum vetustis Codicibus MMS, published by Baluzius, in Vitae Paparum Avenionensium, Paris, 1693. Vol. I, Pages 374, 375 and 386. History of Matteo Villani. Florence 1581. Book I. Chapter LXI. Pages 30 and 31. Abou-Zeid-Abd-er-Rahman Ibn-Khaldoun: History of the Berbers, French translation: Baron de Slande, Algiers, 1586, Vol. IV. Pages 379 and 380. Froissard Jean: Histoire et Chronique Memorable. Paris 1574, Vol. I. Chapter CCXXX. Pages 269, and Chapter CCXLV. Page 311.

punishment by God.[366] Fernandez Nino, however, the loyal collaborator of Peter, who served him up to his death, writes in his renowned report – contained in the Chronicle of Pedro Nino – that the Monarch had selected "a Jew named Samuel Levi as confidant, who taught him to despise great men and to respect the little ones... he separated himself from many, drew his knife and exterminated many in his kingdom. Therefore he was hated by the majority of his subjects." In this Chronicle the preference of the young King for astrology is also spoken of.[367] This fact is politically very important, since in fact the astrologers of Peter were Jews among them Abraham-Abel-Zarzae especially distinguished himself – who influenced his political measures. For before every important measure the astrologers were asked if success was to be hoped for or not. It is interesting in this connection that Peter on the eve of his fall reproached this Abraham in that both he as well as the other astrologers had advised him to conquer Musulman territory as far as Jerusalem. But since things stood far worse than good, it was clear that they had deceived him.[368] It is understandable that, when the Musulmans defended themselves heroically against the Jewish threat and the Jews already controlled Castile, they accordingly wanted to get Peter to conquer the North of Africa as far as Jerusalem. In this way they wished to once again conquer their Islamic enemies with the help of foreigners, in order to perhaps even realise their desired dream of freeing Palestine. This last intention, which they had to abandon when Peter was overthrown, they achieved centuries later, when they were successful in controlling England and caused it to liberate a part of Palestine from the rule of the Arabs. Through astrology it was possible that the Jews controlled the policy of many Kings in times when this superstition was in mode.

The renowned historian Bishop Rodrigo Sanchez, who died in 1471, compares Peter of Castile with Herod,[369] and Paul Hay, the second Chronicler of Bertrand du Guesclin, with Sardanapal, Nero and Domitian.[370]

---

[366] Nicole Gilles: Les Annales et Chroniques de France, Paris 1666. Page 93.

[367] Gutierre Diez de Gamez: Chronicle des Pedro Nino, Count of Buelna, same edition. Pages 14 and 21.

[368] Summary of Kings of Spain. Chapter XC.

[369] Ferrer del Rio: Critical historical investigation of the government of Peter of Castile, edition unanimously recorded by the Royal Spanish Academy, Madrid 1851. Pages 208 and 211.

[370] Paul Hay, Seigneur de Chartelet: Histoire de Monseigneur Bertrand du Guesclin, edition mentioned. Page 93.

The French historian P. Duchesne said in connection with the return of Peter to Castile, when the English troops set him back upon the throne: "Peter came to Castile like a ravening bloodthirsty wolf in a flock of sheep. Before him ran terror, death went at his side, and bloodbaths streamed behind him."[371]

In his general history of Spain the Jesuit Father Juan de Mariana describes the disastrous period of government of Peter the Cruel in the following way: "In this manner the fields and cities, landed estates and castles, the rivers and the sea, were spotted with innocent blood, and everywhere one found signs of violence and cruelty. It is not necessary to assert that the terror of the people of the kingdom was very great. All feared that the same could happen to them, each individual was concerned for his life, and none could be certain of it."[372]

It is worthy of note that this report, written almost 400 years ago, describes with astonishing accuracy the present situation of terror in the Soviet Union and in the other lands under the Socialist dictatorship of Communism. In addition there is an important concordance. In the Kingdom of Peter the Cruel the Jews attained, according to the renowned Jewish historian Bedarride, "the highest point of their power". In the Soviet Union and the other Socialist states the Jews have also reached the high point of their power. This is a remarkable and tragic concordance of situations, which are separated from one another through six centuries.

As in every state, in which the Jews reach "the high point of their power", Holy Church in Castile was persecuted under Peter while the Jews occupied high posts. The consequence of this were energetic protests by the Castilian clergy, which are recorded in interesting documents. Among these is found a work which was already prepared in the lifetime of the monarch, and in which the Chaplain of the Church of Cordoba describes Peter as a "heretical tyrant".[373]

The Holy See broke with this protector of Jews and oppressor of Christians. The Pope excommunicated Peter and declared him in the Church Council as unworthy of the crown of Castile. He released the Castilians and other subjects from their oath of loyalty and invested Henry of Trastamara or the first successor to the throne with the dignity of

---

[371] Duchesne, Teacher of the Infanta of Spain: Short history of Spain. Spanish translation: P. Jose Francisco de la Isla, Madrid, 1827.
[372] Father Juan de Mariana, S.J.: General History of Spain. Madrid, 1650.
[373] Academy for History, Privileges of this Church. Page 18.

king.[374] This made easier the formation of a coalition of the kingdoms of France, Aragon and Navarra, which under the protection of the Pope, undertook a kind of crusade for the freeing of the kingdom of Castile from oppression.

While the Christian clergy and laymen were murdered, taken captive and oppressed in every way, Jewry attained such high regard as never before in Christian Spain. Toledo then was practically the capital of international Jewry, just as in the ensuing time it was to be Constantinople, Amsterdam, London and New York. In this city the powerful minister Samuel Ha-Levi held a Synod or a general Hebrew congress, in which delegates of Jewish communities from the remotest lands participated, in order apparently to admire the new synagogue, which Peter allowed Samuel to build against the orders of the Church.

Witness to this great assembly is given by two inscriptions – veritable historical monuments – in this synagogue, which later temporarily served as a church. From the text of these inscriptions it is revealed that Samuel Ha-Levi himself was the chosen leader, who clearly became the Baruch of that time, which, however, did not prevent that years later au influential circle of his Jewish enemies accused him of having stolen the royal state treasury and as a result hastened his overthrow and death. These envious Jews accused him of having deceived Peter for twenty years, and even occasioned the king to torture him, so that he might confess where the three giant mountains of gold, stolen by him, were to be found. But Samuel died without revealing his secret, and the Chronicler reports further: "And it (his death) caused the King much sorrow, when he learned of it, and upon the advice of these Jews he commanded to bring him all his possessions. The houses of Samuel were searched, and they found a subterranean chamber with three mountains of gold and silver coins, bars and pieces. Each individual one was so high that a man could hide behind it. And King Peter inspected them and said: "If Samuel had only given me the third part of the smallest of these heaps, then I would not have had him tortured. But he preferred to die, without telling me."[375] The fact that Jewish treasurers or finance ministers stole was not new. Many had been deposed for this reason. However, this occurrence shows us that even among the Jews themselves, in spite of brotherhood, astonishing cases of envy and disunity exist, which take a tragic course, like that described here. The Jews, however, continued to exercise their

---

[374] Paul Hay, Seigneur de Chartelet: Histoire de Monseigneur Bertrand du Guesclin, same edition. Book III. Chapter VI. Page 94.

[375] List of the Kings of Spain. Summary in the edition of Llaguno y Amirola of the Chronicle of Pedro-Nino. Madrid 1782.

influence on the government of Peter. Merely the persons were exchanged.

In order to overthrow Peter, he was not only accused of having handed over the government to the Jews, but he was also reproached with being a Jew himself. For King Alfonso XI, who had no male successor, was so enraged about this that he had seriously threatened the Queen, if the next child should again have been a girl. The Queen, in order to save herself, had therefore agreed to exchange the girl with a boy. The son of a Jew was brought, who had just been born, and who now grew up as heir to the throne, without King Alfonso knowing that he, whom they said to be his son, was a Jew. It was asserted in addition that Peter had secretly had himself circumcised when he learned of his Jewish origin, and for this reason also he handed over the government completely and utterly to the Jews. The renowned Chronicler and writer Pero Lopez de Ayala, who was in no way favourably disposed to King Peter, did not expressly mention this suspicion. But the fact that he describes Peter as the legal son of Alfonso XI allows it to be concluded that he did not recognise this accusation. In the same sense historians and Chroniclers express themselves who base themselves on the writings of Lopez de Ayala. If we also hold it to be correct that praise is given to this highly respected Chronicler in respect of this matter, then one must nevertheless take into consideration that he wrote a Chronicle about Peter when Catalina of Lancaster, the daughter of this king, was already married to Henry II, the grandson of Henry of Trastamara.[376] This marriage was concluded for political reasons and was intended to unite the two rival families and avoid future disunity. Since the Chronicle came into being at a time when the Castilian monarchy made efforts to wipe out the stigma of a possible Jewish origin, it is natural that Pero Lopez de Ayala was compelled to keep silent about everything which was connected with this and which could have injured the honour of Queen Catalina.

On the other hand, history has proven to us that the Jews in their striving for world domination are capable of everything, whether it be a matter of replacing a girl child through an Infanta or undertaking any other kind of deception which opportunity offers. However, in the case which we investigate here, the opinions expressed by the defenders of Peter the Cruel seem most probable – Freemasons or Liberals – who assert that the accusation of exchanging of Infantas were made out of thin air, and were spread by Henry of Trastamara in order to justify his claim to

---

[376] Pero Lopez de Ayala in Chapter XIII of the 5th Year of his Chronicle of King Peter says about Catalina: "who is now the wife of the King of Castile."

the throne. However, this fairy-tale was held to be true in Castile and abroad and firmly adhered to in Chronicles of that time.

In the same measure, it seems possible to us that, if it really was a girl in question, that this was invented by the Jews themselves, who surrounded and influenced the young monarch, in order to convert him to Judaism and thus to be able to control him fully.

In favour of this possibility speaks the constant striving of the Jews to control Christian or pagan monarchs for whom they fabricated a Jewish origin. They wished to prove to Francis I of France that he was a Jew, however he laughed at them. Emperor Charles V became for the same reason so enraged that he had the Jews who wished in this way to influence him on behalf of the Synagogue burned. For Charles II of England they even carefully forged a family tree and convinced him to such an extent that he made them some concessions. Even the Emperor of Japan they wished to so deceive and make him believe that he originated from the ten lost tribes, in order to win him for Judaism and thus to control the land of the rising sun. But fortunately the Mikado held them to be lunatics. It is therefore certainly possible that they applied the same methods with Peter and the news seeped through into the hostile camp, where they later used Trastamara as a banner against Peter. However this may be, it is nevertheless evident that Peter, with his murdering of clergy, persecution of the Church and elevation of the Jews, acted more as a Jew than as a Christian, which had the consequence that the story of the exchange of children was believed.

The following Chronicles reveal that Peter was of Jewish origin: the Chronicle from the same period about Peter IV of Aragon, the Chronicle of the contemporary Carmelite Father Juan de Venette, the anonymous Chronicle about the first four Valois, the likewise contemporary Chronicle of Cuvelier among others. It is worthy of note that a century later it is mentioned in a couple of documents – in connection with Salomon-Halevi, the well-known Rabbi of Burgos, who by baptism received the name Pablo de Santa Maria, became priest and later archbishop in the same city – that this prelate was descended from the girl Infanta who was exchanged with the Jewish boy, who was later King as Peter of Castile. The girl Infanta married the father of the renowned Archbishop. The following documents mentioned this widespread rumour: "El libro de los Blasones" (Book of Arms) by Alonso Garcia de Torres (surname Torres), Manuscript Page No. 1306, and the "Recopilacion de Honra y Gloria mundana" (Concerning worldly honour and worldly fame) of Captain Francisco de Guzman, Manuscript Page No. 2046, Excerpt Page 28 and

29.[377] Brother Cristobal de Sánchez assumed as certain, when in 1591 the first edition of his work "Vida de don Pablo de Santa Maria" (Life of Pablo de Santa Maria) was printed, that the renowned Rabbi and later archbishop was the son of the princess who was exchanged for the Jewish boy, who was later king of Castile.[378]

In connection with the exerting of influence by Jews upon the government of Peter – beside the admission mentioned by the "Jewish Encyclopedia" and by respected Jewish historians - it is stated in the Chronicle from that time written in verse by Cuvelier: "He had the bad practice of allowing himself to be advised in all things by the Jews who dwelled in his land. He revealed to them all his secrets and not to his most intimate friends, blood relations or another Christian. Thus the man, who knowingly made use of such counsel, necessarily came to a bad end.[379]

Another Chronicler and contemporary of Peter, who as a second continued the Latin Chronicle of Guillermo de Mangis, asserts that the King and his government were controlled by Jews: "The monarch was reproached in that he and his house were controlled by Jews, who were present in Spain in great number, and that the whole kingdom was ruled by them."[380]

Paul Hay, the second Chronicler of Bertrand du Guesclin, speaks in this connection of the bad counsellors of Peter making difficulties throughout the whole of Castile, committing murders and calling forth dissatisfaction and disconsolation; that they in addition infected the monarch with a general disinclination towards the most highly regarded people in his kingdom and thus destroyed the mutual regard which binds good kings with their subjects and the peoples with their princes, that Peter called in the Church properties in order to reward the ministers for their ill-will, and – so it is stated – rejected his baptism in order to allow himself to be circumcised, and practised countless cruelties, which filled Spain with blood and tears. He combined in his person all the faults of a

---

[377] For information about such valuable manuscripts we have to thank the zealous learned historian J. Amador de los Rios, History of the Jews in Spain and Portugal, Madrid 1876, Vol. II. Chapter IV.

[378] Sitges: The wives of King Pedro. Madrid 1910, Pages 178 and 179.

[379] Cuvelier: Histoire de Monseigneur Bertrand du Guesclin, written in prose by Estonteville, same edition. Page 107.

[380] Continuatio Chronici Guillemi de Mangis. published in "Specilegium sive Collectio Veterum Aliquot Scriptorum qui in Galliae Bibliothecis delituerant", Paris 1722, Vol. III. Page 139.

Sardanapal, Nero and Domitian, and his spirit was controlled by, principally Jewish, favourites.[381]

---

[381] Paul Hay, Seigneur de Chartelet: Histoire de Monseigneur Bertrand du Guesclin, same edition, Book III. Chapter VI. Pages 92, 93 and 94.

THE PLOT AGAINST THE CHURCH

CHAPTER TWENTY-THREE

THE JEWS BETRAY THEIR MOST MAGNANIMOUS PROTECTORS

Besides the murders of Christians during this hated Jewish dictatorship of Peter the Cruel, crimes were committed which caused the whole of Europe to shudder, as for example, the murders of Suero, the archbishop of Santiago, and of Pedro Alvarez, the deacon of this cathedral. The burning of the Abbot of St. Bernard on a fig-tree hastened the excommunication of Peter uttered by Pope Urban V. The announcement of this news nearly cost the representative of the Pope his life. But let us allow Father Joseph Alvarez de la Fuente to speak, whom we have to thank for the following details: "On account of this murder, as I have already said, and because King Peter had driven the Bishops of Calahorra and Lugo from their churches, Pope Urban V sent an archdeacon who was to inform the King of the excommunication. The latter came cautiously in a light galley down the river to Seville and went ashore at Tablada, in the neighbourhood of the city. He revealed to him the Bull from the Pope and escaped down the river with set sails, whereby the tide helped him." The renowned monk asserts that Peter rode into the water and wished to stab the archdeacon, that he was nearly drowned, since the horse became tired from swimming.[382]

During this time many horrible murders were committed. However, we mention here only that of the young innocent and helpless Bianca de Bourbon, the sister of the Queen of France, who was the legal wife of Peter and was taken captive and later shamefully murdered. The Chronicler Cuvelier, a contemporary of Peter, describes the murder of the young queen and gives us the assurance that Peter asked a Jew how he could get rid of the Queen unnoticed. The latter advised him to murder her and even offered to commit the crime himself with other Jews. The Queen was strangled in her own bedroom and left lying on the bed, where

---

[382] Royal Successions in Spain, by Father Joseph Alvarez de la Fuente, Page 79.

she was found dead. And the Chronicler further reports that there Jews killed four servants who wished to raise the alarm and locked in several others. King Peter later asserted that he had not given his approval to the murder, and had the murderers expelled from the land.

However, he only did this in order to justify himself.[383]

Another indisputably true document confirms to us the fact that the Jews were responsible for this rule of terror. This concerns the "Ordenamiento de Peticiones" (Order concerning visits), which was passed by King Henry in the Cortes of Burgos – after he had been proclaimed king in the year 1367. From this we take the following text, which we translate from the old Spanish of the publication by the Royal Academy for History in Madrid. The new king replies in this to the various representatives of the individual classes of the people in the "Cortes" (an organ which was similar to the Mediaeval parliament.)

No. 10. "Further the visits are approved to those who report that the inhabitants of the cities and towns in past times, upon counsel of the Jews, have suffered much evil, injury, death and banishment. The Jews were at that time favourites (i.e. highest ministers or chief counsellors) or officials of the former king. They wished to cause the Christians evil and injury, and the latter therefore begged us to allow neither admittance into our palace nor into that of the Queen nor the Infantas my sons, to Jews, neither that they might become officials, physicians or any other kind of profession.

"We give accord to this request and realise the reason. Never, however, were other kings in Castile begged for the like. And although there are Jews in our palace, we will not accept them in our Council and will not even give them such a great power that they could cause any kind of harm in our land."[384]

One can here observe something astonishing: Henry of Trastamara rebelled against his half-brother and secured himself the moral support of the Pope and the material support of the King of France and other monarchs, in order to overthrow Peter, in that he accused him of having become a rebel, secretly honouring Judaism and having handed over the government of Castile to the Jews. He had in addition hoisted the flag of

[383] Cuvelier: Histoire de Monseigneur Bertrand de Guesclin, same edition. Pages 111-114.
[384] The Cortes [Parliament] of the old kingdoms of Leon and Castile, published by the Royal Academy for History, Madrid 1863, Vol. III. Pages 150 and 151.

freedom and thus obtained the support of the nobility, of the clergy and of the people. Later, when he had triumphed and was crowned King, he acted in exact opposite to his promises and began to employ Jews in his palace.

What had happened during the civil war, that he, who had come to Castile in order to kill Jews, later tolerated them in his palace? What did the Jews do in order to avoid a foreseeable catastrophe and to more or less cut a good figure if the opposite party triumphed? The following historical document solves this problem for us.

In the Jewish Encyclopaedia, the monumental work of modern Jewry, it is stated that Peter surrounded himself since the beginning of his period of rule, with so many Jews that his enemies called his court the "Jews' Court." In addition the Jews had always been his faithful followers.[385] The latter was to be expected, for the young monarch had, as a result of delivering himself to the Jews and bringing the latter to the high point of their power, been able to conjure up the fateful international civil wars which were to cost him the throne and his life. Contemporary Chroniclers and historians, whom one cannot accuse of any Antisemitism, prove to us how false it is to believe that the Jews would always unconditionally keep trust with their ally and friend. On the contrary, they cheated him in the most malicious way, as the Jews usually do with their best friends and protectors. For the Jews count neither the most upright friendship nor proven services or favours, however great these may also be. If it suits their political interests, they are even capable of crucifying those who sacrificed everything to do them a favour.

In his loyalty to the Jews Peter went so far as to apply terrible measures of retaliation against those who offended against them. Pedro Lopez de Ayala, the most important writer and chronicler of that time, reports that Peter, when he went to Miranda del Ebro, "in order to exercise justice, because here people had robbed and killed the Jews, had – with the support of the Court – two men of the city, Pero Martinez, son of Chantre, and Pero Sanchez Banuelos killed. Pero Martinez he had boiled alive in a cauldron and Pero Sanchez roasted alive in his presence. In addition he had still others from the city killed."[386]

---

[385] Jewish Encyclopaedia. same edition. Vol. IX. Word "Spain".
[386] Pero Lopez de Ayala: Chronicle of King Pedro, abbreviated, remark 4 to Chapter VIII of Year XI.

In the fifth year of his rule he showed himself magnanimous and granted mercy, even in favour of those who had striven for the throne. However, this edict of mercy did not extend to persons who had caused injury to the Jews. One should therefore really expect the Jews to have kept faith with him in difficult situations. However, the opposite was the case.

The French Chronicler Cuvelier, who was eyewitness and accompanied Bertrand du Guesclin and Trastamara upon their campaign, writes about the time when, through the tragic defeat of Peter's armies, it became clear that the scales inclined to the side of his opponent. After Peter the Cruel had evacuated Burgos, Toledo and Cordoba, he made his way to Seville. Two of his most valued influential Jewish counsellors, named Danyot and Turquant, agreed with one another to betray him and to hand him over to Henry, as soon as opportunity offered.[387]

Jose Amador de los Rios, the learned writer and historian of the last century, who was favourably disposed to the Jews, openly admits: "It was known in Castile and elsewhere that the Jews themselves let in the Bretons Bertrand Claquins (du Guesclin), when Henry and his supporters appeared before certain cities."[388] (In Spanish the word "juderia" is used here. So were the Jewish communities in Castile called.)

When King Peter learned of this cunning betrayal by his protectors, he was doubtless beside himself. The French Chronicler quoted, who witnessed the events, reports that King Peter, when he learned that Cordoba had fallen into the hands of his half-brother, had a violent quarrel with the two Jews who had resolved to betray him, and said to them: "My Lords, a fateful destiny has caused me to listen to your counsel for years long. You are guilty of the murder of my wife and of the falsification of my laws. Cursed be the hour of the first day when I first believed you, now that I shall be thrown out of my land. Exactly in the same way do I throw you out from my high council and palace. Guard yourselves well, never to come back again and leave the city at once." And the Chronicler continues that the two Jewish counsellors had concluded a secret agreement with Henry of Trastamara, to deliver the city of Seville to him, into which Peter had withdrawn. They agreed with the scribes of the Jewish community in this city that they should let in the troops of Henry of Trastamara through

---

[387] Cuvelier: Histoire de Monseigneur Bertrand du Guesclin, written in prose by Juan de Estonteville in the year 1387. Spanish translation: Berenguer, Madrid 1882. Page 143.
[388] Amador de los Rios: History of the Jews to Spain and Portugal. Madrid 1876. Vol. II. Chapter IV. Page 253.

the Jewish quarter. However, through a beautiful Jewess, who had been his lover and was very fond of him, Peter learned in time of the plans of the Jews against him. Therefore on the next day he left the city and fought through a retreat.[389]

Paul Hay de Chartelet, the second Chronicler of Bertrand du Guesclin, assures us that Peter learned this in Seville from a Jewish concubine who loved him very much and, against the will of her father, informed him that the Jews planned a secret plot together with Henry of Trastamara to deliver the city to the latter. When Peter had received this news, the unfortunate monarch was completely downcast.[390]

Without doubt the Jews had followed their traditional tactics and had provided the King with Jewish lovers in order to keep him better under control. But love is often a double-edged sword. And in this case the love of the girl was stronger than her inclination to Judaism and the fear of reprisals.

If we read these Chronicles, it becomes ever more clear to us how dangerous these unassimilable circles of aliens were, who – as has been proven in the course of time – never kept faith with anyone and always inclined to become the deadly "Fifth Column" in the service of foreign powers, and even then when they harmed their most valuable, fanatical protectors and friends.

These facts show us how the Jews, when they saw themselves threatened through the victory of the Christian people in Castile, under the leadership of Henry of Trastamara, knew how to cross at the right time to the opposing side, i.e. to that of Trastamara, in order to thus transform approaching catastrophe into a triumph. This Machiavellian enterprise was perfected even more by the Jews in the course of centuries, and in our time they no longer wait until their enemies are on the point of victory. If a Christian or anti-Communist opposition threatens to disturb their dark plans, they introduce elements into their ranks which makes them fail, or at least occupy a valuable position in the enemy camp, and give the latter the death blow at the first opportunity.

---

[389] Cuvelier: Histoire de Monseigneur Bertrand du Guesclin, same edition. Pages 143, 144 and 146.
[390] Paul Hay: Histoire de Monseigneur Bertrand du Guesclin, same edition. Book III. Chapter XII. Page 110.

ANTI-COMMUNIST ORGANISATIONS

OF THE FREE WORLD!

Be watchful and defend yourself against the infiltration of Jewish elements into your ranks, for they only give themselves out to be anti-Communists in order to control your movements and to make them fail. Even if they also give you good services, it is only to gain positions.

When Peter was defeated, he fled to Portugal, and from there to England, where he was able to secure the support of the "Black Prince."[391] Supported by the English army and later by the alliance of the Moorish King of Castile. At this stage of the battle there were Jews in both rival camps. They had already discovered the secret of future triumphs: to bet upon two cards, in order to always win. To achieve success with this kind of manoeuvre, the Jews had naturally pretended schisms or divisions in their own ranks, so that attention was not drawn to the fact that one group stood on one side of the combatants and another on the opponents. Thus, after the defeat of Peter at Montiel, they obtained good positions in the government of the victor.

It is astonishing that Henry, in this despicable duel which cost Peter his life, was cynical enough to again call him a "Jew", although the Bastard at that time was bought both through the treachery of the Jews to Peter as also through the gold which the Jewish communities placed at his disposal, and allowed them renewed admittance – in spite of the justified concern of the Cortes of the Kingdom – to his Court. Thus the struggle, which should have ended with a complete victory for the Christians, was cruelly continued up to the end of the century, in the year 1391, with the terrible murders of Jews on the whole peninsula, when it came to an end. Responsibility for the latter was unjustly laid upon the sermons of the Catholic priest Ferrán Martinez. These, however, were only the spark which brought into flame the hitherto withheld alarm of an oppressed people, whom the Jews robbed, murdered and oppressed when they occupied high positions under several governments. For this the irresponsibility of the monarch was responsible, who had willingly given free range to this treachery. The Jewish "Golden Age" in Catholic Spain had dawned as a result. This situation had tragic results and also harmed

---

[391] It must be explained that the chivalrous Prince of Wales, when he was convinced that Pedro had cheated him and the cause which he supported was bad, withdrew his support.

the Musulmans when they made possible the Jewish "Golden Age" in Islamic Spain.

CHAPTER TWENTY-FOUR

JEWISH INFILTRATION IN THE CLERGY

In this chapter the ways and means will be investigated of how the false Jewish mock-Christians usually undertake their infiltration into the clergy.

In order to conquer the Christian world, Jewish imperialism holds it indispensable to control the chief bulwark, the Church of Jesus Christ. Therefore they have applied various tactics – from direct attacks to infiltrations. The weapon preferred by the "Fifth Column" was to bring young Christians descended from Jews into the ranks of the clergy who secretly paid homage to Judaism. After ordination as priests, they were then to rise in the hierarchy of Holy Church – be it in the secular clergy or in religious orders – in order then to utilise the positions obtained in the clergy to the harm of the Church and in the interests of Jewry for its plans of conquest and heretical or revolutionary movements. With this delicate task Jewry makes use of talented young men, who intercede not only very religiously but also mystically and fanatically for the Jewish religion and are ready to sacrifice their life for the cause of the God of Israel and the chosen people.

In Judaism there are many such mystics. And to this the great successes are to be attributed which the theological Imperialism of the Jews has achieved. The child or the youth who enters into the seminary of the Christian clergy knows that he will be undertaking the holiest task, the destruction of the principal enemy of the chosen people, thus of Christianity and particularly of the Catholic Church. He knows that he makes possible with his future activity of destruction and weakening of Christianity the fulfilment of the divine will, and hence the rule of Israel over the whole world will be attained. The false Christian, who in secret adheres to Judaism, believes he is completing a sacred task which in addition secures him eternal salvation. The more damage he can cause the Church as priest, monk, minister, abbot of a monastery, provincial of a province, bishop, archbishop or cardinal, all the more services has he rendered, according to the opinion of the Jews, before God and the chosen people. One can say that this legion of mystics and fanatics was finally successful in bringing to an end the predominance of Holy Church in the Middle Ages, and as a result the revolutionary Jewish-Freemasonic or Jewish- Communist movements of modem time had their way made easier. The Jewish "Fifth Column" in the clergy is thus one of the basic pillars of international Jewry.

The aims of the infiltration of the Jewish mock-Christians in the clergy are clearly laid down in an interesting document which the Abbé Chabauty had published, and which is also mentioned by the archbishop of Port Louis, Monsignore Leon Meurin, S.J. This concerns a letter from the secret leader of the international Jews, who lived towards end of the 15th century in Constantinople, to the Jews in France. As answer to an earlier letter to him from Chamor Rabino de Arles, he gives them in this the desired instructions. This document fell into the hands of the French authorities and Abbé Chabauty had it published. The letter runs literally:

"Beloved brother in Moses, we have received your letter, in which you report of your anxieties of soul and the misfortune which you must bear. We suffer this sorrow with you. The advice of the Grand Rabbis and Satraps of our laws runs as follows:

"You say that the King of France compels you to become Christians. Well then, do his will, but preserve the law of Moses in your hearts.

"You say that they wish to seize your goods with violence. Let you children become merchants, so that through trade they may rob the Christians of their property.

"You say that there is a striving after your life. Let your sons become doctors and chemists, so that they can take life from the Christians without having to fear punishment.

"You say that your synagogues are destroyed. Let your sons become priests and abbots, so that they can destroy the Christian Church.

"You say that you are oppressed in other ways. Let your sons become lawyers or notaries or undertake some other profession which has usually to do with public affairs. Thus you will rule the Christians, you will gain control of their land and avenge yourselves upon them.

"Follow the commands which we give you and experience will so teach you that, although you are now downtrodden, you attain the high point of power."

Signed V.S.S.V.E.F. Prince of the Jews of Constantinople to the leader of Casleo, 1489.[392]

The infiltration of Jewish mock-Christians into the French clergy of that time caused much harm, since it made possible the spreading out of the Huguenot movement in the 16th century. This sect was supported by Jews who pretended to be Christians, and clearly differed from the Lutheran churches which even seized upon anti-Jewish measures.

The purpose of this Jewish infiltration into the clergy is evident: the destruction of the Church from within. What was said in the aforesaid letter has been confirmed to sufficiency in countless trials by the Holy Inquisition against clergy who honoured Judaism. The treacherous activity of the clergy of the "Fifth Column" is indescribably many-sided, yet always directed at the same goal: to passionately defend the Jews or to favour heretical and today, revolutionary openly anti-Christian movements, to weaken the defence of the Church and to attack good Christians – especially the successful defenders of Christianity –, to denigrate and destroy them. Thus they prepare the victory of the Jewish heretical Freemasons and Communist organisations and hope in the future to be able to fully destroy the Church.

The trials brought by the Holy Inquisition against archbishops, abbots, deacons, priests and monks who were secret practisers of Judaism, give a wealth of information concerning the tactics applied by the clergy of the "Fifth Column".

The phenomenon of Jewish infiltration into the clergy has existed as proven since the beginnings of Christianity and was constantly one of the main dangers which Holy Church, not only in the one or other land, but in the entire Christian world, saw facing it. If we wish to investigate this problem in its entire extent, then a work of many volumes would be necessary. We will therefore restrict ourselves to one of the many tragic historical trials of Jewish infiltration into the clergy, which made possible the present triumph of Jewish Imperialism. The following example will suffice, in order to reveal how the Synagogue carried out its infiltrations

---

[392] Archbishop of Port Louis, Mons. Leon Meurin. S.J., Philosophy of Freemasonry. Nos Publishers, Madrid 1957, Pages 222, 223 and 224.

into the Christian clergy, for its tactics were at different times and with different peoples always similar.

The learned Jewish historian Abram Leon Sachar, one of the directors of the Hillel de la B'nai B'rith Foundation, Jewish community leader and later president of the Brandeis University, writes in his work "History of the Jews", in connection with the conversion of the Jews to Christianity in Spain since the year 1391 and with the later results of these conversions, as follows:

"But after 1391, when the Jews were more strongly under pressure, whole communities confessed to the Christian belief. The majority of the new converts eagerly utilised their new status. Hundreds of thousands came together in places from which previously they had been excluded on account of their faith. They entered professions hitherto forbidden them and had admittance to the secret Senate of the Universities. They obtained important state offices and even penetrated into the Church of the all highest. Their power increased more and more with their wealth, and many could thus reckon upon being accepted into the oldest nobility families of Spain... An Italian who lived almost at the same time remarked that the converted Jews practically ruled Spain, while their secret adherence to Judaism destroyed the Christian faith. Like a wedge, hatred stood between old and new Christians. The neophytes were regarded as rogues, as 'infamous' or 'pig dogs.' They were despised on account of their success, their pride and their cynical attitude to Catholic practices . . . While the masses observed with gloomy bitterness the success of the new Christians, the clergy lied about their unfaithfulness and their lack of honesty. It was suspected with justice that the majority of converts were still Jews in their heart. The compulsory conversion had not been able to eliminate a legacy centuries old. Tens of thousands of the new Christians outwardly submitted, went as usual to Church, murmured the prayers to themselves, carried out rites and observed the customs. But their spirit had still not been converted."[393]

It is difficult to aptly comprehend the conversion of the Jews to Christianity who became a veritable "Fifth Column" in the bosom of Christian society. Alarming is the manner in which the Jews gained control of the government posts, of corresponding places in the universities and in all realms of social life and also penetrated into the nobility families and

---

[393] Abram Leon Sachar: History of the Jews, Spanish translation published and edited by "Ediciones Ercilla". Santiago de Chile, 1945, Chapter XVI. 3. "Marranos and the Inquisition." Pages 276 and 277.

even into the sanctuary (all-holiest) of the Church; as the Jewish academician correctly writes, the Jewish infiltration into the clergy.

After recounting how real Catholics grew suspicious when converted Jews, during the baptism of their children, "at once washed away the baptismal mark" from them, this Jewish historian continues:

"It was suspected that they celebrated the Jewish festivals in secret, ate Jewish-foods, maintained friendships with Jews and studied the ancient Jewish science. Reports of countless spies had the aim of confirmation of these suspicions. What son of the Church could have been able to look on calmly at how these hypocrites made merry at the Christian practices and accumulated riches and honours?"[394]

Althis was proved to sufficiency, for the Spanish Inquisition knew best of all how to introduce spies into the Jews' own ranks, who then helped it to discover the most closely guarded secrets, even if they were still so well concealed under the mask of false Christianity. In this lies one of the main reasons for the deep hatred of the Jews towards the Spanish Inquisition and for this reason they have organised against it for centuries long a campaign of slander and blasphemy in the whole world, which has given occasion to short-sighted condemnations and covered the historical truth with dirt.

The Jewish historian Cecil Roth, so very highly regarded in Jewish circles, assures us in his "History of the Marranos", an official Jewish publication of the Jewish publishing house in Buenos Aires, in connection with the same events that even if there were honest converts, nevertheless the majority were in their innermost hearts just as Jewish as previously. In appearance they lived just as Christians, had their children baptised in the Church, but hastened to efface the traces of the ceremony, as soon as they were back home again. They had themselves married by a priest, but this ceremony did not satisfy them, and they carried out yet a second one among themselves in order to render the marriage legitimate. They went often to confession, but their confessions were so unreal, that – so it is said – a priest once begged one of them for a piece of his clothing, as a relic of such a pure soul. Behind this outward concealment they remained what they had always been.

The Jewish historian speaks below of how they carried out the Jewish ceremonies down to the last detail, celebrated the Sabbath as far as was

---

[394] Abram Leon Sachar: same work, same edition. Chapter XVI. Page 277.

possible for them, and often entered upon a marriage with descendants of open Jews.

Then he makes the following interesting revelations: "They secretly attended the Synagogues, for whose illumination they regularly donated oil. They also formed religious communities under the protection of a saintly Christian, with apparent Catholic aims, which they used as pretence in order to be able to carry out their very ancient rites. As far as their race and their faith is concerned, then they were the same as before their conversion. They were one hundred percent Jews, and not only in name. Christians, on the other hand, they were only for the sake of outward form. After the religious hindrances had been cleared away, which had previously blocked the way to them, the new converts and their descendants in social and economic respect, made enormously rapid progress. However much their honesty was doubted, they might nevertheless nowhere be excluded any more on account of their faith. The legal career, the government, the army, the universities, and even the Church were soon filled by more or less doubtful new converts or their direct descendants. The richest married into the high nobility of the land, for only few impoverished Counts or knights could withstand the attractive power of money."[395]

The third remark of the Jew Cecil Roth to the third chapter of this work is very interesting and runs literally: "Jerome Munzer, a German, who travelled in Spain in the years 1494-95, reported that, until a few years previously in Valencia, where later the Church of the Holy Catalina de Siena was built, there was a church which was dedicated to Saint Christopher. Here were found the graves of the 'marranos', i.e., of the false Christians who were inwardly Jews. If a Jew died, they pretended to be in agreement with the rites of the Christian religion and carried in a procession the coffin covered with a golden cloth and image of Saint Christopher. But in spite of all, they washed the body of the dead and buried them according to their own rites. . ." A similar case is said to have occurred in Barcelona, where a marrano, if he said, "Let us go today into the Church of the Holy Cross", meant by this the secret Synagogue which was so named. A classical report about the situation and the hideouts of the marranos of this time is in the history of the Catholic Kings by Bernaldez, contained in Chapter 18.[396]

---

[395] Cecil Roth, History of the Marranos, Spanish translation, Israel Publishers. Buenos Aires, 1946, 5706. Chapter I. Pages 26 and 27.
[396] Cecil Roth: same work, same edition, remark 3 to Chapter I. Page 27.

On the ensuing pages of the already mentioned "History of the Marranos", several examples are given of how it was successful for several of them to attain high positions. The Jew Azarias Chinillo, for example, who upon his conversion took the name Luis de Santangel, went to Saragossa and there studied law. Afterwards he obtained a high position at the court and a nobility title. "His nephew Pedro Santangel became Bishop of Mallorca and his son Martin a judge in the capital. Other members of the family occupied high offices in the Church and in the government of the state." Then the famous Jewish historian enumerates further Jews in Church offices: "Juan de Torquémada, the cardinal of Saint Sixtus was directly descended from Jews,[397] in the same way as the devout Hemando de Talavera, the archbishop of Granada, and Alonso de Orpeza, the head of the Hieronymite Order... Juan the Pacheco, Marquis of Villena and head of the Order of Santiago, who during the rule of Henry the Incapable was sovereign ruler in Castile and tenaciously sued for the hand of Isabella, was descended on both father as well as mother's side from the Jew Ruy Capon. His brother, Pedro Giron, was the head of the (Catholic military) Order of Calatrava, and his uncle was archbishop of Toledo. At least seven of the head Prelates of the kingdom had Jewish blood in their veins. The same was the case with the Chief paymaster... The numerical proportion of converts with their rapidly increasing descendants and far-reaching family connections was very great. In the south of the land it formed – so it is said – a third of the population of the most important cities. Accordingly it must have been three hundred thousand on the entire peninsula, inclusive of the pure-blooded and the half-pagan relations. The former were not so numerous. All in all they represented in the state organism an all-embracing, unassimilable community in no way to be despised. The Jews who had been converted to Christianity, together with their most distant descendants, were known in Jewish circles by the name Asunim, 'Compelled', i.e. persons who were compelled to accept the ruling religion..."

And the Jewish writer continues his interesting report: "A new generation had grown up, which had been born after the conversion of their parents and was naturally baptised in childhood. The position of Church Law could not have been clearer. They were Christians in the truest sense of the word, and the practice of Catholicism placed them equal to every other son or every other daughter of the Church. However, it was known that they were only Christians in name. They publicly supported the new faith only very rarely, while they clung all the more in

---

[397] He must not be confused with Brother Tomas de Torquemada, Grand Inquisitor, as is often the case.

secret to their old one. The position of the Church had become far more difficult than before the fateful year 1391. Previously there had existed countless unbelievers who were easy to recognise and who were made harmless through a succession of systematic government and Church laws. But the same unbelievers were now found in the bosom of the Church and spread out in all realms of Church and political life, often openly derided its teachings and through their influence infected the mass of the faithful. Through baptism they had merely changed from former unbelievers outside the Church to heretics within it."[398]

The words of the authoritative Jewish historian speak for themselves and comments are superfluous. It describes to us in a few words the character and the deadly danger of the "Jewish Fifth Column" in the clergy in the course of centuries up to the present.

Besides their efforts to control the Church from within, by their controlling of the highest offices, the false Christians infected through their influence the mass of the faithful. Thus arose heresies and the Jewish-influenced revolutionary movements.

Jose Amador de los Rios, whom the Jews rightly hold to be one of the most important sources of Jewish history on the Iberian peninsula and whom up to the present only the Jew Cecil Roth equals, says in this connection about the converted Jews: "On the grounds of this improvised demand, they gained control of all state offices and all dignities and honorary offices of the republic. They risked much and attained still more, mixed their blood with the Hispano-Latin in a liberal way, penetrated suddenly into all realms of Christian life and into the highest nobility and climbed with their proud demands up to the steps of the throne itself." "Their inborn lack of shame came to their advantage and they supported themselves upon the well-weighed single-mindedness of their race, whose origin they now proudly and arrogantly sought in the most regarded families of the tribes of Judah or Levi, the representatives and traditional preservers of the priesthood and of the kingdom.

We restrict ourselves now to the converted Jews (as the converts were also called) in Aragon and Castile. One can in fact assert with justice that the Jews, in contrast to the converted Moors who were satisfied after baptism to be respected in the same modest position, advanced themselves in all realms of official life and took up all social positions. In the curacy of

[398] Cecil Roth: History of the Marranos, Israel Publishers. Buenos Aires, 1946, 5706, Chapters I and II. Pages 28-36.

the Pope they sat in his private rooms; at the head of the government, of public property, and of the highest courts of law; in the teachers' chairs and in the rectorate of the universities, as well as in the chairs of the diocesans and abbots. And as spiritual dignitaries they demanded and received from the crown, knights' estates, counties, margravedoms and baronial properties, which led to the noble stamp of the old nobility vanishing. Everywhere and in every respect the calm investigating gaze of the historian falls upon the hectic neophytes. With manifold aspects they offer themselves for rational study and also long fruitful investigations. In all realms of activity and intelligence their initiative was to be traced. The converted Jews became to the same measure statesmen, financiers, lease-owners, soldiers, prelates, theologians, legal scholars, Bible preachers, physicians, merchants, industrial workers and craftsmen, for they laid claim upon all." After this exposition the historian poses the following question: "Should the Spanish race be completely abandoned in the face of the never satisfied ambition which the fortunate combination of the new Christians with Catholicism has called forth among the latter?"[399]

He speaks of the sons of Rabbi Salomon Ha-Levis, who with his conversion took on the name Pablo de Santa Maria and was priest and later archbishop of Burgos. After enumeration of the distinctions which Alvar Garcia de Santa Maria received, it is further expressly stated: "The distinction was allotted to the first born of Pablos, Gonzalo Garcia, who was already invested with the archdeaconship of Briviesca in 1412. In 1414 he was chosen to represent Aragon at the Ecumenical Council of Constance. There he had the fortune that the assembled fathers chose to address him and other noble young men with the difficult, sublime problems which were to be discussed in this high assembly. Alfonso, who was born after Maria, attained the title of doctor when he was already no more than 5 years old and shortly afterwards became deacon of Santiago and Segovia. It is worthy of note that, in this Chronicle, up to his election as archbishop he is always called deacon of the Church of Santiago and Segovia, which proves that he combined both dignities in himself. When he was still very young, Pedro already received the important honorary office of protector of the King."[400]

In the following chapter of the work quoted, José Amador de los Rios comes back once again to the fact that Jews claimed for themselves high offices and says something very revealing in this respect: "In the preceding

---

[399] J. Amador de los Rios: History of the Jews in Spain and Portugal. Madrid 1876. Vol. III. Chapter I. Pages 12, 13, 14 and 16.
[400] Chronicles concerning Juan II, 1420. Chapter XVIII.

chapter we have seen how the converts in Aragon and Castile, through the freedom which conversion brought with it, and by their own education, their riches and their natural daring, had occupied not only all offices of the republic but also social positions, and conquered by storm the highest dignities in the Church, if they were not freely conceded to them."[401]

This felicitously chosen expression "to conquer the highest dignities (offices) of the Church by storm" is interesting, because today it is an actuality. For the "Fifth Column" in the service of Jewry in different dioceses – by its naturally making its influence felt in Rome – has really taken the highest dignities by storm. As a result it becomes completely clear that upon different occasions those who, on the grounds of their virtue and loyalty to the Church, would really have deserved these offices, were not taken into account and treated differently. Preference, however, is given to the clergy who defend Jewry, favour the victory of Freemasonry and Communism, and violently attack the real defenders of Holy Church. In these cases the mechanism of intrigues and influence of the "Fifth Column" has deceived the goodness and sincerity of the Holy See and can therefore record new triumphs, not only through the securing of successors in the Dioceses under control but also in foreign ones, which again injures those who had greater claims to occupy the vacancies. Luckily this kind of manoeuvre has in many cases failed completely and one hopes that in the future, when the truth becomes known and the enemy is unmasked, the "Fifth Column" will have to record greater failures. In addition the Church – as already before – recovered anew from the deadly cunning of the "Synagogue of Satan."

Our Lord Jesus Christ announced clearly and distinctly that the truth will make us free. Therefore we taken the risk of speaking the truth, although this will be highly unpleasant to the clergy and laymen, who secretly confess to Judaism and betray the Church and Christianity.

Concerning Saragossa, the capital of the kingdom of Aragon, the famous historian says the following: "The converts who held themselves to be preservers of the ancient culture of their predecessors, strove not only for the lower offices in the Republic, but also for Church dignitaries." In another passage he provides us with interesting details concerning the connection between a Jewess and the Prince Alfonso of Aragon. The latter fell in love with the daughter of the public Jew Aviatar-Ha-Cohen, who "upon the request of the Prince, first confessed to the faith of the Saviour,

---

[401] J. Amador de los Rios, same work, same edition. Vol. III Chapter I. Pages 20 and 21; Chapter II, Page 88.

before she gave herself to him. With baptism she received the name Maria and presented him with four sons: Juan of Aragon, first Count of Ribagorza, Alfonso of Aragon, who became Bishop of Tortosa and later, at the time of the Catholic Kings, Archbishop of Tarragona, and Feroando of Aragon, Prior of San Juan and Catalonia."[402]

The renowned historian enumerates further concerning converted Jewish families who married into the oldest nobility families. This trial continued for so long until the Holy Inquisition dissolved the old Courts of the faith. The learned writer also mentions the fact that many of these families originating from Jews boasted of going back to David and being directly related to the Holy Mary.[403] One thus sees that they have made use of this trick for five hundred years.

He asserts that the family of La Caballeria was related to Boniface: "Simuel received, as well as Bonafoz, the name Pedro; Achab was called M. Filipe, Simuel-Aban-Jehuda-Juan, Isaac-Femando, Abraham, Francisco; and Salomon, Pedro Pablo. The Jewish name of Luis is not known, since he was baptised very young. It suffices for us to know that Pedro (Simuel) obtained great regard in his spiritual career and became Prior of Egea. Felipe became representative of the Knights and hereditary landed noblemen in the Cortes of the kingdom (a kind of parliament). . . The sons of Fernando (Isaac) had, together with the other converts, a share in the taxing of public income, under the protection of his uncle Luis. Of the latter's three sons, Luis, the firstborn, was chamberlain of the cathedral Church and Juan occupied a position in the same Church."[404]

Different members of the Santa Maria and La Caballeria families were later accused of being inclined to Judaism and prosecuted by the Inquisition. The entire family of Vidal de La Caballeria was burned in Barcelona by the Inquisition, and even Tomas Garcia, the highly regarded jurist and historian, was put on trial. Whoever wishes to investigate further this interesting subject can take for additional reference the work quoted, the so-called "Green Book of Aragon" by Juan de Anchias, which provides interesting details concerning the Jewish infiltration into the clergy, the government and the nobility.

---

[402] J. Amador de los Rios, same work, same edition. Vol. III. Chapter II. Pages 95 and 96.

[403] J. Amador de los Rios, same work, same edition. Vol. UI. Chapter U. Annotation 1. Page 97 and Remark 3, Pages 97 and 98.

[404] J. Amador de los Rios, same work, same edition, Vol. III. Chapter II. Pages 100 and 101.

This valuable document was later published and is found in the National Library in Madrid. In this respect the book which was written by Cardinal Mendoza y Bobilla in the 16th century "Tizon de la Nobleza Espanola" ("Blemish of the Spanish Nobility") is also interesting, which is also preserved in this library.

In conclusion to this chapter we will quote in addition other respected sources and begin with another publication of the Israel Publishing Co. in Buenos Aires. In the work "Israel – A History of the Jewish People" by Rufus Learsi, which was prepared by the author with the "magnanimous support of the Jewish History Foundation Inc," it is expressly stated that: "The universal anger was in fact directed against the new Christians and constantly increased. It was not only assumed that they secretly remained true to their faith, from which they had sworn to have freed themselves, although for the clergy this heresy was the greatest crime. The new Christians called forth through their successes even greater indignation. A too great number had now, since religion no longer prevented them from this, become rich and powerful. They took up high positions in the government, in the army, the universities and even in the Church... All, even the priests and monks, were regarded as heretics and the spite of the people was directed against them, until acts of violence broke out. In the years 1440 and 1467 the rabble rioted in Toledo and many new Christians were murdered and their houses set on fire. Six years later the bloody rebellions against them in Cordoba, Jaen and Segovia were repeated."[405]

It was only natural, that the clergy regarded the descendants of Jews, who belonged to the Church orders, as heretics, and when a half-century later the Spanish Inquisition was founded, this was fully and completely confirmed. On the other hand, the author holds the clergy responsible for the wave of anti-semitism against the Christians of Jewish origin. In order to understand this situation, one must, however, know the motives in all details which led to such proceedings against the marranos.

The Jewish historian Joseph Kastein investigates this motive in his interesting work "History of the Jews" and speaks of the false conversions of the Jews to Christianity: "At first both the people as well as high society regarded the converts as a homogeneous group. Particularly the nobility and the clergy saw in them the result of a victory and at first they were enthusiastically accepted. Countless converts passed through the open doors and obtained admittance into Spanish society and the clergy." In the

---

[405] Rufus Learsi: History of the Jewish People, Spanish Translation, Israel Publishers, Buenos Aires, written with aid of Jewish History Foundation Inc. Chapter XXXVII-6.

following the Jewish historian emphasises that the converted Jews "soon appeared in the highest positions of the clergy." "The converts were accepted with equal rights into Spanish society. However, as a result they did not sacrifice their capabilities. Previously they had been especially merchants, industrialists, financiers and politicians. So now also, only with this sole difference that they belonged to Spanish society. One had compelled them to enter in order to eliminate dangerous foreigners. But now they found themselves inside the house. The problem had only been displaced from the outside into the interior of the social structure."[406]

It is not easy to find such a deep-reaching, painfully exact study concerning the nature of Jewish infiltration into Christian society and the clergy through outward conversion. The Jewish historian ends the chapter with the most contemptuous opinion concerning the utility of baptism for the Jews, by his placing into the mouth of a Jewish defendant the following assertion: "There are three ways of wasting water. 1. To baptise a Jew. 2. To allow it to flow into the sea, and 3. To mix it with wine."

On the following page he continues his study about the new Christians and writes that the converts "supported themselves with their social elevation, in the same way as those who have compelled them to accept the new religion, upon the higher circles of the court, of the nobility and the clergy. They had less the intention to become stronger in the economic respect, but also to attain political and social influence... They had become members of the Church, but not adherents of the faith. The indissoluble connection of a thousand years long religious development compelled them to secretly preserve the indestructible Judaism in their heart and to carry it with them in its deepest form. They went cautiously to work, in order not to be discovered by the adherents of their new religion. They timidly followed all rites and laws, festivals and customs of their own faith and fought in secret for this right, led a double life and each individual bore a double burden." When the Church noticed what was taking place – adds the Jewish historian we quote – "there arose a new battle-cry, that the Church was in danger. The Jews have forcefully obtained admittance into Church and society in order to undermine it from within. The unavoidable, if also absurd consequence of this was, that war was declared on the inner enemy. For this purpose for support, reported the intrigues at the Court, and did everything possible in order to influence high society. The converts, whom the national policy had concerned itself with, became

---

[406] Josef Kastein: History of the Jews, same edition, Pages 290-291.

'swindlers', a vulgar word, which comprises the epithets 'accursed' and 'pig'."[407]

It would certainly not have easily occurred to us to describe so exactly – as the Jewish historian – the essence of the "Jewish Fifth Column" in the bosom of Holy Church and Christian society. Also we could certainly not have explained so well the motives which gave occasion to the creation of the Holy Inquisition Court, which was regarded by the people and its leaders as "aids of Heaven against this evil." Its necessity and value was, however, later denigrated through a campaign of slander lasting over centuries.

In the Jewish-Spanish Encyclopaedia it is stated: "Daniel Israel Bonafou, Miguel Cardoso, Jose Querido, Mardoqueo Mojiaj and others praised the "Swindlers" affair as a method to undermine the foundation of the enemy as a means to shape the struggle against it more elastically." In another passage it is stated of the swindlers: "Queen Esther, who revealed neither her race nor her origin, was held by them to be a prototype."[408]

The description New Christians, which the false Jewish Christians, especially those of Spanish and Portuguese origin, still use today, is also customary among the Musulmans. The Jewish Encyclopaedia which we mentioned cites examples under the word "criptojudios" (= Christians who secretly admit to Judaism): "This phenomenon (criptojudaismo) is still not very old. It appeared in 1838, when the Shah of Persia compelled the Jewish community of Meshed to admit to Islam. Several hundred Jews then formed a community, which was known under the name Dja-did-ul-Islam. The new Musulmans seemingly followed the Mohammedan rites and undertook the usual pilgrimages to Mecca. In secret, however, they practised the religious customs of their forefathers. The members of the community of Dja-did-ul-lslam held religious gatherings in underground synagogues, circumcised their sons, observed the Sabbath, respected the laws of diet and survived the danger to which they exposed themselves. However, later many of them left Meshed and founded two settlements of the sect in Herat, Afghanistan, Merv and Samarkand, Turkestan, Bombay, Jerusalem and even in Europe (London). Through emigration their number in Meshed grew to 3000 and in Jerusalem there were 500 believers. The traveller and orientalist Walter Fischel described the customs and traditions of Dja-did-ul-Islam in his work "A Swindler"

---

[407] Josef Kastein, same work, Pages 291 and 292.
[408] Jewish-Spanish Encyclopaedia, same edition, Vol. VII, Word: "Espana."

(gauner = swindler, rogue, gypsy) in Persia (in Hebrew, 1930).[409] May the English take heed, for many Musulmans who live in London, as well as in the entire Islamic world, are concealed Jews.

---

[409] Jewish-Spanish Encyclopaedia, same edition. Vol. III. Word: "Cripto- Judaismo".

CHAPTER TWENTY-FIVE

A JEWISH CARDINAL BECOMES POPE

The highest aim of the "Jewish Fifth Column" in the clergy has always been to gain control of the Papacy and to place a secret Jew on the chair of St. Peter. For this would make it possible for it to use the Church for the revolutionary Imperialist plans of the Synagogue and to cause harm to our religion. In the year 1130, 832 years ago, Jewry nearly attained its goal. For the investigation of this horrifying chapter in history we have also made use of recognised Jewish and other sources, which are free of Anti-semitism.

The world-renowned historian Fernando Gregorovius — as is known in scholarly circles — and who was in addition extremely favourably disposed towards the Jews, reported about these historical events in his work "History of the City of Rome in the Middle Ages." The first translation into Italian was financed by the city government of Rome, which in addition provided the author with the title of "Honorary citizen of the city of Rome". The following quotations are taken from his work: "Book II. Vol. 2, Chapter III. The Pierleoni. Their Jewish origin. The Synagogue. Peter Leo and his son Peter, the Cardinal. Schism between Innocent II and Anacletus II. Innocent in France. Letter of the Romans to Lothar. Roger I, King of Sicily.

A purely civic schism would necessarily have proved to the world that the German kings were not always responsible for the division of the Church. The wealth and the power of the Pierleoni and still more their great services in relation to the Church awoke in them the hope of making a member of their family into Pope. The astonishing fact that they were descended from Jews and had reached such high regard, gives us opportunity to cast a glance at the Synagogue in Rome."

Gregorovius describes the development of the Jewish community in Rome and then mentions that Benjamin de Tudela, the famous Jew, travelled over half the world to visit all Jewish organisations of his time.

Of the Jews in Rome he says that, at the time of Pope Alexander III, they had great influence in the Papal residence, and he enumerates very intelligent Rabbis, such as Daniel, Geiele, Joab, Nathan, Menahem and others of Trastevere. According to Gregorovius the Jews have only once been persecuted and enslaved in the eternal city. "Their race understood how, on the basis of their slyness, their inventive talent and the power of gold accumulated in secret, to assert themselves against their oppressors. The first physicians and richest bankers were Jews. In their wretched houses they loaned money at usurious interest, and in their book of debts stood the names of the most respected Consuls of Rome and even of the Popes, who were short of money. And from this despised Jewish Synagogue emanated a family of senators who had to thank the usurer for their wealth and their power."

The grandfather of the mentioned Peter Leo, who played an important role in the investiture dispute, also had relations in his capacity as banker with the Papal residence and often helped out with money. He finally allowed himself to be baptised and received the name Benedictus Christianus.

Very soon his son Leo, who with baptism had received the name of Pope Leo IX, could ensure himself an important future, as was fitting for a rich, sharp-minded, bold and ambitious young man. He intermarried with Roman magnates who wished to marry their sons to rich Jewesses, or their daughters to the sons of baptised Jews.[410] Gregorovius assures us that one of his sons, by name Peter Leo, who was the first to bear the surname Pierleoni, "had much influence in Rome and was always asked for advice."

Besides his fortress alongside the Marcellus Theatre, which no doubt his father had built, he also controlled the Tiber Islands situated nearby. Urban II also made him into protector of Castel Sant'Angelo and died — to use the words of Gregorovius — in the house of his creditor and protector. His successors — so it continues — therefore made efforts to obtain the favour of the powerful Pierleoni. However, the people detested him because he was a usurer. The nobility hated him, and we can observe that he, in spite of his friendship with Pope Paschalis, did not ask the Prefecture for his son, because he was of "the new nobility."

The friendship of the Popes, the glitter of kinship, wealth and power very soon wiped away the stain of his Jewish origin, and a short time later

---

[410] Ferdinand Gregorovius: History of the City of Rome in the Middle Ages, Italian translation: Renato Manzato. Turin. Vol. II. Book II. Chapter III. Pages 72 and 73.

the Pierleoni became the most respected princely family in Rome. Leo and his successor bore the title "Consul of Rome" — according to Gregorovius — "proudly and with masterly dignity, as if they were very ancient Patricians." The famous historian adds further that the Pierleoni were Welfs, i.e. were of the Papal party against the German Emperors, for we must not forget that at that time, at least in appearance, they were devout Christians.

The following report by Gregorovius is also very revealing. From this we learn that Pierleoni was buried on 2nd June of the year 1128 with so many marks of honour as never before for a Consul in ancient Rome. Even if the tombs of the Popes of that time were destroyed, then the "Mausoleum of this fat Jew", as Gregorovius calls him in this connection, although he was officially very Catholic, continues to stand. He reports that he "left behind many descendants. These sons of the Ghetto were so unbelievably rich, that one of his sons became Pope and another Patrician of Rome. One of his daughters married Roger of Sicily. This powerful lord had selected a Church post for his son Peter. Would one have been able to refuse him the violet cloak of a Cardinal? Was even the striving for the robes of the Pope to be dared for a son of the Pierleoni? Young Peter was sent to Paris, in order to complete his education. There he belonged without doubt to the students of Abelard. After ending of his study he became a monk of Cluny. This was doubtless the best recommendation for a candidate for the Papal dignity. . . Upon the wishes of his father, Paschalis summoned him back to Rome and named him Cardinal of San Cosmo and San Damian. . . Together with his brother he then accompanied Gelasio to France, returned with Calixtus and became Cardinal of Santa Maria in Trastevere, whence his family originated. Later he became Papal ambassador in France, where he convened Councils, and in England, where he was received by King Henry like a prince."[411]

Holy Church had accumulated experience in the centuries long struggle against the "Synagogue of Satan", and now correspondingly built up its defence. It passed anti-Jewish Church laws which, if followed, would have provided a defence. Unfortunately there were — as we have already seen — monarchs like Witiza, Ludwig the Pious and Peter the Cruel, who submitted to the influence of the Jews and caused the anti-Jewish Church Laws to become ineffective. Thus they protected the principal enemy of Christianity and allowed him to become deeply rooted in the government

---

[411] Ferdinand Gregorovius: History of the City of Rome in the Middle Ages. Ital. Translation: Renato Manzazto, Turin, Vol. II. Book II. Chapter III. Pages 74 and 75.

of the state, which had tragic consequences for the Church as also for the peoples who fell into the hands of the Jews.

These tragedies were, however, locally restricted, for while Witiza or Ludwig the Pious delivered their people to the enemy, the Papacy and other Christian states conducted further the struggle for defence of the Church and Catholicism in a zealous manner. This new situation in the 11th century for the Holy See itself was doubtless the prelude for a universal tragedy, not locally restricted, which was to extend to the whole of Christianity; for the enemy was on the point of conquering the chair of the Church, and this crisis had necessarily to draw the entire Christian world into its effect.

The bitter investiture dispute between Pope and Emperor and the problem of predominance were to offer Jewry the favourable opportunity of advancing to the Holy See, by their offering their valuable services and doubtless revealing themselves as pleasing. In this struggle between Popes and Emperors the Jews began to take decisive side with the party of the Welfs, i.e. for the Pope, who under the existing conditions could not reject this unexpected, seemingly valuable support — also in the economic respect, which was then urgently necessary for the Holy See.

In this trouble, the Church Laws, the results of centuries of experience, were at first forgotten. Through their gainful- seeking adherence to the Popes the Jews had penetrated into a domain which had hitherto been refused to them. The fratricidal struggles among the Christians themselves helped the "Synagogue of Satan" best of all to further their imperialist plans.

This they now attained by their supporting the Church power against the civic. In the 16th century, thus 450 years later, they wished to finally destroy Christianity, by their defending the Kings against the Papacy.

In this case they made themselves indispensable as bankers, and the Pope had to hold to them in order to solve his economic problems. The famous Rabbi, poet and historian, Louis Israel Newman writes in his extremely interesting work "Jewish Influence on the Reform Movements of Christianity" concerning the schism called forth by Cardinal Peter Pierleoni in Holy Church. He attributes to the latter a decisive importance for the development of the so-called Jewish heresy in the Middle Ages, in which Popes, Councils and Inquisition with justice see the origin of all heresies. For the Inquisition proved that the secret Jews, i.e. the Jewish heretics, were the organisers and spreaders of the remaining heretical movements.

The Rabbi quoted states that "the chief factor for the outbreak of Jewish heresy in the 12th century was the election of Anacletus II, one of the members of the Jewish Pierleoni family, as Pope in the year 1130."[412] This confession is extraordinarily important, because it comes from a well-known leader of Jewry and in addition corresponds exactly to reality.

For such a bold stroke must necessarily not only bring about the fall of Christianity, but also certainly very much encourage the Jews, who now believed that everything was attainable for them. The Rabbi mentioned confirms this view in another passage in his interesting work: "Additional proofs of how the rise of Anacletus had effect on the Jews, one can find in the numerous literature about the mystical, Jewish Pope, who in Hebrew legend is called Andreas or Eichanan. It is to be granted that the rise to power of the member of an ancient Jewish family has stirred the Jewish communities in Italy to activity and has led to a powerful confirmation of their own traditions and opinions."[413]

Here the Rabbi mentioned already goes too far and uses one of the chief arguments which the Jews usually advance at their secret meetings in order to prove that their religion and not the Christian is the true one. They assert that the fact that they successfully rose in the hierarchy of the Church up to bishops and cardinals and even reached the throne of St. Peter through all kinds of infamy — even if the Popes in question are really anti-Popes — confirms their opinions and traditions or proves that they can assume that their religion is supported by God.

We will answer this sophistry with an eloquent argument: every human institution which cannot reckon with God's support would already many centuries ago have been controlled through the devilish "Jewish Fifth Column" in the clergy. The latter believed, eight hundred and thirty two years ago, that they had finally conquered the Holy See and had Holy Church in its power. However, this devilish attempt failed then, just as is the case today, eight hundred years later, and that conquest is simply to be regarded as Utopian striving. If Holy Church could not count upon the support of God, it would already have been subjugated by the hellish

---

[412] Rabbi Louis Israel Newman: "Jewish Influence on Christian Reform Movements", contained in Vol. 23 of Columbia University. Oriental Series II. Vol. IV-1. Page 248.
[413] Rabbi Louis Israel Newman, same work, same edition. Book II – 3. Pages 252 and 253.

mechanism of Jewry, which many with Justice hold to be the powerful tool of the Anti-Christ.

Our Lord Christ called Jewry the "Synagogue of Satan", and described the Jews as sons of the Devil. Not only on account of their wickedness, but apparently also on account of the extraordinary power which the Devil lends them. Not in vain are the clergy who support the Jews to the harm of the faith described by the already mentioned Holy Council of Toledo as followers of the anti-Christ, and the Jews were called "Ministers of the anti-Christ" by famous Fathers and Saints of the Church.

This many times supernatural seeming capacity to do evil goes back to the dragon, exactly as John has prophesied in his "Apocalypse". "The Beast and the dragon will be overcome after passing temporary dominance." So was it resolved by God and Saint John prophesies this in the 13th Chapter of the Apocalypse:

"1. And I saw a beast coming up out of the sea, having seven heads and ten horns, and upon his horns ten diadems, and upon his heads names of blasphemy. 2. ... And the dragon gave him his own strength, and great power. 3. ... And all the earth was in admiration after the beast. 4. And they adored the dragon, which gave power to the beast: and they adored the beast, saying: Who is like to the beast? and who shall be able to fight with him? 5. And there was given to him a mouth speaking great things, and blasphemies... 7. And it was given unto him to make war with the saints, and to overcome them. And power was given him over every tribe, and people, and tongue, and nation."[414]

The power, which the dragon lent to the beast, agrees in astonishing manner with the capacity of the "Synagogue of Satan." In addition the latter's power over the Good — as it is written — is transitory. It was also predicted that the Beast, especially in the Communist lands, would utter blasphemies. The interpretation of various Fathers of the Church, theologians and highly-regarded Catholics at different times who equated post-Biblical Jewry with the Beast of the "Apocalypse" seems thus fitting. Reality concords in such astonishing extent with the prophesy, that no doubt seems any more possible.

However, God has also prophesied that the Beast and the dragon, after their temporary victory, will be finally conquered and cast into the fire. This is stated in the 20th Chapter of the Apocalypse:

---

[414] Bible, New Testament of St. John. Chapter XIII. Verses 1-5, 7.

"9. And there came down fire from God out of heaven, and devoured them; and the devil, who seduced them, was cast into the pool of fire and brimstone, where both the beast 10. And the false prophet shall be tormented day and night for ever and ever."

In the Prophecy yet a second Beast is mentioned, whose characteristics concord in astonishing manner with the "Jewish Fifth Column" in the clergy. It looks outwardly like a lamb, however acts like a dragon. It is its task to support the first Beast, as it is the task of the "Fifth Column" to make easier the triumph of the "Synagogue of Satan". In the 13th Chapter it is stated:

"11. And I saw another beast coming up out of the earth, and he had two horns, like a lamb, and he spoke as a dragon. 12. And he executed all the power of the former beast in his sight; and he caused the earth, and them that dwell therein, to adore the first beast, whose wound to death was healed. 14. And he seduced them that dwell on the earth, for the signs, which were given him to do in the sight of the beast, saying to them that dwell on the earth, that they should make the image of the beast, which had the wound by the sword, and lived."[415]

It is really astonishing that Jewry, which was fatally wounded through the Inquisition and the activity of the good, has survived and recovered from its wounds. On the other hand, it is the task of the Beast with the exterior of a lamb to attain that men admire the first Beast. This agrees again astonishingly well with the work of the clergy of the "Fifth Column" which is directed so that believers almost worship the Jews. They pretend to be descended from our Lord Jesus. The latter, however, called them Sons of the Devil, and they are the principal enemy of Holy Church.

One must take into consideration that they who follow the Beast are those "whose names are not written in the book of life" (Apocalypse 17:8) and "whosoever was not found written in the book of life was cast into the pool of fire" (Apocalypse 20.15).

After this parenthesis, which was necessary, in order to prevent that the tragedy analysed here led the timid astray, we continue in synthetic form in the relation of the developing tense drama.

---

[415] Bible. New Testament. Apocalypse of St. John. Chapter XIII, Verses 11, 12 and 14. Chapter XX, Verses 9 and 10.

One saw completely clearly that Cardinal Pierleoni and his supporters made all preparations in order to obtain the Papal dignity, if the ruling Pope died. The cardinals and better orientated clergy of the Holy Church were directly in an uproar, for they were convinced that Pierleoni secretly adhered to Judaism and that, if he ascended the throne of St. Peter, Holy Church, its centuries old enemy, would be delivered to the Synagogue. The accusations against the cardinals mentioned were among others the following: 1. Under the mask of an apparently zealous, honest Christianity he paid homage in secret to Judaism. He concealed this fact behind pious eloquent sermons — for Pierleoni was one of the best preachers of his time. In addition he cloaked his Jewish belief with good works and his impressive work as director and organiser of Church affairs, as Ambassador of the Pope in France, where he summoned Councils, and also as Cardinal. 2. Besides his private property, he collected other riches, which he had robbed from the Church, in cooperation with other Jews. This money was later used for the purpose of bribing the Cardinals and, through intrigues and influence, of making his adherents bishops and cardinals. He had even bought dearly the votes of several Cardinals for the next Papal election.

In the face of this deadly danger, there formed under the leadership of the chancellor Aimerico and Giovani de Cremas a strong anti-Jewish opposition against Pierleoni, in the Holy Collegium of Cardinals. Cardinal Pierleoni was however clearly superior in this bitter struggle, since he was supported by the nobility, which was strongly permeated with Jews and also by the people whom the Jewish Cardinal had brought onto his side with gold and force. In addition he had been cautious enough to control the army.

Since Pierleoni knew that his opponents among the Cardinals accused him of practising the Jewish religion, he sought to quash these accusations through his pious, blamelessly orthodox sermons, his outstanding activity in the most different domains and even — so it is stated — through the new construction of Churches, to punish lies. As a result he deceived clergy and laity and convinced them that the accusations against him were slanders, and Cardinal Pierleoni was in reality an honest Catholic, who was unjustly attacked by envious opponents of the Jews — who wished to see Jews where none were.[416]

---

[416] Vogelstein and Rieger, "History of the Jews in Rome", 1896, Jewish Encyclopaedia and Jewish-Spanish Encyclopaedia, words Anacletus and Pierleoni. Vacandard "Vie de Saint Bernard." Codex Udalrici. No. 240-261. Gregorovius and Newman, same work.

Pope Honorius II was already suffering when he was exposed to the strong counter-pressure of the two groups. When the anti-Jewish Cardinals recognised that the Jew-friendly block of Pierleoni's gained more and more in strength and had the voices of most Cardinals in their pocket, they applied cunning. Upon the urging of the energetic, resolute French Cardinal Aimerico, the Chancellor of the Roman Church, the fatally sick Pope was suddenly conveyed to a monastery, San Gregorio, situated on a mountain. In the midst of the disputes between the two parties, they agreed with Honorius that the new Pope should be chosen by eight Cardinals, who were apparently appointed by the ruling Pope. Pierleoni was also among them. These Cardinals betook themselves to the deathbed of the Pope and awaited the end, in order to be able to choose the new Pope.

Honorius died — as if ordained by divine providence — just at the time when Pierleoni and Jonathan were not present. The six other Cardinals rapidly buried the dead Pope and then in San Gregorio secretly elected the virtuous anti-Jewish Cardinal of Sant'Angelo, Gregorio Papareschi, as Pope, who took on the name Innocent II.

When Pierleoni, who already almost saw himself as Pope, learned that Papareschi, one of his rivals, was already chosen as Pope, he did not, however, regard himself as defeated, but — according to Gregorovius — "went, supported by his brothers Leo, Giordano, Roger, Uguccione and numerous clients, to St. Peter's and forced an entry. He had himself dedicated as Pope by Pietro di Porto, stormed the Lateran, placed himself on the Papal throne in this Church, went to Santa Maria Mayor and confiscated the Church treasure. In the whole of Rome civil war raged, and thousands greedily stretched their hands out for the gold which Anacletus scattered."[417]

Without doubt, Pierleoni, as far as Simony was concerned, was a worthy pupil of his predecessor, the likewise Jewish Simon Magus, and exceeded him where possible on grounds of the centuries long experience which the Jews had gathered. With the most diverse means, he attained that more than two thirds of the Cardinals chose him as Pope, and took on the name Anacletus II. This obese Jew rapidly made himself master of the situation and all the world applauded him, while Innocent II, with his loyal Cardinals, had to flee and withdrew into the Palladium, where the Frangipani protected him. The troops of Pierleoni attempted in vain to

---

[417] Gregorovius: History of the city of Rome in the Middle Ages. Italian translation, Book II. Vol. II. Pages 76 and 77.

storm the Palladium. But since Innocent — as Gregorovius remarks — "foresaw how the gold of the enemy would penetrate through the walls, he fled in April or May to the Trastevere, where he kept himself concealed in the tower of his family. Anacletus in the meantime calmly celebrated the Easter Festival, excommunicated his opponent and replaced the Cardinals, who were opposed to him, through others. Through the fall of the Frangipani, Innocent was without protection, and he was left no other choice than to flee."[418]

Seen with human eyes, everything was lost for Holy Church. The triumph of the "Jewish Fifth Column" in the clergy seemed final, and its centuries long dream of the conquest of the Papacy had finally become a reality. Christianity on the other hand had apparently lost the struggle against the Synagogue.

---

[418] Gregorovius, same work. Same edition, Book II. Vol. II. Pages 76 and 77.

CHAPTER TWENTY-SIX

SAINT BERNARD AND SAINT NORBERT FREE THE CHURCH FROM THE CLUTCHES OF JEWRY

In this case divine providence — as promised — came to the aid of the Church and allowed capable men to come forward, who were resolved to sacrifice everything for the salvation of Catholicism. These leaders recognised at the given moment — through the aid of God — the whole extent of the disaster which had occurred and of the approaching catastrophe and flung themselves fully and completely, with selflessness, highest mysticism and great infectious energy into the struggle against the Synagogue and its supporters. Thus Saint Irenaeus appeared when Jewish Gnosticism threatened to split Christianity. In the same way Saint Athanasius, the great anti-Jewish leader appeared when the heresy of the Jew Arius had almost uprooted the Church, and thus appeared later under similar circumstances Saint John Chrysostom, Saint Ambrose of Milan, Saint Cyril of Alexandria, Saint Isidore of Seville, St. Felix and the archbishop Agobardo, Amolon and many others, who all — illuminated by divine grace — mercilessly combated the Jews, the centuries old enemies of Holy Church and also their "Fifth Column," their heresies and revolutionary movement.

Who would now come to the aid of the Church, since it passed through perhaps the most difficult crisis since its origin? Who would be the anti-Jewish leaders, whom Christ had chosen in this case for salvation of Holy Church?

As usual, God's help was revealed through the appearance of two great fighters: Saint Bernard, Church scholar and Abbot of Clairveaux, and Saint Norbert, founder of the Order which bears his name, and archbishop of Magdeburg, who was related to the German Imperial family.

When Saint Bernard received news of the disastrous events in Rome, he made the rare decision to give up his peaceful quiet life in a monastery,

447

in order to throw himself into a hard, uncomfortable, sorrowful and dangerous struggle, which in addition was already regarded as lost, since the Jewish Pope, thanks to his gold and the support which he continued to receive, was complete master of the situation. Innocent II on the other hand, forsaken and in flight, was excommunicated by Anacletus, and everything seemed lost for him. According to the opinion of important theologians and historians, he could in addition scarcely make his claims valid, since his election did not correspond to Church Law. Saint Bernard took on this already almost lost cause, because he was convinced that it was a good cause and Holy Church ought not in this manner and way to fall into the hands of its worst enemy, Jewry.

He proceeded from the correct standpoint and concerned himself neither with the majority of the 23 Cardinals who had voted for Anacletus, and the six who chose Innocent, nor with how the election had proceeded. In a letter to the German Emperor Lothar he writes among other things: "It is a disgrace for Christ that a Jew sits on the throne of St. Peter's." With this the Church scholar had struck the sore point and alluded to the seriousness of the situation. For it was simply impossible that a Jew, an enemy of Holy Church, was Pope. In the letter to the Emperor it is stated among other things: "Anacletus has not even a good reputation with his friends, while Innocent is illustrious beyond all doubt."

The Abbot Ernold, a contemporary biographer of Saint Bernard, reports that Pierleoni, as ambassador and cardinal, had collected enormous riches, "and had later robbed the Churches." And when even the bad Christians who followed him refused to destroy the golden chalices and crucifixes in order to melt them down, Anacletus had Jews put this plan into action. The latter destroyed the sacred cups and engravings with enthusiasm. These objects were sold, and thanks to this money Anacletus was — as was reported — in the position of persecuting the supporters of Innocent II. Bishop Hubert of Lucca, Andreas Dandolo, the Doge of Venice, the abbot Anselmo of Grembloux and other chroniclers and historians accuse the Jewish anti-Pope on account of this and other grave crimes.[419] In this struggle principally the German Emperor, but also the King of France were of greatest importance, for Germany and France were then the most powerful Catholic states. Saint Bernard, supported by his great friend Saint Norbert, used all his power in persuading the two irresolute monarchs to support Innocent. For this purpose he wrote them

---

[419] Bishop Huberto de Lucca. Chronicle in Codex Udalrici No. 246. Page 425. Rabbi Louis Israel Newman, Jewish Influence on Christian Reform Movements, same edition, Book II. Page 251. Vancardad: "La Vie de Saint Bernard." Article against Anacletus.

letters and undertook all possible steps. Louis VI of France could not make up his mind and had a Council called, which, corresponding to his wish, took place in Etampes.[420] Through his eloquence and his zeal Saint Bernard there attained that the Fathers of the Synod declared for Innocent. He cited the already mentioned grounds and in addition proved that Innocent was the first to be chosen and that this first election would be valid until it was legally annulled, even if later the overwhelming majority of Cardinals had voted for Anacletus. In addition he proved that Innocent had been consecrated as Pope by the competent Cardinal bishop of Ostia. The courage and energy of the heroic Cardinal Aimerico, who had rapidly and secretly buried the dead Pope and thus in somewhat unusual manner hastened the election of Innocent, were now very much of advantage. Holy Church, Christianity and the whole of mankind must be grateful to this courageous, active Cardinal, and maintain his memory, for with his action he began the struggle for the salvation of Holy Church and thus contributed to the salvation of the whole world. If the Jews had been successful in controlling Christianity eight centuries ago, then the catastrophe would have occurred several centuries earlier, which now threatens the globe in terrible forms. Islam was then also threatened through the network of secret revolutionary organisations of Jews — such as those of the "Batinis" and of the "Murderers" — which wished to control and destroy it.

Innocent II had fled from Italy to France and had now, since the Council of Etampes supported his — (so he believed) — already lost cause, hoped once more. Upon the recognition and support of the Council followed the very valuable, temporal support of the King of France, who from now on became the principal mainstay of the legal Pope against his rival, the anti-Pope, as the Synod then described the latter. The French monarch followed the guiding principles of Saint Bernard, and there were no further discussions concerning which of the two elected Popes was the legally justified, but which was the more worthy — as the famous Abbot of Saint Denis, Sugerius, expressed it. In the face of the overwhelming activity of Saint Bernard the skilled diplomacy of Anacletus failed, who praised devout Catholicism and attempted with all attainable means to secure himself the support of the King of France. He pretended excessive piety and based his plans for reform on that he wished to give back to the Church the purity of its first period, which was always a very popular slogan, because it went back to praiseworthy and noble motives. He had

---

[420] It was not possible for us to discover the records and laws of the Council of Etampes. We could only discover incomplete reports and fear that, for reasons easily understandable, they have been lost.

for this reason also taken on the name of the first successor of St. Peter, i.e. of Pope Anacletus I. We are here thus dealing, from all appearances, with one of the first manifestations of that "apocalyptic beast" which outwardly looks like a lamb — i.e. like our Lord Jesus Christ — but nevertheless acts like a dragon. Not in vain was Anacletus held in that time by Saints, Bishops, Clergy and Laity to be the Anti-Christ or, in less crass cases, as forerunner of the Anti-Christ.

The conduct of Lothar, the German Emperor, was to be decisive in this struggle. He remarked quite correctly that this affair concerned the Church itself, and therefore a second Council was called in Würzburg. Here Saint Norbert intervened decisively so that the German Bishops granted Innocent their full support. The almost decisive battle was, however, to be fought at the Holy Council of Rheims, towards the end of the year 1131. This Synod signified a defeat for Pedro Pierleoni, for there the Bishops of England, Castile and Aragon recognised Innocent as the legal Pope and in this respect joined themselves to the French and German bishops, who had already previously recognised him. At this Synod Pierleoni was excommunicated in addition. Concerning this we must recognise that the religious Orders also played a decisive role in this struggle. They then recognised the danger which Jewry represented for the Church, and held Anacletus for the greatest evil which had so far threatened Christianity. Passionately and dynamically, they directed the activity of the monasteries at saving Holy Church from this deadly threat.

Unfortunately at the present day, when Holy Church is threatened to such a high degree by Communism and by the "Jewish Fifth Column" in the clergy, no sign is present for the enormous strength of the religious Orders. These could perhaps save the situation, if they equipped themselves for the struggle. They spend the day with devout services, which are very praiseworthy, but which under the present circumstances prevent them from dedicating themselves to the main task of saving the Church. In our opinion the Orders, when they awake from their lethargy, must take note that today — exactly as in the time of Pierleoni — it is impossible to perform all devout services since these take up their whole time. It would be necessary to abandon a part of these for the moment, in order to have sufficient time for the struggle for the salvation of Christianity. As a result a decisive step would already be taken.

May God, our Lord, illumine the highest Fathers of the Orders and lead before their eyes the necessity of a supreme decisive resolution in this matter! The prayers and the activity of the rules of the Order are very important; however, it is even more important to preserve Holy Church from the Jewish- Communist danger, which threatens to destroy her. Saint Bernard and a great number of monks had to leave their quiet monasteries and disregard the strict rules of their Order (naturally with corresponding permission), in order to go upon the street and save Christianity. And they had success! After the Council of Rheims Pierleoni could still only count on the support of Italy (for the greater part) and especially on that of his brother-in-law, the Duke Roger II or Sicily, who ruled practically the entire peninsula. The marriage of the converted Jewess Pierleoni, the sister of the anti-Pope, nevertheless possessed a value in itself. This marriage, concluded for strategic reasons, now revealed itself as useful. However, in order to finally conquer the Jew on the throne of St. Peter's a military invasion, a kind of crusade, was necessary. Saint Bernard and Saint Norbert persuaded Lothar, the Emperor of Germany, to undertake this. Accompanied by a modest-sized army, the Emperor met together with Innocent in North Italy and advanced unhindered as far as Rome, for many Roman noblemen betrayed Anacletus at the last minute. Lothar brought Innocent to the Throne in the Lateran, while Pierleoni fled to Sant'Angelo and had St. Peter under control. Therefore the Emperor was crowned in the Lateran by Innocent. But since Roger of Sicily then advanced at the head of a powerful army, Lothar had to order a retreat. For this reason the Pope could also not stay in Rome and had to flee. The Jewish anti-Pope was again master of the situation there. Innocent had withdrawn to Pisa and in this city summoned a great Council, in which Bishops of the whole of Christianity and a great number of abbots participated, who played an important role in this struggle. Among them was found St. Bernard, who, as always, conducted the struggle.

A year later Lothar advanced again to Italy, in order to set the legal Pope in Rome and to drive out the Jewish usurper. The conduct of the German Emperor is really worthy of note, for at those moments, critical for the Church, he left to one side his personal interests and the resentments of the Empire on account of the hard investiture dispute, and placed himself fully and completely for the salvation of Christianity.

If only there existed in the present world crisis some men, who imitated this noble conduct, placing behind them personal interests and national requirements and forgot often unfounded spite, in favour of the uniting of all peoples in the common struggle for liberation against Jewish Imperialism and its Freemasonic and Communist dictatorships!

With justice wrote Innocent II to Emperor Lothar during the terrible struggle: "The Church has chosen you — thanks to Divine intercession —

as lawgiver like a second Justinian and has chosen you to combat the heretical infamy of the Jews like a second Constantine."

In this campaign Lothar was in fact successful in defeating Roger and caused him to retreat to Sicily, but he could not take Rome, where to the disgrace of all Christianity the Jewish anti-Pope remained in office. When Lothar left Italy with his armies, Roger of Sicily won it back almost completely, and Pierleoni seemed again to gain dangerously in power. The concern of all Christianity increased more and more, for the power of the anti-Pope again became threatening. Arnulf, the bishop of Liseaux, Manfred, the Bishop of Mantua and other respected Prelates described the latter simply as a Jew. Archbishop Walter of Ravenna called Anacletus's schism "Heresy of Jewish faithlessness", and the rabbi Louis Israel Newman gives the assurance that the party of Innocent held Anacletus for the "Anti-Christ." These opinions were communicated to Emperor Lothar by the Cardinals, who supported the legal Pope. Innocent made into a battle-cry the assertion that the theft of the throne by Anacletus was a "foolish Jewish falsehood." The Rabbi, eager for knowledge, whom we quote, closes his report about the struggle with the following commentary: "The 'Jewish Pope' held his position successfully up to his death on 25th January 1138." This Jewish leader, a very honourable historian, thus admits quite clearly and without reserve or fear that Pierleoni was a Jew and describes him expressly as "Jewish Pope" while he risks at the same time to call Innocent II an anti-Pope.[421]

When the Jewish usurper in Rome was buried with all Papal honours, his Cardinals' collegium — whose members, so it is said, almost all secretly practised the Jewish religion — were concerned with appointing a new Pope or, better, anti-Pope. The choice fell upon Cardinal Gregor, who was named with the approval and support of Roger of Sicily. The new Pope took on the name Victor IV. Saint Bernard had in the meantime through his restless sermons and through the pressure of the German armies for the legal Pope been able to conquer the chief bulwarks of Pierleonis, such as Milan and other Italian cities. Finally the eloquent St. Bernard was also successful in taking Rome itself. During the last days the Jewish anti-Pope had to once again take refuge in St. Peter's and had also occupied the powerful palace of Sant'Angelo. The party of Pierleoni, however, became smaller and smaller and gradually dissolved, so that for the new anti-Pope

---

Victor IV the situation was practically untenable. Thanks to the eloquence of Saint Bernard, he surrendered.

In this episode we encounter anew the tactics which play the decisive role for Jewry in all its political struggles: a Jewish party, or one controlled by Jews, attempts, if it believes itself lost, to prevent that the imminent defeat becomes total destruction or catastrophe by surrendering at the right time to the enemy and begging him for mercy. Or it negotiates the permission to be able to retain the highest possible positions by its promising subjection and loyalty. If this Jewish power remains preserved from destruction, it often retains valuable posts in the new government of the victor. However, it does not give thanks for this, but in secret instigates conspiracies, in order to gain powers again, to extend them in time and at the given moment to carry out the treacherous stroke which destroys the blissfully trusting, great-hearted enemy who gave the ungrateful opponent, instead of destroying him when it lay in its power, the possibility of gathering new strength and recovering for a new blow. This has been repeated again and again in the history of the struggles between Christians and Jews for more than a thousand years and was one of the principal reasons for the re-enlivement of the Synagogue after its great defeats. Unfortunately, however, the time had come, when the roles were changed.

Giordano and the other brothers of Pedro Pierleoni pretended to repent and legged for forgiveness, abjured all heresy and reconciled themselves with the legal Pope. With their hypocrisy they touched the heart of Innocent II and Saint Bernard, who magnanimously pardoned them. Instead of casting them down, the Pope left to them their positions at the Papal court. Later he even honoured them through homage and offices in the intention of achieving a stable permanent uniting of the Church. He attempted to win over the Jews with extreme kindness, so that they would perhaps become ashamed through such great-heartedness, and finally honestly repent.

On the Church level Innocent proceeded more energetically. In 1139 he called a Ecumenical Council, the second of the Lateran, which rejected the teachings of Arnaldo de Brescia and Pedro Bruys and simultaneously declared the actions of Anacletus as illegal and deposed all priests, bishops and cardinals. To put it briefly, all clergy who had been appointed by

Pierleoni were declared to have lost all their consecrations,[422] above all particularly those who were regarded as schismatics. The Generality regarded those as schismatics who tolerated heretics and such of Jewish origin among themselves, in a word, all who in a concealed manner adhered to Judaism. Thus the Holy Father purged the clergy of secret Jews of the "Fifth Column", purified the hierarchy and made with one blow all Jewish infiltration into the clergy impossible, which was naturally carried out under the protection of the "Jewish Pope" — as the renowned Rabbi Newman calls him. The liberality of the Pope in the political domain towards the defeated Giordano Pierleoni and his brothers was to become fateful for the Holy See. It must be remarked that Saint Bernard had certainly influenced the Pope in this policy of forgiveness. The former believed, in his over-great kindness, that Holy Church could perhaps soften the hardened hearts of the Jews if it pursued a different policy. Saint Bernard admittedly combated the schisms and heresy of the Jews, but exercised extreme caution and did not wish that they should be persecuted or any harm done to them. Put in another way, he wished to tame wolves with kindness.

As always the Jews abused the kindness of Saint Bernard and proved irrefutably that it is impossible to make wolves into obedient lambs. The occurrences of the past century have proved this and forced the Holy Church to proceed energetically and often mercilessly in her struggle against the Jews. The bonfires of the Inquisition were largely the consequence of the liberal policy of forgiveness. The tolerance and kindness preached by St. Bernard had failed lamentably.

---

[422] Lateran Council II. Law 30. Collected work: Acta Conciliorum et epistolae decretales, ac Constitutiones Summorum Pontificum, Studio of Joannis Harduini S.J. Ed. Paris 1714. Vol. VI. Part II. Page 1207 ff.

CHAPTER TWENTY-SEVEN

A JEWISH-REPUBLICAN REVOLUTION

IN THE 12ᵀᴴ CENTURY

Several Popes had previously liberally tolerated the Jews at the papal Court, had acted towards them in a friendly manner and had used them as bankers. The consequence of this was the schism at the time of Pierleoni, which had almost destroyed Holy Church. The kind liberality of Pope Innocent II towards the family of the converted Jew Giordano Pierleoni were to embitter the last hours of the latter and cause the Papacy great harm in the political domain.

Five years after the death of the Jewish Anti-Pope, his brother Giordano used the valuable positions and aids which he had preserved thanks to the kindness of his opponents, and prepared in secret a revolution which, if it had not been defeated, would have had incalculable consequences. The conspirators proved their great political talent and worked out a fighting programme which was extremely attractive for the Roman people. Indeed, it was perhaps the only one which possessed sufficient attractive power, in order at a time, when the religiosity was very great, to move the nobility and the people in a movement of rebellion against the highest Pontifex of Christianity. With this battle plan or this battle platform, as we would call it today, the Pierleoni proved that they were capable of carrying out training and preparing future norms for the "Fifth Column" in the clergy, not only on the religious but also on the political front. The movement led by Giordano Pierleoni reminded the inhabitants of the "Eternal City" of the glorious republic when Rome was ruled by the patricians and the people and not by autocrats, and had thus become the first nation of antiquity. Intensive personal labour was carried out. The glittering Roman Senate was recalled and the contrast shown between that glorious time of the Republic and the condition of enfeeblement in which the State found itself in the 12th Century. It was necessary that the Romans made efforts to rise again and made Rome once more in a political, military and economic respect the first city of the world. Then the Romans set through their will and their laws in the whole world. Unfortunately the temporal power of the Pope was a hindrance. All Christians respected the Pope, but he should be no hindrance for the rise and enlargement of Rome. He must therefore restrict himself to his religious functions and allow the city to make efforts to recover its former glory and to take up again the form of government which had made possible this glorious past.

The Roman nobility, which — as we have seen — was fairly undermined through its Jewish relationship (inter-marriage), and the rest of the inhabitants of the city were intoxicated by these sermons and gradually joined themselves to the movement led by Giordano Pierleoni. In the year 1143 this had become so strong that, with a kind of coup d'Etat, he was able to eliminate the "City Prefecture", which had been diminished in authority through the propaganda of the conspirators. In addition, the movement did not recognise the temporal power of the Pope over the city, summoned the Senate to the old Capitol and proclaimed the Roman Republic under the leadership of the renowned Patrician Giordano Pierleoni. Thus this Christian descended from Jews, whose honesty of belief was dubious, repaid the forgiveness of Pope Innocent II and of Saint Bernard and the permission to be able to retain his wealth and his position, which he now used to lead this new revolution to success. But that is in fact the law of life. Every magnanimity and tolerance which one exercises towards a wolf gives the latter the opportunity of devouring the sheep.

The heroic meritorious Pope Innocent II died embittered, without having experienced the triumph over this painful rebellion. His successor, Celestine II became Pope for five months. He had to take refuge in the fortress of the Frangapini, while the nobility and the people of Rome censured the Pope and cheered the Republic, the Senate and the new lord of the situation, Giordano Pierleoni. The next Pope, Lucius II, attempted with the help of some noblemen who had remained true to the Church, to free himself from captivity and to conquer the Capitol. However, he was mortally wounded by a stone thrown by the mob of Pierleoni and died eleven months after he had been consecrated as Pope. So was strengthened the power of Giordano Pierleoni and his band over the new Republic. Under such difficult circumstances a modest monk was elected and consecrated as Pope, who had lived apart from the world in a monastery on the outskirts of Rome. When he became Pope in the year 1145, he took the name Eugene III. Immediately after his election the revolutionary forces attempted to persuade him to approve the Republican Constitution and to recognise the Senate. However, the Pope refused and therefore had to flee from Rome. That is also the reason, why he was consecrated in a monastery outside the city. Afterwards he went to Viterbo, where he proved himself as very energetic and excommunicated the revolutionary leader Giordano Pierleoni and the members of the Senate, while the mob under the latter's protection stormed the palaces and fortresses of the cardinals and noblemen who were for the Pope, and committed cruel murders of Christians who kept faith with the Holy See. That liberal forgiveness, which the renowned Pope Innocent II had shown to the Pierleonis, made it possible for the latter to win great political power, which not only represented a serious threat for the Church, but also seriously endangered the life and the property of the Cardinal, and manifested itself in treacherous murders of the disciples of the Church. Without doubt liberality towards the Godless, especially towards Jews, can lead to a serious danger for the good. However, the farmers had remained true to the Pope and together with various landed nobility supported them in the besieging of the city, to which he cut off the supply of provisions. So the rebels were finally compelled to negotiate with the Pope. They recognised him as authority under the condition that he recognised the Republican Constitution and the Senate, whose dispositions should be restricted to the city government. Through this agreement Pope Eugene III could set up his residence in Rome in the year 1145.

This was, however, only an armistice, which the Jews as usual used for gathering strength in secret, winning greater power, and then renewed their attacks. When the revolt broke out a second time, a new leader of the popular masses, by name Arnaldo de Brescia, was involved. The Holy Father had to leave Rome again, and a renewed intervention by St. Bernard in his favour was not heeded by the mass of the people of Rome, whom the revolutionaries had influenced. Arnaldo de Brescia supported the movement of Giordano Pierleoni. From the pure political realm, where it had taken its beginning he went over, however, to the religious, accused the Cardinals of avarice and arrogance and asserted that they enriched themselves at the expense of the people. The Pope he described as a bloodthirsty creature and hangman of the Church, who understood how to fill his pockets with money that he had robbed from strangers. In addition, he asserted that Holy Church was no Church but rather a den of robbers. Neither the Church nor the clergy had the right to claim property which legally belonged to the laity and especially to the Princes. Thus he skilfully stirred up the ambition of the monarchs and nobility, to appropriate the property of the clergy. The Pope had to flee to France, which, apart from the German Empire, supported Holy Church most magnanimously and was her chief bulwark in the struggle against Jewry. There the warlike Pope secured the support of King Louis VII of France and gathered together an army, at whose head he marched to Italy and advanced as far as the gates of Rome. Therefore Roger of Sicily offered him every support, in order to re-establish his regard. During this year the Norman magnate had really changed. He had married a sister of Pierleoni and applied his whole power in favour of the Jewish Anti-Pope, as well as tolerated the Jews and Musulmans at his court, whose influence there was very great. But the Jews as always misused the protection granted them and the positions they had attained as a result, until finally Roger of Sicily recognised the Jewish danger. He therefore altered his policy and attempted to destroy Jewry. In addition he applied the outworn, ineffective method of compelling the Jews to conversion through laws. At all events, after Roger of Sicily had offered the Holy Father his help, having changed his earlier policy, the Pope naturally accepted his support. Supported by the troops of the Normans he entered Rome on 28th November 1149. Unfortunately the revolutionaries had the people of Rome completely in their hands and gave themselves out as their liberators. Scarcely seven months later the Pope had to leave the city anew in all haste and withdraw to Anagni, where he died in the same year as the great St. Bernard.

After the brief period of office of Anastasius IV the English Cardinal Nicholas Breakspeare, the Bishop of Albano, was elected as Pope. When this famed, energetic Pope ascended the throne of St. Peter, the position of the Church in Rome was catastrophic. The revolutionaries under the leadership of the Jew Giordano Pierleoni had the city in their hands and carried out treacherous murders, even on pilgrims, who on account of their faith travelled into the capital of the Catholic world.

With his speeches Arnaldo de Brescia aided the progress of the revolution and it began to extend threateningly to the whole of Italy. The daring of the revolutionaries even went so far as to severely wound Guido, the Cardinal of Santa Prudenciana. This made the measure full, and the Pope resolved to proceed against them in a radical way. For the first time in history he uttered an "Interdict" against the city of Rome, as a result of which all religious ceremonies were stopped. Although the people had also allowed themselves to be deceived by the leaders of the revolution, they were nevertheless very religious, and the majority now left the inciters in the lurch. Simultaneously the Pope utilised in a masterful way the support which Friedrich Barbarossa, the new German Emperor, had offered him. As condition for his crowning he should put down the rebellion and deliver to him Arnaldo de Brescia, which he did when his troops captured Rome. As usual the Jews set all levers in motion, in order that the Pope spare the life of Arnaldo de Brescia. But with this warlike Pope, who was himself fully conscious of the danger, their intrigues were of no avail. If in fact they had been successful, the plotters would have been in the position to continue their revolution in the future, in the manner that had already occurred.

Under mandate from the Pope the Emperor had Arnaldo taken prisoner and delivered him to the Prefect of Rome, who had him hanged, his corpse burned and the ashes scattered in the Tiber. As the Pope had acted in an unexpectedly energetic way, the rebels in Rome were seized with fear, and finally the desired peace was restored in the city and its environs.[423] Holy Church had not wished to use any force against her foes. The latter, however, had abused her kindness, spread anarchy and created such great desolations and committed countless crimes, that the energetic English Pope understood that it was necessary to suppress the evil in order to protect the life and the rights of the good, although the deputy of Jesus Christ was against the use of force. The Church of Rome now pursued a new policy. The wolves were to be destroyed, so that the sheep could be saved. Not the Pope – as Jewish writers and their supporters have asserted – but the "Synagogue of Satan" is responsible for this change in policy. The latter compelled Holy Church through their conspiracy, their heretical-revolutionary movements, their crimes and the anarchy they provoked, to seize upon fully effective defensive measures. In conclusion to this chapter we must still make clear that Arnaldo de Brescia had gone in his youth to France, where he became a pupil of the heretic Abelard, who imparted to him his destructive doctrines. Concerning Abelard it must be said that he defended the heresy of the Jew Arius and was therefore condemned. In addition the teachings of Abelard about the Jews are very interesting. Rabbi S. Raisin assures us that Abelard, the most popular teacher of that time, said among other things: "One must not lay guilt for the crucifixion of Christ onto the Jews." Abelard attacks in addition the authority of the Church Fathers[424] and was in general favourably disposed to the Jews.

On the other side there exists no doubt that, if Pope Innocent II had not purged the clergy of Holy Church — by deposing all clergy, including the Bishops and Cardinals who were for the Jewish Anti-Pope and had received consecration from him — of the members of the "Fifth Column", then Holy Church would perhaps have been subjected to the

---

[423] L. Duchesne: Liber Pontificalis, Vol. II. J. M. Waterich: Vitae Romanorum Pontificum, Vol. II, Rabbi Louis Israel Newman: Jewish Influence on Christian Reform Movements, Gregorovius: Geschichte der Stadt Rome im Mittelalter, Book II. Vol. II. Llorca-Garcia Villoslada- Montalban, S. J., History of the Catholic Church, Vol. II. Otto de Frisinga: Chronicle. Vol. VII.

[424] Rabbi Jakob S. Raisin, op. cit., Chapter XVII.

pressure of the revolutionary movement which we have investigated in this chapter or would have fallen a victim to the cunning attack of the heretical secret organisations which the false Christians, who secretly practised the Jewish religion, had founded in the entire Christian world. If the members of the "Fifth Column" in the decisive moments of this struggle had still occupied their posts in the College of Cardinals or in the Bishoprics, they would have worked together with the revolutionaries of the heretical sects in order to destroy the highest hierarchy of the Church. The purging by Innocent saved Christianity during the following decades from a direct catastrophe. Concerning the revolutionary activity of the Jewish-Italian family of the Pierleoni it is stated in an official document of the Synagogue, word for word in the quoted Jewish Spanish Encyclopaedia: "Pierleoni, a respected Roman family in the 11th-13th century. Baruj Leoni, financier of the Pope, had himself baptised and took on the name Benedict Christian. His son Leo was the leader of the Papal party which supported Gregory VII. The son of Leo, Pedro Leonis (Pierleoni), was also leader of the Papal party and defended Paschal II against the German Emperor Henry V. His son Pierleoni II was promoted Cardinal in 1116 and in 1130 elected as Pope. Lucrezia Pierleoni had inscribed on the socket of her statue her family connections with the royal houses of Austria and Spain. In spite of baptism and of mixed marriages the Pierleoni were connected for centuries long with the Jewish community."[425]

In a highly regarded and above all not anti-Semitic work there is a brief reference to the false Jewish Christians of the Pierleoni family who set up strategic norms more than eight hundred years ago, which often repeated themselves and were decisive for the triumphs of the Jews then and also in later centuries. These norms are:

I. It is necessary to introduce oneself into the Church and political hierarchy and to gain influence through financial support.
II. To infiltrate the Catholic and Conservatives parties, in order, after the leadership has been attained, to make the cause fail.
III. With mock-Christianity, to deceive not only intelligent but also such brilliant Popes as Gregory VII, who in addition — as we have already elaborated in another passage — was a radical energetic enemy of the Jews.
IV. Make one's services indispensable, as for example through the defence of Pope Paschal II against the Emperor, as a result of which the Jews obtained favourable laws and the Cardinal's hat for one of the

---

[425] Jewish-Spanish Encyclopaedia, same edition, Vol. VII. Word Pierleoni. Page 452.

Pierleoni. The latter was later to bring about the terrible schism in Holy Church, which we investigated in the preceding chapters, and was close on gaining complete control of the Church.

V. Finally, a relationship was to be invented with the royal houses of Spain and Austria. As a result incautious rulers were again and again deceived, who granted the Jews protection and valuable political advantages always to the harm of the Christian nations and of the defence of mankind against Jewish Imperialism. In addition, it is revealed that in Italy and in the whole world a family descended from Jews, in spite of different baptisms, mixed marriages and their seeming Christianity, remained bound for centuries to the Jewish organisations.

CHAPTER TWENTY-EIGHT

QUINTESSENCE OF THE JEWISH REVOLUTIONS. SECULAR ATTACKS ON THE TRADITION OF THE CHURCH

Rabbi Benjamin of Tudela, in his famous: "Itinerary", manifests that the situation in the Islamic World is magnificent in the Twelfth Century, with the reign of The Prince of the Captivity giving his title to the Rabbis and Cantors of the land of Sinar or Chaldea, of Persia, Khorasan, Sheba or Arabia Felix (Yemen), Mesopotamia, Alania, Sicaria, as far as the mountains of Georgia, as far as the Gihon River, Tibet and India. All those synagogues received, according to the illustrious traveller, his permission to have Rabbis and Cantors, who went to Baghdad to be solemnly installed in their orders and to receive their authority from the hands of The Prince of Captivity, called by everyone "Son of David."

On the contrary, in the Christian world, in the same Twelfth Century, another outstanding authority of Judaism said: "These are the days of exile in which we now are, and we have neither King nor Prince in Israel, but we have the dominion of the Gentiles and their Princes and Kings."[426] In reality, according to the data we have, The Prince of the Exile (Diaspora) had jurisdiction only over the Hebrew communities of the East; those of the West, although in close alliance with the former, were governed by communal councils and general synods of directors, one of which we have seen took place in Toledo. But the interesting thing is the confession of the said Rabbi in pointing out that, in the Twelfth Century, the Jews dominated the Gentiles (among whom they include us Christians) and their Princes and Kings. This was a sad reality, not only in the East, but likewise in the West. Jewish Imperialism, as confessed by the distinguished

---

[426] James Finn. "Sephardim or The History of The Jews in Spain and Portugal", London, 1851, Pages 216 to 219.

Rabbi, had already made enormous progress in its task of dominating the Gentile nations. It is true that in Christendom, in certain kingdoms and seignories in accordance with the Canons of the Church, the Jews were forbidden access to the offices of government, but, for one thing, some monarchs disobeyed the Canons, and for another, those who adhered to their mandates, could not prevent the clandestine Jews, under cover of generations of false Christianity from away back, from infiltrating by well organized plans into the offices of government in France, Germany, Italy, England and other countries of Christendom, as they likewise got themselves into the laity and the religious orders, reaching to the hierarchy of the Church. Judaism in those times already had a gigantic invisible power which penetrated everywhere, without the Popes, Emperors and Kings being able to avoid it.

Nevertheless, this occult power encountered serious obstacles in its attempt to obtain a rapid domination of the Christian world. In the first place, the monarchy and nobility in which the title was inherited by the first born, made the task of the Jews secretly to scale the supreme authority of the State with rapidity, very difficult. They could gain the king's confidence, get to be ministers, but it was almost impossible for them to become kings. In the second place, their position in the royal government was somewhat insecure, and they were liable to be removed at any time by the monarch who appointed them, thus bringing down a dominion brought about by many years of preparation and effort. On the other hand, the princes of the blood royal could only wed princesses of the blood royal, thus safeguarding the headquarters of these States with a wall of blood, which made it impossible or almost impossible for a plebeian accession to the throne. Under these conditions no matter how much the Israelites were able to infiltrate into the government offices of the Christian society, the wall of blood impeded their attaining the throne. Something similar occurred during several centuries with the nobility. Notwithstanding, as we have already seen, the Hebrews in some exceptional cases succeeded in penetrating that wall of blood of the aristocracy, which resulted disastrously for Christian society, for, with mixed marriages with members of the aristocracy, they succeeded in achieving important positions from which they supported their schisms and revolutions.

But the blooded aristocracy was, especially in some countries, an exclusive case, difficult to penetrate by the plebeians, so that in order to infiltrate it and control it, for example in England, the Israelites were obliged to work for several centuries. By contrast, in other places such as Italy, Spain and France, they achieved in a few decades great progress in the penetration of the aristocracy, although the Inquisition upset their conquests which were greatly reduced. Nevertheless, during the Eighteenth and Nineteenth Centuries they were sufficiently powerful to facilitate the triumph of their Masonic-Liberal revolutions which overthrew the monarchies.

In one way or another, the nobility presented a barrier of blood which, in many countries, obstructed the infiltration of the Hebrews into the upper spheres of society. Hereditary monarchy presented the principal obstacle for the Jews, disguised as good Christians, in capturing the offices of chief of state.

Although whenever they could they attempted infiltrating into royalty, in almost every case they failed, with the exception of Ethiopia, where they succeeded in installing a Judaic dynasty, and in England, where it is said they have already judaized royalty.

It is understandable that the Israelites of the Twelfth Century should not want to await the fruition of a long and frustrating labour of centuries, consistent with the progressive infiltration of the royal and noble dynasties; for that reason, without ceasing for a moment their attempts to do so, they nevertheless thought out a more rapid way to reach the desired goal: the destruction by revolutionary means of the hereditary monarchies and blooded aristocracies and the substitution of Republics for these regimes, thus making it possible to scale the offices of chiefs of state quickly and with little difficulty. That is why the revolution organized in Rome by the Jewish Giordano Pierleoni, which reached quickly the highest office of government in the small republic, is of such importance. Although this revolution was not directed against a king, by this coup de main, which in a few days placed him in the apogee of power, the brother of the Jewish anti-pope had shown universal Judaism how to penetrate and destroy in short order that barrier of blood presented by hereditary monarchy. In some of the heresies of the Middle Ages, in addition to the Reformation of the Church, there was projected the overthrow of monarchies and the extermination of the aristocracies; and in modern times they have been succeeding in doing so, raising the flag of Democracy and the abolition of privileged classes.

Nevertheless, the attempt to achieve so many goals with a single blow, only succeeded in the Middle Ages in uniting the kings, the nobility and the clergy, who, as long as they remained united, defeated the revolutionary intentions of Judaism. Faced with these failures, they finally understood that it was not possible to achieve at one stroke so many ambitious objectives. The Hebrews have always had the great characteristic of being able to profit from the lessons of the past; for that reason, in their new revolution, which began in the Sixteenth Century, they no longer attacked simultaneously the kings, the nobility and the clergy, but, on the contrary, attempted to reform and dominate the Church with the help of monarchs and aristocrats in order later to overthrow these with new revolutionary movements.

Another obstacle which interfered with the rapid domination of the Christian peoples by the crypto-Jews, was the Holy Church, its clergy, its hierarchies and, above all, its Religious Orders. It is understandable that for these false Christians, judaizing secretly, it entailed a great sacrifice to infiltrate the clergy, especially the Religious Orders, without having a real vocation, and solely for the purpose of controlling the hierarchies of the Church in order to prepare its ruin. If they did it and continue doing it, it is because they have a paranoiac mystique and fanaticism, but doubtless a more rapid solution entailing fewer sacrifices must have seemed to them preferable. Faced with the impossibility of destroying the Church, due to its roots among the people, they chose to attempt a revolutionary Reformation by heretical methods, while it was yet possible to destroy it completely. Therefore, the heretical sects organized by the secret Jews from the Middle Ages until this day, among other objectives, always favoured the following:

1. First, suppression of the monastic Orders, whose vows of poverty, communal life, hard discipline, and difficulty in satisfying their sexual appetite, made difficult their infiltration. Incontrovertible documents, among them the Inquisitorial Processes, demonstrate to us that the crypto-Jews, in different times, achieve dangerous penetration in the Monastic Orders which it was important for them to infiltrate, as, for instance, at one time the Dominicans and Franciscans, and later, the Jesuits, and others as well, demonstrating that the Judaizers as well as the Christians were capable of major sacrifices for their cause. But undoubtedly for subterranean Judaism the most convenient way was to destroy these difficult barriers, by achieving in some way or other the dissolution of the Religious Orders.
2. Suppression of celibacy among the clergy. Although the records of the Inquisition show us that the crypto-Jewish clergy always had a way of having their women clandestinely with the help of their coreligionists (Jews), or of introducing into the Christian clergy young crypto-Jews with homosexual tendencies who did not have that problem, for undercover Judaism, wearing the mask of Christianity, it was much more convenient to contrive a revolutionary reform of the Church which

would do away with the celibacy of the clergy. That is why, wherever they could in an heretical movement, they abolished clerical celibacy.

3. Suppression of the hierarchy of the Church. The actual hierarchy is difficult to achieve; albeit the Jewish fifth columnists have reached the pinnacle, it is also true that this work has always been very difficult and slow. Holy Church has gradually, with time, been accumulating natural defences in its own institutions; that is why, in those heretical movements of the Middle Ages and the Renaissance, which were controlled by the Jews, the ecclesiastic hierarchies were suppressed, being substituted by Councils of Presbyteries and by a kind of religious democracy. It is clear that in the Soviet Union, where they have absolute dominion, they (the Jews) have no great interest in suppressing the hierarchy. Having assassinated the independent bishops, they have replaced them with Jews placed in the Dioceses, according to various writers. Under these conditions, the hierarchy also serves them by giving them a more secure control over the churches.

But in the Middle Ages, and later in the time of the crypto-Jews Calvin and Zwingli, the situation was different; in those times the shortest road to domination of the Christian churches was by the revolutionary suppression of the ecclesiastical hierarchy, because, in this way, any crypto-Jew could elevate himself to the leadership of the Church, without having to go through the long and uncertain process of rising from presbyter to pope.

That is why in the Protestant monarchies they fought bloodily against the Episcopal Churches, attempting to establish those of a Presbyterian character; and, if they failed in their endeavour, it was because of the support given by the kings to the former.

The fact that the monarchs played a decisive part in the appointment of the bishops, if it did not completely prevent it, at least hampered the infiltration of the crypto-Jews into the Protestant Churches, as was also the case with the Orthodox Churches of Eastern Europe. The control of the kings over them (the churches) saved them for several centuries from falling under Judaic dominion.

The Jews had been for centuries infiltrating secondary positions of command in both Church and State, but, commencing with the Eleventh Century, they felt themselves strong enough to decide to scale the highest posts, resolving then that if it could not be done by slow and difficult infiltration, they would do it by rapid and impressive revolution. In order to accomplish this it was necessary to destroy the obstacles preventing it, by revolutionary reform of religious, political and social institutions.

This plan could not be executed by Israelites identified as such, who practised their Judaism publicly, since the Holy Church and the Christian monarchies had, over the centuries, created ecclesiastical and civil laws which prevented their access to the governing positions of society; and, although this legislation was violated by some monarchs, it remained in effect in most Christian States. Besides, in cases where (this legislation) was forgotten, giving right of way to the Jews to the peaks of power, as in the example we examined in Castile, the redeeming Crusades, organized by other monarchs under the auspices of the Holy See, saved the situation.

But the clandestine Jews certainly were in a position to attain these objectives. Identified with the other inhabitants of a region by baptism, their subterranean Judaism, transmitted from father to son, from one generation to the other, was becoming less visible, until already in the Eleventh Century it was impossible to detect it in the Christian States in which a very secret Judaism existed in many families which appeared to be Christian for generations back, some of which, although in small numbers, had managed to keep the tides of nobility acquired in the manner we have already analyzed. The great majority of these secret Jews belonged to a social class which was arising: the bourgeoisie (yeomanry), in which they were without a doubt the most powerful element and, above all, the best organized and the richest. It cannot, therefore, be considered a coincidence that, as the yeomanry grew in power, Judaism was increasing its potentialities for dominating the peoples.

To understand the decisive strength the Jews had in Medieval Yeomanry, it is necessary to take into account that in some cases they monopolized commerce and in others played the principal role in its control, that of the bankers and usurious money-lenders.

At the same time, the sons of Israel formed a good percentage of the artisans.

4. Another thing that disturbed exceedingly those undercover Judaizers disguised as Christians was the veneration they had to render to the images of Christ, the Virgin Mary and the Saints. The business of having to go so frequently to churches filled with images was most repugnant to the crypto-Jews, not only because of their religious convictions which consider such adoration as idolatry, but also because of the hatred they have for the Virgin Mary and for the Saints,

especially those who distinguished themselves as anti-Jewish leaders. The most odious thing of all for these false Christians was to be obliged to have their own homes filled with images in order to avoid suspicion from their Christian neighbours and friends. Therefore a form of worship devoid of images was, for these undercover Hebrews, much more comforting, so, whenever they could, in their heretical movements, they abolished the veneration of images. Nevertheless, there are instances of Christian churches, already under their control, in which they cannot yet accomplish this for fear of hurting the peoples feelings. But we have good reason to believe that they will do so as soon as they can do it without losing control of the masses.

5. Another of the objectives of the crypto-Jewish action in Christian society was to suppress what is now called "anti- Semitism", because they realized that, as long as the Christian were aware of the danger of the Hebrews for them, for the Holy Church, and for the Christian nations, they stood a better chance at defending themselves against the conquering action of Jewish imperialism, provoking, as they did provoke, constant defensive reactions which would continue to cause the failure of the Synagogue's attempts at dominion now and again, as was the case at that time. On the other hand, if the Holy Church and the Faithful lost this sense of their peril, they would have less chance of defending themselves against their dominating action. That is why, in the first millennium, and especially in the Middle Ages, one notes a tendency to achieve the transformation of the Christian mentality and that of the authorities of the Church and State intended to change their anti-Semitism into a philo-Judaism, a plan which originated those constant pro-Jewish movements organized by the Hebrew fifth column infiltrated into Christian society and the clergy of the Church.

Thus we see obtruding in many of the Medieval heresies these philo-Jewish tendencies, defended with ardour by many of the most distinguished great heretics of Jewish stock, a phenomenon which was repeated in various Protestant sects of Unitarian or Calvinist origin in the 16th and 17th Centuries, sects which were denounced by the Spanish and Portuguese Inquisitions as enterprises secretly controlled by the occult Jews disguised as Christians.

But how achieve all the foregoing if the doctrine of the Fathers of the Church, of the Popes, of the Ecumenical and Provincial Councils and of the principal Saints of the Church condemned the Jews in some way or another? Did it have to be embraced by loyal Christians? The Israelite conspirators solved this problem by "cutting through the live part" of the branch and including in their heretical programs ignorance of the

Tradition of the Church as a source of revelation, and maintaining that the only source of the Truth is the Holy Bible. This war to the death against tradition was renewed by the crypto-Jewish clergy, that is, by the worthy successors of Judas Iscariot, whenever they could, repeatedly from the 11th Century until now, with a perseverance worthy of a better cause; achieving their first success in the Protestant Reformation. With this fierce (bloody) struggle against the traditions of the Church, the Judaists and their agents, infiltrated in the clergy, strove to throw out the anti-Jewish doctrine of the Fathers of the Church, the Popes, and the Holy Councils, in order to instil in Christianity a philo-Jewish thesis which facilitates the work of The Synagogue of Satan in achieving dominion over the Church as well as the Christian People. In all this there is astonishing coincidence in all the heretical sects of Jewish origin which arose between the 11th and the 20th Centuries.

On the other hand, as in the rituals and liturgy of the Church there were included frequent allusions to Judaic perfidy, the crime of deicide, etc., in order that the clergy might have constant and frequent reminders of how dangerous was the mortal enemy and be prepared to defend their flocks (sheep) against the ambush of the fiercest of wolves, the first accomplishment of heresies of this type was the suppression of all these anti-Jewish allusions from the Liturgy and the Ritual, which is a very significant fact.

Removing from the sacred tradition all authority as fountain of revealed truth, there remained as such only the Holy Bible, and, although the New Testament has many allusions to the wickedness of the Hebrews, the only thing left for the Jews to do was to attempt to falsify the Holy Gospels, suppressing in them those concepts odious to the ears of the Israelites. And, incredible as this may seem, in some heretical sects they have gone to the extreme of truly falsifying certain portions of the New Testament, alleging that the Vulgate is an apocryphal bible which falsifies the original documents.

6. Another of the proposed objectives, with the change in Christian ideology from an anti-Semitism of centuries to a philo-Semitism, was to repeal all civil and canonical laws which impeded the action of the Jews, in order to gain dominion of the people, especially of the Hebrews who lived, and live, identified as such, that is to say, of the publicly admitted Jews. By this is meant those who could achieve what they call the liberation of the latter would have to be the clandestine Jews, who, upon achieving by infiltration or revolution the control of the Christian governments, could repeal the laws which prevented their Hebrew

brethren, open practitioners of their sect, from participating in the dominion of Christian or gentile nations. In the Middle Ages, the underground Jews had some isolated and fleeting successes; and only commencing in the 18th Century were they able to emancipate their brother Jews (publicly avowed Jews) with the help of Freemasonry.

7. Another of the maximal aspirations of the Hebrews has been that of appropriating the wealth of other peoples. Elsewhere we have seen how they gave this pretension theological basis, affirming that it (wealth) is the product of the will of God. By means of usury, they were able, during the Middle Ages, to achieve in part this goal and accumulated gigantic wealth with cruellest plunder. Even in some of their Medieval heresies they already preach communism, the abolition of private property and the general expropriation of the properties of the Church, the nobility, royalty, and the Yeomanry.

Their expropriation of the rising yeomanry did not affect the Jews, since the only ones to suffer were the Christians and the Gentiles, since the Israelites, controlling the new communist regime, in their hands rested the riches of kings, clergy, nobles and Yeomanry. However, experience showed the Jews that the wish to achieve so many objectives all at one stroke only succeeded in uniting all those affected, resulting in violent defensive reactions against them, which altogether succeeded in smashing their revolutionary intentions. They learned that they could not defeat all their enemies at once; and in the following centuries they preferred achieving their great revolution piece by piece, dividing the enemy camp and making use of one part to attack the other, until they gained their objective, little by little, but at a safer pace.

But these sinister ends of the Judaic revolutions have been carefully concealed from the masses, which have always been deceived with attractive programs designed to carry them along, making them believe that the heresy or revolution is a movement arising from the people themselves, for their benefit, to establish democracy and liberty, to suppress the abuses and immoralities of the clergy or the civil authorities, purify the Church or the State, end tyranny and exploitation until the earth is converted into a paradise. The crypto-Jewish leaders have always been masters of deceit; dragging with them the people with a beautiful program, whereas, in secret, they are planning something quite different. This clever stratagem has always been another of the keys to the success of the Jewish heretics and revolutionary leaders. The universal fact that the Israelites, under cover of Christianity or some other religion, are scattered among the people, using their own names without anyone suspecting they are Jews, that is, foreigners planning conquest, has made their heresies and revolutionary movements seem to spring from the people themselves.

True, in the Middle Ages the Hebrew origin, recent or remote, of many false Christians was still remembered. This permitted the clergy, monarchs and aristocrats to trace the Jewish origin of these revolts and these sects. But, as centuries passed, the origin of these families was forgotten. They, for their part, did everything possible to erase the memory of their Jewish descent until one fine day nobody suspected that, under the appearance of a pious Christian, was concealed an undercover Jew who conspired constantly against Church and State. And who never missed an opportunity to organize revolts and conspiracies, which, in such circumstances appear to spring from the people themselves and to be internecine wars between members of the same nation, while being in fact real wars inflicted upon an people invaded in the worst manner, against disguised invaders, deliberately utilizing for this purpose a large portion of the same people caught in the nets of the fifth columns by clever revolutionary plans. Very fine programs with which they make their future victims believe that, by helping them, they are labouring for their own betterment and that they are fighting for the improvement of their political, social and religious institutions. This has been the deception of all the crypto-Jewish subversive movements since the 11th Century and until our times; and this has also been the cause of the victories of the Israelite deceivers and swindlers, in guise of being sincere redeemers of the people, saviours of the nation or reformers of the churches. Initiating a revolution with the highest and noblest ends in view in order to take it later into the most perverse objectives, has been the traditional tactics of Judaism for nine hundred years. Naturally, these unwary people, entrapped by the deceitful leaders and by programs as fake as they are attractive, one day become aware of the criminal deceit, but sometimes this occurs when there is no longer any remedy and the betrayed ones are either annihilated or enslaved, suffering the consequences of their ingenuousness.

If we analyze the cases of the heretics of the Middle Ages, comparing them with the crypto-Jewish or above-board Jews, revolutionary leaders of the present days, we are frequently confronted with individuals who have known how to surround themselves with a hypocritical aspect of kindness and sincerity, with an aura of sanctity, such that anyone not familiar with Judaic fables will wind up believing he is actually face to face with a true Apostle, when in reality they are false prophets and false apostles, against whom we were thoroughly warned by Christ Our Lord and by Saint Paul, who knew better than anyone else what Judaic hypocrisy was capable of. Add to this that their crypto-Jewish gang which assists them knows how to cover them with incense to consolidate their good name and prestige, converting them into actual fetishes to gain the unconditional support of the people, later using their influence in favour of the Judaic plans for dominion and their subversive enterprises.

In the records of the Spanish Inquisition, it can be seen how the new Christians, Judaizing, would give one another prestige in order to elevate them to positions where they dominated the old Christians (Spaniards of Visigoth and Latin blood) and how they managed to pass off as good Catholics men who, being clandestine Jews, cursed the Holy Church in secret.

In few words we have just summed up what we could call the quintessence of Hebrew revolutionary movements from the 11th Century on. Whoever desires to dig deeper into this theme and learn it thoroughly must study the Archives, not only of the Pontifical Inquisition, but also of the Spanish and Portuguese Inquisitions, which we have enumerated elsewhere, since those institutions were able to penetrate the innermost secrets of undercover Judaism and of the heretical and revolutionary movements it concocted in secret, since these Inquisitions had the means of making the most secretive Jews talk and forcing them to reveal their greatest secrets. In addition, they utilized another system of great utility for this purpose.

MAURICE PINAY

CHAPTER TWENTY-NINE

SECRET JEWRY AND THE HERESIES OF THE MIDDLE AGES. THE ALBIGENSIANS

It is a significant confirmation that, particularly in the regions of the Christian world where a great percentage of the population were Jews and the Israelites were most influential of all, the most important heresies and heretical movements in the Middle Ages without doubt won the greatest power.

Mostly they began as protest movements against the apparent immorality of the clergy, against Simony and the accumulation of riches by the clergy. They demanded a return to the poverty and asceticism of the first Christians and attacked the apparent oppression and tyranny of the Popes Kings and Nobles. The Church hierarchy should be abolished. Since they were against the priests, their religious leaders much resembled the Rabbis of Judaism, who are not actual priests but religious and political leaders, who lead the same life as the other Jews, from whom solely their calling as Rabbis distinguishes them. In several heretical movements the social- revolutionary aspect was especially important, for they also revealed the tendency to free the poor and they often showed strivings to set up a Communist government.

In all heretical movements, however, it is rather noticeable that they are begun with programmes which are very enticing for the people but are gradually deflected towards aims which no longer have anything at all to do with the original ones which were successful in binding the beginners. In a word, cheating was at the bottom, which is characteristic of all revolutionary movements of Jewish origin.

The Archbishop, Bishop of Port-Louis, Monsignor Leon Meurin, S.J., says citing Hurer in his work "Innocent" (p. 50):

"In France in 1184 a carpenter, named Durad, pretended to have had a vision of the Virgin Mary. For this reason he gathered a large number of fellow citizens around him, under the name of the Brothers of the White Cap. He applied all principles of heresy and wished with all strength to take by force the highest power. He pretended to wish to create the State of equality of primitive men, in which all must be externally equal. Every worldly or spiritual power was declared to be harmful. His supporters worked out a pact of brotherhood, in order to prepare the sudden rule of their sect. The new thing about this sect, to which all elements opposed to order joined themselves, was the fanatical zeal of their supporters and promoters. However, the support given by the Jews was nothing new."[427]

This is the absolute limit! To use a vision of the Virgin Mary to influence the masses and then to make this influence felt in the founding of a sect, which wishes at one stroke to abolish the existing order and to found a new one with similar principles as those of present-day Communism.

Bishop Lucas de Tuy, a Chronicler from the 13th century, writes that "the heretical teachings found admission with the Princes of the State and the Judges of the cities through their Jewish relatives and friends."[428] With good reason the 3rd and 4th Ecumenical Councils issued an Order from the Lateran and Pope Innocent NI, which divided the Jews from the Christians, so that they did not infect the latter with their rebellious teachings. The rabbi Louis Israel Newman writes in his already mentioned and valuable work "Jewish Influence on Christian Reform Movements" on page 135: "The presence of the Jews in southern France favoured the rise of liberal thought", and on page 136 he states: "Simultaneously with the increase of liberal thought in southern France gradually developed a more liberal conduct in the face of the Jews . . . This circumstance favoured Jewry in Provence and not only gave heresy an upward trend in general, but made it possible that the Jews and Judaism also contributed decisively to the development of heterodox movements, and caused, wherever heresy prospered, diverse Jewish tendencies and groups to arise."[429] On page 137 it is stated: "Not only the scholarly Christians but also Jewish researchers — among them Levy — have observed that the decline of hostility against the Jews went hand in hand with the opposition against

---

[427] Archbishop, Bishop of Port Louis, Monsignor Leon Meurin, S. J.: Philosophie der Fremaurerei, Ed. Madrid 1957. Book I. Chapter XI, Page 169.
[428] Bishop Lucas Tudensis: De altera vita adversus Albigensis errores, Vol. NI, 3.
[429] Rabbi Louis Israel Newman: Jewish Influence on Christian Reform Movements, published as Book XXNI of the "Columbia University Series". New York. Columbia University, printed 1925.

the 'Secrets' of the Church, which offended reason, and the visible abuses in Church circles."

In the ensuing, the interesting rabbi Newman gives proof for his facts and mentions that the Jewish writer Leeb, in his work "La Controverse Religieuse," pages 25-26, also alludes to the fact that a relationship exists "between Jewish activity and the religious movement in Languedoc."[430] St. Bernard for his part describes in his letter No. 241 his stay in Languedoc and laments that there "the Churches are regarded as synagogues, and the sanctuary of the Lord is no longer holy."[431] In the monumental work of Spanish Jewry, the Spanish-Jewish Encyclopaedia, it is stated expressly: "From the 11th to the 13th century the regions in southern France most affected by heresies enjoyed a material and spiritual well-being such has never yet again been encountered in the Christian world and can only be compared with the cultural rise of Moorish Spain. There the Roman Church became more and more corrupt and the clergy more and more worldly. This called forth in all strata of the population a great number of rich Jewish communities that were respected by the rulers and the people. . . In addition a mutual tolerance was practised, which in Europe was no longer possible until the Enlightenment. The Jews had admission to public offices, were active in the land and community government and respected in academies and schools. They lived together peacefully with the heathens (gentiles) who frequently shared table with them and even jointly celebrated the Sabbath. Jewish rabbis, physicians, scholars, bankers, merchants and farmers cultivated close contact with their Christian colleagues and mutually influenced each other on the cultural realm. It was thus only natural that the Jews, with their original Bible, powerfully supported the anti-Papal movements which, in spite of their different teachings, were united in the struggle against the falsification and distortion of early Christianity through the Church."[432]

It is strange how the Jews regard the mutual tolerance between Hebrews and Christians which — according to their assertions — prevailed in regions where the Jewish influence was very great, and which is only comparable with the tolerance at the time of the Enlightenment. The fact must be alluded to that the Jewish-Christian brotherhood and the mutual tolerance which then degenerated into a powerful support for the anti-Papal movements, bloody revolutions and murder of Christians, was also a prelude at the time of the Enlightenment of the French revolution

---

[430] Rabbi Louis Israel Newman, same work, same edition. Book N, Page 137.
[431] St. Bernard. Letter 41.
[432] Jewish-Spanish Encyclopaedia, same edition, Vol. NI. Word "Cristianismo" [Christianity].

for the murders of Catholic priests and laymen, which the Freemasonic Jacobins exerted under the control of the Jews — as we have already proved. Through the apparent tolerance and the peaceful coexistence, as they now call it, the Jews desire namely not only to attain freedom of movement, in order to be able to control the Christians and their political and religious institutions. The terrible revolution, not only against Church but against the existing social order in general, which could be prepared in the shadow of this apparent tolerance in the 17th and 18th centuries, proved clearly what these clever, seductive demands signify for the Jews.

The writer Dr. Hesekiel Teyssier, who bases himself among other sources on the handbook of Freemasonry, supported by Condorcet, describes the important Albigensian revolution in the following words: "They formed a giant group, to which belonged citizens, soldiers and even such important personages as the King of Aragon, the Count of Tolouse, the Count of Toix, the Viscount of Beziers and Carcassonne . . . they apparently gained great public power. Their theological theory was the deadly Dualism. In the social sphere they strove for anarchy. This occurred in the 13th century. The Pope and the kings soon learned about it. . . Since they saw themselves discovered and held themselves to be powerful enough, they called for rebellion and made a revolution which put that of 1792 in the shade, and which had its headquarters in Albi. Hence also the name 'Albigensians'. Their weapon was terror, common ownership, the independence of men from every authority, hatred for social institutions and especially for the Church.

"They revealed their secrets only to persons whom they had previously subjected to long, difficult examinations, and laid a duty upon them of maintaining secrecy even to their relatives. Their leaders were unknown to the masses, likewise the signs of recognition by speech and manner of agreement. (Condorcet, "Manuel Maçonnique").

"The Albigensians were protected by powerful magnates and instigated fires, caused devastations and committed countless hideous crimes. With armies of a hundred thousand men they plundered the cities and above all destroyed the churches and monasteries. Every kind of crime was familiar to them and delighted them. The peoples were seized by terror."[433]

Thus ended the peaceful coexistence of Jews and Christians in southern France. In order to defeat this widespread revolution which threatened to destroy the whole of Christianity, the Papal Inquisition had

---

[433] Dr. Hesekiel Teyssier, same work, same edition. Pages 126 and 187.

to be introduced and a great crusade organised by Pope Innocent NI. This army of a half million soldiers, which belonged to the most powerful of that time, was able to defeat the revolution after a long bloody war. The revolutionaries in their most radical regions strove for the collectivisation of property, i.e. Communism Another was that they skilfully understood and understand how to turn to their own advantage all shortcomings of the ruling government and the immorality of respected clergy and politicians, so that they then get themselves to be regarded as reformers of these shortcomings and correctors of this immorality. Thus they secure the support of the people, which is later deceived. If in fact the existing order is once abolished, the Jewish liberators usually fall into worse shortcomings and greater immorality than those which they pretended to correct. In the Spanish Encyclopaedia "Espasa Calpe" it is recognised that, among other things, the immoral conduct of many clergy has favoured the development of the heresy of the Albigensians:

"One of the first acts of these heretics was a robust opposition to the clergy, upon whom they could let loose the hatred of the people, for certain clergy left much to be desired with regard to their knowledge and virtue . . . the people sided with the heretical party."[434]

The anti-Catholic historian Henry Charles Lea confirms this and writes: "From the other side we hear that the principal arguments were based on the pride, the avarice and the impure mode of life of the clergy and prelates."[435] Even if these attacks are also much exaggerated, then we nevertheless all know that, in relation to the conduct of life of various clergy, they were certainly well justified. In this case also — as always — the Jewish plotters skilfully used the faults, the bad conduct or the immorality of the civil or church personages of a ruling government, in order to arouse the people against them and the government. In order to prevent the victory of the Jewish rebellions, it is therefore indispensable to moralise our own ranks and to avoid that the enemy on grounds of the real shortcomings can justify his rebellions and can deceive the masses.

This was also the opinion of St. Bernard, Francis of Assisi, Santo Domingo de Guzman and the Popes Innocent N and Innocent NI, who then fought bitterly against the corruption of the clergy and through this truly purifying work triumphed over the heresies of their time, by their

---

[434] Encyclopaedia Espasa Calpe, same edition, Vol. IV, Word "Albigensians", Pages 157 and 158.
[435] Henry Charles Lea: A History of the Inquisition of the Middle Ages, New York, 1958. Chapter N. Page 61.

taking from them one of their principal rallying-cries to gain supporters and spread their heresies.

In the official publication of the respected Jewish historian N. Leven, intended for internal use by Jewry, "Fifty Years History. The Universal Jewish Alliance." (25 copies in Japan paper and 50 copies in Dutch linen, numbered 1-75), which was intended for highly-regarded Jewish leaders, it is stated word for word:

"At the beginning of the 13th century the Church faced the heresy of the Albigensians, which had arisen in southern France. The Albigensians are not the only Christians who attack the Church and its dogmas. On the other side also there are unbelievers. For this the Jews are guilty; the Albigensians received their instructions from them, and many a one admits that the Jewish doctrine is to be preferred to the Christian. The Jews are the founders of heresy. The church recognises this, and therefore the Jews alarm it. They were destroyed in material aspect, but in all their spiritual power they have received no harm. . . Pope Innocent III, who strove for domination over Europe, encountered in this little people (Israel) a hindrance which he had to overcome. At the commencement of his period of office he wished for neither the death of the Jews nor their compulsory conversion. He hoped to be able to triumph over them through humiliation and leniency. The Pope directed his attack against the Albigensians. South France is conquered with blood and fire. The Jews are thrown into one pot with the Albigensians and die with them. . . . When in 1197 he took over the Pontificate, he had forbidden the crusaders to rob the Jews and to convert them with force. In 1209 they were confused with Albigensians and cut down with them. . . The Council of Avignon later obligated all Barons and free cities under oath to remove the Jews from all positions and services with Christians and to compel them to practise the Christian religion."[436]

The last refers concretely to the false Christians who were secretly given up to Judaism. Admittedly then Holy Church forbade the conversion of the Jews to the Christian religion by force. However, the Christians of Jewish origin who practised the Jewish religion in secret were certainly very well compelled to abandon this and to honestly confess to their official religion. One thus wished to exterminate the "Fifth Column." On the other side it is not remarkable that, together with the Albigensians, many Jews lost their lives, for they were indeed the instigators and

---

[436] N. Leven: Cinquants Ans d'histoire. L'Alliance Israelite Universelle, 1860-1910. Ed. Paris 1911. Vol. I, Pages 7 and 8.

founders of this heresy and therefore lived together with the heretics. In addition it is recognised in this important Jewish work that the Jews were also the instigators of other heresies and unbelief.

The historian Vincente Risco reveals that: "In Provence and in Languedoc, under the rule of the Earls, the Jews enjoyed great well-being and influence. They had positions and public offices and even occupied the stewardships and exerted a real influence on the Christians in philosophy and religion. Therefore several Jewish authors assert that they were responsible for the origin of the heresies of the Catharsians and Albigensians."[437]

The learned Rabbi and writer Lewis Browne writes: "If the truth were known, then one would know that the instructed Jews in Provence were partly responsible for the existence of this Freemasonic sect of the Albigensians. The doctrines which the Jews have spread for centuries long in all nations must positively undermine the power of the Church."[438]

However, it is known that the heresy of the Albigensians therefore became a serious danger for Christianity, because many southern French nobles supported it and even led this enormous movement of revolution which caused blood to flow in streams and true Christians and devout priests to be murdered.

Jules Michelet, the renowned Gallic historian of the previous century, who was one of the directors of the French spiritual archive, establishes in his monumental work "French History": "It was amongst the nobles of Languedoc that the Albigensians found their principal support. This 'Judaea of France', as it has been called, was peopled by a medley of mixed races, Iberian, Gallic, Roman and Semitic." The nobles there, very different from the pious chivalry of the North, had lost all respect for their traditions, and Michelet expressly asserts: "There were few who in going back did not encounter some Saracen or Jewish grandmother in their genealogy."[439]

No particular importance is attached to the existence of a Saracen grandmother, for the Musulmans in France generally converted sincerely to Christianity. The matter of a Jewish grandmother in a family tree is, on the other hand, very serious, for all Jews regard it as a duty to be fulfilled

---

[437] Vincente Risco: History of the Jews, Barcelona 1960. Book 5, Chapter II, Page 306.
[438] Rabbi Lewis Browne: Stranger than Fiction, New York 1925, Page 222.
[439] Michelet: Histoire de France, Vol. III. French edition, 1879. Pages 10-19.

fanatically, to guide their children to the Synagogue, be it only concealed, if it is publicly impossible. In fact the Count Raymond VI of Toulouse and the Count of Comminges among others were repeatedly accused, at the time of this terrible revolution, of being only apparent Christians and in secret practising the Jewish religion. Both Counts supported the heresy very assiduously.

The cautious English historian Nesta H. Webster confirms the assertions of Michelet, and adds in addition that then: "The South of France was a centre from which went forth much of the basic occultism of Jewry as well as its theosophical dreams."[440] She writes in addition: "The Comte de Comminges practised polygamy, and, according to ecclesiastical chronicles, Raymond VI, Comte de Toulouse, one of the most ardent of the Albigensian Believers. had his harem. The Albigensian movement has been falsely represented as a protest merely against the tyranny of the Church of Rome; in reality it was a rising against the fundamental doctrines of Christianity—more than this, against all principles of religion and morality. For whilst some of the sect openly declared that the Jewish law was preferable to that of the Christians (Graetz, 'History of the Jews', III, p. 517), to others the God of the Old Testament was as abhorrent as the 'false Christ' who suffered at Golgotha; the old hatred of the Gnostics and Manicheans for the demiurgus lived again in these rebels against the social order. Forerunners of the seventeenth-century Libertines and eighteenth-century Illuminati, the Albigensian nobles, under the pretext of fighting the priesthood, strove to throw off all the restraints the Church imposed."[441]

The famous Rabbi Louis Israel Newman, mentions certain anti-biblical doctrines of the Cathars, the forerunners of the Albigensians, and writes later in his work "The Jewish Influence on the Christian Reform Movements," on Pages 173 and 174 of the edition quoted: "The chief dogma of Catharism, namely the dualism of God, has a parallel in certain aspects to Jewish tradition. . . In spite of strict monotheism, there existed in Judaism an original Dualism, which was founded on declarations of the Haagadah and even on apocalyptic allusions in the Old Testament. . . During the period of flowering of Catharism we encounter a sharpening of the Jewish discussion about Dualism, in the contemporary 'Cabbala'." And on Page 176 it is stated: "Between the ideas of the Cathars and of the Cabbala exact parallel passages can be found."

---

[440] Nesta H. Webster : Secret Societies and Subversive Movements, same edition, Chapter IV. Page 75.
[441] Nesta H. Webster, same work, same edition, Chapter IV. Page 75.

One must not forget that the heresy of the Albigensians not only goes back to the Cathars but also, exactly like the latter, retains the theological dualism.[442]

The influence of the Jewish Cabbalists on the Cathars and Albigensians and on their theological Dualism is recognised by distinguished Jewish writers. On the other hand, it seems evident that Jewry unscrupulously introduced into the movement of the Albigensians, and especially among their foot soldiers, an apparent anti-Jewish ideology in which Jehovah was frightfully slandered; just as today they show no scruples in spreading atheism in Communist lands.

But this is understandable. Since in Europe then the great mass of Christians was strongly disposed against the Jews, they could not be awakened through a pro-Semitic movement, but, in order to capture them it was necessary to surround the sects, especially in the lower strata, with an atmosphere, which caused the incautious to believe that the Jews were not participating in the movement. The best suited means for this was to slander Jehovah, to renew the Gnostic theories which identified him with the maleficent Demiurge, and to take over the teachings of the Manicheans. Since the leaders of the sects were in addition secret Jews who pretended to be Christians, it was not easy to recognise at first sight — as centuries later with Freemasonry and the conspirators — that many of them were Jews, since they had disguised themselves very well and had taken on their Christian origin, their Christian baptismal and surnames according to the religion.

Holy Church not only discovered that the sect was directed by secret Jews, but also that this ideology, apparently anti-Jewish in the lower spheres, was little by little being transformed in the higher circles, to such a point that the Jewish law, i.e. the Jewish religion, was asserted to be better than the Christian.

Also in the Freemasonry of the 18th century the ideology of the founders was gradually altered, always according to the different grades. The latter joined an official Christian association, which seemingly refused Jews admission in its ranks. However, gradually the ideology was altered through lectures, addresses, liturgy, ceremonial and special instruction in the different degrees, always according to how the Freemason rose, and anti-Semitism, which ruled in the then society, was transformed into pro-

---

[442] Rabbi Louis Israel Newman: Jewish Influence on Christian Reform Movements, same edition. Pages 173-176.

Semitism. So it was successful for the secret Jews, who gave themselves out as Christians, to create legions of allies among the Freemasons, who were ready to organise the liberal revolutions, to pass laws, which emancipated the public Jews and placed them equal to the rest of the population politically and socially, and to abolish the Churches — and civil laws, which for centuries had represented the principal bulwark of Christian society. When the secret Jews had brought the anti-Jewish disposition to silence through Freemasonry and liberalism in the society of the 18th and 19th centuries, they dropped the pretence and left out from the Freemasonic constitutions the articles which forbade the Jews admission in the organisation. Soon afterwards the leading places were occupied by Jews, who openly confessed to their religion. Several free men, like Benjamin Franklin, were astounded and alarmed about this invasion.

In conclusion we will add an interesting revelation concerning the principles of the Albigensian heresy, which Rabbi Jacob S. Raisin makes in his work "Gentile Reactions to Jewish Ideals": "The revolution against the hierarchy was especially strong among the Albigensians. They appeared for the first time in Aquitania in the year 1010, and in 1017 we have evidence of a secret society in Orleans, to which ten priests of a church and a father confessor of the Queen belonged. A short time later we find them in Luttich and Arras, in Soissons and Flanders, in Italy and also in Rome, where many nobles and the people enthusiastically joined them. One called them good men (Bonhommes)."

And the rabbi quoted continues: "In spite of the repression ordered by the Church, the heretics remained stiff-necked, continued to preach their doctrines and were able to win over several archbishops and noblemen."[443] The details given by the zealous rabbi are very interesting and give us an opportunity to allude to one of the tactics which the Jews use in the founding of their revolutionary movements in Christianity. These movements consist at first of a group of secret Jews who give themselves out to be Christians. Hence it appears as if there are in this circle no Jews, but in reality it consists only of such. In addition they usually provide the secret society or the public movement with Catholic, Protestant or orthodox priests, always according to the religion of the land in the individual cases. This is easy for them, for through the "Fifth Column" in the clergy they have at their disposal priests, prebendaries or clergy of high rank. This measure should make possible that the true Christians believe with their admission into the association that it is the matter of a good

---

[443] Rabbi Jacob S. Raisin, "Gentile Reactions to Jewish Ideals," Chapter XVII, Page 454.

cause, which indeed a devout prebendary or a respected cardinal belongs to. The clergy of the "Fifth Column" are thus in this case used as birds of decoy, in order to capture the incautious. Thus the heresy of the Albigensians began with prebendaries and even a father confessor of her Majesty the Queen. Afterwards bishops honoured the secret gatherings through their presence, in order to allow it to appear as a good cause and thus to easier capture the naive people. The same method was used centuries later with Freemasonry, which as a result up to their lowest grades appeared to be a Christian institution and humanitarian society. Their lodges were occupied with priests, prebendaries and even with clergy of highest rank. Thus Jewry could mislead the Church and the Christians for a long time and guide thousands of the disillusioned to the sect. The secret Jewish clergy were principally responsible for this deceit. They were aggressive Freemasons, who served as bait to capture the incautious.

When the Holy See and the monarchies noticed this swindle, the Pope excommunicated the Freemasons. However the brotherhood had everywhere obtained such a great power, that neither the Church nor the monarchs were successful in holding up the onslaught which pulled away with it, for the initial ties had revealed decisive results. The secret Jews in England and the U.S.A. still represent Freemasonry as a Christian institution, and in its lowest strata as a humanitarian association. They even make outcries, which have nothing to do with politics, so that the chivalrous Anglo-Saxons, when they have once made the oath, remained caught in the mouse trap and unconsciously serve Jewry as pliant tools. Thus the "Synagogue of Satan" maintains its rule over two great powers. With Communism the Jews apply similar methods. There are secret Jewish priests in the clergy of the Catholic Church. In the Protestant and orthodox churches, which have joined the Communist parties, they attempt to lead Christians astray and to convince them that Communism is not all too bad and that alliances could be made with it. It is the task of these Jews to lull the free world to sleep, so that it neglects its defence and to weaken the anti-Communist resistance of the peoples, whose shepherds these priests wish to be, in order to introduce the final triumph of Jewish Communism. The tactics applied at the time of the Albigensians in this respect are today essentially the same. The higher the "Fifth Column" rises in the hierarchy of the clergy, all the greater harm can it cause Christianity in every respect. Also among the members of the present day existing Jewish-Christian brotherhoods we find hypocritical and seemingly devout clergy of the "Fifth Column" who through their membership of these organisations deceive and entice many good-willed personages of the Church. Since they do not know the secret aims of these brotherhoods — which make the Christian members into satellites of Jewry — they join themselves to these. As a result, the believers are naturally led still more astray and these organisations can capture them more easily and then make use of their activity to serve the "Synagogue of Satan" and to oppress the patriots who defend the Church and the peoples threatened by Jewish imperialism.

CHAPTER THIRTY

THE JEWS AS MOST DANGEROUS ENEMIES OF THE CHURCH. THE WALDENSES

Then in the 12th century Jewry attempted to gain control of the Papacy with help of the Jewish cardinal Pierleoni, and the sect of the Albigensians also prepared in secret the greatest revolution of the time. Through this Christianity was to be destroyed, and simultaneously in secret other sects were founded, which wished to master all Europe, abolish the existing order and destroy Holy Church. Jewry thus restricted itself not only to organising one sect, one revolutionary movement, but caused secretly several, differing from one another, to arise. The ideologies and principles were different and suited to satisfy the taste of all. If one did not agree with the programme, the dogmas or the confessions of faith of one sect, then perhaps the others would convince him. And if one sect failed, another would triumph.

At all events they supported each other mutually in secret, even if also following apparently opposing and. incompatible programmes. Thus Jewry began to apply another of its tactics: not to trust to the victory of one single organisation, but to found many organisations with different and even contrasting ideologies, which did justice to the most diverse wishes and opinions. The Jews do the same today. They found Christian-democratic parties, extreme Right parties — without the name playing a role —, Centre parties, socialist, anarchistic and Communist parties, as well as Freemasonic, Theosophical and Spiritualist organisations, Rotary Clubs, Boy Scouts Organizations and many others. It would require too much space to mention all those which — as well-known writers have proved — are controlled by international Jewry. Thus the Synagogue can control men of the most different tendencies and ideologies, watch over Christian and gentile peoples and drive onward their plans for world rule.

Before we investigate other heretical sects which participated together with the Albigensians in this great Jewish revolution in the 12th century and which nearly conquered Europe and destroyed Holy Church, we will quote highly regarded Jewish sources, which provide us with details about the role which the Jews played in the heresies of that time.

The Jewish-Spanish Encyclopaedia mentions the attitude of the Church to the mediaeval heresies and confirms the assertions of priests and writers of most different epochs, who made the assurance that "the Jews were the fathers of the heresies." Then it is stated expressly:

"In the same way as the Inquisition, it accused the Jews of having instigated the mediaeval heresies, and all heterodox movements were for the Church the result of a Jewish conspiracy, and the instigators and leaders Jews."[444] It is clear that neither Holy Church nor the Inquisition lied. In addition they had sufficient proofs to base their assertions upon.

The rabbi Lewis Browne writes in addition in his interesting "History of the Jews," in a chapter with the title "The Disunion of the Church" and the subtitle "The Help of the Jews in the Protestant Reformation": "It is more than only a thorn. Since the Synagogue was represented in all Christian lands, it had the effect everywhere like a network of small swords, which injured the self-satisfaction of the Church. This explains the fact that the Church allowed the Jews no pause to rest. It was her most dangerous foe, since everywhere it wandered, it promoted heresies."[445] This learned Rabbi expresses not only completely openly the greatest of all truths, by his describing the Jews as the worst enemies of the Church, but also gives us the solution to what was for many a great mystery, i.e. the rapid spreading of the mediaeval heresies, later of freemasonry and finally of Marxist Communism, over the individual lands. Since there have been Jewish organisations all over the world for many centuries, which have the effect of "a network of small swords," being represented in all lands through influential personalities and having everywhere a great financial power, it is naturally an easy thing for them to spread with astonishing rapidity every revolutionary, public and secret movement or every other kind of connection and to provide it with international regard. Only an institution like the synagogue, which has been rooted for centuries in all parts bf the world, could provide so many perverse movements rapidly with an international character. As a result it has attempted and still attempts through its favourite weapon, deceit, to rule the peoples and to make freedom impossible. In connection with another of the great

---

[444] Jewish-Spanish Encyclopaedia, same edition. Vol. III, word £Christianity."
[445] Rabbi Lewis Browne: The Story of the Jews, Jonathan Cape Limited. London 1926. Chapter XXIX. Page 207.

heretical movements, which in the 12th century, threatened to tear down the existing social, political and religious order, we will once again quote very highly respected Jewish sources.

Rabbi Jacob S. Raisin writes about the Waldenses: "Another heterodox group went back to Waldo, a rich merchant from Lyons. He diligently studied the Bible and commissioned two priests to translate it into French. The rich young man had the wish to set the counsels of Jesus into deeds and divided his wealth among the poor and also among those from whom he had acquired it, and praised poverty (1175). Many men of the city followed his example, and the poor of Lyons — under this name the Waldenses were known — were imitated not only in North France, but also in Spain and Italy."[446] The motto of this sect could thus not be more attractive, especially for the poor population strata, who as always were in a majority. The appearance of holiness and purity, with which its leaders surrounded themselves, was extraordinarily captivating. All this caused the revolutionary power of the movement to become enormously great. It is understandable that, with such a pure, clean and, for the lower classes, so beneficial exterior, great masses of believers were captured. However, later the poison made itself perceptible. The same rabbi writes:

"For these devoted pupils of the Ebionites the Roman Church was 'the scarlet woman' of the Apocalypse, and its idolatry (revering of Holy Images) was the same as the cult which they had displaced."[447] Up to then, however, everything alluded to a movement of unblemished purity, which was led by men who divided their wealth, followed exactly the rules for perfection of our Lord Jesus, and fought against the immorality of the clergy, for which reason they — as they pretended - compared the Church with the "scarlet woman" of the Apocalypse. It is natural that great masses allowed themselves to be deceived by this appearance and joined the heresy.

On the other hand, their doctrines departed less from the orthodox than that of the Cathars and Albigensians who were Gnostics and Manicheans, and would therefore be more easily accepted by the masses. Who would even suspect that behind so much beauty was also concealed a renewed dark attempt on the part of the Jews to control Christian society?

---

[446] Rabbi Jakob S. Raisin: Gentile Reactions to Jewish Ideals. Same edition. Chapter XVn. Page 455.

[447] Rabbi Jakob S. Raisin: GentUes Reactions to Jewish Ideals Same edition. Chapter XVN. Page 455.

We quote once more the "Jewish-Spanish Encyclopaedia," that official work of Jewry, in which the later course of this apparently purely humanitarian movement of the Waldenses is described: "The Waldenses, a sect which arose in 1170 in Lyons under the leadership of Peter Waldo, represent that aspect of the Jewish movement which also later the protestants Huss, Münzer, Zwingli and other reformers of later centuries made use of. This heresy took on a considerable extent and stretched from Lyons and Provence up to Lorraine and south Belgium in the North and Hungary and Moravia in the East. It is certainly not by chance that it arose in Lyons, as also the sect of the Passagii in Milan, since the two cities were great centres of Jewish life and influence. The Waldenses' Bible, which is preserved in some copies (MS Cambridge, 14th century, and Grenoble) contains no less than 32 Jewish books. It was read at the secret gatherings under the direction of the preachers or ancients (one assumes that this word originates from the Hebrew). The Waldenses also held themselves to be the 'real Israel', or, as their leader Muston expressed it, 'Israel of the Alps'. Comba and Muston spoke of Exodus and the scattering of the faithful. Peter Waldo is the 'Moses of this little people which migrated from the land of slavery' and 'the father, the Abraham of Israel of the Alps, before he became Moses.' The Ancients of the Waldenses sent missionaries to Italy 'in order to call for repentance and to feed the lost sheep of Israel in the valleys of the Alps.' The Ancients themselves, who were well skilled in the sciences, the languages and scripture, compared themselves with the Ancients of Israel, whose communities consisted of the Israel of the Alps, and whose Levites and Judges they were."[448]

The tactic of the Jews of accusing their enemies of what they themselves do, attained its peak in the attacks of the Jewish heresy of the Waldenses against the absolute anti-Jewish tradition of Holy Church. As the rabbi Louis Israel Newman assures us, it was asserted that "the tradition of Holy Church was the tradition of the Pharisees." This reproach is frequently made by heretics. The Waldenses of Lombardy asserted that their separation from the Roman Church was justified, for it was no longer the Church of Jesus Christ but was ruled by scribes and Pharisees."[449]

Later on Page 236 and 237 of the work mentioned, the rabbi, in connection with the personal relation between Jews and Waldenses, states that "cities, as for example Lyons and Metz in which the Jews were

---

[448] Jewish-Spanish Encyclopaedia, same edition, Vol. III. Word "Christianity".
[449] Rabbi Louis Israel Newman: Jewish Influence on Christian Reform Movements, same edition. Page 229.

powerful and influential, were also important centres of the Waldensian heresy." And he asserts: "Not only during the 12th and 13th century did the Jews and Waldenses join together." On Page 238 of the work quoted it is finally stated:

"It is not only evident that a personal relationship existed between the Jews in Provence and the Waldenses in the 13th century, but in the 15th century also the Hussites were frequently in contact with the Jews, and the Hussites and Waldenses were directly and indirectly connected with one another. During the 16th century, before and after the Reformation, the personal relations between Jews and Waldenses became strong. . . And as late as the 19th century we find the Waldenses and Jews associated, not in intellectual relations, but in governmental ones. Thus, on 13th September 1849, in Italy, a ministerial committee was founded which was to regulate anew the special government of Waldenses and Jews."[450]

In conclusion we will quote an interesting revelation of the Jewish historian Gerson Wolf. The latter asserts that the Jews in the 15th century were accused of having conspired together with the Hussites and Waldenses against the then government.[451] This Jew was prosecuted by the Austrian government on account of his book "Democracy and Socialism", which reveals revolutionary tendencies.

One finds valuable details concerning the said Jewish conspiracy in a report which is contained in the Protocols of the Theological Faculty in Vienna, and in fact in the Protocol of the 10th January 1419. Those who are interested in investigating still further this Jewish-Hussite-Waldense conspiracy in the 15th century, which wished to abolish the existing order, can refer to the original mentioned.[452]

---

[450] Rabbi Louis Newman, same work, same edition. Pages 236-238.
[451] Gerson Wolf: Studien zur Jubelfeier der Wiener Universitat, Ed. Vienna. 1865. Pages 22-23.
[452] Protokolle del Fakultat fur Theologie der Universitat Wien, MS "Protokoll vom 10 Jan. 1914."

MAURICE PINAY

CHAPTER THIRTY-ONE

THE GREAT POPE GREGORY VII
(HILDEBRAND) DESTROYS A JEWISH
THEOCRACY IN NORTH ITALY

A nother movement provoked by the members of the "Fifth Column" in Christianity was that of the Passagii, the Sabbatarians or the circumcised. These sects naturally made the greatest progress in North Italy and South France, i.e. in the regions of Europe, where the Synagogue was then particularly strongly represented. These sects can be regarded as the left wing of the manifold revolutionary movements of the secret Jews in the 12th century against Christianity.

In order that the reader can form an idea of this revolutionary movement, we will take over word for word in the following interesting passages from the already mentioned "Jewish-Spanish Encyclopaedia": "The Sects of the Passagii, of the Sabbatarians or circumcised, arose in Lombardy, where Jew-friendly erroneous beliefs had always found favourable ground. Approximately between the years 884 and 1058 there ruled over Milan and neighbourhood a theocracy founded by Angilberto de Pusterla and Jose de Ivres, which held faithfully to the Old Testament. Its sanctuary in Caroccio received the Bundeslade. The people was ruled by captains (judges) and Levites (priests), and its entire political and spiritual life bore the imprint of the Old Testament, as later with the Baptists and the Puritan communities in Europe and the New World. This theocracy was at once overthrown after Gregory VII became Pope. The Jews in Lombardy occupied a leading position in it. The Pierleoni family, who provided the Pope Anacletus II (1130-1138) and from which one queen, the wife of Roger II of Sicily came, has made itself a name in history. The Jewish influence in Lombardy was so great that in many cities Christians honoured the Sabbath (Saturday) instead of Sunday, and even the Cathars in this region accepted parts of the Old Testament in contrast to the Provencals. Arianism had left behind deep traces in North Italy, and its tolerance towards the Jews favoured their position and at the same time prepared the climate for countless anti-Papal sects, among whom stood out the Jewish. Without doubt the most important, that of the Passagii, was strongly influenced by the flourishing Jewry in Lombardy."[453]

One must read this paragraph over again before one grasps its entire importance in every respect. Here we will limit ourselves to seeing in it a further proof that tolerance towards the Jews, as is admitted in the Encyclopaedia, prepared the climate for countless anti-Papal sects – as the Jews called them. This tolerance towards the deadly enemy thus signifies giving him freedom of action, so that he can destroy the Church and rule the Christian peoples.

On the other side Gregory VII, one of the most important Popes of the Church, the famous Hildebrand, has given us an example of how one should proceed against Jewish rule. When he entered the Pontificate, he at once began to fight and suppress the Jewish theocracy on Christian soil in North Italy.

Oh, if only all of us in our struggle against the Communist and atheistic forces, which are led by the same foe whom Gregory VII destroyed, would behave in the same way as this great Pope! Concerning the confession of belief of the Passagii, it is stated in the Jewish Encyclopaedia mentioned: "Their teaching prescribed the literal following of the Law of Moses, the Law of circumcision, the diet instructions, feasts, etc. However, sacrifices, in agreement with the then Rabbinical teaching, were rejected... They recognised Jesus and the New Testament, which they attempted to bring into harmony with the Old Testament, so that the latter became in time most important of all, according to the extent – it is assumed – that Jewish scholarship increased."[454]

Here the Jewish Encyclopaedia gives us a revelation which yet again confirms the development of this tactic. The movements are introduced with some demands which are suited to capture the Christians and pagans (Gentiles). Afterwards there is a gradual alteration, in the same measure as those captured are prepared to accommodate themselves to this development. Great as Jewish influence may then have been in North Italy, it was naturally nevertheless difficult to induce at the first attempt the Christians, who knew that the Apostles had lifted the Jewish Law and given preference to the New Testament, to join a sect which represented

---

[453] Jewish-Spanish Encyclopaedia, same edition, Vol. III, Word "Christianity".
[454] Jewish-Spanish Encyclopaedia, same edition, Vol. III, Word "Christianity".

the exact opposite and did not recognise the teaching of Paul and the Apostles. The more the "Jewish scholarship" of the Neophytes increased on the basis of the instruction given by the sects, the more members were prepared to be convinced of the opposite. The rescinded Law of Moses was declared as valid and the Old Testament given privilege over the New. As a result a decisive step was taken on the way to the ideological influencing of Christians through the Jews and their control through Jewish Imperialism.

But let us allow the Synagogue to speak further through its quoted monumental work: "The Passagii universally believed in general that the Jewish Law was better than the Christian and naturally rejected the dogma of the Trinity. In this sense their leader Bonacurso declared, 'They (the Passagii) say that Christ, the son of God, was not equal to the Father. Father, Son and Holy Ghost were not a single God, no single being', and Muracon asserts: 'Thus it is said, Christ was a first, pure creature, i.e. God created Christ.'"[455]

Rabbi Louis Israel Newman writes in his work "Jewish Influence on the Christian Reform Movement" about the Passagii: "The sects of the Passagii visibly represent the Jewish aspect of the heterodox movements in Christianity of the 12th and 13th century. Particularly when the Catholic Church seemed strengthened, violent protest movements began, which placed its authority in question. In the 12th century arose many sects, which in spite of all efforts to destroy them, maintained themselves."[456]

Whoever has not occupied himself thoroughly with these questions, confuses these sects of Jewish Christians and the circumcised who celebrate the Sabbath and follow the Law of Moses in all rigour, with the false Christians who are Jews in descent and practise their religion in secret. The latter are described in the terminology of the Inquisition as Jewish heretics.

However, the Papal Inquisition with its effective methods of investigation exactly laid bare the difference. Although it was known that the Passagii, Sabbatarians or circumcised were controlled by the Jews and practised a religion which stood closer to Judaism than Christianity, the Inquisition separated them clearly from the actual Jews. The archive of the Inquisition in Carcassonne (South France) supply us, among other things,

---

[455] Jewish-Spanish Encyclopaedia, same edition, Vol. III. Word "Christianity".
[456] Rabbi Louis Israel Newman: Jewish Influence on Christian Reform Movements, same edition, Page 255.

with the proof that the Holy Office was very well informed about this. The Inquisition asked the captive Jews or the false converts from Judaism, who were called "relapsed", "How does the circumcision of Christians differ from that of the Jews?" ("Quomodo circumcidunt christianos aliter quam suos? Interrogatoria ad Judaeos.")[457] Further enlightenment concerning this point is given us in a treatise about the heretics written in the 13th century, in which the appropriate differentiation is made: "Take ye to knowledge that the Jews circumcise their own sons in other manner than the grown-up Christians who confess to Jewry. With the latter they cut only a semi-circle into the upper skin, while with their own sons they cut a whole circle."[458]

As we will investigate still more thoroughly in a sequel to this work, the Jewish religion is very racially conscious, destined only for the chosen people. The new-converts at the door, i.e., the gentiles, who are converted to Judaism, are always kept remote from the real Jewish organisations and used only as satellites and common tools of the really pure-blooded Jews in lower organisations. Although they look like Jewish communities and synagogues, they are nevertheless simple mouse-traps for the incautious, who are controlled by secret pure-blooded Jews, and the naive adherents or pure Jews are radically excluded from the circles where decisions are made about the important affairs of Jewish imperialism. The pantomime Jewish organisations are watched over by pure-blooded Jews who give themselves out as new-converts or spiritual Jews, and so it appears that these organisations rule themselves. However, they do not know that they are influenced by a secret circle of pure-blooded Jews who belong to these communities, watch over them in different manner and use the new-converts simply as tools of Jewish Imperialism. They do the same with the Freemasons and Communists. They make the unwary believe that they belong to the elite which directs the affairs of the Synagogue, so that they fight with the greatest dedication for the cause.

---

[457] Archives of the Inquisition of Carcassonne, quoted by Domingo José Vaissette in his Histoire Génerale de Languedoc, Vol. VIII, Preuves de vol lii. c. 987-88.

[458] Tract. de haers. pauper. de Lugd, Anon., in Edmundo Martene, v.c. 1794.

CHAPTER THIRTY-TWO

THE JEWISH "FIFTH COLUMN" IN THE RUSSIAN ORTHODOX CHURCH

B efore Jewry took root in Russia, the Jews had become powerful in the Ukraine. Their revolutionary activity was suppressed, and the consequence of this was that many of them were apparently converted to the Christianity of the Greek- Orthodox and later to the Russian-Orthodox Church. As with Catholicism, they were also in these churches the spreaders of the heretical-revolutionary movements.

Concerning one of these revolutionary organisations which shattered the Russian church and Christianity, the "He-brew Encyclopaedia" studied by us reports the official work of Jewry. The sect was spread by the Passagii. In the Encyclopaedia it is stated literally: "The concealed Jewish nucleus of the Passagii revealed itself in the development of its doctrine with the 'Shidovstvuyushtchiye' (Judaizers) in Russia in the 15th century. This sect, whose first apostle was the Jew Shkariya of Kiev who even won over the princes and the highest clergy of Moscow, believed that Christ had still not come, and, if he came, then not as son of God, as essence, but through his good deeds like Moses and the Prophets'."[459]

As one can see, this sect first spread itself in the Catholic world and was then introduced by a Jew into the Russian- Orthodox Church. Other sects, on the other hand, such as those of the Cathars, arose apparently in the Byzantine Empire and were later spread in Christianity. How serious this crisis was, can be recognised from an assertion of the Jews in their Encyclopaedia mentioned, where it is stated that the heresy provoked by a Jew in the middle of the 15th century, i.e. approximately five hundred years ago, gained to its side the greatest part of the orthodox clergy of Moscow. Also under the word Rusia (Russia) in Volume IX of the "Jewish-Spanish Encyclopaedia" this powerful heretical movement is

---

[459] Jewish-Spanish Encyclopaedia, same edition, Vol. IX. Word "Rusia" [Russia].

mentioned, and it is asserted that the Church "attributed it directly to the influence of Jewish preachers", and other sources see a connection between it with the sects of the Sabbatarians which were very widespread in south and east Europe during the time of the Reformation, and concerning which the Jewish Encyclopaedia affirms that they had "unquestionable nexuses with Judaism". Accordingly this monumental work of the Synagogue quotes the opinion of Dubnovs: "At the same time there arose in Moscow, as result of secret Jewish propaganda, a religious movement, which is described as Jewish heresy. According to Russian chronicles, its founder was the learned Jew Sjaria (Zejarya), who, together with several fellow believers, emigrated from Kiev to the old Russian city of Novgorod. During the religious unrest then prevailing in Novgorod, the new sect of the Strigolniki (named after their founder Carp Strigolnik) had come into existence in this city, who announced the lifting of the Christian rites and did not recognise Christ as God. Zejarya approached various representatives of the orthodox clergy and was able to convert them to Judaism. The leaders of the rebels of Novgorod, the priests Denis and Alexei, went in 1490 to Moscow and there converted a great number of Greek-Orthodox believers. Some of them even had themselves circumcised. The Jewish heresy soon took firm root among the Moscow nobility and in court circles. To their adherents belonged also Helene, the daughter- in-law of the Grand Prince.

"The Bishop of Novgorod Henadio declared the spreading of the Jewish sects to be dangerous and made courageous efforts to root them out in his diocese. In Moscow the struggle against the new doctrine was exceedingly difficult. However, there also it succeeded in finally blocking their further progress thanks to the vigorous efforts of Henadio and other righteous stalwarts. Upon decision of the Church Council of 1504, and upon command of Ivan III, the chief rebels were burned alive and their supporters taken prisoner or concealed in monasteries. Through these measures the Jewish heresy was destroyed."

And the quoted Jewish Encyclopaedia closes with the following interesting commentary: "However, the Jewish tendencies did not completely die out in the Russian people and occasionally made themselves perceptible centuries later in a way and manner which disturbed the imperial government."[460]

The Jewish "Fifth Column" in the Russian-Orthodox Church later gained in strength through the following mock conversions of the Jews to

---

[460] Jewish-Spanish Encyclopaedia, same edition, Vol. IX. Word, "Rusia".

Christianity. In the 17th century apparently many Jews were converted to Christianity and pretended to be good Christians. But in their innermost heart they remained secret Jews and hated the Russian tradition. These secret Jews were known in Jewish circles by the name Shobatnik. Several studies were made of them. Chachem Joseph Israel Benjamin, the famed Jewish leader, compiled, for example, the historic data about the Shobatnik and published it in Tiemsan, Algeria, under the title "Four Years War of the Poles against the Russians and Tartars, 1648-1652." The Czar Nicholas 1 attempted to solve the Jewish problem, but made the tragic error of compelling the Jews to be converted to Christianity. The catastrophic result was an enormous number of mock-conversions. The Jews displayed in public a dishonest Christianity, while in secret they were as Jewish as before and had their sons ordained as priests, infiltrating them into the hierarchy of the Orthodox clergy, just as their crypto-Jewish brothers had done in the Catholic and Protestant clergy.

One must, however, recognise that the Czars, the Orthodox Church and the Russian people in equal degree violently opposed the Jews penetrating into Russia. Although the latter at first came in great masses, especially at the time when Russia conquered a great part of Poland, the Orthodox Church, the state and the people continued to fight heroically against the Jewish communities, which became as numerous as no others in the world. With the aid of international Jewry the Jews were finally successful in triumphing at first in the March revolution of 1917 and later in the Bolshevist October revolution. The help of the Jewish "Fifth Column" in the Russian Orthodox Church was thereby decisive. It would otherwise have been impossible for such a weak Communist party, which in a land with a total population of a hundred million inhabitants had only a few thousand supporters, to triumph so easily and quickly. It triumphed because the members of the Jewish "Fifth Column" possessed the key positions of the parties of the Right, of the Centre and of the extreme Left, sabotaged the defence of traditional Russia and with evil-willed intrigues destroyed and brought into discredit those who could have saved the country. At the decisive moment the Jew Kerensky and his accomplices handed over power to a band of Jewish criminals, who tyrannised the Russian people from then onwards.

As soon as the Jewish band under Lenin imposed their bloody dictatorship in Russia, it had archbishops, bishops, priests and clergy of all ranks who held firm to their faith, murdered and replaced them with Jews in the Soutane, as intellectuals who have fled from the lands ruled by the beast have informed the free world. These Jewish Communists in priestly garb (in the sequel to this work we will prove, that they do in fact exist) snatched to themselves the patriarchate and the Bishoprics of the heroic old Russian-Orthodox Church. Although the latter favoured the schism of Constantinople to the harm of our Catholics, it must nevertheless be recognised that it fought bitterly to preserve the nation from falling into the hands of the "Synagogue of Satan". As the exiled bishops of the real orthodox Church of the "Free World" have informed us, today both the Patriarch of Moscow as also the remaining clergy are Communist agents in priestly robes, who use their holy office in order to carry on Bolshevist propaganda, in order in various ways and means to make easier the triumph of Communism. They wished to weaken the defence of the free world and to deceive it with the myth that Communism does not persecute the Church and that a peaceful coexistence is possible with atheistic Marxism. As we already know, with this coexistence only the intention is followed, of causing the Holy Catholic Church to conclude an alliance with the anti-Christ, in order to demoralise the activity of the Russian exiles and the patriots in Poland, Hungary, Rumania, Yugoslavia and the other tyrannised lands and to nullify the efforts of those who fight persistently and tenaciously to free their states from the bloody criminal yoke of the Jewish Marxists. This pact with the Devil would finally also demoralise the Christians in the U.S.A. who, in spite of high taxes, make great sacrifices in order to finance the defence of the free world.

The American people, which is already weakened through the treachery of many rulers, would be completely demoralised if it noticed that Holy Church threw its sheep into the gullet of the wolf and concluded a league with the Devil.

This is the plan for the next Ecumenical Council. As we have experienced, they will then make use of the Communists in the Soutane, who have illegally appropriated the offices in the Russian-Orthodox Church, as well as of the World Church Council, which controls a great part of the Protestant Churches. Protestant patriots of the USA have repeatedly accused the World Council of Churches in the press of treachery against Protestantism, the U.S.A. and the Free World, for its policy was clearly directed to a pact with the Kremlin and the betrayal of the Free World. However, we are convinced that God will allow His Holy Church to continue to exist and will once again cause the rancours of the dragon of Hell and its synagogue to fail. At the Council a new Athanasius, Ambrose, John Chrysostom or St. Bernard will appear and at a critical moment cause the failure of the dark plans of Jewish Communism and its "Fifth Column" in the clergy, even if they believe they already have the Council under their control and break out into a cry of jubilation. They claim to be able to cause the Council to approve reforms which would finally ruin the Church and would allow international Communism to triumph.

Among other things, they wish to attain that the ban against Communism is lifted and peaceful coexistence with the anti-Christ is approved. The Jewish bands of the Kremlin and their clergy of the "Fifth Column" wish that the Soviet authorities should suddenly liberate bishops and priests imprisoned for years, in order to then lead them in triumphant procession through Rome. Exaggerated good-will letters to the Pope and the Holy Council from the side of the Communist authorities and other proofs of friendship shatter the resolution of the Fathers of the Council to continue to fight against Communism and are intended to cause them to approve the policy of peaceful coexistence, which Jewry and its satellites wish to force upon the higher clergy of the Church. The Communists know how to negotiate and in exchange for a few gestures, which shows good will, to obtain in exchange the destruction of the Church defence against Marxism and to attain that a peaceful coexistence is made possible, which shall only occasion Holy Church to no longer fight against atheistic Communism, so that the latter can more easily rule the world. For relatively insignificant concessions they wish to attain essential advantages, which secure to them the victory over the free world. Why do they not abolish the atheistic materialism of Communism if they really wish to conclude peace with Holy Church? Why do they not release the Catholic Poles and Czechoslovakia from slavery, withdraw Soviet troops from these lands and allow free elections? Why do they not do the same with the remaining Christian nations which they have subjected? Why do they not abandon the anti-Christian and anti-religious propaganda which takes their faith from the true Christians? But they wish that the hands and feet of the Church are bound in practice and that the "Red Beast" is able to gradually consume the whole world. In exchange they make a few gestures which show apparent good will but stand in no relation to the concessions which they demand. A learned Rumanian academician, who fled to the west from the Communist tyranny, gives us a valuable report about the present position of the Russian-Orthodox Church, which we reproduce below.

"Among the thousands of priests whom the Jews have murdered in Russia are:

The Archbishop Veniamin of Petrograd
The Bishop Pantelimon of Polosky
The Bishop Nokodim of Bielgorodsky
The Archbishop Grigory of Katharinenburg
The Archbishop Tihon of Voronej

The Archbishop Vladimir of Kiev
The Bishop Mitrofanis from the province of Arkanghelsk
The Archbishop Vasily from Chernikovsky
The Bishop Makarie Orlovsky of the Russian Bishopric in the North
The Archbishop Andronik of Perm
The Bishop Amborzie of Viatka
The Bishop Ermoghene of Tobolsk
The Bishop Grigorie of Novgorod
The Vicar Isidor of Novgorod
The Bishop Pimin of Turkestan
The Bishop Efrem of Vladivostok
The Bishop Laurentius of Nijinovgorod."

In the same way as the Churches, all monasteries, seminaries and printing works of the Church were closed. The entire Church organisation was destroyed and every Christian cult forbidden. Religion (naturally not the Jewish) was regarded by the Jews, as Lenin had said, as the "Opium of the People". After everything had been destroyed and many millions of Christians were murdered, "the tyrants of Communist Russia considered it convenient to again seemingly reintroduce freedom of religion, in order to deceive the still free Christian peoples and to diminish the hostility of Christians towards the Communist regime.

The murderers of the Kremlin (continues the Rumanian Traian Romanescu in his report) found among themselves a capable man, who could play the role of "Patriarch of Moscow," and provide the impression that the Russian-Orthodox Church again created "Patriarchs". But the latter is no Christian. "The Patriarch Alexei is in reality called Rubin. He is a Jew from Odessa in the Ukraine, and his family there owned a transit house in the harbour before the revolution. The present Russian-Orthodox Church is only a secret tool of the Communist regime and its representatives abroad, just as the Russian-Orthodox Bishops in North America, Paris and Jerusalem are members of the Soviet secret service and are just as dangerous as the Soviet spies who come to the West as diplomats."[461]

This representation of facts, which we have taken from the work "The Great Jewish Conspiracy" of the Rumanian academician Traian Romanescu, brings before our eyes how the Jews at first murdered the true Christian Bishops in masses, in order then to hand over manu militari the direction of the Russian-Orthodox Church to the "Jewish Fifth Column."

---

[461] Traian Romanescu: The Great Jewish Conspiracy, same edition, Pages 222 and 223.

It is thus not remarkable that the members of the "Fifth Column" in the Catholic clergy can easily come to an agreement with their secret Jewish brothers in the Orthodox clergy. The scandalous events which await us in the next few months can only surprise those who do not know what goes on behind the scenes, to use the aptly chosen words of Benjamin Disraeli.

CHAPTER THIRTY-THREE

THE JEWS SPREAD THE CULT OF SATAN

Adolf Jakob Franck, a Jewish leader of the past [19th] century, writes in his interesting work about the "Cabbala" in connection with Jewish demonolatry (worship of demons): "If in Judaism traces of dark superstition are present, then one must above all seek the cause of the terror which it inspires through its devil worship."[462]

The confession that there has existed a Devil worship in Judaism is therefore so valuable, because it comes from an important leader of the synagogue who was no less than Vice-president of the Israelite Church council in Paris, the highest Jewish authority in France, collaborator in the "Israelite Archives" and assistant director of the Imperial library at the time of Napoleon III.

The Jews spread the Lucifer cult at first in various Gnostic sects and later through the secret Luciferian and Satanic sects and chiefly through the devilish magic which is universally known as Black Magic. Their doctrines go back to the Jewish Cabbala, and their chief diffusers were at all times the Jews. The most perverse phenomenon of this magic is the adoration of the Devil. It must be made clear that some circles of Jewish Cabbalists with their secret gatherings have really honestly worshipped Satan. Without doubt, however, most Jews who spread Satanism have not held this terrible superstition to be true and have only used it as an effective means to disrupt Christian society and prepare its destruction by their declaring evil to be good and conversely.

The Jews in an unexampled infamous way and manner made use of the motto: "The end justifies the means." How better in the Middle Ages could they have been able to demoralise Christian society than to cause it to worship Satan and to despise God? As one sees, the wickedness of the

---

[462] Adolf Jacob Franck: La Kabbale en la Philosophie religieuse des Hebreux, Page 151.

Jews knows no bounds. Not in vain did Our Lord Jesus call them "Sons of the Devil" and described the synagogues as "Synagogues of Satan."

Satanism was another "octopus arm" of that great Jewish revolution in the 12th century, which in many respects was so terrible or even more terrible than that of modern time.

The English writer Nesta H. Webster writes: "Towards the end of the twelfth century Luciferianism spread eastwards through Styria, the Tyrol, and Bohemia, even as far as Brandenburg; by the beginning of the thirteenth century it had invaded western Germany." In addition this writer asserts that it spread out as far as Italy and France.[463]

It must be pointed out that, at the time of the crusades and afterwards, thousands of Jews in Germany and Central Europe were apparently converted to Christianity and in these lands took on usual family names. As a result, they joined themselves to Christian society and strengthened the Jewish "Fifth Column".

Upon this invasion of false converts followed as usual the spreading of heresies and revolutionary movements, among which Satanism played an important role.

In Bohemia the false converts had flooded over the Church and this land, like South France and North Italy, became a veritable centre of heretics. Later the same occurred there as today in Switzerland, which became the cradle of the Jewish Protestantism of Calvin and Zwingli, which differed from the nationalistic and in many cases anti-Semitic Protestantism of Martin Luther.

Eliphas Levi describes the conjuration ceremonies of Hell, pointing out that those present "must unconditionally dishonour the ceremonies of their religion and debase the most holy symbols. This method attains its high point in the polluting of the Holy Sacrament. The secret host was fed to mice, pigs and toads, and disgraced in an indescribable way and manner."[464]

In the course of centuries there have again and again been scandals when it became known that Jews or converts or even Christian clergy, who

---

[463] Nesta H. Webster: Secret Societies and Subversive Movements, same edition, Chapter IV, Page 76.
[464] Arthur E. Waite: The Mysteries of Magic, Page 215.

were secret Jews, used hosts (Hostien) to commit terrible pollutions at their secret gatherings. Through magic the Jews, in their great hatred towards Christ, were successful in inducing many Christians infected by the teachings of the Satanists to do the same.

Nesta H. Webster, quoting Deschamps, writes: "That science of demoniacal arts, of which the Jews were the initiators" and in which cannot be ignored the Jewish 'Cabbalists' in some form or other in any comprehensive analysis of the situation.[465]

Eliphas Levi, an authority whom no one can accuse of anti-Semitism, asserts: "The Jews who believed most of all in the secrets of the 'Cabbala' were in the Middle Ages almost exclusively the grand masters of magic."[466]

Another personality whom one cannot accuse of making common cause with the Catholic Church is Voltaire. He accused the Jews of spreading Black Magic and in his work "Henriade" describes a revolting ceremony, in which the devilish name is named together with the name of the Eternal in the same breath: "The priest of this temple is one of those Jews who were respected as world citizens..." etc. And in a footnote to this splendid sentence he adds: "It was universally customary that the Jews gave themselves up to magical actions. This old superstition goes back to the secrets of the 'Cabbala,' whose sole preserver the Jews regard themselves."[467]

Nesta H. Webster closes after a calm thorough study: "Demonology in Europe was in fact essentially a Jewish science."[468]

Monsignore Meurin, the archbishop and bishop of Port Louis quotes Leo Taxil and the Cabbalist handbook of Brother Constant, 30th Grade of Freemasonry, and writes: "'This report confirms the opinion of almost all authors who have dealt with this devilish magic, that all branches and practices of sorcery have their origin in the Jewish Cabbala."[469]

Since the Jews were without doubt the founder and secret leaders of Freemasonry, they also introduced into some freemasonic organisations

[465] Nesta H. Webster, same work, same edition.
[466] Eliphas Levi. Dogme et Rituel de la Haute Magie, 1961, Chapter IV, Page 78. Vol. II, Page 220.
[467] Voltaire: Henriade.
[468] Nesta H. Webster, same work, Chapter IV. Page 80.
[469] Mons. Leon Meurin, S.J. Archbishop, Bishop of Port Louis: Philosophy of Freemasonry, same edition, Page 230.

the cult of Lucifer. This is proved by Leo Taxil, who has employed himself thoroughly within this material. Concerning the 20th Grade (degree) of certain rites he writes: "The Prince of the Tabernacle is now prepared for the freemasonic revelation, for in the 20th degree of the Grand Patriarch he has worshipped a glittering star on a golden cloud, which was described to him as morning star or also as Lucifer, and hears the summons of the President: 'Be like the morning star, who announces the day; bring the world light, in the holy name of Lucifer, dispel the darkness'."[470] Concerning the purpose which the Jews follow with this reversal of values, the renowned, learned Jesuit, Archbishop and Bishop of Port Louis writes the following: "As our readers know, the Jewish Cabbalists have reversed the value of words, in order to turn away their followers from the truth. Thus, for example, God signifies Satan and Satan God. Good is Evil. Virtue is vice and vice is virtue. Truth is lies and lies are truth. Light is darkness and darkness light. Revelation is obscurantism and obscurantism is revelation. Religion is superstition and superstition religion."[471]

---

[470] Leo Taxil: Les Fréres Trois Points, II. Page 126.
[471] Archbishop, Bishop of Port Louis, Mons. Leon Meurin. S. J. Philosophy of Freemasonry, same edition, Page 232.

CHAPTER THIRTY-FOUR

THE CHURCH AND THE CHRISTIAN STATES BUILD UP THEIR DEFENCE AGAINST THE GREAT JEWISH REVOLUTION OF THE MIDDLE AGES

In the face of the revolutionary activity of this network of secret societies led by Jewry, which endangered Holy Church, the Christian states and the whole existing order of that time was threatened and set about building up an effective defence. Several Popes were effective one after the other in this task, and especially the great Innocent III, Domingo de Guzman, Francis of Assisi, the 3rd and 4th Ecumenical Lateran Councils and other provincial synods distinguished themselves.

The most astounding thing about the matter is that, in the organisation of this effective defence, a free-thinker, an unbeliever and bitter enemy of Pope Innocent III participated, since he realised that Europe was close to falling into the bloody claws of the Jews and their heresies. We are speaking of the German Emperor Frederick II, who on the one side fought against the Papacy, but on the other side was so spiritually with his time and far-sighted and correctly evaluated the great deadly danger which hung over the European nations. Frederick II was perhaps more concerned to save his people than the Church, but fortunately he was conscious of this deadly threat and did not disturb the work of defence, but supported it energetically and successfully. May all German patriots, who today fight against the beast, follow his example, and even if there are also unbelievers among them, may they not nevertheless strike out on the false disgraceful path of the Nazis and turn against the Christians. The edicts of Emperor Frederick formed to a great extent the foundations for the Inquisition court and were later recognised by the Popes. The decisive intervention of this unbelieving enemy of the Papacy proves to us that not only was the Church threatened but Europe itself, and that the Inquisition court was indispensable for preserving Europe from falling under the rule of Jewish Imperialism. Our present situation is just as serious as in the 12th century, even more dangerous if one reflects that today neither the hierarchy of the Church nor the civil rulers pay heed to the danger and arm for defence, as if they wore a bandage before their eyes, or as if a similar crisis like that occasioned by the Jewish Cardinal Pierleoni was played out in the high hierarchy, which apparently is much undermined by the "Fifth Column", which resolutely with all means scatters sand in the eyes of those who could save the Church and Christianity.

Before we investigate the defensive measures adopted against Jewry and its heresies in the Bulls of various Popes and in the 3rd and 4th Ecumenical Lateran Councils, we will in this chapter briefly summarise these measures.

Since the Jews sought with all means to destroy Europe and did not allow the smallest opportunity to escape them in order to conquer and subjugate the Christian peoples, measures were naturally seized upon to prevent these aliens and traitors from causing further harm.

The most important thing was to prevent their close connection with the Christians, for only thus could they deceive them and infect them with decomposing doctrines. For this purpose the laws of the Holy Church Councils were to be strictly followed, which had already arranged this division over centuries. These laws were in fact in force, but in several regions had fallen into oblivion, and it sufficed to summon the civil and religious authorities to observe them. Later new laws were passed by the Ecumenical Councils, which declared universally authorised and obligatory the prescription that the Jews should wear a sign on their clothing, so that the Christians could recognise them and protect themselves from deception and deceit. If a Jew who wore the sign attempted to preach a heresy or the overthrow of the social order, no one listened to him, for they knew that they were dealing with a deceitful Jew, about whose falsity the faithful were constantly warned from the pulpit. The clergy were reminded through the ritual and the liturgy, where there were repeated references to Jewish falsehood. Among this fell the entire revolutionary heretical activity, the infiltration into the clergy of the Church and completely generally the wickednesses which distinguished the actions of the Hebrews in Christian society. Accordingly for defence the obligatory Ghetto was erected and the Jews compelled to dwell in a fixed part of the city. They were forbidden to live with the Christians and to pervert them with their destructive doctrines and intrigues. For the same reason they were excluded from the craftsmen's guilds, the rising universities and fundamental institutions of Christian society, which were thus freed from their domination. As a result, the Jews were prevented from abusing to bring to a successful conclusion their frequent conspiracies against Holy Church and against the unfortunate peoples who had opened their frontiers to them and had bade them hearty welcome.

Put briefly, the Church and its shepherds set themselves to fulfil their duty and to preserve their sheep from the cunning wolf, just as Christ commanded. At the present time, the "Fifth Column" in the supreme hierarchy of the clergy wishes to attain that at the current Vatican Council II certain reforms - which it represents as apparent improvements — are approved, which are intended to deliver the sheep to the wolf. For in secret they wish to make easier the victory of Communism and prevent the peoples from defending themselves against the imperialism of the Jews and their perverse conspiracies. They attempt to achieve that vague theses about uniting of the peoples or churches are set up by the Council, which later Communism, Jewry and its accomplices and agents in the Catholic clergy can misuse. While Holy Church and the Christian states undertook the former mentioned measures in order to make impossible the revolutionary activity of the public Jews or nevertheless at least to make it difficult, their attention was also especially directed at the problem of the secret Jews (Jewish heretics) and their revolutionary movements (various heresies).

Since the secret Jews appeared in public as honest Christians, lived outwardly as devout Catholics and even joined themselves to the clergy, in the course of centuries their Jewish origin had fallen into oblivion, and it was therefore very difficult to discover it. Since they were represented in all realms of religious, political and social life, they were far more dangerous than the Jews who publicly admitted to their religion. On the other side, the heretical sects also founded by them were just as secret as their Judaism, for the heretics lived outwardly like Catholics. Their organisations and gatherings were strictly secret. Like their concealed leaders, the secret Jews everywhere undermined Christian society, without the Church or the state being able to prevent it. Only when the conspiracy was ripe and strong enough in order to carry out the decisive stroke, did the sect cause one of those bloody revolutions to break out which caused mediaeval society to shudder. If it had not been completely defeated, then the catastrophe which faces the world today would already have occurred several centuries earlier. This sore must be expunged, if the peoples wish to live in peace, the Church and Christian society to save themselves, and the nations not to fall into the hands of the Jews. Everyone understood that one could only proceed against this network of secret organisations with a likewise secret organisation, which would destroy all arms of the octopus and especially the head, clandestine Jewry. Thus the institution of the Holy Office of the Inquisition was set up.

At first the Popes left the hearings to the Bishops. Since, however, the Prelates were concerned with affairs in their dioceses and little time was left to them, they could not devote sufficient time to this task. Experience taught that the Bishops' Inquisition was ineffective, since in addition it lacked the required coordination. Secret Jewry had spread over the entire Christian world, and likewise its revolutionary heresies. The enemy represented a supranational or international — as we call it today — organisation, and it was therefore impossible to combat it with local institutions. The civil courts could on account of the reasons mentioned not attain the intended goals, for they were not in connection with the corresponding authorities in the other states. As a result it was impossible for them to carry out a general repressive action, indispensable against such a foe.

With this splitting up of Christianity into several states — some of them dumbly rivalling with one another — the Papacy was the sole connecting link, the sole super-national institution which could face such a sizable enemy. The Papal Inquisition was therefore unconditionally necessary.

At first various Bishops, instigated by the clergy of the "Fifth Column" opposed this measure. But fortunately then the "Fifth Column" was less powerful than at the time of the Pierleonis and could not prevent the setting up of the Papal Inquisition. The examining judges were delegates of the Pope and the directorship was finally taken over by a Grand Inquisitor. Thus an organisation was created which could defeat the foe. It could also have destroyed it, if upon various occasions the Jews had not utilised the natural kindness of the Popes and abused their good faith, in order to achieve general pardoning for the secret Jews and heretics. The latter later destroyed with one blow the strenuous work of the Inquisition completed over many years. The secret Jews skilfully utilised the goodness of the Popes, in order to preserve themselves from greater catastrophes and to gather strength for a new onslaught. Because it would forgive them again and again, the secret synagogue, after the Holy Papal Inquisition had preserved Europe and Christianity for three centuries from Jewish rule, was able to deliver the blow at the beginning of the 16th century which shattered Christianity and made it possible for Jewish Imperialism from then on to make greater and greater progress and finally to threaten Holy

Church and all peoples of the world with atheistic, murderous, tyrannical Communism.

As a result of that, the problem was attacked from all sides, the defence by the Inquisition was so effective for three centuries long. Experience had taught the Church that many rebels were of right faith, so that it was impossible to accuse them of heresy. However, in a strange way, in spite of their orthodoxy they provided the heretics and revolutionary movements with such valuable support that they frequently caused the Church and the Christian peoples more harm than the real heretics. In one word, these individuals worked in the ranks of the true believers together with the heretics and in favour of heresy. In our 20th century language we could say that they were a "Fifth Column" of heretical sects in the ranks of Catholicism. And still more, they bragged about their orthodoxy, in order to obtain better positions in Catholic society or in the hierarchy of the Church, which they accordingly used to carry on successful espionage for the heretics or to cause the Church injury, by their providing valuable services to the sect to which they belonged.

These individuals, who were in fact not actual heretics, but supported heresy and its adherents in some kind of form, were described in the Church Laws and by the Inquisition as "Accomplices of the heretics" or "Accomplices of the heresies." Their crime could be punished in the case of clergy with immediate deposing or imprisonment, confiscation of property or even with death, always according to the harm which they caused Christian society and the Church. Here we are not only concerned with a religious affair, for it was not a question of proving if the individual was orthodox or heterodox, but it was far more a pure political problem, for it had to be investigated whether the priest or layman had supported the heresy or the heretics in some kind of form. With this step the Church and the princes hit the sore point and began to dam up the revolutionary movements of Jewry and even to fully overthrow them, for then already the secret of Jewish successes was the activity of the "Fifth Column", i.e. the accomplices of the heresies. The later remained unconditionally orthodox and rose in the hierarchy of the Church, in order to there stand by Jewry and its heresies and simultaneously with intrigues and condemnations to eliminate the true defenders of the Church. At the end of the 12th century, Holy Church and the Christian states suppressed the "Fifth Column" in all severity and could yet again, even if also only for another three centuries, defeat its deadly enemy.

In our time, on the other hand, these accomplices of heresies — cardinals, bishops and clergy of all ranks — while they boast with their orthodoxy, contribute in different ways to the advance of the Freemasonic and Communist revolutions and betray the Church and their fatherland, without their being deposed on account of their criminal activity. Simultaneously they attack with inexplicable rage the Catholic rulers who defend their lands against Communism, Freemasonry and Jewry, or condemn and discredit the anti-Communists who try to really fight against a Red dictatorship.

This was the principal reason for the successes of the Freemasons and Communists in the Catholic world. For since these successors of Judas Iscariot were not punished, their power becomes greater and greater, and they are already threatening to gain power over the entire Church. At the time of the Papal Inquisition, they were without doubt locked up, deposed from the priestly office, and in some cases reduced to the position of laity, in order to be executed. Only if freed from the "Fifth Column" could Christianity successfully ward off all attacks of the enemy. However, the defensive work of Holy Church and the Christian states was still not at an end here. There were individuals who were neither heretics nor accomplices of the heretics, but concealed them. These simple protectors, be they clergy or laymen, were severely punished. As a result, the defence of the Church and the Christian states was enormously strengthened. For when the priestly accomplices and protectors of the heresy were deposed and energetically punished, there were fewer cases of archbishops, bishops or clergy of all ranks who supported the revolutionary heretical movements, since they knew that they would lose their positions and be severely punished. At the present day an archbishop can support unpunished Freemasonry and Communism and betray the Church, for he knows that, although he aids a bloody freemasonic or Communist revolution to victory and is therefore responsible for the subsequent murders of priests and the persecution of the Church, he will continue to occupy his comfortable Bishop's seat as if nothing has happened. We, who wish to save the Church, should reflect upon this.

THE PLOT AGAINST THE CHURCH

CHAPTER THIRTY-FIVE

AN ARCHBISHOP AND SEVEN BISHOPS ARE
ACCUSED OF WORSHIP OF LUCIFER

So that the reader can form an idea of the alarm of the people in Europe on account of the heretical movements because of the reasons previously mentioned, we will reproduce here the opinion of the anti-Catholic historian Henry Charles Lea, who was an enemy of the Inquisition. He refers to an abbot from Langres, who was accused of heresy and whom the Pope handed over to the archbishop of Sens and the bishop of Nevers for examination. Two years later he excused himself in Rome with the following words: "He had fear at the appointed time to place himself before his judges, for the people was so much against the heresies and burned not only all heretics but also all suspects. He therefore begged for the protection of the Pope and for permission to repent of his guilt in Rome. Innocent sent him back again and commanded that the prelates should provide him a letter of conduct and grant him protection until his case had been appropriately decided."[472]

These and similar facts allow it to be discerned that the demands of the Popes and princes to the people, to combat the heresies and reveal the heretics, even made difficult the harmful work of the clergy who aided these revolutionary movements, for in spite of their church offices they ran the danger of being burned alive by the mass of the people.

In this position naturally the clergy of the "Fifth Column" which had previously betrayed unpunished the Church and made easier the progress of the Jewish revolution, had to withhold their hand. Thus the "Fifth Column" had very much less opportunity to cause harm to the Church and the Christian states.

---

[472] Henry Charles Lea: A History of the Inquisition of the Middle Ages, same edition. Vol. I. Page 307.

515

For the Church, a priest, who hypocritically supports the heresies and revolutionary anti-Christian movements was and is more dangerous than a layman. For the priest has, on account of his respected position, greater possibilities to harm the Catholic cause. Therefore the Church and Civil Law made it a duty of all the faithful to immediately denounce heretics as well as accomplices of heresies, including priests of every rank.

The writer and historian, H. C. Lea, who was against the Inquisition, quotes in this respect a very revealing case: "In the year 1318 Jean de Drasic, the bishop of Prague, was summoned to Avignon by Pope John XXII, in order to answer the accusation of being an accomplice of heresy brought against him by Frederick von Schonberg, Abbot (Stiftsherr) of Visegrad. The accusation ran that the heretics were very numerous and that among them were found an archbishop and seven bishops, who each had three hundred pupils. As far as their belief is concerned, they must have been simultaneously Waldenses and Luciferians."[473]

As we see, a zealous abbot fulfilled his duty and accused at the right time that bishop of Prague, not because he was a heretic but an accomplice of heresy, i.e. because he gave himself out to be orthodox but supported the revolutionary movements. Therefore Pope John XXII, who fought against the Jews and heretics of all kinds, had the traitorous bishop arrested and sent him to Avignon, where he faced the accusation. The confirmation is also interesting, that – as also emanates from the complaint handed in by the devout abbot – there were in that region an archbishop and seven bishops who were Luciferians, i.e. who worshipped Lucifer. From this we see that the problems which Christian society had then to solve were as weighty as the present, with the sole difference that then both Holy Church and the Christian states defended themselves successfully against the enemy, while today those Communist bishops and cardinals or clergy who aid Communism and freemasonry could severely damage the Church and the peoples who believe in her and trust in her. One must recognise that Pope John XXII is worthy of all respect and all praise, for in this case, as also in others, he proceeded rapidly and energetically without discrimination against the clergy who practised treachery against Holy Church. He understood that a Luciferian bishop or accomplice of the Luciferians could cause greater harm than a simple layman. Just as today also a prelate who supports Communism can cause greater harm than a civic leader.

---

[473] Henry Charles Lea; Histoire de l'Inquisition au Moyen Age, Translation into French by Salmon Heinach, Paris 1901, Vol. III. P. 515.

Lea then clearly elaborates that the Waldenses and Luciferians had shaken hands in spite of their different ideologies, and the Luciferians hoped that Lucifer would rule one day.[474]

This strange connection of two sects with such contrasting ideologies is comparable to the present agreement between different so-called Catholic and Socialist-Marxist parties who carry on a very suspicious game. The aim is the same. Jewry has always excelled in uniting different ideologies, in order to be able to control individuals of the most opposed disposition and diverse tastes. When they proceed against the good and wish to collect forces for the victory of their revolutions, they are compelled to conclude remarkable alliances, which often become a stumbling-block for those who do not know the secrets of Jewry. The fact is that the associations of parties of different tendencies are controlled by a secret power, concealed Jewry.

Jean de Drasic, the bishop of Prague and accomplice of the heretics, appears to have been a worthy predecessor of the Archbishop Beran of Prague, the Primate of Czechoslovakia. When the Communist Gottwald carried through his coup d'état, in order to introduce the Bolshevist dictatorship in Czechoslovakia, he received — to the consternation of the clergy and the Catholics of the land — the Red Leader with a Te Deum in the cathedral. In this way, and by forbidding Christians to fight against the Communist regime, he effectively contributed to strengthening the victory of the Socialist dictatorship. Even if a great part of the Czech bishoprics were horrified at the treachery and later rose against the Archbishop and Primates, the confusion which all these events had called forth in the conscience of the Catholics led to the victory of Communism. Since then Czechoslovakia has been tyrannised by the Reds, who also murdered a great number of priests and Christians.

How can it be right that, through the mode of action of treacherous priests, the true clergy are murdered and taken captive and Holy Church is persecuted? But Beran paid for his treachery. After the Communists had made use of him, they threw him into prison. What has the "Fifth Column" in the clergy to expect from a Socialist regime, in which leaders of the Soviet revolution like Trotsky, Zinoviev, Kamenev and thousands of others were later murdered by their Jewish brothers Yagoda, Beria and Stalin? It is painful to recall the mode of action of an archbishop and primate of our days. But it is even more painful that, through the

---

[474] Henry Charles Lea, same work, French translation. Vol. II. Page 515.

Communist victory which he aided, so many faithful priests were murdered and the Church in Czechoslovakia was so infamously repressed.

Here we come back once again to the virtuous Pope John XXII. His zeal to defend the faithful against the cunning of the Devil is clearly shown in reference to Juan Muscata, the Bishop of Krakow, to whom the meritorious Pope imparted a severe reprimand, not because he was heretic or accomplice of the sectarians, but simply on account of his "indulgence and neglect, which had the effect that the heretics in his Diocese had become courageous."[475]

It is easy to understand that Christians and mankind would never, with such Popes, have stood before such a catastrophe as today. Also it would then have been avoided that so many souls were lost to the Church and so much blood was shed among the Christian peoples. It may appear strange that there were bishops and archbishops who were Luciferians or accomplices of the Luciferians, just as it also appears remarkable today that there are cardinals or bishops who are secret Communists or support atheistic Communism, even when they are themselves of right belief. What possibilities had then a man who entered very young into the priestly class, rose in the hierarchy up to archbishop or cardinal and passed his whole life in the service of Christ, to succumb to such confusions? What kind of interest could he have had then to support the cause of Luciferianism, and today to help the victory of the atheistic, priest-murdering Communism to victory? This problem was thrown up by the Christians of all times. The enemy could assert that the Luciferian errors were the truth and the Church was in error, and therefore many priests of the highest ranks supported the former. However, this is not only completely absurd, but we have already explained and proven through facts that the Jewish fanatics in the clergy in fact gave themselves out as Christians, but in the bosom of the clergy carried out the most perverse sabotage in favour of Jewish interests or their revolutionary activity. On the other hand, this is the normal activity of all "Fifth Columns" in the world. The most important among them is that of the secret Jews, because it exists already a thousand years and is represented everywhere in the world. When the Inquisition was able to successfully investigate cases of this kind, it transpired that these priests of high rank who spread the most terrible heresies or supported them, were secret Jews or in our modern language priests of the "Fifth Column" of Jewry. That is really the most logical explanation for many, astonishing and scandalous cases.

---

[475] Henry Charles Lea, Same work, French translation. Vol. II, Page 515.

We are certain that, if today there existed a court with such effective methods of examination as the Inquisition then, it would be known that many of those cardinals, archbishops, abbots, prebendaries, priests and monks are Jews, who so expressly and zealously — even if also hypocritically — aid the progress and triumph of freemasonry and of Communism or so fanatically and successfully defend the Jews, as they have never done in the case of Holy Church. It is difficult to understand that men who have devoted their whole life to the sacred calling of the priest could aid in good faith such objectionable, openly criminal movements opposed to the Christian faith and every moral norm. The most logical thing is that it is a question of a couple of those Jewish plotters who favour these movements and who belong from their youth on to the clergy as members of the "Fifth Column."

If a Jew (Pierleoni) could become cardinal and could conquer the throne of St. Peter's, then it is not remarkable that those who rise today in the hierarchy of the clergy use their office to facilitate the victory of the Jewish revolutions and to destroy the defence of the Church, just as their predecessors in the Middle Ages have done and as was proven by the Inquisition and the civil and church authorities of that time.

In fact it was more the activity of the treacherous priests than those of the aggressive heretics which compelled the Holy See to set up the effective Papal Inquisition. The Pope perceived that the heretics represented the greatest danger for the Church and the Christian peoples and especially dangerous were those who remained apparently orthodox or supported the revolutionary movements.

Henry Charles Lea, the renowned historian of the Inquisition, who bases himself upon Chronicles, Archives and contemporary documents, asserted: "It was diversely said that the Inquisition was founded on 20th April 1233, when Gregory (IX) published the Bulls and made the persecution of heretics the principal task of the Dominicans. Really the direct cause seems to have been the punishment of priests and other clergy who were accused of supporting the heretics and teaching them how they could escape examination by concealing their faith and feigning orthodoxy..."

The other Bull is directed against the abbots and monks of the "Order of the Inquisitorial preachers." Allusions are made to the damned sons who defend heresy, and then it is stated further: "Therefore shalt thou and every other who have power where they preach, if they do not upon admonishing leave off from this defence (of heretics), and rob the clergy of their privileges, proceed against them and the rest without mercy, in case of need request the lay order to aid and overcome all hindrances without consideration by means of Church censure."[476]

---

[476] Ripoll 1, 45, 47- C. 8-8. Six v. 2. - Gregorius P.P. IX, Bulls Ille humani generis, licet ad capiendos - Pothast. Nr. 9143, 9152, 9235, Archive of the Inquisition of Carcassone [Deat XX-21 and 25] quoted as Henry Charles Lea, A History of the Middle Ages, New York, Vol. I Chapter VII. Pages 328 and 329.

CHAPTER THIRTY-SIX

THE 3ᴿᴰ LATERAN COUNCIL EXCOMMUNICATES AND DEPOSES BISHOPS AND PRIESTS WHO SUPPORT HERESIES OR FAIL TO OPPOSE THEM ENERGETICALLY

The Pope had struck a sore point. A special organisation had to be created, which uncovered the traitorous activity of the seemingly orthodox clergy who in different ways and means supported the revolutionary movements, which then revealed themselves as heresies. For this he made use of a group of idealistic fighters, who were exclusively to devote themselves to the combating of the revolutions. First of all he chose the Dominican monks, to whom later the Franciscans were added.

The prelates were busy with the affairs of their Dioceses and had not enough time for this kind of activity. The same held for the secular clergy. On the other hand the idealistic monks of the Dominican and Franciscan orders, who had made a vow of poverty and zealously defended the Church and Christianity — a remarkable fact in the then clergy, which in general was apathetic and complacent as also in our time — were suited for the great struggle of the Church against the Jews and their heresies.

These monks, who had abandoned the world and riches, the Jews with their principal weapon, bribery, could not bring under control, in order to destroy the defence which the remaining peoples had built up against them over the course of centuries. The Jews were successful in buying for themselves at enormous prices favourable prescriptions from kings, nobles and respected members of the secular clergy. However, the Pope was certain that their attempts with the monks, who in addition had praised poverty, lived in communities without every luxury and were subjected to strict chastity and sacrificial discipline, would fail. The resolution of the

Holy See could not have been cleverer and more appropriate. In addition, Francis of Assisi and Santo Domingo de Guzman had founded their meritorious orders in order to preserve Holy Church from the catastrophe threatening it and had for this purpose provided it with a corresponding organisation. Admittedly there existed previously a Bishops' Inquisition and also a kind of Papal one, but Henry Charles Lea asserts correctly that the final Papal Inquisition arose through the Bulls which commissioned the beggar monks with it.

Another pressing problem related to the monks, who filled the whole day with prayers and activities which were prescribed to them by the rules of the order, and spent their whole time with these devout duties, so that they could not effectively fight against the anti-Christian forces. The Popes grasped this serious problem and allowed the Inquisitor monks to specialise in this kind of activity and to spend the necessary time on conducting the deadly struggle against the Jews and their satellites of other heresies, even if as a result the time for prayers and the rest of the duties laid down by the rules of the order became very much contracted. This skilled measure placed legions of monks directly in the service of defence of the Church. Their activity was decisive for their victory over the forces of Satan.

In addition the Pope gave the Inquisitor monks full authority, so that they could overcome the resistances, which were always enormously large, since the "Jewish Fifth Column" in the clergy did not allow itself to be overthrown without violent resistance. He also gave them the possibility of receiving support from the lay class (laity), i.e. the civil authorities, so that if necessary it could be attained with force what was not possible through persuasion. As is known, Francis of Assisi and Santo Domingo de Guzman founded their beggar orders in spite of the resistance of certain bishops and contributed effectively to perfecting this distinguished defensive-network, which preserved Holy Church and the European peoples, during the three centuries when the Popes in general maintained this condition, from being subject to Jewry.

It is, however, noteworthy that besides some suspect bishops who were against the founding of the Franciscan and Dominican orders and also later against the institution of the Holy Inquisition, the overwhelming majority of prelates — full of virtue and zeal for the defence of Christian order — furthered the origin of these institutions and welcomed them. It is only natural that the "Jewish Fifth Column" in the clergy has attempted to prevent Holy Church from building up a defence which should destroy and prevent the "Fifth Column" from causing further harm. But all lies, cunning and slander of the "Fifth Column", all their efforts and intrigues before the Popes and the Councils to prevent such a defence and to denigrate and to destroy the true defenders of Europe and Christianity, failed completely in face of the firm conduct of the well-orientated Popes Innocent III, Gregory IX, and John XXII. Hence the embittered struggle could once again end with the victory of Holy Church and the defeat of the synagogue.

In order to discern the great importance of this victory, we need only to compare the gloomy 12th century and the first years of the 13th century, which were distinguished through anarchy, bloody internal struggles, the devastating crusade against the Albigensians, dark plots and constant crimes of the secret Jews and their tools, the heretics, with the rest of the 13th century, which after the lasting victory of Catholicism passed with justice into history as the "golden era of the Church". This was possible due to the effective defensive measures which the European peoples carried out, under the leadership of the Holy See, in the struggle against the "Synagogue of Satan". If these measures had not been effected, the 13th century would have taken on the disastrous features of the gloomy 20th century, when Jewry and its present day heresies, freemasonry and especially Communism, are close at hand to strangle humanity with their claws. Also the activity of the laity was very dangerous for Holy Church and Europe. They pretended, to be unconditionally orthodox and in some cases even enemies of heresy, however stood secretly in connection with it and supported the sectarians and their revolutionary enterprises in the ranks of the orthodox, to whom they caused great harm.

The accomplices of the heretics were without doubt the forerunners of those apparently strict Catholic worldly leaders who at the present day pretend to be loyally bound to Holy Church and utilise Christian-democratic or Catholic and Right parties, to whom they give the most diverse names, in order to promote the triumph of freemasonry and Communism. They even make use of the meritorious Catholic Action, in order to carry through their most Godless activity. At that time, these kinds of traitors who committed the crime of "helping heretics", even though they passed themselves off as Catholics, were vigorously combated by Holy Church as "partisans of heresy", just like clergymen who adopted the same behaviour. The great, renowned 3rd Lateran Council, which began in 1179 in the Basilica of the same name, approved in its Law XXVI a series of measures for prevention of a close association of Christians and Jews.

It was emphatically affirmed that it was necessary to separate the Christians from the Jews, since one only allowed the latter to live among the Christian peoples "out of humanity". Not only were the heretics punished, but also the pseudo-orthodox who supported or concealed them. In Law XXVII it is stated about the heretics: "That they no longer keep their wickedness secret but publicly spread their error and influence the simple and the weak. They and their defenders and protectors are banned, and we forbid anyone to take them into his house or do business with them. Whoever takes this guilt upon himself, will be excommunicated and can receive neither under the pretence of our privileges; nor through approval or from another reason receive sacrificial gifts of a Christian burial."[477]

One thus sees that not only heretics were punished with excommunication but also all who supported or concealed them, laymen and clergy alike. This law imposed punishment for these criminals without regard to their standing or the circumstances.

The Catholic leaders, therefore, who fight in their lands to avoid being subjugated by freemasonry or Communism, are constantly betrayed. Again and again ostensibly Catholic leaders, clergy or laymen stab them in the back, men who pretend to serve the Church, but in reality promote in a hypocritical but effective way and manner the triumph of the freemasonic or Communist revolutions, or work for the dictatorships which these heretical sects could set up in many Christian states. If the anti-Communist, anti-Freemasonic and anti-Jewish leaders of Catholicism do not attack the internal enemy with the same energy and efficacy as the outer, they will finally be subjected to the "Fifth Column."

Therefore it is not only necessary to unmask the false Catholics in the press or pamphlets publicly, but an organisation must also be created which collects proofs from which is revealed that they are accomplices of Freemasonry or of Communism. Action must then be brought against them by the Church courts on account of heresy or, if their orthodoxy does not allow this, because they are accomplices of heresy, i.e. accomplices of Communism or of Freemasonry. If the trials are published in the press in a seemly way and a commission sent to Rome with the mandate of establishing the truth, the destructive activity of this "Fifth Column" in the clergy would be hampered, and as a result it will be avoided that the good are consumed by two fires: the Jewish Left and the

---

[477] Acta Conciliorum, et Epistolae Decretales, ac Constitutiones Summorum Pontificum. Studio P. Jeanni Harduini, S. J., Vol. VI, Part II.

secret Jewish Right, which supports this Left. All political parties who defend their respective nations should therefore make special efforts, if they do not wish to fall victim to the traditional technique of the pincer movement which secret Jewry has already used for a long time. It may therefore not be tolerated that one people after the other comes under the rule of the Jews and the patriots and real defenders of Christianity are cut down. The parties should have technical advisors for the Church law, for there are countless laws of different Councils and Bulls of the Popes upon which they could support their accusations against the imitators of Judas.

At the conclusion of this Canon XXVII there is in addition a terrible punishment decreed, not only against the clergy who support the heretics, but also against those who simply "do not energetically oppose them." This punishment consists in immediate dismissal from their offices, including episcopal sees when it is a matter of Prelates. In the sacred canon it is stated concerning the heretics mentioned: "But the bishops and priests who do not energetically show resistance to them shall be deposed from their offices, until the Holy See has mercy on them."[478] That is the conclusion of the 3rd Lateran Council, one of the most renowned Ecumenical Councils approved by the Church. If already at this Council the Bishops and Clergy who did not energetically oppose the heresies were dismissed from their offices, what punishment do those cardinals, bishops and clergy then deserve who not only show the Freemasonic or Communist heresies no resistance, but even support them in the most diverse way and manner, as well as those chiefly responsible for the successes of Jewish freemasonry and of Jewish Communism in the last centuries and are the secret immediately effective weapon of those sects, who make possible their successes? Today Christianity, if it wishes to save itself, must seize upon the same defensive measures which freed it then. If it does not do this, we are facing a certain catastrophe. It must also be stressed that the monastic orders could again play the same role in the salvation of Holy Church and of Christianity. These legions of men, who have sacrificed everything in order to serve God, can be today as in the Middle Ages the deciding factor in the victory of the forces of good. The difficulty, however, is again the same: the strict rules of the Order and prayers take up the greatest part of their time or, better said, almost all their time, and they have therefore no opportunity to participate in the struggle against the "Synagogue of Satan" and its new heresies, Freemasonry and Communism. We recognise the values of these rules and prayers. But not only the Holy Church but the whole world is on the brink

---

[478] Acta Conciliorum et Epistolae Decretales, ac Constitutiones Summorum Pontificum, same edition. Vol. VI, Part II.

of the abyss, and we are of opinion that today, as at the time of the Lateran Councils, the moment has come to make a heroic resolution. It is today urgently necessary that the rules of the order be altered as then, so that the monks can devote a part, and, if possible, the greatest part of their time to the active struggle against Communism, Freemasonry and the "Synagogue of Satan", just as the Franciscans and Dominican- Inquisitor monks did in the Middle Ages, and later the Jesuits.

At a time when the world is on the point of perishing, when Holy Church is threatened by destruction and the monastic orders see themselves facing the danger of extinction, it is impossible that those numerous legions of most important men, who are ready to give all for God, are crippled, without participating actively in a struggle whose outcome is vitally important for themselves. Their direct participation in this new crusade could be decisive, especially if one bears in mind that that religious order is already in itself an international organisation, and that the enemies of Christ, His Church and of mankind are also organised on an international basis, and only such organisations could effectively combat them. May God our Creator provide the superiors and all other Fathers of this Order with the courage to make a decision which does justice to the circumstances, and adjust the rules of the orders to the requirements prevailing today. Naturally they will encounter cunning energetic resistance from the Jewish "Fifth Column" in the clergy and especially from the crypto-Jews infiltrated into these Orders, whose characteristic activities are perceived to a much greater extent in those which the Synagogue fears, as for example the Society of Jesus, and to a lesser extent in others. Today, as in the 12th and 13th century, the good must make zealous efforts to overcome all hindrances, and doubtless God will stand by the faithful who courageously and resolutely tackle this noble task, even if they, like Santo Domingo de Guzman and Saint Francis of Assisi, are defeated. In the sequel of this work we will — as always — on the basis of documents and sources of penetrating proof, investigate details about the infiltration of secret Jews into the monastic orders and reveal the harm which they have caused to the defence of the Church, and especially to the Jesuits.

THE PLOT AGAINST THE CHURCH

CHAPTER THIRTY-SEVEN

THE GREAT POPE INNOCENT III AND THE FAMOUS 4ᵀᴴ LATERAN COUNCIL IMPOSE AS A GOOD AND A DUTY WHAT THE JEWS CALL RACISM AND ANTI-SEMITISM

Pope Innocent III, who is recognised with justice as one of the greatest Popes of Holy Church, undoubtedly played a decisive role in the struggle to save it from the devilish Jewish revolution in the 12th century; and at the same time he made possible the flowering of Christianity in the 13th century which is rightly called the golden age of the Church. But in order to achieve all this, it was first necessary to really fight and conquer the principal enemy of Christianity and of all mankind, the "Synagogue of Satan", and in this realm the renowned Pope distinguished himself as with all his holy actions. It is therefore not remarkable that the Jews in their spite heap the meritorious Pope with poisonous disdain.

The Jewish leader Moses Hess, forerunner of Zionism, collaborator of Karl Marx, from whom he later separated, and who like the latter exerted a decisive influence in the Jewish world of the past century and in the development of Socialistic Jewry, writes concerning Innocent III in his work "Rome and Jerusalem" as follows: "Since Innocent III conceived his devilish plan to destroy the Jews, who at that time made Christianity accessible to Spanish culture, and compelled them to sew a disgraceful mark on their clothing, which under the rule of Cardinal Antonelli led to robbery of a Jewish boy, Rome became an unconquerable well-spring of poison against the Jews."[479]

---

[479] Moses Hess: Rome and Jerusalem. Translated and edited by Rabbi Maurice J. Bloom. New York, 1958. Beginning of Foreword of Author, on Page 7.

It is, however, important to remark that the same thing happened with Pope Innocent III as with many devout men who do not know the extent of Jewish wickedness. Through the intrigue of the Jews who speak of injustice and cruelty and assert that the Jews were not so bad as made out to be, they finally believe that it is not justified to fight them, which in reality was only a natural defence of the peoples attacked by them. Thus Innocent III ascended the throne full of sympathy for the Jews and in 1199 passed a succession of statutes for protection of the development of the Jewish cult and of the legal foundations of their life, their person and their property. With this policy the idea definitely played a role, which first St. Luna had, that one should not make the life of the Jews impossible by compelling them to convert to Christianity. Afterwards Jewry became more fearful and dangerous. It was to be preferred that they were publicly Jews and not false Christians who destroyed the Church from within. This idea ruled the policy of several Popes who practised tolerance towards the open Jews and provided them with a certain protection, while on the other side they combated with fire and sword the Jewish Christians who were secretly linked to their old religion, undermined Christianity and threatened to destroy it. But as in the case of Pius IX and other Popes, the traitorous schemes of the Jews and the proof that they were the instigators of the heresies forced Innocent III to alter his first well-meaning policy.

Like many things painful experience must have taught this great Pope, in order to bring him within a few years to replace his original policy of protection of the Jews with this "devilish plan to destroy the Jews" which respected and authorised Israelite Moses Hess attributes to his Holiness. At all events Innocent proved at the 4th Lateran Council that he was ready to combat them with the necessary energy, in order to save the Church.

In order to attain these goals, to organise the defence of Holy Church against the deadly enemies through a corresponding reform in a balanced way and to solve the problem of the Holy Land and other important questions, he summoned a new Ecumenical Council, the 4th Lateran, which up to the present day illuminates the conscience of Catholics. Besides the prelates, abbots and priors, who participated in this, the Emperor of Constantinople, the kings of France, England, Aragon, Hungary, Sicily, Jerusalem, Cyprus, as well as respected princes and ambassadors of other states were present. This general Synod was opened on 11th November 1215.

How widely those innovations and reform of the Lateran differ from those which the representatives of the interests of Jewry and of Communism wish to set through at the forthcoming Vatican Council!

While the former tended to strengthen the Church in her struggle against the synagogue and its heresies, those who now hatch Jewry and Communism plan, by means of their agents in the higher clergy, to destroy the fundamental traditions of Holy Church, to make impossible to Catholics every defence against Jewish Imperialism, and to open the gates to Communism. All this naturally under the deceptive cloak of outwardly clever but deceitful demands, which have the purpose of concealing secret aims which pursue the aforementioned purpose. Under the pretence of fighting for the unity of peoples and of Christians – sublime demands which we all call good – the "Fifth Column" in Holy Church wishes to provide false bases which shall in the future make possible the victory of its age-old foes. They are not so concerned with modernising the Church, adapting it to the modern time and abolishing obsolete traditions which no longer have any justification for their existence, but they wish particularly to destroy the traditions which are the strongest support of the Church and which protect her best against the spite of her enemies. We do not oppose the reforms which make easier the fulfilment of the task of the Church and strengthen her against her worst enemies, atheistic Communism and Jewry. But we view these apparent reforms as a deadly danger, since they are directed at the opposite, i.e. the defeat of the Church in the face of these enemies who are also enemies of free mankind.

The 4th Lateran Council gave universal force to the measures approved by the provincial Synods, to the effect that Jews must be marked so that they might be distinguished from Christians. Thus it is ordered in Canon LXVIII: "So that they cannot escape or misuse this harmful mixing through a similar error, we determine that all of both sexes, in every Christian province and at all times, must distinguish themselves publicly from the other peoples through their clothing, as Moses also commanded them."[480] This Lateran Council has always most of all called forth protests and furious outbreaks by the Jews against Holy Church. Thereby they do not pay heed to the Law of Moses, which they pretend to follow so zealously, in which it is commanded them to make themselves distinguishable by their clothing, as the Holy Synod asserts. The Jews follow the Law of Moses only insofar as it appears convenient to them and do not follow what does not please them. If they are so very enraged about Holy Church on account of this Law, they must logically also be dissatisfied with Moses, who commanded it to them. But this commandment of divine providence must have its good reasons. Whoever

---

[480] "4th Council of the Lateran," Canon LXVIII. Collection of Acta Conciliorum et Epistolas Decretales ac Constitutiones Summorum Pontificum. Compiled by Pater Joannis Hardulni. S. J. Paris, 1714, P. 70.

belongs to a really honest good organisation can be proud of wearing a uniform which honours him before all the world as a member of this institution. If on the contrary he belongs to a godless association, the uniform is naturally a sign of disgrace before all people. One thus sees that the command which God laid in the mouth of Moses was based on His eternal foresight and wisdom. For, if the Jewish nation followed his commandments and acted honestly, this sign on their clothing would be occasion for honour and pride. If on the contrary they acted badly and faithlessly, then it would be a sign of shame and dishonour and would warn the other peoples of the cunning of this godless sectarian people, which was admittedly chosen by God but on account of its wickedness became the "Synagogue of Satan." Canon LXIX confirmed the preceding Church laws and determined that the Jews should be excluded from the government offices, since they had the possibility as a result of ruling the Christian nations in a secret way and means. In this holy law it is stated: "LXIX. So that the Jews do not occupy public offices. Since it is all too absurd that the slanderers of Christ have power over the Christians, the Council of Toledo has already passed corresponding Statutes. On account of the boldness of the transgressors we renew them here in this chapter and forbid that the Jews occupy public offices, for as a result harm is caused to many Christians. If anyone tolerates this, he is, if denunciation is at hand, to be judged by the provincial council (which must take place yearly) with appropriate severity. Simultaneously the society of Christians in trade and other things is refused... And with shame he must leave the office which he irreverently assumed."[481]

One thus sees that in this law the strict prescriptions for the division between Jews and Christians are confirmed, since coexistence, on account of the dishonesty and the godless intentions of the Jews, was always so fatal to Christians.

Canon LXVII wished to suppress the Jewish tendency — as we have already elaborated – to rob the Christians of their goods, which they usually attained in the Middle Ages through unscrupulous usurers. In this respect it is stated in this law: "LXVII. Concerning the usury of the Jews. The more the Christian religion is harmed through the extortion of the usurers, all the more increases the infamy of the Jews, and in a short time they destroy the goods of the Christians.

---

[481] "4th Council of Lateran". Canon LXIX. Collection of Acta Conciliorum et Epistolas Decretales ac Constitutiones Summorum Pontificum. Compiled by Pater Joannis Harduini S.J. Same edition, Vol. VII. Page 70.

"So that they are not all too gravely burdened by the Jews, we dispose through a Synodic decree that: if the Jews under any kind of pretence carry on extensive excessive usury with the Christians, the Christians affected by this shall take as much from them until the excessive burden is completely repaid. Also the Christians, if an appeal is proposed by the Church censure, shall carry on no trade with them.

"And for the princes we add that the Christians for this reason may not be harmed, but they far more should attempt to prevent the Jews from such crimes."[482]

As we see, this undisputed document from the records of the Lateran which alludes to the falsehood of the Jews who in a short time destroy the property of Christians, confirms yet again the Jewish tendency of snatching away their goods from Christians and pagans, which goes back to the Sacred Books, the "Talmud" and the "Cabbala". The synagogue has been for nearly two thousand years less a temple for worship of God, but rather more the headquarters of the most dangerous, most powerful criminal band of all times. There exists no doubt that the remaining people have a natural right to defence, as they are also justified in protecting their wealth from every other robber band. No one can take this right from the peoples, not even the clergy of the "Fifth Column", who serve God less than the interests of Jewry. How different is this Holy Lateran Council from other apparent Councils which contradicted the doctrine and the traditional norms of the Church and have been in reality heretical councils, as for example those which were admittedly called by a Pope, but were subjected to the Arian heretics, as that summoned by Witiza which we investigated in the preceding chapters. At the Lateran Council the divine dedication was clearly to be traced, for the vitally important traditions were heeded and some innovations introduced, but which only had as goal to defend the sheep against the cunning of the wolf and to combat the latter, who had principally taken shape in Jewry and its heretical movements.

Canon LXX is directed against Christians who were Jews in secret, and it is stated in this that, even if they allowed themselves to be voluntarily baptised, they did not lay aside the old man (i.e. the earlier personality) in order to become a new one. "Retaining the remains of the earlier rite, they mix the Christian religion with it. Cursed be the man who enters on two ways, who shall wear no clothes of linen and wool. (Deut. 22.) We decree

---

[482] "4th Council of Lateran". Canon LXVII. Collection of Acta Conciliorum et Epistolas Decretales ac Constitutiones Summorum Pontificum. Compiled by Pater Joannis Harduini S. J. Same edition. Vol. VII Page 70.

that these shall be suppressed by the Prelates of the Church if they practise their old rites in any kind of form, so that those who confess to the Christian religion out of free will thereby maintain a worthy compulsion."[483]

It is interesting how this Sacred Canon concords with the assertion of an authorised Jewish scripture quoted by us, that the swindlers or secret Jews had two personalities, the visible, public, Christian one, and the concealed Jewish. This diagnosis is thus visibly correct, since it is recognised by respected personalities of both disputing parties. On the other side one clearly sees that at this time the job of repressing these delinquents belonged to the bishops, i.e. the so-called Bishops' Inquisition, which confirms the opinion of Henry Charles Lea that the Papal Inquisition arose only several years later. In addition it is dear that the revelations of many Jewish writers are inaccurate, who assert that the Jewish mock-conversions to Christianity were compelled, as here it is clearly a matter of voluntary conversions and this point is emphasised, which proves that even at that time the false conversions of the Jews were not compelled but were resolved upon because they were favourable to the interests of Jewry. This is also easily explainable, for these apparent conversions gave them great possibilities to introduce themselves into Christian society and into the clergy, to undermine its foundations and to make easier its destruction. Among other things the renowned Pope Innocent III and the authorised Lateran Council defined the doctrine of the Church and the norms to be followed. Many patriots who defend their nations or the Church against Jewish Imperialism and its Freemasonic or Communist revolutions are accused of race hatred and anti-semitism. If this renowned Pope had lived in our time and the no less renowned Council of the Lateran had taken place today, they would undoubtedly have been accused as Nazis and condemned on account of race hate and anti-semitism by those cardinals and prelates who, like those who then supported the worshippers of Lucifer and other Jewish heresies, stand today in the service of the enemies of Christ and His Holy Church. Therefore the aims planned in secret assemblies of the synagogue and of Communism are so dangerous, which wish to have the next Vatican Council condemn race hatred and anti-semitism. For if the Jewish solution is entered into, Holy Church could seem to contradict itself and assert that what it had previously held to be good is now bad. This carries the serious danger that the confidence of the faithful in it is shattered. But that is a

---

[483] "4th Council of Lateran." Canon LXX. Collection of Acta Conciliorum et Epistolas Decretalis ac Constitutiones Summorum Pontificum. Compiled by Pater John Harduini. S. J. Paris 1714. Vol. VIII, Page 70.

matter of indifference to the agents of Jewry in the higher clergy, since they particularly wish that the religious faith of Catholics is shattered and the churches gradually stand empty. We are certain that the Fathers of the Council, as far as this is concerned, will proceed with greatest foresight and will study exhaustively the Papal Bulls, the Ecumenical Councils, the doctrine of the Fathers and Saints, who held the struggle against the Jews for good and necessary, in order not to envelop themselves in contradictions which fatally damage Holy Church. They will doubtless have to overcome the violent resistance of the "Jewish Fifth Column" in the clergy which has stretched out its powerful feelers after the bishops' offices and the cardinals' collegium. But we believe that in this, as on similar occasions, the good will triumph over the evil with the help of God.

CHAPTER THIRTY-EIGHT

MONKS, NUNS AND PRELATES

AS SECRET JEWS

James Finn, the English historian of the past [19th] century, writes in his work "Sephardim or the History of the Jews in Spain and Portugal" about the Jews living in both lands as false Christians: "They took on heraldic surnames, gained the Knights Cross, became bishops and even judges of the Inquisition, although they remained Jews at the same time. Orobius declared that he had come to know Jews in Amsterdam who did penance in the synagogues for their brothers, who in Spain pretended to be Franciscans, Dominicans and Jesuits."[484]

This work was published by the Yard Printers in the Anglican St. Paul's Cathedral and confirms to us the assertions of Jewish authors, who assert that the secret Jews attached themselves to the Dominican orders in order to later introduce themselves into the Holy Office of the Inquisition and to spy upon the secret organisation, which was to destroy and cripple them or at least to render their activity ineffective from within. This is another of the traditional tactics of the synagogue: they introduce themselves into the secret organisations which they should fight, in order to allow no possibility to arise of effectively struggling against Jewry. Thus they behaved with the Czarist Okrana and – so it is asserted – also with the Gestapo.

The secret Jewish infiltration into the offices of the judges of the Inquisition, as is stated in the English work mentioned, gave Jewry the opportunity of causing the struggle of the Holy Office against secret Jewry to remain without effect. In his famous "History of the Marranos" the authorised Jewish writer Cecil Roth reports to us the remarkable history of a secret Jew who entered the clergy as brother of the Order and also practised the cult which the synagogue dedicated to the brother Diego de

---

[484] James Finn. Printed by J. G. F. and J. Rivington, St. Paul's Church Yard, London, 1841.

la Asuncion, a secret Portuguese Jew. This cult was particularly strongly spread in the city of Coimbra. Concerning this Roth writes: "There were a considerable group of new Christians there (Marranos) who belonged to the famous university, and all or almost all remained true to the belief of the fathers. Their leader was Antonio Homen, one of the most talented men of the educated society of his time... Great grandson of Moises Boino (the good), merchant and Jewish physician in Oporto... He was brought up by his mother Isabel Nunez de Almeida, who belonged to an old Christian family. Jesuits educated him, and he studied at the university of his home city, where in 1584 he matriculated in Church law. In 1592 he obtained a position in the faculty. During the great plague in the year 1599, he provided valuable services, which brought him spiritual livings. In order to enjoy these, he entered into the Holy Order... In 1614 he became professor of Church law at the university. As such, he had an incomparable reputation. Various of his treatises are preserved as manuscripts. On the occasion of the proposed canonisation of Queen Isabella of Portugal, he was requested to give his attitude in 1612. Simultaneously he attained great regard as preacher and father confessor... When he had reached the high point of his fame as theologian, Antonio Homen nevertheless became spiritual leader of the Jewish group in Coimbra, to which various very respected personages of the university belonged. Among these were: Andres d'Avelar, lecturer in mathematics, author of various scientific works, and monks like Homen..."[485]

Then the Jewish historian whom we quote enumerates the respected professors of the university who belonged to the circle of false Catholics and reports further that a member of the Jewish circle "Francisco de Gouves, who was born in Lisbon, was promoted after brilliant studies as Lecturer in Church Law at the university of Coimbra and was also appointed as archdeacon of Vilanova de Cerveira. In addition he occupied still other lesser offices. He had already written an important book and would in a short time publish further ones. The Inquisitor General valued him greatly and particularly recommended him to the Pope."[486]

With an anti-Semitic Inquisition like the Catholic one then in Portugal, the events reported to us by the Jew Cecil Roth reveal how the leader of the secret Jews of Coimbra concealed his secret Jewish activity and joined himself to the clergy of Holy Church, i.e. obtained an influential position in the enemy organisation and in this manner even became Professor for

---

[485] Cecil Roth: History of the Marranos, Israel Publishers. Buenos Aires, Chapter VI, Pages 117 and 118.
[486] Cecil Roth: History of the Marranos, Israel Publishers, Buenos Aires, Chapter VI. Pages 117 and 118.

Church Law and made himself a name as preacher and father confessor. Imagine to yourselves a secret Jewish blasphemer who, in his capacity as monk, utilises the confessor's chair for espionage! This is monstrous, but countless documents, both Jewish as well as Christian, report to us an abundance of similar cases. This was one of the reasons why many religious orders were compelled to approve the so-called Statutes for purification of the blood, in which entry into these Orders was forbidden to Catholics descended from Jews, for one had many proofs that almost all remained secret Jews. Naturally the Order of the preacher monks applied the Statute for purification of the blood in the strictest way. For since they were experienced in the struggle against Jewry, they recognised this necessity clearer than the others. As we have already seen, and authorised Jewish writers confess, however, the Jews succeeded in entering into these Orders and becoming judges of the Inquisition.

This was without doubt to be traced back to the fact that, even if in the Spanish and Portuguese Empire everyone had to provide a family tree of several generations, a great number of secret Jews were not established and this for the simple reason, because many false conversions, as we have already seen, had taken place already at least a thousand years before the working out of these family trees, and it was practically impossible to go back to such distant times.

When therefore in Portugal, Spain and their dominions, Jews were not identified in spite of the family trees going back six or more generations, one can easily conceive what may have occurred in Nazi Germany, where it was restricted to investigating only three generations. It is conceivable that countless secret Jews belonged to the Nazi government as Aryans.

The facts have proved that, in the wide overseas regions of the Spanish and Portuguese Empire, Jews were discovered by the Inquisition both in the higher clergy as also in government officials and in other realms of social life, who appeared like old Christians, i.e. as pure Catholics of Jewish origin who had everywhere admittance and also the right to occupy every kind of leading positions. We come back again to the reporting by the Jewish historian Cecil Roth concerning the organisation of the secret Jews in Coimbra (Portugal), where it is expressly stated: "Other persons also, who were connected with the university, belonged to the secret group, among whose members were found a half dozen clergy, several prominent physicians and countless priests.

"They held their religious services (the synagogue) regularly in a house of Largo das Olarias in Coimbra, and two dozen people, among them various students of the university, participated in these. They were conducted by a certain Diego Lopez da Rosa, and Antonio Homen seems to have acted as Rabbi.

"The secret was finally betrayed. On the 24th November 1619, the Inquisition took Homen captive and sent him to Lisbon, where he was to be put on trial. After four and a half years in prison, he was condemned to death as a 'stiff-necked, unbelieving heretic.' On 5th May 1624, he was executed by the garrotte at a public ceremony. He had not wished to confess his guilt at any price, and his body was burned, while eight lesser members of the circle (of whom one died in prison) were handed over to the worldly authority for lesser punishment. To the group belonged two priests. . ."[487]

In the following the Jewish historian quoted gives interesting details, and about Antonio D'Avelar, another Jew of the group, he writes: "His two sons and four daughters (three of them were nuns) were put on trial, because they adhered to Judaism... The scandal had a wide echo. On 30th April 1629, the Portuguese courts turned to Philip III and instructed him that, at recent burnings of heretics carried out by them, besides three monks and various Jesuits, three abbots from Coimbra had also been involved. A further six – all of whom had been appointed by the Pope – were in prison. The King was therefore requested in future to approve no livings to new Christians (i.e. Catholics of Jewish descent) or to allow them to enter the Holy Order."[488]

The report of this renowned Jewish historian makes clear to us how a seemingly zealous monk, Professor of Church Law, famous preacher and father confessor, was not only leader of the secret Jews of Coimbra, but, as it appears, even a Rabbi of the secret synagogue in a private house. It is also revealed to us that to the secret group belonged monks, nuns, Jesuits and even abbots of the respected Church chapter.

For six centuries the Inquisition, with its effective methods of locating and uncovering such secret Jewish organisations and their infiltrations into the clergy of Holy Church, destroyed them and put them out of operation. But when the Papal and then also the Portuguese and Spanish Inquisition were abolished, the Church and Christian society saw themselves robbed of the institutions which had defended them against the disastrous

---

[487] Cecil Roth, same work, Chapter VI, Page 110.
[488] Cecil Roth: History of the Marranos, Israel Publishers, Buenos Aires, 1946-5706. Chapter VI, Pages 119 and 120.

infiltrations and activities of the "Jewish Fifth Column." Thus it was possible that, from this moment on, enormous progress was made by the secret Jewish revolutions, since they now, in order to triumph, could reckon with a veritable swarm of clergy as accomplices. These made easier at first the victories of freemasonry and today those of atheistic Communism. Christianity and the whole world have need of new institutions which are adapted to modern times, but which must be equally as effective or even more effective than the Inquisition, in order to protect mankind from the strivings for conquest of Jewish Imperialism.

In the publication mentioned of the Jewish publishers in Buenos Aires, this secret Jewish infiltration into religious convents is openly admitted. In this connection it is stated: "One could set up a long list of nuns and monks who suffered under the Inquisition or have ended their lives as Jews", and in the first footnote to the same page it is stated: "The family of Manuel Pereira Continho must be mentioned, whose five daughters were nuns of the cloister de la Esperanza in Lisbon, while his sons lived in Hamburg as Jews under the name Abendana. Among other remarkable Church personages of the 17th century in Spain must be mentioned the famous dramatist and novelist Juan Perez de Montalvan, the friend of Lope de Vegas, priest and notary of the Holy Office."[489]

Some of the priests of the "Fifth Column" burned by the Inquisition are regarded by international Jewry as martyrs, as for example the famous monk Diego de la Asuncion, about whom the Jewish historian Cecil Roth writes the following: "One of the most outstanding martyrs of the Portuguese Inquisition was Diego de la Asuncion, a young Franciscan monk, who was born in Viana in 1579. He had in his veins only a small percentage of Jewish blood. It was impossible for him to keep his intentions to himself. Since his situation was dangerous, he attempted to flee to England or France, but was taken captive on the way. Before the Inquisition Court he voluntarily confessed everything which he was accused of, and at first pretended to repent, but later altered his conduct and proudly confessed himself to be an adherent of the law of Moses. On 3rd August 1603, he was burned alive as a twenty-five year old in Lisbon. A number of Jews in Lisbon founded an association in his memory which, in order to remove all suspicion, was called the "Brotherhood of Saint Diego," and which maintained a perpetual light in front of the Ark of the Law of a synagogue, in a place of greater religious freedom. Thus the

---

[489] Cecil Roth: History of the Marranos, Israel Publishers, Buenos Aires, 1946-5706.

blood of a sacrifice fructified and strengthened the faith of the secret Jews."[490]

At the time of the Inquisition, the technical organisation of the Holy Office frequently discovered the members of the "Fifth Column", who in the Church today conduct themselves as they wish, without anyone preventing it. The defence of Christianity is destroyed or crippled, the internal enemy causes all possible harm and rapidly brings us towards Communist slavery. On the other side, one sees that a small percentage of Jewish blood suffices for a Christian man to be a secret fanatical Jew who gives his life for this dark cause.

The Jewish historian mentioned speaks once again about the Catholic but secretly Jewish nuns and writes: "To the 231 persons who were condemned, in Portugal, in the eight years from 1619 to 1627, to public burning as heretics, belonged fifteen doctors of the university, two of whom were professors, eleven additionally academicians, twenty lawyers and the same number of physicians and notaries, and in particular 44 nuns and fifteen priests, of whom seven were abbots."[491]

In other cases, the career of the priest serves the secret Jews for the purpose of not having to confess to the real priests. This device is especially of importance for the confession of children who, on account of their age, are unable to conceal a secret and therefore, during the first years, are true Christians and do not know that their parents secretly belong to Judaism. If then the children at the age of thirteen or later are prepared for the secret introduction into Judaism, it may happen that for many of them the Christian faith is already rooted, and that they naturally wish to ask their father confessor for advice. It would thus be very dangerous if the father confessor of youth were a real priest, who obtained knowledge of the great secret of clandestine Jewry and sounded the alarm, watched strictly over the confessing child, made it attentive to the Jewish error and could strengthen it in the Catholic belief. If, on the other hand, the father confessor is also a Jew, he can be decisive for the final resolution of the vacillating child. At the time of the Inquisition this was a vitally important problem for the new Christian families, for every child was obligated, under threat of excommunication, to denounce to the Holy Office every attempt of the parents to introduce it into Judaism. And every indiscretion of the boy towards the father confessor could have the

---

[490] Cecil Roth. Same work. Same Edition. Israel Publishers. Page 116.
[491] Cecil Roth: History of the Marranos, Israel Publishers, Buenos Aires. 1946-5706. Chapter IV, Page 74.

consequence that the latter convinced him that he must reveal this to the Inquisition, which represented a serious danger for the entire family. In this sense the Jewish writer quoted, Cecil Roth, writes in the American edition of his work mentioned, which was published by the "Jewish Publication Society of America," that an English Jew "who died in 1890 in the U.S.A.", had said about the secret Portuguese Jews: "Many families were, including those of merit, Jews, and in different districts the Jewish families were very numerous. Often then a monk, so that he could take confession from the families in the neighbourhood."[492] In another place we will report more elaborately how other Jewish writers describe the procedure of how to introduce the young generation of secret Jewish families into Judaism, who were baptised and during their childhood had lived as Christians. At a suitable moment they are introduced in an imposing, gloomy ceremony into the dark sect of Judaism.

Concerning the strict control that the Inquisition exerted over the Christians of Jewish descent and over the population in general in order to unmask secret Jews, reports to us the respected Jewish historian Frederick David Mocatta, who in the previous century was President of the "Jewish Historical Society of England," in his work written in 1877, "The Jews in Spain and Portugal and the Inquisition": "The unfortunate Jews, outwardly the most devout of the entire Catholic population, followed in all secrecy the laws of their old faith in spite of the great danger linked with it. The traitors had on grounds of their denunciation such great advantages and the suspicion was so easily believed, that no one escaped with whole skin if the servants of his house, secret enemies or incautious brothers had slandered them. In spite of the greatest caution the new Christians were not secure from showing an inclination to Judaism. Their clothing, suits and especially their food were carefully watched over."

The Jewish historian mentioned further reports, that it was observed how they practised the Catholic rite, how they behaved on the Sabbath and Jewish festivals, that their expressions and gestures were zealously observed and often an unconscious action was denounced. Then an official of the Holy Office, called by the relatives, appeared at the door in order to fetch his victim, whom he kept in prison for months, years or perhaps forever. "So one generation of secret Jews followed upon the

---

[492] Cecil Roth: A History of the Marranos, Jewish Publication Society of America, Philadelphia, USA, 1932, Page 359.

other. They mixed with all social strata and occupied all State posts and especially Church offices."[493]

This strict superintendence was carried through, although the secret Jewish clergy, in order to arouse no suspicion in general, pretended to be anti-Jewish. For any defence of the Jews would have sufficed for the Inquisition to regard them as suspect, to accuse them of practising the Jewish religion in secret, and to put them on trial in order to discover the truth. In our time the secret Jewish clergy defend the Jews unpunished, for there is no Inquisition or a corresponding modern institution that has investigated and revealed the dark practices of Jewry.

In another passage of his work the president of the Jewish society for historic studies in England asserts: "In fact the converts adapted themselves outwardly to the Catholic confession of faith, took on new names, filled their houses with crucifixes, holy images and other Christian symbols and went regularly into the Church..." Then he closes by remarking that, despite everything, many were discovered by the Inquisition.[494]

One can easily imagine how difficult it was under these circumstances for the secret Jews to effectively develop their revolutionary movements. In addition, the Inquisition had to be abolished or made harmless before the first revolutionary attempt could have positive and lasting results.

One of the most renowned anti-Jewish works of the 17th century was the famed "Sentry on the tower of the Church of God." The author was the virtuous Franciscan monk Francisco de Torrejoncillo, the Prior of various Franciscan monasteries including, among others, that of St. Bartholoma of Valencia de Alcantara, our Holy Virgin of Rocamador and our Holy Virgin of Montecelli del Hoyo; he had also been clerk with three different provincial fathers. In his quoted work he writes expressly about the secret Jewish priests: "In the monastery of St. Hieronymus, says Velazquez, they once cheated one of the monks and chose him as Prior and Prelate. Secretly he carried out his rites and ceremonies, until he was discovered by the Inquisition, taken prisoner and publicly burned. From then on great Laws and Statutes were introduced in this monastery and in the entire Order, that none of this race should be admitted.

---

[493] Frederick David Mocatta: The Jews in Spain and Portugal and the Inquisition, London 1877, Page 96.
[494] Frederick David Mocatta, same work, same edition. Page 29.

In the kingdom of Murcia a superior or prefect of a religious order preached all day zealously the Law of Christ and at night he went out with another Jew, who was door-keeper in his foundation, in order to teach the Law of Moses to the Jews of a house. Many of them were burned with their teacher and others died in prison."[495] Here we have another scholar of the scripture, i.e., secret rabbi, who, in order to conceal his true character, became at first monk and then superior of the Order, which made it possible for him to secretly practise his activity as rabbi. But the Inquisition knew very well, that the greatest danger lay in the higher clergy, watched over them all, and finally discovered that the devout superior of the religious Order was a secret Jewish leader, and also discovered his parish children, who were burned or met death in prison.

And Father Torrejoncillo further reports: "If a man wished to become Prelate, then he told others that he did not wish to, and since the others saw that he apparently rejected it, they gave him the office. Accordingly, he confessed, that he was a Jew."[496]

These revelations of the famous protector of the Franciscan Order compel us to explain a fact which other writers confirm and is also corroborated through documents from the time of the Inquisition. The rules of the monastic order, to refuse the offices to those who strove after them, were set up to the greatest part in order to prevent the secret Jewish infiltration. However, they were skilfully evaded by the Jews, which even today is still the case. The best God-fearing men do not strive in reality after such dignities, while the secret Jewish monks act as if they are not interested, but provide skilled teamwork in order to obtain these positions and even gain control of the leading positions in these religious Orders, in whose control they are most interested. The same occurs with the Bishops' offices, for the best, most virtuous and most devout priests are not concerned with gaining Bishops' seats and often refuse to accept them when they are proposed for them, in contrast to the Jews, who mutually support one another and through the influence of their own in Rome easily rise in the hierarchy of the Church.

When the Inquisition still existed, it suppressed this infiltration as far as possible and even put famous archbishops and bishops on trial, who had been seduced to practising Judaism in secret. But when this defence of Christianity was destroyed, nothing any longer held up the infiltration of

---

[495] Brother Francisco de Torrejoncillo: Sentry against the Jews on the tower of the Church of God, Madrid, 1674, Pages 195 and 196.
[496] Brother Francisco de Torrejoncillo, same work, same edition. Page 196 and 197.

the "Fifth Column" into the supreme hierarchy of the Church. For this reason there are so many cardinals, archbishops, bishops, abbots, presidents of an Order for the province, abbots, etc., who in inexplicable manner support the enemies of the Church, for it is a matter of Jews, of freemasonry or of Communism. If we wish to prevent this situation degenerating into a catastrophe, the competent authorities must build up at the right time a new defence against these infiltrations and against the otherwise traitorous activity of the "Fifth Column."

The educated member of the Franciscan Order reports further in his quoted work: "A treasurer of Holy Church (Cathedral) of Cordoba, pretended to fall into ecstasy in a solemn procession. A short time later he was burned, and his figure and insignia are today exhibited in this Holy Church.

Since that time extreme caution was exercised that no new Christian should occupy an office. Another was vicar of the Bishop of Cordoba and set the entire Holy Church into confusion with prosecutions and dispute among the old Christians. With matters in dispute, which he had to decide as judge, he always gave judgement in favour of the new Christians. For it is ordered in their law that one shall support the other against the Christians. However this may be, everything undertaken against the Christians is just, even if it is a matter of killing us."

Concerning this Pharisee, Father Torrejoncillo reports in addition the following: "With the midday or evening meal the Jews wish to have the best place, and in the Church they also wish to have the best seating places. In Valladolid there was another new Christian in a monastery, who there instigated great dispute among fifteen noble pupils. Therefore some have thought that the old custom had begun in the monastery of the Holy Cross, in memory of them (the Jews), as is described in the fifth Chapter of this book."[497]

The most serious danger of the new Christians, who overthrew everything and brought their children up from infancy as Jews, is made clear through the following report of Father Torrejoncillo: "During confession a priest asked a child, in connection with the fast obligation, for his name. The child answered: 'Are you asking me for the name which I have at home or outside?' 'I ask about the name you have at home.' And the child said: 'My home name is Abraham and the other Francisquito'."[498]

---

[497] Brother Francisco de Torrejoncillo, same work, same edition. Pages 192-198.
[498] Brother Francisco de Torrejoncillo, same work, same edition. Page 111.

It is thus understandable that the false Christian families, who do homage to Judaism, undertake the introduction of their baptised children, who have been educated as Christians, into the Synagogue only at an age when they are no longer incautious and they always attempt to give them a secret Jewish father confessor. In addition they subject themselves before their acceptance into Jewry to a succession of examinations, which prove that they are capable of preserving the most closely guarded secrets. Through experience all these methods were perfected in the course of centuries, which the Jews use all over the world, and since there exists no Inquisition or like organisation that defends the people and watches over this devilish sect, the danger today for the Jews is very small.

The uncertainty of the peoples about this problem has this consequence: that the natural lack of caution, which occur again and again, is not noticed. Here in Spain we have, for example, experienced something remarkable: A member of the Catholic Action, which was very much against Franco and for Gil Robles, once said to us: "I am a zealous, apostolic, Jewish Catholic." When we asked him what he meant by Jewish, he became excited and said: "I have made a mistake, a slip of the tongue, I wished to say Roman. Well, you see, one often says one thing in place of the other." (Jewish in Spanish = marrano, Roman = romano, very similar words). The Jews are naturally men like us all and no gods, and they constantly commit indiscretions. But since the people know nothing of all this and on the other side there exists no organisation that can discover and destroy this godless sect, these indiscretions are overlooked.

In Spain and Hispanic America, the secret Jews of the 20th century jokingly say to one another, "Catolicos Apostolicos Marranos" (Catholic apostolic Jews) instead of (as is correct) "Catolicos Apostolicos Romanos" (Apostolic Roman Catholics), and naturally the power of custom allows them to commit such indiscretions, but today, due to the reasons mentioned, they have no importance.

In the monumental work of modern Jewry, the Jewish- Spanish Encyclopaedia quoted, it is stated: "The monasteries are full of Jews. Many of the abbots, Inquisitors and bishops also are descended from Jews. Many of them are in the bottom of their heart convinced Jews, even if they also, in order not to have to abandon worldly goods, pretend to believe in Christianity."[499]

---

[499] Jewish-Spanish Encyclopaedia, same work, Vol. IX. Word "Sefardies" [Jews of Spanish origin]. Page 512.

As one sees, this quotation from an official work of Jewry concords with other no less credible sources. We will deal in the sequel of this work, on the basis of undisputed documents and sources, with the tragedy of Jewish infiltration into the Protestant clergy, but here we will make some allusion in advance, which particularly draws our attention to it and proves that the problem of the "Jewish Fifth Column" in the clergy is a general phenomenon that concerns all confessions. In this connection it is stated expressly in the monumental Jewish work, quoted by us, under the word "Holanda" (Holland): "Many new Christians turned, from 1566, to Calvinism and other reformed doctrines. It is, for example, known that a certain Marco Perez, of Jewish descent, was president of the Calvinist Church Council of Antwerp."[500]

This proves that it is not a question of a tendency but of a clear striving for domination, for this Church Council was the highest Calvinist Church Council in Antwerp, and in fact a Jew was president, i.e., the highest authority.

These Jewish infiltrations into Christianity had at times dangerous consequences for the Christian rulers. In the Jewish Encyclopaedia quoted by us, another interesting revelation is made. Under the name "Gaden Stephan", alias Daniel or Daniela Yevlevich, it is stated: "Physician at the court of the Czar, in the 17th century... altered several times his religion and finally entered into the Catholic men's association of the Greek Orthodox Church... he was cruelly murdered on account of his friendship with the Bojars, who planned the overthrow of the Czar."[501]

In addition, this official work of Jewry provides us with the following other details: "Alexei Protopop, Russian priest and one of the leaders of the Jewish sect in Kiev, Novgorod, Pakow and Moscow (1425-1448). Was apparently pupil of caraita Zejarya. Ivan III, Grand Duke of Moscow, appointed him as director of the Cathedral of the Ascension in Moscow, where he succeeded in converting countless personages of the court and of the Church."[502]

Concerning the Jew Bar Hebraeus, whose Christian name was Gregor Abul Faradesh, it is stated in the Encyclopaedia: "Historian and dignitary

---

[500] Jewish-Spanish Encyclopaedia, same edition. Vol. V. Word "Holanda" [Holland]. Page 284.

[501] Jewish-Spanish Encyclopaedia, word "Gaden" etc. Vol. V, P. 25.

[502] Jewish-Spanish Encyclopaedia, same edition, Vol. I, Page 157.

of the Syrian Church, of Jewish origin, see Bar Hebraeus."[503] Under the name "Bar Hebraeus" it is then stated: "Bar Hebraeus (Gregor Abul Rafadch or Abu-al- Faradch), Superior of the Church of Jacob in Syria, historian, philosopher, theologian and physician, was born in 1226 in Melitene and died in 1286 in Maraga, Persia. He was the son of Aaron, a converted Jewish physician and became Bishop of Guba (1246) and Aleppo (1253) and in the year 1264 director of the Jacobus Church in Persia. He wrote countless books in Arabic and Syrian about history, philosophy, medicine, grammar, biblical commentaries and a book with histories and chronicles, which contains anecdotes and simple proverbs, of which a part refers to the wise Jews. In 1889 E.A.W. Budge translated this book into English."[504]

In another passage, it is stated in this monumental work of Jewry: "Abraham Rabbi, prior of the barefoot monks, new convert, burned in 1270."[505]

Alexander Michael Solomon, converted Jew, first Anglican Bishop in Jerusalem religiously educated in Germany, studied the rabbinical sciences and in 1820, when he went to England, was confirmed in the Synagogue of Plymouth as cantor. In 1825 he was baptised appointed superintendent of the English clergy and of its men's associations in Syria, Mesopotamia, Egypt and Abyssinia.[506]

We will not tire the reader with numerous data that we have at our disposal concerning this material. After what has been said already, he can nevertheless form an opinion concerning the universal spreading of the "Jewish Fifth Column" in the clergy and also concerning the deadly danger that it represents not only for the Catholic Church but also for the whole of Christianity. In conclusion to this chapter we will mention a regrettable fact. In some lands, where the Protestant and Orthodox patriots heroically fight against the Communist infiltration into their churches, the former commit the fault, when they have noticed that certain dignitaries of the Catholic Church aid Communism to victory, of accusing Catholicism in general of what only the members of the "Fifth Column" in the clergy do. This conduct is unjust and the same would be the case if we Catholics conversely were to accuse the Protestants and Orthodox, who are to the

---

[503] Jewish-Spanish Encyclopaedia, Word "Grecia" [Greece], Vol. V, Page 152.
[504] Jewish-Spanish Encyclopaedia, same edition, word "Bar Hebraeus". Vol. II. Collection 2. Page 76.
[505] Jewish-Spanish Encyclopaedia, same edition, word "Abraham Rabi." Vol. I. Page 43.
[506] Jewish-Spanish Encyclopaedia, same edition. Word "Alexander Michael Solomon", Vol. I, Page 211.

greatest part anti-Communists, of betrayal, which the members of the "Fifth Column" in the clergy and the leadership of the orthodox and Protestant Churches daily commit on their chosen fatherland and the free world. We real Christians, who are also necessarily anti-Communists, must therefore recognise, that the Catholic Church, as also the Protestant and Orthodox Churches to the same extent, fall victim to the destructive activity of the same enemies. The "Synagogue of Satan", which through its infiltrations into the clergy of the different churches furthers the triumphs of the Communist, atheistic revolution, which in secret is directed by the synagogue itself. The fact that we are threatened by the same danger and the same enemy, should allow ns to see the necessity to apply our powers in common against the enemy. As long as we remain divided through religious, racial or national hatred, the Jews will conquer us one after the other until they have enslaved us all, as they have done with the unfortunate peoples under Communist rule. For self-preservation we must therefore unite our forces and as an organisation represented in the whole world fight against the foe. Only thus can we counter with prospect of success an enemy, who at present solely and alone hinders the true Christians and pagans on account of the disunity among us, and rules not only the world but the entire planet. If we unite, we will become much stronger than they, easily defeat them and be able to secure the salvation of Christianity, of independence and of well-being of our peoples. Victory or defeat can thus depend on our unity or disunity. Our alliance in the political realm is relatively easy to bring about; for, if we are not blind and wish to save ourselves, we must regard it as urgently necessary.

As far as the unity of all Christians in the theological domain is concerned, then it seems — even if it is an apostolic ideal, which encourages us all — very difficult for the one and attainable for the others. In every case it is clear that if we Christians, Catholics, Protestants and Orthodox form an alliance in the political sphere against Jewish Imperialism, its Communist revolution and its "Fifth Column" in our Churches, then this struggle against the materialist atheism of Communism is the best preparation for a greater approach in the theological sphere, through a friendly discussion, which allows us all to discern the truth. How different is this Christian striving for unity from that of the agents of Jewry and of Communism in the Vatican clergy, which they wish to spread at the next, Second Vatican Council!

Under the pretence of uniting Christians, they attempt to destroy the traditional foundations of Holy Church, the foundation of its most important defence against the Jewish- Communist revolution, so that atheistic materialist Marxism can easily rule the Catholic world. The same goals are followed by analogous so-called Christian unity movements, which are led by secret Jewish members of the "Jewish Fifth Column", who are also secret Communists and control many Protestant Churches. In these cases simply the sublime ideal of Christian unity is utilised for the dark purposes of somehow furthering the victory of the Jewish-Communist revolution. In other cases they wish to control the Churches, which they do not rule, through those national or world church councils, in order upon diverse ways and means to favour the triumphs of Communism and to attack, by denigration, the patriots who defend their peoples against the beast.

Also among Protestants and Orthodox there are efforts for uniting of Christians against Communism. Fortunately, there are many Protestant pastors and dignitaries who desperately fight with Christian zeal to free their Churches from the "Communist Fifth Column".

The same is the case with the Orthodox Churches. In order to be able to form an idea of the violent dispute in this domain, we will reproduce what the renowned orthodox Bishop Alejo Pelipenko says concerning this in his work "Communist Infiltration into the Christian Churches of America" (Buenos Aires Edition, 1961, Page 232): "And if the Patriarch of Moscow works together with all kinds of sectarians, who in reality fight the priests of Christ, supports the spiritualists who are not even Christians for they do not recognise Christ as God and do not believe in the Resurrection, why should we Orthodox not work together with our Catholic Brothers and fight together with them against the forces of Hell? We must keep before our eyes that if, under the constant attacks of the Kremlin and of the Patriarch of Moscow, unity is lost and the power of the Catholic Church diminished, none of the Orthodox Churches will remain free, but would be enslaved by Moscow."

Thereupon he writes concerning the "ICAB" (Iglesia Catolica Apostolica Brasilena) (= Apostolic Catholic Church of Brazil), which is ruled by the Orthodox Church of the Kremlin: "I have reflected upon all this with the publication of this book. I have trustworthy information about the harmful work of the ICAB not only for the Catholic Church but also for the entire Brazilian people, and I have not only the right to write and speak openly, but for me this is a sacred duty. May many others follow my example and join themselves together in an anti-Communist Front. Why does power always lie only in unity?"

Assault on the Independence
and Freedom of the Peoples

As we will investigate extensively in another volume of this work, the League of Nations and the Organisations of the United Nations are, in spite of their noble ideals, controlled in fundamental points by Jews and Freemasons who occupy the bureaucratic key positions and also sit in many national representations of States, whereby the most diverse ideologies and Communist, anti-Communist or neutralist tendencies are followed. In all three camps the Jews and Freemasons take up important positions, for they introduce themselves secretly everywhere they can and utilise all these key positions, in order to further the triumph of Jewish Imperialism and its Communist revolution or to attack the important patriotic governments that Jewry does not control. Thus the League of Nations and the UNO, which could have done much good to preserve world peace and to promote the progress of mankind, have failed, for frequently they are used by Jewry, Freemasonry or Communism for purposes which do not justify their existence.

However, the ideal of Jewish Imperialism has always been to found a world state, which would make it possible for it to control the states which could not be conquered. One of the measures which seems indispensable to Jewry for the preparation of such an ambitious plan, is the setting up of a world police under the control of UNO, which has power in every state and — so they say — should serve for securing world peace and unity among the peoples. These apparent goals are only intended to conceal the real ones. These are: (i) to have a new "Fifth Column" of Jewry in the Christian and pagan states, which is fully supported by the UNO, for it must be an effective organ within this organisation; (ii) to use the world police for espionage against the states which Jewish Imperialism does not control. For this police will be controlled by Jewish, Freemasonic or Communist agents, like almost all bureaucratic organs of the UNO, even if these agents also seemingly represent the most diverse political tendencies, from the Right to the very Extreme Left, and thus pursue the centuries-old tactics of the Synagogue.

As one sees, the possession of this world police, which in the hands of UNO is a satellite of the Synagogue, would be one of the most important measures that the Jews could take in order to destroy the remaining independence and freedom of the peoples. We will discuss this matter further in the sequel of this work.

Jewry wished to make the League of Nations, as also later the UNO, into that Super-State which had sufficient full powers to make an end to the independence of the peoples. But the resistance of many nations, who zealously defend their sovereignty, compelled Jewish Imperialism into recognition of this sovereignty, in order in these state alliances to join together most or all states. For many of them would not have participated in these organisations if their independence might have suffered. Therefore Jewry saw itself compelled to equip these two super-state organisations with limited executive powers. All this was provisionally accepted, in order to gradually give greater authoritative powers and finally to fully abolish the sovereignty of the states. One of the preparatory steps to this goal is the planned world police, which shall have the right to exercise its power in the most different states of the world. They wish to use — so they assert — their powerful influence in the Vatican in order to attain that this proposal is drawn into a document, and thus becomes the doctrine of the Church. In the same way they wish to bring it about that the Holy See is transformed into a kind of satellite of the "Synagogue of Satan" and even serve them as a mouthpiece, if it appears purposive, so that in the name of Holy Church proposals or definitions of doctrine are made that directly or indirectly favour the political plans of international Jewry. For to this shall also belong naturally the plans that are connected with the condemnation of patriots who fight against Jewish Imperialism, or with measures which somehow make easier the victory of Marxist Socialism and the policy of the Kremlin. These Jewish projects seem to us not only satanic, but also monstrous and prove once again that, in the same way as the Scribes and Pharisees constantly led our Lord Jesus into temptation and wished to entice into a trap so as later to have arguments in order to kill him, the descendants of these Scribes and Pharisees have taken over the methods of their forefathers and attempt to constantly place traps in the way of the highest Church dignitaries so that they, if they fall into these traps, can bring forward arguments against them which they need in order to degrade Holy Church and prepare its disintegration. Under the present Pontificate, the "Synagogue of Satan" behaves as at the time of the secret Jewish anti-Pope or satellites of Jewry, for it believes it has almost everything in its hand. But it does not reckon with the support that Our Lord Jesus has always granted His Holy Church and which has always condemned the hellish conspiracies of the Synagogue to failure. At the time of Pius IX, for example, the Jewish- freemasonic forces had already struck up a cry of triumph. They even boasted that this Pope was a freemason. But Our Lord God illuminated at the right time the Vicar of Christ, who finally opened his eyes and recognised the infamous intrigues of Jewry.

One of the measures which clearly allow the change in his policy to be discerned, was the frequent enclosing of the Jews in the ghetto. Upon other occasions the Pontificate had always been represented by secret Jewish cardinals. But in these cases the support was always revealed which God showed His Holy Church, in that He illuminated other Church dignitaries and gave them strength so that they could organise the Holy Councils and convince the Fathers of the necessity of not recognising the descendants of Judas Iscariot as Pope, and to declare them to be anti-Popes and – as in the case of the Pierleonis – to declare null and void their actions, declarations relating to doctrine and investiture of priests, although they had sat for many years or a whole life on the throne of St. Peter in Rome and had been elected by a two-third majority of the cardinals. The case of another well-known Pope, who at first on 1st April 1412 summoned the Holy Council of Rome and later in 1413 the Ecumenical Council of Constance, is also revealing. At the seventh session on 2nd May 1413 he was declared by the general Holy Council to be a rebellious, incorrigible rebel and Simonist, and at the 12th sitting of 29th May it was added to these earlier accusations that he was a notorious Simonist squanderer of goods and rights of many Churches, repellent on account of his revolting unnatural morals, stiff-necked and guilty of many other crimes. The Holy Council finally deposed him as Pope and took from him every power. All this was attained, as in the case of the Pierleonis, with military aid, which various powerful Christian heads of state provided the Holy Council. The latter understood that it was a duty to save the Sacred Council and their lands from the danger hovering over them. The history of Holy Church shows that the divine assistance has revealed itself in a very varied manner but was finally always revealed against the infamous spite of the enemy. Not in vain did Our Lord Jesus promise men that "the powers of hell should not rule over them."

CHAPTER THIRTY-NINE

JEWISH-FREEMASONIC INFILTRATION
INTO THE JESUIT ORDER

In the "Jewish Spanish Encyclopaedia", Limborch is quoted as follows: "In Amsterdam and elsewhere there are Augustinians, Franciscans, Jesuits and Dominicans, who are Jews."[507]

As we have been able to discern, the secret Jews usually strive for all positions of the secular clergy and the monastic orders. In reference to the latter we must, however, still mention their preference to attach themselves to and control those orders which are most dangerous of all for their infamous plans, since they could make them ineffective through their control. When, in the 13th century, the Templar Order signified a great danger for them, they entered it and finally in all quietness conquered the highest positions, brought it away from its goals and used it against the Church and the Christian monarchies. This was a real catastrophe, and the Papacy and the Christian monarchy rapidly intervened, dissolved the Order and had the Grand- Master executed, in order to preserve Christianity from a catastrophe. In the Middle Ages they preferred the infiltration into the Orders, who worked out the plans for the Papal Inquisition, in order to make the latter's struggle harmless. Since, however, the Franciscans and Dominicans exactly knew the Jewish problem and were masters in the struggle against Jewry, they were nevertheless able, as we have seen, to assert themselves.

In modern times the meritorious Society of Jesus has fought most of all against the Jewish revolutionary enterprises, freemasonry, spiritualism, theosophy, Communism, etc. This is to be attributed to the fact that many of their members are not subjected to such strict rules and prayers and have the necessary time to devote themselves to political-social struggles.

---

[507] Jewish-Spanish Encyclopaedia, same edition, Vol. II. Word "Sefardies", Collection 2, Page 512.

Naturally the Jews, since the founding of the holy work of St. Ignatius, have attempted to introduce themselves there in masses.

It is known that the Jesuit Order at first played a decisive role with the counter-Reforms, which made it possible that Poland and other states were won back for Catholicism. Although very soon the new Christians flooded over this land and gained control of the key positions, the true Jesuits still fought heroically against the Jewish threat and attained that a Statute was approved, which, as also with another Order, refused admittance into the Society of Jesus to descendants of Jews. Even today, there is a statute which forbids admittance into the Order to Jews up to the third generation. However, it is no longer heeded, for if today one investigates the family tree of the false secret Jewish Catholics of our days, it can be to the greatest part proved that they are descended since ten or more generations from Christians, which is to be traced back to the false conversions of their forefathers before this point in time.

Until now we have seen by means of recognised Jewish or Catholic sources that the presence of traitorous Jesuits, who secretly practised the Jewish religion, was at various times a frequent occurrence. In the following we will now, even if only summarised on account of the expediency of this work, investigate this regrettable occurrence.

Among other things, the Jewish Jesuits have attempted with intrigues to bring away from its goal the meritorious Society which was founded for the defence of the Church, and to occasion it to exactly the opposite, i.e., instead of combating the enemies of the Church to fight against its best defenders. Naturally the secret Jews, who pretended to be Jesuits, first of all set the Society against the sole bulwark of the Church, the Inquisition. This we will prove by means of Jewish sources, who enjoy the greatest regard in the modern synagogue.

In the "Jewish-Spanish Encyclopaedia", it is stated under the word "Bahia" concerning the false Jewish Christians in Brazil: "It is highly probable that in Bahia, since its foundation, there were secret Jews, for the Portuguese needed settlers for their possessions in the Western Hemisphere and made use of the suspect new Christians. Many other Jews emigrated to Brazil in order to escape the Inquisition. Also in the trade with African slaves they played an important role, since it became necessary to introduce workers more capable of resisting the climate for the heavy plantation labour than the natives. Besides Jewish planters, manufacturers and merchants there were also some physicians. During the first centuries of the Portuguese settlement, the Jews lived relatively free in

Bahia in spite of the activity of the agents of the Holy Office in Lisbon. The authorities represented economic and fiscal interests for the capital and were tolerant in living together with the Jesuits, who were then against the Inquisition. The Jews secretly held religious services and maintained rabbis."[508]

In this case the organisation of St. Ignatius, founded for the defence of the Church against her enemies, was led astray and occasioned to be exactly the opposite, to oppose the Inquisition, which represented the principal defence of the Church and to tolerate its enemies. Here also we see once again the participation of the Jews in the hated slave trade, which in the preceding centuries was one of their most productive occupations.

The present day false Jewish Christians in Brazil, whose forefathers captured the unfortunate negroes, who really deserved a better fate, like wild animals or sold them like cattle, proceed in a really shameless way when today they lead the Socialist and Communist movements in Brazil and give themselves out to be liberators of the negroes or Mulattos of the population, when they brought their forefathers in chains and made them into slaves. The Brazilian negroes and mulattos must open their eyes and recognise that the same evil powers who condemned their forefathers to hated servitude, now lead them towards the worst slavery of all, Communism, and deceive them with enticing means of liberating them and creating a paradise for them. They did the same with their forefathers who were cheated by the secret Jewish slave dealers and believed their lying promises in the hope of being led to a better life and one fine day awoke with the chains of slaver when it was too late to free themselves.

Let us select one of the many cases in Brazil, for to this land we have hitherto devoted little space in this work. This terrible struggle took place a hundred years later than that which we have just investigated. The details we take from another authorised source of Jewry. The most renowned historian of the present, Cecil Roth, writes in his "History of the Marranos" concerning the suppression of the secret Jews in Brazil by the Holy Office and continues as follows: "In this time a ray of hope fell through the clouds. An Interregnum in the office of the Grand Inquisitor from 1653 to 1673 admittedly did not influence the activity of the Court, but diminished certainly its regard. Meanwhile Antonio Vieira, the great Jesuit, who had earned the surname Apostle of Brazil, had taken over the defence of the new Christians in Brazil. He pressed Juan IV to abolish the disappropriations and to erase the still existing differences between old

---

[508] Jewish-Spanish Encyclopaedia, Vol. II, Word "Bahia". Pages 42 and 43.

and new Christians. Through his free expression of opinion he engaged upon a feud with the Holy Office. After three years of imprisonment (1665-67), his writings and he himself were formally condemned. Through his experience with the terror of the Holy Office his sympathy increased with the oppressed. He went to Rome where, in the citadel of Christianity, he attacked the Portuguese Inquisition as a godless court not influenced by devoutness, which condemned the innocent just as often as the guilty and was the enemy of the best Christian interests. The Society of Jesus – afflicted on account of the treatment of one of its most regarded members – supported his cause. Encouraged through the change of events, the new Christians turned to the throne on account of definite reforms, including the free pardon of those prosecuted and the replacement of the Inquisitorial procedure through a more humane form customary in Rome. For such modest concessions they offered to pay 20,000 Cruceiros yearly, to send 4000 soldiers to India and each year 1200 as reinforcement and a further 300 in event of war. The Inquisition protested energetically, but the application was supported by many great men of the kingdom and even by the faculty of the University of Coimbra (which, as we have seen, was flooded with secret Jews) and personally supported by the Archbishop of Lisbon. It was thus approved and sent on to Rome for final decision. There Francisco de Azevedo, the representative of the new Christians, together with Vieira, prepared a sharp denunciation, and allowed it to be seen that the Portuguese Inquisition was only a means of repression, enriched itself through extortion and was out for the last blood of every new Christian. The latter – so they asserted — were all zealous Catholics, who, because they denied, i.e., denied Judaism, were condemned or were pardoned on grounds of a false confession. After a long struggle, the new Christians won. On 3rd October 1674, Pope Clement X took over control of the activity of the Portuguese courts and ordered that the most important cases should be transferred to Rome. Since the Inquisitors refused to cooperate on the following investigation, under the pretence that thereby the secrets of the trial could come to light, an interdict was uttered against them and on 27th May 1679 they were finally deposed from their offices. The easing was not of long duration, for on 22nd August 1681 the deposing was already annulled, after a couple of reforms of no further importance had been resolved. The resumption of activity in Portugal was celebrated with triumphant processions and carnival lights. In January of the following year, the first burnings of heretics took place again in Coimbra. Upon this followed a few months later the burning of four persons in Lisbon on, 10th May, three of them alive, because they did not repent. To the latter belonged a lawyer of Aviz, Miguel Henriquez (alias Isaak) da Fonseca, who had himself called Misael Hisneque de Fungoca, Antonio de Aguiar (alias Aaron Cohen Faya) from Lamunilla in the neighbourhood of Madrid, and Gaspar (alias Abraham) Lopez Pereira, who were all lamented by the literates in Amsterdam as martyrs."

The renowned Jewish historian reports further concerning the burnings of several secret Jews as heretics, and the Jewish researcher describes the high point of this terrible struggle as follows: "This resumption was given expression in September 1683 through a command that all persons who had been pardoned on account of membership to Jewry, must leave the kingdom in the impossibly short period of two months. They should in addition leave behind their children who were younger than seven years until they proved that they lived in their new home as true Christians. The rapid increase of the communities on grounds of the dispersion in that time was partly to be traced back to this measure, which first became invalid when the war with France broke out in 1704."[509]

Later this and other renowned Jewish historians assert that, despite everything, secret Jewry in Portugal and Brazil survived, i.e., the repression through the Inquisition was able to be avoided. The case particularly investigated by us is an important example of how the Synagogue, against the intentions of St. Ignatius of Loyola and the other meritorious founders of this order, has utilised the Society of Jesus in order to destroy the defence of Holy Church. It also makes the serious fact clear to us that a bad Jesuit or a group of wicked Jesuits let themselves into an unjust struggle against the real defenders of the Church and later drew in the entire Order by that they utilised the noble spirit of solidarity of the meritorious society towards non-members. With all respect and high regard for the Jesuit Order, we allow ourselves to give warning of such manoeuvres which frequently occur in this disastrous time.

In addition the special interest of the "Synagogue of Satan" to introduce itself into the Society of Jesus and to control it, is proved in an official work of freemasonry, which we have just received from one of those groups of devout Latin American clergy, who, out of the noble striving to save Holy Church, provided us with the extensive South American Bibliography, which is so inestimably valuable and useful for the rapid preparation of this work and to spare us expensive travels and the search for Bibliography, which would have considerably delayed the publication of this work. We speak of the "Abbreviated Encyclopaedic Dictionary of Freemasonry", which was written by the freemason of the

---

[509] Cecil Roth: History of the Marranos. Spanish Translation, Israel Publishers. Buenos Aires. Chapter XIII, Pages 257, 258 and 259.

33rd degree (grade), who under the name Pascalis or Pascualis writes expressly:

"Pascalis or Pascualis (Martinez) Jewish theosopher and renowned enlightener, leader of the sects of the Martinists . . . founded a school of the Cabbalists, made in 1754 talk about himself for the first time as founder of a philosophic-spiritual, Jesuitical rite, which he described as a rite of the chosen Coons... It is revealed from his writings that the doctrine of Martinez Pascalis goes back to the Cabbalist tradition of the Jews."[510]

In connection with this rite, it is stated in the freemasonic dictionary under the term "Elegidos Coons", word for word: "Chosen Coons. Description for a philosophic-spiritual, ultra- Jesuitical rite, which was founded in 1754 by a Portuguese Jew named Martinez Pascalis. Coons means priest in Jewish."[511]

Concerning the repeated attempts of Jewish freemasonry to introduce itself into the Society and to control it, another source gives us information about this freemasonic rite created for this gloomy purpose. It is stated in the official encyclopaedic dictionary of freemasonry under the term "estricta observancia" (strict observance): "Estricta observancia. Description for a rite which had split up into many others and represents the most perfect expression of the Templar system in freemasonry. This rite was the third freemasonic innovation of the Jesuits, who stirred up the hope among their supporters to come into the possession of the riches of the old Templars. The chronological history of the Grandmasters corresponds to that of the generals of the Society of Jesus. The rite of strict observance was finally set up in Germany, between 1760 and 1763, by the brother Karl Gathels, the Baron of Hund, who to the six grades of the Order at first determined added yet another. The rite was organised in the following seven degrees: pupil, companion, master, Scottish master, novice, Templar in three classes: Eques, Socius and Armiger, and Eques professus."[512]

---

[510] Lorenzo Lady Abrines M ∴ M ∴ 33rd degree of the old taken-on Scottish Rite. Short Encyclopaedic Dictionary of Freemasonry, 2nd edition of the Compania General de Ediciones, S.A., 22 Nov. 1960. Mexico. D.F. Collections 1 and 2, Page 349.

[511] Lorenzo Lady Abrines. M ∴ M ∴ Degree 33 of the old taken-on Scottish Rite. Short Encyclopaedic dictionary of freemasonry, same edition. Collection 1, Page 156.

[512] Lorenzo Lady Abrines: Dictionary of Freemasonry, same edition, Collection 2 and 1, Pages 182 and 183.

The fact that, since his grounding in this Rite which was intended to control the Jesuits, a new Grandmaster was also chosen if a new general of the Order was appointed, shows the tenacity of Jewry and its satellites, freemasonry, to introduce themselves in the Holy Work of St. Ignatius and to control it.

On the other side is the special wish to make this freemasonic rite in connection with the Templar Order very significant. We must not forget that the Templar Order was founded in order to defend Holy Church against its enemies. The "Synagogue of Satan", however, gained entry into it until the secret Jews occupied the leading positions, then brought it away from its original aims and made it become a serious danger for the Church and the Christian peoples. One must also bear in mind that, in the prosecutions against the Templars, the effort was revealed to skilfully conceal themselves, for, although the Christian Order was watched over by the enemy, it remained in its official outward realms bound to Holy Church, even if also in secret circles the easier controlled Catholic Templars were seduced and their religious faith gradually taken from them, until they had finally become secret satellites of Jewry. The infiltrations of the Synagogue and of Freemasonry into the Society of Jesus followed visibly the same aims, for this freemasonic-Templar rite of the Jesuits wishes apparently to make the Society of Jesus into a new Templar Order with retention of its outer official structure is then finally secretly ruled by the enemies of the Church and then used in order to destroy its defenders and with the purpose of making easier the victory of Jewry and its satellites, freemasonry and Communism. From the valuable Freemasonic document, which we study, it is revealed that even other schismatic rites of Freemasonry, which were for this reason called mixed rites or also controlled by the Jewish Cabbalists, were organised in order to influence the meritorious work of St. Ignatius of Loyola and to control it. Accordingly it is stated under the expression "Clerigos de la estricta observancia": "Clergy of the strict rule of the Order. Title for a Jesuitical mixed rite, which was formed by Cabbalists, Alchemists, Black Magicians and members of the Society of Jesus."[513]

This is apparently a Freemasonic rite, which emanated from a schism of the "Rite of the strict rule of the Order", which, as is stated in the dictionary of Freemasonry mentioned, was subjected to schisms. Both rites are of Jewish origin and we must allude to the fact that in Judaism frequently inner dissensions occur, which are reflected in the schisms

---

[513] Lorenzo Lady Abrines: M ∴ M ∴ Degree 33 of Scottish Rite. Short Encyclopaedia Dictionary of Freemasonry, same edition, Collection 2, Page 113.

which every Jewish party calls forth in the Freemasonic organisation, which at first is ruled by the Jewish cell, but then later passes through its own split. It is not further remarkable that to this Freemasonic rite, which is intended to control the Jesuits, Black Magicians belonged, for we have indeed already proved that the Jews were the most principal spreaders of the Lucifer cult and of Black Magic. On the other side, it was revealed, through many prosecutions of Templars, that in secret circles of the Order the devil was worshipped, even if the open outward structure of the Templar order appeared additionally so Catholic and orthodox as in good old times.

The hair-raising facts, which we describe and have taken from official works of Judaism and of Freemasonry, allow us to clearly recognise the devilish stiff-neckedness of the "Synagogue of Satan" in infiltrating itself into and controlling the Society of Jesus, which in modern times was for it the most combative, most dangerous Catholic Order, in order then to use it against Holy Church, just as it did circa seven centuries ago with the Templar Order.

But what interests the Catholic world certainly most of all is how far Jewry could realise its intentions to make the Society of Jesus into a satellite. Since today, however, there are no Holy Inquisitional Courts or a like institution which could discover this with effective methods, no balanced investigation in this sense is also possible to us. However, certain facts allow it to be concluded that a traceable process of Judaisation is in progress in some domains of the Order of St Ignatius. There are Jesuits who, to the harm of Christianity, defend the Jews and the "Synagogue of Satan." Others favour with any disposable means the enemies of the Church instead of combating them, while on the other side they attack cruelly and in an anti-Christian way the defenders of the Church, especially those who successfully and tenaciously fight against Jewry, Freemasonry and Communism. Others again further the victory of the Freemasonic and Communist revolution, perform tenacious disruptive work against the few Catholic governments which there are in the world. In addition – and that is the most remarkable thing in the affair – the good fighting Jesuits who fortunately still exist in great number, when they defend the Church against her enemies, especially against Jewry, Freemasonry or Communism, are in an inexplicable way and manner opposed hostilely in the Order by other Jesuits themselves, who stir up rancour against them for so long until they make them harmless or can attain that the superiors forbid them to fight further against the enemies of the Church. In other cases we see well-regarded very intelligent Jesuits, who on grounds of their great capacities could do much good for the Society and Christianity, set back and practically eliminated. As a result, the Order and Holy Church loses the opportunity of using these so valuable capable men. All this gives the impression as if the enemy already sat deeply in the meritorious work of St Ignatius.

But we are convinced of the fact that the Jesuit Order can still save itself from the cunning of its enemies, for the majority of members are honest upright Catholics who entered the Order in order to serve God. If the members, who secretly belong to the "Jewish Fifth Column" and their Freemasonic accomplices were able at times to make progress with their attempts to conquer this fortress, it was only because they proceeded highly secretly and always with the most skilled deceit. We believe honestly, through warnings and the unmasking of the enemy, that the honest Jesuits will, with our modest aid, prosper, so that they can save the Society from a possible catastrophe. As the reader will have remarked, we quote in these last chapters details from official sources of Jewry and of Freemasonry, who cannot be accused of any Antisemitism or fanatical clericalism. Whoever wishes to carry out further research in this sphere as to what methods the secret Jewish monks and nuns have applied at various times, in order to exert their practices in the strict life of the cloisters, can deepen their knowledge in the archives of the Holy Inquisition, which we mention in another part of this work.

In the Archive of Torre do Tombo in Portugal and that of Simancas in Spain, in that previously mentioned in Italy, France and other lands of the world, we find the handwritten original records of countess trials of the Holy Office against Jesuits, Dominicans, Franciscans and monks and nuns of various other religious Orders — among them even abbots and dignitaries of the Order — who were led over and confessed to have secretly paid homage to Judaism in the peaceful life of the most strict cloisters. All this would appear unbelievable to us if, in addition to those admissions from the Jewish and Freemasonic side, the existence of thousands of Inquisitional prosecutions were not able to be quoted which with many details confirm this terrible fact. From these trials are revealed the revolutionary activity and the terrible secret blasphemies of those monks and nuns, who apparently lived with holy dedication according to the rules of their religious Order, against Our Lord Jesus and the Virgin Mary.

In conclusion to this chapter it seems to us necessary to draw the attention of the organisers of patriotic organisations and political parties to the danger that the Jews and Freemasons join themselves to these organisations, finally control or ruin them. Many simpletons believe that the infiltration by such enemies is not important. Others, no less naive, are of the opinion that it would be easy to hold up this invasion. Those who with regrettable naiveté believe the one or other, must reflect that the Catholic clergy and the religious Orders are from diverse reasons far more rigid institutions, into which it is more difficult to penetrate than into simple political parties or associations. If it was successful for Jewry, even at the time of the Inquisition, which particularly wished to prevent this by all means, to infiltrate into the Church institutions, the Synagogue will be able to influence political or social associations even more easily, since they demand neither vows of chastity, poverty and obedience, nor strict monastic life, absolute discipline and all the rest, which in the religious orders have nevertheless held up the deadly infiltration of the enemies of mankind, even if it could not prevent it entirely.

The leaders of political movements should thus prevent by all attainable means that the Jews, Freemasons or Communists enter into their ranks, for, if they are not successful in this, the enemy can bring these movements to ruin. We can make the assurance that the possibility of the triumph of a political Christian or pagan association is to the greatest part dependent upon whether it triumphs before the Jewish, Freemasonic or Communist infiltration can prevent this. The necessity to eliminate the Christians of Jewish origin rests upon the fact, proven in the course of centuries, that by far the majority of mock-Christians, are Jews in secret, as we have proved by means of indisputably credible documents and sources in this work.

We have here to do with a sad political truth, which has been proved to sufficiency, and not with racial prejudices, which we as Christians in no way foster, and as followers of Jesus Christ all men are for us equal before God and the law. It is one thing, however, to have no racial prejudices, but quite another to allow oneself to be surprised knowingly by the Fifth Column of an enemy who wishes to enslave and destroy us. If we wish to defend ourselves against such an invasion, we are simply making use of our natural right to justified self-defence.

CHAPTER FORTY

CONSPIRACIES AGAINST HISTORY

AND THE RITES

The Jews have made the falsification of history into one of the great — perhaps the most important of all — secrets of their successes. Without this, Jewish Imperialism would not have been able to control almost the whole world, but would perhaps have been defeated by the threatened institutions and peoples, as it also repeatedly occurred in the Middle Ages, when Holy Church and the Christian nations recognised the enemy who laid in wait and could defend itself against him. Particularly the Church and worldly chronicles and historic studies provided this knowledge and described the true origin of the earlier attempts of Jewry to control the Christians, to rob them, to gain control of their governments, to destroy Holy Church, to call forth schisms, to organise degrading heresies or to conspire against the Christian peoples.

Since they recognised the historic truth, the Christian and pagan generations could always identify their principal enemies, take heed before them and bring about the failure of their renewed revolutionary plans for rule. On grounds of the knowledge of historic truth, the priests and dignitaries of Holy Church could exactly recognise that the most bitter enemy of Christ and of Christianity was satanic Jewry, and were thus in the position to defend the Church against all its cunning. For in order to destroy an enemy, one must first recognise him. There is nothing more dangerous than an enemy who can conceal his hostility or his identity, for in these cases he can destroy his victims with decisive surprise attacks. If the victim does not know the aggressive plans of his enemy, he is incapable of preparing a defence or even of recognising the necessity for this. Not to mention the fact that the presence of the enemy may not even be known.

Jewish Imperialism grasped this at the right time and therefore it applied enormous powers in a succession of heretical-revolutionary movements and in intentions of political conquest, even if these were also bloodily defeated with great losses for the 'Synagogue of Satan". These unfortunate events have taught them to apply a part of their energy really attentively to a long-lasting work of organisation, in order to falsify the worldly and religious history of the Christians and to cleanse them all from that is connected with conspiracies, attacks or revolutionary movements of the Jews and finally to attain that in the historical texts every allusion to the participation of the Jews in these enterprises will be left out, which they carry out for centuries, and prepare with a tenacity and energy which would be worthy of a better cause.

For examination of these assertions one can for the sake of studies compare the version of the mediaeval chronicles and historical books and those edited at the present concerning the same factual content. In the comparison one will be able to establish without difficulties, that in the present version every single reference of the mediaeval chronicles to the participation of the Jews in plots, rebellions, crimes, treachery against the King and of the land in question, etc., have been left out although nevertheless the modern historical texts should give again the truth, as this is revealed from the sources upon which they support themselves.

The same is the case with the historical texts of Holy Catholic Church. The clergy who are interested in this kind of investigation should make a thorough comparison between the histories and chronicles of the Church, the writings of the Fathers, the Bulls and the records of the Councils, which were written between the 1st and 15th centuries A.D. concerning events of the time and the edited historical reports in our time We can predict to them in advance that they will be astounded at the mysterious omissions in the modern Church histories of all allusions to the intrusion of the Jews in the heresies and against the Church and the movements directed by the Popes or their cooperation with crimes and conspiracies against the Christian peoples, which are present in the old chronicles and documents, which serve as basis. Naturally, in the history books of different lands errors occur about one or other fact. But it is highly strange and revealing that in all or almost all modern texts — a remarkable coincidence — that particularly all reports existing in mediaeval history books, chronicles and documents concerning the revolutionary, harmful interference of the Jews into the historical events of the time were left out. It would be ridiculous to hold that such a universal and persistent circumstance must be due to chance or to some kind of magic which from the historical texts caused only one line to vanish concerning social activities. In fact, the knowledge of this should have made the succeeding generations watchful, so that they defended themselves against Jewry. One thus sees that in the course of centuries an organised work was performed, in order to leave out from the new historical sources everything which could damage the plans for world conquest of the Jews.

Every serious researcher can affirm that this mutilation of the Chronicles and history books becomes more frequent and general, the more the Jews and principally the false converts to Christianity joined themselves to Christian society and gained in influence in it. As far as Church history is concerned, then, the conspiracies increased when the current of secret Jewish new Christians became greater, who introduced themselves into the clergy of Holy Church in order to gain control of her from within or to disintegrate her through schisms and heresies. Thus, for example, we can observe that up until the 11th century A.D. in the Chronicles and Documents the harmful, destructive participation of the Jews in social events and also all other interesting historical events are mentioned. From the 15th century onwards there are historical texts written by Christians and even by Catholic clergy, whose authors were in general converted Jews or descendants of converts, in which carefully the allusions to the wickedness of the Jews were left out. In these texts every revelation concerning the participation of the Jews in various events was left out and it was even attempted to falsify certain factual contents.

The more the secret Jewish historians and chroniclers descended from false converts to Christianity mutilated the historical texts and chronicles of their time — and that is what is serious about the matter — the real Christian historians, who went the most simple way, supported themselves on these already mutilated sources, without consulting the older more credible documents, which represented the events without evil-willed omissions. Thus one can establish that even in the 19th century, scarcely a Church or lay historian, even when it was a matter of well-believing persons, gives details about the harmful activity of the Jews in the past centuries. We are in the sad situation of having to reach back to the Jewish history books destined for internal use by the Synagogue, in order for the greatest part to reconstruct the true history of Holy Church.

In the face of the indisputable fact that both Church history, which is studied in the seminaries, and secular history, which is studied in the schools and universities, are incomplete and distorted and in them all that is missing which can give an idea of the most tenacious and very worst enemies of the Church and of mankind. It is urgently necessary that those particularly make efforts who are in the financial position to do so, in order to finance the work of researchers who are free of all suspicion of being accomplices of Jewry, so that they reconstruct the real history of

Holy Church and also the true history of Europe. In this way, future generations, both civil and ecclesiastical, will throw off the blindfold obscuring their eyes and be in constant alert, ready to defend against the new attacks and conspiracies hatched by the enemy.

In the Liturgy and the rites of Holy Church there are constant references to the danger of the Jews, to their falsity and their infamous hatred for Christ and His Church. This warning greatly disturbs the Jews, for it signifies a constant drawing of attention to something which the Jews wish to efface in the memory of Christians: their infamy and danger, from which everyone must take great heed. For this reason they now wish to undertake an unbelievably bold step and to use the next Ecumenical Council in order, with the help of their "Fifth Column" in the bosom of Holy Church, to carry out a total reform of the Church, to alter the liturgy and the rites and to leave out all allusions to the infamy and danger of the Jews.

With this the Jews and their accomplices in the clergy wish to throw even more sand in the eyes of Christians and Church dignitaries, who then, when they no longer know the principal foe of the Church, have no opportunity to defend themselves. Thus can Jewry easily continue its unexpected advances for enslavement and destruction of the Holy Church of Christ and of mankind.

One must bear in mind that all zealous clergy who have carefully worked out the Liturgy and the rites, and Holy Church, which in the course of centuries has made these part of itself, had good reason for certain, very clear allusions to the Jews. When Holy Church accepted them, it has in no wise erred, as those assert, who support Jewry, but as divine institution has performed the correct decision. In addition, there exists the plan to abolish tradition as source of revelation, as we already investigated in other chapters and alluded to the fact that the chief aim of this infamous manoeuvre is to abolish the highly anti-Jewish determinations in Bulls and Council Laws, and to abolish the doctrine of the fathers as doctrine of the Church, even if other reasons are given for this.

CHAPTER FORTY-ONE

ERRORS OF THE NAZIS AND IMPERIALISTS

When Russia was conquered by Communism, millions of Christians were murdered by the Soviet Jews, and in Hungary and Bavaria, towards the end of the 1st world war, Marxist coups d'Etats took place. Europe was justly disturbed. It saw itself directly threatened by subjection and enslavement through the seemingly irresistible Red avalanche, especially on account of the complicity of the secret Jewish government in London and the victory of the separatist tendencies in the U.S.A.

The visible predominating participation of the Jews, not only in the Communist revolution in Russia, but also in the revolutions in Hungary and Germany, opened the eyes of many European patriots and allowed them to recognise that the Red conspiracy was a tool of Jewish Imperialism. Russian monarchist writers had already warned the world, and subsequently Frenchmen, Rumanians, Spaniards, North Americans, Germans and others from various parts of the world and of different race and religion have drawn attention to the same danger. When it appeared as if Europe had been conquered by Jewish Imperialism and its Communist revolution, various patriotic organisations arose on the old continent and attempted to save their lands from the danger threatening them. They would perhaps have been successful in this, if the most important group, the National Socialist Workers Party of Germany, had not arrived upon false paths, which caused this European revival to fail sorrowfully.

All peoples have the right to justified defence against the attacks of Jewish Imperialism. If the Nazis had limited themselves to saving their people and Europe in the face of the deadly threat, no one could reproach them and perhaps they would have had success with such a praiseworthy enterprise. Unfortunately, into the National-Socialist movement imperialistic, aggressive tendencies against other peoples and races crept in. Even the Jewish racial hatred would not have been dangerous if it had remained limited to seizing upon internal measures for the betterment of its race or racial union. Even mixed marriages with the Jewish people could be forbidden, without that we protested against it. What causes Jewish race hatred to be unacceptable and dangerous, is its aggressive imperialist tendency to conquer and to enslave other peoples and is made authoritative to the harm of the legitimate rights of other races.

The same holds for the Nazi race hatred. No one can deny the great capacities of the Nordic race and refuse the German people the right to improve the good qualities of its race, or better expressed, of the complex of races. No one can also dispute its right to defend itself against Jewish Imperialism, and less still Holy Church which for nineteen centuries long has fought tenaciously and heroically against the cunning of the "Synagogue of Satan". But it is not permissible that a nationalism or a so-called race hygiene strikes out upon imperialist paths and injures the legitimate rights of other peoples or sets itself up above them. The unjust invasion of Poland, the repellent Pact with Russia to divide the Polish territory, the violent conquest of Bohemia and Moravia, the attacks against neutral peoples, the over-estimation of German superiority and the under-estimation of the quality of other peoples, which the Nazis so greatly promoted, and which damaged so much their relations with their allies, were only a logical consequence of the Imperialist racial hatred which the National Socialist movement subjected itself to, and in a certain aspect is very similar to the Imperialist race hatred of the Jews.

Another serious consequence of the preceding were the events in the Ukraine, where the Germans were received as saviours, and which could have been one of their most loyal, most valuable allies against the Kremlin, but soon became an enemy on grounds of the policy of conquest and subjection which the Nazis pursued in this land, for instead of as liberators they came as cruel conquerors.

With the race hatred of the Nazis one must certainly very well distinguish between the purely defensive and the aggressive or Imperialist aspect. They first wished to drive the Jews from government posts and in general from valuable positions, which they occupied in German society. The Nazis only did what Holy Catholic Church has ordered upon various occasions during the last fourteen centuries as a measure to preserve Christianity from the conquest and revolutionary activity of Jewish infiltration.

The writings of the Church Fathers as well as various Papal Bulls and Council Laws give us evidence of the struggle of Holy Church, in order to depose the Jews from public offices and leading positions in the Christian states, since they have always utilised these in order to destroy Christianity and to subjugate the Christian peoples.

We have already investigated how the Church applied all possible means and even attempted to keep the Jews remote from the social and family life of Christians. For this reason we could also not criticise this aspect of the Nazi race policy, for we would as a result blame Holy Church, and as Catholics we could not do this. On the other hand, the aggressive Imperialist aspect of Nazi race hatred is absolutely to be condemned and rejected. For if the so-called Nordic race with its great scientific, artistic, and political talent is to preserve, cultivate and apply its outstanding talents to the well-being and service of other races, as the Nazis wished.

With such a mode of thought it is incomprehensible that this alliance between Nazi Germany and the Japanese Empire could have been honest and effective, for the Japanese Nationalists also founded their movement for freedom upon a racial Imperialism, which was just as extreme and dangerous as the Nazistic, and wishes to aid the yellow race to world domination under the leadership of the Japanese. With this fateful ideal in mind they attacked China and fell upon other peoples. How under these circumstances could the two Imperialists work together loyally and successfully? To this lack of cooperation on the part of both allies their defeat in the last world war is to be attributed. Even if the Jew Roosevelt, as respected North American patriots have proved, did everything in order to encourage the Japanese attack upon Pearl Harbour, then nevertheless the Japanese government, if it had not had such insane Imperialist intentions, would not have fallen into the trap, which international Jewry had laid for it.

As we already said in another passage, all great peoples of the world have unfortunately inclined to Imperialism and the subjugation of other peoples in favour of their own. The Assyrians, Chaldaeans, Persians, Greeks, Carthaginians, Spaniards, Portuguese, Turks, Dutch, French, English, Russians and North Americans did the same in this respect.

In connection with Imperialism, we could repeat the divine sentence of our Lord Jesus: "He who is without sin amongst you cast first the stone." All men, without difference of race or religion, must understand that every new Imperialist enterprise is not only unjust but is also suicidal, for in face of the deadly threat hovering over all religions and peoples of the world from Jewish Imperialism and its Communist revolution we have no other choice — as our elementary self-preservation instinct tells us — than at least to join together in the political realm. For only through the uniting of the peoples and the alliance of all religions can a coalition come into existence which is strong enough to save us and mankind from the Jewish-Communist slavery threatening us all to the same measure.

This great alliance can only be concluded, if a real feeling of brotherhood exists among the peoples and a respect of the natural right of each individual.

It would be fateful and catastrophic if the movements for freedom against Jewish Imperialism and its Communist revolution, which arise in different nations of the world, became Imperialist nationalisms. For then the defence of the peoples would be impossible, which at these moments is so necessary, in order to triumph over Jewish Imperialism. We would once again fail with this perhaps last opportunity, in order to save ourselves, for the Jews and their Freemasonic and Communist satellites would skilfully utilise every Imperialist tendency of an anti-Jewish liberation movement, in order to set the threatened peoples against it, just as was the case in the last world war.

This is a decisive moment in history, and we have only a few years to liberate ourselves from Jewish-Communist slavery. The liberation movements which in several countries fight against Jewish Imperialism, should understand that today such conduct is suicidal and should therefore zealously fight, not only to liberate their peoples from the Jews, but to also unite in a brotherly way with similar liberation movements, so that the whole of mankind can be freed, including naturally the unfortunate peoples, who are already subjected by Red totalitarianism. The Imperialist Jews would be defeated by a closely allied world. But their victory over a mankind split up on the political realm in national, racial or religious rivalries is certain.

National and racial rivalries should be laid aside by way of peaceful negotiations. Differences of opinion in the religious domain should be decided in an honourable, peaceful, theological discussion, which in the long run gives the right to those who deserve it, but prevents that these antagonisms degenerate into religious wars or violent conflicts, which always make impossible a political uniting of the peoples, which is so neces-sary, in the first place to eliminate the threat by Jewish Imperialism and later to secure world peace, which is indis-pensable for the progress and maintenance of the human race.

We have already mentioned another tragic fault of the Nazis, who in their struggle against Jewish Imperialism made no difference between the ancient chosen people, which provided us with our Lord Jesus, the Holy Virgin Mary, the Prophets and Apostles, and the sons of the Devil, as Jesus called the sectarians of the "Synagogue of Satan" who denied Him, crucified Him and have bitterly fought His Holy Church in the course of centuries. With this erroneous thesis the theoreticians of Nazism take up an anti-Christian conduct, which was to make impossible the traditional highest Christian union of Europe against Jewish Imperialism and thus also prevented the victory.

Whoever is still so simple as to believe that Christianity can easily be destroyed without divine help, should at least see the facts as they are. For if the mighty Roman Empire was not successful in three long centuries of merciless persecution, if the criminal Jews in the Soviet Union did not achieve it in 45 years of bloody terror, then still less will any modern Imperialism be successful, which in addition must still simultaneously conflict with the secret, enormous power of international Jewry.

We stand at the edge of an abyss, and the unbelievers and even the adherents of anti-Christian tendencies must, if they are not blind to the threatening danger, understand that we must all lay aside our dislikes and our national or religious resentment and must organise a common defence against the deadly enemy threatening us all. If we continue to think in terms of national hatred, revenge for injustice done and religious rivalries, we will all perish in the ever increasing onslaught of Jewish Imperialism and its Communist revolution. We must therefore all make efforts to bring about this unity, which is so necessary in order to save ourselves. In this chapter we decline to comment upon the slaughtering of the Jews by the Nazis, for we deal with this in the 3rd and 4th chapter of the part of this book which bears the heading "The Synagogue of Satan".

We should condemn for ever the war between the individual states, because it is first of all catastrophic for all and secondly aids the totalitarian Imperialism of Jewry most securely to the final victory. We must ally ourselves against Jewish Imperialism and also liberate our own peoples and all the others who are subjected by Jews, so that after victory over the worst form of Imperialism which has ever existed in the world — which hypocritically preaches peace but constantly furthers war — all lands of the earth can form a world organisation which, with respect for the legitimate rights of all, secures world peace, promotes the truth and the progress of mankind, and raises the living standard of all men, especially that of the economically weak strata, as high as possible and simultaneously fights to bring men nearer to God, the beginning and the end of the whole Universe.

The failure of the League of Nations and of the UNO is — as we shall investigate further in the 2nd volume of this work — to be traced back to the fact that both institutions, even if they announce the noblest most humanitarian aims, are controlled by the secret power of Jewry and Freemasonry and are used to promote the victory of the Imperialist plans of the Synagogue.

We anxiously call upon the patriots in the U.S.A. and England, that in the liberation of their nations from the Jewish yoke they may not enter upon the suicidal path of Imperialism. We make the same summons to the heroic-minded President Nasser of Egypt and the patriots of the other nations of the world who fight for the same goal.

The struggle for Arab unity is without doubt just. But if it is achieved, it must not pass over from nationalism to Imperialism. For by this it would give the Jews of the world the wonderful opportunity of suppressing Arab Nationalism, just as they did with Marxist Imperialism, which unintentionally gave the Synagogue the opportunity to destroy nationalistic Germany. The National Socialists hampered for a time Jewish Imperialism and had raised the living standards of the working classes in astonishing degree.

Thus the revival of Germany achieved in a few years was once again destroyed through the Imperialist ambitions of the very same creators of the revival. The great peoples and leaders easily become egocentric through repeated success in their important enterprises and often devote themselves to suicidal Imperialist intentions. Let us think, for example, of Napoleon, who snatched rule over the French revolution from the dark forces of Jewry, made it into a really national undertaking and completed the miracle of making a destroyed anarchistic France into the most important military power of the world. If Napoleon had not allowed himself to be led by his unlimited Imperialist ambition, then his work would have been of longer duration. The successes give the leaders and peoples a feeling of superiority, which drives the one or others to a kind of delusion of grandeur and causes them to forge Imperialist plans which finally leads them to collapse, especially in times when Jewish Imperialism utilises all these situations in order to stir up all the other peoples to struggle and war against those powers and leaders who disturb or endanger the plans for domination of the "Synagogue of Satan".

CHAPTER FORTY-TWO

POPES, CHURCH FATHERS AND SAINTS
COMBAT AND CONDEMN THE JEWS

The great Pope Gregory VII, the renowned Hildebrand, the great reformer and organiser of the Church, writes in a letter to King Alfonse VI of Castile in the year 1081: "We exhort your Royal Majesty not to further tolerate that the Jews rule Christians and have power over them. For to allow, that Christians are subordinated to Jews and are delivered to their whims, means to oppress the Church of God, means to revile Christ himself."[514]

However, this great Pope was strictly opposed to forcing the Jews to baptism, for he knew how dangerous false conversions were and seized upon measures to avoid this kind of error and protected the Jews against the immoderate zeal of some fanatics. Pope Gregory VII fought uninterruptedly to prevent that the Jews ruled the Christians, for--as he said--this came close to a repression of Holy Church and elevating of the "Synagogue of Satan." But in addition he asserted that to please these enemies of Christ, meant to revile Christ himself. What would the members of the "Fifth Column" say to this, who at present do exactly the opposite of what Pope Gregory VII ordered? The same thing, which was asserted by this renowned Pontifex--one of the most renowned of the Church--is championed today by those who fight against Jewish Imperialism and for this reason are called anti-Semites, i.e., to prevent that the Jews rule the Christians and as a result vilify Christ and His Church and cause grave harm to the Christian nations. St. Ambrose, a Bishop of Milan, and great Church Father, said to his flock, that the Synagogue "was a godless House, a collecting place of wickedness and that God Himself had damned it."[515]

---

[514] Pope Gregory VII. Regesta IX. 2.
[515] St. Ambrose, Bishop of Milan, Great Church Father, Epistle XI to Emperor Theodosius.

And if the host of Christians on grounds of the faithless conduct of the Jews could not hold back their rage and burned a synagogue, St. Ambrose allowed them to enjoy his full support and said in addition: "I declare that I have set the synagogue on fire or have at least given the crowd the mandate to do it... And if it is said against me, that I should not have personally set the synagogue on fire, I answer that it was burned through the judgement of God."[516]

We must also not forget, that St. Ambrose of Milan is recognised in Holy Church as model bishop and on account of his Christian neighbourly love is held to be worthy of imitation. This proves that neighbourly love must not be used to protect the evil powers.

Holy Thomas of Aquin, who knew the danger of Jews in Christian society, held it to be correct, to allow them to live in eternal servitude. A semitophilic writer complains about this and writes as follows: "Aquinas based himself upon the standpoint of that time, that they should live in eternal servitude."[517] This opinion of St. Thomas of Aquinas is completely justified. If the Jews, in every land in which they live, constantly instigate conspiracies upon command of their religion, in order to conquer the people which magnanimously offered them hospitality, and they in addition fight to rob it of its goods and to destroy its religious belief, there is no other choice: either they must be expelled from the land, or they be allowed to live there, but in hard servitude, which binds their hands and prevents them from doing so much evil.

Another great genius of the Church, Duns Scotus, the Doctor Subtilis, went still further than Thomas of Aquinas and proposed to Christianity a solution of the Jewish problem on the basis of the complete destruction of this devilish sect. In this aspect a renowned Rabbi complains that Duns Scotus "Instigated the forceful baptism of Jewish children and that parents who refused to be converted should be brought onto an island, where they could practise their religion until the prophecy of Isaak concerning those remaining, who wished to return, was fulfilled. (4.22)"[518]

---

[516] St. Ambrose, letter mentioned.

[517] Malcolm Hay: Europe and the Jews, Boston 1960. Chapter IV, Page 91.

[518] Rabbi Jakob Salmon Raisin: Gentile Reactions to Jewish Ideals, same edition. Chapter XIX. Page 525.

As one sees, the idea of banishing all the Jews in the world onto an island, where they should live alone, without being able to harm the remaining peoples, originates not from Hitler but from one of the most renowned authorised Church Fathers.

Saint Louis (Ludwig), King of France, exemplary in his saintliness and Christian love of the neighbour, who was so magnanimous as to give back a conquered king the regions conquered by him, which no one in that time did voluntarily, was of the opinion that the Jews, if they mocked the Christian religion, should have a sword thrust as deeply as possible into their body.[519] In order to understand the standpoint of Saint Ludwig (Louis), one must bear in mind that then every revolutionary action and conspiracy of the Jews against the Christian nations then principally expressed itself in heresies or attacks on religion. This is understandable in a time when the religious problem was fundamental and all political affairs were subordinated to it. Jewish Imperialism has also still preserved a highly religious foundation in our time, as we have already elaborated earlier.

St. Athanasius, the great Church Father, asserted that "the Jews were no longer the people of God but were Lords over Sodom and Gomorrah."[520]

Saint John Chrysostom, another great Church Father, reports concerning all the misfortune which occurred to the Jews at different times: "But the Jews say that men and not God had brought them all this misfortune. But exactly the opposite is the cause, for God has occasioned it. If they (the Jews) make men responsible for this, then they must remember that they, even if they had risked it, would nevertheless not have been strong enough, if God had not so willed it."[521] St. John Chrysostom defined approximately fifteen hundred years ago clearly and distinctly the nature of the Jews and described them as "Nation of criminals," "Lustful, robbers and avaricious false thieves." Later the great Church Father makes the assurance in connection with the traditional Jewish tactic of lamenting that men declare war on them and destroy them, and of always representing themselves as innocent victims: "Always when

---

[519] Rabbi Louis Israel Newman: Jewish Influence on Christian Reform Movements, New York, 1925, Pages 61 and 62.

[520] St. Athanasius: Treatise concerning the incarnation, 40, 7.

[521] Saint John Chrysostom: Sixth Sermon against the Jews.

the Jews say to you: Men have waged war upon us and have conspired against us, answer them: men would not have waged war upon you, if God had not allowed it."

Saint John Chrysostom even supports himself upon another point of the Catholic doctrine, that "God hates the Jews,"[522] because God hates Evil, and the Jews after they had our Lord Jesus crucified, became the greatest evil. The renowned Saint in general defends the thesis, that "a man crucified by you was stronger than you and has destroyed and scattered you." and asserts that the Jews must continue to be punished for their crimes until the end of the world. The terrible events in this century, where the Jews erected their Communist dictatorship, have confirmed what Saint John Chrysostom asserted over fifteen hundred years ago, namely, that the Jews are a band of thieves and murderers, and it is understandable that the just punishment of God is frequently bestowed upon them for their bloody misdeeds. In our days the assertion of this great Church Father, that they always--when God punishes them, destroys them or causes the misfortune prophesied in the Holy Bible to come upon them--make the rest of mankind responsible for the terrible occurrences which they have provoked through their own crimes.

The renowned Bishop of Meaux, Bossuet, writer and sacred preacher, whose position is known in the history of Holy Church, likewise fought the Jews energetically and cursed them from the pulpit: "Accursed People! Your visitation shall pursue you up to your most remote descendants, until the Lord becomes weary of punishing you and at the end of time takes pity on your wretched remains."[523]

As one sees, the renowned Catholic theologian was of opinion that at the end of time only a wretched remnant of Jewry would remain and was of one opinion with Saint John Chrysostom and other Church Fathers concerning the catastrophes which the Jews must suffer on account of their murder of God and their wickedness. In his "Addresses Concerning History" and in various sermons Bossuet repeatedly described the Jews as "accursed race," upon whom "divine punishment" has come and will

---

[522] Saint John Chrysostom: Sermons against the Jews. Malcolm Hay: Europe and the Jews, same edition, Page 30 and 31.

[523] Bossuet: Sermon for Good Friday, Complete Works, Vol. II. Page 628.

always "be destroyed by the other peoples of the world."[524] He also gave the assurance, that "the Jews were hated by God."[525] If this devout wise Bishop, a genius of the Catholic Church, had lived in our time, he would also have been accused by the secret Jewish clergy of racial hatred and Antisemitism.

Like all Church Fathers Bossuet knew the Jewish falsehood very well. If the Jews had not behaved in a criminal way in the course of centuries since the crucifying of the Lord, no one would accuse and condemn them on account of their wickedness. Through their mode of action they are solely and alone responsible for the all-sided reaction against them. If a man does not wish to be regarded as a murderer and thief, then he only needs to abandon this kind of crime. But if he robs, kills or conspires, it is not remarkable that the peoples affected reproach him with his crimes. However, the Jews are shameless enough to protest and to raise a great outcry, because their own conspiracies and manifold crimes against other men and nations are held against them. One must have inherited the pharisaic hypocrisy, in order to tear the priestly garb into fragments, when the truth is spoken into one's face.

The Holy Pius V, another great saint of the Church, who is renowned on account of his devoutness and Christian neighbourly love and was simultaneously one of the most highly regarded of Popes, gave energetic expression to his opinion--alarmed by the revolutionary action of the Jews--that the Jews should be compelled to wear a visible mark, which distinguished them from Christians, so that the latter could protect themselves from their destructive preaching. In the Bull of 19th April 1566 he confirmed the determinations of the earlier Papal Bulls and Holy Councils and ordered that all Jews should wear as distinguishing mark a cap for men and a simple sign for women: "3. In order to make an end to all doubt concerning the colour of the cap and the sign of the women, we declare that the colour must be yellow." Then he commands the Prelates to publish the Bull and to maintain this, and continues: "5. All worldly princes, lords and judges do we exhort, and implore for the mercy of Jesus Christ's sake and utter to them for this forgiveness of their sins, to support in all the foregoing the patriarchs, primates, archbishops and bishops and

---

[524] Bossuet: Discours sur l'Histoire Universelle, Part II, Chapter XXI. Jules Isaac "Jesus et Israel". Page 372.

[525] Bossuet, quoted by Malcolm Hay: Europe and the Jews. Same edition. Page 174.

to further them, and the transgressors with worldly punishments and judgements."[526]

Since in addition the Jews gained power in the Pontificate states through deceit and usury of the real estate, this Pope, recognised as a Saint, saw himself compelled to issue the Bull "Cum nos nuper" of 19th January 1567, in the second year of his Pontificate, and to confirm the earlier Popes, by that he forbade the Jews to acquire real estate, and compelled them to sell these within a short period. If in this respect they once more did not pay heed to the Papal Bull, these real estates were to be confiscated from them. From this interesting document we take informative parts: "Since we a short time ago renewed the orders of our predecessor Pope Paul IV against the Jews and among other things ordered that the Jews both in our city Rome as also in other cities, districts and places, which stand under the worldly rule of the Holy Roman Church, must sell the properties (real estate) in their possession to Christians within a period fixed by a judge. And if these Jews do not carry out this or the preceding, we order that they be punished by the judges as rebels and as guilty of the crime of lèse majesté, according to the manner of the crime determined by us, our Vicar or other official. And the Christian people shall show them mistrust in accordance with our judgement, of the official and judge."

In another part of the Bull the Pope orders in connection with the deceit which the Jews had committed, that: "Since we, as is necessary, wish to remedy this deceit and wish to ensure that that ordered by us had its effect voluntarily, with full understanding and in exercising of the apostolic powers, we withdraw from the Jews and their rule (and recognize no right or claim) all properties, which the Jews have in their possession in this city Rome or other places of our domain of rule."[527]

One can imagine, how great the usury and swindling of the Jews and the sale of properties must have been, that this devout virtuous Pope saw himself compelled to make these measures for defence of the Christians. One must not forget, that Pope Pius V is one of the Popes who

[526] His Holiness Pope Pius V, Bull Romanus Pontifex, 19th April 1566. Compiled in Bullarum Diplomatum et Privilegiorum Sanctorum Romanorum Pontificum. Taurinensis Editio, Turin, 1862. Vol. VII. Page 439.

[527] His Holiness Pope Pius V. Bull "Cum Nos Nuper" of 19 Jan. 1567. Compiled in Bullarium Diplomatus et Privilegiorum Sanctorum Romanorum Pontificum, Taurinensis Editio, Turin, Vol. VII. 1862. Page 514 ff.

distinguished himself most of all through his recognised holiness and therefore was also declared holy by Holy Church. If he had lived in our disastrous time, he would have been condemned by the Church dignitaries in the service of the "Synagogue of Satan," of race hatred and Antisemitism and, if possible, even have been included among the war criminals of Nuremberg; for in our time the "Fifth Column" condemns all who defend their peoples or Holy Church against the political or economic Imperialism of the Jews.

But the Holy Bulls and their carrying out could not alone hold up the wickedness of the Jews, who in all lands which show them hospitality, become a deadly danger for Christian and pagan peoples. At that time this Pope--exemplary in holiness and devoutness--had enough energy in order to attack the problem radically and undertook thorough measures. On the 26th February 1569 he announced the thunderous Bull "Hebraeorum Gens" and expelled the Jews from the Pontificate states. On account of the inordinate length of this work we only reproduce parts of this valuable document, which seem to us most important of all. In this sense the holy Pope says: "The Jewish people, which was once preserver of the divine Word, participated in the heavenly secrets and exceeded so much in favour and dignity the other peoples, fell down later from its height on account of its faithlessness, so that in its period of bloom ungratefully and faithlessly condemned its Redeemer undignifiedly to shameful death. But Christian devoutness came to terms from the beginning with this unanulled fact and allowed that it settled far more comfortably in its bosom . . . In spite of this its godlessness with the stamp of all possible repellent arts has taken on such forms, that it becomes necessary for the salvation of our own, to prevent such a sickness with force through a quickly effective healing method. If we look away from the countless kinds of usury, through which the Jews have everywhere sucked the property of the needy Christians, then we give judgment that they are visibly protectors and even accomplices of thieves and robbers, who cause the stolen and embezzled goods to come to another or hitherto wish to conceal them. Many desire, under the pretence of their own business affairs, the houses of honourable women and destroy them with shameful flatteries. And the most damaging thing in the matter is, that they attract through prophecy, magical incantations, superstition and witchcraft many incautious and sick people to the deceit of the "Synagogue of Satan" and boast of being able to predict the future, where treasures are concealed and secret things. In addition we know and have exactly investigated, how in an unworthy way this revolting sect misuses the name of Christ and in what measure this is harmful for those who are judged in this name and whose life is threatened through their deceit. On account of this and other grave things, of account of the gravity of the crimes, which unfortunately from day to day more and more increase in our cities, and since we are in addition of the opinion, that the race mentioned, with exception of unimportant groups in the East, is in no way of value for our Republic . . . We order in the following that in the time limit of 3 months from the publication onwards all Jews of both sexes in our entire worldly realm of justice and in the appertainent towns, districts and places, the same in those of the 'domicelli,' of the Barons and other worldly property Lords, including those who only have power, mixed power, power over life and death or any other jurisdiction and freeing-- must leave these regions without grace."

Since the Holy Father Pius V knew that the Jews all over the world usually evade in diverse ways and means such expulsion edicts and, in order to avoid in this case, that they did not respect the statutes of the Holy Bull, he ordered in the same, strict punishments for those, who did not leave the land in the appointed time: "2. After this time limit shall all at the present or in future, who dwell or wander into that city of the region of justice mentioned, in every district or place also of the 'domicelos,' barons, property lords, or other already mentioned, be affected, their property confiscated and handed over to the Siscus, and they shall become slaves of the Roman Church, live in eternal servitude and the Roman Church shall have the same rights over them as the remaining lords over slaves and property. Excepted are the cities Rome and Ancona, where the Jews will be tolerated, who now live there, so that the formerly mentioned memory remains awake, the negotiations with the East and the mutual trade are continued, under the condition that they respect our Church Laws and those of our predecessor. If they do not do this, they shall suffer all punishments, which are ordered in this law, and which we renew in this document."[528]

The Holy Bulls bring an important innovation in reference to the expulsion of Jews from the Christian states, during the earlier centuries. As we recall, the Jews were given the choice, to be expelled or to be converted. The consequence of this was, that the majority, in order to escape expulsion, apparently confessed to Christianity and represented a greater danger for the Church and the Christian states. Holy Pius V without doubt knew this and simply ordered the expulsion from the

---

[528] His Holiness the Pope Pius V. Bull Hebraeorum Gens of 26 Febr. 1596. Compilation in Bullarium Diplomatum et Privilegiorum Sanctorum Romanorum Pontificium. Taurinensis Editio, Vol. VII. Page 740, 741 and 742.

Pontificate states, without leaving them the way out of conversion, which they had always evaded. As one sees, this holy Pope knew the Jewish problem better than many worldly and clerical dignitaries before him; but also in his case pressure was exerted on His Holiness, so that he excluded Rome and Ancona from the expulsion, so that trade with the east was not damaged. The Jews thus once again made use of this means, in order to partly evade the expulsion. Another renowned Saint and an important figure in the first centuries, Saint Gregory of Nysa, who played such an important role in the philosophic defence of the Christian faith, accuses the Jews in his famous "Prayer for the Resurrection of Christ": "Murderers of the Lord, Murderers of the Prophets, enemies of God, men who hate God and despise the Laws, Enemies of grace. Enemies of the faith of your fathers, advocates of the Devil, race of blasphemers, slanderers, mockers, men with clouded spirit, Pharisee breed, collection of Devils, sinner, infamous men, casters of stones, enemies of honesty."[529]

Undoubtedly not even Hitler has in so few words expressed so many accusations against the Jews, as sixteen hundred years ago this holy Bishop of Nyasa, the brother of the great Church Father St. Basilius, who was also canonised like the latter on account of his capacities. And if he drew the Jews into the prayer mentioned, then he wished like many other Saints to warn the Christians to be on their guard against this band of thieves and murderers whose strength lies only in the lack of knowledge of Christians of their danger, and this lack of knowledge the member of the "Fifth Column"--clergy and laymen--wish to promote further, so as in the protection of this lack of knowledge to make possible the successes of Jewry. Therefore is it so easy to establish the identity of the secret Jews in the Catholic Action or in the clergy and to recognise them, for when it is a question of the Jewish danger, they assert with suspicious constancy that it does not exist, that it is a myth, an invention of the Nazis or some other unimportant fable. As a result they only wish to conceal and defend the band to which these false Catholics belong in secret, who often as descendants of the Pharisees make an exhibition of their devoutness and adherence to our Church, while on the other side they seek to prevent that it defends itself against its principal enemy.

In the struggle against Jewry for defence of Christianity Pope Gregory IX published on 5th March 1233 his famous Bull "Sufficere Debuerat" from which we take the following: "It ought to have satisfied the faithless Jews, that Christian devoutness accepted them again solely and alone from

---

[529] St. Gregorius von Nysa: Aratio in Christi resurrectionem. Page 685.

goodwill. They, who persecuted the Catholic faith and have denied the name of the Lord. They do not give thanks for the concessions, forget the deeds of good will, pay back this kindness with godlessness and in return for the concessions they despise us. As was thus ordered at the Council of Toledo and was confirmed at the general Council, no preference may be given to the blasphemers of God, for it is completely absurd, that such should have power over Christians. Nevertheless they are entrusted with public offices, which they utilise to the harm of the Christians. They have in addition wet nurses and women servants in their own houses where they devote themselves to indescribable things, which with those who know of them, call forth revulsion and horror. Although at the general Council mentioned it was disposed that the Jews of both sexes at all times and everywhere should be distinguished from others through their clothing, nevertheless in Germany the confusion becomes ever greater, since they distinguish themselves through no clothing piece. As it is repellent, that that which was reborn through the water of baptism, is spotted through the practices of the faithless and their activity and the Christian religion is attacked through the power of the false (which would happen), if the blasphemer of the blood of Christ has the liberated in service, we order for all our brothers in the Bishopric, absolutely to suppress the mentioned and similar blaspheming of the Jews in your dioceses, churches and communities, so that they do not dare to raise their necks bent under eternal servitude, in order to revile the Redeemer. In addition they should avoid through greater strictness, that they in no way risk to discuss their practices with Christians, so that discussions of this kind give the ignorant no opportunity to slip away through error, which is to be hoped will not occur. For this you should, if necessary, turn to the worthy law for support."[530]

As one sees, Pope Gregory IX complains bitterly about the ingratitude of the Jews, who answer kindness with reviling, and poison the conscience of Christians, persecute the Catholic faith, place themselves against the Christians when they occupy public offices, and carry out actions which are despicable and terrible. In short, they do the same as always in the course of the past nineteen hundred years. Therefore it is very praiseworthy that the determinations of the Council of Toledo, which were confirmed through the Ecumenical (Lateran), were carried out, the Jews excluded from public offices and that they should live in eternal

---

[530] Pope Gregor IX, Bull Sufficere Debuerate of 5th March 1233. Compilation of the Bullarium Diplomatum et Privilegiorum Sanctorum Romanorum Pontificum, Taurinensis Editio, Vol. III. 1233, Page 479.

slavery. The wild beast is laid in chains as a result, so that it can cause no harm. One sees that this time in Germany, where the laws of the Councils mentioned were not fulfilled, the beast was freed, and caused harm in the shadow of tolerance.

The Popes thus lead the defence of Christian society against the Jews, and that should really be their actual task, to defend their sheep against the cunning of the wolf and not to deliver them to it. May the Jews only not come and make the Church responsible for what has occurred to them in the course of history, for they provoked this action through their ingratitude and their Imperialist activity. Without doubt Holy Church had and has like the peoples attacked always the right to defend itself in a correct way. If the Jews do not wish to bear the consequences of their attacks, they must cease them.

When Pope Martin V ascended the Papal throne, he was influenced by the intrigues of the Jews, who represented themselves as victims of the Christians and now followed a policy of tolerance fateful for Christians. Therefore the Pontifex Maximus soon saw himself compelled, even if only seemingly, to alter the course, since the clergy dissatisfied with his policy urged him to this.

Whatever the reason may have been for the change in the conduct of the Pontifex Maximus, his renowned Bull "Sedes Apostolica" gives an idea of how the Jews accepted the protection, which this Pope granted to them for a time. The Bull mentioned goes back to his policy of good-will towards the Jews, and then it is stated further: "However, we received a short time ago through credible reports knowledge to our great alarm, that various Jews of both sexes in Cafas and over cities, lands and places overseas, which fall under the jurisdiction of Christians, are obstinate of mind and, in order to conceal swindling and wickedness, wear no special sign on their clothing, so that they are not recognisable as Jews. They are not ashamed to give themselves out as Christians before many Christians of both sexes of these cities, districts and places mentioned, who could not in fact identify them, and consequently commit shameful things and crimes, among others the crimes of Zachi, Rossi, Alani, Minfredi and Anogusi, who are baptised according to the Greek Rite and as Christians buy as many persons of both sexes as is possible to them, then godlessly sell them further at a tenfold price to the Saracens and other unbelievers, and bring these persons as wares into the land of the Saracens or unbelievers."[531]

But the ingratitude of the Jews finds even clearer expression, if one reads what Jewry writes officially in its already quoted Encyclopedia concerning Pope Martin V: "The friendly conduct of Martin was probably to be for the greatest part attributed to the rich presents, which agents made to him. Without immediate payment nothing was wished from him. With the corresponding amount everything was easy to attain. "At the Papal court friendship ceased, if the money runs out," wrote the German ambassador at the Vatican. Whatever the motive for the Papal good-will may have been, the fact is that it was continued under Eugen IV (1431-47) in spite of some hostile Bulls, which to a certain extent confirmed the old Jewish legislation. Especially his "Dudum ad Nostram" was hostile and contributed to creating a Ghetto atmosphere for the Jewish community. He saw himself compelled to give way to the pressure of the Spanish clergy and of the Council of Basle."[532]

Even if one believes that the Jews bought Pope Martin V with gold, then they ought to have kept silent out of a natural feeling of gratitude and not sully his honour in such a way as they do even in an Encyclopedia through corresponding allusions. At all events, in this as in other cases the pro-Jewish policy of a Pope--contrary to the laws of the Ecumenical Councils, of the Bulls and the doctrine of the earlier Popes and Church Fathers--had once again catastrophic consequences and brought the Church and all Europe in the middle of the 15th century close to disaster.

Martin V through his giving way to a half extent, unchained the beast, which through the energetic policy of the earlier Popes and Councils had been laid in chains, and simultaneously Jewry in Europe once more gained an enormous power. The great secret Jewish revolution of the Hussites, which one believed to have ended in Constance, took on giant proportions, and threatened to destroy the Church and to swallow the whole of Europe.

The alarm of the world bishoprics against the Pope increased in a form which aroused concern, and the thesis, that the Ecumenical Council stood

---

[531] Pope Martin V. Bull Sedes Apostolica. 1425. Compilation of Bullarium cit. Vol. IV. S. 1425.

[532] Jewish-Spanish Encyclopedia, same edition, Vol. VIII. Word "Papas" [Popes] Page 347.

above the Pope, gained more and more in strength. For it was said, that a man could easier fail than the entire Bishopric, and that in addition the support which God granted Holy Church, became effective through the Council and not through the Pope. Under these circumstances his Holiness was pressed to fulfill the determination of the Council of Siena and to summon a new Ecumenical Council in Basle.

It is understandable, that in this situation, as Juan de Ragusa says, the mere word Council horrified the Pope enormously. (In inmensum nomen concilii abhorrebat)[533]

When the Pontifex had already summoned the Council and it was on the point of assembling, Martin V. suddenly died, and the ship of Holy Church steered upon a stormy sea under the leadership of Eugen IV, who suffered from the consequences of his predecessor.

The Synod of Basle supported the thesis approved at the Council of Constance, that the Ecumenical Council receives its power direct from God and represented the disputing Catholic Church. For this reason everyone of the faith and also the Pope was compelled to obey it in all questions of belief, the elimination of schisms and in Church reform. In addition it was ordered, that every Catholic and even the Pope, who did not respect the resolutions of the general Synod, should be correspondingly punished and that the Council could not be dissolved by the Pope.[534]

At the Council of Basle not only the doctrine approved in Constance was confirmed but it was also refused the Pope to appoint new cardinals during the duration of the Synod. The situation worsened, when the Pontifex Maximus dissolved the Council and subsequently recalled the decree of dissolution, in order to later lift it again. The Council on its side condemned the Pope and deposed him.

In the midst of this storm the Hussite revolution in Europe which was organised and financed by the secret Jews made shattering progress. All seemed lost for the Church, when divine providence as always stood by her through the work of extraordinary men, who saved her from her fate and were not only able to strengthen her unity but also to completely

---

[533] Juan de Ragusa: Monumenta Conciliorum generalium saeculi XV. Vol. I. Page 66.

[534] Juan de Segovia: Historia gestorum generalis synodi Basiliensis.

defeat the "Synagogue of Satan" and its great revolutionary movement in the 15th century. Among these clergy a simple Franciscan, Juan de Capistrano, particularly distinguished himself, who led the tremendous struggle, which had as consequence the complete victory of the Church over Jewry. This devout Franciscan fought the beast with his sermons and also with the sword, which he thrust into the throat of the dragon, until he had conquered it. Therefore the Jews call him the "scourge of the Jews." But we can make the assurance, that this is saying too much-- St. Juan de Capistrano was the most energetic, most successful, anti- Jewish leader of Catholics after our Lord Jesus and the Apostles. The desolation which he called forth in the "Synagogue of Satan", is regarded by various Jews as the worst of all. But Holy Church has already passed its final judgement on this fighter and canonised him.

St. Juan de Capistrano, who saved the Church and Europe in the 15th century, deserves to be regarded by the patriotic organisations, who at present fight against Jewry, as a guardian saint. In heaven he, who won a similar struggle, will be the most valuable interceder with God and apply himself for those who follow his holy footsteps and in the present fight to defend the Church and their nations against the Jewish Imperialism of the "Synagogue of Satan."

St. Augustine, the great Church Father, asserts and proves in his treatise on the Psalms, clearly and distinctly, that the Jews and not the Romans killed Christ.[535]

Meliton, Bishop of Sardes in Libya and one of the most revered figures of the Church in the 2nd century, asserted: "But the Jews--as it was prophesied--rejected the Lord and killed him. Even if his death was predicted, then nevertheless his guilt was voluntarily recognised. They are lost, but the faithful, to whom Christ preached in hell, and those upon earth, participate in the triumph of the Resurrection."[536]

St. Hippolyte of Rome, a contemporary of Origen, makes the Jews responsible for their misery and misfortune. He was a martyr of Holy Church and was canonised.[537]

---

[535] St. Augustine: Treatise on the Psalms, Psalm 63, Verse 2.

[536] Prof. John Quasten, Patrologie, Madrid, 1961, Vol. I, Page 232.

[537] Prof. John Quasten. Patrolegie. Same edition. Vol. I, Page 470.

Saint Thomas of Aquinas recognised the necessity of placing the Jewish beast in chains, so that it did not cause further harm, and declared in his teaching: "The Jews must according to the Statute of the general Council, wear a distinguishing mark. The Jews may not retain what they have appropriated through usury and are obligated to raise up again those who have destroyed. The Jews live in eternal servitude on account of their guilt. The Lords can therefore take away from them everything and leave them only what is necessary for life, unless it is forbidden through the Holy Laws of the Church."[538]

Without doubt the members of the "Fifth Column" who wish to condemn the antisemites, would also bring Saint Thomas of Aquinas into the accusation box.

In his treatise "Adversus Judaeos" Tertullian brings grave charges against the Jews. In "Scorpiase" he asserts that "the Synagogues are the starting points for persecutions of Christians" and in "Ad Nationem" he mentions, always in connection with the events eighteen hundred years ago, but which coincide astonishingly with those of the present day: "From the Jews issue the slanders against Christians."[539]

All these blasphemous and slandering campaigns are used today as 1800 years ago especially by the false Christians or those who have gained important positions in the clergy, in Catholic or worldly associations or in the parties of the Right, in order to destroy the anti-Communist and anti-Jewish leaders. From the secret gatherings of the synagogue emanated today also as eighteen centuries ago the Christian persecutions, which are especially directed against those who successfully fight against Communism or Jewish Imperialism.

Jaime Balmes, the renowned philosopher of the past century, accused the Jewish merchants in France and Spain of importing Calvinist Bibles in French wine bottles, in spite of the zeal of the Inquisition.[540]

The great Church Father, St. Augustine, himself held certain slaughters of Jews for a punishment of God and made the assurance that many Jews

---

[538] Thomas de Aquinalis: Opera Omnia, Ed. Pasisills, 1880 tabula 1 a-o, Vol. 33, Page 543.

[539] Tertulian: Adversus Judaeos, Escorpiase, Ad Nationes.

[540] Jaime Balmes, S.J.: Protestantism in comparison with Catholicism, Vol. I, Page 466.

were later crucified, because they crucified Christ. Thus Titus during the siege of Jerusalem had 500 Jews crucified daily.[541]

Origen also accused the Jews, of having nailed Christ to the cross.[542]

Pope Paul II refers in his Bull "Illius Vides" of 12th October 1535 clearly to the Jewish falsehood and condemns the Christians, who pay homage to Judaism in secret. From this important Bull we take the following paragraph: "We have received knowledge that in the greatest part of the Kingdom of Portugal several converts from Jewish falsity-- called new Christians-- return to the Rite of the Jews."[543]

Pope Paul IV says in his renowned Bull "Cum Nimis Absurdum" of 12th July 1555: "It is too absurd and pointless that the Jews, whom their own guilt condemns to slavery, under the pretence that Christian piety suffers and tolerates their coexistence, pay back the mercy received from Christians. Accordingly it is ordered in the holy Bull, that the Jews must wear the determined distinguishing mark and should live in Aljamas (ghettos).[544] This renowned Pope likewise speaks of Jewish ingratitude and of the necessity of causing them to live in servitude and mentions how they attempted more than four hundred years ago to rule over the

Christians and used the magnanimous hospitality, which those show them who tolerate them in their regions. As consequence of this he passed the command to enclose them in Almajas and ordered that they must wear the famous distinguishing mark, so that they could be identified. If this famous Pope had lived in our time, he would have undoubtedly been accused and condemned by the members of the "Fifth Column" on account of race hatred and anti-semitism.

---

[541] St. Augustine, Great Church Father. Quoted through Brother Francisco de Torrejoncillo. Sentry against the Jews on the tower of the Church, same edition, Pages 175-176.

[542] Origen: De principiis, Vol. IV, 8.

[543] Pope Paul III. Bull Illius vices of 12th October 1535. Carolitificum. Amplissima Collectio. Rome 1739-1753. Vol. IV, Part I., Cocquelines: Bullarium, Privilegiorum ac Diplomatus Romanorum Pon-Page 132.

[544] Pope Paul IV. Bull Cum nimis absurdum of 12th July 1555. Caroli Cocquelines, same Bullarium, same edition, Vol. IV. Part I. Page 321.

More than seven hundred years ago, Pope Innocence IV declared in his important Bull, "Impia-Judeorum-Perfidia" as follows: "The divine falsity of the Jews, from whose hearts our Saviour did not tear the veil on account of their enormous crimes, but caused them to still go blind, as is just, do not pay heed that Christian pity only accepts them out of mercy and patiently bears coexistence with them, and commit acts of shame, which set those who hear of them, in astonishment, and fill those with terror, who receive report of it."

Since this Pope assumed, that the "Talmud" and other secret books of the Jews incited them to every possible wickedness, he ordered in this same Bull, that they should be burned publicly. "In order to confuse the false Jews."[545]

Nicholaus IV, one of the Popes, who fought with the greatest energy against secret Jewry, passed against the Jews his famous Bull "Turbate Corde", in which he exhorted the Inquisitors, clergy and worldly authorities, to proceed with zeal against them and also against those who defend, favour or conceal them. This Bull was one of the firmest foundations of the Holy mediaeval Church in the struggle against the "Jewish Fifth Column" in Christianity, whether it was now a matter of clergy or laymen or they were recognised as secret Jews or their accomplices or protectors. Thus anyone needed only to protect a secret Jew or heretic, in order to be prosecuted by the Papal Inquisition. One will understand, that while the Popes gave their support to the determinations of these and similar Bulls and the already studied Laws of the Councils of the Lateran, the Jews found it difficult to penetrate into the Christian citadel. Only when Martin V and Leo X did not heed these Bulls and Councils, could the "Synagogue of Satan" at first transiently and later more definitely, divide Christianity.

From this interesting Bull ("Turbate Corde") we take the following: "With troubled heart we hear and bring to mind that many of those converted from the error of Jewish blindness to the light of Christian faith, have fallen back into their former falsehood. Also many Christians have denied the Catholic faith and exchanged it for the Jewish rite, which must be condemned proceed with emphasis against all who make themselves guilty of this crime, against the heretics and their promoters, protectors and defenders. As far as the Jews are concerned, who have occasioned

---

[545] Pope Innocence IV. PP., Bull Impia Judaeorum perfidia of 9th May 1244. Caroli Cocquelines. Same Bullarium, same edition. Vol. III, Page I, Page 298.

Christians of both sexes to their revolting rite or draw them over, they must be punished as they deserve."[546]

The Jewish authors explain that these Christians converted to Judaism were in general descendants of the converts who were baptised in childhood and were later secretly introduced into Jewry.

Since we must close this work, we see ourselves compelled not to quote from countless Bulls of the most famous Popes, which condemn repeatedly Jewry or which represent an important episode in the enormous centuries long struggle of Holy Church against the Jews. In the following part of this book we will study further important documents. We leap over in a moment a great space of time and place ourselves almost in the present. In the following we will reproduce what Jewry says officially in its quoted Encyclopedia about Pope Leo XIII, a genius of modern time: "Leo XIII (1878-1903) was one of the most famous Popes, but never forgave the Jews, that they supported Italian and European Liberalism in general. He placed them equal with the Freemasons and usual revolutionaries and supported the anti-Jewish reactionaries in Austria and France."[547]

Here we have once again the firm conduct in the defence of Holy Church and of the Christian world by one of the greatest Popes of all times, who clearly knew the Jewish problem exactly and made the Jews responsible for Freemasonic activity, which played an important role with the Liberal revolutions.

The elaborations in this and the remaining chapters of this volume suffice in order to prove that the members of the "Fifth Column" in the clergy, by their condemning race hatred and anti-semitism, wish to bring into the accusation box not only our Lord Jesus and the Apostles but also the Church Fathers, the most renowned Ecumenical and provincial Councils and the most respected Popes--to put it briefly, the entire Church. Their infamous intentions are incited through the ignorance which unfortunately prevails in the clergy, which does not know the true Church history. These Judas Iscariots of the 20th century believe under shield of this ignorance to catch in their mousetrap the most devout and

---

[546] Pope Nicolausa IV. Bulle Turbate corde of 5th Sept. 1288. Caroli Cocquelines, same Bullarium, same edition, Vol. III, Part II, P. 52.

[547] Jewish-Spanish Encyclopedia, same edition, Vol. VIII. Word "Papas," Folio II on Page 351.

good-willed Church dignitaries. But we know that divine providence will prevent such a terrible crime and will never allow, that its Holy Church is silently condemned by its own dignitaries. We have-- following the example of St. Bernhard--held it necessary to contribute with our grain of sand, so that the victory of the conspiracy will be prevented, according to the old motto: "God helps those who help themselves."

The mere fact, that the Holy Chair would contradict the doctrine established by Holy Church in the way and manner revealed by us and would declare, that the "infamous Jews" are loved by God, as the "Synagogue of Satan" plans in the shadows, as well as give way and conclude an alliance with them, which neither our Lord Jesus nor the Apostles, nor Holy Church did in almost twenty centuries, would be not only a visible degradation and simultaneously condemnation of the doctrine and the policy of our Saviour, of the apostles, the Popes, Saints and Councils, who fought so much against the "Synagogue of Satan", but would bring the Church into a false position. Her enemies could then prove, that, what she once held for bad, is now good, and what was once black, is now white, which would have catastrophic consequences as one can easily imagine. But this cannot occur. The faithless Jews, who already believe they control the Holy Chair and base themselves upon a group of cardinals and prelates, which is strong enough in order to destroy the essential tradition of the Church and to open the doors to Communism and to carry out reforms, which prepare the decline of Christianity and hasten the fall of the free world, do not reckon with the fact that God supports His Holy Church, among whose dignitaries a present day Ireneus, Athanasius, Chrysostom, Bernhard or Capistrano will arise, who with help of divine providence, will once again save her from the storm.

CHAPTER FORTY-THREE

JEWISH-CHRISTIAN BROTHERHOODS,
FREEMASONIC LODGES WITH A NEW STAMP?

The Jews have murdered millions of Christians in the Communist states and still do it today. They have imprisoned millions more and enslaved them. Everywhere they organise revolutionary movements and civil wars, which constantly call forth cruel bloodshed. And since all criminals have a panic-stricken fear of punishment, they attempt by squandering millions of dollars in the Free World to avoid that the natural anti-Jewish revolution becomes strong, which prevents the triumph of the Communists through an effective attack at their head, and in order to additionally make it impossible for them to punish the guilty and to prevent that they cause mankind so much evil.

In order to prevent that mankind can defend itself effectively against its deadly enemies, they found brotherhoods or associations for Jewish-Christian friendship with enormous expenditure of money in all countries. In the Communist world it is not necessary to squander money upon such bagatelles, for every Christian attempt at defence against the Jews is explained as Antisemitism and punished by the Soviet Courts as also by those of the Satellite states as counter- revolutionary crime and in grave cases punished with death or in lesser ones with long imprisonment.

In the U.S.A. even mixed churches have been founded, where Jews and Protestants unite. The same is now intended with some modifications, to be transferred to Catholicism with help of the secret infiltration into the clergy, which allows them to have dedicated agents there.

Generally these Jewish-Christian brotherhoods or associations are founded under the twofold protection of a Jewish rabbi and of a Catholic cleric. In fact, they flatter and deceive many priests and dignitaries of the Church, win them over with attentions and presents or exert pressure upon them in different manner and compel them to give way, without many knowing the real intentions, which they pursue with these Jewish-Christian brotherhoods or associations. But it is beyond doubt, as the Holy Inquisition and all dignitaries of the Catholic Church established, who have learned the problem in the course of centuries, that all priests and dignitaries who constantly join in the game of the "Synagogue of Satan," must be suspected as being secret Jews; for whoever supports the worst enemies of Christ and even denies the truth and deceives the Christians must be one of those Jewish enemies of Christ, even if he also conceals his wickedness with the soutane or even the cardinal's hat. If one assumes of an individual, who constantly supports a band of thieves and murderers, that he belongs to the band or is at least their accomplice; then it is also logical, that those who, in the clergy, even set their churchly career at stake by their supporting the wickedest band of criminals and thieves which has ever existed in the world, be held to be members of the dark band. With aid of their accomplices in the clergy, who deceive many of the true faith, it is successful for the Jews, to found these Jewish-Christian brotherhoods, whose apparent harmless aims among others, are as follows: "I. To teach Jews and Christians, with mutual respect and honest friendship, to maintain brotherly relations to one another. II. To further a better understanding and mutual respect between Jews and Christians. III. To strengthen the spiritual approximation between Jews and Christians. IV. To promote the knowledge of the mutual confessions of faith, traditions, culture and ways of life. V. To strive for brotherly love in both groups, which rests upon learning to know each other mutually and constant intercourse." And then it is declared in astonishing manner: "VI. Parallel to the already mentioned intentions, Judaism and Christianity should unite in their spiritual ideals their forces against the constant offensive of present day materialism, which unites the spiritual or ideal values, which we Jews and Christians have always asserted in the course of centuries", etc.

These aims are apparently admirable and suited to capture well-meaning people who do not know the Jewish problem, however in secret they conceal deceit and lies, the favourite weapons of the sons of Israel. A fair dose of cynicism is necessary in order to assert that the Jews must unite with the Christians in order to fight against present day materialism. For, as was already proved in this work, the Jews are the principal spreaders of this materialism. No less cynical must one be in order to declare that the Jews wished for brotherly relations with the Christians. This they must first prove and free the unfortunate Christians, whom they have imprisoned both in the Soviet Union as also in the other Communist states and caused to live in hard servitude, and cease to murder them. In reality the Jews and their accomplices in the Catholic clergy wish to capture the incautious with these Brotherhoods and make them into satellites of Jewry, so as later to use them as tools for attacking and destroying the anti-Communist or Nationalistic

Catholic organisations, which defend their country and their religion from the blows of Communism, of Freemasonry and in general from the secret Jewish power, which directs the two already mentioned organisations. Against facts there is no argument: From the report No. 5 of the year 1960 according to our calendar and 5720 of the Jewish calendar, which was published by the Jewish-Christian Brotherhood in Costa Rica, from which we take some of their very brotherly and harmless aims, we now give the following information about their activity and that of similar brotherhoods.

Costa Rica: "Pater Idoate reports to us concerning anti-semitic movements and retaliatory actions, February-March 1960. 1. the antisemitic movements, which have appeared regularly and periodically during the last months in different parts of the world, have also occurred hesitantly and artificially in our beloved Costa Rica. 2. The Jewish-Christian Committee has resolved to speak out publicly against them. Our President (the priest Francisco Herrera) sent to the press a declaration of principles by a party, from which a not only unjustified anti-semitic conduct emanates but which is also contrary to the ordinations of God and Christian demands. 3. This protest of our brotherhood in the name of their President, had a great effect upon society in Costa Rica and called forth a succession of magnificent manifestations in support of the unjustly attacked Jewish cause."

Uruguay: "The Jewish-Christian Brotherhood in Uruguay has sent various interesting newspaper cuttings from Montevideo, which illustrate in a detailed way the splendid demonstrations of solidarity, which took place there in large theatres, in order to reject the anti- semitic manifestations."

It thus becomes clear what the real aim of these Associations of Jewish- Christian rapprochement is: to capture the greatest possible number of Catholics, who are to serve the Jews as blind tools in combating and destroying the political movements of other Catholics in defence of their country, the Church and mankind.

These associations are similar to the former Freemasonry lodges; for there also the brotherhood of the peoples, peaceful coexistence of the various confessions of faith, a friendly Jewish-Christian rapprochement was discussed, but in reality the domination of the Jews over Christians was achieved.

Also in the Freemasonic lodges the Jews made use of Catholic priests, abbots, bishops and even cardinals, who as Freemasons served as bait, so that honest Catholics fell into the trap. The years pass, but the classical tricks of Jewry remain the same.

In the same way and manner they fooled the incautious with the enticements of Freemasonic banquets and feasts with glittering speeches about friendship and brotherhood, while the Jews, who secretly directed Freemasonry, used these masses for infamous aims and could reckon with the Freemasonic Catholic clergy, who stand in service of Jewry, exactly as upon the clergy, who today lead these apparent movements of Jewish-Christian friendship.

Finally in these societies of Jewish-Christian rapprochement and friendship, it is assured that the Jews explain their religion and their thought to Christians and show them books and brochures--even forgeries of the "Talmud", so that the naive Catholics do not regard the Jewish religion as something bad but as equally as good or even better than the Christian. The Jews swindle them, just as the Freemasonic Jews did with the neophytes of the first Freemasonic degree, to whom they introduce a harmless doctrine, which has nothing to do with that which they follow in the highest grades and still less with the real intention of the Jews, who direct this Freemasonic sect. This intention is never revealed to the Christians, who serve them as satellites and tools.

The Jew was always the father of lies. It is only incredible that there are so many simpletons, who always fall again and again into his net.

CHAPTER FORTY-FOUR

FRIENDLY JEWISH-CHRISTIAN APPROACHES

If Holy Church concludes an alliance with Jewry, then it would contradict itself and lose its respect in the eyes of the faithful, since it would offend against the determinations of other Councils of the Church, Bulls of the Popes, who define the doctrine and unified theses of the Church Fathers, as we have already seen. But in the following we will investigate whether it is not at least possible to come to a rapprochement with Jewry and if possible to at least conclude an armistice in this thousand year old struggle. When we spoke of the conversion of the Jews, we have already seen how they use such a sublime striving of the Church only as cunning propaganda in Catholic circles, in order to create an atmosphere of sympathy. In its protection they then attempt to attain through deceit, concessions which may certainly seem harmless at the moment, but have fateful consequences for Holy Church and the Christian world. It is not far away, when the Jewish agents in the hierarchy of the Church will raise anew at the next Ecumenical Council the problem of the conversion of the Jews and as a result create an atmosphere of sympathy, which makes it possible for them to seduce the Holy Synod to resolutions, which are extremely dangerous for the future and the constancy of Holy Church.

As one has experienced, they attempt to put through a kind of Statute, in which the relations between Jews and Catholics shall be laid down, on the foundation that the Jews do not attack Holy Church and the Christians do not attack Jewry. [But although] such a proposal may seem clever for those who are not familiar with the Jewish problem and especially for those who do not grasp it in its entire range, but are also timid and hence tend to form their image of the world according to their own wishes on the basis of a beautiful peace, in which the so mighty Jewry allows Holy Church to live peacefully and would not fight against her. At least now must we learn from history and recall to ourselves that Jewry never keeps its alliances, swindles everyone and promises what it has no intention of keeping and concludes agreements which it violates as soon as it is favourable, solely and alone to weaken its opponent.

The classical tactics of Communism, which in fact consists in never fulfilling its agreements or alliances, is only one revelation of the Jewish policy of lies and of swindling. This is also not remarkable, for Marxist Communism was conceived by Jews, organised by Jews, directed by Jews and is the greatest work of modern Jewry. If no one, who holds himself to be rational, believes the word of a Communist or trusts to agreements and armistices with the Communist because their fatal consequences are already known; with equal or even greater justice must every armistic, peace or agreement with Jewry be regarded as useless, since it is the father of Communism and the instigator of its false policy, which distinguishes itself by not fulfilling international agreements.

From Jewish sources one knows that it is only desired to attain with this statute planned in dark synagogues and high circles of Freemasonry, that the relations between Christians and Jews are regulated and that it will be laid before the next Ecumenical Council by the agents of Jewry in the higher clergy, so that Jews and Christians obligate themselves not to mutually attack each other, and thus the hands and feet of Catholics will be bound in the defence of their nations or their Christian families against the destructive activity of Jewry, which on its side apparently does not attack the Church and Catholics directly, but will do it with its classical system of casting the stone and concealing the hand. For this it uses Freemasonry, Communism and other revolutionary sects, which serve this purpose. Put briefly, while the "Synagogue of Satan" will continue to attack Catholicism and the Free world through their Freemasonic, Communist, etc., sects and will hypocritically announce that it has nothing to do with this and that it is innocent of their deeds, it will be successful for it to bind the hands and feet of Catholics, so that they do not even have the possibility of defending their natural human rights against the Jewish conspiracy, which -when once the Christian defence is crippled- finally destroys everything. While therefore the Christians held the time limit agreed upon, the friendly rapprochement or the concluded peace, they were violated by the Jews, who would use the self-chaining of the Catholics in order to easier control them and to be able to attain their goal- -the destruction of Holy Church, the annihilation of its clergy and the enslavement of mankind.

All these Jewish wiles are to be traced back to the fact that they have become alarmed at the anti-Communist movements which have arisen in the U.S.A., in Latin America, in all countries of Europe, in the Islamic world, in the other states and especially in North America. If these movements unite, they can save the world from the Communist danger and Jewish rule, for many are aware that behind Communism,

Freemasonry and behind every action which is directed at the destruction of Christian civilisation, stands Jewry as head of the octopus, which must be destroyed, if one wishes to effectively defeat the arms - Communism, Freemasonry, Socialism and the other sects. For if the head of the octopus is not attacked, the arms can grow again.

The knowledge of the existence of these political defensive movements which, in many places, especially in the U.S.A.--in spite of constant slanders which the Jewish press and propaganda sling against them, which describes them either as Fascistic, clerical or Nazistic--take on significant extent, disturbs Jewry most of all, so that efforts are being made by it for a world-wide campaign not only in the bosom of the Catholic but also of the Protestant or other-thinking confessions and in other social domains. This movement will apparently conclude alliances between Jews and Christians bring about apparent approaches between the one and other, which could deceive only the believing Christians and men in general concerning the character of the real head of the conspiracy, so that they avoid attacking it and the latter can lead with force to the final victory: the ultimate triumph of Jewish-Communist slavery.

History has shown us, that if the head of the dragon, i.e., Jewry, is effectively attacked and destroyed, this has neither time nor possibility while on the defensive to organise revolutions or to successfully carry out its destructive activity. Thus the Jews who wished to survive had neither time nor rest in the critical moments of the Visigoth repression to organise heresies. The same was the case in times when they were effectively repressed through the Inquisition and Jewry had to vanish. In order to be able to conveniently carry out their revolutionary activity the Jews must be certain that no one attacks them, and they avoid losing energy and money for their own defence, which they need for the revolutionary action in enslaving of the world. Therefore they have sought means and ways so that they do not attack the Christians in their own defence and have conceived all these cunning proposals of rapprochement and Jewish-Christian friendship, mixed societies, non- aggression pacts, etc.

If in the apparent attempts of Jewry to attain a reconciliation between Jews and Christians one saw only a slight possibility of honesty, of getting to know one another better and of sitting at the negotiating table in order to clear friction out of the way and at first to attain an approach and a lasting peace, we would be the first who accepted this proposal of understanding and of peace. Naturally this must not in any form contradict the statutes of the Popes, Church Fathers or of the Holy Councils. But unfortunately one knows only too well, and we have also proved it in this book, that Jewry always uses this apparent good will and these offers of friendship or rapprochement in order to weaken and cripple the defence of those who allow themselves to be deceived by its promises and fall into the traditional centuries old trap.

If anyone doubts and believes that this criterion is exaggerated, then we give them the possibility of experiencing it themselves. If the Church dignitaries who serve the "Jewish Fifth Column" in the Church as tool stand for a rapprochement and that non-aggression pact which is intended to promote the peaceful relations between Jews and Catholics, it would first be essential to examine the honesty of Jewry and to demand in relation to possible negotiations, revealing proofs that the Synagogue is really resolved not to attack Holy Church or the Christian nations, and also not to violate the natural rights of the peoples or to attempt to destroy Christian civilisation. If Jewry in this respect gave clear proofs of its honesty, negotiations could be carried on with some prospect of success. But there is only one way for Jewry to prove that it really wishes for a reconciliation, close approach and peace: It must be prepared to immediately put into effect the following measures:

I. Effective dissolution of Freemasonry all over the world and abandoning of its anti-Christian action.
II. Effective dissolution of the Communist, Socialist-Marxist parties and those controlled by Freemasonry, which fight in order to undermine Christian institutions and to lead the Christian states openly or secretly into the Socialist dictatorship of Jewish Communism.
III. Direct holding of free elections in Russia, Poland, Cuba, Czechoslovakia and the other Christian lands which are cruelly tyrannised by Jewish Communism, as well as in China, where thousands of Christians live under repression. Direct reform of the constitutions of these states, re-establishment of freedom, among other things of freedom of religion, cessation of atheistic and materialistic propaganda, with which the Jews poison the conscience of the young generation of Christian families.
IV. Immediate withdrawal of the Jewish-Russian troops from the east European lands which they have occupied.

If the Jews proved through the really honest carrying out of these measures, that they long for a friendly approach to Holy Church and to Christianity in general, we would be the first who wished that negotiations be opened for bringing both sides together, and we would give congratulations on this most important step on the way to world peace. This would prove that finally the hearts of the Jews were softened, as prophecy of their future conversion to the religion of our Divine Redeemer.

But if they on the contrary come with their deceit and make the assurance that Communism is not a Jewish cause, that there are Communist and anti-Communist Jews, that they neither control nor lead Freemasonry and that they cannot prevent that these sects continue to attack Holy Church; if they say that they can do nothing in order to liberate the Christian peoples from the Jewish-Communist yoke, through which the Christian Churches are also destroyed and persecuted; then one will clearly see what the Synagogue intends with its apparent approaches, with an armistice and a mutual Pact, which is intended to establish the Christian-Jewish relations. Then it would be clear that with this lying proposal they solely and entirely wish to bind the hands of Catholics, so that they do not attack the head of the dragon (Jewry), while its claws (Communism, Freemasonry, Socialist parties, etc., etc.) continue their destructive work against Holy Church, Christianity and the Free World.

"Non praevalebunt." It stands written in the divine Gospel that the gates of Hell shall not triumph. It lies in us to defend ourselves; and with God's help we will do it.

APPENDIX

S tatistical information on the organisations in the Communist government of the Soviet Union, the Party, the Army, the Police and the Trade Unions.

COMMISSARIAT OF THE INTERIOR (1918)

(High officials of this Commissariat)

1. Ederer, President of the Soviet of Petrograd; Jew.
2. Rosenthal, Security Commissar of Moscow; Jew.
3. Goldenrudin, director for propaganda of the Commissariat for foreign affairs; Jew.
4. Krasikov, Press Commissar of Moscow; Jew.
5. Rudnik, Vice-President of the Commissariat for health; Jew.
6. Abraham Krohmal, first secretary of the Commissariat for the accommodation of refugees; Jew, alias Saguersky.
7. Marthenson, director of the press bureau of the Commissariat for internal affairs; Jew.
8. Pfeierman, Chief Commissar for Communist police of Petrograd; Jew.
9. Schneider, Political Commissar of Petrograd; Jew.
10. Minnor, political Commissar of Moscow; American Jew.

COMMISSARIAT FOR FOREIGN AFFAIRS

(Higher Officials)

1. Margolin, director of the pass office; Jew.
2. Fritz, director of the Commissariat for foreign affairs; Jew.
3. Lafet (Joffe), Soviet ambassador in Berlin; Jew.
4. Lewin, First secretary of the Soviet embassy in Berlin; Jew.
5. Askerloth, director of the press and information offices of the Soviet embassy in Berlin; Jew.

6. Beck, Ambassador Extraordinary of the Soviet government in London and Paris; Jew.
7. Benitler (Beintler), Soviet ambassador in Oslo; Jew.
8. Martius, Soviet ambassador in Washington; German (?).
9. Lew Rosenfeld (Kamenev), Soviet ambassador in Vienna; Jew.
10. Vaslaw Vorovskv. former Soviet Ambassador in Rome up to the year 1922, who was murdered by the former Czarist officer M. A. Kontrady on 10th May 1925 in Lausanne; Jew.
11. Peter Lazarovich Voicoff, Soviet Ambassador in Warsaw up to 7th June 1927, when he was murdered by a young, Russian; Jew.
12. Malkin, Soviet Consul in Glasgow (Scotland) in the year 1919; Jew.
13. Kain Rako (Rokevsky), President of the peace Committee of Kiev; Jew.
14. Manuilsky, first adjutant of Rako and at present leading Communist ruler in the Ukraine; Jew.
15. Astzumb-Ilssen, first legal advisor of the Soviet Commissariat for foreign affairs (1918); Jew.
16. Abel Beck, Consul General in Odessa; Jew.
17. Grundbaum (Cevinsky), Consul General in Kiev; Jew.

HIGHER OFFICIALS IN THE SOVIET ECONOMIC COMMISSARIAT (1918)

1. Merzvin (Merzwinsky), first trade Commissar; Jew.
2. Solvein, Secretary of Merzvin; Jew.
3. Haskyn, general secretary of the Soviet trade Commissariat; Jew.
4. Bertha Hinewitz, assistant of Haskyn; Jewess.
5. Isidor Gurko (Gurkowsky), second trade Commissar; Jew.
6. Jaks (Gladneff), Secretary of Gurko; Jew.
7. Latz (Latsis), President of the trade council; Jew from Latvia.
8. Weisman, secretary of the trade council; Jew.
9. Satkinov, government counsellor of the Peoples Bank of Moscow. Russian.
10. Jaks (Brother of the other), government counsellor of the Peoples Bank; Jew.
11. Axelrod (Orthodox), government counsellor of the Peoples Bank; Jew.
12. Michelson, government counsellor of the Peoples Bank; American Jew.

13. Furstemberg (Ganetsky), Commissar for the government of "Soviet-German" trade affairs. In reality he was the contact man of the Jewish revolutionaries of Russia, and the Jewish banking group of Kuhn-Loeb & Co., New York; Warburg, Stockholm; Speyer & Co., London; Lazar Freres, Paris, etc., which supported the Communist revolution of Russia by way of the Rheinisch-Westfalische Syndicate for the Bank-system in Germany with money contributions.

14. Kogon (one of the Kaganovich brothers), first secretary of Furstemberg; Jew.

HIGHER OFFICIALS OF THE COMMISSARIAT OF LAW (1918-19)

1. Joseph Steinberg, brother of Steinberg who is the titulary Commissar; Jew. He occupies the post of first "Peoples" Commissar.
2. Jakob Berman, President of the revolutionary court of Moscow, Jew; probably the same Jakob Berman, who is the present director for the Communist party in Poland.
3. Lutzk (Lutzky), Court Commissar of the "Peoples" military forces; Jew.
4. Berg, Court Commissar of Petrograd; Jew.
5. Goinbark, Director of the department for formulation of laws; Jew.
6. Scherwin, First Secretary of the "Peoples Commune" of Moscow; Jew.
7. Glausman, President of the Control Commission at the Commissariat of Law; Jew.
8. Schraeder (Schrader), Chief Commissar of the Supreme Court of Moscow; Jew.

HIGHER OFFICIALS OF THE COMMISSARIAT FOR PUBLIC EDUCATION

1. Groinim., Commissar for the lands in the south of Russia; Jew.
2. Lurie (brother of the President of the Supreme Soviet of trade), director of the department for elementary schools of the Commissariat for public education; Jew.

3. Liuba Rosenfeld, directress of the theatrical section of the ministry for public education; Jewess.
4. Rebeca Jatz, secretary of the above-named; Jewess.
5. Sternberg, director of the department for sculpture of the Commissariat for public education; Jew.
6. Jakob Zolotin, President of the government council of the Institute for Communist education; Jew.
7. Grünberg, Commissar of instruction for the northern lands; Jew.

OFFICIALS IN THE ARMY COMMISSARIAT

1. Schorodak, personal advisor of Trotsky: Jew.
2. Slanks, personal advisor of Trotsky; Jew.
3. Petz, personal advisor of Trotsky; Jew.
4. Gerschfeld, personal advisor of Trotsky; Jew.
5. Fruntze, supreme commander of the Communist southern armies; Jew.
6. Fichmann, chief of general staff of the Communist armies of the North; Jew.
7. Potzern, President of the Soviets (Government Council) of the West front; Jew.
8. Schutzman (Schusmanovich), military advisor for the district of Moscow; Jew.
9. Gübelman, Political Commissar for the military district of Moscow; American Jew.
10. Leviensohn, Law Counsellor of the Red Army; Jew.
11. Dietz, political advisor for the military district of Vitebsk; Jew.
12. Glusman, military advisor of the Communist brigade of Samara; Jew.
13. Beckman, political Commissar of the district of Samara; Jew.
14. Kalman, military advisor of the Communist military forces of Slusk; Jew.

HIGHER OFFICIALS IN THE COMMISSARIAT FOR

HEALTH

1. Dauge, Vice-Commissar of the Commissariat for health; Jew.
2. Wempertz, President of the Committee for the fight against venereal diseases; Jew.

3. Rappoport, Director of the pharmaceutical department of the Commissariat; Jew (later political Commissar of Petrograd).
4. Fuchs, Secretary of Rappoport; Jew.
5. Bloschon, President of the Committee for the struggle against infectious diseases; Jew.

MEMBERS OF THE SUPREME SOVIET (SUPREME COUNCIL) FOR PEOPLES TRADE (MOSCOW 1919)

1. Rosenfeld (Kamenev), President of the Trade Soviet for Moscow; Jew.
2. Krasikov, Vice-President of the Trade Soviet of Moscow; Jew.
3. Abraham Schotman, Director of the Trade Soviet of Moscow; Jew.
4. Heikina, secretary of Schotmans; Jewess.
5. Eismondt, President of the Trade Soviet of Petersburg; Jew.
6. Landeman, Vice-President of the Trade Soviet of Petersburg; Jew.
7. Kreinitz, Director of the Trade Soviet of Petersburg; Jew.
8. Abel Alperovitz, Commissar for the iron foundry system of the Supreme Trade Soviet; Jew.
9. Hertz (Herzen), Commissar for the transport system of the Supreme Trade Soviet; Jew.
10. Schilmon, secretary of Hertz; Jew.
11. Tavrid, President of the Commissariat for the harvesting of the sunflower seed oil; Jew.
12. Rotemberg, President of the Commissariat for coal-mining, which is subject to the Supreme Trade Soviet; Jew.
13. Klammer; President of the Commissariat for the fishing industry; Jew.
14. Kisswalter, President of the Commissariat for the economic reconstruction; American Jew.

MEMBERS OF THE FIRST SOLDIERS AND WORKERS COUNCIL OF MOSCOW

1. Moded, Council President; Jew.
2. Smitdowitz, President of the workers commission; Jew.
3. Leibu Kuwith, President of the soldiers commission; Jew.

COUNCIL MEMBERS

4. Klautzner, Jew; 5. Andersohn, Jew; 6. Michelson, Jew; 7. Scharach, Jew; 8. Grünberg, Jew; 9. Riphki, Jew; 10. Vimpa, Latvian; 11. Kiamer, Jew; 12. Scheischman, Jew; 13. Lewinson, Jew; 14.Termizan, Jew; 15. Rosenkoltz, Jew; 16. Katzstein, Jew; 17.Zenderbaum (Martov), Jew; 18. Solo, Latvian; 19. Pfalin, Jew; 20. Krasnopolsky, Jew; 21. Simson, American Jew; 22. Schick, Jew; 23. Tapkin, Jew.

MEMBERS OF THE CENTRAL COMMITTEE OF THE SOVIET COMMUNIST PARTY (1918-1923)

1. Gimel (Sujanov), Jew;
2. Kauner, Jew;
3. Rappoport, Jew;
4. Wilken, Jew;
5. Siatroff, Jew;
6. Grabner, Jew;
7. Diamandt, Jew.

MEMBERS OF THE CENTRAL COMMITTEE OF THE FOURTH CONGRESS OF THE SOVIET WORKERS AND PEASANTS

1. Jankel Swerdin (Sverdolov), Committee President, Jew.

COUNCIL MEMBERS

2. Cremmer, Jew;
3. Bronstein (not Trotsky), Jew;
4. Katz (Mamkov), Jew:
5. Goldstein, Jew;
6. Abelman, Jew;
7. Zünderbaum, Jew;
8. Urisky, Jew;
9. Rein (Abrahamovich), Jew;
10. Benjamin Schmidowitz, Jew;

11. Tzeimbur, Jew;
12. Riphkin, Jew;
13. Schirota, Jew;
14. Tzernin Chernilovsky, Jew;
15. Lewin (Lewinsky), Jew;
16. Weltman, Jew;
17. Axelrod, (Orthodox) Jew;
18. Lunberg, Jew;
19. Apfelbaum (Zinoviev), Jew;
20. Fuschman, Jew;
21. Krasicov, Jew;
22. Knitzunck, Jew;
23. Radner, Jew;
24. Haskyn, Jew;
25. Goldenrubin, Jew;
26. Frich, Jew;
27. Bleichman (Soltntzev), Jew;
28. Lantzer, Jew;
29. Lishatz, Jew;
30. Lenin, Jew on mother's side.

MEMBERS OF THE CENTRAL COMMITTEE OF THE FIFTH CONGRESS OF THE SOVIET SYNDICATE

1. Radek, President, Jew.

MEMBERS

2. Ganitzberg, Jew;
3. . Knigknisen, Jew;
4. Amanessoff, Jew;
5. Tzesulin, Jew;
6. Rosenthal, Jew;
7. Pfrumkin, Jew;
8. Kopnig, Jew;
9. Krilenko, Russian;
10. Jacks, American Jew;
11. Feldman, Jew;
12. Bruno, Jew;
13. Rozin, Jew;
14. Theodorovich, Jew;

15. Siansk (Siansky), Jew;
16. Schmilka, Jew;
17. Rosenfeld (Kamenev), Jew;
18. Samuel Kripnik, Jew;
19. Breslau, Jew;
20. Steinau, Jew;
21. Scheikman, Jew;
22. Askenatz, Jew;
23. Sverdin, Jew;
24. Stutzka, Jew;
25. Dimenstein, Jew;
26. Rupzuptas, Latvian;
27. Schmidowitz, Jew;
28. Nachamkes (Steklov), Jew;
29. Schlichter, Jew;
30. Peterson, Jew;
31. Sasnovsky, Jew;
32. Baptzinsk, Jew;
33. Valach (Litvinov), Jew;
34. Tegel (Tegelsky), Jew;
35. Weiberg, Jew;
36. Peter, Lithuanian;
37. Terian, Armenian;
38. Bronstein, Jew;
39. Ganlerz, Jew;
40. Starck, Jew;
41. Erdling, Jew;
42. Karachen, Jew;
43. Bukharin, Jew;
44. Langewer, Jew;
45. Harklin, Jew;
46. Lunacharsky, Russian;
47. Woloch, Jew;
48. Laksis, Jew;
49. Kaul, Jew;
50. Ehrman, Jew;
51. Tzirtzivatze, Georgian;
52. Longer, Jew;
53. Lewin, Jew;
54. Tzurupa, Latvian;
55. Jafet (Joffe), Jew;
56. Knitsuck, Jew;
57. Apfelbaum, Jew;

58. Natansohn (Babrof), Jew;

59. Daniel (Danialevsky), Jew.

THE POLICE CHIEFS. C.E.K.A. (CHEKA) (1919)

1. Derzhin (Derzinsky), Supreme Chief of the C.E.K.A. (CHEKA); Jew.
2. Peters, Sub-chief of the C.E.K.A.; Lithuanian.
3. Limbert, director of the ill-famed Tagansky prison in Moscow, where a great part of the Czarist aristocracy and many former ministers, generals, diplomats, artists, writers, etc., of the old regime were murdered. Limbert is likewise a Jew.
4. Vogel, Executive Commissar of the CHEKA; Jew.
5. Deipkyn, Executive Commissar of the CHEKA; Jew.
6. Bizensky, Executive Commissar of the CHEKA; Jew.
7. Razmirovich, Executive Commissar of the CHEKA; Jew.
8. Jankel Swerdin (Sverdlov), Executive Commissar of the CHEKA; Jew.
9. Janson, Executive Commissar of the CHEKA; Jew.
10. Kneiwitz, Executive Commissar of the CHEKA; Jew.
11. Finesh, Executive Commissar of the CHEKA; Jew.
12. Delavanoff, Executive Commissar of the CHEKA; Jew.
13. Ziskyn, Executive Commissar of the CHEKA; Jew.
14. Jacob Golden, Executive Commissar of the CHEKA; Jew.
15. Scholovsky, Executive Commissar of the CHEKA; Jew.
16. Reintenberg, Executive Commissar of the CHEKA; Jew.
17. Gal Pernstein, Executive Commissar of the CHEKA; Jew.
18. Zakis, Executive Commissar of the CHEKA; Lithuanian.
19. Knigkisen, Executive Commissar of the CHEKA; Jew.
20. Skeltizan, Executive Commissar of the CHEKA; Armenian.
21. Blum (Blumkin), Executive Commissar of the CHEKA; Jew.
22. Grunberg, Executive Commissar of the CHEKA; Jew.
23. Latz, Executive Commissar of the CHEKA; Jew.
24. Heikina, Executive Commissar of the CHEKA; Jew.
25. Ripfkin, Executive Commissar of the CHEKA; Jew.
26. Katz (Kamkov), Executive Commissar of the CHEKA; Jew.
27. Alexandrovich, Executive Commissar of the CHEKA; Russian.
28. Jacks, Executive Commissar of the CHEKA; Jew.
29. Woinstein (Zwesdin), Executive Commissar of the CHEKA; Jew.
30. Lendovich, Executive Commissar of the CHEKA; Jew.

31. Gleistein, Executive Commissar of the CHEKA; Jew.
32. Helphand (Parvis), Executive Commissar of the CHEKA; Jew.
33. Silencus, Executive Commissar of the CHEKA; Jewess.
34. Jacob Model, Chief or the Communist "Peter and Paul" troop for mass repression; Jew.

PEOPLES COMMISSARS OF PETROGRAD

1. Rodomill, Jew.
2. Djorka (Zorka), Jew.

EXECUTIVE COMMISSARS OF THE CHEKA OF PETROGRAD (1919-1924)

1. Isilevich, Jew.
2. Anwelt, Jew.
3. Meichman, American Jew.
4. Judith Rosmirovich, Jewess.
5. Giller, Jew.
6. Buhan, Armenian.
7. Sispper (Disperoff), Jew.
8. Heim Model, Jew.
9. Krasnik, Jew.
10. Koslowsky, Pole.
11. Mehrbey, American Jew.
12. Pawkis, Lithuanian.

MEMBERS OF THE SUPREME COMMISSARIAT FOR LABOUR IN MOSCOW

1. Benjamin Schmidt, Peoples Commissar; Jew.
2. Zencovich, Secretary of Schmidt; Jew.
3. Raskyn, General secretary of the labour Commissariat; Jew.
4. Zarach, director of the supply department for workers; Jew.
5. Woltman, second Commissar of public workers; Jew.
6. Kaufman, assistant of Woltman; Jew.
7. Goldbarh, President of the Commission for public works; Jew.

8. Kuchner, first advisor of the Commissariat for public works, Jew.

COMMUNIST COMMISSARS AND OFFICIALS IN THE PROVINCES

1. Isaak Latsk, Supreme Commissar of the Don Republic; Jew.
2. Reichenstein, Peoples Commissar of the Don Republic; Jew.
3. Schmulker, secretary of the above; Jew.
4. Levinson, President of the Don Soviet; Jew.
5. Haytis, Commissar for Siberia; Jew.
6. Dretling, President of the Soviet of Kiev; Jew.
7. Ziumperger, assistant of the above; Jew.
8. Zackheim, President of the Soviet of Jaroslaw; Jew.
9. Sheikman, President of the Soviet of Kazan; Jew.
10. Willing, President of the Soviet of Orenburg (present day Chicakow); Jew.
11. Berlin (Berlinsky), President of the Soviet of Sizrn; Jew.
12. Limbersohn, President of the Soviet of Penza; Jew.
13. Somur, Trade Minister of Transcausasia; Jew.
14. Schultz (Slusky), President of the Soviet of Tavrida; Jew.
15. Herman, President of the Soviet of Tzarinsk; Jew.
16. Rotganzen, President of the Soviet of Bielatzerkowski; Jew.
17. Lemberg, secretary of Rotganzen; Jew.
18. Daumann, President of the Soviet of Narwsky; Jew.

EDITORS OF THE COMMUNIST NEWSPAPERS "PRAVDA", "EKONOMICHENSKANYA ZIZIN" AND "IZVESTIA"

1. Najames (Steklov), Jew;
2. Jacob Golin, Jew;
3. Kohn, Jew;
4. Samuel Daumen, Jew;
5. Ilin Tziger, Jew;
6. Maximo Gorky, Russian;
7. Dean, Jew;
8. Bitner, Jew;

 9. Kleisner, Jew;
10. Bergman, Jew;
11. Alperowich, Jew;
12. Laurie (Rumiantzeff), Jew;
13. Brahmon, Jew;
14. Grossman (Rozin). Jew;
15. Abraham Torbeth, Jew.

EDITORS OF THE COMMUNIST NEWSPAPER "TORGO-PROMISLEVNOY GAZZETTY"

1. Abel Pretz, Jew;
2. Rafalowitz, Jew;
3. Gogan, Jew;
4. Bastell, Jew;
5. Grochmann, Jew;
6. Bernstein, Jew;
7. Moch, Jew;
8. Abraham Salomon Emanson, Jew;
9. Goldenberg, Jew;
10. Slavensohn, Jew;
11. Benjamin Rosenberg, Jew;
12. Schuman, Jew;
13. Kulliser, Jew;
14. Goldman, Jew;
15. Jacob Giler (Gilev), Jew.

EDITORS OF THE COMMUNIST NEWSPAPER "DIE FAHNE DER ARBEIT" (BANNER OF LABOUR) (1920)

1. Schumacher, Jew;
2. David (Davidov), Jew;
3. Jarin (Yarolavsky), Jew;
4. Lander, Jew;
5. Samson Lewin, Jew;
6. Steinbeck, Jew;
7. . Bilin, Jew;
8. Evron, Jew.

EDITORS OF THE COMMUNIST NEWSPAPER "VIOLA TRUVAS"

1. Katz (Kamkov), Jew;
2. Jacks, Jew;
3. Eisenberg (Poliansky), Jew.

MEMBERS OF THE COMMISSION FOR THE ARREST OF SYMPATHIZERS WITH THE CZARIST REGIME

1. Muraviov, President, Russian.

MEMBERS

2. Salomon, Jew;
3. Edelsohn, Jew;
4. Goldstein, Jew;
5. Gruzenberg, Jew;
6. Tanker, Jew.

MEMBERS OF THE CENTRAL OFFICE OF THE HIGHER TRADE SOVIET

1. Rabinovich, Jew;
2. Weinberg, Jew;
3. Larin, Jew;
4. Galalt, Jew;
5. Kreitman, Jew;
6. Zupper, Jew;
7. Krasnin, Russian;
8. Alperovitz, Jew.

MEMBERS OF THE CENTRAL BUREAU OF STATE CONSUMER BODIES

1. Sidelgenim, Jew;
2. Heikinn, Jew;
3. Lubomirsky, Russian;
4. Kritzer (Krozov), Jew;
5. Tanger, Jew;
6. Kinstung, Jew.

MEMBERS OF THE CENTRAL COMMITTEE OF ARTISANS SYNDICATE

1. Ravetz, Jew;
2. Zmirnov, Russian;
3. Gitzemberg, Jew;
4. Davidson, Jew;
5. Brillante, Jew.

REPRESENTATIVES OF THE RED ARMY ABROAD

1. Sobelsohn (Radek), Soviet military representative in Berlin; Jew.
2. Neinsenbaum, military representative in Bucharest; Jew.
3. Bergman, military representative in Vienna; Jew.
4. Abraham Baum, military representative in Copenhagen; Jew.
5. Bergman, military representative in Vienna; Jew.
6. Alter Klotzman, military representative in Warsaw; Jew.
7. Abraham Klotzman, Adjutant of the former; Jew.

MEMBERS OF THE HIGHER JUDICIARY CORPS

1. Katsell, Jew;
2. Goldman, Jew;
3. Walkperr, Jew;
4. Kasior, Jew;
5. Schnell, Jew;
6. Schorteil, Russian;
7. Zercov, Russian;
8. Schmidt, Jew;
9. Blum, Jew;
10. Rudzistarck, Jew.

PROFESSORS OF THE "SOCIALIST" ACADEMY OF MOSCOW

1. Skentenberg, Jew; 2. Nadezda Krupp (Krupskaya, i.e. the wife of Lenin, likewise Jewess not Russian as generally asserted), Jewess; 3. Kraskowsko, Jew; 4. Gleitzenr, Jew, lover of the second wife of Stalin, for this reason shot in 1932, although in the affair he was made to appear as "supported of Trotsky", Jew; 5. Keltsman, Jew; 6. Schutzka, Jew; 7. Schirolla, Finnish Jew; 8. Rotstein, Jew; 9. Reisner, Jew; 10 Josif Rakovsky, Jew; 11. Jacob Lurie, Jew; 12. Rozin, Jew; 13. Pokrovsky, Russian; 14. Karl Levin, Jew; 15. Gimel (Sujanov), Jew; 16. Budin, Jew; 17. Ehrperg, Jew; 18. Nemirovich, Jew; 19. Coikburg, Jew; 20. Rapport, Jew; 21. Grossmann, Jew; 22. Fritz, Jew; 23. Najamkes, Jew; 24. Ludberg, Jew; 25. Dand (Dauzewsky), Jew; 26. Goldenbach (Riazonov), Jew; 27. Kusinen, Finn; 28. Weltman, Jew; 29. Salomon Olansky, Jew; 30. Ursiner (Ursinov), Jew; 31. Gurovich, Jew; 32. Rosa Luxemburg, German Jewess; 33. Elchenkoltz, Jew; 34. Tzerkina, Jewess; 35. Gatze, Jew; 36. Moises Ulansk, Jew; 37. Broito (Broitman) Jew.

MEMBERS OF THE SUPREME SOVIET OF THE DON COMMITTEE

1. Polonsky, Russian; 2. Rosental, Jew; 3. Krutze, Jew; 4. Bernstein (Koganov), Jew; 5. Zimanovich, Jew; 6. Klasin, Latvian; 7. Otzkins, Jew; 8. Wichter, Jew; 9. Kirtz, Jew; 10. Liphsitz, Jew; 11. Bitzk,Jew.

MEMBERS OF THE AID COMMITTEE FOR THE COMMUNISTS

1. Ethel Knigkisen, Jewish woman Peoples Commissar.
2. Goldman, secretary of the above; Jew.
3. Rosa Kaufman, assistant of the above; Jewess.
4. Pautzner, director of the Aid Committee; Jew.
5. K. Rosenthal, Chief of the central office of the Aid Committee; Jew.

SOVIET TRADE REPRESENTATIVES ABROAD

1. Abraham Shekman, Trade representative in Stockholm with the banks Warburg and Nye Bankon; Jew.
2. Landau, Trade representative in Berlin; Jew.
3. Worowski, Trade representative in Copenhagen; Jew.

PEOPLES JUDGES IN MOSCOW

1. Jakob Davidov, Jew; 2. Paul Bitzk, Jew; 3. Jakob Adokolsky, Jew; 4. Joseph Beyer, Jew; 5. Abraham Gundram, Jew; 6. Kastariaz, Armenian; 7. Beniamin/Aronovitz, Jew.

PERMANENT COMMISSARS AT DISPOSAL OF THE SUPREME SOVIET OF MOSCOW

1. Tziwin (Piatinsky), Jew; 2. Gurevich (Dan), Jew; 3. Silberstein (Begdanov), Jew; 4. Garfeld (Garin), Jew; 5. Rosemblum (Maklakowsky), Jew; 6. Kernomordik, Jew; 7. Lowenshein, Jew; 8. Goldenberg (Meshkowski), Jew; 9. Tzibar (Martinov), Jew.

MILITARY ADVISORS OF THE COMMUNIST GOVERNMENT OF MOSCOW

1. Lechtiner, adviser of the military Soviet of the Caucasian army; Jew.
2. Watsertish, Commander of the West Front against Czechoslovakia; Jew.
3. Bruno, Special advisor for the East Front; Jew.
4. Schulman, second advisor of the Moscow government (Council of the Peoples Commissars) for the East Front; Jew.
5. Schmidowitz, Commander of the Communist military forces in the Crimea; Jew.
6. Jack, second commander of the forces in the Crimea; Jew.
7. Schnesur, third commander of the same army; Lithuanian.
8. Meigor, Chief of the military Soviet of Kazan; Jew.
9. Nazurkoltz, Commissar of the military Soviet of Kazan; Jew.

10. Rosenkeltz, Commissar of the military Soviet of Kazan; Jew.
11. Samuel Gleitzer, Commissar and Commander of the Soviet trooping school for the frontiers (frontier guards); Jew.
12. Kolman, commander of the military Commune of Moscow; Jew.
13. Katzmer (Lazimov), Adjutant of the above; Jew.
14. Dulis, military advisor of the Soviet government; Jew.
15. Steinger, military advisor of the Soviet government; Jew.
16. Gititz, political Commissar for the military district of Petrograd; Jew.
17. Dzenitz, political Commissar for the 15th Communist brigade; Jew.
18. Bitziss, commander of the military district of Moscow; Jew.
19. Gecker, commander of the Communist army of Jaroslaw; Jew.
20. Mitkatz, military advisor of the government for the military district of Moscow; Jew.
21. Tzeiger, Commander of the military Soviet of Petrograd; Jew.

MEMBERS OF THE COMMISSARIAT FOR THE LIQUIDATION OF PRIVATE BANKS

1. Henrick, special Commissar of the government; Jew.
2. Moisekovak, assistant of the above; Jew.
3. Kahan, Controller-general for the private bank depots; American Jew.
4. Jacob Giftling, technical advisor of the Commissariat; Jew.
5. Nathan Elliasevich, second technical advisor; Jew.
6. Sarrach Elliasevich, assistant of the above; Jewess.
7. Abraham Ranker, advisor of the Commissariat; Jew.
8. Plat, Jewish advisor; Latvian.
9. Abraham Rosenstein, Jewish advisor; Jew.
10. Lemerich, advisor of the Commissariat; Jew.

MEMBERS OF THE LINGUAL SCIENCE DEPARTMENT OF THE PROLETARIAT

1. Beniamin Zeitzer, Jew; 2. Pozner, Jew; 3. Maxim Gorky, Russian; 4. Alter, Jew; 5. Eichenkoltz, Jew; 6. Schwartz, Jew; 7. Berender, Jew; 8. Kelinin, Jew; 9. Hadasevich, Jew; 10. Leben (Lebedeff), Jew; 11. Kersonskaya, Jewess.

How many leading posts of the new Jewish-Soviet State have been occupied by Gentiles and how many by the descendants of Abraham, is shown by the following statistics.

1. Members of the first Communist government of the Mesed (Council of Peoples Commissars).
2. High officials, who belong to the Commissariat for Internal Affairs.
3. Higher officials of the Commissariat for foreign affairs.
4. Higher officials of the trade Commissariat.
5. Higher officials of the justice Commissariat.
6. Higher officials of the Commissariat for public schools.
7. Officials of the Commissariat for armed forces.
8. Higher officials in the Commissariat for health.
9. Members of the Supreme Soviet for Peoples trade.
10. Members of the first Soldiers and Workers Councils of Moscow.
11. Members of the Central Committee of the Soviet Communist Party.
12. Members of the Central Committee of the 40th Congress of Syndicates of Soviet Workers and Peasants.
13. Members of the Central Committee of the 50th Congress of the Soviet Syndicate.
14. Directors of the CHEKA police in Moscow.
15. Peoples Commissars in Petrograd.
16. Executive Commissars of the CHEKA police of Petrograd.
17. Members of the higher labour Commissariat.
18. Communist Commissars and officials in the provinces.
19. Editors of the newspapers "Pravda", "Izvestia", and "Ekonomichenskaya Zizin."
20. Editors of the Communist newspaper "Torgo-Promislevnoy Gazzetty."
21. Editors of the Communist newspaper "The Banner of Labour."
22. Editors of the newspaper "Vola- Truva."
23. Members of the Commission for the arrest of sympathisers with the Czarist regime.
24. Members of the Central Bureau of State Consumer Bodies.
25. Members of the Central Bureau of the Higher Trade Soviet.
26. Members of the Central Committee of artisans Syndicates.
27. Representatives of the Red Army abroad.
28. Members of Higher Juristic Corps.
29. Professors of the Socialist Academy of Moscow.

30. Members of the Higher Soviet of the Don Commissariat.
31. Members of the Aid Commission for the Communist.
32. Soviet trade representatives abroad.
33. Peoples Judges of Moscow.
34. Permanent Commissars at disposal of the Supreme Soviet.
35. Military advisors of the government of Moscow.
36. Members of the Commissariat for the liquidation of private banks.
37. Members of the Lingual Science department of the Proletariat.[548]

---

[548] Traian Romanescu, La Gran Conspiración Judía, pages 143-161.

THE SUPREME ROMAN PONTIFFS

St. Peter of Bethsaida in Galilee, Prince of the Apostles, who received from Jesus Christ the Supreme Pontifical Power to be transmitted to his Successors, resided first at Antioch, then at Rome for twenty-five years where he was martyred in the year 64, or 67 of the common reckoning.

END OF PONTIFICATE, A.D.			
St Linus, M.	76	St Sixtus III	440
St Anacletus or		St Leo I (the Great)	461
Cletus, M.	88	St Hilary	468
St Clement I, M.	97	St Simplicius	483
St Evaristus, M.	105	St Felix III or II	492
St Alexander I, M.	115	St Gelasius I	496
St Sixtus I, M.	125	Anastasius II	498
St Telesphorus, M.	136	St Symmacus	514
St Hyginus, M.	140	St Hormisdas	523
St Pius I, M.	155	St John I	526
St Anicetus, M.	166	St Felix IV or III	530
St Soterus, M.	175	Boniface II	532
St Eleuterius, M.	189	John II	535
St Victor I, M.	199	St Agapitus	536
St Zephyrinus, M.	217	St Silverius, M.	537
St Callistus I, M.	222	Vigilius	555
St Urban I, M.	230	Pelagius I	561
St Pontian, M.	235	John III	574
St Anterus, M.	236	Benedict I	579
St Fabian, M.	250	Pelagius II	590
St Cornelius, M.	253	St Gregory I (the	
		Great)	604
St Lucius, M.	254	Sabinianus	606
St Stephen I, M.	257	Boniface III	607
St Sixtus II, M.	258	St Boniface IV	615
St Dionysius	268	St Deusdeditus or	
		Adeodatus I	618
St Felix I, M.	274	Boniface V	625
St Eutychian, M.	283	Honorius I	638
St Caius, M.	296	Severinus	640
St Marcellinus, M.	304	John IV	642
St Marcellus I, M.	309	Theodore I	649
St Eusebius, M.	309	St Martin I, M.	655
St Melchiades, M.	314	St Eugene I	657
St Sylvester I	335	St Vitalian	672
St Mark	336	Adeodatus II	676
St Julius I	352	Donus I	678
Liberius	366	St Agathonus	681

St Damasus I	384	St Leo II	683
St Siricius	399	St Benedict II	685
St Anastasius I	401	John V	686
St Innocent I	417	Conon	687
St Zozimus	418	St Sergius I	701
St Boniface I	422	John VI	705
St Celestine I	432	John VII	707
Sisinnius	708		
Constantine	715	John XII	964
St Gregory II	731	Leo VIII	965
St Gregory III	741	Benedict V	966
St Zachary	752	John XIII	972
Stephen III	757	Benedict VI	974
St Paul I	767	Benedict VII	983
Stephen IV	772	John XIV	984
Adrian I	795	John XV	996
St Leo III	816	Gregory V	999
Stephen V	817	Sylvester II	1003
St Paschal I	824	John XVII	1003
Eugene II	827	John XVIII	1009
Valentine	827	Sergius IV	1012
Gregory IV	844	Benedict VIII	1024
Sergius II	847	John XIX	1032
St Leo IV	855	Benedict IX	1044
Benedict III	858	Benedict IX	1045
St Nicholas I (the Great)	867	Sylvester III	1045
Adrian II	872	Gregory VI	1046
John VIII	882	Clement II	1047
Marinus I	884	Benedict IX	1048
St Adrian III	885	Damasus II	1048
Stephen VI	891	St. Leo IX	1054
Formosus	896	Victor II	1057
Boniface VI	896	Stephen X	1058
Stephen VII	897	Nicholas II	1061
Romanus	897	Alexander II	1073
Theodore II	897	St. Gregory VII	1085
John IX	900	B. Victor III	1087
Benedict IV	903	B. Urban II	1099
Leo V	903	Paschal II	1118
Sergius III	911	Gelasius II	1119
Anastasius III	913	Callistus II	1124
Landus	914	Honorius II	1130
John X	928	Innocent II	1143
Leo VI	928	Celestine II	1144
Stephen VIII	931	Lucius II	1145
John XI	935	B. Eugene III	1153
Leo VII	939	Anastasius IV	1154
Stephen IX	942	Adrian IV	1159
Marinus II	946	Alexander III	1181
Agapitus II	955	Lucius III	1185

Urban III	1187	Adrian VI		1523
Gregory VIII	1187	Clement VII		1534
Clement III	1191	Paul III		1549
Celestine III	1198	Julius III		1555
Innocent III	1216	Marcellus II		1555
Honorius III	1227	Paul IV		1559
Gregory IX	1241	Pius IV		1565
Celestine IV	1241	St Pius V		1572
Innocent IV	1254	Gregory XIII		1585
Alexander IV	1261	Sixtus V		1590
Urban IV	1264	Urban VII		1590
Clement IV	1268	Gregory XIV		1591
B. Gregory X	1276	Innocent IX		1591
B. Innocent V	1276	Clement VIII		1605
Adrian V	1276	Leo XI		1605
John XXI	1277	Paul V		1621
Nicholas III	1280	Gregory XV		1623
Martin IV	1285	Urban VIII		1644
Honorius IV	1287	Innocent X		1655
Nicholas IV	1292	Alexander VII		1667
St. Celestine V	1296	Clement IX		1669
Boniface VIII	1303	Clement X		1676
B. Benedict XI	1304	B. Innocent XI		1689
Clement V	1314	Alexander VIII		1691
John XXII	1334	Innocent XII		1700
Benedict XII	1342	Clement XI		1721
Clement VI	1352	Innocent XIII		1724
Innocent VI	1362	Benedict XIII		1730
B. Urban V	1370	Clement XII		1740
Gregory XI	1378	Benedict XIV		1758
Urban VI	1389	Clement XIII		1769
Boniface IX	1404	Clement XIV		1774
Innocent VII	1406	Pius VI		1799
Gregory XII	1415	Pius VII		1823
Martin V	1431	Leo XII		1829
Eugene IV	1447	Pius VIII		1830
Nicholas V	1455	Gregory XVI		1846
Callistus III	1458	Pius IX		1878
Pius II	1464	Leo XIII		1903
Paul II	1471	St Pius X		1914
Sixtus IV	1484	Benedict XV		1922
Innocent VIII	1492	Plus XI		1939
Alexander VI	1503	Pius XII		1958
Pius III	1503	John XXIII		1963
Julius II	1513	Paul VI,		
Leo X	1521			

BIBLIOGRAPHY

P. ABEL: Die neue freie Presse, Vienna 1898.

ABJAR MACHMAU: Translation by Emilio Lafuente y Alcantara: Collection of Arabic works of history and geography. Real Academia de la Historia. Madrid. Vol. I.

ABODA SARA: 26b. Tosephot.

ACADEMIA DE LA HISTORIA: Privilegios de dicha Iglesia. Cortes de los Antiguos Reinos de Leon y Castilla. Madrid. 1863.

RICARDO C. ALBANES: Los judios a traves de los siglos.

ALMANACH DER FREIMAURER (Almanach of Freemasons), Leipzig 1884.

P. JOSEPH ALVAREZ DE LA FUENTE: Succession Real de Espana.

JOSE AMADOR DE LOS RIOS: Historia de los Judios de Espana y Portugal. Madrid 1875.

AMOLON: Treatise against the Jews. Published by the "Patrum Maxima" library.

ARCHIVO GENERAL DEL ESTADO: Proceso de Luis de Carvajal el Mozo. Published by the Mexican Government, 1935.

ARGENTINE-HEBREW SOCIETY: Los Judios. Su Historia. Su aporte a la cultura. Buenos Aires 1956.

ARIO: Thalia.

JAIME BALMES, S.J.: El protestanismo comparado con el catolicismo.

BALUZIUS: Vitae Paparum Avenionensium, Paris 1693.

BARRUEL: Memoires pour l'Histoire du Jacobinisme.

BATIFFOL: Les sources del l'histoire du Concile de Nicee. Edition of 1925.

LEROY BEAULIEAU: Israel among the nations.

BEDARRIDE: Les Juifs en France, en Italie et en Espagne. Published by Michel Levy, Paris 1961.

BENAMOZEGH: Israel und die Menschheit (Israel and Mankind).

DIE HEILIGE SCHRIFT (Holy Scripture). Paul Pattloch Publishers, Aschaffenburg.

BIBLIA. Ed. SCIO.

CARLO BO: "E ancora difficule dire ebreo". Periodical L'Europeo, Milan. 26.8 1962.

BOSSUET: Good Friday Sermon and Talks about World History.

BULLARIUM DIPLOMATUM ET PRIVILEGIORUM SANCTORUM ROMANORUM PONTIFICUM. Taurensis editio, 1739-1754.

BULLETIN OFICIEL DU G.O. DE LA FRANCE. Oct. 1922.

CAPEFIGUE: The great Financial manoeuvres.

JOSE MARIA CARO (Cardinal), Archbishop of Santiago and Primate of Chile: El misterio de la Masoneria. Difusion Publishers.

CAVALLERA: Le Schisme d'Antioche. Cambridge 1938. CHANIGA

CIVILTA CATTOLICA. Periodical of the Society of Jesus in Rome. Volumes of 1898 and Number 1870 from the year 1928.

CONTINUATIO CHRONICI GUILLELMI DE NANGIS. Published in "Specilegium sive Collectio Veteerum Aliquot Scriptorum qui in Galliae Biblothecis delituerant." Paris, 1723. Vol. III.

CORTES DE LOS ANTIGUOS REINOS DE LEON Y CASTILLA. Published by the Academia de la Historia. Madrid 1863. Vol. II.

CRONICON MESSONIQUE E CRONICON SEBASTIANI. "Espana Sagrada." Vol. XIII.

CUVALIER: Historie de Monseigneur Bertrand du Guesclin.

ALFONSO DE CASTRO: El problema judio. Actualidad, Mexico 1939.

RENZO DE FELICE: Storia degli ebrei italiani sotto il fascismo. Einaudi. Turin 1961.

DUQUE DE LA VICTORIA: Israel Manda. Latino-Americana Publishers. S.A. Mexico.

HUMBERT ODE LUCCA (Bishop): Cronica en Codex Ul-darici.

DE LUCHET: Essai sur la Secte des Illumines.

JUAN DE MARIANA, S.J.: Historia General de Espana. Madrid 1650.

LEON DE PONCINS: Les forces secrètes de la revolution. F. . .M . . . JUDAISM. Fax Publishers. Madrid.

JUAN DE RAGUSA: Monumenta Conciliorum Generalium Saeculi.

P. DESCHAMPS, CARDINALE MATHIEU. Monseigneur Besson and others: The secret societies and human society.

JUAN DE SEGOVIA: Historia gestorum generalis Synodi Basiliensis.

C. DE TORMAY: Le livre proscrit.

FRAY FRANCISCO DE TORREJONCILLO: Centinela contra los judios puesta sobre la torre de la Iglesia de Dios.

DUCAY DE TUY: Cronicon Era 733.

GUTTERRE DIEZ DE GAMEZ: Cronica de Pedro Nino Conde de Buelna. 1445.

DUCHESNE: Compendio de la historia de Espana. Spanish translation by P. Jose Francisco de la Isla. Madrid 1827 and Liber Pontificalis. Paris 1955.

JOSEPH DUNNER: The Republic of Israel. Published in October 1950.

EBEN HA ESER, 6 and 8.

E. EBERLIN: Les juifs d'ajourd'hui.

ENCICLOPEDIA ESPASA CALPE.

ENCICLOPEDIA JUDAICA CASTELLANA.

EUSEBIO: Vita Constantini.

MAURICE FARA: La Masoneria al descubierto. Published by "La Hoja de Roble." Buenos Aires.

FERRER DEL RIO: Examen historico critico del Reinado de don Pedro de Castilla. Madrid 1851.

D.G. FOATTA: L'ebreo: ecco il pericolo. Prato 1891. FORUM JUDICUM.

JEAN FROISSARD: Histoire et Chronique Memorable. Uaris 1574.

FUERO JUZGO. Published by the Real Academia Espanola. Madrid 1815.

P. GAXOTTE: The French Revolution.

GEVATKIN, Studies of Arianism.

NICOLE GILLES: Les Anales et Chronique de France. Paris 1666.

GOUGENOT DES MOSSEAUX: Le Juif, le judaisme et la judaisation des peuples chretiennes.

GRAETZ: History of the Jews. Published by Jewish Publication Society of America, Philadelphia 5717. 1956. Vol. II.

FERDINAND GREGOROVIUS: History of the city of Rome in the Middle Ages. Turin.

LEON HALEVY: Survey of the history of the Jews.

JOANNES HARDUINI, S.J.: Acta Conciliorum et epistolae decretales ac constitutione Summorum Pontificum. Paris 1714.

MALCOLM HAY: Europe and the Jews. Boston 1960.

PAUL HAY SEIGNEUR DE CHARTELET: Histoire de Mon-seigneur Bertrand du Guesclin, Paris 1666.

MOSES HESS: Rome and Jerusalem. Translation and published by the Rabbi Maurice J. Bloom. New York 1958.

HOERET WAND: The Four Great Heresies. Edition 1955.

BERNARD HUTTON: French periodical Constellation, Number 167 of March 1962.

IBN-EL ATHER: Cronica El Kamel.

IBN-KALDOUN: Histoire des Berberes. Translated from the Arabic into French by Baron de Salane. Argel 1852.

INQUISITIONS ARCHIVE OF CARCASSONE, quoted by Vaissette in "Histoire Generale de Languedoc."

INTERNATIONAL FREEMASONS congress of Brussels in the year 1910.

ISRAELITE ARCHIVE, 1864.

JULES ISSAC: Jesus et Israel. JEBAMOTH.

JEWISH ENCYCLOPEDIA. GOSPEL OF JOHN.

SALVATORE JONA: Gli ebrei in Italia durante il fascismo, Milan 1962.

RICARDO JORGE: Os Cristianos novos en Portugal no seculo XX. Samuel Schwartz, Lisbon 1925.

MONS JOUIN: Le peril judeo maconnique. 5 volumes. 1919-1927.

KABALA AD PENTATEUCUM.

KADMI-COHEN: Nomades (essai sur l'ame juive) 1929.

LEON KAHN: The Jews of Paris during the Revolution.

JOSEF KASTEIN: History of the Jews.

W. KOCH: Comment l'empereur Juliane tacha de fonder une Eglise paienne.

LABRIOLLE: La reaction paienne. 1934.

R. LAMBELIN: Las victorias de Israel.

LATAIS: Terror rojo del 10 de Noviembre, 1918.

RUFUS LEARSI: Historia del pueblo judio. Israel Publishers, Buenos Aires.

LES CAHIERS DEL L'ORDRE. Nr. 3-4 1926.

N. LEVEN: Cinquante ans d'histoire: L'Alliance Israelite Universelle, 1860-1910. Paris 1911.

ELIPHAS LEVY: History of Magic.

B. LLORCA, S.J., GARCIA VILLOSLANDA, S.J. y F. J. MONTALBAN: Historia de la Iglesia Catolica, Madrid 1960. Volume I.

PEDRO LOPEZ DE AYALA: Cronica del Rey don Pedro.

ESTEBAN J. MALANNI: Communismo y Judaismo. La Mazorea Publishers. Buenos Aires 1944.

MALINSKY Y PONCINS: La Guerra Occulta. Milan 1961.

MATTER: Histoire du Gnosticisme. Edition of 1844.

MARCELINO MENENDEZ Y PELAYO: Historia de los Heterodoxos Espanoles. Consejo Superior de Investigaciones Cientificas. Madrid 1946.

GOSPEL OF MARK. GOSPEL OF MATTHEW.

PROSPER MERIME: Histoire de don Pierre. Paris 1848.

MONS. LEON MEURIN, S.J. Archbishop of Port Luis: Simbolismo de la Masoneria and Filosofia de la Masoneria. Nos Publishers. Madrid 1957.

DEAN MILMAN: History of the Jews. Everyman's Library II. Edition.

LOUIS ISRAEL NEWMAN (Rabbi): Jewish Influence on Christian Movements Reform. Vol. XXIII. Oriental Series Columbia University. New York.

ALFRED NOSSIG: Integrales Judentum (Integral Jewry).

ORIGENE: De Principiis.

OSSERVATORE ROMANO. Newspaper of the Vatican. Edition of 19.4.56.

ISIDORE PACENSE: Cronicon.

G. PANANZI: L'ebreo attraverso i secoli e nelle questioni della moderna societa. Treviso 1898.

HUNTLEY PATERSON: History and Destiny of the Jews. New York 5712, 1952.

PIKE: The morality and the dogma in the Scottish Rite.

JOHANNES QUASTEN: Patrologia.

RAGON: Maconnerie Occulte.

JACOB S. RAISIN (Rabbi): Gentile Reactions to Jewish Ideals. Philosophical Library, New York, 1953.

REVUE INTERNATIONAL DES SOCIETIES SECRETES. Pars. Nr. 2. from the year 1913.

DR. RHLIENG. Catholic priest: Die Polemik des Abbinismus (the polemic of Abbinism).

ADOLPHE RICOUX: L'existence des Loges de Femmes. Paris, Tequi Publishers 1891.

VICENTE RISCO: Historia de los Judios. Zurco Publishers. Barcelona 1960.

R.I.S.S. Nr. 8. 1926.

TRAIAN ROMANESCU: La Gran Conspiracion Judia. Third edition. Mexico 1961.

PAUL ROSEN: Satan.

ERNESTO ROSSI: II Manganello e l'aspersorio. Florence.

CECIL ROTH: Storia del popolo ebraico. Silvia Publishers. Milan 1962, and Historia de los marranos. Israel Publishers, Buenos Aires 5706, 1946.

ABRAM LEON SACHAR: Historia de los Judios. Ercilla Publishers. Santiago de Chile 1945.

SALLUSTE: Les Origines secretes du bolschevisme: Henry Heine e Carlo Marx. Jules Tallandier Publishers. Paris.

SAN AGUSTIN: Tratado sobre los salmos.

SAINT ATHANASIUS: Espistola de Morte Arri. Historia Arianorum and Monachos and Contra Arianos.

SAINT AMBROSIUS, Bishop of Milan: Epistle XI to the Emperor Theodosius.

SAINT BERNHARD: Epistola 241.

SAINT GREGORIUS, Bishop of Tours: Historia Francorum.

SAINT GREGORIUS NACIANCENUS: Oratio I et Juliano.

SAINT GREGORIUS OF NYSSA: Oratio in Christi resurrectionem.

SAINT JOHN: Apocalypse.

SAINT JOHN CHRYSOSTOM: Sixth Sermon against the Jews.

SAINT PAUL: Letter to Titus. Thessalonia epistle.

SAINT THOMAS OF AQUINAS: Opera omnia. Pasisillis Publishers.

SAINT PIUS., P.P.: Bull. Romanus Pontifex. 19.4. 1566.

P.V. SELLERS: Eustatius of Antioch and his place in the early Christ doctrine. Cambridge 1928.

SHABBATH.

SEFER-HA-ZOHAR: Translation of Juan de Pauly. Paris. Ernesto Leroux. 1907.

HIS HOLINESS GREGORY VII: Regesta IX.

HIS HOLINESS GREGOR IX: Bula Sufficere debuerat.

HIS HOLINESS LEO XIII: Encyclica Humanum Genus. 20.4. 84.
SITGES: Las mujeres de Rey don Pedro.
WERNER SOMBART: Die Juden und das Wirtschaftsleben.
SOZOMENO: Historia Eclesiastica.
TALMUD: Soncino, London.
JUAN TEJADA Y RAMIRO: Coleccion de Canones de todos los
Concilios de la Iglesia de Espana y de America. Madrid. 1859.
TERTULIANO: In Apologet, Book V, and Orosio, Book VII, Scorpiase,
Ad Nationes and Adversus Judaeos.
J. ET THARAND: Causerie sur Israel, 1926, Marcelle, Lesage.
RODERICUS TOLETANUS: De rebus Hispaniae; Rerum in Hispania
Gestarum.
LUCAS TUDENSIS: Cronicon en Hispania Ilustrata.
UNIVERSITY OF VIENNA: Protokollbuch der Theologischen Fakultat
(Protocol book of the theological Faculty). Protocol of 10.1.1419.
VACANDARD: Vie de Saint Bernard. "Codex Uldarici".
VON HAUGWITZ: Memoirs.
VERMIJON: Rivelazioni d'interesse mondiale. Rome 1957.
VOGELSTEIN AND RIEGER: History of the Jews in Rome. Edition of
1896.
WILLIAM THOMAS WALSH: Philipp II. Edition Espasa Calpe.
Barcelona.
J. M. WATTERICH: Vitae Romanorum ab exeunte saeculo IX usque ad
finem saeculi XII. Lipsia 1862.
NESTA H. WEBSTER: Secret Societies and Subversive Movements.
Boswell Publishing Co. London 1924.
WESTFALISCHER MERKUR. Newspaper of Minister. Nr. 405 of 6.10.
26.
RABBI WIENER: The Jewish Food Laws.
GERSON WOLF: Studien zur Jubelfeier der Wiener Universitat, Vienna
1865. (Studies to the jubilee centenary of the Vienna University).
JOHN YARKER: The Arcan Schools.

OTHER SOURCES AND REFERENCES

ADDISON, A.--Rise and Progress of Revolution, 1801.
AMERICAN JEWISH COMMITTEE BUDGET, 1953-1954.
AMERICAN MERCURY--Money Made Mysterious, 1958.
ANONYMOUS--Judaism in Action, 1964.
APIONUS--The Bolshevist in Ancient History. A
RCAND, Adrian--The Key to the Mystery.
ARCAND, Adrian--La Republic Universelle.

ARMSTRONG, George W.--Third Zionist War. A
RMSTRONG, George W.--World Empire.
BARDECHE, Maurice--Nuremberg ou La Terre Promise, 1948.
BARRUEL, Augustine--Memoirs of Jacobinism.
BARRY, Colman J.--Readings in Church History.
BASKERVLLE, Beatrice--The Polish Jew.
BATSELL, W. R.--Soviet Rule in Russia.
BEATY, John--The Iron Curtain Over America.
BELLOC, Hilaire--The Contrast.
BELLOC, Hilaire--The Jews.
BELLOC, Hilaire--Characters of the Reformation.
BELLOC, Hilaire--The Path to Rome.
BELLOC, Hilaire--Cromwell.
BELLOC, Hilaire--The Servile State.
BENSON, R. H.--Lord of the World, 1955.
BENTWICH, Norman--The Jews in Our Time.
BERGER, Elmer--The Jewish Dilemma.
BERLE, Adolph A.--The World Significance of a Jewish State.
BERNIER, M. Flavien--Le Juifs et le Talmud.
BERNALDEZ, Andres--Historia de los Reyes Catolicos.
BIENENFIELD, F. R.--The German and the Jews.
BLANCHARD, Charles A.--Modern Secret Societies.
BOEPLE, E.--The Grave Diggers of Russia.
BRASOL, Boris--Balance Sheet of Sovietism, 1922.
BRASOL, Boris--Socialism vs. Civilization, 1920.
BRASOL, Boris--World at the Crossroads, 1921.
BRITISH WHITE PAPER--Russia No. 1 (1919) A Collection of Reports on Bolshevism in Russia.
BRITISH PEOPLES PARTY--Failure At Nuremberg.
BRITTON, Frank--Behind Communism, 1965.
BROPHY, Rev. Edward F.--The "Brotherhood" Religion, Is It Anti-Christian?
BROWN, Bernard J.--From Pharoah to Hitler ("What is a Jew?"), 1933.
BROWN, Bruce H.--The World's Trouble Makers, 1981.
BROWNE, Lewis--How Odd of God.
BROWNE, Lewis--Stranger Than Fiction, 1925.
BUJAK, Franciszek--The Jewish Question in Poland.
BUTLER, Eric D.--The International Jew.
BUTLER, Eric D.--The Red Pattern of World Conquest.
CAHIL, E.--Freemasonry and The Anti-Christian Movement.
CAHIL, E.--The Framework of a Christian State.
CAMPBELL, Byram--American Race Theorists, 1952.
CARR, Wm. G.--Pawns In The Game, 1966.

CARR, Wm. G.--Red Fog Over America, 1964.
CATHOLIC BOOK CLUB--The Persecution of the Catholic Church in the Third Reich, 1942.
CHAMBERLAIN, Wm. H.--Foundations of the Nineteenth Century.
CHERODANE, Andre--The Mystification of The Allied People.
CHESTERTON, A. K.--Sound The Alarm.
CHESTERTON, A. K.--The Tragedy of Antisemitism.
CHESTERTON, A. K.--The New Unhappy Lords, 1965.
CHESTERTON, G. K.--The End of the Armistice.
CHESTERTON, G. K.--The New Jerusalem.
CINCINNATUS--War! War! War!, 1940.
CLARKE, Dr. John H.--England Under the Heel of the Jew.
CLAVEL--History of Freemasonry.
CLIFFORD, Hon. R. C.--The Application of Barruel's Memoirs of Jacobinism to the Secret Societies of Ireland and Great Britain.
COHEN, Israel--A Racial Program for the Twentieth Century.
CORRIGAN, Raymond--The Church in the 19th Century.
CORTI, Egon--Rise of the House of Rothschild.
CORTI, Egon--Reign of the House of Rothschild, 1923.
COTTER, Hilary--Jewish World Strategy Made Plain.
COTTER, Hilary--Cardinal Mindszenty, The Truth About His Real Crime.
COUGHLIN, Charles E.--By The Sweat of Thy Brow.
COUGHLIN, Charles E.--Am I An Anti-Semite?
COUGHLIN, Charles E.--An Answer To Father Coughlin's Critics.
DANIEL-ROPS, H.--The Church in an Age of Revolution, 1789-1870.
DAY, Donald--Onward Christian Soldiers.
DEANE, J. B.--The Worship of the Serpent.
DE HECKLINGEN--Israel, Its Past, Its Future.
DE HECKLINGEN--Juifs et Catholiques, 1939.
DEL MAR, Alexander--A History of Money in Ancient Countries.
DEL MAR, Alexander--Usury and The Jews.
DE PONCINS, Visc. Leon--Histoire de la Revolution Espagnole, 1938.
DE PONCINS, Visc. Leon--La Mystererieuse Internationale Juif, 1943.
DE PONCINS, Visc. Leon--Le Problem Juif Face au Concile, 1985.
DE PONCINS, Visc. Leon--Espion Sovietique sous la Monde, 1961.
DILLING, Elizabeth--The Plot Against Christianity.
DILLON, Mgr. George E.--The War of Anti-Christ Against The Church.
DILLON, E. J.--Ourselves and Germany.
DILLON, E. J.--The Inside Story of the Peace Conference.
DISRAELI, Benjamin--Coningsby.
DISRAELI, Benjamin--The Life of Lord George Bentick.
DISRAELI, Benjamin--Endymion.
DISRAELI, Isaac--Charles I--(2 volumes).

DWOWSKI, M.--Foundations of Nationalism.

DOMVILLE, Barry--From Admiral to Cabin Boy.

DON BELL REPORTS--The Falling Away and the Coming of the Anti-Christ.

DON BELL REPORTS--Methods of Survival if the Red Terror Should Strike--Vol. I & II.

DOUGLAS, C.H.--The Realistic Position of the Church of England.

DOUGLAS, C. H.--The Land of the Chosen People Racket.

DOUGLAS, C. H.--The Brief For The Prosecution.

DOUGLAS, C. H.--Program for Third World War.

DUNLOP, D. M.--The History of the Jewish Khazars, 1954.

DUPANLOUP, Bishop of Orleans--A Study of Freemasonry.

EDERSHEIM--Life of Jesus, Vol. I, and Vol. II.

EDERSHEIM--Jewish Social Life.

ELMHURST, Ernest--The World Hoax.

ENGLE, Roy--The Jew Menace.

ERBERLIN--Les Juifs d'aujourd hui.

EYMERIC, Nicholas--Directorium, Inquisitorium, 1578.

FABIUS--Rothschild Money Trust.

FAHEY, Rev. Denis--The Mystical Body of Christ and the Reorganisation of Society.

FAHEY, Rev. Denis--The Mystical Body of Christ in the Modern World.

FAHEY, Rev. Denis--The Kingship of Christ and Organized Naturalism.

FAHEY, Rev. Denis--The Kingship of Christ and the Conversion of the Jewish Nation.

FAHEY, Rev. Denis--The Rulers of Russia and the Russian Farmers.

FAHEY, Rev. Denis--The Rulers of Russia.

FELLOWS--Mysteries of Freemasonry.

FENELIDTH, Maurice M.--Children of the Martyr Race.

FIELD, A. N.--The Truth About the Slump, 1963.

FIELD, A. N.--All These Things, 1963.

FINKELSTEIN, Louis--The Pharisees.

FORD, Henry--My Life and My Work.

FORD, Henry--The International Jew.

FOUARD, Abbe Constant--Saint Peter and First Years of Christianity.

FOWLER, George B.--Analysis of the World Revolution.

FRASER, John--The Conquering Jew.

FRAZER, James--The Golden Bough, 1900.

FREEHOF, Rabbi S. B.--Race, Nation or Religion?

FRITZ, Ludwig--Crime of Our Age.

FROMER, Dr.--The Nature of Jewry.

FROST, J.--The Secret Societies of the European Revolution.

FRY, L.--Waters Flowing Eastward.

GAEBELEIN, Arno Clemens, D.D.--The Jewish Question.

GALTER, Albert--The Red Book of the Persecuted Church.

GINZBERG, A.--Transvaluation of Value.

GOFF, Kenneth--Hitler and the 20th Century Hoax.

GOSTIC, Ron--The Architects Behind World Communism; Zionism in the Middle East, 1960.

GOULEVITCH, Arsene--Czarism and Revolution, 1962.

GRANDMASION, Leonce De--Jesus Christ.

GRANT, Madison--Conquest of a Continent.

GRAVES, Philip--The Land of Three Faiths.

GRISAR, H.--Martin Luther, 1964.

GUI, Bernard--Practica Inquisitionis Heretice Pravitatis, Douais, Paris, 1886.

GWYNNE, H. A.--The Cause of World Unrest.

GYGES--Les Juifs dans la France d'aujourd'hui.

HAMILTON, William--Salute The Jew.

HANNA, Walton--Darkness Visible, 1952.

HANNA, Walton--Christian by Degrees, 1954.

HEAD-JENNER, H. C.--The Real Origin of the Balfour Declaration.

HECHT, B.--Perfidy.

HECHT, Ben--A Jew in Love.

HEADINGS--French Freemasonry Under The Third Republic.

HECKETHORN--Secret Societies of All Ages.

HEINZ, Heinz A.--Germany's Hitler.

HENDRICK, Burton--Jews In America.

HERTZL, Theodore--The Jewish State Diaries.

HIGGER, Michael--The Jewish Utopia.

HIRSCHFELD, K. J.--Hadst Thou But Known.

HOBART, Mary E.--The Secret of the Rothschilds.

HUBER, Canon Lipot--Jewry and Christianity.

HUDDLESTON, Sisley--Diplomacy and War.

HUDDLESTON, Sisley--France: The Tragic Years.

HULL, Rev. Ernest, S. J.--Thirteen Articles on Freemasonry.

HUNT, Rev. C. Penney--The Menace of Freemasonry to the Christian Faith.

HURT, Walter--Truth About the Jews.

HUTCHINSON--Spirit of Freemasonry.

INTERNATIONAL COMMITTEE OF THE RED CROSS. Regarding factual appraisal of the conditions of German Wartime Concentration Camps. (1) Report of the International Committee of the Red Cross on its Activities during the Second World War (3 volumes, Geneva, 1948).

(2) Documents sur L'activite du CICR en faveur des Civile detenus dans les camps de concentration en Allemagne, 1939-1945 (Geneva, 1946), and

(3) Inter Arma Caritas: the Work of the ICRC during the Second World War. (Geneva, 1947).

INQUIRE WITHIN--Light Bearers of Darkness.

INQUIRE WITHIN--The Trail of the Serpent.

JAMES--Dark Scenes of History.

JEFFERIES--Palestine The Reality.

JEFIMOW, Alexey--Who Are The Rulers of Russia?

JENKINS, Newton--The Republic Reclaimed.

JENSEN, B.--The "Palestine" Plot.

JENSEN, B.--The Satanization of "Russia".

JENSEN, B.--The UNO Fraud.

JENSEU, B. and MASSON, P. R.--Hitler's Policy Is a Jewish Policy.

JOHNSON, Frank--The Octopus.

JORDAN, Colin--The Fraudulent Conversion, 1955.

JORDAN, David--Unseen Empire.

JOUIN, Msgr.--Le Perile Judeo-Maconnique.

JOUIN, Msgr.--Review Internationale des Societes Secretes.

KALLEN, Horace M.--Zionism and World Politics.

KAMEN, Henry--The Spanish Inquisition, 1966.

KELLEY, Francis C.--The Book of Red and Yellows.

KELLEY, Francis C--Mexico, The Land of the Blood Drenched Altars.

KENNEY, Rev. Michael, S.J.--No God Next Door.

KENNEY, Rev. Michael, S.J.--American Masonry and Catholic Education.

KRANSNOFF, P. N.--From Double Eagle To Red Flag.

KNONECZNY, Feliks--On the Plurality of Civilisations.

KNUPFFER, George--America, Russia and the World.

KNUPFFER, George--The Struggle for World Power.

LA HODDE, Lucien De--The Cradle of Rebellions, A History of the Secret Societies of France.

LA HODDE, Lucien De--History of the Secret Societies and of the Republican Party of France, 1830-1848.

LAMBELIN, Roger--The Victories of Israel. LANE, E. H.--The Alien Menace.

LAZARE, Bernard--Anti-Semitism.

LEA, Charles--A History of the Inquisition in the Middle Ages.

LEESE, Arnold--The Jewish War of Survival.

LEESE, Arnold--Gentile Folly, The Rothschilds, 1966.

LEO XIII--The Human Race (Humanum Genus).

LEO XIII--Review of Our Pontificate. LEO XIII--Annum Sanctum (Encyclical).

LEO XIII--In Ipso (Encyclical).

LEONARD, Bernard F.--The Book of Destiny, 1955.

LEVINGTON, John--Key To Masonry, and Kindred Secret Combinations.

LEWSOHN, Ludwig--Israel.

LILIENTHAL, Alfred--What Price Israel?, 1953.

LILIENTHAL, Alfred--There Goes the Middle East, 1957.

LILIENTHAL, Alfred--The Other Side of the Coin, 1965.

LLORENTE, Juan--Historia Critica de la Inquisition de Espana.

LOPEZ, Robert and I. W. Raymond--Medieval Trade in the Mediterranean World.

LUTHERAN RESEARCH SOCIETY--The Sedition Case, 1953.

LUTHER, Martin--The Jews and Their Lies.

MAMEROVS--Iesat Nassar.

MARIANA, Juan--General History of Spain.

MARK, Jeffrey--The Modern Idolatry.

MARR, Wilhelm--The Victory of Judaism over Germanism.

MARSCHALKO, Louis--The World Conquerors, 1965.

MARSDEN, Victor E.--Jews in Russia.

MARX, Karl--A World Without Jews, 1959.

MATHEZ, J. A.--Le Passe, Les Temps Presents et La Question Juive (Eng. summary in the same volume).

MAZZINI, Joseph--Life and Writings of Joseph Mazzini.

McCULLAGH, Francis--Red Mexico.

McCULLAGH, Francis--Bolshevik Persecution of Christianity.

McCULLAGH, Francis--Prisoner of the Reds.

McFADDEN, Louis T.--Speeches of Congressional Record, 1930-1934.

MENENDEZ y Pelayo, M.--Historia de Los Heterodoxos Espanoles, Madrid, 1917.

MENUHIN, Moshe--The Decadence of Judaism in Our Time, 1965.

MILIUKOFF--Bolshevism--International Danger.

MOCATTA, Moses--Faith Strengthened.

MORGAN, William--Freemasonry Exposed and Explained.

MOURRET, Fernand--History of the Catholic Church (in 8 volumes).

MOUNIER, J. J.--On The Influence Attributed To Philosophers, Freemasons, and to the Illuminati, on the Revolution of France.

MUNGER--Way To Zionism.

MURCHIN, M. G.--Britain's Jewish Problem.

NEILSON, Francis--The Makers of War.

NETCHOVOLODOW, Gen. A.--Nicholas II and the Jews.

NEWMAN, Rabbi--Jewish Influence on Christian Reform Movements.

NEWTON, Francis E.--Fifty Years in Palestine.
NILUS, Serge--It Is Near, At The Door.
NODIER, Charles--History of the Secret Societies of the Army and of the Military Conspiracies.
OECHTERING, J. H.--Short Catechism of Church History.
O'GRADY, O.--The Beast of the Apocalypse.
OLIVER--Antiquities of Freemasonry.
OLLIVIER, George--L'Alliance Israelit Universelle.
OLMSTEAD, A. T.--History of Palestine and Syria.
PATKIN, A. L.--The Origin of the Russian-Jewish Labor Movement.
PATMONT, Louis A.--The Mystery of Iniquity.
PAYSON, Seth--Proofs of the Real Existence, and Dangerous Tendency, of Illuminism.
PEARSON, Roger--Race and Civilization.
PENDLEBURY, J.--Web of Gold.
PETROVSKY, D.--Russia Under The Jews.
PHELPS, J. W.--Secret Societies, Ancient and Modern.
PINKNEY, George--Jewish "Anti-Communism," 1956.
PIKE, Albert--Morals and Dogma.
PIKE, D. W.--Secret Societies, Their Origin, History and Ultimate Fate.
PITT-RIVERS, George--The World Significance of the Russian Revolution.
PLAYFAIR--History of Jacobinism.
POPE-HENNESY, Mrs. Una--Secret Societies and the French Revolution.
PRANAITIS, Rev. I. B.--The Talmud Unmasked, 1965.
PRESTON--Illustrations of Freemasonry.
PREUSS, Arthur--A Study in American Freemasonry, 1908.
QUEENSBOROUGH, Lady--Occult Theocrasy.
RAMSAY, A. H.--The Nameless War.
RAPPAPORT, A.--The Pioneers of the Russian Revolution.
RAUCHNING, Herman--Germany's Revolution of Destruction
RAUCHNING, Herman--Hitler Speaks.
RAWLINSON--Origin of Nations.
REED, Douglas--Far and Wide.
REED, Douglas--From Smoke To Smother.
REED, Douglas--Insanity Fair.
REED, Douglas--Disgrace Abounding.
REED, Douglas--Somewhere South of Suez.
REED, Douglas--Nemesis?
RICCIOTTI, Giuseppe--Life of Christ.
RICCIOTTI, Giuseppe--Paul the Apostle.
RICE, Cecil Spring--The Letters and Friendship of Sir Cecil Spring-Rice.

REEVES, John--The Rothschilds, The Financial Rulers of Nations.
ROBERTS, Glyn--The Most Power.
ROBISON, John--Proofs of a Conspiracy Against All Religions and Governments of Europe.
ROGERS, Arthur--The Palestine Mystery.
RASSINIER, Paul--Le Mensonge D'Ulysse.
RASSINIER, Paul--Ulysse Trahe Par Les Siens.
RASSINIER, Paul--Le Veritable Proces Eichmann.
RASSINIER, Paul--Le Drame Des Juife European.
ROTH, Cecil--Jews in the Renaissance, 1959.
ROTH, Cecil--A Life of Menasseh Ben Israel, 1934.
ROTH, Cecil--A History of the Marranos.
ROTH, Samuel--Jews Must Live.
RULE, W. H.--History of the Inquisition, 1874.
SABATINI, Rafael--Torquemada and the Spanish Inquisition.
SAINT-AULAIRE, Comte de--Geneva Contra La Paix, 1937.
SAMUELS, Maurice--You Gentiles.
SANCTUARY, Col. E. N.--Are These Things So?
SCHAFF, P. H. and W. Wace--A Select Library of Nicene and Post Nicene Fathers.
SCOTT, Walter--Life of Napoleon Buonaparte.
SEARCH, R. E.--Lincoln Money Martyred.
SELIANINOV, A.--The Secret Power of Masonry.
SHULCHAN ARUK.
THE SISSON REPORT. SHULCHAN ARUK-
SMITH, W. E.--Christianity and Secret Societies. SOKOLOW, Nahum--History of Zionism.
SOKOLSKY, George E.--We Jews.
SOMBART, W.--The Jews and Modern Capitalism.
SPIRIDOVICH, A. C.--History of Bolshevism.
SPIRIDOVICH, A. C.--The Secret World Government.
SPIRIDOVICH, A. C.--The Science of Political Foresight. ST.
BENEDICT CENTER--Our Glorious Popes, 1956.
STEHLN, J. P.--Traditions of the Jews.
STEED, Wickham--The Hapsburg Monarchy.
STEED, W.--Through Thirty Years.
STODDARD, Lothrop--The Revolt Against Civilization.
SALLUSTE--Marxism and Judaism.
TALMUD, Babylonian--Preface by M. Rodkinson.
TEMPERLEY, H. M. V.--History of the Peace Conference in Paris.
TENNEY, Jack, Sen.--Zionist Network.
TENNEY, Jack, Sen.--Zion's Fifth Column.
TENNEY, Jack B.--Cry Brotherhood.

TENNEY, Jack, Sen.--Zion's Trojan Horse.

TENNEY, Jack, Sen.--Anti-Gentile Activity in the United States.

THORKELSON, Jacob--Rescue The Republic.

THYSSEN, Fritz--I Paid Hitler.

TORMAY, Cecile--Outlaw's Diary. (Revolution, Vol. I; The Commune, Vol. II), 1923.

TROCASE, F.--Jewish Austria.

U.S. DEPT. OF STATE--National Archives, Decimal File, 1910-1929, No. 861.40161/325.

U.S. HOUSE DOCUMENT--House Document, No. 1868, 65th Congress, 3rd Session. Papers related to the Foreign Relations of the U.S. 1918--in 3 volumes--Russia.

U.S. HOUSE DOCUMENT--Investigation of Un-American Propaganda Activities in the U.S.--Special Committee on Un-American Activities House of Representatives. 78th Congress. Second Session on H. Res. 282, 1944 (Volumes I, II, III).

U.S. SENATE DOCUMENT--Subcommittee on the Judiciary of U.S. Senate 65th Congress, Vol. 3, German and Bolshevik Propaganda.

U.S. STATE DOCUMENT--Senate Document No. 62, 66th Congress, 1st Session, 1919--Vol. III.

U.S. ROHRBERG COMMISSION--Commission of Inquiry.

U.S. AMERICAN INTELLIGENCE SERVICE DOCUMENT--Also published by Documentation Catholique of Paris.

U.S. THE NATIONAL ARCHIVES OF THE UNITED STATES-- Record Group 120: Records of the American Expeditionary Forces. Report of June 9, 1919 and Report of March 1, 1919, Capt. Montgomery Schuyler.

U.S. THE NATIONAL ARCHIVES OF THE UNITED STATES, 1934- - Department of State Decimal File, 1910-1929, file 861.00/5067. Summary of Report No. 9 of July 16, 1919, from the Directorate of Intelligence (Home Office), Scotland House, S. W. 1, entitled "A Monthly Review of the Progress of Revolutionary Movements Abroad."

U.S. SENATE--Committee on the Judiciary--The Church and State Under Communism. A Special Study prepared by The Law Library of the Library of Congress for the Subcommittee to investigate the administration of the internal security act and other internal security laws of the committee on the Judiciary United States Senate.

Part I--The U.S.S.R.

Volume I Parts II and III--The U.S.S.R. Volume II Rumania, Bulgaria, Albania. Volume III Yugoslavia.

Volume IV Lithuania, Latvia and Estonia.

Volume VI Hungary, Czechoslovakia, German Democratic Republic.

Volume VIII Communist China.

Volume IX North Korea and Democratic Republic of Vietnam.
U.S. SENATE--Committee on the Judiciary--Communist Exploitation of Religion. Testimony of Rev. Richard Wurmbrand, May 6, 1966.
VAN NOORT--Dogmatic Theology, Vols. I and II.
VIERECK, George--The Kaiser on Trial.
WADDELL, Laurence Austine--The Makers of Civilization in Race and History.
WAITE, Arthur--The Holy Grail.
WALSH, Wm. T.--Isabella of Spain, 1935.
WALSH, Wm. T.--Philip II.
WALSH, Wm. T.--Characters of the Inquisition, 1940.
WARNER, George--The Jewish Spectre.
WEBSTER, Nesta H--Secret Societies and Subversive Movements, 1924.
WEBSTER, Nesta H.--Surrender of an Empire, 1931.
WEBSTER, Nesta--World Revolution, 1921.
WEBSTER, Nesta--The Socialist Network, 1926.
WESTON, Warren--Father of Lies.
WIERNIK, Peter--History of the Jews in America, New York, 1931.
WILCOX--Russia's Ruin.
WILLIAMS, Ariadna Tyrkova--From Liberty to Breast-Litovsk.
WILLIAMS, Maj. Robert H.--The Anti-Defamation League.
WILLIAMS, Maj. Robert H.--Know Your Enemy, 1965.
WILLIAMS, Maj. Robert H.--The Ultimate World Order.
WILSON, R. McNair--The Mind of Napoleon.
WILTON, Robert--Russia's Agony, 1919.
WILTON, Robert--The Last Days of the Romanovs, 1920.
YEATS-BROWN, F.--European Jungle.
YOCKEY, Francis Parker--Imperium, 1965.
YORKE, Onslow (William Hepworth Dixon)--Secret History of the Internationale.
ZIFF, W. B.--The Rape of Palestine.

CPSIA information can be obtained
at www.ICGtesting.com
Printed in the USA
BVHW081900190123
656623BV00008B/508